ORIENTATIONS

ORIENTATIONS
Collected Writings by

PIERRE BOULEZ

edited by
JEAN-JACQUES NATTIEZ

translated by
MARTIN COOPER

Harvard University Press
Cambridge, Massachusetts

1986

Originally published in French by
Christian Bourgois éditeur as *Points de repère*, 1981, revised edition, 1985

© Christian Bourgois éditeur, 1981, 1985

Translation © Faber and Faber Ltd
and the President and Fellows of Harvard College, 1986

Library of Congress Cataloging-in-Publication Data

Boulez, Pierre, 1925–
Orientations.

Translation of: Points de repère. 2e èd.
Includes index.
1. Music – Addresses, essays, lectures.   I. Nattiez,
Jean Jacques.   II. Title.
ML60.B796P613   1986   780   85–27317
ISBN 0–674–64375–5

Contents

Part Two: Exemplars

Translator's Note

This English edition of *Points de repère* is based on the second, revised French edition of 1985 and includes two items – 'On Musical Analysis' and 'Kandinsky and Schoenberg' – that were not in the first edition (1981), and three items not in either French edition – 'Stravinsky: *The Rite of Spring*', 'Oriental Music – A Lost Paradise?', and 'Technology and the Composer'. The introductory essay, 'On Reading Boulez', has been specially written for the English edition by the editor, Jean-Jacques Nattiez. There are two omissions to declare: an introduction to the catalogue of the Gaëtan Picon exhibition at the Centre Pompidou in April 1979, and 'Une Écurie pour Jarry' which is to be found on pp. 19–24 of *Boulez on Music Today*, translated by Susan Bradshaw and Richard Rodney Bennett, London, Faber, 1971. All the translations have been made directly from the texts in *Points de repère*, with the exceptions of 'Berlioz and the Realm of the Imaginary', translated by David Noakes, and 'Stravinsky: *The Rite of Spring*', translated by Felix Aprahamian, both of which are gratefully acknowledged. The arrangement of the essays is sometimes different from that in *Points de repère*, particularly within Part Two, where it was felt that the reader would find it more illuminating if Boulez's writings on, say, Berg or Messiaen were grouped together rather than dispersed under such subsections as 'Occasions Fragmentaires' or 'Le texte et sa réalité'.

A number of original essay titles have been changed for the same reason as section titles and that of the collection as a whole. French and English readers have different systems of intellectual reference, so that a title that is both natural and informative to the French reader may well seem obscure if translated literally. The original French titles of the pieces are given in the source footnotes. Any explanatory footnotes that I have thought it necessary to add are marked [M.C.].

The orthography of the original texts (some all in lower case) has been preserved, but very long paragraphs have sometimes been subdivided.

MARTIN COOPER
Richmond, 1985

On Reading Boulez

JEAN-JACQUES NATTIEZ

Orientations is the most extensive collection of writings by Pierre Boulez yet published. It follows three previous books, *Notes of an Apprenticeship* (1968), *Boulez on Music Today* (1971), and *Conversations with Célestin Delièbe* (1975).[1] *Notes of an Apprenticeship* is a selection from articles written between 1948 and 1961, while *Boulez on Music Today* includes the first two chapters of a larger project – an elaboration of the courses given by the composer at Darmstadt between 1959 and 1961 – which never materialized (other important material from that project is now printed in the present volume). In *Conversations with Célestin Delièbe*, the edited transcript of a long interview, Boulez reflects on his career up to 1974, the year in which he returned to France to assume the directorship of IRCAM (Institut de recherche et de coordination acoustique/musique). In 1966 it was decided that there should be a further volume of essays taking over where *Notes of an Apprenticeship* left off, and this was the object of *Orientations*, the first French edition of which appeared in 1980 under the title *Points de repère*. A second, fuller edition came out in 1985, and it is on this, as explained in the Translator's Note on p. 9, that the present book has been based.

The choice of these essays was deliberately as catholic as possible, and apart from a few very minor texts we have included virtually everything written by Boulez from the fifties up to 1980 on which we could lay our hands, including unpublished texts. All the big moments in Boulez's career are therefore covered. Part One is concerned with Boulez as a composer; Part Two with his activities as a conductor; and Part Three with the part he has played in different musical institutions. Interviews – which would make a book in themselves – have not been included, with a few exceptions – a 1974

---

[1] The full publication details are: *Relevés d'apprenti/Notes of an Apprenticeship*, trans. Herbert Weinstock (Paris, Seuil, 1966/New York, Knopf, 1968); *Penser la musique aujourd'hui/Boulez on Music Today*, trans. Susan Bradshaw and Richard Rodney Bennett (Paris, Gonthier, 1963/London, Faber, 1971/Harvard University Press, 1971); *Par volonté et par hasard/Conversations with Célestin Delièbe*, trans. anon (Paris, Seuil, 1975/London, Eulenburg, 1976). Other publications include *Rencontres avec Pierre Boulez* by Antoine Goléa (Paris, Juillard, 1958). For the latest bibliography, see *Pierre Boulez: Eine Festschrift*, ed. Josef Häusler (Vienna, Universal Edition, 1985).

interview in which Boulez sums up earlier works discussed in the foregoing pieces (p. 199), a 1967 interview about oriental music (p. 421), and parts of a Montreal interview (1971) edited by the author for inclusion here (pp. 116, 464, 467). There are no texts concerning IRCAM, or connected with IRCAM after 1974, since that would have involved making premature judgements about a venture that is not yet complete.

Like *Notes of an Apprenticeship*, *Orientations* follows no systematic plan. But although Boulez may occasionally have expressed doubts as to the usefulness of writing *about* music (pp. 80, 105), he and Schoenberg are probably the two twentieth-century composers who have written most, thus joining the line of writer-composers that goes back to Schumann, Berlioz and of course Wagner. Right at the beginning of his career we find him musing on 'The Composer as Critic' (1954):

> As a first approximation in tracing the evolution of any art, we can establish various fluctuations, some gradual and others violent. On the one hand there are periods during which a language is being established, its potentialities explored; and these are on the whole periods of stability marked by a certain primordial peace guaranteed by the quasi-automatic nature of what is happening. On the other hand there are periods of destruction and discovery, with all the accompanying risks that have to be taken in responding to new and unfamiliar demands. In the first period there is not much critical writing apart from a few turgid polemical pieces of no more than passing interest; but in the second there are passionate discussions of fundamental problems raised by the weakening of automatic responses, the impoverishment of means of expression and a diminishing power of communication.

Boulez's writings belong, of course, to the second category – which doubtless explains their paradoxical nature. Everything he has written has been linked to some occasion – a first performance, a lecture or the interpretation of some important work – and can be properly understood only by reading it in that context. Owing to their occasional nature they have no single format, and a record review will be found next to a serious piece of thirty pages; a technical analysis of his own works will be followed by a brilliant and definitive discussion of general ideas. And there are gaps, of course: he has not written about everything he has composed.[1]

However varied in character these pieces may be, they are all concerned with fundamental questions that constantly recur throughout his career, revealing a most unusual single-mindedness, both theoretical and practical.

---

[1] After 1966 he seems not to have written systematically about his own works, preferring interviews. The appearance of all Webern's works on record produced from him no more than an anthology of Webern quotations. And there is still no major overall document dealing with what already appears to be going to be his masterpiece, and probably also one of the major works of the century, *Répons*.

This is what gives them their value and what we shall try to establish here. Furthermore they are unique among writings about music and are couched in an original style that is hard to define. The author is quite clearly a composer, a thinker and a writer, and the reader is repeatedly confronted by an assortment of polemical, theoretical and poetic ideas. In fact musicologists do not often find themselves engaged in polemics; writers who speak about music avoid technical questions and not many musicians write at all. Boulez indulges in polemics when it is a question of attacking the mediocrity of musical institutions and the musical life they foster, or of answering critics who have failed to understand the necessity of serialism. He enters the world of theory when he is looking for the foundations of a universal musical language that will provide answers to problems that the twentieth century has not yet solved. And finally he shows himself to be a poet by the individuality of his style, which has both the beauty and the cutting edge of a flint fragment. Now and then we come on sentences that could well become aphorisms: 'A work exists only if it is the unforeseeable become necessity' (p. 126), or, the phrase of a natural writer, 'A man must be born anew every day to be himself.'[1]

Part One of *Orientations* is subtitled 'The Shaping Imagination' and is concerned with Boulez the composer, which activity directs and justifies all other aspects of his life. It begins with 'Fundamentals', a group of texts of courses given at Darmstadt and lectures given between 1959 and 1961. The first three of these define an aesthetics of music, and the next three are about notation and form; these latter were originally intended by Boulez to have formed the basis of four additional chapters in *Boulez on Music Today*, the published version of which eventually included only two chapters ('General Considerations' and 'Musical Technique') preceded by an 'Interior Duologue'.[2] This first group is rounded off by 'Periform', a later text, which is an inspired piece of 'thinking aloud' about the meaning of form.

The second group, 'Seeing and Knowing', is about the relationship between composing and teaching. The first piece, 'The Composer as Critic' (p. 106), was written when the concerts of Domaine musical (since 1954, Concerts du Petit Marigny) were being started, and appeared in the review *Domaine musical*, which was supposed to provide the theoretic background to the programmes, but ran to only a single number. In it Boulez explains the need for a link between reflection about music and actual composition, in his case a constant need, as is shown by his writings, his initiation of the review *Domaine musical* (published in 1954 by Editions du Rocher under Pierre

[1] In an interview published in *Le Monde*, 23 December 1976, not reproduced here.

[2] The original German version of *Penser la musique aujourd'hui* was called *Musikdenken heute 1*. The additional material has now been published as *Musikdenken heute 2*, trans. Josef Häusler, Mainz, Schott, 1985.

Souvtchinsky), and more recently in the series 'Musique/passé/présent' published by Christian Bourgois, with Pierre Boulez and the present writer as co-editors.

The second piece, 'Demythologizing the Conductor' (p. 113), is a kind of declaration of intent in connection with the analysis and composition classes that he was to give at Basle between 1960 and 1963, and that were to include analyses of *Wozzeck*, Stockhausen's *Gruppen*, Webern's *Second Cantata* and one of the movements of *Pli selon pli* among other works. Boulez has not in fact published many analyses, except that of *The Rite of Spring* (*Relevés d'apprenti*, pp. 75–145). His big analysis of Webern's *Second Cantata* was never more than sketched, so that what he says *about* analysis in the following piece ('On Musical Analysis', p. 116) tells us much, expanding and completing the remarks already made in '. . . Auprès et au loin' ('Near and far') in *Relevés d'apprenti* (particularly pp. 187–93).

For Boulez the minutiae of the analytical process could never be an end in themselves but rather, as in the 'explication des textes' used in French schools, a method of grasping the underlying dialectic of a piece of music and isolating the fundamental principles that govern its organization and working. This is important because what Boulez has to say about analysis, though it may not occupy much space here, helps us to understand the basic nature of the other pieces in the book, whether they deal with his own music or that of others. General – even abstract – ideas play a larger part than empirical details, so that as a writer Boulez is a communicator of ideas rather than of technical information. This may sometimes prove disappointing to composition students, but it is no doubt a peculiarity of his writing that explains its popularity with non-musicians, who find it both interesting and enjoyable. If you ask Boulez, 'Can you give us the series?' he replies, 'What good would that be?' (p. 117). The only exception is to be found in 'The System Exposed' (p. 129) where Boulez is uniquely indiscreet about the series in *Polyphonie X* and *Structures* for two pianos.[1] The text published here is taken from a series of letters exchanged by Boulez and John Cage between 1948 and 1951, in which each tried to convince the other of the legitimacy of his own attitude. 'The Teacher's Task' (p. 119) is another Darmstadt lecture and is a cool account of Boulez's ideas about the master–pupil relationship and the difficulty of teaching composition: 'The ultimate object of analysis is self-definition by the agency of another' (p. 123).

The third group, 'Frenzy and Organization', shows us how Boulez in fact undertakes this task of self-definition. In the past each of his major works was accompanied by a theoretical 'justification', and in these pieces he pushes his passion for anonymity to such a point that he generally avoids

---

[1] Compare the mass of details here with what Boulez had thought fit to publish on the subject of these same two works in his 1952 article 'Eventuellement' (*Relevés d'apprenti*, pp. 152–73).

mentioning even the names of the works concerned. Hence the patchwork of *Relevés d'apprenti*, in which 'Propositions' (1948) dates from the days of *Sonatine*, the First Piano Sonata and *Visage nuptial*; 'Recherches maintenant' (1954) refers to *Structures I* (1957), 'Aléa' (1957) to the Third Piano Sonata (1956–7), 'Son et verbe' to *Poésie pour pouvoir* (1958), 'Eventuellement' (1952) to *Polyphonie X*, *Structures I* (1951–2) and *Etude sur bande* (1951–2), etc. ... Here 'Sound, Word, Synthesis' (1958) (p. 177), which includes part of the text of 'Son et verbe', and 'Poetry – Centre and Absence – Music' (1962) (p. 183) treat in a general way the relationship between poetry and music but deal largely, though not specifically by name, with the composer's experience while writing *Poésie pour pouvoir* (1958) and *Pli selon pli* (1957–62). In addition to the letters to Cage already mentioned, this group includes Boulez's important lecture (1961) on his *Deuxième Improvisation sur Mallarmé* (p. 155) (which was to become the third piece of *Pli selon pli*), the sleeve-note that he wrote for the record of *Pli selon pli* (p. 174), and a long article (p. 143) on the Third Sonata (1956–7), which forms an indispensable pendant to 'Aléa' in *Relevés d'apprenti*. All these pieces have the great merit of informing us in concrete detail about Boulez's ideas on the subject of chance in composition – a 'chance' that is very controlled and does not alter the fact that the work that finally emerges is the result of *choice*. In the 'Interview with Dominique Jameux' (p. 199), dating from 1974, these masterpieces of the 1960s are reviewed in retrospect.

Adding these to the essays already published in *Relevés d'apprenti* we may well wonder whether there are any of Boulez's major works that he has not discussed in print. *Le Marteau sans maître* is scrutinized in connection with Schoenberg's *Pierrot lunaire* in the piece called 'Speaking, Playing, Singing', which is included in Part Two of the present collection (p. 330). But generally speaking, since *Pli selon pli* Boulez does not appear to have felt the need to explain his major works in print. Instead he has used the interview, and those with Deliège are indispensable as a complement to our knowledge of Boulez through his own statements. It would need a montage of different interviews to cover the latest period, from *Rituel in Memoriam Bruno Maderna* (1974–5) to *Répons* (1981). But there may well be a good reason for this silence if we consider that the Third Sonata (1956–7), the *Livre pour cordes* (1958), *cummings ist der dichter* (1970), *Eclats/multiples* (1970) . . ., *Explosante-fixe* . . . (1972), *Notations* (1980) and *Répons* (1981) are all unfinished, or 'works in progress'. *Polyphonie X* (1950–1) has been withdrawn from circulation, and neither *Poésie pour pouvoir* (1958) nor . . . *Explosante-fixe* . . ., both of which make use of electronic techniques, satisfies the composer. There are very clear references throughout this collection to the different problems at the root of these unfinished works, chief among them being the crisis in the language of music after total serialism had proved a dead end (1949–52) and the lack of technical means for adapting the actual sound material (whether electro-acoustic or instrumental) to Boulez's demands as a composer. The diagnosis was clear as long ago as 1954: 'Get rid of a number of prejudices about a Natural Order; rethink our ideas about acoustics in the light of recent experiments; face the problems arising from electro-acoustics and electronic techniques – that is what we now need to do' (*Relevés d'apprenti*, p. 185). And that, in fact, was to be the programme of IRCAM, though not until exactly twenty years later. In the meantime Boulez became a conductor.

Boulez studied conducting in the first place in order to raise the standard of professional performances of twentieth-century music and to propagate that music more effectively with the general public. These years, 1954–66, were the great years of the Domaine musical. There is, however, no getting away from the fact that he composed relatively less as he became increasingly active as a conductor and eventually achieved an international reputation. At first he conducted theatre music for the Barrault–Renaud Company, then at the Domaine musical, but in 1963 he enlarged his scope by conducting *The Rite of Spring*. He studied conducting (often by simply watching) with Hermann Scherchen (see p. 499), Hans Rosbaud (p. 513) and Roger Désormière (p. 500). His name was associated with a string of spectacular operatic productions that have since entered operatic history as part of the process of purging and renovating the whole genre, both musically and dramatically. They include *Wozzeck* first at the Paris Opéra, produced by Jean-Louis Barrault, and then at Frankfurt produced by Wieland Wagner (both 1966); *Parsifal* at Bayreuth from 1966 to 1970, again with Wieland Wagner; *Pelléas et Mélisande* at Covent Garden with Vaclav Kašlik and Josef Svoboda (1969 and 1971); the 'centenary' *Ring* at Bayreuth with Patrice Chéreau, from 1976 to 1980; and the first performance of the completed *Lulu*, also with Chéreau, at the Paris Opéra in 1979.

At the same time as he was immersing himself in opera Boulez became the head of a number of internationally famous orchestras – principal guest conductor (1969–70) and musical adviser (1970–1) of the Cleveland Orchestra, principal conductor of the BBC Symphony Orchestra (1971–5) and musical director of the New York Philharmonic Orchestra (1971–7). Little wonder, therefore, if the second part of this book, 'Exemplars', is so extensive.

Each time that he undertook the conducting of an opera (whether it was *Wozzeck*, *Pelléas*, *Parsifal*, the *Ring* or *Lulu*) he produced at least one major text, in some cases more than one; and these were all studies in depth. His sleeve-notes for records are shorter, but no less interesting for that reason (works by Berlioz, Mahler, Debussy, Stravinsky, Webern, Berg, Varèse, Bartók). As a prominent musician and writer, he was much in demand for prefaces (Wagner, Mahler), obituaries (Schoenberg, Désormière, Wieland Wagner) or radio and television talks (Messiaen).[1]

The question has been how much of all this writing to publish here. Boulez composed less during these years when he was so deeply engaged in conducting and organizing, as we have said; but even while he was organizing others, his mind was always on his own affairs or, to be more exact – on the problems of the contemporary composer.

Why did he take an interest in Mahler, whose aesthetic might seem to be so far removed from his own? Because in Mahler he recognized the influence of the performer on the composer and could observe what a composer can gain from performance. Berlioz? In 'Bruno Maderna: A Portrait Sketch' (p. 523) we find ourselves back with Berlioz's concern with the positioning of instruments in the orchestra: this enables us to 'infer . . . present day solutions for contemporary creation' (p. 219). And the same is true of all the composers whom Boulez has either conducted or discussed in print. Wagner's criticisms of the musical establishment of his day prefigure those of Boulez, here included in Part Three. And when, in speaking of *Parsifal*, he talks of 'time-weaving', the fusion of horizontal and vertical, or the contrasts between solo instruments and instrumental groups in the orchestra could he not in fact be speaking not only about Webern, but also about *Rituel* or *Répons*? Boulez is interested in works of the past for their 'harmonic resonances', for what they can teach us that is relevant to today's music. 'Would these same masterpieces indeed still continue to arouse our interest unless they continued to express our subjective feelings?' (p. 474).

Boulez's subjective feelings, then – and the question arises, 'Does what he writes about other composers tell us about himself?' It is a striking fact that the categories he uses in speaking of Wagner, Mahler and Debussy are generally speaking the same – the ductility and malleability of motives, i.e. their adaptability to different tempi; the fluctuation of tempi; the transition from one tempo to another; the dialectic between different instrumental blocks that serve as markers to the listener, and the fluidity of the musical discourse; refinements of texture; subtle differentiations of dynamics. These are all things that we have, in fact, already *heard* in *Le Marteau sans maître* and *Pli selon pli*.

Boulez's tie with the past is a quite specific one. He never turns to the past

---

[1] As well as writing newspaper articles and giving interviews, Boulez also took part in a large number of broadcast or televised interviews, and to list these would be an enormous undertaking. Here we have printed only two broadcasts, both on Messiaen, and in each case Boulez prepared the script beforehand. Dominique Jameux's *Boulez* – which will be published by Faber and Harvard – contains a list of the ten broadcasts that Boulez did for the BBC with Barrie Gavin. This does not include his lectures or his public presentations of music – the 'Perspective Encounters' and 'Rug Concerts' in New York or the lecture concerts at IRCAM in 1980, 1981 and 1982, available on ten cassettes produced by Radio-France.

to borrow actual stylistic ideas, but rather to learn about *principles* – not the manifest style itself but the *idea* on which that style is based. Hence his dislike of neo-classicism with its archaic borrowings (p. 349), his rejection of the various kinds of genre music quoted by Berg, and his lack of interest in musical anecdote of any kind. He is not concerned with Bartók the folklorist, and he does not actually hear the bells in *Ibéria*. If, in fact, we are to speak of 'intellectualism' in Boulez's case, this is where it lies. 'What do we find fascinating in Cézanne's *Montagne Sainte-Victoire*? – the capturing of the landscape, the painter's obsession, – or the "order" he established?' (p. 76). This attitude is something quite fundamental in Boulez, and it explains his particular, very selective interest in early twentieth-century artists and the order in which he rates them.

As he says on several occasions, the big five come first. Stravinsky has his place among them[1] thanks to his rhythmic innovations,[2] though the rest of his language is still too close to diatonicism. Schoenberg invented the series, but Boulez accuses him of treating it as a 'super-theme' and casting it in nineteenth-century rhetorical moulds, whereas for Boulez the series is a *principle* that should organize the work at every level. When he first started writing, in 1948, he rejected Berg and all his works; but in 1974, after conducting *Wozzeck*, he said, 'I have learned to discover the labyrinths of Berg's music after surmounting the emotional obstacle that separates us.' That is pure Boulez – ready to forget the persistent romanticism of Berg's gestures and to concentrate on his passion for symmetry (this is worth comparing with what he says here of his own Third Sonata and *Pli selon pli*), his ability to reconcile the 'number' opera and the through-composed, and his taste for musical cryptograms. Webern, of course, is discussed in detail in *Relevés d'apprenti*, but is in fact an omnipresent model – for his abolishing of the opposition between horizontal and vertical, for his way of mapping the space of a composition, and for his organizing of a whole structure on a single principle, as Bach did in *The Art of Fugue*. While Boulez enjoys conducting Bartók's music, he has actually written very little about it. It is not, of course, Bartók's neo-classical works that interest him, but his instrumental expertise, his setting of chromaticism against diatonicism and his skill in development and in counterpoint.

What, then, of Debussy – and Varèse, and Messiaen? It is late Debussy that interests Boulez most – *Jeux* and the piano *Etudes* (p. 312) – on account of the development techniques based on a matrix of intervals. Though he wrote a handsome obituary appreciation of Varèse (p. 497), he does not like

---

[1] Or had. In a recent essay ('Un bilan?' in *Stravinsky, Etudes et témoignages* présentés et réunis par François Lesure, Paris, Lattès, 1982, pp. 55–65) Boulez seems to be saying goodbye to Stravinsky: 'I seem to have nothing more to say to the family, nor they to me . . . I just can't be interested any more.'

[2] Studied in detail in 'Stravinsky demeure' (*Relevés d'apprenti*).

Varèse's sectional way of writing, his treatment of rhythm as an autonomous element or his method of isolating blocks of harmonies. It is Varèse's strength that he admires, his assertion of the actual material of the music, his refusal to use themes, and his supple use of tempi. And finally Messiaen, for whom he certainly has the respect due to a master, one who developed rhythmic reflection (*la réflexion rythmique*) in new directions, thus opening the way to total serialization, though Boulez found him too eclectic and his taste more than doubtful ... Subjectivity admitted, therefore – 'Do we never want to remodel the faces of those to whom we feel in some way drawn to suit ourselves?' (p. 507). Boulez might say, 'I am the future of Stravinsky, of Schoenberg and of Webern.' And that is not unimportant, for once we read the past with reference to ourselves, there is a great temptation to suppress it.

A number of themes recur throughout the book like *Leitmotivs* – the horror of remembering (in the case of Désormière), the commendation of amnesia (directed against Stravinsky's neo-classicism), the fascination with anonymity (his own Third Sonata), the disassociation between the composer's life and his work,[1] and the refusal to provide keys to his music. 'It is essential for any creative artist ... to burn ... his first attempts' (p. 403). And this subject inspired some of Boulez's most lyrical outbursts: 'What a delight it would be for once to discover a work without knowing *anything* about it ... Shall we ever make up our minds to disregard contexts and to forget the time factors so relentlessly insisted upon by the history books? Shall we ever manage to ignore the circumstances, banish them from our memories and bury them in oblivion and take the interior essence of a work as our only guide?' (p. 261). Embark on works without sophisticated forethought (pp. 317, 396), discover them immediately from the text, forget (for instance) all the familiar talk about Debussy's 'misty dreaming', reveal in *Pelléas* the theatre of cruelty and fear (p. 314), and burn one's library (p. 449). There is a great deal about 'fidelity' in interpretation: he speaks of *quartering* Webern, of irreverence (p. 482), disrespect and plundering the past (p. 403), making a clean sweep of it. Just when musicology has begun triumphantly to 'restore' performances of baroque and early music Boulez makes no bones about saying, 'There is no such thing as *truth*' (p. 403). If he performs works of the past, his chief object is to show the potential novelty in even the most familiar work. And his attitude to *analysis* is the same (*crimen laesae musicologiae*!) – 'Inferences that are false but full of future possibilities are more useful than those that are correct but sterile' (p. 122). There is no point in trying to reconstitute the private, labyrinthine workings of the composer's mind, that 'indestructible kernel of darkness' (pp, 83,

---

[1] There was something no doubt involuntarily ironical in asking Boulez to write a preface to a biography of Mahler and to review Cosima Wagner's *Diary*.

294), that permits neither knowledge nor analysis. All that is necessary is to understand the work's own dialectic and, before all else, to be able to draw conclusions from it for the future.

Meanwhile we should make no mistake about the importance to Boulez of the composer's work. The feverish preparation below ground is none the less *work*: it involves the craftsman, without whom nothing would emerge. This insistence on the composer's poetics – one might almost reverse it in that way – seems to have discounted the other pole of composition, perception. And it is useless for Schaeffer and creators of *musique concrète* (renamed first 'electro-acoustic' and then 'acousmatic' music) to complain of this, as they did particularly when total serialization was the fashion. With Boulez, however, the passion to communicate is so strong that he can never really forget that music is meant to be heard – strange as it may seem! First, though, the foundations of the new language must be discovered, even at the risk of making mistakes. There are occasional signs of Boulez's growing interest in problems of perception, and particularly in the idea that a new work, by its language and its form, creates its own specific listening conditions, especially types of moment-to-moment listening (p. 178), as in *Jeux* – something that will not be overlooked by the composer of *Répons*.

Boulez's constant desire to claim descent from a carefully picked genealogy of composers, coupled with his often violent refusal of tradition as such, makes it clear that the fundamental category that articulates all his thinking is that of time. In the first place, *historical* time – as shown in this passage, written in 1963, which explains the whole way in which he thinks:

> I shall never tire of saying that personality starts with a robust critical perspicacity that forms part of the gift itself. Any vision of history actually implies, from the first moment of choice, a sharpness of perception in judging the 'moment', and that perception is not explainable in exclusively logical terms ... It is the gift that enables him to clarify what appears to be a confused situation, to discern the lines of force in any given epoch, to take an overall view, to grasp the totality of a situation, to have an intuitive hold on the present and to apprehend its structure on a cosmic scale – that is what is demanded of any candidate who aspires to the title of 'seer'.

And Boulez does not hesitate to look into the future. In 1964 he wrote, 'Who can in fact envisage any future for music without its own solution imposing itself with all the force of a law? A pleasant utopia indeed and something to look forward to' (p. 66). And later, in 1971, 'Everyone's ambition is, roughly speaking, to *remain a presence* in the affairs of his day and in future utopias' (p. 521). 'The "desire for immortality" is nothing new, among poets especially', and he himself expresses it (p. 329). There is absolutely no doubt that Boulez has a latent, secret wish to round off the history of music at the same time as carrying it forward and giving it a further impetus. Anyone who interprets a historical evolution in terms of his own becomes a Hegelian.

A vision of history, then. The rhythmic innovations introduced by Stravinsky, Messiaen and Varèse are incompatible with what these men preserve of traditional syntax, just as Schoenberg's morphological innovations are incompatible with his outdated rhetoric. At the beginning of the twentieth century the different parameters were out of phase with each other. The composer's *critical responsibility* consists in first being aware of the fact, then avoiding dead ends and finally discovering ways to achieve new syntheses. To borrow the mystic's vocabulary, we might say that Boulez needed only a very short time (somewhere between 1945 and 1950) to receive the *revelation* of what this evolution of twentieth-century music meant. What may well seem obvious to us today (though not perhaps so obvious to some!) was far from obvious at a time when Webern was virtually unknown. Boulez then 'programmed' himself for the rest of his life, very much as Wagner did between 1843 and 1849, in Dresden. What strikes us is the durability and stability of his principles and his way of stating them. The trajectory – a favourite word of his – of his life is straight, deviating only in order to avoid obstacles . . . To borrow a phrase of Paul Veyne's, Boulez *constructed* his own *plot* of musical history and has never modified it. He chose his own ancestors who, leaving the composers aside, include a number of painters (Cézanne, Klee, Kandinsky, Mondrian), and a great many writers (Baudelaire, Mallarmé, Proust, Joyce, Kafka, Musil, Genet, Char, Michaux). Not a bad selection.

His vision of history also explains Boulez's dislikes, which can be reduced roughly to two. First, the return to archaisms – and this puts paid to the neo-classicism of Stravinsky, let alone that of Hindemith or Henze – and to neo-romanticism, and to neo-expressionism.[1] Then anything that suggests a *retreat* on the part of the composer – such as we witnessed among yesterday's avant-garde composers, who made a 'virtue' of their congenital inability really to create and to communicate and boasted of their position as 'marginal' composers. Boulez is not a revolutionary so much as 'an orderly anarchist', as has been well said by Jameux,[2] a man who creates a disturbance in order to establish the truth in which he believes. He rejects the facile pleasingness of electro-acoustic music inasmuch as it has shown itself incapable of forming the basis of any language and/or solving the problems of concert-giving; musical theatre;[3] improvisation; and pure chance, to which he prefers 'indeterminate choice', or a series of different possible versions (p. 146) creating a flexibility of form to match the relative nature of the new

---

[1] See for instance his recent interview with Jonathan Cott, 'On New Music', *New York Review of Books*, 28 June 1984, pp. 14–15. (French version in *Le Debat*, No. 33, January 1985, pp. 140–5.)

[2] Dominique Jameux, *Pierre Boulez*, Paris, Fayard, 1984, p. 270.

[3] Cf. his interview with Zoltan Pesko in *Melos*, September–October 1973.

components of the musical language (p. 155). Between these poles –
structure/chance, discipline/freedom – there must be a traffic, and this
demands flexibility, malleability, ductility, all *temporal* categories once
again.

There are matters on which Boulez has changed his mind, but in each case
it has been in order to recover fundamental principles that transcend temporal contingencies. Berg is a good example, Boulez swallowing Berg's
neo-romanticism and penetrating his labyrinthine mind. Other examples are
opera – where he and Wieland Wagner revealed the possibilities of a new,
simplified theatrical style and its attendant problems (the relationships
between music and singers, orchestra and stage) – and general serialization,
in his discussions of which it is often not difficult to divine a certain amount
of self-criticism (pp. 68, 76–7). In *Répons* he embarked on the same search
as he had initiated twenty years earlier, in 1950, only having at last possessed
himself of the technological equipment for which he had always been longing.

Here Boulez's intellectual and artistic course, his 'trajectory', comes full
circle. This sense of history, his fashioning of his own development from a
small number of basic principles, is repeated in his actual works, musical
time being not only that of history but also that of the processes of artistic
creation and of its products as they appear.

At one point in *Orientations*, where Boulez is talking of himself and
Wagner, he alludes to what was the fundamental theme of *Penser la musique
aujourd'hui*, smooth and striated time (pp. 86–7, 271). These cannot be
separated in watertight compartments, as antithetical, but must be regarded
as two poles of a continuum. The transition from one to the other he
discovers, or rediscovers, in Wagner (*Tristan*) (p. 227) and Debussy
(*Ibéria* – the passage connecting the second and third pieces) (pp. 319–20);
and the same is true of tempo fluctuations, again in Wagner, in Debussy's
rubatos, and also in Varèse (p. 371). Musical time is therefore also the
time that 'elapses' as a work develops and proliferates from a central,
initial cell or kernel. This applies equally to the subject of *The Art of Fugue*,
the basic intervals of Debussy's *Etudes*, the *Leitmotivs* of the *Ring* and
their transformations, as they unfold in 'historical' time from *Rheingold*
to *Götterdämmerung*, and to the organization of a work at every level,
morphological and rhetorical, based on unified serial principles. It is a
proliferation of this impressive kind that we can trace in Boulez's work
as well as in his life. In his orchestral *Notations* (1980) he develops material
that he had not touched since 1945; and in the same way *Répons* (begun
in 1981) represents the true completion of earlier works unfinished (the
Third Sonata, *cummings ist der dichter*, *Eclats/Multiples*) or problematic
(*Poésie pour pouvoir*, ... *Explosante-fixe* ...). Primarily, however, it is
an answer to the crisis of general serialization in the 1950s. We must
therefore understand in a literal sense the observation that Boulez makes

in *Par volonté et par hasard*: 'The different works that I write are basically no more than different facets of a single central work, with a central concept' (p. 63).

Répons is clearly this single, total work which, in a sense, cancels all the others and makes the completion of the unfinished ones pointless. Why is this so? Because the works that did not come to term encountered a complex of linguistic and technical problems. The composer's invention did not dispose of the necessary technical means, and the absence of those means inhibited that invention. And this, I believe, is the other fundamental point for Boulez, beside his preoccupation with time – the impossibility of separating *material* from *invention*.

This is certainly the most long-standing of Boulez's ideas. In 1951 we find him writing (in an essay about Bach, and it was not by chance that he was discussing this 'legendary ancestor'): 'In Webern the *sound clarity* is achieved by the generation of the structure from the material. By this I am alluding to the fact that the architecture of the work is derived directly from the manipulation of the series' (*Relevés d'apprenti*, p. 17). It is really necessary to read the whole page, but any reader who is interested can refer to it. Boulez's summing up of the position in 1957 ('Tendances de la musique récente', in the same book) ended with these words: 'Such observations are still premature: we are only on the road to making such music a reality' (p. 231) – the music, that is to say, arising from 'a choice of material based on its intrinsic structural qualities' (p. 230). 'What can we do but turn to the machine?' (p. 229). 'Perfected apparatus, easy to use, such as is necessary for works like these, has not yet been constructed' (p. 231). But it will be one day, and that is why Boulez, after a certain date, felt the urgent need of an institution.

This brings us to Part Three of these *Orientations* and Boulez's career as a conductor. In other men's music he discovered the same problems that he faced in his own, just as the shortcomings of musical institutions concerned him both as composer and as conductor. Four of the pieces printed here recall the fighting spirit that he showed in organizing the Domaine musical concerts – presenting model performances of twentieth-century classics, properly rehearsed; establishing links with certain works of the past; appealing to a more widely based public – in fact *communicating*. This was followed by the quarrel with Malraux, at that time Minister for Culture in the de Gaulle government, who had simply ignored Boulez's carefully thought out suggestions for the reorganization of French musical life, and appointed Marcel Landowski, a perfectly respectable composer but of the second rank. The document in which Boulez gives his reason for saying 'no' to Malraux is uncharacteristically violent in tone (p. 441): 'I am therefore on strike against the whole of French musical officialdom' (p. 443). Nor was it only French musical institutions that aroused his anger. We have not included here the interviews in which he demanded the burning down of opera houses and changes in the rituals of concert-giving.[1]

The language of the other pieces in this third part is less incendiary but they all reflect Boulez's chief concerns at this period of his life. It is very important to notice that in the long lecture, which he gave on 13 May 1968, 'Where are we now?' (p. 445), he coupled two points – the need for a new, universal language, as always, *and* reflections on the whole question of musical institutions. Here and in the following pieces, which date from 1970 to 1977, we find him pondering the nature of 'concerts', the organization of orchestras, the architecture of concert halls (which he would like to be adaptable), programme building and public relations, the inability of existing instruments to satisfy the *imaginative* demands of contemporary composers, research in new (and especially electronic) techniques and the necessity for collaboration between musicians and scientists. His solution to all these problems was the creation of an independent research institute modelled on the Bauhaus, and so the idea of IRCAM was born; and since Boulez never abandons any project without realizing it, IRCAM opened its doors in 1974. It was surely not by chance that his first public mention of the idea in France seems[2] to have been on 13 May 1968, an historic date for all Frenchmen of the present day, since it was the day that saw the most formidable demonstrations against the de Gaulle government all over the country. Boulez may have had his reservations about the 'mouvement de mai', but all his thinking at this period surely had something in common with the upsurge of expansive, utopian feeling of those days – change concerts, change relations between players and audience, change music . . . change life, in fact! 'What I want to do', he was still writing in 1972, 'is to change people's whole mentality . . .'

It is outside our scope here to estimate how far IRCAM has in actual fact realized the basic ideas expressed by Boulez between 1968 and 1974. We may well wonder[3] what remains of the 'contacts' between American orchestras and audiences that Boulez hoped would be maintained after his contracts had expired (p. 483). There is, however, one tangible result that can be identified and evaluated, *Répons*, which will doubtless be finished in the

---

[1] 'Sprengt die Opernhäuser in die Luft', *Der Spiegel*, No. 40, 1967; 'Das Ritual der Konzerte muss geändert werden', *Süddeutsche Zeitung*, 18–19 October 1969.
[2] In fact Boulez had been approached in 1966 (Jameux, op. cit., p. 218) by the Max Planck Gesellschaft to create a musical research institute. We may even go back as far as 1951 when Boulez, in presenting some of John Cage's pieces for prepared piano, observed, 'At Los Angeles Cage tried to set up a centre for musical research where musicians and engineers could carry on acoustic experiments of every kind, including electronics' (unpublished material). Was Cage perhaps a distant originator of IRCAM?
[3] Cf. Jameux, op. cit., pp. 212–13.

near future, though as yet we have only the first part. This work is the incarnation and amalgamation, as it were, of all the 'themes' dealt with in *Orientations*, for in it we have a work created from a basic material by which it is organized at every level, morphological and rhetorical. This has been made possible by the invention of a machine, the 4X, able both to generate in real time the proliferation of the original material so that the composer can make his various choices as he goes along, and can also be used directly in a performance, thus creating a *dialogue* between traditional instruments and electronic devices and freeing performers from dependence on tapes. This is in fact a new *instrument* able to produce musical *material* that satisfies the demands of an *imagination* thanks to an *institution* that has made it possible to invent and make use of the machine and to put on the expensive concerts that demonstrate its effectiveness. All these – IRCAM, the 4X and *Répons* – must be considered as the direct results of Boulez's original demand for an alliance between material and invention, an idea that had occurred to him as early as 1951 when reflecting on two Bach chorales.[1]

Thus Boulez appears – to use a phrase of the historian Fernand Braudel – as a musician 'de longue durée', 'far-reaching' in every sense, capable of conceiving musical evolution, his own career, or the growth of an individual work over a long period of time. The striking feature of this trajectory is not so much the diversity of the areas covered as the singleness of the aim. In the last piece in this book he writes, 'What may well have seemed a pointless sidetrack and a dangerous dispersion of energy has been simply the multiple manifestation of a single central obsession – the need to communicate this mystery, or at least fragments of the mystery that one thinks one has discovered oneself' (p. 526).

Multiple activities, then – composer, essayist, lecturer, conductor, teacher of analysis, teacher of conductors, organizer of concerts, director of a research institute – Boulez has been them all. At each period of his life the same varied activities recur; whether at the Domaine musical, in Baden-Baden, in the USA or at IRCAM he has always spent his time composing, commenting, explaining, communicating – and always in the service of a single idea, his vision of the evolution of the language of music and his search for new ways of furthering it.

First and foremost, then, he strikes us as a *whole* person. Few musicians except Wagner have made such a mark on all aspects of musical, and para-musical, life; and there are very few today who combine a comprehensive view of the history of the musical language with – as a rider to this – a passion to recover, in a contemporary idiom, the lost cohesion of tonality after the progressive disassociation of parameters in the music of Stravinsky,

---

[1] 'Von Himmel hoch' and 'Vor Deinem Thron tret' ich hiermit', cf. *Relevés d'apprenti*, pp. 22–3.

Schoenberg and Berg. We have seen Boulez's whole thinking, as we can follow it in these *Orientations*, converging on his present work.

We can also follow the development of his ideas in the other field of expression in which he has not yet found the answer to all his problems, vocal music. The evolution of Boulez's ideas about the relations between music and the human voice has been both more uneven and also more ambiguous, particularly in the case of opera. There is no difficulty as long as it is only a question of instruments and the voice, and in fact *Pli selon pli* provides the answer – it is possible to combine the two on the *structural* level (pp. 177–82). With *Sprechgesang* matters become rather more complicated. What exactly did Schoenberg want? *Le Marteau sans maître* is in fact Boulez's answer to the problems of *Pierrot lunaire* (p. 330). As far as opera is concerned, Boulez had no real interest in it before he met Wieland Wagner (p. 244), and had even denounced the degeneracy of the whole form. But first Wieland (p. 240), and then Chéreau, showed him the possibility of co-ordinating stage and orchestra, and he then pointed to the need for exploring new lyrical forms (p. 485). Reading *Orientations*, we catch glimpses of what could well be Boulez's next major work after *Répons*, a project which may well give the lie to *Wozzeck* being 'the last opera'. For a long time he has dreamed of setting a libretto by Jean Genet, and since Genet is no longer writing, Boulez and Patrice Chéreau have discussed an operatic adaptation of Genet's *Les Paravents* (*The Screens*). He has already thought about the structure of the work and how he could use *la lutherie électronique*. Boulez may have chosen *Les Paravents* because it contains a striking image to which he has referred on several occasions (as on p. 495) – that of the dead breaking through paper screens ... Death, was that all?

There is in fact a certain concern with death throughout Boulez's music and his writing – the 'Tombeau' of *Pli selon pli, ... Explosante-fixe* ... in memory of Stravinsky, *Rituel in Memoriam Bruno Maderna* and the 'funeral march' in *Répons*[1] – not to mention the memorial or obituary notices for the men who have been landmarks in his life – Steinecke, founder of the Darmstadt courses; Varèse; Scherchen and Rosbaud, the great conductors; Adorno; Strobel, who invited him to the Südwestfunk at Baden-Baden; Maderna. These pieces are all to be found in the second half of Part Three.

The place that death occupies in Boulez's mind may very well be simply that of a counterpart to his enormous activity. There are, in fact, two ways of approaching totality, the absolute – the positive, which means a maze of activities all directed to a single aim, and the negative, that irreversible suspension of time ('Zum Raum wird hier die Zeit' – 'Here time becomes

---

[1] According to Jameux, op. cit., p. 442.

space') which gives final and eternal form to that maze, the edifices and the undertakings of a lifetime.

In this the main outline of Boulez's ideas recalls another great twentieth-century explorer, Lévi-Strauss, who has always seemed to me basically a writer and a poet. At the end of *L'Homme nu* (*The Naked Man*) we find him meditating, against the background of his ethnological knowledge, on the great opposing forces that appear in all mythologies, and in life itself, and are resolved only in nothingness:

> The basic opposition, root spring of all the others in which mythologies abound, is the one that Hamlet states in the form of an alternative, which already implies too credulous an attitude. For between being and not-being human beings have no choice. A force of mind, which is part and parcel of his essential being and ceases only with his disappearance from the scene of the universe, forces him to accept two contradictory pieces of evidence, the collision between which makes his brain reel and, in order to counter the shock, generate an endless series of further, secondary distinctions. These never resolve the initial contradiction, but simply reproduce and perpetuate it on increasingly smaller scales ... (p. 621).

If a reader of *Orientations* were to ask me what I considered to be the fundamental characteristic of Boulez's thinking I should not have any hesitation in saying, 'The binary principle on which it is organized.' It is this instinctive cast of mind that gives these *Orientations* their individual character. Even a more or less random list of pairs of 'palpable categories', without any regard for context, will reveal the general lines along which Boulez's mind works – material/invention, past/future, choice/chance, discipline/freedom, strictness/improvisation, rational/irrational, order/disorder, necessary/unpredictable, deliberation/surprise, firmness/flexibility, precise/imprecise, conscious effort/free proliferation, stability/transformation, kernel/development, continuity/discontinuity, partitioning/through-composing, construction/destruction, striated/amorphous, macrostructure/microstructure, global/local, definite/indefinite, centrality/absence...

The possible explanation of this persistent 'binary' habit of mind may be found in the fact that it is the quickest and most direct way of approaching the *totality* of any subject. Not that this perpetual dialectic in Boulez's thinking denotes actual opposition between any two pairs. Like every dialectician, Boulez is able to transcend his own contrasts, by making *transitions* (for example from striated to smooth time) and by making fluctuations in tempi, but most importantly in the actual character of his works. It is here, in his music, that chance alternates with necessity, and it is in the irreversible lapse of duration time that all these contrasting ideas are actually incorporated, poetry uniting with music and conventional instruments with electronic devices. It is here that we find structures and contradictions finally and indissolubly linked, allowing on occasion for the necessary margin of flexibility. And the works themselves are marked by this same dualism, whether it be in their binary organization (First Sonata, *Structures* for two pianos, Third Sonata); in their forms, e.g. the constant use of the versicle and response of traditional antiphony (*Structures Ia*, *Structures II*, *Rituel* and most certainly *Répons*); in their basic plan (*Constellation/Miroir*, *Antiphonie*, *Doubles* the mirror of *Domaines*, No. 9 of *Le Marteau* as the double of No. 5); in the frequent dialogue between soloist and groups (*Domaines*, *Rituel*, *Répons*), or between conventional instruments and electronic devices (*Poésie pour pouvoir*, . . . *Explosante-fixe* . . ., *Répons*).

And so we are left with Boulez's musical works, where contradictions are faithfully resolved and the transitoriness of things overcome, but which must themselves inevitably be abandoned to an uncertain future.

*   *   *

The selection and annotation of the material is based on a bibliography published by Jean-Pierre Derrien in 1970 (*Musique en jeu*, No. 1, pp. 125–7), and Josef Häusler's German editions of Pierre Boulez's writings: *Werkstatt-Texte* (Frankfurt, Propyläen, Verlag Ullstein, 1972) and *Anhaltspunkte* (Stuttgart–Zürich, Belser-Verlag, 1975). Further references have been drawn from Michael Fink's bibliography (*Current Musicology*, No. 13, 1972, pp. 135–50) and from the article 'Boulez' by G. W. Hopkins in the *New Grove*. Dominique Jameux's *Pierre Boulez* (Paris, Fayard, 1984; currently being translated by Susan Bradshaw for publication by Faber in England and Harvard in America) has been of constant use in verifying the biographical details in this preface. Footnote references are always, to the best of my knowledge, to first publication. The order of the pieces in the second French edition (1984) has been slightly modified in this English edition in accordance with the well-judged suggestions of Patrick Carnegy (see explanation in the Translator's Note on p. 9); and there are three additional texts. I should like to express my thanks to the Music Faculty of Montreal University for their assistance in the transcription of Pierre Boulez's letters to John Cage. My thanks are also due to all those who have helped me to locate, discover and collect these pieces; Nancy Hartmann and Astrid Schirmer of IRCAM; Brigitte Marger of the Ensemble Intercontemporain; Suzanne Tézenas, President of the Domaine musical; Josef Häusler and David Noakes, respectively the German and American translators of Pierre Boulez, who provided me with texts that had not appeared in French; Philippe Albèra, who told me of a text that did not appear in the first French edition of this book; and finally Pierre Boulez himself, who placed his personal archive at my disposal.

PART ONE
The Shaping Imagination

FUNDAMENTALS

I

Aesthetics and the Fetishists[1]

It is a well-known fact that many lovers of culture are disinclined to any change in their habits, unwilling to give up of their own accord the tastes inculcated in them as children. This is an attitude capable of statistical demonstration, something needed in order to counter the mass of fallacious arguments often produced by such people in order to justify the poverty of their intelligence and taste by ostensibly rational means. In the face of such shameless bad faith nothing will do but a definite refutation, if only to cut these talkers down to size.

We belong to a generation generally unwilling to discuss aesthetic problems as such, and it is not so long ago that I myself launched a vigorous campaign against a number of expressions commonly bandied about on every occasion, relevant or otherwise. Among these phrases those that particularly turned my stomach were 'cosmos', 'human', 'man's communion with the world', 'on the human scale' – all employed with nauseating frequency in the discussion of matters themselves either contemptible or at best trifling in importance. To us the older generation seem to have pursued aesthetic 'summations' with an almost frantic eagerness, producing a host of 'schools' and 'groups' distinguished from each other only by vague poetic principles as poor in definition as in content. This monstrous appetite reached terrifying proportions between the two wars, and the years between 1920 and 1940 produced a veritable crop of slogans – they really do not deserve to be called aesthetic aims or plans – to conceal the pathetic absence of true invention. The name of Bach was invoked and there was talk of some ideally purified 'classicism'. Others took refuge in 'the cult of the fairground and the music-hall', or in 'functional' music (the so-called *Gebrauchsmusik*), in music for the masses and so on, all dishes so laboriously concocted that they turn the stomach. And what was beneath all these fanciful shifts except a determination, a really remarkably persistent determination, whatever form it took, to avoid facing fundamentals? Camouflaged beneath all these

[1] 'L'esthétique et les fétiches', revised text of a lecture given in 1961. Published in *Panorama de l'art musical contemporain*, ed. C. Samuel, Paris, Gallimard, 1962.

different and fundamentally meaningless phrases lay an idea of 'style' totally mistaken from the very beginning and really devoid of all meaning. We have witnessed too many bankruptcies in this field to miss the salutary warning that they contain against any return to errors of this kind. We are now aware of the fundamental mistake of concealing beneath the word 'style' a dichotomy between form and content, technique and expression. This distinction, which was a favourite with aestheticians of the old school, has been proved to be groundless and furthermore quite inapplicable to the actual facts of musical language. It is no more than a purely academic distinction bitterly insisted on by official traditionalists who have lost all contact with reality.

Music is an art that has no 'meaning': hence the primary importance of structures that are properly speaking linguistic, given the impossibility of the musical vocabulary assuming a simply communicative function. I do not need to insist on the double function of language itself, which on the one hand serves for direct, day-to-day communication while forming on the other the basis of intellectual and – more especially – poetic elaboration. The use of words by a poet clearly differs fundamentally from that by two persons engaged, for example, in an everyday conversation. In music, on the other hand, 'word' and idea are identical.

What is music then? It is at the same time an art, a science and a craft. 'Art' is a convenient abbreviation for 'means of expression': this must be the only point on which everyone is agreed without preliminary discussion. It is with the words science and craft that misunderstandings, and hostilities, begin. There can, however, be no denying that a musician is both an intellectual and a craftsman. If people call me an intellectual, I cannot take it as an insult, however offensively intended – very much the opposite! I have never really understood why it should be thought the first duty of a musician, and particularly a composer, to relegate his intelligence to a place among the dangerous, if not actually pernicious, accessories of his personality. He surely has the same right as his other 'colleagues in creation' to use his mind. If a poet is allowed to question himself, there can be no reason that I can see why a musician should not be allowed his 'meditations'. It is certainly true that he has no specific gift for the easy handling of language; but even so, and although his speculations may be clumsily directed, he cannot in all honesty be refused the right to indulge in them, or to call on the methods of analysis to assist him.

On the other hand there is no fear of his forgetting that he is also a craftsman, particularly if he is concerned in the performance of his own works. Conductors and performers prepared to risk themselves among the (so-called) mysteries of contemporary music are so few and far between that the composer, whether he likes it or not, has to summon up the courage to take the plunge himself. This is, in fact, the best of all schools; for direct, personal contact with the raw material of music can only improve his mastery of the art. He will discover for himself that music has no real existence except in direct communication. How many non-professionals are able to read a score? Only a tiny percentage, of course; and yet, if the truth be told, compositions should never be judged except by concrete experience. Scores, then, are diagrams that it is imperative to 'realize' – to bring into concrete existence, that is to say – if an audience is to have an effective share in the ideas elaborated by the composer. In fact I adhere to these three aspects of music – as art, science and craftsmanship – which I regard as indissolubly linked in a single, complex unit.

Having stated my own position, I can now enumerate the principal arguments that the unrepentant fetishists bring against it. These gentry do not bother to vary their tunes, which are repeated virtually unchanged during some six centuries of musical evolution in Western Europe. I will state them bluntly in order to expose the poverty of their quality:

1   Too much science, no sensibility (too much art, no heart)
2   Desire to be original at all costs, hence artificiality and exaggeration
3   Loss of contact with the public owing to excessive individualism
4   Refusal to accept history and the historical perspective
5   Lack of respect for the natural order

This meagre litany drones on from century to century, for our fetishists are unfortunately loath to change their idols, though these have not so far proved very effective. Can it be that they are in fact impotent? In primitive societies, according to the ethnologists, there are some tribes that turn and rend fetishes that have failed to answer their prayers, and choose new ones, in the hope that these will have learned by experience and will dispense their favours more scrupulously than their predecessors. It seems that our civilized world is more easily contented, since our medicine-men go on shaking the same old rattles regardless of their proved inefficacy.

Let me take them one by one.

Too much science, no sensibility

Music is a science as much as an art. How is it possible to study the history of music except, primarily and essentially, through the evolution of its forms, its morphology, and its syntax? How can a musicologist determine the co-ordinates of a work without first studying its morphology? In the case of Western Europe it was the invention of polyphony that was the great revelation: *organum* – the technique of two-part counterpoint, that is to say – is the basic phenomenon that initiated an irreversible process of evolution specific to the Western European tradition. The musical history of the Middle Ages may be described as the progressive adoption of a certain number of principles held in common. There is no need to insist on the precise differences between *ars antiqua*, *ars nova*, the beginnings of the 'imitative' style, the gradual elaboration of polyphonic laws. The salient features of the story are all related to morphology, to syntax and to rhetoric. What can we see besides? Modality insensibly becomes tonality and rhythm evolves on a parallel plane. The preponderance of vertical control determines the laws of tonality as we find them manifested in Rameau's *Traité de l'harmonie* and in Bach's '48'. Tonality in turn produces its own forms, a fixed framework within which the hierarchy of values is determined by a kind of Copernican order. As time passes, tonal functions are progressively downgraded until they are totally suppressed, as is the case today. The rhythmic system undergoes a parallel transformation. The Greek metres, which had served as a basis in the early years, are gradually dropped in favour of a variable metrical system partly adapted from non-European models. This short historical survey provides firm evidence to prove that it is absolutely impossible to describe the facts of musical evolution without taking into account all its stylistic components.

I cannot remember which of the ethnologists it was who said that 'from the design of an amphora it is possible to reconstitute a whole civilization': but this amounts to an assertion that the most precise characterization of any civilization is to be found in the aesthetic qualities of its products, the curve of its arabesques, its preference among colours. This is a recognition of the degree to which 'morphology' is important in the general history of civilization.

Linguistic studies follow exactly the same pattern. How is a Greek text dated, for instance? Generally speaking by the study of its grammatical features, and secondarily by the historical references it contains. It is by this same study of grammatical features that we can date a musical composition, at least approximately. There are not many musicologists who maintain a live contact with contemporary music without going back on the basic principles of musicology and refusing to face their logical consequence. It is amusing to observe how the majority follow scientific principles, as we have defined them, in their historical studies but promptly abandon those principles when it comes to the music of today, because they do not and cannot understand it. They do not even try honestly to follow the principles on which their studies are based. The attitude of these censors, who grandly claim the right to pass judgement on the music of today without first turning their attention to the evolution of the musical language, is in fact beneath contempt.

The first fetish to be destroyed is that of the 'creative message'. Only too often we hear or read that the quality of a work depends first and foremost on 'what the composer has to say', regardless of the means he may choose. What are we to understand by this phrase? And how in fact can a composer conceive his 'message' without a morphology – a formal scheme – capable of communicating it to the listener? This whole concept of an abstract 'message' is in fact no more than a cheap sophistry, employed only to conceal a profound misunderstanding, or indeed complete ignorance, of the circumstances of a particular historical period and, more generally, of the means of expression at the composer's disposal. This sort of myopia is a relic of romanticism in its pathetic final stages, and it reveals an inability to understand the real relationship between vocabulary and expression. I must admit that any sensibility that catches cold at the slightest draught of intellectual air seems to me to be in a pretty poor way.

Desire to be original at all costs, hence artificiality and exaggeration

It is generally agreed that evolution has become increasingly rapid, and that the world is desperately pursuing novelty whereas earlier generations were content for much longer with a language that had arrived at a certain stage in its development, and originality – within certain conventions – was regarded as a kind of extra bonus. Even the dreaded 'scientific' arguments have been adduced to prove this: 'In a mere hundred years we have passed from the horse to the jet plane, whereas the horse had sufficed from the remotest past until the nineteenth century. We find a dramatic similarity in the case of music which, in a hundred years, has passed from Beethoven to Webern.' Quite apart from the fact that 'at a given distance a number of different mountain ranges form a single horizon' this way of looking at history suggests a nostalgia for a 'paradise lost' that really belongs to the province of psychoanalysis. It certainly has only the most tenuous connection with reality.

As I see it, history is divided into periods of evolution and periods of mutation, or, in other words, periods of conquest and periods of stabilization. History is not a well-oiled machine that advances smoothly along rails composed of masterpieces, as they would have us believe. There was bitter fighting between the champions of *ars nova* and *ars antiqua*, and feelings ran just as high when, in Monteverdi's time, the pure polyphonic style of the madrigal was replaced by the *aria accompagnata*. Nearer our own day the writings of Rameau and Jean Le Rond d'Alembert are a reminder of the violent differences of opinion aroused by the theory of tonality, very like those aroused later (and even today) by the new principles of serial organization. At every point in history where there has been a mutation in the vocabulary of music we discover evidence – almost, as it were, geological evidence – of bitter disputes. Without going into more detail I will remind you of a few of the most celebrated instances – the decretal of Pope John XXII against *ars nova* (1324), condemning the polyphonic treatment of plainsong, the hocket and *cantus lascivus*; Canon Artusi's attack on Monteverdi; the duels between Rousseau and Rameau, Pfitzner and Schoenberg. All those who suffer from a nostalgia for the past as a 'paradise lost' react violently against a future that seems to them to be a terrifying nightmare.

We really must accustom ourselves to the fact that there are periods of mutation in the history of music, and that these periods question the very principles that, after much discussion, have been generally accepted and then, by sheer reiteration, have gradually lost their vital significance. The evolution of any language obeys the universal law by which energy dimin- ishes; there is an entropy in the successive systems that have established themselves during the course of centuries. This evolution, however, was for long considered as a kind of absolute progress, and the style of an older generation was regularly taken to be demonstrably inferior to that which replaced it. The history of ecclesiastical architecture is one instance, among many, of this belief in 'progress'. As is well known, Romanesque wall paintings were often covered with stucco, and many Romanesque churches actually destroyed or mutilated, when the Gothic style triumphed. The Renaissance regarded Gothic buildings as barbarous, and so it went on until the nineteenth century. More generally speaking, each period believed that its predecessors were still clumsy, that its own means of expression were more beautiful and more nearly perfect and that the future would produce a beauty of the same kind and even nearer to being 'absolute'. This belief was so naïve, so innocent and so little handicapped by the idea of 'an artistic heritage' that it was actually productive rather than otherwise.

It was the same with music. Each age spoke with a certain condescension of its predecessors, believing them to be the 'primitives' of its own, more advanced art. Eighteenth-century comparisons of Lully and Rameau are a good example of this mentality. Nobody would then have dreamed of questioning this idea that music grows increasingly richer and progresses indefinitely towards a kind of future Eldorado. Nowadays it would not be easy to adopt such an exclusive attitude. We have learned to regard the relationship between our own means of expression and those of the past as a kind of evolution rather than as an asymptotic progress, and we can no longer be accused of an arrogant attitude towards the past. Furthermore it is not only our attitude to the past of our own culture that has changed, but also our relationship to non-European cultures, as forming part of a collective whole. There is no longer any place in a demonstrably relative universe for the idea of progress as a kind of one-way movement.

A Gregorian melody is unquestionably more complex than a tonal melody, since its structural pointing is much more subtle. We cannot speak of a 'progress' from monody to polyphony, only of a shifting of interest that enriches one element and impoverishes another, gain in one area compen- sating for loss in another. Regarded in this way, there is a marked resembl- ance between this 'robbing Peter to pay Paul' and the transformation of creative energy. In the same way tonality replaced the modes because it was able to answer more pressing needs, such as the extension of universally applicable norms; but this was only by sacrificing the wealth of individual characteristics belonging to the modes. From one point of view modal music was in fact more closely differentiated than tonal. But the rational appeal of tonality (and particularly the consequent codification of vertical, i.e. harmonic, relationships) and the new possibility of generalizing – even standardizing – musical relationships was essential to the further development of the art. Without tonality music might well have either become repetitious or else declined into a kind of mannerism overwhelmed by sterile complications. The serial principle, which is that of a hierarchy established anew in each work, and not a pre-existing system like that of tonality, has given the contemporary composer the ability to create musical structures that are constantly evolving, though it is only by sacrificing the power of immediate generalization characteristic of tonal functions. It is worth observing, by the way, that scientific thinking has evolved in exactly the same way. Contemporary writers on science differ radically from their predecessors in their attitude to 'the laws of nature', for instance, and even to such 'abstract' subjects as pure mathematics. We should therefore be fully aware of our responsibilities and recognize that we are in fact links in an evolution that will continue through us.

There is a further point important to remember – that we in the West no longer live in our own closed cultural circuit. The phrase 'musée imaginaire', coined by André Malraux, achieved its wide popularity because, I believe, it expresses a deep and widespread feeling that knowledge of the arts – and particularly the plastic arts – has been strikingly extended both historically and geographically. It is no longer possible for the West to make an exclusive claim to creative intelligence, and any remaining illusions of this kind bring disastrous sociological consequences. The mere fact that music was for a long time more difficult to export than paintings and sculptures explains the fact that less attention has been paid to this aspect of non-European cultures. Now, however, recordings and tapes and the visits of artistic companies from – among other places – Japan, China and Bali have actually confronted us with the music of civilizations that we once rashly called 'primitive'. Their extreme refinement clearly comes from ideas and principles very unlike those of the West, but just as logical and coherent and quite as capable of 'expressiveness' and 'beauty'. After all, we must remember that our own language, though it needs no justifying to us, makes quite a different impression on other civilizations.

Comparison of our own music with that of other cultures must surely make us wary of talking about the 'eternity' or 'supremacy' of any of our musical laws. Their value is relative, in time as well as in space; and they may be reduced, in fact, to the best method discovered, at a given time and in given circumstances, of organizing a language coherent enough to be effective and flexible enough to give maximum expression to the intellectual and emotional potential of the age concerned. An obsession with originality at all costs is a kind of supplementary fetishism, by which those who have no deep understanding of musical evolution try to force the pace of the necessary and inevitable transformation of traditional techniques.

Loss of contact with the public owing to excessive individualism

A great deal of nonsense has been talked about the artist's so-called 'ivory tower'. This is a favourite theme with so-called conservative champions, and the gap between the composer and his public always crops up in even the shortest interview or questionnaire. The example always quoted is that of the royal courts of the eighteenth century where, we are assured, there was no problem of communication between composer and listener. The humblest amateur was capable of understanding the style of the day and the same language was shared by all alike, including kings. Those were the heroic days, they say, when Frederick gave Bach the famous 'royal theme', though they forget to mention that it was Bach, not Frederick, who actually composed *The Musical Offering*, while, as for the theme itself, the history of its various transformations has never been clearly established . . .

The real facts cannot be reduced in this way to a formula, and the relations between the individual and society cannot really be classed in this fetishistic manner, as immediate and direct. Seen less simplistically, the truth is that individual and society differ in their degree of development. Every age expresses itself through the individual most able himself to assume the historical responsibilities of the society of which he forms a part. It may therefore happen that society does not immediately recognize itself in its own representative, just as a sitter may fail to recognize himself in an artist's portrait of him, in which he fails to discover the familiar traits of what he believes to be his own face. (Such failures go back at least as far as Rembrandt and are by no means confined to modern painters.) If we pursue the comparison, society rejects the individual responsible for this 'portrait' and refuses to accept his angle of vision, his 'point of view'; and this leads to resentment and hostility on both sides. Bitter though this disagreement may be, it is, I believe, only a question of the two parties being 'out of phase' with each other, and the next generation will fairly soon correct the unhappy relationship between society and the individual. So much so that it will seem hard to believe that any age could fail to grasp immediately the deep ties existing between society and the individual who has succeeded in 'transfiguring' it. It is impossible for us to imagine the end of the nineteenth century without such names as Debussy, Cézanne, Van Gogh, Mallarmé, Rimbaud and so forth, who seem to us the perfect expression of their age. But we are in fact reversing the situation as it was experienced by such men during their lifetime. It is in individuals who were in practice refused general admiration, and in some cases even any corresponding social recognition, that we find the true portrait, or model, of an epoch. Society may refuse to accept them in their lifetimes, or may rehabilitate them only in old age, but in either case will become identified with them willy-nilly.

Let me return for a moment to my earlier comparison. Like the archaeologist with the fragment of amphora, so we too discover the essential picture of an age by picking up a handful of names. Proust observed that, when we look at the portraits of the past, what strikes us most is their way of dressing, the manner in which they wore their hair or trimmed their moustaches; and that such things strike us so forcibly that we find it difficult to distinguish a nobleman from a workman or an ordinary citizen from an artist, because their distinguishing features are outweighed by those that they have in common. It is exactly the same with individual artists who, at first sight, seem to be complete strangers to the society surrounding them. However eccentric their attitudes may seem, however violent the controversy aroused by their works, however flagrant the distortions they may have permitted themselves, all that we are aware of in historical perspective is – as Proust puts it – no more than their clothes and the way they wear their hair or their moustaches. So what, in the end, remains of the fetish of 'excessive individualism'? However much he exaggerates, an individual reflects the age in which he lives. There is not, to my knowledge, anything exaggerated about mediocrity. The only passion shown by the mediocre is their determination to defend ruins, nor have they ever truly characterized or revealed anything whatever.

Refusal to accept history and the historical perspective

I have said enough about the importance of the evolution of language to make it unnecessary to return to that point. I must add only that today's new discoveries easily take their place within the perspective of history, but that perspective must be a living one and not one that is frozen in academic commonplaces. For the fundamental question we must ask ourselves is where the true tradition is to be found. As Theodor Adorno wisely said, there is more tradition in the *Bagatelles* of Webern's opus 9 than, for instance, in Prokofiev's *Classical Symphony* – by which he meant that reproducing a model from the past is meaningless compared with drawing the consequences implicit in the language inherited by the artist. You may know the story of the painter who was asked which great figure in the history of art had exercised the greatest influence on him and answered, wittily enough, 'It is not history that influences me, but I who influence history.' That was of course a joke, but a joke that reflects an important attitude to historical perspective. There is, in fact, a dialectical relationship between history and the individual, history certainly providing the individual with a challenge but the individual in his turn refashioning history, which will never be quite the same after him. A 'genius' is both prepared by history and also unexpected. He is prepared because it is impossible for him to be independent of the age in which he lives. As Malraux said, a man becomes a painter by looking at pictures and a musician by listening to music, for it is impossible to become a musician from nothing. The difference in the paths pursued by different civilizations proves this. A child who is familiar from an early age with the traditional Chinese theatre apprehends the phenomenon of 'music' in quite a different way from one whose auditive faculties are first stirred by Bach, Mozart and Beethoven. This conditioning is inescapable, whatever efforts may be made to escape from it. However wide the perspective in which we may view other traditions and however deep our knowledge of them, we cannot avoid the fact that Western music is rooted in our very beings and our experience, since it was the whole conventional system of Western music that first attracted us and stirred our reactions. We might perhaps symbolize the relationship between a creative artist and tradition by a kind of propulsion from within, and by means of, a certain milieu. Let me quote Pierre Souvtchinsky's formulation of the matter:

> Perhaps it is useless to apply any other method to the history of the arts than that which we apply to political and social history. It is even more true of the arts that their history must be understood both as an uninterrupted process and also as a sequence of discontinuous and distinct facts and events. Even if we allow due importance to the role played in the development of genius by social and technical evolution, if we view the phenomenon of 'culture' as a dialectical process that is apparently continuous, and if we recognize to the full the importance of the milieu and the age as both determining the creative formation of one generation and acting as a stimulus to the formation of the type and mentality of the next, it is still essential to recognize that, despite all such 'preparation', the appearance of a great creative artist is always something unexpected, something unpredictable.

It is easy to find support for this theory. Take the example of Debussy – totally unexpected, though 'prepared', 'conditioned' by Wagner. Debussy's vocabulary is unthinkable except as springing from Wagner's chromatic evolution, just as his aesthetic is unthinkable except as a violent reaction against Wagner's. It is Debussy who is Wagner's true 'heir', not the composers who copied the *Ring*. The similar affiliation of Webern and Mahler is equally surprising and equally significant.

It is this quality of unexpectedness that defeats the fetishists, because they lack the instinct, the necessary antennae. Their idea of historical evolution is very far from the facts of the case. Their lack of imagination makes them unable to conceive of history except as a kind of egg in which they long to enclose themselves, but unfortunately history does not take into consideration their museum tastes. Imagination, 'the queen of the faculties', will always make fun of fetishisms, will understand how to interpret tradition and will thus provoke the 'creative shock' of which Souvtchinsky speaks. Far from being a refusal of history, the unpredictable and the unforeseen are its most radiant manifestations.

And now for the last of the 'fetishists'' charges:

Lack of respect for the natural order

This is really a question of authority, even theology! If this famous 'natural order' really existed, it would be found in every civilization, and this is something very far from being the case. Each civilization has elaborated its own musical theories based, of course, on the facts of acoustics but with numerous adjustments and corrections, since the facts alone are far too complex to reduce to practical proportions. It would even be possible to write a history of music based on the different theoretical 'corrections' of acoustical data employed by different cultures. Without going outside Europe for examples, we have only to examine the theoretical works that have appeared as landmarks in the history of our own Western music, and we shall discover that musical theory varies in direct relationship to acoustics, as is shown by the succession of hypotheses that have dominated the musical scene since the eighteenth century. Scientists are quite willing to recognize this as far as scientific laws are concerned, as one of them – Léon Brouillin – has shown:

> When do we claim to 'know' a physical phenomenon? We have this flattering impression, in fact, when we are able to imagine a model that, in accordance with already tested laws, will successfully 'explain' results that we have observed in a new series of experiments. To understand a phenomenon, therefore, means to bring it into line with what we already know . . . The 'laws' that suggest themselves to the scientist's imagination give results that are correct within certain limits. Any attempt to extrapolate too far from them will reveal divergences that necessitate a revision and correction of the 'law' concerned, and this often means a complete changing of the model . . . To speak of natural laws as though they existed absolutely, independent of man, is a kind of confidence trick. Nature is something far too complex for the human mind to grasp. We observe isolated fragments of it and then imagine representative 'models' that are simple enough for us to make use of.

Brouillin goes on to emphasize 'the essential part played by the human imagination in the invention (and I deliberately refrain from using the word "discovery") and formulation of scientific laws'.

The situation in the case of acoustics is almost precisely identical, as many examples from the past will show. You have only to read d'Alembert to discover that the tonal system is adapted from the laws of acoustics as formulated in his day, an adaptation involving a formidable number of approximations, as we know. Neither the minor triad nor equal temperament are 'natural' so much as familiar to our ears. The difficulty of reconciling the human voice, in particular, with 'natural resonance' troubled both Rameau and d'Alembert, whose explanations remain very largely on the academic level. The theory of tonality is in fact both natural and artificial and simply demonstrates the character of the eighteenth-century scientific imagination.

Today we have at our command not only the whole body of 'natural' sounds but the vast area of electro-acoustic sound sources, and it is therefore difficult to imagine why the laws of natural resonance should remain an article of faith. Acousticians themselves do not hesitate to reconsider radically the problems arising from their experiments, and their solutions provide the composer with his. What other attitude is logically possible? What authority can decide that one theory should be eternally preferred to another? Is there any inquisitor so sure of his case that he can attempt to exorcize a *diabolus in musica* both so tenacious and so protean in form? What answer do these musical theologians give to scientists who maintain that 'to speak of natural laws is a kind of confidence trick'? Why not be honest and admit that they are clinging to the familiar in order to preserve the 'flattering impression' that they 'understand'. To go on from there to promulgate dogmas is a temptation too strong to be resisted. We can answer them by adapting Paul Valéry and saying, 'We musical systems are now aware that we are mortal.' A Roland for an Oliver!

Every system is simply a working hypothesis for the solution of the problems confronting an individual epoch, a working hypothesis that will be replaced by another once the old hypothesis has proved insufficient at any given point. Of one thing we may be certain: that the creative imagination will never fail to provide the 'models' of which Brouillin speaks. The periods of evolution and mutation will be determined either by extrapolating from the laws of one system or by a radical revision involving the creation of a new system.

All things considered, it is oddly paradoxical to talk of misplaced arrogance when describing what is actually no more than an awareness of the limitations of the creative artist. Those who preach about the 'natural order' are driven by some congenital blindness to misunderstand the most elementary laws of thinking and to hurl major excommunications, which are effective only in their own eyes. Some of their remarks, qualified by a kind of bitter superiority or by the brusque finality of a sergeant major's orders, really exhibit more passion than intelligence. 'Serial technique will never enter ... practical music' (it might almost have been 'the kingdom of heaven' reserved for the elect, to whom they never for a moment doubt that they themselves belong) ... 'Serialism has already been out of fashion ... for forty years' (tonality is more than two centuries old, but one contradiction more or less hardly matters) ... 'We shall soon see a return to tonality.' (What a relief it will be for them to have been right all the time, and finally to see the prayers of the righteous answered and the wicked punished! They will be able to say, 'Order reigns in Warsaw!' like the Russian general reporting the putting down of the Polish revolution of 1830.) Well, there will certainly never be a return to tonality. We shall probably move towards some kind of expanded serialism; but not being gifted with prophecy, I cannot say anything more precise than that. And in any case what a ghastly bore it would be if we knew the course that history will take! So let the Pharisees maintain their hot line with the Almighty and put the cosmos in their pockets! Unless they have recourse to social and political coercion, none of their precautions will succeed in capturing the order of nature! Woyzeck suspected the truth when he said 'mit der Natur ist's was ander's' and Hamlet too, with his 'There are more things in heaven and earth, Horatio,/Than are dreamt of in your philosophy.'

What remains to be said? Nothing, except perhaps, to admit that all argument is fruitless when faced with the fetishists who proclaim tradition, nature, the human heart, moderation, 'keeping in touch', perspective, order, moderation, 'keep left, but not too far', moderation in originality, propriety, clarity and once again moderation – the moderation of eternal laws, of imprescriptible rights, moderation, moderation, moderation . . . I really must stop. Let these whirling dervishes enjoy their palinodes, as they go on turning, like demented tops, in the narrow circle of their petty obsessions. Let us meanwhile cross that threshold over which there stands inscribed the title of René Char's *Poème pulvérisé* – 'Comment vivre sans inconnu devant soi?' 'How can one live with no unknown before one?'

2

Taste: 'The spectacles worn by Reason'?[1]

Of all the natural gifts taste is the most easy to recognize and the most difficult to explain. It would not be what it is if it could be defined, since it judges matters that are not in fact capable of being judged, serving – if such an idea is permissible – as a pair of spectacles to reason. It would be something like a charade to banish the word itself, and a charade that would be very difficult for the spectators to guess!

This ingenious effusion occurs in an article written for the *Encyclopédie* by Jean-Jacques Rousseau who, as you may remember, himself had a good 'tincture' of music, to use a popular expression of those days! But Rousseau was not content with this *mot* and attempted to discover a more exact definition of taste. 'Everyone', he says, 'has his own individual taste by which he establishes his own private scale of values among the things that appear to him good and beautiful'. In that case, of course, we should really abandon the discussion without more ado and this lecture would lose its point. Whatever we may do, whatever arguments we may use, we shall never – unless we are grossly intolerant – succeed in preventing anyone from having their own 'private scale of values'. You like the mountains, I like the sea; you like red wine, I like fish – it is a matter of taste! The very vagueness of what we mean by such remarks can very easily threaten our goodwill towards our neighbour.

And before I go any further, I must make a digression. What on earth, you may well be asking, made me choose this subject of 'taste'? I know that it is very French, and that only a Frenchman would allow himself to get entangled in the search for such a will-o'-the-wisp as 'taste', a search that is notoriously a fool's errand. No one has talked about 'taste' for years. Romanticism killed the very concept, which is purely intellectual and restrictive, totally incompatible with genius, which laughs at rules and taste, whether it be good or bad! The word really belongs to the eighteenth century and it is not surprising that you have to dig out the *Encyclopédie* in order to

---

[1] 'Le goût et la fonction', lecture given at Darmstadt in 1961. Published in *Tel quel*, Nos. 14 and 15, 1963, pp. 32–8 and 82–94.

discuss so antiquated and obsolete a notion. Well, I admit that it is indeed a long time since the days when Shakespeare was described as 'barbarous' and lacking in art and Jean-Jacques – once again! – allowed himself to speak of 'such remains of barbarity and bad taste as the porches of our Gothic churches, which only remain as a disgrace to those who went to the trouble of building them'. That proves at least one thing: that the taste of the age has changed. The Romantics' passion for the Gothic style and the horrors of so-called 'ecclesiastical' furniture have rather cooled our own feelings about the Gothic. In fact there are now some art historians who use terms very like those used by Jean-Jacques when they speak of the Gothic, only now it is in order to sing the praises of the Romanesque. In exactly the same way Greek art was abandoned for that of Sumer or the Tomayas, and Raphael's star paled beside that of Piero della Francesca, which began to glow with quite a new light. The list of such revolutions in taste is in fact endless.

I admit that taste often comes down to that 'good taste' which is the pretty, satin-lined coffin in which triumphant academicism tries to bury taste. But I am not prepared to watch these amiable academic Procrustes racking and chopping whatever does not fit their mediocre, 'average' standards. I would even go so far as to say that I regard 'good taste' as the direst of calamities, because it leads inevitably to artistic creation being considered as a branch of *haute couture*, a kind of 'special scents' department. We in France are too familiar with the harm done by this hedonistic approach – art as a refined form of sensuality, that is to say – not to be immune to that particular danger. Not that clothes and scent are to be despised: that kind of philistinism is merely stupid. Elegance is no more to be despised in music than in poetry. I like the sense in which mathematicians and physicists use the word 'elegant' when they apply it to a process of reasoning, a hypothesis or a proof. There is nothing frivolous in that kind of elegance, which is simply the ultimate manifestation of a difficulty mastered, the easy grace that conceals the very existence of difficulty. Elegance in this sense is a proof of 'good taste' that we can willingly accept, since it is in fact simply an extreme form of precision.

Here, then, we are faced with a number of different ideas, which, far from bringing us nearer to an exact definition of taste, make our task all the more difficult, because each of these ideas is double-edged. Is my taste inextricably linked to that of the period in which I happen to live? Or can I make my own personal contribution to its formation? Am I the victim of my age's good or bad taste? Am I to revolt and simply to analyse objectively all these criteria, which, it seems, I shall never succeed in mastering? Are we really so certain of what 'elegance' itself actually represents? According to Rousseau, 'One listener will value melodic simplicity while another will attach importance to signs of unusual workmanship: and each will give the name of "elegance" to his favourite "taste".' This seems only to complicate matters and to cause still further misunderstanding. Perhaps any further investigation of the matter is useless, and indeed at first sight it appears that it can only add to the existing confusion. This specious objection was foreseen by Rousseau, who says that differences of opinion 'come sometimes from differences in the dispositions of the individual's organs of perception, sometimes from his character – which inclines him to be more aware of one charm or one shortcoming than another – sometimes from differences of age or sex, which incline his interest one way or another. Since in every case the individual has only his own taste to set against his neighbour's, quarrelling on the subject is pointless.' Quarrel, then, we will not, but follow Rousseau's good advice in the matter. Yet how familiar such fruitless quarrels are: 'Stendhal is the man for me!' 'No, Balzac!' 'Mozart is the man for me!' 'No, Beethoven!' Does this mean that I incline to be tolerant in such matters? Not really! – for we are inclined to forget that the issue at stake in such quarrels lies quite outside any questions of quality, and that a great number of works simply do not come up for consideration owing to their inferior quality, which automatically eliminates them.

If this throws at least some light on the matter, it is still far from wholly clear. Rousseau says quite categorically: 'There also exists a general taste upon which all well-educated people are agreed; and it is to this alone that we can give the name of taste without any qualifications.' Does that perhaps bring us nearer to an answer? As both philosopher and musician, Rousseau seems to be approaching it when he writes that 'for the sufficiently educated there are matters on which agreement, and the reasons for that agreement, will be virtually unanimous: these are matters that are subject to rules'. Is that perhaps the solution to which we were coming? Agreement once reached on the rules to be observed and the canons of beauty, we shall have no difficulty in defining taste ... or, for that matter, in having it. The codification of beauty is an ancient ambition, and Aristotle has a numerous progeny. It would be so convenient to be able to rely on eternal principles and to finish once for all the discussion of what beauty, truth and naturalness are, and what they are not ... Unfortunately, however, we have seen that standards change and, however august they may be, fall victims to the law of entropy. As we know, 'What is true one side of the Channel ...' Both historically and geographically all the principles of aesthetics are variable, and the most one can say is that there are as many 'tastes' as there are canons of beauty. It is merely shifting the question and shirking the answer if we simply put the whole matter within the wider framework of different cultural evolutions, with which it is of course closely linked.

Though we may fail to isolate taste, can we hope at least to describe the 'man of taste', a concept that demands looser definition and less rigid criteria? According to Rousseau, 'Among the things that the artist and the connoisseur are agreed in finding good or bad, there are some in which they will find it impossible to find any rational and universally compelling justification for their opinion; and such opinions are the province of the 'man of taste'. There we have at least some negative indications, which suggest that the man of taste is a sort of creature gifted with a sixth sense that makes it unnecessary for him to give reasons either for his admiration or his disapproval. Shall this be the solution, then – simply declare myself a man of taste when I want to criticize any point of view that I consider mistaken? If so, I shall have to face considerable opposition. As we all know, common sense and taste are the most evenly distributed of all faculties – no one will admit to thinking that he has less common sense than his neighbour, and no one will consider it other than a gross insult if he is asked to admit to any inferiority in matters of taste. Try asking anyone, in any situation, however monstrous, whether he considers that his behaviour is in bad taste, and his face will immediately express either indignation, contempt or pity. If one admits to any small area of bad taste, one considers it as a very venial sin, something that one rather cultivates as being of no consequence, rather like a hobby at most. But in all the important, major matters of life one's taste is impeccable. It is no use, therefore, putting our confidence in this definition, since every individual with any right to a judgement considers himself also entirely within those rights in exercising his 'taste'. He has his; communities and nations have theirs. Who is the monster with such a high opinion of himself that he will declare his judgement superior to that of everyone else when, as we have seen, it is impossible for anyone to produce 'rational and universally compelling justification'? No one would dream of making such a claim.

How, then, are we to discover those who have more taste or less taste, or indeed those who may be said to be 'more or less' men of taste? In the case of such a democratic quality, is there perhaps a democratic approach to the question? Rousseau was of course a precursor of the Revolution and the Republic, and this is what he has to say: 'If unanimity is hard to find, the explanation lies in the fact that all men are not equally well educated, or in fact "men of taste", and that their priorities among natural beauties are often determined, arbitrarily, by prejudices of habit or education.' 'Natural beauties' is a very eighteenth-century term. Are we still so sure that they in fact exist? I suspect that, even more than 'taste', the word 'natural' has been ruthlessly expunged from our vocabulary and that we should find great difficulty in reintroducing it. Meanwhile we cannot help feeling trapped between 'matters that are subject to rules' and 'natural beauties'. In Rousseau's day, of course, there was a strong conviction that the best rule was the one that imitated 'Nature' . . . since then, though, 'nous avons changé tout cela'. We believe, very reasonably as it seems to me, that these famous rules are a means of putting us into the closest possible touch with the models that, for the moment, provide the best possible description of 'Nature'. Many of the eighteenth century's most cherished illusions have 'fled for ever', as sentimental song writers used to say. And so we believe that beauty – natural or otherwise – is a matter of arbitrary convention, of habit or education, as witness Jean-Jacques himself, with his talk of 'Gothic barbarism'!

Nevertheless Rousseau did leave us sceptics a final argument, though it is one that reveals either an excessive confidence in democracy or an exaggeratedly low opinion of the human race. He produces from up his sleeve, as it were, a method that would certainly delight the organizers of referendums and the statisticians: 'It is possible to go on for ever discussing "taste", because there is in fact only one that is true: but I can hardly see any other way of concluding the debate except a show of hands, if we are not ready to acknowledge Nature's silent prompting.' As far as he was concerned, this was an interested vote since it was to achieve the defeat of Rameau, whom he could not bear, and to proclaim the superiority of Italian music to French. Anyhow, we now know our fate, we blasphemers who refuse 'Nature' – the question of taste is to be decided by a show of hands. It is not really so odd, since it is what happens in fact at every concert, though on that occasion hands are clapped rather than raised. What else is applause but a community voting the ratification of its own taste? Every Tchaikovsky-lover at a Tchaikovsky concert is celebrating the cult of himself. He recognizes his own taste in that of the composer, congratulates himself on it, and when he applauds is applauding himself. Do we not do the same ourselves? We consider ourselves members of an élite whose tastes we share, and this complicity makes us applaud the same works. Our applause may contain a note of irony, but it is still ourselves that we are applauding. Go against the taste of whatever public it may be and you will be hissed. No one will bother to recognize his own taste in yours. Everyone who disagrees with you will make very sure that you are aware of the fact, and will insist that if your taste dominates the acts, his shall be represented in the entr'actes. It is no use your producing any number of proofs to convince your opponent, he will not listen to you, taste being outside the range of 'rational and universally compelling justification'.

Whether we approve of this form of democracy or not, it is an undeniable fact. Rousseau is quite clear about the matter: 'In fact, genius creates, but taste selects.' You have been warned, therefore. No genius will protect you from the working of these universal laws and their extravagant ratification. What, is genius not to be master of his own taste as he is of the universe? In whom are we to put our trust, then, since our scale of values (in fact, our 'taste') is determined by one genius after another? We must imagine some kind of *famulus genii*, like the *genius loci*, in order to rescue taste from hands powerful enough to break it: 'Too rich a genius needs a severe critic to ensure that he does not abuse his wealth. Great things may be achieved without taste [we are back to Shakespeare again] but it is taste that makes them interesting.' How, precisely? We are not told.

Once again we have come very near to an answer, but not reached it. How the great inventions of genius can be 'made interesting' by taste seems to be the first and most important question. Is it in fact possible to separate genius from taste? Is not taste an integral part of genius? For the moment let us content ourselves with this magic effect of taste without examining it further. Before we finish with Rousseau, however, let us bear in mind that this faculty – which bears a close resemblance to the old physicists' *phlogiston*, that element which was believed to 'burn by burning' – in fact unites composer, performer and public by means of a kind of initiation:

> It is taste that enables a composer to grasp the ideas of the poet and a performer to grasp the ideas of the composer. It is taste that provides each with what he needs in order to decorate and bring out the full sense of these ideas, and taste that enables the listener to respond emotionally to all these accepted proprieties.

Why not be honest and call these 'accepted proprieties' conventions? What is this quality which now seems to be becoming a mystery in the celebration of which public, interpreter and composer are invited to join in a common rite? It must be a very strong philtre, a very compelling code that can dominate the members of a group in this way and compel them to conform! Must it not in fact be something fundamental if it is able to correct genius itself – not in jest, either, but with at most a smile – and to serve as the password between composer and public? We must not exaggerate, however: we have not yet finished this article from the *Encyclopédie* or come to the end of our surprising discoveries. Remember that Rousseau was profoundly convinced that the order of natural beauty is superior to all others, and that the human heart responds more spontaneously the more deeply it is aware of Nature. He ends with a warning to observe the greatest prudence in the matter:

> Taste is not identical with sensibility. Great taste is by no means incompatible with a frigid temperament, and there are people who are insensitive to charm in a work of art, though carried away by real passion. It appears that taste is more concerned with the small expressions of feeling, and sensibility with the large.

Here, all of a sudden, we find the merits of taste reduced from those of a censor of genius to 'small expressions of feeling'. This is indeed a labyrinth beset with precipices! We may notice, however, two points that may perhaps be regarded as firmly established –

1 the rules governing any extended work, the principles observed, the conventions bounding it
2 the yield that we may expect from creative invention

Working from these we can try to define what we mean by taste, and this would incline us primarily to corroborate Rousseau's first definition, when he speaks of taste as 'the spectacles worn by reason'.

Composition is an activity that involves a large number of established conventions – mental, aesthetic and practical. The degree of evolution attained by the civilization to which we belong determines the systems of reference necessary to our existence, and we are therefore unavoidably influenced by society. Our role as individuals depends on our valuation of these conventions, on how far we accept or refuse them; and this in turn depends on the historical epoch in which we happen to live, a variable that I do not propose to discuss here. The individual may find the age in which he lives sympathetic or antipathetic, but newly established conventions will spread to a group which will in all probability increase in size. There too, there may well be downgradings, and it is by no means certain that those who contribute most to effecting a change in taste will not be remembered for that rather than for their aesthetic creed. We must therefore beware of making swift generalizations and of attaching 'taste' directly to works themselves when in fact it may simply mark the *shifting value* attached to works.

It remains true, however, that taste is a matter of convention, that it is confirmed or rejected by succeeding generations, that it may be forgotten or resurrected according to whether the original conventions that determined a work lose or regain their effective power. All works are essentially connected with the taste of the age that produced them, and from this point of view the whole production of any age is bound by the general conventions of that age, and is therefore an expression of the same 'taste'.

There now arises the question of quality, since works are not remembered simply because they are manifestations of some particular taste, except in the case of vanished civilizations, every product of which becomes a historical document. The further removed an age, the more difficult it becomes to judge the quality of its products, except for those who have made a special study of that age. It is almost, if not completely, impossible for the non-specialist, whose knowledge of the conventions of that age is incomplete or non-existent, to distinguish masterpieces from secondary works. This is particularly so if we have only fragments of a civilization, in which case there is no means of judging whether those fragments represent what is finest or most characteristic. Ethical considerations may produce further complications and are sometimes a barrier to appreciation. We judge any period by our own criteria and our own conventions. In fifty years' time Mayan sculpture and architecture will certainly be appreciated in a manner quite different from that of today, but they will never be contested as witnesses – documents in the highest sense – of a certain vision of the world as a whole, a system of thought establishing a link between the various products of Mayan civilization, which it justifies, even glorifies, and links together.

So far we have deliberately ignored the word 'function', and stuck to Rousseau's 'rules' and 'conventions'. The moment has now come to speak of function in order to generalize our point of view. What in fact are these rules and conventions to which we keep referring but structural functions? All revolutions in the history of the arts have come from functional changes or changes of functional direction. By this we understand not only the intrinsic functions of a means of expression, but also the function of this means of expression in a given society, the one being closely allied to the other. Every society gives birth to its own ceremonial and rituals according to its hierarchical structure, its religious or secular practices and its conception of diversion, or 'play' in the widest sense. The concert-hall is thus conceived as the setting for a rite, a 'Temple of Taste' as it might be . . . The form and the site of the ceremonial impose on music certain determining functions, which act as very precise limitations to musical taste, so precise indeed that changes in taste can clearly be related to changes in the function of music in a society. There is no doubt that a musician can influence the direction in which taste evolves, but it is equally true that his taste is subordinate to that of the age in which he lives. In other words, there is no such thing as *absolute* taste, but there are functions that determine taste, complex functions of environment and conditioning, and our reactions spring directly from them. 'Genius' consists, in this first phase, in a maximum awareness of these functions that bind the artist to society. After that it is of small importance whether, in his later developments, the artist finds himself 'in phase' with his age or not. He may identify himself as closely as possible with that age, in which case his creative powers will adapt themselves exactly to the circumstances in which he finds himself. He may, either by conscious analysis or by unconscious intuition, go beyond what seems to be the general character of his age and thus reveal functions that are latent; or equally he may deliberately view that age in historical perspective and see local and temporal functions in a wider context. In fact an artist may either identify himself with the taste of his age, go beyond them, or project them on the past.

It need hardly be said that these different attitudes are not to be found thus neatly docketed in the case of each individual artist. There is no necessary sequence from past to future, or inversely, which would denote either constant progress or constant deterioration, and an artist may well change his attitude during his career. Unfortunately there is a common tendency to regard an artist's work in these simplistic, black-and-white terms, and generally as arguments *ad hominem*. Fluctuations in an artist's attitudes may well be quite irregular and unforeseeable, accidents of taste or in fact different avatars of his personality. In every department of expression each of the three attitudes mentioned above has produced excellent – and also deplorable – results, whether it be anticipating the future, adhering closely to the present or forming a synthesis (only too often illusory) with the past. Examples are not hard to find. Take, for instance, the case of artists who have gone down to history as precursors, men who have intuitively sensed the movement of history in choosing their means of expression, and in many cases sensed it with quite extraordinary precision. Without them their art would certainly have developed differently. What do such artists lack? What is it about them that, despite their having sensed in advance the taste of our own age, still leaves us unsatisfied? Why in fact are they 'precursors' and not 'cursors' – like the weights in Roman scales? They are, in fact, 'lacking in weight', to use a common expression. They cannot be taken as standards by which to measure the age in which they live. Even so, their directives serve a good purpose and set in motion mechanisms more powerful than their own; and their claim to fame lies in their conscious or unconscious ability to foresee the manner in which taste would evolve. In this sense it really is possible for a mouse to bring forth a mountain. Their works, and their manner of thinking, are built on premises whose conclusions will be fully drawn only in another biological element.

Satie is the perfect example of this kind of 'jobbing' precursor. Many of the ideas that guided him for much of his life proved right, and it was only when he was disorientated by the sudden overestimation of his works that he began to lose his sense of direction, like some insect blinded by too bright a light. Even so, and regarding him in the most favourable light possible, it was not Satie who modified the taste of his age but Debussy, who, taking into account certain of Satie's discoveries, enormously enriched them with a formal logic, giving them stylistic coherence and true aesthetic direction. In this way Debussy's taste was infinitely more organic than Satie's. Singularity is here something quite different from the irresistible force of coherence. Thus it appears that there is a subtle dialectical relationship between taste and value; but singularity and originality are separated by a gulf like that which separates a home industry from full-scale manufacturing. We should however not forget that a home industry may well develop into manufacturing; and any neglect of this truth – which may be considered as a precept – can involve the individual in personal restrictions leading ultimately to a kind of asphyxia. Taste, in the context of artistic creation, is certainly a powerful force, but it will lose rather than gain from the artist's interest in tastes other than his own. In fact it might almost be said that the greatest geniuses are those who have, as it were, imbibed all the various 'tastes' of their day and transcended them in their own.

As soon as I say this I am aware of a number of exceptions that occur to me – those meteoric personalities who have simply imposed their own taste, and with maximum effectiveness! Perhaps, therefore, we should say that there are two kinds of genius, but that I personally am attracted primarily by the former, though often envious of the latter!

There are a great many instances of poets or musicians whose taste is perfectly adapted to that of their contemporaries, because the nature of their work corresponds exactly with the demands of the day and therefore has a proper social function. We do not need to envy them, we who have grown up as a race of *poètes maudits* – by which I mean that we spent our youth in that atmosphere of injustice and abuse which the greatest artists of the previous generation encountered because their works ran counter to contemporary taste. The list is a long one, running from Edgar Allan Poe to Webern, and including Cézanne; and it provides striking evidence of a violent break in the history of taste. I hope later to suggest the attitude that our own generation should take towards this problem of the 'de-phasing' of taste. For the moment all I want to say is that it seems to me quite exceptional for a work, or the complete output of such an artist, to be good even when it totally fulfils its sociological function and supplies exactly the demands of its epoch. Greek and Elizabethan drama do, I admit, present very striking examples, without going further afield. Although what the Greeks and Elizabethans most admired in these works is often what we admire least – and I shall no doubt be reminded of the difference between what is lasting in a work and what is ephemeral – it still remains a most remarkable fact that, even taking into account a number of flaws, these works, which entirely satisfied the taste of their age, continue very largely to satisfy our own.

Can it be that after all there are some constant factors in taste in addition to the many variables? The answer, I believe, is an unhesitating 'yes'. Any comparison of different literatures, and of means of expression in general, will reveal the fact that beneath very different appearances taste is characterized by a number of strongly marked constants. These depend primarily on reactions to human existence, shared by all human beings, and on similarities that exist between all forms of society. Whether it is a question of the individual or of society as a whole, the transcending element enables us to appreciate works of the remote or recent past that do indeed express that past, yet in some way or other transcend it. The immanent element in such works, which will depend on contingencies of thought as much as those of social forms (two closely interdependent factors), will present a barrier to the appreciation of works belonging to another age; but that barrier will seldom prove insurmountable, though the demands it makes will sometimes be high.

Hitherto I have deliberately refrained from speaking about works belonging to cultures other than our own. Our lack of fundamental background information makes it impossible for us to have more than a very partial understanding of such works, even if they do not constitute a completely closed book. Here we are often faced with a deliberate intention to restrict the appreciation of certain speculations and artistic forms to a closed society able to decipher them only by means of certain definite 'keys', a pleasure in fact reserved for the few; so that, whether by sheer accident or by the actual disappearance of such 'keys', these works will never communicate to us their beauty and their meaning but will remain permanently inaccessible. Further investigation will show that such a taste for the esoteric is characteristic of certain societies, indelibly colouring all their art forms with its special function. We can neither reconstitute nor fully comprehend that function, which is the carefully protected taste of one social or religious caste. In such a case taste is directly linked to the ethical system of which it forms a part, and can perhaps hardly be called taste.

I will not venture on speculations about the Pythagoreans, since I lack the qualifications needed to speak with authority on the subject, but I should like to quote Indian music as an example of what we have been saying. We are quite able to appreciate the immediate exterior of Indian music, its 'artistic' beauty so to speak; but a full appreciation of it is impossible without understanding its precise symbolism and its religious or metaphysical implications. Listening to Indian music we are aware of what may be called its surface, but quite unable to judge of what lies below that surface, and our 'taste' is severely restricted by our lack of education or illumination. Approaching the matter from the reverse side, can we even be sure that ritual function does not abolish 'taste'? Our experience of Gregorian chant suggests that it does: to detach the chant from the ritual of which it forms an organic part, and to judge it simply as music, needs a considerable effort on our part and one further complicated, as we have seen, by the remoteness of this music in time. Such examples show that taste can be considered as a single aesthetic category, but that ethics and metaphysics sometimes play an important, if not a primary role in the matter. I will not venture further in a field in which I feel uncertain of myself and ill-qualified to speak. But although this is a matter for specialists, I have felt obliged to mention something that seems to me of such capital importance.

Returning to our main subject – the composer's attitude to the tastes of his contemporaries – I will now discuss my third category: the artist who integrates functions that are local and temporal with functions that are more general. Here the name of Berg immediately occurs to me as a good instance. His best works are a résumé and a synthesis of his romantic inheritance. When I speak of projecting the present on the past, I am not of course referring to the various types of 'neo' – whether it be classicism, romanticism or anything else of the kind – or to academicism in general. Such sham syntheses are simply using the forms of the past employed to flatter the public's taste for reminiscence, a rather low taste at that. In order to excite that taste and provide it with pleasurable exercise, already existing objects are deliberately concealed, not enough to disturb the listener but just enough to provoke his salivation – a manoeuvre exactly parallel to certain erotic practices designed to arouse ... shall we say tired hearts ... but unfortunately not to be found in the inventory of the Divine Marquis! Berg's method is something entirely different from this perversion of taste, and it consists of synthesizing romantic taste by removing it to the second degree, as in Valéry's 'je me voyais voir', 'I saw myself seeing'. When an artist succeeds in this feat of alchemy and enables a whole generation 'to see itself seeing itself', we are gripped by the clarity of vision that it presupposes, as in certain chapters of *Ulysses*.

You will remember that we said that these three attitudes were not incompatible in the same artist – an identification with contemporary taste, an anticipation of future taste and a projection of contemporary taste on the past. And it is certainly true that though there may be a general line of evolution in an artist's development it will include many cross-currents. Some artists begin their careers adhering closely to contemporary taste and then gradually move on to a vast projection into the future. Their works move increasingly into unknown territory and terminate, as it were, in steep cliffs. They not only outstrip contemporary taste and anticipate that of the future, but even incline to transcend all categories of taste. Theirs may be called a Promethean attitude linked, on the individual plane, with the esoteric, which is the reserve, as we have seen, of a specially privileged and educated minority. Such works, which represent the supreme and sublime achievement of a lifetime of effort, will never be appreciated by any but a minority. No aesthetic function will ever link them, historically or geographically, to the tastes of the majority, who will revere them precisely *qua* mysteries that few will seek to understand in order to appreciate them fully. Other artists develop along a mere fluctuating general line and project contemporary tastes on the past only in order to direct them with greater force into the future – an attitude that is no less Promethean than the other – and achieve the same results. Others again, gifted with some strange prophetic sense, step intuitively from the future to the present and find themselves in total and explicit accord with their contemporaries. There is in fact no limit to the number of individual reactions to the tastes of contemporary society.

In order to arrive at any conclusion in the matter, however, we must be clear that there is an element of transcendence in taste. There is no such thing as absolute taste, of that we can be sure: but inasmuch as taste tends towards this absolute ideal, it can be only by transcending any single geographical or historical culture. Hence taste may be said to have a double nature or, to quote Pierre Souvtchinsky, it may be said to be 'explicable and inexplicable, definable and indefinable, determinable and indeterminable'. 'Immanence and transcendence are synchronized and indivisible in it.' 'Balance is perpetually being disturbed and restored.' Any work may achieve universality and become a prototype of 'taste' in proportion to the degree to which it satisfies this dialectic of immanence and transcendence.

An artist's attitude to this fundamental problem will reveal deep-lying traits of his character and the direction in which his natural enthusiasms lie, both in general intellectual interests and in his special field – in other words his psychology and the form that his education has taken. If we push the argument a little further, we may perhaps be able to isolate the part played by the artist's personality in his work. According to Rousseau, 'genius creates, but taste selects'; yet how is one to conceive the exact role of this severe 'censor', which 'makes great things interesting'? Taste, it would seem, is synonymous with discernment or critical sense; or, if not exactly synonymous, extremely similar, distinguished only by a certain element of irrationality generally absent from discernment and critical sense. We shall get a rather closer view of the question if we analyse the actual process of composition.

In composing the artist makes use of an ordered complex of morphological and syntactic functions, and this immediately involves questions of taste. We alter the disposition of some sound complex because it seems to us to 'sound badly'. We omit an instrument from some passage because it seems out of place there; we avoid some rhythmic figure because we find it commonplace or vulgar, or because it involves clashes of pitch. We employ one dynamic level or choose another according to which seems the better suited to the text. These are only a few examples of the composer exercising his 'taste'. Is the choice of one solution rather than another dependent simply on his taste, good or bad? Whether the result is good or bad it is a manifestation of his choice, which is in effect the ability to reject an infinite number of other solutions in favour of the one adopted.

Is taste, then, something resembling 'style'? Not at all! It is quite possible to write without taste but in a very definite style or, equally, to write with taste but to have no style. This notion of 'taste' is really devilish, you may say: the moment you think that you have pinned it down, caught it at last, it turns up again mockingly in some other quarter. Taste is, I admit, protean in form; but among all these examples of it, there is none that can be disallowed, even in the matter of style. What in fact is 'style' but writing within a network of functions as limited in their intrinsic potentialities as in their historical effectiveness! Although the music will suffer, it is quite possible for 'taste' to ignore this so-called network and to concern itself simply with uncoordinated functions, elements free of any morphology or even syntax. In the same way a style may be perfectly coherent and the network of functions that it implies may be clearly established, but there will be no real integration of taste unless the composer has taken care to justify both vocabulary and syntax according to criteria that are applicable generally, not in this single instance alone. So you see that style without taste and taste without style are not inventions of mine, but very real entities, whose existence could be easily attested by a multiplicity of examples. Am I then to suppose that taste is a kind of 'hyper-function' of style? If so, we are getting very close to a proper definition, at this morphological and syntactic level, which is, I hasten to add, only the initial stage.

I can now try to explain how I conceive of this 'hyper-function'. It will involve a number of extremely fragile relations, which you may well consider ill-founded but which I believe to be undeniably existent. Style, seen as a network of functions, is basically a rational phenomenon – though I say 'basically' because the formation of a style certainly involves a number of irrational elements. Perhaps you are beginning to think that I say a thing only to contradict it in the next sentence? I hope you are wrong, and that although our progress may involve a number of zigzags, it really is progress; we are simply observing, as we go along, how every positive definition conceals a number of possible negations but thereby becomes correspondingly wider. An idea is seldom categorically 'this' or 'that' but is better described as 'this, *but* that' – it contains within it irresolvable contradictions, which enrich the dialectic. For this reason I am constantly on my guard against calling things 'black' or 'white', something that is very rarely possible and even then likely to be proved shatteringly wrong a moment later. I am trying to approach as closely as possible, and with a full awareness of inherent contradictions, a very complex phenomenon.

But let us return to style – rational in principle but admitting of many irrational elements. Taste, on the other hand, seems to be eminently irrational; and that is why it is the subject of endless discussion that never issues in any closer agreement, for the very good reason that no argument can be conclusive in the field of the irrational. Remember at the same time that taste is by no means entirely irrational, since some of its criteria are definable by the strict application of formal logic. Taste, then, is an irrational category allowing of certain rational elements; and if we compare taste and style, we shall, I believe, discover the secret of their relationship, which is by no means a simple one. The irrational elements of the one are linked to the irrational principles of the other, the rational elements of the latter to the rational principles of the former. Shall I give you an exmple? A composer's use of any form of sound-complex is guaranteed, stylistically speaking, by the function of that complex in the field of morphology – guaranteed moreover by its overall function as determined by syntax. What remains is the irrational element, namely the choice involved in giving this complex the position and the form most appropriate to any given moment of a work. This is a totally irrational question decided by 'taste', though taste must be backed by a rational phenomenon, i.e. the relationship of the complex in question to the laws of acoustics. Is this example enough to convince you that taste and style form a kind of double revolving spiral? I could easily find other examples, some more obvious and some more subtle; but having stripped down the mechanism of the system of functions, I think that we can go on with our exploration.

As you will remember, we are still engaged in the field of morphology and syntax, what I have spoken of as 'elementary phenomena'. Rhetoric and form are going to present us with the same problems, and ones that I believe to be even more important. A lack, or an error, of taste here can have catastrophic results. A momentary failure of taste in the morphology of a work, for instance, may be regrettable but can be satisfactorily compensated in a number of ways. On the other hand a failure of taste in the matter of form is the worst of all things, and that is why I insist in my rejection of certain writers on musical subjects – because their form shows an unfailing lack of taste. Literary works are often marred by *rhetoric* that is vulgar, commonplace, tasteless, whereas in the plastic arts, it is to *forms* that we apply these adjectives. This suggests that each of these specialized arts has its own sensitive point – rhetoric in literature, form in the plastic arts. Meanwhile, both rhetoric and form are closely linked with taste, as morphology and syntax are linked by a kind of 'hyper-function' to characteristics crossed as regard to function. The rational elements in taste will be applied to the rational principle of a form, while the rational elements of a form will appeal to the irrational principle of taste. It is for this reason, I believe, that no form is justified by the mere logic of its unfolding, still less by any distributive hierarchy. A form may well be impeccably organized and yet totally lacking in taste because the irrational phenomena to which every form is susceptible have not been taken into account.

Looking back, then, we can see that as applied to morphology, syntax, rhetoric and form, taste is to be imagined as a kind of delicately balanced alchemy, integrating rationality and irrationality in an unstable amalgam. The point of equilibrium, which is the critical point, is impossible to determine in any general sense: it will vary with each individual case. Our grounds for despair – or perhaps our grounds for hope? – are that we cannot lay down precise rules for achieving that transmutation of the base metal of sound into the gold of a unique, indestructible work of art. This alchemy retains all the old prestige associated with the word, for it remains a secret to which we have not found the clue, even for our own personal purposes. We must not lose heart, but we should always remember that this irrational element is found in all categories, independently of each other; so that we are not guaranteed against a tasteless form by the fact that our morphology is in perfect taste, and our rhetoric may very well contradict our syntax. In fact, any work that we undertake demands a perfect synchronization of taste and also the necessary independence of each of the different planes on which it is worked out. Taste must be both independent and co-ordinated in its function; and that function must be both analytical and synthetic.

Have we at last said all that needs to be said about this protean monster? No, not yet, for I should never forgive myself if I left this aspect of the subject without pointing out that, in addition to independence and co-ordination, there are also detail and overall character, a pair that is similar though from a quite different standpoint. Independence and co-ordination concern the various stages of composition as an art, while detail and overall character are concerned with the activity as a whole. Not for nothing do we speak of 'being unable to see the wood for the trees' when a composer or a performer pays so much attention to individual detail that he loses sight of the work as a whole. A taste for detail does, in fact, often militate against the overall view of a work, and those who concern themselves primarily with that overall view may often neglect detail. Here we find ourselves faced by yet another alchemical process, quite as delicate as the former. When and how are we to decide on the point of equilibrium between taste in the work as a whole and taste in detail? The only answer is a practical one, and it is to be found by consulting the works in which this difficult fusion has in fact been faultlessly achieved. Once again, we shall not discover any way of codifying something so intangible. All the necessary conditions may be present and that irreplaceable something may still fail to materialize. In that case there is nothing for it but to start again . . .

Are we to stop there and say that 'the intrusion of the irrational into organic functions constitutes the whole problem of "taste" '? I do not think so, for I believe that we have still not mentioned one large area in which taste is exercised. Hitherto we have looked at music from the inside. Should we not now change our point of vision and look at it from outside? You may well be wondering whether there are such things as extra-musical functions that concern taste. Well, there certainly are, and to neglect them is to threaten the other functions. Like the fairy in *The Sleeping Beauty* who was not invited to the christening of the princess – in this case, the work – they will not fail to provide the spindle that pricks the princess and sends her to sleep. Only in this case no prince will appear to wake her. What in fact are these dangerous functions? They are of two kinds. The first relates to the ambivalence of the environment, and the second to the actual functional character of the elements used by the composer, whether these are in direct or indirect relation to the realization of a work or related with a definite aesthetic purpose.

By its very material music is brought into contact with other inorganic phenomena by numerous ambivalences in its structure. These ambivalences are therefore inherent in two structures and will be real in the one and potential in the other (according to a definition that I have made elsewhere). They will be real in the more pregnant, and potential in the less pregnant of the two structures. The category in which events are organized as subjectively real can be destroyed and rendered potential by an ambivalence that falsifies these events and 'distracts' them, in the literal sense. It follows that these events are literally false to their category, deserting their proper function and assuming others. Nor is this limited to individual musical events: it can apply equally well to superstructures. The task of taste in this case is to decide exactly the real or potential functions and the dangers of the different forms of ambivalence.

A good example is that of 'noise' and 'sound'. There is a relationship, of course, between organized sound and noise, and this relationship is ambivalent in many ways, particularly at the present time when – for reasons which I will not go into now – the concept of 'sound' has been deliberately enlarged and made more complex. It is precisely this greater complexity that is in danger of giving music references to everyday life and the inorganic world, to which it refers us by ambivalent structures. Any phenomenon of this kind will, as it were, perforate the musical context, the external reference being more powerful than the musical function properly so called: the 'noise' makes a *potential* appearance in the musical organization, whereas we feel it to belong more *really* to the inorganic world, which falsifies it and makes it false in itself. This, of course, is one of the most extreme cases; but there is another that I can quote, which is the exact opposite.

A traditional chord will falsify a structure in exactly the same way, because its traditional reference will certainly be stronger than its immediate reference to the structure in question. These two examples show that taste is here concerned with style, but at the second degree – namely by reference. Does that mean that once the reference is forgotten coherence will be re-established? No, I do not think so. As long as objects or structures are in any way attached to the extra-musical world – to the accident recorded as such under this double aspect – they will not be absorbed by music. Their centrifugal force is so strong that they will, on the other hand, degrade the work in which they appear by their often peremptory insistence on autonomy. You will understand from this that taste plays an important part in the choice of objects really capable of being integrated into a musical structure. I believe that whether material of this kind is good or not depends not only on its intrinsic quality, but on how far it is capable of adaptation and integration. Indeed, to think otherwise seems to me extremely naïve. At moments the taste required in the choice of this kind of material may seem comparable to that demanded by morphology. It is, however, a quite different taste that is engaged in the choice of pure material that is not in any way elaborated on the plane of a work's overall structure.

The second point that concerns us is taste as applied to the functional character of phenomena deliberately related to each other by the composer. This is a further stage of what we have just observed. For if the material itself has a functional character, so have other major organized elements in direct relationship with music – by which I mean words. It seems to me that composers show an insufficient care in their choice of means – may even sometimes show mere simple-mindedness – if they use words without regard to some technique based on their meaning, if they employ gestures regardless of their natural function or use an instrument either unaware or regardless of its specific character. History suggests that attitudes of this kind can produce only works that are either mannered or inconsequent. We may have a soft spot for all those *Batailles*, *Cris* and *Oiseaux* of the French polyphonic age, but a very little of them goes a long way. Nobody can fail to find the *Pandemonium* in Berlioz's *Faust* ludicrous; with its 'diff! diff! merondor Irimiru Karabano', which inspires laughter rather than terror. Everyone's first reaction to the *poèmes-collages* of the surrealists is to smile, and it very soon becomes clear that they are in fact a lot of fuss about nothing. Can it really be that the 'Angel of the Strange' is just one of these gaudy toys? In actual fact the Angel of the Strange is a much more disturbing character who makes his appearance only when genuine subversion is in the air. Perhaps we may be more fortunate with the Angel of the Droll? Why not, indeed, always provided that the two angels are clearly distinguished (a *distinguo*, mind you, that is not at all scholastic). If we are promised a *paradis artificiel* and a rabbit is then produced out of a top hat, we shall certainly find this a feeble sort of magic in response to the question. As for *Gebrauchsmusik*, there is not much hope of it having any future: all that is necessary is to get a number of highly skilled workmen to carry out a piece of manual labour – how touching to make oneself intelligible to the working classes in this way! But seriously speaking, what is the point of going on with this rigmarole? In the most advantageous cases, however, only a slight shift is needed for every element to regain its functional character. Particularly in the matter of language and gesture, an action or a description to establish their function could effect the co-ordination needed in the case of para-musical or para-linguistic elements, and these 'para' categories would be then fully justified.

Am I now asking 'taste' to play the part of a magician? Not at all. In the case I have been describing taste selects from the sum total of events those that are interrelated and provides them with their ultimate justification, which is 'spectacle'. By this I mean spectacle in the widest sense, the sense in which Mallarmé used it in sketching his *Livre*. In this sense 'spectacle' is something much more than mere exterior action: it involves the ordering of performers and the decisions of a 'producer'. I have the highest hopes of this spectacle, but what taste it presupposes! And what a mass of preliminary obstacles and tests to surmount! Taste will then be identical with the ultimate function – the ordering of the universe.

Good! Let us now come down from the clouds and establish some conclusions which will give us all food for further thought prompted by these rambling considerations of 'taste'. Anyone led by my title to expect something polemical, some kind of *syllabus errorum*, will be disappointed. We left Torquemada in the cloakroom, and there he will remain. If at this last moment the devil, hoping to fan a spark of malice, reminds me that there have been deliberate provocations of taste, my answer is that they are soon over and done with. Satie included typewriters in his orchestra; Webern did not. The surrealists shouted in the street and Joyce shut himself up with old Irish songs and Italian operatic airs. Which has proved the greater provocation? Which is the provocation recorded in the pages of history other than in a footnote? The transcendental, perhaps, you will say with an ironic smile? Yes, I shall reply, also with a smile, the transcendental! But I should like to tell you what I think about 'the revolution in taste': accept it as it comes, accept it as an hypothesis, no more than that! Lenin, who altered the whole style and taste of revolutions, used to say, 'Communism is the soviets plus electricity.' I shall be very happy to adopt the same well-authorized opinion about the revolution in taste. There are often explosions of anarchy, and very welcome they are. But without electricity – that is to say, without the organization of the aesthetic economy and the sociology of forms – everything rapidly deteriorates, as the number of abortive revolutions shows. In matters of taste I am, like Lenin, a convinced partisan of the 'soviets', but to no less a degree of 'electricity' – or in other words, of taste and function!

Have I convinced you? Will you even take taste seriously, let alone tragically? Nobody mentions it and I felt sorry for the poor neglected creature. Is it never mentioned because people think of it as a natural, familiar gift whose existence there is no point in admitting, or as a disgraceful disease to be discussed only in vague terms and behind closed doors? I really do not know! I have spoken of it quite openly and proved, I think, that I am not encumbered by the superficial distinctions of 'good' and 'bad' taste – which amount in fact to 'good' and 'bad' usage, or simply a conversation between people of education. Have I even been concerned with convincing you? As I said at the beginning, nobody is perfectly convinced of his neighbour's good taste, and nobody believes his own taste to be bad. I have often used the words 'protean', 'chameleon', 'phlogistic'. So I think the best thing is to think of this evening as though it had never existed, as something like taste itself, impossible to grasp, present everywhere and nowhere. In talking to you this evening I can now in fact admit that the first aim of my lecture was to fulfil my 'function' with 'taste'.

3
Putting the Phantoms to Flight[1]

I suppose that all members of our generation have the gravest suspicion of the words 'aesthetic' and 'poetic', and I am curious to know the origin of that suspicion. Is it something purely accidental or does it spring from a profound reaction? What can have made us so deeply suspicious, to the point of rejecting all aesthetic speculation as dangerous and pointless and thus confining us (just as dangerously) to a single interest – technique, 'getting on with the job'. Can it be that we have been so sure of our 'poetic' goal that we have felt no need to think about it in detail? If so, has this been a question of overconfidence, lack of confidence, lack of interest or simple carelessness? Have we been unwilling to commit ourselves to a territory so notorious for its mirages, in the belief that the technique of the language of music was better suited to our powers of formulation? Has it been lack of 'culture', or a mere reaction against the ramblings of a precarious philosophical system? Or has it been quite simply the fear of appearing inferior to intellectuals better armed for fighting, a large part of which consists also of armed juggling?

There has been something of all these in the unwillingness, the lack of confidence (or aggressive refusal, which comes to the same thing) to face problems that are in fact fundamental. It must be said in our favour that our attitude of simple abstention has not been wholly wrong. Ah!, you are going to say, so now you are going to blame someone else for your failure, are you? Well, it is not possible to give an exact account of our weakness or our tardiness; and there can certainly be no question of excusing them as so many purely unconscious reactions. Even so, let me explain what we have felt: it may not justify, but will at least be an attempt to explain our attitude.

During the years immediately preceding our arrival on the musical scene there was so much aesthetic speculation that it confused the actual situation. Only think of the endless clichés and slogans that were first current and then

---

[1] 'Nécessité d'une orientation esthétique', from a course of lectures given at Darmstadt in 1960. Published in the *Mercure de France*, April–May 1964, Nos. 4 and 5, pp. 623–39 and 110–22.

obsolete, then put back into circulation in a slightly different form, and finally forgotten. I say clichés and slogans, because it is impossible, in retrospect, to take such numerous and ephemeral things seriously. It was not so much a question of ideas as of fashions launched every year by *littérateurs* who dictated, like the big fashion houses, lengths, numbers of folds, pleats, cutting straight or on the cross, according to the season and the demands of a very varied clientele. In most cases it was vaguely musical *littérateurs* who launched these 'collections' of their favourite composers. Their competence in the matter was so tenuous that the reasons for their different choices were pretty superficial, even if we do not count the more or less 'historic' judgements that will certainly become the laughing-stock of history.

No, I am not going to accuse these *littérateurs* of warning us off the path of aesthetic speculation by their example. I am not animated in any way by a spirit of revenge; and I am the first to acknowledge that the best things written about the powers of music have been written in fact by poets, and that not only because they are further removed from the actual task, the toil and sweat of composition, but because they are able to express in words what they feel when they hear a work. I am not forgetting that Baudelaire (on Wagner), Hoffmann and Balzac wrote about the aesthetics and the significance of music in a way that no composer could ever have written, even if his opinions were exactly the same as theirs. In our own time Henri Michaux has shown himself to be a clear and far-sighted analyst of certain musical 'modes of being' of which he has a profound intuitive understanding. These he describes with the verbal precision of a master, and we can only say, with envy, 'Yes, that is just what it is!' In this field of what Baudelaire spoke of as *correspondances*, we musicians are beaten from the start and we can compete only at the risk of exhibiting our inferiority.

We therefore have no resentment in principle against writers speaking about music: we merely defend our own territory when we feel that it is threatened by the inexpert. For every writer who actually assists the composer, there are a large number who gaily add to the present confusion. And to return to the situation of which we were speaking before, some of our immediate predecessors can claim to have achieved records in aestheticizing, though it is hard to know what caused this unnatural appetite, and why the speculations that once enjoyed universal currency in the world of music now seem so totally 'dated'. It would be an interesting study, given the documentation, to pinpoint exactly the origins of this inflation, the sources of this epidemic. Much information could be gleaned from certain books and monographs, and there would be little difficulty in distinguishing between the composer who responded to these changing directives and those who went on their way regardless of each season's new fashions – a sort of geography of artistic creation, in fact. An analysis of this kind has never been attempted, nor is it my intention to embark on anything of the sort here, as what I have in mind is something much less specialized in interest. The whole situation at that time concerns me now for one very good reason: I simply want to discover what caused the consequent bankruptcy of ideas. I am quite convinced, in fact, that this bankruptcy had the effect on our generation of a solemn warning. Even if our first reaction was simply a more or less unconscious reflex, an instinctive distrust, the position in which we found ourselves led us to explain our own reactions, and so brought us to question the justification of all aesthetic philosophizing and to give – as it were in our own despite – a negative answer to that question.

In our despair we wanted to consider nothing but the technique of composition; and yet, once certain urgent linguistic problems had been solved, practical music-making made our excessive suspicion of all theorizing impossible. Our instinctive timing cannot in fact have been wholly absurd, as it seems to me, since it enabled us to overcome a major antinomy and to disregard a number of paralysing contradictions.

If we consider the different aesthetic approaches of any generation one fact becomes obvious: that the tendency of any work, its real significance, had been deliberately chosen before any consideration of the vocabulary to be employed. This, if you come to think of it, is a fairly common experience – that the artist thinks that he need only give his inspiration sufficiently precise meaning and the means will follow automatically, without his having to give too much thought to the matter. This belief, which is rooted in the obstinate survival of romanticism in its most degraded form, implies that 'inspiration' automatically guarantees quality of language. We are only too familiar with the privileged place occupied by 'sincerity', as though that eminent virtue, by its very purity, atoned for ignorance and weakness of all kinds. If the composer's sincerity in the pursuit of his aims guarantees a work's validity, the idiom of that work and the way in which it is organized are of secondary importance. Any consideration of actual idiom, which is rejected as a handicap and an intolerable imposition, can then only weaken 'inspiration' and destroy the composer's vision of his work. Any concern with purely technical matters would in that case deny the pure intention of realizing the composer's ideal. How often one has read, or listened to, composers' explanations of what they set out to do, most of their sentences beginning with, 'What I wanted to do was . . .' Actually explanations of this kind are simply excuses for failure in achievement. If, as I think we must admit, there are some things that one must not 'want to do', or that it is essential to 'know how to want', music (and in fact all artistic creation) is one of them, for it demands not only the 'wanting' but also the 'doing': and the only way that leads from 'wanting' to 'doing' is 'knowing'. Any ignoring of technique and its importance brings a fearful vengeance with it, nothing less than a mortal disease inherent in the work. If you simply adopt a traditional technique, which has a purely factitious, illogical, decorative relationship with the facts of the historical situation, all your vital energies will be absorbed and exhausted by the sheer stylistic exercise, and the result will be . . . a whited sepulchre.

Aesthetic thinking divorced from considerations of technique can lead only to bankruptcy: the musical idiom is in such a case nothing more than a kind of ingenious simulation or a banal gesturing, a question of temperament. What interest can there be in these individual efforts to obtain relief? Their poverty is as striking as their feebleness, their eclecticism and their lack of conviction, and they only confirm our profound belief in the importance of technique. No composers who have produced solid, durable works that stand up to critical examination have ever minimized the importance of this choice, or ever treated style as a kind of garment that can be changed out of boredom or caprice (fashion, circumstance, or even subject). Without exception they have regarded this choice as an integral part of their musical nature.

From the very outset our generation was determined to restore to its proper place this problem of technique, which had been despised, ignored, corrupted and distorted. We considered this the most urgent of our tasks and one on which not only our own future, but the whole future of music depended. (Who can in fact envisage any future for music without its own solution imposing itself with all the force of a law? A pleasant Utopia indeed, and something to look forward to!) And so we reversed the existing system of priorities, of whose faults we were only too aware, and laid down the following principle: that the composer's primary consideration must be the actual technique of his musical language; and I believe that the validity of this principle will be sufficiently guaranteed by what I am about to say. Was this overriding concern with technique destined in fact to stifle all expression? (And I should explain that I am using the word 'expression' in a less specialized sense than that in which it is used by those whose attachment to 'expression' is fanatical, even maniacal.) Were we not set on a course that could lead only to what might seem to be a perfect 'technological' rationality but was in fact a monumental absurdity? It would be an understatement to say that we went very near to this absurdity on many occasions. Looking back on this 'ride to the abyss', I can see that more than once we crossed into the territory of the absurd without in other respects any awareness of a mass of contradictions, many of them of a hair-raising nature. The cases in which we dragged our intellectual anchors were sometimes spectacular and sometimes not, but in the majority of cases they arose from our lack of any real aesthetic applicable to the linguistic developments in our music. Once again we come on the explanatory ritual formula, 'What I wanted to do . . .', only now it was not a justification of some 'poetic' decision, but an attempt on the composer's part to explain himself in terms of morphological or syntactic ideas, involving a mass of 'structural' description employed as a smoke screen to conceal the work itself. You have only to read some of the notes or prefaces published by composers to realize their implication of a failure to deliver the actual goods themselves. It is very easy to ridicule these effusions, and indeed they deserve it. They reveal a description in words of *ideal* models that never materialized *in fact* – or, more accurately, the materialization did not succeed in transcribing the imagined model.

While we are on this subject, I should like to say something about this itch to write commentaries, to give verbal descriptions of what the composer has imagined in his own mind. It seems probable that a composer embarks on such things as a substitute when his imagination of a work has not been complete, anticipating the full realization of his ideas in a spate of rhetoric. Like a sorcerer creating his power by ritual incantations that excite the sense of vision, the composer (in the most favourable instances) specifies his aims and tries to give a material existence to his *idea* by enclosing it in a network of descriptions, in order to facilitate his own grasp of it. If he persists in such descriptions after the actual act of creation – when the work is finished, that is to say – this is an absolute proof that he has failed to realize his idea. The need to explain has not been destroyed by accomplishment, and once again we are reminded of the gulf that separates *wanting* from *doing*. There are plenty of examples in the lives of composers, plenty of instances in which a composer will justify some procedure in a composition as long as the composition itself is not there to provide its own irrefutable evidence. Once the composition is completed, all verbal commentary on it vanishes, or takes on a retrospective character. A composer may very well tell us the history of a work, how it originated in his mind and the sources from which it sprang. He may succeed in explaining the necessity of its existence and its particular nature, but he will no longer try to describe it from the inside, because the time for such 'transcription' has passed.

Is this tantamount to saying that I regard the composition of a work as being simply the realization of a model glimpsed in a moment of blinding lucidity? Is it enough to see in imagination a superb model and then to set to work, with every means at my command, to give it a material form? Can the birth of a work really be so easily compared – as is often done today – to a moment of conception followed by a long, difficult and painful pregnancy? This comparison may be satisfactory from the point of view of morality, but it implies a certain number of naïve assumptions, which we shall be identifying in greater detail in the course of examining the springs of musical thought.

For the moment let us be content with registering one fact: that regarding linguistic problems in music as an overriding concern, and giving them priority over the creative sense, has produced no better results than the reverse procedure. Both have equally led to a sort of exhaustion of the imaginative faculty. The intention still remains more remarkable than the actual achievement – hence both the persistence of composers in accompanying their works with explanatory texts and the uselessness of those texts, which cannot provide convincing evidence. (It seems to me essential that a composer's intention must be perceptible before investigation and analysis demonstrate that intention to the intellect. This primary importance of perceptibility is certainly a hallmark of what we call 'masterpieces': the awareness of their quality establishes itself at different levels, and they defy analysis in the sense that the listener's unconscious is as fully aware of that quality as is his conscious mind. We know how such a work satisfies us while remaining ignorant of why . . . and surely the same is true of the composer himself. He may be able to explain what he has done without being able to give an exact account of the impulse that led him to do it, or the urgency of that impulse.)

The priority given to 'treatment' – the manner in which the composer actually handles his material – has led to abuses and ultimately to an intellectual stalemate; for we now find ourselves faced once again with those very problems of 'aesthetics' that we were determined to avoid – rashly, as it has turned out. Our own weaknesses have proved even more decisive than those of the older generation (now relegated to the purgatory of history) – and forced us to make a choice. Moreover, since we have mentioned the historical component, had we not in fact made aesthetic decisions without intending to do so or being aware of the fact? Our predecessors left musical history at a certain point in its development. According to them the wish to compose meant making a critical judgement of their own position and taking a personal decision in view of this analysis of the situation from the point that they had reached. I feel sure that I shall be accused of presumption: how, given the complexity of contemporary music, can I possibly feel myself qualified to make decisive value judgements? Well, in the first place I could plead the unrestricted liberty of individual choice and insolently declare my judgement to be as good as the next man's (insolence sometimes pays a direct dividend, but not often for longer than a single season), show a determination to insist on the force of my reasoning and the validity of my judgement – though I have the impression that shock tactics of this kind would not be effective for long. There would be talk about my aggressiveness and then the whole matter would be forgotten . . .

Is the situation today, then – or was the situation yesterday, for that matter – so complicated as to render any discrimination totally impossible? Have we really got to have recourse to that famous and mysterious 'posterity' as the only guarantor of any clear and definitive judgement? Have we really no choice beyond vague personal convictions based on a narrow field of 'elective affinities'? Must we regard a whole era of history exclusively from the angle of an eclectic taste, an assortment of pleasures ranging from the austere to the frivolous?

It is only in appearance that the situation is so complicated. Every age has a superficial covering of light, low-lying cloud easy enough to disperse by those who possess any 'solar' warmth (is such warmth a privilege of heroes, or of gods?) and a constitutional antipathy – an 'allergy' – to muddle. I shall never tire of saying that personality starts with a robust critical perspicacity that forms part of the gift itself. Any vision of history actually implies, from the first moment of choice, a sharpness of perception in judging the 'moment', and that perception is not explainable in exclusively logical terms. It is all part of that faculty which makes the poet a 'seer', as Rimbaud used to insist so energetically. It is the gift that enables him to clarify what appears to be a confused situation, to discern the lines of force in any given epoch, to take an overall view, to grasp the totality of a situation, to have an intuitive hold on the present and to apprehend its structure on a cosmic scale – that is what is demanded of any candidate who aspires to the title of 'seer'. I have deliberately avoided the word 'simplification', for simplification is the great danger with misguided proselytizers. Such people are always inclined to confine themselves to a single aspect, as it were, when portraying a historical era, and to model the face of history to suit their own convenience in order to discover – or if necessary to invent – a genealogy that either suits their own book or protects them from hostile scrutiny. And there is always the danger of contradictions that are overemphatic or ludicrous. Of course we are all acquainted with those bird's-eye views of history that achieve the momentary addition of a hitherto uncertain candidate to history's roll of honour: but in such cases the manipulation of history is so naïve and so obvious that it is hardly worthy of comment. Equally common are examples of history written with a number of convenient short circuits that eliminate everything outside a narrow orbit of vision – what might be called Procrustean historical writing, the results of which are no less horrifying than those of the old legend. No, history must not be rewritten to suit the individual historian: simplifications of this kind are ludicrous and the ideas they propound are forgotten as soon as they reach the public. When I speak of clarifying the present situation, it is not simplifications of this kind that I have in mind, but a prevision of what the future will show to have been merely seminal and what will have proved truly lasting.

And who, you may well ask, is going to assure me that you are not mistaken and that the absolute terms in which you make your very clear judgements are in fact justified? At the most it amounts to a bet, which you will either win or lose, but the bet is your own personal concern and you should not try to impose a risk that you have agreed, even demanded, to take on anyone who does not feel called upon to take it. For there must be no illusions on this score, if you please: nothing you can do can prevent me from seeing your personal choice as an operation in which chance plays a part. What chance? Well, the chronology of the various encounters in your life and even the chronology of that chronology. How am I to believe in such things as inevitability and destiny once I have observed the number of fortuitous circumstances that have contributed to the historic 'casting of the die' in your own case? Has not history in any case often proved wrong about itself, and have we not witnessed the most improbable rehabilitations after almost incredible intervals of oblivion? If collective opinion is so vacillating over such long periods, how can an individual like yourself claim instant infallibility? These are the questions that I ask myself, questions the force of which I try to ignore. For in the first place why should not I claim 'the right to be wrong', a claim that has already been sovereignly vindicated? That is assuredly a simple and swift means of escape. On reflection I can see no reason why I should not make this bet quite openly, with no sense of shame and with all the privileges of a planned risk. Yes, of course circumstance plays an undeniable part in all lot-casting. In fact there is *one* circumstance that may, indeed must, become *the* circumstance. Judgement and vision will imply reconsidering, revising and correcting genuine mistakes or failures to understand, and these can never be entirely obliterated because, originally, they contained part of the fundamental truth. I can only affirm my absolute belief in this, for no proof is possible: it is in fact itself, essentially, already the act of creation. Since I exist only in relationship to my past, the choice – the 'bet' – is a basic gesture ensuring me my place in a historical succession, quite apart (for the moment) from the worth of what I represent. Self-definition is a long way from self-realization.

Once this initial choice has been made, whether by instinct or by hard work, you have already accomplished a task closely related to aesthetic choice, to poetic decision. Your orientation cannot be determined simply by sentimental or intellectual attraction, simply by logical necessity or the need for security. Your very affinities, the very action of choosing, constitute a revelation of yourself to yourself, a proof of your own existence, an experience of your own personality. It may not be easy to disentangle the more intellectual interest, in which reason plays a greater part than instinct, from immediate, intuitive attraction, in which instinct is stronger than reason; but it is still possible to observe a difference between spontaneous acceptance and conscious conviction. Is one of these more vitally important than the other? In a sense it is, for in the last resort there must be a kind of deep hunger, a persistent demandingness in our recognition of another artist. If we are simply attracted by a work or a composer, there is always a danger of our critical faculties being blunted and of our therefore overlooking qualities that do not immediately entice us, but are none the less valuable.

History, and more especially recent history, furnishes us with instances of choices that are difficult not only to make but even to formulate. Surface appearances have been so intricate and positions sometimes so hard to define that it has been necessary to be doubly alert and on one's guard in searching for the first real indication of a new situation. Our vision has been impeded, particularly by the distorted relationship between technique and poetics, and by the difficulty of finding a place for a new composition within an existing tradition. Both of these account for many fatal errors of judgement. In certain circumstances of creation and performance many works have made a false impression, and this has had to be 'rectified', as one rectifies the apparent crookedness of a stick in water. In some works novelty – and often interest itself – has been unequally distributed. There have been cases in which the composer's vocabulary has constituted the main interest of the work, while there has been nothing to learn from his form. Or, vice versa, the form has been fascinating and highly instructive but the actual style of the music too traditional to hold the attention for long. In another instance rhythmic or instrumental innovations might repay prolonged study, which, however, has revealed only too clearly the weakness of the composer's overall vocabulary. Or again it might be that a composer's grammatical innovations were of profound importance, but the poetic conception of his work pretty 'dated'.

These few examples will show how easy it has been to miss an important point in the contemporary development of music, and to have relied simply and solely on instinct could have only magnified the discrepancies of which I was conscious in other men's attitudes. Moreover the fact that certain aspects of contemporary music have been for so long and so persistently underrated and ignored, for purely emotional reasons and without a moment's reflection, has served us as a warning against giving our own reflex reactions too much latitude. This even inculcated a kind of discipline in our enthusiasms, if the two words can be compatible in the same sentence (or the same person) . . . Of course we committed errors of judgement and faults of taste, and there was on occasion a note of sophistry in our appreciation; but none the less sooner or later we have been justified by events, and the balance sheet has eventually been drawn up accurately. (After all, reality always wins in the end. We can number some tough characters among our predecessors, men whose continued *existence* it would be perfectly useless to deny. Aggressive attitudes to history do not pay high dividends. Most of them spring from sheer bad temper and are therefore of no more than psychological rather than general interest.)

Music is in a state of permanent revolution, and do not forget that there are time-bombs as well as the bombs that explode immediately. Or is that too terrorist a point of view? To employ a less explosive terminology we can recognize the existence of certain works and certain composers whose influence is not necessarily felt immediately. I am not speaking of the extreme cases in which a composer's music simply remains unknown, but of works and composers whose fame is uncontested. It sometimes happens that certain aspects of a composer's music remain as it were submerged for a time, and only then emerge into the general consciousness. The way this happens is often curious and unexpected, involving relationships hitherto impossible; but the result is an unmistakable fact. We cannot therefore claim an absolute knowledge of all aspects of the present even when we accept it *in toto*; and yet this lacuna in our information is filled by our intuition, which corrects any remaining inaccuracies of detail. For when we speak of 'knowledge', this does not necessarily imply possessing a precise inventory of all the technical details, which remain for the most part linked to the personality of the composer, and thus unusable as such. (It is their inability to 'distance' themselves from their model and his personal gestures, their lack of judgement, that makes so-called 'epigones' caricatures in matters of critical selection.) Any composer's working procedures are, as such, perfectly adapted to the invention of that composer: and it is of course essential to examine them closely enough to ensure a real knowledge of the grammatical laws that they obey. This is an elementary stage which cannot reveal the meaning of the work (which, after all, we do not have to discover) and still less its grammatical motivation. It looks as though all works of the past that fail to bear fruit fail because it is only the exterior characteristics of their morphology that are studied – which implies a kind of 'mannerism' – and nobody concerns themselves with internal structure, the work's real *raison d'être*. This amounts to saying that a vocabulary only needs to be described, whereas in fact it demands to be legitimated. It is only from this legitimation that we learn the composer's thought and can thus derive inspiration and real strength. For once that legitimation has been established, our strength is not simply a pale reflection of the other composer's: we have as it were transmuted his strength so that it serves as a base for our own, which is distinct in nature, origin and quality.

Thus although we may have reservations about any investigation in depth, we must recognize that in the study of any composition it is, in the last resort, motivation rather than facts that we are trying to ascertain, although the only key to that motivation is provided by those facts. Any study not directed towards discovering a composer's *thought*, in its widest context, would be barren. Who could otherwise be capable of deduction? Only by a sufficiently 'abstract' view of individual details and procedures is deduction made possible and these details and procedures *reduced* to an initial generative act of the composer's. And so we are forced to return to examining those aesthetic decisions which determine the use of any given technical system. It is no use objecting that this is a purely personal matter. Collective choices and rejections operate in the same way. Each age has what may be called its own collective 'harmonic resonances'. The collective preferences of any historical period arise from a set of similar data which can claim parallel solutions. The famous 'points of similarity' linking one epoch to another are nothing other than hallmarks of a choice established and recognizable in an infinite variety of individual choices.

We are conditioned by our past collectively as well as individually, and what influences us is not any pure technique or any abstract thought, but the relation of that thought to that technique – in other words its realization. How then are we to explain the fact that some composers mistrust the morphological approach to the point of neglecting it completely, while others have an allergy to all aesthetic ideas? We have only to look about us to see the harm, the irreparable damage caused by this state of affairs. Just as there are abuses of scientific language, so there are numerous caricatures of philosophical language, and in each case we can spot the same ridiculous lack of simple competence. What is called the 'mathematical' – and is in fact the 'para-scientific' – mania is a convenience because it gives the illusion of an exact, irrefutable science based on precise facts: it appears to be presenting objective facts with the maximum of authority. This is a return to the medieval concept of music as a science demanding a scientific, rational approach: everything must be defined as clearly as possible, demonstrated and formed on models already existing in other disciplines based on the exact sciences. What a pious illusion!

In the first place we must take into account the musician's lack of experience in the scientific vocabulary, in the use of which he exhibits neither ease nor skill, invention nor imagination, not to speak of the imprecision of that vocabulary itself or the gaps in his knowledge of it. And even supposing his use of its concepts and terms to be perfectly correct, he does no more than go from one sterile plagiarism to another, impoverishing the language of science without enriching that of music. One can only smile at the diagrams and treatises that consist of a mad collection of permutations totally devoid of interest. Such parallels with scientific procedures remain hopelessly superficial because they do not spring from any musical thought. All reflections on musical technique must be based on sound and duration, the composer's raw material; and imposing some alien 'grid' on these reflections can result only in a caricature. No examination of different forms of permutation will convince us of the quality of the result when these permutations are realized in the substance or the structure of a musical work. What guarantee can there possibly be that a figured scheme, carefully described to the last detail, can – simply as such – support the whole weight of a musical structure? Who can prove to me that numerical laws, however valid in themselves, will remain valid when they are applied to categories that they do not govern? Surely these intricate sophistries are a total absurdity, and indeed almost sublime in their craziness.

Number-fanatics of this kind belong to the same class as those who preach the Golden Number and esoteric ideas about the 'power' of numbers. In the last resort they are all concerned with the same thing, finding and deciphering 'secret affinities' in the universe. Nowadays magic is out of fashion and would be regarded as a handicap, but in fact such people do assume the 'mysterious powers of numbers' in a way that carries little more conviction than that of their medieval predecessors. What is more, this juggling with numbers surely reveals a lack of confidence, an impotence and a lack of imagination. Numbers represent a safe refuge from the undependable, incalculable imagination and provide a form of rational reassurance, a cloak (quite genuinely assumed) for the lack of self-confidence in the much more demanding field of pure invention. In its commonest form this play with numbers is simply a routine that can be carried on without any creative faculty whatever. Given a basic material, I can 'manipulate' it straightaway and be sure of obtaining results, thus gaining the impression of having invented something, whereas all that I have been doing is rehearsing a catalogue to the point of exhaustion.

In fact, therefore, the majority of 'scientific' minds in music are really hardly more ingenious than Jarry's Monsieur Achras, who collected polyhedra. It remains to be seen whether the interest of such 'polyhedra' is inexhaustible . . . I cannot, for the life of me, see the need for them!

If we can dismiss number-juggling as the sign of a quite unusual feebleness of imagination and thought, how does the matter stand with philosophy? In the musical world philosophy has had a very bad press for some time owing to the quick turnover of ideas at the end of the last century, when hardly a note was written without being related to some intricate philosophical system. This gave musical philosophizing a bad name; and though poetics, feeling and sensation were allowed, philosophic ideas were mercilessly excluded until some innocent smuggled them in again, only in less ponderously professional form. But they have not had much success, it must be admitted, and their employment has resulted in some really wonderful nonsense. Systems of thought in themselves perfectly coherent have been studied through the keyhole (we must suppose that the key was not in fact in the lock . . .) and 'consequences' have been drawn that are not remarkable for their rationality. What are those who indulge in such speculations trying to disguise? It is certainly not lack of imagination, as in the other case! They show plenty of imagination, or at least they go through the motions of imagining. But are those motions alone enough? Apart from them the 'attitude' is refreshingly new: but what is an attitude unless it is reflected clearly and accurately in the actual musical material? It really amounts to no more than a stimulating subject for discussion. Only an actual mastery of the language carries conviction, not just putting forward ideas on how that language should be used: and mastery implies thorough technical knowledge, without which there is no getting beyond 'the idea of an idea', or, in Valéry's words, 'I saw myself seeing myself.' You may remember Louis Aragon's rude comment, in which he relegated this kind of obligatory narcissism to the borderland of mental paralysis:

> Almost all his phrases conceal this play of reflections, employed in order to give the impression of depth . . . All we see is a succession of M. Valérys looking into the same mirror, discovering nothing, seeing nothing but the same banal images of himself and repeating, 'I saw myself seeing myself', as he might have said, 'I saw myself, I saw myself . . .' rather like a one-way street. Very much as though he were saying, 'I was bored stiff, I was bored stiff, I was bored stiff . . .'

The resemblance seems all too close.

Philosophical and scientific ideas are equally useless when misapplied. In each case misapplications arise from the same weakness, a weakness of the purely musical imagination aggravated by submitting the data of music to wholly alien systems of ideas and priorities. This amateurish approach there-fore gives a kind of legal status to a misapprehension which is both honest and sincere. We must reject, without too much sentiment, these sham solutions whose charm lies in the fact they often present facets of what is undeniably the truth. I believe that music warrants its own individual field of study and must not be submitted to mere arrangements of fundamentally alien methods of thought, which have in fact proved a dangerous threat to the freedom of musical thought.

This does not mean that I am deliberately hostile towards all interference or communication between music and the outside world. Far from being an isolationist of this kind, I recognize that contact with other disciplines can be extremely fruitful, in introducing a different order of vision and providing us with glimpses of what we should never have dreamed, stimulating our inventiveness and forcing our imagination to a higher degree of 'radioactiv-ity'. But influences of this kind can be only by analogy rather than by any literal application, which has no foundation in fact. As I see it, the most important level at which this fertilizing process takes place is the very deepest, namely that of thought-structures – the imagination adapting outside resources to new purposes in a kind of fertilizing process. There are certain discoveries, philosophic and scientific, that have first to be trans-posed before their significance is fully realized, and this transposition cannot be effected by any mere juxtaposition or parallel application. What I am really saying is that in the composer's imagination these different external 'acquisitions' assume an exclusively musical form and become specifically and irreversibly musical concepts.

For instance, the idea of permutation, which has been so grossly abused, is in fact meaningful only in certain clearly defined circumstances. In any other context permutation remains a collection of figures with a 'cladding' of sounds, durations or whatever it may be, but having nothing to do with musical *essence*. Similarly indeterminacy is justified only on an explicit basis – in fact when it rests on clearly defined musical functions, lacking which we find ourselves in the realm of the arbitrary and immediately threatened by inflation. The phenomenon of music requires a special kind of thinking, though how to describe that phenomenon presents a problem. Can the mechanism of creation be apprehended so easily? From without, creation often seems to be something particularly resistant to the mental grasp, and none of the multifarious explanations that have been attempted carry much conviction. It is worth observing that composers who have expressed their views on the subject have sometimes flatly contradicted each other. Are they in fact the best qualified people to provide a verbal description of a state of affairs that it is their business to communicate by quite other, non-verbal means in their possession? In the last resort, is the actual knowledge of how artistic creation 'works' – its mechanism – needed by the composer in order to 'live', i.e. to put into effect the necessary choices?

Musical creation is generally considered from the point of view of the ends pursued, and not in its functioning as such – as is shown by the simple but formidable question, 'What did you want to express?' The usual joke answer is of course, 'Nothing' – or 'Nothing but myself'. In that case what is 'myself'? Does it mean that I am consciously describing myself by means of music, or that my music describes me more or less without my knowing it? Are what are generally known as 'temperament' and 'personality' responsible for the style in which I transmit what I want to? Am I conscious of what I want to 'express', and if I mean to express something, does that something need to be defined before it is described? Must I set out with a fixed goal in sight, or am I at leisure to encounter on the road what will, in retrospect, turn out to be the motive of my search and to give it significance?

To try to give absolute answers to these questions – the Answer, as it were – would be wrong, I believe, because there are as many answers as there are days and seasons. It may be already some consolation to remember that these questions of 'meaning' and 'expression' are very much the bane of other disciplines also, painting for instance. What do we find fascinating in Cézanne's *Montagne Sainte-Victoire* – the capturing of the landscape, the painter's obsession, or the 'order' he established? Or in the case of non-figurative painting, is it the geometry of the different masses, the relationship of the colours, the painter's personal fingerprints or the characteristic gestures of his style? Are we in fact sure of *understanding* what we see? Are we aware of some message that refuses to be defined?

A further lesson in prudence is provided by the very diversity of the works produced by the same individual. It is not hard to understand how a writer can keep a diary at the same time as he is writing a play, or that the two activities demand different techniques. On the other hand the different possibilities open to the composer are not generally taken into account, although they have always existed; and the varied pattern of his evolution is thus ignored, his activity reduced to a kind of standard regime with a single network of obligations. This gives rise to a great number of misunderstandings. There are in fact two points to consider: the genesis of a work and its character.

To be perfectly honest, each work originates in a unique way, and this applies even to the original idea, which very seldom recurs to the composer under the same aspect. What in fact is the stimulus to compose? Well, it may be an entirely abstract formal idea, quite divorced from any 'content', in which case the intermediary processes needed for its realization will gradually present themselves to the composer's mind, so that the original overall plan will reshape itself by means of a number of subsidiary 'local' discoveries. Alternatively the stimulus may come from some purely instrumental feeling, a sound-picture demanding certain types of writing, which will generate the musical idea best suited to produce the desired effect; and in that case the outer envelope will have to find its own suitable content.

Again, it may be some linguistic enquiry, which will lead to the discovery of forms of which the composer had in the first place no idea, or the use of certain instrumental combinations that had not at first occurred to him. The outline and sense of a work will sometimes be quite clear to the composer from start to finish, while in other cases actual starting points may be ill-defined and become clear only after a long and difficult working-over. Or again the initial plan may be so modified during the course of composing that the composer has to go back and 'recalibrate' the whole piece.

It is only very seldom that the composer finds himself in the presence of a world that he has glimpsed, like Schoenberg, in a single flash of heightened awareness, a world he then has to bring into actual existence. This 'theological' aspect of the composer's task is more an aspiration than a fact ('. . . and you shall be like gods'), since it implies a most improbable degree of knowledge. Henry Miller is probably nearer the truth when he describes himself drawing a horse that gradually becomes an angel: 'Very well, let's make a start! That is the great thing – so let's start with a horse.' As the work progresses there are a number of incidents that suggest provisional conclusions: 'If it doesn't look like a horse when I've finished, I can always turn it into a hammock.' From horse to zebra, from zebra to straw hat with the help of a man's arm, a bridge rail, some stripes, some trees, some clouds over a mountain that turns into a volcano, then a shirt, some odd things that look like cemetery railings and then an empty space 'in the top left-hand corner':

> I draw an angel . . . a woebegone angel with a sagging belly and wings on umbrella ribs. He seems to be overrunning the framework of my ideas and hovering mystically over the wild Ionian horse which can no longer by any stretch of the imagination become a man . . . If you set out with a horse, stick to it – or else get rid of it altogether.

Like drawing, painting offers plenty of fresh surprises: and in the finished picture there are stories, inventions, legends, cataclysms . . . But no!

> You see only the pale-faced blue angel frozen by glaciers . . . you see an angel and a horse's crupper. Hold on to them then, *they are meant for you*! . . . The angel is there like a piece of filigree, guaranteeing your perfect vision . . . I might ransack mythology to find an explanation of the horse's mane . . . abolish the whole thing . . . *But there is no removing the angel. I've got a filigree angel.*[1]

It is to be feared that we sometimes start with the angel and get the filigree horse (who is far from being a Pegasus!).

Whatever may be said about the passage from original intention, vision,

---

[1] Henry Miller, *Black Spring* (London, John Calder, 1965) 'The Angel is my Watermark', from pp. 54–66. The French word *filigrane* means both 'filigree' and 'watermark'. [M.C.]

intuition (even commission) to finished work, we must never forget that the field of invention is wider than is generally supposed. The composer too can pass from fresco to easel-painting, from play to poem. But whether he is writing chamber music or a big choral or orchestral work, his viewpoint will not only be modified by the scale of the work: it will change qualitatively according to the radical difference between his various projects. In one case his chief concern will be to establish contact – visual as well as auditory – with an audience, while in the other he will be entirely preoccupied with personal reflection. Technical criteria will alter according to the introvert or extrovert character of the work. The idiom of a predominantly reflective piece will generally be complex and so exclusively self-related that it borders on the esoteric and is in danger of being fully grasped by only a small number of 'partners' of whose competence in the matter the composer can be sure. On the other hand, a work written with the public in mind will not be exploratory in character, and the composer will not embark on any voyage of self-discovery in this case. His music will be simple to apprehend and will be enjoyed by a larger circle of listeners, though this does not mean that it is in any way superior.

A composer's evolution is reflected in the graph of his works – by which I mean that it can be followed in his various changes of style and, more importantly, that a composer's relationship to his own idiom can never remain a constant. A composer will go through periods of conquest and discovery. His fundamental concern – the exploration of new possibilities in every area of his field – will lead him to write a number of 'chaotic' works that are less confident, and may well be less polished, than others, but will have a powerful effect in destroying routine and will be more remarkable for their effect on the future than for their relationship to any tradition. Such works are for the most part reflective in character and answer the composer's profound need to exercise his vital inner self, though there are in fact plenty of reflective works that are not directly exploratory. At other times a composer will go through periods of establishment and organization, when he needs to investigate further the discoveries that he has made, to widen and generalize their meaning and to collect them into a consciously organized synthesis. During such periods of apparent 'rest' his music will seem more polished and masterly and will be more immediately satisfactory-seeming, even though it may lack the illuminating power of his other pieces. Sudden or accidental mutations will follow periods of slow, deeply reflective evolution.

Am I making it clear, I wonder, how impossible it is to submit the phenomenon of artistic creation to any one, single kind of analysis? Remember, too, that composers depend on the age in which they live and that conditions them; and that history itself presents periods of sudden mutation and periods of slow evolution. When any logical and coherent system gradually decays, there is an extremely active search for new materials; and this search is undisciplined and chaotic in character, quite as much concerned with destroying the old world as with constructing the new. Once this storm of anarchy has blown itself out, the process of organization starts again, this time on new principles that eventually lead to the establishment of a new coherent system, which in its turn begins to admit exceptions, that is to say to decay ... When these two phenomena corroborate each other, individually and collectively, they produce periods of maximum agitation or maximum repose in the history of music ...

We have come a long way from aesthetic choice, but we were obliged to take this long way round in order to put the whole problem in the right perspective and to determine its true co-ordinates. We have examined the composer's uncertain, shifting position and the difficulty of establishing his motives and methods. We have seen how easy it is to lose one's way with analogies borrowed from other disciplines which, though perfectly equipped for their own purposes, present a dangerous temptation to the musician, who must follow his own, purely musical path. It is no less difficult to reconcile choice of technique with aesthetic intention, since there is always a temptation to favour one of the two at the other's expense. Finally we do not possess the specialized vocabulary needed for this specifically musical undertaking, and we are clumsier than we could wish in our use of the existing vocabulary ... It begins to look, in fact, as though any further study of the question were something in the nature of a bad bet! Let us make the attempt nevertheless and try, if only for practical reasons, to disentangle the apparent contradictions that beset us, to make a scientific survey of the field.

How are we to set about this task in order to reach even passably satisfactory conclusions? The logical way seems to be to start from the basis of all aesthetics – that famous philosophical 'doubt' which, if we apply it to the totality of any musical project, will provide a firm starting point and rid our minds of a number of existing handicaps. We will forget for the moment all the traditional concepts and reconstruct our ideas from basically new data, which will open up a hitherto unexplored field of aesthetic choice. If we grant that this choice is nowadays made at too late a stage in the process of composition, we shall then try to show that, in order to be valid, it must be present at the very outset and must relate to phenomena for which it is generally not held responsible. In this way we shall define the characteristics of this choice and the different levels at which it takes place, from elementary morphology to overall form and from considerations of semantics to those of poetic intention. We shall then try to pin down what is to be meant by 'style' and how the different components of style are to be defined. In doing this we must try to broaden our point of view as much as possible, first by studying the relationship between the style of the individual composer and that of his age, and then by examining how these two intimately connected phenomena interact. Finally we shall find ourselves considering the sense of the work itself, its significance for the composer and its compre-

hension by the listener – the interior and exterior faces of a single phenomenon. On the way we shall ask questions about communication, as lying
at the root of all comprehension; and communication plays an even more
important part in music than in the other means of expression, because
music is irreversible in time. We shall be speaking therefore of the aesthetics
of concert-giving and of listening; and the stricter our enquiry becomes, the
closer we shall find ourselves to the kernel of the matter, a nut so hard that it
cannot be cracked – namely, the collective justification of the individual
aesthetic undertaking. This will bring us eventually to the end of the cycle,
for we shall then be discussing the permanence of this justification, i.e. the
profound ambiguity of all compositions and the relative nature of their
existence, which brings us back to the 'absolute' choice involved in each
individual instance, a reference established at the outset of our decision,
viewed historically,.

This is no mean undertaking, but it forms a cycle that is far from being
merely artificial and will enable us to make a complete study of musical
thinking. Does this mean that we shall succeed in grasping the exact experience of the composer? This actual experience is difficult for anyone to
imagine unless he has actually shared it, although its importance can be
clearly judged. In the last resort it is presumptuous to develop ideas about
music, which are in danger of doing a disservice to their object by the mere
fact of diverting attention to themselves while forming no intrinsic part of
music itself. We have already observed that there is no lack of such ideas
about music and that in fact they reflect the point of view of 'outsiders'.
Poets, for example, will describe mental associations and formal analogies (I
am not speaking of merely pictorial imagery) and these, despite their brilliance, do not go to the heart of the 'mystery' but simply describe its effect.
We may well appreciate this gift of the poet's, and be grateful for it, and still
refuse to admit his success without qualification; for in fact the ultimate
question eludes his magic. On the other hand we are in a position to state
more specifically 'musical' ideas – ideas not *about*, but *in* music. Even so, are
we any nearer to grasping the effect, the 'radiation' of this 'mystery'? We do
not wish to make any impossible claims, and there comes a point in our
knowledge at which ambition surrenders. We know very well that we have
not grasped the *idea* of music simply because we have thoroughly investigated our ideas *in* and *about* music.

As we have already said, we do not consider musicians to be in the best
position for undertaking this enquiry. They are too concerned with actual
practice, too deeply involved to be aware of what may be called the
'cryptography' of the language of music. Music forms such an integral part of
their daily existence that they lose their sense of perspective and their ability
to 'distance' themselves, so that some problems are really beyond their
grasp. If the composer could express in words his obscure instinct to communicate and felt the need to transcend verbally the contradictions that

make him a creative artist, then he would be not a musician but a writer. (Thus E. T. A. Hoffmann's best musical compositions are certainly not the ones he actually wrote but the ones of which he gives 'ideal' descriptions in his books; and the same is true of Nietzsche.)

The musician arrives at the *idea* of music only by means of music itself, which is his own personal means of communication, the only medium that is his by right and in which he can express his conviction with maximum force, the only medium in which he is irrefutable. This is a fundamental fact that we should never forget – indeed it should be inscribed above every reflection in this very book. The specific strength of the composer lies in the 'non-significance' of music, its lack of 'meaning', and we ourselves must not lose sight of the fact that it is the phenomenon of sound that is of primary importance: 'living' this order of human existence is the very essence of music. We musicians feel neither humble, nor beaten before we start fighting, nor do we in any way regret our inability to reach our sources by more than one path. After all, one has to know one's powers in order to make the best use of them and to avoid the confusions that prejudice one's clarity for vision. It is not a question of seeking for some kind of alibi simply in order to rid ourselves of a number of different nightmares; if it were, our search would result in nothing but useless commentaries, which would very soon be forgotten. What we wish to do is to put ourselves at the very heart of those questions which are always being asked and never receive an answer, that is to say at the vital centre of musical creation.

There is always a temptation, not for the musician himself but for those who discuss his work, to express what we may call 'outside' opinions; and whether the alibi is a poetic, a philosophical or even a political one will depend on circumstances and on individual cases. It always appears as though the majority of these 'outside' commentators were embarrassed by music's lack of 'meaning' and felt obliged to give it some definite aim, without which it would have no social purpose and would in fact deserve to be called no more than an 'ornamental' art, as has often been done. We can only repeat that music cannot undertake the task of expounding rational ideas; it supports none of these or, alternatively, supports them all indiscriminately; but it goes against its own nature if it attempts concepts that are totally alien to it. It can, on the other hand, undertake the qualification of our ideas, their emotional character and their ethical content. This is particularly true when there is a generally accepted system of conventions, so that certain musical situations automatically evoke certain mental situations by means of associative reflexes. If this system of conventions disappears or the meaning of the conventions is for some reason lost, we are unable to decipher that particular code of ideas to which the music specifically refers. At most we shall be left with certain effects that imitate spontaneous human reactions, which do not change whether they find some form of expression or not! Since the communication of ideas is outside the sphere of music, this is not an alibi on which we shall pick in order to discover any sense or necessity in musical thought, and we reject in advance any arguments that may be brought forward in this field. We refuse the idea of music as propaganda of any sort, because this is absolutely alien to the very aims of music; and by 'propaganda' I do not mean simply what is generally understood by that word but all ideology of any kind.

You may well be thinking that although I have laid special emphasis on the inability of music to express anything but itself, and have recognized that it is essentially a 'mystery', yet here I am trying to analyse, with a minimum of logic, this extremely irrational phenomenon. (Remember the goose that laid the golden eggs . . .) Am I not afraid of finding, quite literally, nothing at the heart of this 'mystery', or at any rate nothing that has not already been formulated by more illustrious thinkers than I? Above all have I no fear of destroying my own spontaneity, of drying up the springs of my own musical vitality by trying to 'prospect' them? Does not this unrestrained desire for knowledge carry with it, automatically, a terrible curse? Is there not something unhealthy about such curiosity, something destructive in this ambition – this determination at all costs to purloin secrets destined to remain buried in the deepest recesses of consciousness? (Once again the goose with the golden eggs, with hints of Greek tragedy and the Bible . . .) Well, to be honest, these fears do not worry me; and I believe that a deliberate campaign should be waged against the idea that 'inspiration' is damaged by intellectual activity, even if inspiration is understood in the most fulminatory, oracular sense! Surely my own complex nature is sufficient to face these different situations, or rather to adapt itself to these apparently incompatible states? I must admit that I am not much impressed by people who are frightened by the smallest hint of investigation, who consider that there is an absolute taboo on exploring knowledge in depth and prefer once and for all to be guided by instinct. This belief in – or rather subjection to – instinct does not seem to me to be a sign of either health or strength, but simply a terror of finally losing a vigour that is already on the wane. One must be able to 'recuperate', as people say nowadays.

Am I not, perhaps in the last resort, questioning the artist's principal virtue – imagination? Is the imagination permitted to acknowledge boundaries and to exhibit a sudden timidity in situations of which it had better, for its own sake, remain unaware? I do not think that the imagination loses anything by self-awareness in certain circumstances: in fact it can only gain in confidence and strength. We must not be afraid of carrying through this investigation in depth right to the end: if our powers of invention are not strong enough, then such investigation will reveal the fact of their weakness, and if they are sufficiently strong, then they will draw further strength from our study. Does the explanation of caution lie in the fear of sacrilege, or is it not perhaps in the fear of not being able to 'recompose' the mystery once it has been unveiled? Could it be that we take alarm at seeing ourselves 'liquidated' (or perhaps 'spirited away') and having to live with our own nullity? When we force ourselves to look clearly at such fundamental problems as these, we are pledging ourselves to a formidable undertaking: for if the Sphinx refuses to answer, what will happen to me, to my poor little answers and my vain curiosity? Of course it is never pleasant to scrape the bottom of one's own personality and to face one's own inescapable limitations; but it is worth while pursuing the experiment to its logical conclusion, for this will immunize us against those weaknesses that are not actually insurmountable and will reinforce our conviction. Having once passed through this crucible, our imaginations will have less to fear from the phantoms that assail them. There can be no question of mistrusting the mystery of creation and if, in the last resort, we do not succeed in unravelling all its threads, we can always cut them ... following an illustrious precedent ...

I should like finally to quote an excellent remark of André Breton's about the composer's personality – one that I have quoted elsewhere. I am convinced that in every great composer (every great creator, in fact) there is an 'indestructible kernel of darkness'! He can never destroy this even if he should want to: it is the deep and inexhaustible source of that 'radiation' which will unfailingly resist every purely rational approach. He can degrade it only by either plundering, forgetting (which implies hating), or deriding it. I put my faith in this 'kernel of darkness', which will still subsist after every momentary flash of illumination.

4

Time, Notation and Coding[1]

... hence the idea of abandoning as far as possible all representation of the objects of theory and designating such objects by symbols, defining the entities studied exclusively by means of their relationship to each other. [Roger Martin]

In this connection I should like to say something about graphic transcription, i.e. notation, which can at present be of two kinds – based either on neumes or on mathematics, according to the co-ordinates of plane geometry.

Both methods of transcription, 'neumatic' and 'structural', employ the same system of co-ordinates. This is defined in the one case by the temporal abscissae moving from left to right, from the first beat to the last: and in the other by pitch structure, from low to high for the different frequencies. Even if these co-ordinates are not entirely explicit, they are in every case subjacent. 'Neumatic', that is to say linear, notation is a regression from symbolic notation, which consists of figures represented by a system of conventional symbols. 'Neumatic' notation has no such coded and figured symbols, but consists simply of a line traced on the surface of the paper and referring implicitly to the space–time co-ordinates mentioned above.

Now the logical evolution of any language must – and historically speaking always does – take the following form: ideas that are more 'general' and more 'abstract' at every stage replace those of the foregoing period. Thus the logical evolution of music appears as a series of 'reductions', the different basic systems forming a decreasing succession in which each one is slotted into the one that precedes it. Dialectically speaking, however, and taking into account the more 'general' and 'abstract' notions, which represent a *restriction*, or *reduction*, of previous notions, the new formal system becomes correspondingly wider than the old and in a sense subsumes it. In this way, to take an example, tonality represents a generalizing of the more

---

[1] 'Temps, notation et code', text of a lecture given at Darmstadt in 1960. The author intended to use it as a basis for an additional Chapter 3 of *Penser la musique aujourd 'hui* (*Boulez on Music Today*), but it was not included there and is previously unpublished. See explanation on p. 13.

particularizing modal system. Tonality generalizes the idea of modality by introducing the principle of transposition, at the same time impoverishing the older system by abolishing all the truly 'particular' characteristics of the modes. These characteristics, once integral to the modes, were in fact completely disintegrated by the new principle of general transposability.

In the same way it might be said that with such a 'generalizing' and 'abstracting' principle as permutation, for instance, the idea of the series subsumes all the other principles that have preceded it, including modality and tonality. A scale may be considered to be a series, in a restricted sense, but one with stronger, more particularizing properties than the twelve-note series; and in the same way the different modes may be said to have arisen by a simple process of circular permutation. Historically, therefore, we may lay down that no intuitive system is ever abandoned until the discovery of some method by which a study of that system can be reproduced in terms of the new 'order'. This series of logical-mathematical operations (called reductional reproductions) is *limited* in number, the order in which they occur is *necessary* and their outcome is *irreversible*, so that – for instance – there can never be a return to modal conceptions of music.

To return to 'neumatic', or 'linear' notation and its historical necessity. This was the first, unsophisticated attempt to transcribe the musical phenomenon of singing; and the association between note and word was so intimate that in the earliest neumatic texts the vocalized syllable and the pitch or the melisma described were amalgamated into a kind of ideogram. Gradually this ideogram became closer to actual musical reality by the progressive use of the co-ordinates that we still use today – from left to right to indicate movement in time and from bottom to top to indicate changes in pitch.

Proportional notation represented a great advance, in that it initiated a coherent formal system by which duration could be indicated 'without the physical need of paper', as it were. The new system subsumed the old, in that the new, 'proportional' notation, with its ability to generalize, could account for everything represented by the old neumatic notation, with its 'particularizing' features. The reverse of this is not true: it is not possible to substitute neumatic notation for proportional, because the former is only a particular instance of the latter – namely an instance of the formal symbol (figured code) being transcribed on the paper proportionally to its value. Furthermore the mass of shifting and ambiguous symbols in neumatic notation was replaced by a body of more restricted, more 'abstract' symbols by means of a proper reductive process. Of course we owe many of the rhythmic gems of the *ars nova* to the earlier neumatic system of notation.

To sum up, then, graphic notation does not completely cover the area covered by symbolic notation: it represents a regression from the general to the particular, and a return to the ideogram would be a further retreat. Any logical and coherent notation in the future will have to include what it replaces and will have to subsume our present symbols, the neumatic symbols and the ideograms. Until such a system is invented, any graphic notation will only constitute a regression, at best a literal, graphic transcription of a situation that can be translated into symbols. It will be no more than a sheet of figured values, as it were a reproduction on paper squared in millimetres.

Psychologically and physiologically speaking, however, we should naturally expect the eye to help the brain rather than the brain to be activated by the eye. In fact the structure of the brain offers far greater possibilities for analysis and information than the nervous structure of the eye, the brain constituting a powerful agent of *measurement* whereas the eye is no more than a rough *calculator*. The brain's *measurements* subsume those of the eye and its approximations are more precise. The *measurements* made by the eye, on the other hand, are rougher, and there is a wide margin of uncertainty in their approximations – even error, in fact, depending on the degree of precision demanded. It is clear that here too any return from brain-measurement to eye-measurement represents a regression, with a corresponding increase in the element of approximateness; and any such regression is essentially anti-historical.

Lastly, any exclusive use of a notation entirely dependent on paper surface seems to show an ignorance of the true notion of musical time. Any notion of graphic transcription gives preference to a vague, amorphous idea of time and completely disregards the idea of time as a pulse, 'striated' time. We shall be seeing later how richly rewarding this dialectic of time and notation can be if consciously used.

We have three reasons, therefore, for considering exclusively graphic notation as totally regressive:

1   it does not use proportional symbols
2   it appeals to less delicate brain structures (thus leading to rougher approximations)
3   it takes no account of any *overall* definition of musical time

What I have said should not lead you to suppose that I reject all graphic solutions: on the other hand, I have sometimes made use of them myself. For there is another confusion to be avoided, namely that which arises from the failure to distinguish between graphic notation properly so called and the actual presentation on the page, designed to emphasize certain formal relationships. I shall return to this question of how music is presented on the page when I come to speak of form. For the moment I will restrict myself to 'neumatic' notation, which must be employed only with a full awareness of what it can achieve. As we have seen, its scope is narrower and more *approximate* than that of proportional symbolic notation. Our present task is to discover a still more general system that will subsume earlier systems by means of more extensive and more abstract elements. Until that discovery is made, we must use the two existing systems, having regard to their specific characteristics: the neumatic system, relying on the eye, being the less precise, whereas the proportional system takes into stricter account the element of duration, of which it provides our minds with an idea more immediate than that provided by figured proportion with its element of guesswork. On the other hand the neumatic system is better suited to the representation of *smooth* [*lisse*] or *amorphous* time and the proportional system to *pulsating*, or *striated*, time. Of course, as I have said before, I regard the two categories – *smooth* and *striated* time – as capable of reciprocal interaction, since time cannot be *only* smooth or *only* striated. But I can say that my whole formal time system is based on these two categories and *on them alone*. They may act on each other by osmosis, thus following a biological process. The abstract of this biological process must conform exactly to the process in order to reflect it faithfully.

It is even possible to make conscious use of the discrepancy between notation and realization – i.e. use this coded grid, which is what notation is – in order to initiate an interaction between composer and performer, whether the performer is conscious of this or not. Let me first explain this 'circuit' between the two, which can be formulated thus:

A   the *composer* originates a *structure* which he *ciphers*
B   he *ciphers* it in a coded *grid*
C   the interpreter *deciphers* this *coded* grid
D   according to his decoding he reconstitutes the *structure* that has been transmitted to him

It is clear that ciphering in code followed by deciphering constitutes the whole problem of notation, with all its potential uses; and I am convinced that this ciphering plays a role in actual composition, the course of which it may affect. By 'structure' and 'coding' I mean *overall* structure and *local* coding, since local structure and local coding are part of the same mental operation. It is impossible to generate a local object or a local structure *in the abstract*; in however elementary form I may conceive it, I am obliged to put it in code even to transcribe it (in fact the code also has to serve as an 'alphabet'). Thus the more I elaborate these local structures, the greater the importance the coding acquires.

This importance was so great to Stravinsky that he concentrated all his attention on a coding so precise that it obliged the performer to reproduce the composer's message as exactly as it was originally communicated to him. Coding in the romantic era, on the other hand, was fairly loose, and the performer could *interpret* the composer's message. The coding of the message was not designed to provide him with high-precision information, and the message was therefore reproduced with varying degrees of approximation. We can thus see that, historically, the search has been for ever finer grids in order to ensure the maximum precision in transmitting the composer's message. The idea of the composer capitalizing the different capacities of different codings has arisen hitherto only in very primitive forms, and has never been integrated into any formal system of composition. The composer may deliberately employ an ambiguous coding system; but this ambiguity – still in accordance with the composer's instructions – may either be felt as such by the performer or, on the other hand, it may direct his performance.

In the first case composer and performer agree to 'play' with the coding; the performer consciously reproduces the messages intended by the composer: the coding is a complicity between the two. In the second case the composer knows that his coding cannot possibly be deciphered by the performer, whose reproduction of his message will therefore be defective. The performer, on the other hand, is simply faced with the problem of this deciphering and must try to transmit the message as faithfully as he can. In other words, the margin of error beyond which he is working must be made increasingly smaller, though it will always exist and can never be reduced to zero. In this last case, as we were saying, it is the sheer *difficulty* of deciphering the code that is the problem, the difficulty of performing extremely complicated rhythms or large and small intervals at the same set speed, etc. 'Beyond possibility' does not mean an 'impossible absurdity'. 'Beyond possibility' means that the composer has carefully considered the limits of the difficulty involved and knows that beyond a certain point he can count on a performance that is only more or less approximate. 'Absurdity' means writing something that lies quite outside the general possibilities of the instrument or the performer.

Let me give you an example of absurdity. I take a certain duration and give it an irregular irrational. I follow this with a duration different from the first and give it another irregular irrational (also different from the former one) to which I add still another, different, irregular irrational. This implies a mental operation that I am totally incapable of performing, even approximately, because in a single instant I have to think three different temporal planes, subjacent temporal pulsations that are never expressed as such. Only two of them can be really 'thought', and the third has therefore to be realized purely mechanically – by which I mean the following. When the action of one's hands is concerned with the complete co-ordination between pulsation (or its subdivisions) and its actual *realization*, a special mental control operation is not necessary: the pulsation is transmitted directly to the player's fingers, the physical action of playing a certain number of notes being sufficient to establish the rhythm of the musical figure.

In the case quoted above I have to think the original pulsation, then calculate the second pulsation in relation to the first, and after that calculate the second in relation to the third. The first two operations can be carried out instantaneously, the first pulsation being taken as a *state* subjacent to the calculation of the third (that is to say a beat, a speed of development), but the second cannot become a *state* and thus abolishes the first. What is more, when I change note values, I have to re-relate to the first pulsation the duration of the first note value and its proportion to the second that I have to play; and then repeat all the previous operations. This is in fact a *basic absurdity* in terms of the structure of the human mind.

The position needs to be only slightly changed in order to make it possible to realize this hugely difficult example – still impossible as a total reality but intelligible to the eye, with a fair degree of approximation. All I need to do is to take the relationship of the basic duration to the first irrational group, so as to give myself a different tempo on each occasion. At this tempo, and following the unitary co-ordinates of this tempo, I calculate the speed of the irrational group, and this gives me a succession of tempi – or states – subjacent to the calculation of the second pulsation. These irrational values can become purely mechanical if, as I said earlier, there is complete co-ordination between the secondary pulsation and its realization by the performer. In this case I have reduced the whole to a single mental operation, namely the co-ordination of successive states of *striated* time. These successive states are quite difficult to establish exactly, and there will always be a margin of inexactitude because reflexes are less sharp, vaguer – almost to the point of indecision, in fact – in the case of a *state* than in the case of an action. But can this margin be noticeably reduced by a determined effort to improve one's reflexes in reaching a temporal *state*?

This example is designed to demonstrate the fundamental difference between an impossible absurdity and a difficulty that is beyond the limit of possibility. In the second case you are basing your reasoning on mental categories and what they can and cannot achieve. In the first case you have simply ignored those categories and your proposition is therefore meaningless.

I have spoken of notation as the coding of structure, and it is in this form that it plays a role in the elaboration of local structure, and actually affects that structure.

We must consider notation therefore as a means, and not as a principle, of creation. I would say that in the expression 'transcribed structure' (or notated figure) it is the 'structure' that is the primary element, while the qualifying adjective refers only to the coding of that structure. You cannot in any case take the actual coding as the message that is to be transmitted, although the coding may be thought of as capable of influencing that message.

5

Form[1]

I should like to begin with an observation of Claude Lévi-Strauss's, which I have already quoted elsewhere: 'Form and content are of the same nature and amenable to the same analysis. Content derives its reality from its structure, and what is called *form* is the "structuring" of local structures, which are the content.'

History provides plenty of evidence to prove this: musical form has varied in exact proportion to variations in 'local structures'. I can only observe once again that the serial system has therefore of necessity meant the search for new forms capable of structuring the new 'local structures' produced by the serial system. The universe of serial thought being essentially a *relative* universe, there can be no question of fixed, non-relative forms. We have seen that the generation of networks of possibilities, which are the raw material for *l'opérateur* – to use a significant term of Mallarmé's – has from the outset tended increasingly to produce a material that is constantly evolving. Among the most characteristic examples, from the vertical angle, are the series of variable density, which exhibit the mobility sought at the outset. Given series of this kind, we can only work towards connections that are constantly evolving, and in the same way this morphology will be matched by a correspondingly non-fixed syntax. Formerly the position was quite different, and the composer was working in a universe clearly defined by general laws that already existed before he embarked on his composition. From this it followed that all 'abstract' relationships implicit in the idea of form could be defined *a priori*, and thus give rise to a certain number of schemes or archetypes that existed ideally before being realized in any actual work. Composing amounted to choosing an exact scheme. These schemes gradually ceased to have any real meaning, thanks to the evolution of musical vocabulary and morphology, and their function as regulators came to contradict the material that they were supposed to regulate. This whole

---

[1] 'Form', text of a course given at Darmstadt in 1960 and intended as a basis for an additional Chapter 4 of *Penser la musique aujourd'hui*, but not included there and previously unpublished. See explanation on p. 13.

scaffolding of 'schemes' had eventually to make way for a new conception of form as something that could be changed from one moment to the next. Each work had to originate its own form, a form essentially and irreversibly linked to its 'content'.

It has therefore become exceedingly difficult to speak of form in general, since it is not really possible to examine it apart from the aspects that it assumes in individual works. At best we can hope to distinguish a number of general principles of organization.

In the first place there are two kinds of local structures: what we call *static* structure and *dynamic* structure (corresponding roughly to what we have called *amorphous* and *striated* time). In what sense can a structure be called static? In the sense that it presents – statistically speaking – the same quality and the same quantity of events in its unfolding. This *static* quality is entirely independent of the *number* of events, whose constant density is their important feature. Static structure may admit of a large range of all kinds of note values, or a small range; it may be based on extreme, though constant, selectiveness or on a complete absence of selectiveness – but all these criteria must of course remain virtually constant. On the other hand *dynamic* structure presents an evolution, sufficiently large to be perceptible, in the density of the events that succeed each other, and in their quality. This *dynamic* quality, like the static quality mentioned above, is entirely independent of the frequency, the number of these events; dynamic structure involves a selectiveness that may vary in strictness but is always evolving, i.e. the criteria of this selectiveness are perpetually changing.

Let me explain these positive and negative criteria. In order to make an initial selection in the indeterminate, amorphous universe it is essential to have a capacity not only for choice but also for refusal, refusal being quite as important as choice. For instance, I may choose a certain series of sounds for the positive act of writing signs in sound-space: this is a positive choice. At the same time I may refuse to employ, for example, some part of the register, and this is a negative choice. Of course I am considering these negative and positive criteria, choice and refusal, as complementary, since my refusal to employ some portion of the register may equally be said to be my choice of the register-minus-the-portion-that-I-have-refused. But when we speak of 'choice' and 'refusal' we must not ignore the psychology of the composer, or indeed of the listener. Let me give you an example. A listener is more aware of the absence of some part of the register from a given passage than he is of the phenomenon 'register-minus-something'. And this awareness is such that when the composer, as it were, lifts the ban on that 'something', the listener experiences the introduction of that 'something' as a *positive* action, because it involves the appearance of something of which he had been formerly *deprived*, in the literal sense of the word.

Static and dynamic local structures are therefore determined as follows:

QUALITY

Static

1 constant criteria of selection (referring to the restricted automatism of relationships)
2 absence of selective criteria (tending to a total automatism of relationships)

Dynamic

changing criteria of selection (moving towards a total exclusion of the automatism of relationships)

This gives rise, according to circumstances, to:

QUANTITY

Static

fixed density of events: weak $\rightarrow$ strong

Dynamic

mobile density of events: strong $\rightarrow$ weak

This gives us a complete picture of what may be called the characterology of a local structure. I must remind you once again that I have been considering here only extreme situations, the movement from static to dynamic being natural, and thus included in this description.

We therefore have two quite distinct phenomena, the quality of the events in a structure and the quantity of those events. The two must be carefully distinguished in order to avoid the misunderstandings that arise from the common confusion of the two.

On the other hand the criteria of selection for each component of the musical event, not only morphologically but also syntactically speaking, are applicable in the following manner:

morphology $\rightarrow$ **Initiation/Distribution**
syntax $\rightarrow$ **Production/Placing**

It is therefore on these criteria of selection that the dialectic of the succession, or connecting, of local structures will be built; and these criteria of selection are decisive in the incorporation of local structures in that main, overall structure that we call *form*. The ensemble of these criteria of selection may be called the *formants* of an overall structure. We know what acoustic formants are – selected and 'privileged' frequencies that give a fundamental its character by means of its related harmonics. The criterion of *density* will play something like the role of the intensity of each of the frequencies that constitute the 'formant'. None of this, of course, must be regarded as anything more than an analogy between a concrete structure and a mass of abstract notions.

The *formants* – or the sum total of the criteria of selection – in a large structure are the only originators of the perceptible 'points' or 'areas' that make it possible for a form to become articulate, as well as determining the physiognomy of the points and areas thus articulated.

How do we arrive at any judgement of overall structure? From what premises do we start? Formerly the perception of any form was based *a priori* on direct memory and on an 'angle of hearing' (as we speak of 'angle of vision'). That perception is now based on what may perhaps be called 'para-memory' and the angle of hearing is *a posteriori*.

Until recently Western European music, with its strong pre-established hierarchy underlying every actual composition, had elaborated a skilful system of markers, or reference points, within an initially given form; there were of course surprises – that is to say, exceptions – but generally speaking the element of surprise depended precisely on the fact that most people were familiar with a number of the formal schemes employed by the composer. Actual memory played an important part in judging these formal schemes – in the case, for example, of entirely self-sufficient themes or easily recognized figures, especially if these were short, immediately striking and repeated fairly often. Repetition ('recapitulation') was plainly designed to support perception by 'sedating' it with memory. Furthermore, just as the eye has a general field of vision in the case of classical architecture, the ear had an 'angle of hearing' that could be verified at crucial moments in a work by means of reference-points or 'markers'. This was the process characteristic of classical Western music: actual memory of real objects and 'angle of hearing' checked at major points in the structure – in other words, an *a priori* awareness of the formal schemes employed by the composer, a sort of common fund shared by the musical consciousness of a whole society.

How has the situation changed during recent years? One feature has been the placing of these 'markers' at increasingly irregular intervals – making them, in fact, more difficult to 'mark' – in order to keep the listener's attention more alert. The conclusion to be drawn from this is that the evolution of form, 'marked' in this way, must end in an irreversible phase when criteria of form are established according to systems of differentiated possibilities. Let me give you an example. If in any given system of possibilities I employ a certain number of criteria (negative or positive) and then later employ the same system of possibilities but with criteria slightly different from the first, I shall have two classes of musical objects, identical in origin but different in aspect. In order to recognize them, I shall have recourse to what they have in common, properties that I will call potential since they are not directly explicit; and it will therefore be a 'para-memory' that compares the two objects presented. On the other hand, since formal schemas today are no longer preconceived but are created, as it were, *ambulando*, in a sort of time-weave [*temps tressé*], it is impossible to be aware of the form until it has been actually described. During performance the listener travels through the music following a kind of graining process [*fibrage*] – comparable to the 'grained space' [*espace fibré*] of ensemble theory – noting as he passes the 'markers' provided by the criteria of form. He will therefore not be conscious of the form, and his 'angle of hearing' will be established only *a posteriori*, when the form has been completed. It is clear that the two perceptions are fundamentally different.

on the one hand: real memory of real objects
on the other hand: potential memory ('para-memory') of classes of
                      objects
on the one hand: 'angle of hearing', *a priori* awareness
on the other hand: 'angle of hearing', *a posteriori* awareness

It is therefore important that the *formants*, or ensemble of determining criteria, should be chosen with precision in order to direct, or orientate, the local structuring that they govern. Thus the local structure must first be assigned its 'register' and will then be assigned its 'intensity' by establishing the density of the events it contains. The order of these local structures, their classification and their density demand serial criteria of wider dimensions, so as to impose the order of their succession, of their diagonal relationships or their simultaneity. Thus, in order to determine the overall form, the same mode of *thinking* (though not the same *modes of application*) will prevail throughout the passage, from the morphological microstructure to the rhetorical macrostructure. In the following order we find:

criteria of placing of the local structures within the overall structure →
criteria of producing the local structures →
criteria of disposing the internal structures →
criteria of originating the elements of these internal structures →

By means of this scheme *everything* is possible within a coherent system of formal logic, and everything is originated consistently – from closed forms, totally determined, to open forms and total indeterminacy. The essential strength of this overall organization resides in the fact that, in order to originate an overall form of any kind whatever, I need no *accident* foreign to it, nothing for which it is not itself, however remotely, responsible. I find the *accident* at the conclusion of a logical and coherent deduction: it is not the point of departure from which I set out to organize it according to syllogisms that are apparently correct but have no fundamental connection with it, except factitious numerical connections – a factitiousness rooted in the ambiguity of the properties of numbers.

Take an opposite example, and suppose that I allow all these organizations to be dictated by pure chance. In that case I shall not obtain a form but a mere sampling of local structures, with *amorphous permutations*, and these local structures may, or may not, be able to support the functions of transformation (or determining criteria) dictated by chance. In order to plan an extreme example of this kind I should have to use local structures that can be made to succeed each other without any errors of syntax or morphology; and local structures also capable of supporting *all* the transformations supposed by the determining criteria. I have never met a work in which all these conditions were fulfilled. On the other hand local structures follow the normal law of large numbers. That is to say, some can be successfully linked and others involve syntactical and morphological solecisms when linked. Some prove amenable to the transformations imposed on them by the determining criteria; others do not – still in accordance with the law of large numbers. The composer has therefore failed in his task, since the universe that he has created lacks all coherence. In the ideally perfect case that I have supposed – in which *all* links and *all* transformations by determining criteria are controlled by the composer (not, presumably, one by one, but rather class by class and group by group) – his knowledge of the universe he has created would not be structure by structure; he would be complete master of its coherence. The difference between these two operations should now, I think, be clear.

I attach great importance to this idea of *formants* as applied to overall structure; in the first place because it is the extension of an organic principle, and secondly because it has the merit of giving a clear account of something as abstract as the articulation of overall form. It does this without having anything in common with traditional classical schemas, or with simple empirical ideas that cannot be formed into a synthesis. Furthermore, I believe this idea to be sufficiently malleable to establish an order without imposing a restriction; and it also allows all the oppositions between free (or mobile) and strict (or fixed) form, using these terms in a sense parallel to that in which we speak of free and strict writing.

Free (or mobile) forms present a delicate problem. The moment that you are dealing with a number of performers it is hard – for psychological as well as technical reasons – to allow them initiatives or responsibilities. The greater the number of performers and the greater their lack of special skills, the less is it possible to control the 'operations' within a mobile form. Bearing in mind some of the conditions of performance, I prefer to think of mobile form as a *material* form, i.e. to regard it as a 'possible' score serving as a basis for one or more 'fixed' scores chosen from the multiplicity of possibilities. I quite realize that this contradicts the principle of the whole thing, but only at first sight, since musicians will have gradually to accustom themselves to this way of thinking. In chamber music, for instance, the difficulty does not arise; but in any ensemble the possible margin of error must be calculated and borne in mind when determining in advance the 'mobility' of the work, i.e. the margin of error must either be included in that mobility or else that mobility must be limited by the margin of error. The problem is therefore not as insoluble as it appears at first.

I should like to add further that different 'formants' of a structure may take as reference a homogeneous or a non-homogeneous time. On the other hand they may be conceived simultaneously, i.e. immediately, in function of their combination; or they may be conceived quite independently of their distinction and only later mounted, according to their salient characteristics, which involves working with what may be called a kind of precast material.

I have, as you see, attempted to define form as a group of concepts rather than as a gesture. (If I come to need a gesture, it will find a place within this group of concepts.) Finally it seems to me that I have resolved the antinomy between form as something thought and form as something experienced; since the concrete deductions on which it is founded, within a coherent system of formal logic, demonstrate that it can be experienced only by being thought. And that, today is surely an important antinomy to have resolved.

6

Towards a Conclusion[1]

I have been trying in these talks to expose the foundations of a real methodology of composition, from the morphological stage to that of overall form.
I have treated some points in greater detail because they are of more topical
interest; in fact it seemed to me essential to cut anecdote to a minimum and
to demonstrate plainly that gesture, if repeated, leads to gesticulation. I
have never thought gesticulating intelligent, any more than I have felt
impelled to drop my intelligence when engaged in making music. In any
case, I have really tried to find a deductive method that will enable me to
explain and to account for my actions as a composer, and I have not been
content to draw up catalogues of samples or simply to describe how I set
about composing any one of my works. This has led me to demand of my
listeners a considerable amount of abstract reflection on the categories and
classification of the different problems that have arisen, and I admit that this
has not always been easy. But why, I asked myself, should we musicians not
be as mentally agile and rigorous as other intellectuals?

As far as methodology is concerned, I cannot allow that it should be
arrived at entirely irrationally. That, to my mind, suggests refusing responsibility for one's own acts and the rigorous training (or *askesis*) necessary for
anyone willing to assume such responsibility – a refusal that may come either
from fear or from incapacity. This situation seems to me to lie at the very
heart of contemporary musical life, and rather than turn my back on it I have
thought it better to face the problem and consider the possibility of achieving
a coherently organized musical universe. Although I have admitted that I
would not accept the irrational as sole guide, I certainly do not exclude the
irrational from all musical activities, for without the irrational music would
cease to exist. Building the universe within which we are to evolve on logical
principles does not in any sense mean restricting the sum total of purely
intuitive psychological means at the musician's disposal for *ascertaining* the

---

[1] 'Conclusion partielle', text of the last course at Darmstadt in 1960 and intended as a basis for
a Conclusion to *Penser la musique aujourd'hui*, but not included there and previously
unpublished. See explanation on p. 13.

efficaciousness of any particular form, for *discovering* certain means of expression and *integrating* them in the process of composition because they are genuinely interesting. It is easy to believe that any composer who reduces his musical procedures to a formal system is submitting his brain to 'a shrinking and desiccating process rather like that "reduction" (so called in fact) that certain Indian tribes practise on the severed heads of their victims'. Daniel Lacombe, who wrote that, is a mathematician, and he goes on: 'This idea of a Jivaro-style obsession with logic may well be common enough among the anti-logicals,but it still belongs to the world of myth and carries with it the corresponding significances, whether these be implicit or explicit.' So the argument that music is sterilized if it is 'reduced to a formal self-sufficient system and robbed of any contact with reality' is invalid. In fact it is no more than a reflex defence mechanism of minds too poor to admit of any easy co-existence between their own irrational feelings and a rational universe. This is a weakness and by no means a mark of superiority.

Why all these analogies with mathematical method, you may well be asking. I have never established any direct relationship between music and mathematics, only simple relations of comparison. Because mathematics is the science with the most developed methodology at the present time, I have taken it as an example that may help us to fill the gaps in our present system. I have tried in some way to lay the foundations of a methodology of music which must be detached, as such, from the methodology of mathematics with which I have tried to establish an analogy. Each discipline has its own proper objects and methods, and its aims are specifically and exclusively its own. The last thing I want to do is to introduce any misunderstanding on this point and then to be told that I am 'reducing' musical functions to mathematical functions. Others have in fact done this and shown thereby that they are not aware of the specific nature of each of these two universes.

On the other hand, you may very well ask whether this formal system, elements of which I have been trying to explain during these last few days, is an intellectual preconception or linked to my own musical experience. Experiencing and theorizing are plainly two sides of a single event, the one bright and the other dark. We start with an experimental elaboration of certain concrete events, and our elaborations suggest a number of laws, which we then arrange in a coherent system. Armed with this system we return to our experiment, which will give us either a better system, i.e. one that gives a better account of the musical events that we have in mind – or a more robust system that subsumes the first. And we may well have to return more than once to the task ... There is therefore no question of a rigid, *a priori* system. It is simply a matter of the best immediately available provisional solution leading to a better – or at least more inclusive – further provisional solution. There can surely be no more fruitful dialectic between actual experience and pure speculation. My thought does not in such a case 'gesticulate', make gestures: it progresses steadily along a path solidly paved with facts it has previously established.

We may say in conclusion that in discussing new schemas, new structures and new musical propositions in general, we should follow the same procedure as that used in discussing any other intellectual proposition and ask ourselves three fundamental questions: What does it mean? Is it intellectually valid? Is it of any use? Take, for example, a new structural possibility. If it has any meaning, it will almost always prove valid in its own context; and there is no need to insist on its practical use. Some lines of enquiry often prove unrewarding because these three fundamental questions have not been asked at the outset. I should like to end this series of talks with a quotation from one of Rimbaud's famous letters to George Izambard and Paul Démeny: 'Our task is to arrive at the unknown by the *regulation of all the senses.*' It is by a long, immeasurable and reasoned *regulation* of all the senses that the musician becomes a *seer*.

7

Periform[1]

A conference on form?

Well, why not?

A bold assault on such a subject argues considerable assurance about 'the rest' ... How unwise to embark on such a dangerous investigation!

Perhaps the least important of the elements lacking is an actual subject?

In any case there is at the moment no question of a conference on that 'subject' ('starting from ...')

So there we are embarking on the raft of form, with plenty of provisions (such as phrases, words, instructions), on a highly educational cruise ...

I cannot honestly say that I feel very inclined to pay my fare in the form of a useful contribution to the numerous questions that we shall have to consider.

I feel no temptation to go back to the Flood, and no genius shows any willingness to whisper in my ear any vindications, either definitive or provisional. If genius there be, he finds me more inclined to undertake some roaming commission than to pontificate.

As motto, I will borrow my own words: 'A revolution must be dreamed quite as much as engineered.'

I don't want to show any reluctance to admit the truth of that dictum, but I shall take my time over dreaming revolutions and meanwhile count on others to provide a rich supply of solid, robust, substantial discourses, while I confine myself to observations that demonstrate the versatility, the humour and the fantasy of my mind.

So much by way of introduction!

Form, or as Jarry might have put it, 'the word' ...

Or another quotation – Webern on Hölderlin: 'Living means defending a form.' I am willing to accept sole responsibility for what I deduce from that, and I shall start by inverting it and say, 'A form means defending life' or in more egocentric terms, 'Form means defending one's life.'

---

[1] 'Periforme'. In 1965 a congress on 'form in contemporary music' was held at Darmstadt and the proceedings were published in the *Darmstädter Beiträge zur neuen Musik*, No. 10. Boulez's text, though announced for a future issue, did not appear there, but in *Lettres françaises* (16 June 1966) without reference to the original context.

I should be quite happy to conjugate a musical destiny – or any other destiny, for that matter: we must not be cliquish! – on a formula such as this:

```
  I           form
 you   trans  form
  he    de    forms
```
Racine, I would call 'proteiform' . . .
```
              formal
              formalism
              formation
           information
           informal
              formula
          unformulated
              formulary
              formulation
              formant
              etc.
```
Not forgetting . . . :
```
              formidable!
```

(on principle I am not excluding imposture)

I remember an aesthete better known for his brilliance than his prudence once admitting in a confidential moment (among a host of other confidences of all kinds) that he really preferred 'the forms of life' to 'the life of forms'.

I might scramble Hölderlin and Cocteau together and say, 'I prefer defending the forms of life to defending one's life in forms.' A wonderful programme, and quite enough to keep generations of brilliant humanists busy!

Unfortunately this is not a conference on humanism, and I cannot therefore pursue all the possible lines of thought that this aphorism suggests. (And speaking of humanism, I find this key word is often used by ideologists as a weapon against formalism; but the way in which they use it is rather like the way people use meteorological language when talking about trivialities . . .)

Form – a key word for a key subject – perplexes me.

The harder you try to pin it down, the more it eludes you; the more you try to isolate it historically, the more unreal it becomes.

The less you talk about it, the more it keeps cropping up; the more you discuss it, the less you agree about it.

There are questions that one finds oneself endlessly repeating; they echo each other until the echo becomes indecent:[1]

---

[1] This comment arises from an untranslatable pun in the French on 'qu'est ce *que*' (queue).

what is form?

what is . . .?

what . . .?

Is virgin forest a form?
Quite . . .
Imagination, then, is also a form.
Will that convince anyone?
I do not think so. But the further I advance, the more I doubt the virtues of conviction – she is really a not very interesting widow.
So I will adopt the Rimbaud–Infernal method:

One evening I sat Form (with a capital F of course) on my knee. (Why not? There's nothing indecent in that!) And I found her bitter (which has certainly happened to a number of people, even if they had never before dared to sit Form on their knees) – And I gave her a dressing-down. (I should be willing to bet that the people who have behaved in this irreverent way are much less numerous.)

I could go on with my parody of the poem, but it would be no more than a scholastic exercise . . . a dead form in fact!
Winter or spring, it would bring us no more than 'the idiot's dreadful laugh'. . .

Tournons toujours
autour . . .
de la plus haute tour.

Form:
is it a gesture, an accident? a series of gestures, a series of accidents?
is it a chance encounter?
is it a discipline?
is it a truth to be discovered or reinvented?
is it a concept? an act of the will?
is it a pattern in the maze, inherited from one generation to the next?
is it an organized maze?
is it a revelation?
or an illumination?
or a shock?
is it a doubt?
is it an adjustment by feel?
is it a mystery that keeps on reforming within the evidence itself?
is it . . . a black sun?

We are questioning questions . . .

In the footsteps of the old alchemists – and it won't do.

For better and for worse the old patterns have lost their reality, so we must just accustom ourselves to the unavoidable vacuum and put in its place . . . precisely what *are* we to put in its place? Isn't that the question?

Form, that pretty philosophers' stone which they all find it such fun to search for – all those big, serious, well-behaved, studious children. Will they find it – yes or no?

I am making comparisons, engineering collisions – perhaps these are embryo forms?

Can I abide by my eventual conclusion or must I include what I saw in advance?

How far am I going to mislead the interpreter of dreams? Do I have to hand over the keys needed to understand? Or am I allowed to shut myself up in the fortress of my imagination?

'How easy it is to write, how difficult it is to compose.'

No exclamation mark, please. It could be the heading of a chapter, an entirely objective one. Pushed to its logical conclusion as description, form would probably play the part of spectrum analysis . . . an altogether spectral part, you might even say!

Who will recount the labours of transmutation, the pangs of transsubstantiating forms? Perhaps one day, if I feel a greater gift for describing phantoms . . .

Can the unusual juxtaposition of an umbrella, a sewing machine and an operating table create a form? Stupid question and not, at first blush, really a necessary one, though there are times when one might feel that it was topical . . .

Form: a key word [*maître-mot*], I wrote. By a typing error I wrote 'mître-mot' and I could go on forever: *maître-mot, mot de maître*; *mître-mot, mot de pître*; *piètre-mot*; *maître-sot* . . .[1] (*Sinbad the Sailor* . . . and so on, *à la Joyce!*)

Let's go on with our argument *per absurdum*:

I do not defend a form, therefore I am not alive. Right?

Or, 'I am alive, therefore I defend a form.' Righter?

Or more commonly, 'I am alive, therefore I don't have to bother about defending a form' (unless it's a question of a political crusade, in which case . . .).

Has even an anchorite ever said, 'I am concerned with defending a form, therefore I am not alive'?

(If such an anchorite existed, we should have at all costs to find him and bring him to this congress, now. He might well be able to give us some

---

[1] *mître*, mitre or chimney-pot; *pître*, fool, jester; *piètre*, tramp, vagabond; *sot*, idiot.

interesting unpublished information. But perhaps he would look at us in silent commiseration and leave without further explanation, with our hunger for knowledge still unsatisfied. And we should be even more reduced than before to the patient assembling of umbrellas and sewing machines on operating tables!)

On principle, the first thing that I do is to live; or at least I do my best to, though I am not sure that it is as easy as is generally supposed and as people say. Yes, I live; but I am interested in acquiring knowledge. What is a human being without knowledge? No more than an animal . . . And so, long live learning!

Armed with my small parcel of knowledge, the first thing I do – to be original – is to get rid of it as quickly as I can, following the advice of all the best masterminds, whom I would not dare to disobey in such an important matter!

So there I am moving in a zigzag.

Am I going to hurry to pick up my small parcel again, in order to gain control of the situation? Or am I going to allow myself, quite deliberately, to be guided entirely by the fever that possesses me and make ecstatic diagrams of my own creative energy? The problem of problems.

How am I to form – let alone formulate – myself? I am my own engineer and what I have to do is to pin down the lightning! (The comparison, *hardiesse oblige* . . . is not altogether inapt.)

Language is an alchemy still full of feints and fictions . . .

Rereading what I have written elsewhere, I find it extremely serious and very much to the point. This for instance:

> Form and content are of the same nature and amenable to the same analysis. Content derives its reality from its structure, and what is called *form* is the 'structuring' of local structures, which are the content.

(I did not write that, of course, but Lévi-Strauss, the eminent ethnologist, whom I quoted merely for my own purposes.) Is that the inexpressible verbalized and written down? Have our ecstasies been trapped at last?

It was certainly a real attempt . . .

As I read on, I come upon things whose *naïveté* I find in retrospect delightful. This, for instance:

> It has become exceedingly difficult to speak of form in general, since it is not really possible to examine it apart from the aspects that it assumes in individual works. At best we can hope to distinguish a number of general principles of organization.

That is admirably guarded, and I should say the same today and with even greater emphasis, since I still find certain subjects hard to 'confer' about.

Even so, I did manage to dissect a number of structural aspects without entirely abandoning the hope of reaching thereby the Promised Land of definition.

The road was certainly a dusty one and there were times – many of them – when its dustiness proved disconcerting, in the most literal sense. And yet one would risk one's life in any desert in order to reach that Promised Land. Now and then the tables of the law exert a mixture of fascination and repulsion that acts as a great spur to the bold explorer . . .

Here is another passage:

> The conclusion to be drawn from this is that the evolution of form, against the references, must end in the notion of irreversible time when criteria of form are established according to systems of differentiated possibilities . . . [I shall] therefore not be conscious of the form, and [my] 'angle of hearing' will be established only *a posteriori*, after the form has been completed . . . I find the *accident* at the conclusion of a logical and coherent deduction.

(I grant that last sentence a certain quality of oddity, if nothing more; and I suppose oddity is a virtue that I may indulge in now and then, if I want to.)

> I have, as you see, attempted to define form as a group of concepts rather than as a gesture. (If I come to need a gesture, it will find a place within this group of concepts.) Finally, it seems that I have resolved the antinomy between form as thought and form as experienced; since the concrete deductions on which it is founded, within a coherent system of formal logic, demonstrate that form can be experienced only by being thought. And that, nowadays, was surely an important antinomy to resolve?

Don't read any further!

We have had enough of the written word, of transcriptions and translations and quotations, both lapidary and arabesque! Let us leave the dense maze of mortared words and wander freely among the structures improvised the moment the word leaves the speaker's mouth.

8

The Composer as Critic[1]

Speaking of Delacroix's writings about painting, Baudelaire observed, 'His certainty of being able to *write* on his canvas what he had in his mind was matched only by his concern at not being able to *paint* his thoughts on paper.' And he quotes Delacroix's own words on the subject: '"The pen," he used often to say, "is not my *tool*; I feel that my thinking is right, but I am alarmed by the demands of the 'order' that I am obliged to obey. Can you believe that having to produce a page of writing will give me an attack of migraine?"'

Even though the critical writings of creative artists are of minor importance compared with their masterpieces, they are still haunted by this need to obtain a clear picture of their own field and of their own investigations in that field. A creative artist may never express his essential self in these critical essays, analyses and general theoretical writings, but these may turn out to be a critical commentary, or a kind of incantation murmured over a new work as it comes to birth. The common concept of the theory and the practice of an art as existing in watertight compartments is part of the old academic tradition that tries jealously to preserve similar distinctions between form and content, 'studies' and finished 'works'. It seems, though, that in fact the position of the creative artist is not so simple as such academic distinctions would suggest; and that pigeon-holing his different activities in this way is inadmissible if we consider for a moment all the possible and probable interventions of the imagination alone.

We must bear in mind one very important fact: that the coincidence of the two activities – the critical and the creative, as we may call them provisionally – can never in any case be fortuitous. That is to say, this double phenomenon of realization and reflection depends not only on the individual artist's personality but also on the epoch in which he lives. As a first approximation in tracing the evolution of any art, we can establish various fluctuations, some gradual and others violent. On the one hand there are

---

[1] 'Probabilités critiques du compositeur', *Domaine musical*, International Bulletin of Contemporary Music, No. 1, 1954, pp. 1–11.

periods during which a language is being established, its potentialities explored; and these are on the whole periods of stability marked by a certain primordial peace guaranteed by the quasi-automatic nature of what is happening. On the other hand there are periods of destruction and discovery, with all the accompanying risks that have to be taken in responding to new and unfamiliar demands. In the first period there is not much critical writing apart from a few turgid polemical pieces of no more than passing interest; but in the second there are passionate discussions of fundamental problems raised by the weakening of automatic responses, the impoverishment of means of expression and a diminishing power of communication. Anyone who recalls Rameau's numerous writings and the furious controversies they started will realize that our own times, with all their literature of recrimination, are by no means unique in their frantic pitting of one theory against another.

There are endless discussions about music nowadays. 'Serialism' and 'atonality' are the chief questions debated; and the poor 'twelve-note system', furiously buried almost daily and the object of gloomy prophecies for many years, remains 'toujours debout' – still standing – like the famous Golden Calf. The most irrefutable proof of its vitality lies in the frequency of these attacks: cut off one of its heads and ten grow in its place, while critics thunder and composers fulminate and composer-critics go on explaining with intellectual ardour or exhausted nervous systems. The battle is waged (literally) with 'ideas', or figures, or simply with categorical assertions: irrefutable arguments are exchanged and each side treats the other with contemptuous pity. The comic character of all this journalistic in-fighting soon palls for its sheer lack of intelligence, and what will survive of all this balderdash except clear statements based on actual experience of the works themselves? It is only from these that we can hope eventually to build up an idea of constructive criticism that complements the activity of the creators. This might make a valid, positive contribution to the development of a language and a system of poetics; and it would remain, having once accomplished its aim, as a simple historical document – and one absolutely essential in order to obtain a definitive picture of the present age.

As things stand at the moment, there is only one attitude possible: to refuse to be put out by the veterans and the deaf who will continue to call honesty disrespect, courage presumption and independence arrogance. These gentry are small fry who reduce the discussion to their own level, which is pretty low, and to their own capabilities, which are non-existent. It is beneath our dignity to answer them. What else have we to face apart from this solid block of the Establishment? Has it never occurred to anyone that the composer might have asked himself the very same questions that arise in the listener's mind, might have set them rather like mantraps before embarking on some particular line of argument? If so, why should there be any reticence about a composer trying to trace the path of his own progress?

And, above all, what would be the most sympathetic and effective aspects of such an attitude? We can make a few investigations in this field and determine a few cardinal points without claiming to arrive at any dogmatic conclusions, which would only have the effect of making the existing confusion worse confounded.

The first and most immediate form of criticism is a reflection (no punning on 'reflex', please.) In his 1846 *Salon* Baudelaire wrote:

> I sincerely believe that the best criticism is the amusing and poetical variety, and not the cold and algebraical, which, under the pretext of explaining everything, exhibits neither hate nor love and deliberately divests itself of 'temperament' of any kind. A picture is the artist's reflection of nature, and the best criticism will be the reflection of that picture in an intelligent and sensitive mind. Thus the best account of a picture may take the form of an elegy or a sonnet. Only this kind of criticism is meant for volumes of poetry and for poetically minded readers.

This specious argument might seem to err primarily on the side of humour; and yet this form of criticism – if anyone can formulate it – is far superior to all other actual forms, which are simply more or less degraded versions of it. Indeed this impressionist, 'reflecting' criticism is the commonest of all; and it is the quality of the 'reflector' and the impression that leave so much to be desired, and the poetic quality that is unfortunately totally absent, since we do not suffer from a plethora of good poets. The fault lies in this absence of poetic genius, which is a bad start in this particular poetic game.

If we acknowledge our weakness as regards sonnet and elegy, we must resign ourselves to not passing from one masterpiece to another as in some subtle – and magic and miraculous – play of mirrors: a fantastic progression easy to imagine but very seldom realized, for the simple reason that exceptional artists are rare birds in this sort of field. What, then, is the first qualification in Baudelaire's eyes?

> As for criticism proper, I hope that philosophers will understand what I am going to say – that in order to be just, i.e. to possess a *raison d'être*, a critic must be partial, passionate, political, by which I mean wedded to an exclusive point of view, but a point of view that takes in the greatest number of horizons . . . individualism, of course: demanding of the artist simplicity and the sincere expression of his own temperament, with all the aids of his professional skill . . . A critic must be passionate in fulfilling his task, since one is no less a human being for being a critic, and passion links temperaments that are analogous, and raises reason to new heights.

That passage is full of snares, illusions and mirages. No one can be partial or passionate at will; and, as for individualism, it leaves room for every kind of *pons asinorum*. Only one thing is absolutely clear – Baudelaire's absolute ban on sexless eclecticism.

If we take this as our first negative term and imagination as our second positive term, it seems possible to determine what is meant by criticism that is 'rational and impassioned'.

Criticism of a composer – to speak of what concerns us specially here – is in fact primarily the critical analysis of one human being by another. From the technical point of view tricks are never convincing and nothing will compensate a keen observer for any deceptions or disappointments that he may encounter. On the other hand an immediate, spontaneous admiration will be only strengthened by the study of any work that has no blemishes, one in which (to quote Baudelaire again) the maximum of resource is wedded to an exceptional temperament. Thus the composer will choose his co-ordinates and at the same time gauge exactly what he expects of them. If he is clear-sighted enough, he may even be able to judge in advance the swift decline of works that have enjoyed a short success (with audiences whose taste is, for a number of ambiguous reasons, suspect). He may be able to foresee which contemporary reputations the future will confirm, and why at the moment these composers' works can be appreciated by only a small number of listeners. What he is in fact doing is forming for himself the picture of an era in decline. I do not mean gambling, betting on posterity's verdict. A bet hardly comes into the matter, if he regards it as no more than an intelligent amusement, with no risks involved. In his own case, however, this discrimination is of vital importance, and if he is too weak to undertake this 'examination of conscience', so much the worse for him. He will have an easy run, hopelessly prejudiced and obsessed by tradition and finally so overwhelmed by the inanity of what he is doing that he loses all hope.

In 'examining his conscience', however, he must not be content with any easy, accommodating scale of values. He will need a great power of assimilation, as well as a perception and a taste that depend on his possessing an active and enquiring imagination. Without that curiosity there is nothing to be got from any score, however much discussed in any number of insipid and inconsequent commentaries. The only really effective critic will be one who is capable of directing and sustaining a reflected image, and the vitality of his criticism will be determined by the deformations arising from the personal quality of his vision. Bar-by-bar accounts of a work are suspect, it is true; but there is a transcendent kind of criticism that is based on technical analysis, no doubt, but reveals such a mastery of the vocabulary that it can afford the generalizations and syntheses forbidden to the short-sighted. Another essential element in criticizing a composer is a basic 'lack of respect' (a philosophical 'doubt') and I do not mean by that the vague, anarchistic (and quite ineffective) 'lack of respect' that is often fashionable and consists of nothing more than amusing sallies that miss their mark because they have no real relationship to the object. Squibs of this kind have often been let off by innovators or revolutionaries whose chief innovation and unique revolution has consisted in an altogether exceptional lack of intelligent reflexes. 'Lack of respect' in this sense belongs primarily to the commercial-traveller mentality, and is coupled with an altogether exceptional uninformedness; it is really a euphemism for the formidable kind of stupidity that we know by the name of philistinism. The philistine is quite unaware of the liberties that he takes and would never dream of 'taking' them. That is the whole difference between the 'lack of respect' that is allied to philosophical 'doubt', and a vaguely libertarian cast of mind. 'Lack of respect' can be expressed by a maximum of radical questioning: it starts with doubt and ends in certainty, in the establishment of a hierarchy of values that will determine the new situation in which composers of the future will find themselves. But a certain Monsieur Descartes has thrown sufficient light on this point to make further insistence unnecessary.

From this it is quite clear that criticism, whether formulated in words or not, is an indispensable part of composition. Whether he actually writes it down or not, it is the composer's 'logbook', and the fact of writing a logbook is simply the expressing in words of another activity, and not really the reverse side of a double activity. Thus the insistence on distinguishing creative artists from theorist-artists turns out to be no more than hypocritical nonsense invented by the impotent to protect their fellow cripples.

Nevertheless, this single activity – expressed doubly – may reveal that dual nature of which Baudelaire speaks in his great essay on Delacroix. He speaks there of

> great artists possessing a double character, which makes them, as critics, spread themselves with particular delight in praising and analysing the qualities of which, as creators, they themselves stand in most need, qualities that are the antithesis of their own.

And later he says,

> Why go in search of what one already possesses almost to excess, and how is it possible not to praise what seems to us more rare and more difficult to acquire? This is always the case with creators of genius, whether painters or writers, whenever they apply themselves to criticism.

This might be said to correspond very closely to the development of any creative artist, the musician as well as Baudelaire's painter and writer. In youth he feels the need to define his own personality, to see where his strength lies, to put his finger on his strong points and develop these to their highest potential. Once he has done this, he will clearly have achieved a certain stability, and that very stability will cause him a further anxiety – how is he to avoid simply exploiting those 'strong points' which threaten to stifle him by the very luxuriance of their growth? To forget or deny one's own personality and to wander aimlessly with no logical consistency is not a good plan, and people are often mistaken when they speak of an artist 'renewing himself'. The majority understand it to be a conscious chameleon trick, a kind of Bogomoletz serum graded according to the patient's age, something out of science fiction. But in fact it is an experience that is fruitful only if one bears in mind that 'self-renewal' involves having exactly the same 'lack of respect' for oneself as one had in the first place for one's predecessors. Lack of respect for himself broadens the artist's field of vision without completely demagnetizing his compass. It is an undeniable fact that if he questions all his own procedures, he becomes obsessed by the characteristics most foreign to himself, the most difficult to acquire – even perhaps the most atrophied.

An artist is in fact brought by his observation in other men's work of qualities that are the complement of his own to a sort of self-criticism, to use a word much in favour nowadays. On the other hand it would be exaggerated to ask a composer to give an exact definition of his artistic desires or his morphological researches – in fact a perfect critical definition of himself. It cannot be denied that, were this possible, his work itself would be doomed, short-circuited from the outset by the fact of being totally unnecessary. An artist's critical analysis of himself can never claim to be anything more than an instrument, to be used for the selection and preparation needed in developing a work and for correction at those times when the artist loses the last semblance of confidence in his own conviction. But how far can this critical analysis be exercised without danger? To reinforce imagination and not to dry it up? This is a personal matter about which it would be foolish to generalize: the gift itself is part of this faculty. Let us simply say that every vital work of art seems to demand of the artist a steady refusal of complacency.

These opinions may be seen as profoundly contrary to the spirit of an age in which 'spontaneity' is always – and particularly in France – being held up as the ideal: 'producing music as an apple tree produces apples'. That expression comes from Saint-Saëns, as it happens . . . but Baudelaire, in his 1859 *Salon*, speaks of the artist lacking both soul and instruction, 'a simple *spoiled child*'. His diatribe against 'the *spoiled child*'s indecent little idiocies' is as true today as it was then. We still suffer from the ghastly racket of the dreadful degenerates whose total unawareness makes them innocent of the filth they produce. We cannot expect to rival Hercules' hygienic exploits in the Augean stables, but we do have a right to demand a minimum of discretion in the display of idiocy:

> The disrepute into which the imagination has fallen with them, their contempt for all that is truly great, their exclusive love (no, that is too good a word) – their exclusive concern with their *métier* – these, I think, are the chief reasons for the depressed condition of artists today.

Looking at our own times, let us suggest that creation be indissolubly linked to constructive criticism, remembering at the same time both the dangerous grandeur and the daunting limitations implicit in the idea. And one last quotation from Baudelaire:

> Since all art is always beauty expressed by the feeling, the passion and the dreams of individuals – that is to say, variety in unity or different faces of the Absolute – criticism is every moment bordering on metaphysics.

And Paul Klee answers in his *Pedagogical Sketchbook*, 'Everything is known by studying its root, prehistory is learned from what we see ... Mystery begins, once we reach a higher plane.' And so we come to have a still deeper reverence for talent and imagination and to recognize that, as we were saying earlier, the work of criticism will be a kind of spell to make a work germinate. As for the headaches that Delacroix mentions, we can only trust that they will not be severe enough to kill the inclination to practise this double solution of that active madness which we know as 'the desire for self-expression' – for that, in the last resort, is what it is.

9

Demythologizing the Conductor[1]

neither dictator nor artisan!

it is high time to *demystify* the word 'specialist', which provides too convenient a way out for people anxious to escape without too many scruples from today's musical facts, to monopolize history and 'the past' and to turn it into a rather mawkish sauce for queasy stomachs!

no less urgent a task is the *demythification* of the personality of the conductor, who plays the *chef* (is it *d'école* or *de cuisine?*) all too often to the detriment of contemporary events, denying (or rather disowning) his essential *raison d'être* – and still more commonly to the detriment of the reputation of works that, by a little shuffling, have become identified with his own personal reputation.

neither oracle nor flunkey!

to be avoided, then, at all costs, both the cleverly disguised amateur and the blinkered professional: two plagues equally formidable and leading to parallel disappointments, identical defeats and similar catastrophes. they distort knowledge; they refuse solidarity; they bring about confusion and provoke misunderstanding; they retard unification, warp vision, drain the vital flow of communication.

in the matter of contemporary development: every new point requires a knowledge, a background, a reserve of expedients.

(present-day works increasingly present problems which are as much acoustical as dramatic. yet the appearance of these difficulties was not sudden, still less surreptitious: they match a number of extended ideas whose origin can be found in the most important of the works written since 1900. if student conductors are not made aware of these early stages of contemporary music, it is small wonder that there are terrible gaps in their understanding of today's music!)

a quick glance at these new points of interest:

---

[1] 'Alternatives', opening statement at the Basle courses, 1960.

non-metrical gestures imply a perfect training in the most complex metrical gestures;

a free acoustic demands a particularly subtle understanding of the traditional acoustic;

the ability to control an 'expanding' music can be acquired only by an absolutely accurate hearing of a 'fixed' score.

it would be pointless deliberately to neglect the basic strata of investigation and then to ask the composer for his approval, to demand the player's confidence, to claim and require the approbation of the public, while allowing – as often happens at present – none of them any previous awareness of your convictions, your abilities or your powers.

as for the music of the past: to believe that codification is a function of distance in time is an initial contradiction that very few avoid. on the other hand, there is an aesthetic of physical demonstration that overshoots the mark – in other words, the conductor's control of his body is no substitute for intellectual training!

intellectually, the conductor must have a clear conception of a work: of the music itself, its background, its harmonic resonances, which change from one period to another, its constant factors, and the reasons for its durability. a mere exterior dramatization, by means of a more or less appropriate miming will give no account of any style, any emotion, any form; instead of mediating between the work and the listener, such miming simply substitutes a vulgar byproduct, which slurs the work's intelligibility and comprehension. this dialectic of the present in the past, and the past in the present, with an essential implication of the future – this is the fundamental demand that should be satisfied by all interpreters.

when alban berg was asked what he demanded of an opera house he used to say, 'give the operas of the classical repertory as if they were contemporary works . . . and vice versa.'

this wish was expressed on 12 september 1928 (admittedly in a review called 'music and revolution') and we are still a long way from fulfilling it in any branch of musical life.

neither messiah nor sacristan!

might not this dichotomy in the 'repertory' be due to a still more dangerous dichotomy between creation and performance? thought on one side of the line and action on the other. the headless woman and the cripple! an odd sort of fable.

without feeling nostalgic about a unity that has disappeared, the earthly paradise said to have been lost by the apple of specialization, we may legitimately consider some dilemmas useless, and even harmful.

there is inevitably a 'magic' element in the relationship that must be established between a work and its performers through the agency of the conductor/medium; not every creative idea necessarily possesses the power of transmitting itself independently – or independently enough – of any performing plan. purely psychological phenomena are involved, and these have very little to do with the search for 'truth' for its own sake; professional skills, too; in fact, a specific gift directed towards specific ends.

nevertheless, without demanding an impossible ideal in the distribution of interest, we do come to wish for a stronger current between the two poles of the magnetic field of musical activity.

to restrict oneself to prophecies of doom / to sail grandly through the palace of shadows; to pontificate and to dream / to 'realize' and to get on with the job; to exclude / to be excluded – can we not spare ourselves misleading trivialities of this kind, since none of them can obviate the necessity of choosing?

in the last resort the alternative may be stated – with the indispensable dash of bitters – as

neither angel nor animal!

10

On Musical Analysis[1]

I believe that our analysis, particularly of the Second Viennese School, has too often been of the 'B–A spells BA' variety. We must not forget that the Viennese School – and especially Webern, who was the most extreme instance – represents an extremely narrow and rigorous passage of musical history, each note being determined by an absolutely decisive logic. It is obviously easy to make a word-by-word, letter-by-letter analysis of the kind of structure in which there is only a single solution from one moment to the next, and given such simple principles, the solutions themselves are also simple.

What is much more important in this case is the dialectic of composition, and this has very seldom been examined. What may be called figured, or 'ciphered', analyses of this music are legion, but studies in depth are very rare; and it is these that are needed. In the classics, too, identifying a first theme, a second theme and a gradually resolving conflict is not really very rewarding. Anybody can do it and a beginner can draw up an account of this kind. What is rewarding is to observe the dialectic of events, to obtain a bird's-eye view of the whole procedure and see how a composer contrives to formulate his thinking by means of such a system – that really does open up many more lines of enquiry. Finally, what must be analysed in a number of complex works is not, essentially, the way in which the composer arrives at his formal structures or different musical objects, but much rather the actual relationship between these structures and objects – for instance the relationship that may exist between the expression of a form and the content of the composer's thought. If all you have in mind is stripping down a vocabulary, you will very easily fall into a sterile mannerism, as has in fact often happened. The history of such mannerisms is too often simple repetition. If a composer's vocabulary is extremely expressive, extremely significant in itself, the general rule seems to be that commentators are content to observe

[1] 'Question d'héritage', based on an interview with Maryvonne Kendergi (19 March 1970) published with the title 'Pierre Boulez interrogé' in *Cahiers Canadiens de Musique*, Spring–Summer 1971, pp. 31–48. Revised by the author in 1980.

its exterior features and aspects; and when the commentator's thought is no longer active in originating his various schemas, he easily falls into mannerism, because it is only the external results of those schemas that are grasped. The essential thing is to penetrate the deepest level of the composer's procedure. I have often been asked about my own works: 'Can you give us the series?' Or, 'Can you give us the principle?' What use would that be? Far the most important thing is to observe the existence of points shared by different structures, and to mark the different areas of a work composed of such-and-such characteristics; to see how, in one section, certain features are avoided only to be concentrated in a future development; to follow, for instance, the interferences that may arise between forms or structures. That is the fruitful kind of analysis and quite as important as searching for the 'why' and the 'how' of a work.

During my short spell of teaching, and particularly towards the end of it, my interest during my courses was no longer in note-by-note analysis. What concerned me was analysis by means of overall form, or *Gestalt*. I took the basic structures of a work and studied – and made my students study – the transformation of these primary ideas, the ways in which they could be developed. Note-by-note analysis I left to students, working from these essential data. I was particularly interested, for example, in the principles of ambiguity in Webern's last works where the notion of time is, in the last resort, the ultimate junction between what may still be called counterpoint and harmony but is better described as a phenomenon due to the transition from time o to time n in the placing of the musical events. When you have lines succeeding each other according to certain data within successive time, you have counterpoint, or even canon. When you return to time o – and in fact superimpose the musical lines on each other – you have a simultaneous, vertical result, i.e. harmony. The interesting thing to decipher is this transition from time o to time n, not the canonic structure of the passage, which even the most academic of musicians could observe. The importance lies in detecting the composer's conception and grasping the element of ambiguity introduced simply by this function of time. That is how I understand analysis, not making collections of letters and syllables, which I consider a useless pastime. You do not analyse a novel by using words as markers, nor do you decipher its construction by elementary grammatical analysis. You know that sentences are constructed according to certain models and do not need to verify this in the case of every sentence you read, provided that you know what logical construction is. The interest of the novel lies in the linking of events and phenomena. Analysing *Wozzeck* with my students, studying Stockhausen's *Gruppen*, or presenting one of the pieces of my own *Pli selon pli*, what I tried first and foremost to do was to emphasize the large formal structures and the reasons governing their existence and their relationship.

As far as I am concerned, vocabulary-analysis is an elementary phase, useful but restricted, and the student must be able to pass on from that to the more general plane of musical objects, local structures and overall formal relationships. Failing this, analysis remains an academic exercise, perfectly painless but perfectly pointless.

II

The Teacher's Task[1]

There is nothing novel in the observation that for the last few decades there has been a certain amount of confusion in the teaching of music. What may be called the handing on of the craft of music has become quite simply inadequate compared with what it used to be. Nor is this inadequacy confined to music, which enjoys no privilege in this respect, as anyone will realize who has read Cézanne's correspondence and the remarks that he makes on the subject to his contemporaries. He used to complain bitterly that he was not taught his craft as it used to be taught in the sixteenth century, and he particularly envied Titian, for whom there were no secrets, no difficulty in learning the skills of his predecessors. Cézanne had to work hard to achieve results that would in those days have seemed absolutely natural. This was sixty years ago and we are no nearer to solving the problem.

What is in fact taught at a conservatory? A certain number of traditional rules, very limited in date and geographical provenance; after which any student wanting to enter the contemporary field must, as it were, jump with a miniature parachute, taking his life in his hands. How many are brave enough to make that jump? And how many feel strong enough?

In principle all instruction should be based on historical evolution; there should be no obligation to make a specialized study of musicology, but a knowledge of texts of the past, recent or remote, should form a foundation. The literary texts of the past are much easier to come by than the musical scores of the same date, and the same is even more plainly true in painting. Music is so bound up first with notation and then with the technique and construction of the different instruments that once the means of transmitting it become out of date so does the music itself. For example, texts of medieval music are few and far between and generally meant for specialists and scholars. Anyone who wishes to revive this music in the concert hall has to make transcriptions that more or less restore its original appearance. At the present time conservatories do not base their curricula on a knowledge of

[1] 'Discipline et communication', lecture given at Darmstadt in 1961 and published, against Boulez's wish, and under the title 'Down with Disciplines!' in *Les Lettres Nouvelles*, February–March 1964, pp. 63–79.

these texts, starting instead with the codification – at an arbitrarily chosen moment in history – of grammatical principles that are the outcome of several centuries of musical evolution. In most cases there is not even any explanation of their historical or aesthetic *raisons d'être*: they are taught simply as articles of a creed that it would be impious to question. In fact they resemble fetishes and a curse will descend on anyone who refuses to acknowledge them. What, I ask you, have intelligence and understanding of the phenomenon of music to do with the handing on of a number of taboos from one generation to the next?

Of course no one can be a walking encyclopaedia. A student overloaded with learning would not know where to turn, and his memory would be stronger than his intelligence. I accept that, and I do not expect him to know the complete history of a perfect chord from the trope to the present day. Musical grammar should primarily be taught in its presentday form as regards both morphology and syntax. But there is a point in knowing precisely how this grammar arose in the first place, how it has evolved and what are its future potentialities. What I insist on is that grammar should be taught in its present form. After all, we are not taught seventeenth-century French grammar on the grounds that it represents a high point of classical elegance. But that in fact is what happens in music. We learn, in particular, contrapuntal techniques that have remained absolutely unchanged since the eighteenth century, and then have to reconcile as best we can that stage of technical development with what we observe a century later. The only innovator in this field of ideas is Olivier Messiaen whose *Vingt Leçons d'harmonie*, published in 1939, dealt with the evolution of harmonic style from Monteverdi to Debussy.

This whole problem raises the important question of inheritance. It is often said that some composer has 'inherited' the qualities of some other composer. What does this 'inheriting' mean? And, in so far as it means anything, what is transmissible and what is not, either individually or collectively? I mean what, from the individual point of view, can one hope to transmit oneself from among the things that one has inherited? And, collectively, what is directly transmissible, or not, in the historical context?

As far as the collective angle of vision is concerned, time makes some phenomena obsolete and metamorphoses others. There is a constantly evolving dialectic between the immediately obvious and the permanent, and this makes any prophesying about the relationship between history and actual historical works pure guesswork. And what is the deciding factor? In the first place every age interprets the work of the past personally – both individually and collectively. In this connection I have spoken of the 'harmonic resonances' of an age. The successive points of view, which change from one age to the next, suggest that the 'historical heritage' is something entirely relative. Some work, or some part of a work, may have had a decisive historical influence at a given moment in time and later lost all its importance and with it any real claim to be considered a living force in our cultural heritage. Examples of this are too numerous to quote. Can it be no more than a question of taste? No, taste forms only part of these judgements. It is primarily a question of utility, as we can see in our own generation from our attitude to the music of the three composers of the Second Viennese School. Why was it Webern who was really the first to be, so to speak, 'pounced on' by composers? Because he produced a radical solution of grammatical and stylistic problems that desperately needed solving and did so by means of a clear methodology that established the premisses of a new dialectic of musical language. Why did not Berg exercise the same influence despite his more obvious links with the immediate past? It was for that very reason – because it was much more difficult in his case to distinguish what was really novel in his music. This had already been clear with the generation of the twenties and the thirties, which rejected Schoenberg because of his romanticism but was generally speaking incapable of drawing the basic lesson of Schoenberg's language. They confused his aesthetics, which were indeed old-fashioned, with the incidents of his vocabulary and his grammar. In Berg's case we may be sure that, with the stylistic principles of our age settled and established, his future influence will be freed of all the contingent elements in his expression, his 'expressionism'; and that we shall in fact profit from his work, by transposing the basic contradictions, which provide the key to that work, out of the phenomena from which they sprang.

Every age obeys certain general lines of force that are not specifically musical but form part, whether we know it or not, of major movements of thought: this is an indisputable fact. In a clearly defined situation of this kind is any 'handing on of the craft' possible? In fact is it ever possible? This is a question of capital importance. Our first awareness of music as such can take the form only of an awareness of music already in existence, i.e. the music of the past. Even more importantly, any awareness of the craft of music can be only an awareness of the craft of our predecessors. There can be no musical gift, however dazzling, of which this is not true. No craft can be invented *ex nihilo*; like our digestive organs, this gift transforms into organic life the elements that it needs. The organism chooses what it needs as food, reacting more favourably to some foods than to others. If we push the comparison still further, we may ask whether a young organism is itself capable of distinguishing between what nourishes it more effectively and what less. Left to itself, it will flounder and may equally well encounter what suits it best or what proves harmful and sterile. Hence arises the necessity for an intelligent training in order to avoid pointless experiments and gropings in the dark. You may say that no such experiments and gropings are pointless, that there is in fact no better way of establishing a spirit of independence. At a certain very high level I entirely agree with you; but below that level I would maintain that the immature intelligence of the ordinary student makes him waste a great deal of time and may even set him on a totally false path in search of the best way to harness his vital powers. 'Teaching' means both discipline and also communication. In fact teaching is the communication, by means of discipline, of some practical knowledge. There are therefore three problems:

1   Is a technique to be taught?
2   Are ideas to be transmitted?
3   Are personalities to be formed?

I have stated these three questions impersonally; but for the last year I have been forced to put them to myself in the most direct and personal form possible. Having never taught before, I have found myself faced with a number of basic questions that I have tried to answer in the first place purely practically. But not content with these pragmatic solutions, I have embarked on more general reflections and asked myself these three questions: Am I to teach a technique? Am I to transmit *my* ideas? Am I to form (if not actually to mould) a personality?

I have no difficulty in answering 'yes' to the first two, but I am still much more doubtful about the third, and likely to remain so.

As regards teaching a technique, I satisfy a student's wish by providing him with two methods of investigation, analysis and criticism, which includes self-criticism. I believe that these two methods are inseparable, and that they form a major element in all teaching. It is not that I attach such primary importance to the descriptive analysis of a work, however complete; it has been shown that analysis of this kind, which is not difficult to assimilate, can often lead to academicism, which is perhaps the worst of evils. But even the most passive kind of analysis trains the mind and gives it a certain flexibility; all that we have to guard against is the flexibility that becomes pure acrobatics and useless virtuosity. Once this flexibility has been achieved, the most important task, as I see it, still lies ahead: I mean analytic *interpretation*, which is where the really interesting work begins.

Interpretation is the touchstone that shows whether a work has been comprehended and assimilated: but it would be mistaken to demand of it nothing more than these justifications. Once any phenomenon, however embryonic, is discovered in a score, the student must apply his intelligence and his logical faculties to deduce its possible future consequences. He must in fact extrapolate, and this is primarily a question of intuition, creative intuition. I would even go so far as to say that analysis assumes, or rather reveals, the chief concerns of the composer in any work under discussion. Returning to the same work some years later he may well become aware of inferences that had hitherto escaped his notice. I would almost say that inferences that are false but full of future possibilities are more useful than those that are correct but sterile. A composition is sometimes no more than an excuse for introspection. The ultimate object of analysis is self-definition by the intermediacy of another. I cannot do better than quote Michel Butor's essay on Baudelaire:

> There may well be people who will say that, having set out to talk about Baudelaire, I have managed to talk only about myself. It would certainly be truer to say that Baudelaire has been talking about me – *he is talking about you*.

This is the kind of investigation that I try to inculcate in my pupils. In a word, I want them to reach a point at which the masters of an earlier age speak to them about themselves. It is not an impossible ambition; and indeed I feel convinced that it is the quickest way to acquaint pupils with their own powers.

Using this double-sided mirror of analysis, I try to give their technique greater precision by means of criticism, self-criticism in fact, and that is not always easy! As far as possible, I employ Socrates' favourite method and make a pupil use his own critical faculties, otherwise his mind easily becomes idle and fails to react with the necessary authority, speed and severity. What will be the object of this criticism as applied both to the works of the past and to the pupil's own? In the first place style, form and aesthetic presuppositions; and by 'criticism' I do not mean a negative attitude, but a positive estimate of the virtues and failings that can reasonably be expected in any work. Criticism of this kind is directly related to analysis, of which it forms an integral part. It is comparatively easy to analyse the strong and weak points of an accepted work, but much more difficult in the case of one's own. That is perhaps the most ticklish part of composition, for whatever precautions one may take, it is hard to gauge the exact effect of structures and forms – to estimate, for instance, the relation between structure and time, form and its various elements, etc. In criticizing his own work, a composer must have enough self-confidence to be able to judge the real facts; and it is precisely at this point that working with a class can be an advantage. When a single individual feels unsure about certain points, a second opinion can be of considerable use, even if only as representing a different reaction. This means a kind of 'triangulation' of a work and then drawing the necessary conclusions.

We have now described the easiest part of teaching. Easy in principle, that is, because it in fact demands great flexibility in application, each temperament reacting to its own constituent elements and each individual possessing – even in this purely technical area – his own psychological make-up, which the teacher must know. Analysis and criticism clearly answer fundamental, objective needs, and in this field the 'transmission' from teacher to pupil has every chance of being as faithful as possible. Anyone who has ever taught seriously, for however short a time, will know what 'writing' [*écrire*] means – an elementary step not to be underestimated as a necessity, nor overestimated in importance.

The next step in teaching already involves 'cases of conscience' but these, I think, can generally be solved positively without too much difficulty. I now come to my second point: am I to transmit my ideas?

The highest praise for any 'master' is to be called liberal. Time and again we hear that so-and-so was unique because, far from destroying his pupils' personalities, he encouraged them and left them free to develop on their own. If I am asked whether I approve of this liberality, I do not hesitate to say, 'No, I do not.' A pupil does not come to you to be allowed to flounder about on his own, but in the hope (even if unexpressed or disappointed) that you will impose a discipline by which he will acquire things that he lacks. Do you consider yourself, then, as a kind of animal trainer, you may ask. No, the constraint – or rather the discipline – of which I am speaking has nothing to do with animal training. But liberalism, or what goes by that name, is most deceptive and is, to me, the opposite of real teaching. It is no good being liberal with people who are not yet formed, because they themselves hesitate about what direction to take. Liberalism of this kind is more often than not a sign of impotence, of an inability to teach, or else of a lack of interest in the problems of those who turn to you for advice. What makes me want to transmit my own ideas is the fact that, by explaining how I arrived at them, I shall be indicating a method; it is not that I have any wish to draw up a list of universally applicable procedures. A method that I have found good may well spark off a number of quite different reactions and lead a student to look for alternatives, and that is what I consider important in forming an individuality. And how do I set about 'transmitting', or at least giving a general idea of my own ideas? Well, there are two ways. The first of these is to enlarge on the various possible reactions to the historical situation of music today, attempting to form a critical judgement on general issues. The second is to use interpretative analysis, such as I have described above, to activate the mechanism of the student's creative faculties.

It is no easy task to shape another person's judgement; it is already hard enough to form one's own, and that is always subject to revision. The whole area is a perpetually shifting one and it is mad to attempt to impose rigid and definitive norms. We know only too well the result of such sacrosanct opinions about history and the present situation – the death of evolution, and in fact the exact opposite of my attempt to introduce a student to the idea that all historical phenomena are by definition relative.

I then move on to methods of comparison founded, as far as possible, on objective realities. Comparative methods of this kind involve a fairly close evaluation of historical and contemporary realities and this sometimes lays me open to a charge of intransigence; but is not truth by definition intransigent? Any ideas I may have on the present necessity for certain methods, developments and inductions are discussed and justified by clearly stated arguments, and I always point out that any situation arising from different co-ordinates will lead to quite different results, which I am quite unable to prophesy. In forming a pupil's judgement I always emphasize and return to the idea of relativity and the impermanence of any means involved. I hope in this way to free a student's mind from the prejudices that can easily build up in the present methods of teaching, and to make him really think about the situation in which he finds himself. This may be considered a dangerous method, which the strong-minded will resist and the weaker brethren will swallow only too easily. That is true, but it seems to me preferable to allow any student capable of a useful reaction to progress in his own way rather than provide him with crutches, which can do nothing but result in the atrophying of his own powers.

At the same time as I am forming his judgement, it will be my duty – and this is something really positive – to use interpretative analysis to activate the mechanisms of his creative faculty. 'Genius', it has often been said, 'is an infinite capacity for taking pains', and patience is indeed needed, in the sense that the mechanisms of creation do require training if they are to acquire strength and the ability to react with precision when necessary. Creative mechanisms that cannot be reduced simply to inspiration can still be thought of as simple gymnastics: developing them exclusively in either of these two directions shows a complete lack of any sense of reality. Creative mechanisms are nothing without imagination, but they are also nothing without the training that immeasurably strengthens them and perpetually enriches the means at their disposal. One of the most important tasks is to stimulate a student's imagination by providing him with *material markers*. He must be helped to make good use of his imagination, a faculty that cannot be of any great use to him unless he has learned to make use of obstacles as a springboard. Thus the important thing is to be able to transmit to a student a way of interpreting analytically the starting-points that he has himself created. Once he has mastered this, he will be able to reconnoitre his own territory, because he will have found the means needed to explore and exploit it. If I were to do this entirely for him, I should not be doing him any service. For the most part I content myself with analysing his powers for him and making him fully aware of them – after which it is essential that he should be allowed to go his own way, even if he is hesitant at first. Otherwise he will never have the courage to make the initial effort.

It will be clear by now that far from applying constraint on my own part, I see it as something that a student must apply to himself. This, as I see it, is the only profitable method, the only active way for him to get to know himself and to know music. That is why I have no hesitation in transmitting my own ideas – or in other words putting him in the presence of my own personality and thus, I hope, creating in him the desire to form his own personality, and one absolutely independent of mine. I believe this to be a more effective method than the old idea of a 'liberal' teacher, which did not really achieve very much.

Then 'personality' – the 'Open, Sesame!' of all teaching. I have felt able, as you see, to give quite positive answers to the first two of the three questions – about imparting a technique and transmitting my own ideas – but in answering the third I must confine myself to expressing hopes. All that I believe myself capable of doing with a student's personality is to give it an edge or – what comes to much the same thing – to stimulate it. To judge from my own experience in the clear perspective of seventeen years, no personality was in fact created among any of my fellow classmates. To claim to create personalities is in any case a caricature of the very meaning of teaching. It is impossible to *direct* a personality without making a *disciple*. However the teacher himself may feel, there will always be disciples who will be content to repeat what he has said, and they are a most detestable race. There have been too many examples of the harm such people can do for us not to be warned of this ridiculous phenomenon. No strong personality who reacts intelligently and profits from a master's advice will ever permit 'direction' of this kind. His pride would, very rightly, make this impossible and his reflexes will never allow themselves to be broken by another's will. In any case manoeuvres of this kind are quite pointless, history being (as we know) notoriously 'unforeseeable' despite the continuity of the historical context. If I may be allowed to quote myself: 'A work exists only if it is the unforeseeable become necessity.' In the same way the student, or 'pupil' in the best sense of the word, will be as unexpected to himself as to his master. There may be surprises that have incalculable consequences and arise from encounters or formulations that do not at first seem of any particular importance. The relationship between the intelligence of a master and that of his pupil seems to be that of a detonator, the implicit mass in the pupil being detonated only by the intellectual substance of the teacher. But the power of this detonation bears no relation to that of the actual detonator, and its mechanism may be set in motion without the detonator's knowledge. I had this experience myself when I was working with Olivier Messiaen. There were phrases and points of view that he expressed quite incidentally but which were perhaps among those that struck me most forcibly and are still vividly present to my mind. This is a phenomenon that is not specific to teaching but part of the whole mechanism of the influence of the non-self on the self. Nobody can predict his own creative reflexes, properly so called. A great part is played by the imagination, which is the most irrational of all our faculties. Why should our imaginations carry us at some given moment in one direction rather than another? This is a complex problem and difficult to explain: all that one can say is that the unconscious plays an incalculable role. If I am unable to define the resources of my own imagination, how much less can I define those of another individual's imagination, with all its different approaches, byways and explosions? This is an open admission of the limitations of all teaching, and to face them honestly in this way seems to me not so much a confession of weakness as the recognition of a mystery.

With some of the pupils who come to me I feel quite exceptionally awkward and out of touch, and there are some problems in which I can only describe my reactions, leaving the individual to do his own spadework. A simple conversation, not necessarily about music, will sometimes reveal points of contact; and I have spent whole afternoons of conversations and discussions that had no immediate relevance but proved among the most fruitful of all, since they brought up things that each pupil found relevant to his own problems and attitudes. Too detailed a study of one particular work may result in a loss of interest because the problems involved are too specific and reduce the discussion to purely practical questions. These must of course be carefully gone into, but general ideas must not be neglected; and they will play a very important role in the case of students who are already advanced in the actual practice of composition.

It is clearly very hard to adopt any general attitude towards one's pupils, and there will always be moments of embarrassment when it is essential to make real contact with a pupil while remaining within the limits of a definite discipline. In fact I often think that in these circumstances the best father is the one who, like Jean-Jacques Rousseau, takes his offspring straight to the Foundlings' Hospital, where he will at least be sure of neither spoiling them by his own faults nor tyrannizing them in his desire to give them an impossibly strict education. It is enough for him to have begotten them, which is in itself something. It would perhaps be not too much of a paradox to say that the best educator is the bad father.

In every discipline it is the practical element that can be taught exactly, what the teacher has acquired by his own personal experience: that presents no insurmountable difficulty. What is absolutely incommunicable is imagination, and one must therefore resign oneself to two facts: first, that about the existence of the imagination nothing can be done; and, second, that there exists a law of large numbers to which there is nothing to do but to submit. As in the case of wines, there are good years, bad years and – by far the greatest in number – indifferent years. Quality itself, and its transmission, is a purely chance phenomenon. There have been many cases of an indifferent master with a brilliant pupil and a brilliant master with indifferent pupils. It has been so in the past, is so now and always will be so. Quality and quantity are two phenomena over which a teacher has absolutely no control. You may well ask me why I, with my lack of belief in the virtues of teaching, have accepted such a dangerous honour and such a burden. My answer is that although I do not believe that personalities can be created by teaching, teachers are of the very greatest importance to the personalities that do in fact exist. What really arouses my scepticism is the placid kind of teacher who believes that he can spend a quiet life teaching a number of recipes for composition and soon finds himself surrounded by a host of epigones. The teacher's highest task, as I see it, is not to radiate confidence and conviction. Any gratitude a pupil may in later life feel towards a teacher is for having increased his own inclination to scepticism and his dissatisfaction with himself; and by this I do not mean sentimental questionings and vague dissatisfaction, but radical questioning and permanent dissatisfaction. (Both Descartes *and* Trotsky – why not?) This questioning and dissatisfaction will undermine all hitherto accepted principles and will leave plenty of room for novel constructions. In fact the best pupil from my point of view will be the 'bad' pupil, the one who takes nothing on trust! The relations between a bad father and a bad son are, in the last resort, the warmest possible. When each is free to choose his own path, there will be no question of being loaded with prejudices and affectations that are in the last resort useless.

As Hamlet says, there are a number of different ways of seeing a cloud – 'a camel, a weasel, a whale . . .' – and so I should like my fundamental lesson to be simply this: an imagination that allows you to order your own musical universe. I can give you the necessary tools, develop your skill in using them and direct the aptitude of your muscles and your faculties; but bear in mind that if you lacked imagination when you came to me, you will still lack imagination when you leave me. And if you ask me whether you are gifted or not, I shall always give the same answer: ask yourself that question – you are the best judge. I always think of the subtitle of Nietzsche's *Also sprach Zarathustra* – 'a book for everyone and for no one'. I can say the same of my role as I see it: the advice I give is for everyone and for no one. You are at liberty, like Hamlet, to see a cloud as a camel, a weasel or a whale, and, whatever you say, I shall not contradict you. What, then, is the middle term between discipline and communication? It always comes back to the same thing, which means everything and nothing: freedom. I will be neither a paternalist nor a dictator of ideas but I will – if I am allowed to – organize your dissatisfaction. You are free to hold it against me or to refuse. My teaching is equally remote from magic and bookkeeping but we shall at most have established a disinterested encounter, and for me that is the fairest of fair dealing.

12

The System Exposed[1]

POLYPHONIE X

There are seven groups of seven instruments: two groups of woodwinds, one of brass, two of percussion: first group, pitched percussion (piano, xylophone, harp, drums); second group of unpitched percussion (skin, metal, wood); and finally two groups of strings. The whole is based on the transformations of a single series, the mechanism of which is shown below.

Series of twenty-four quarter-tones:

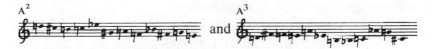

which divides into two series of semitones:

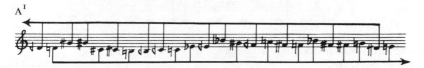

If I now take series A^2 and diminish the intervals by a quarter-tone –

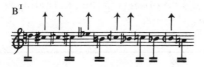

---

[1] 'Le système mis à nu', from two letters to John Cage (1951). Previously unpublished French texts kindly communicated by the Archives of Northwestern University, transcribed by Françoise Toussignant. The second was published in English, without a title, by John Cage in *Transformation: arts, communication, environment*, 1952, Vol. I No. 3, pp. 168–70. This translation appears below.

– I get a defective twelve-note series of quarter-tones that can be used only on transpositions of its notes. By transferring quarter-tones I reform this series in semitones, and this gives me –

I go through the same procedure with series A³ and this gives me C¹ and C².

Next I take series A² and augment the intervals by a quarter-tone. This gives me:

which, in semitones, gives me:

Using the same procedure with series A³ I get E¹ and E².

From the four series B², C², D² and E² in semitones I make an ideogram by taking the notes common to all four:

With this series, F¹, I reconstitute two quarter-tone series with F¹→ and F¹→± a quarter-tone, and observing the alternating semitone/quarter-tone implied by my series A¹, thus :

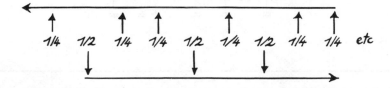

thereby obtaining two forms: F² and F³ which complete the cycle.

I therefore have three complete series of twenty-four quarter-tones (A¹, F² and F³); four defective series of twelve quarter-tones (B¹, C¹, D¹ and E¹); two semitone series (A^2 and A^3 [components of A^1]); four derivative semitone series (B^2, C^2, D^2 and E^2); their ideogram (F^1 [component of F^2 and F^3]).

The general structure of these polyphonies is therefore organized by the deduction of their series.

Rhythmically I make use of seven organizations, based on a cell:

Three basic,
or simple rhythms

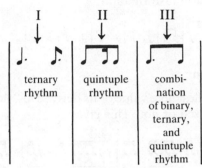

Four compound,
or combination rhythms

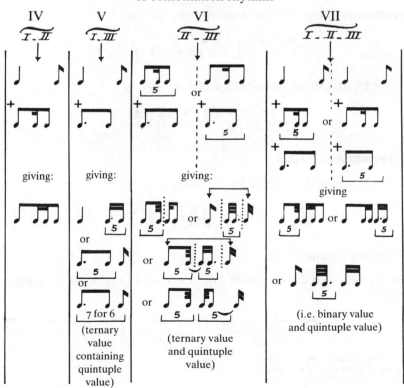

Each of these simple rhythms is submitted to seven series of transformations.

Take, for instance, rhythm I:

(a) Simple transformation

By adding a dot; augmentation by reducing note values; regular or irregular diminution, irrational transformation:

(b) Expressed rhythm

By means of the smallest note value or its derivatives, the dot of the original rhythm being expressed or not. This gives

(c) Hollowed rhythm

Introduction of the syncope, but only one struck:

or with the dot struck and the rest inverted:

(d) Demultiplied rhythm

Multiplication of the rhythm by its principle:

(e) Divided rhythm

Decomposition of the rhythm in expressed values taking its principle into account:

(f) Rest rhythm

In a non-retrogradable rhythm one pole of the rhythm being replaced by the corresponding rest, in all forms. This gives

or fb   or fc   or fd   or fe

In a retrogradable rhythm pivot cell or symmetrical cells.

(g) Rest rhythm

In a non-retrogradable rhythm, the other pole of the rhythm being replaced by the corresponding rest. This gives

or fb   or fc   or fd   or fe

In a retrogradable rhythm, the pivot cell and a symmetrical cell, or a symmetrical cell.

Next:
Non-retrogradable rhythms
These I make retrogradable by adding to them one of their value, which gives

α   or

Then I start with α and apply the same transformations to the whole cycle   β   γ   δ   ε.

    Retrogradable rhythms I make non-retrogradable:

thus   becomes   or

Then I obtain further:
    from retrogradable, non-retrogradable:

from non-retrogradable, retrogradable:

etc. in symmetrical or asymmetrical augmentation.

For a cell that is initially fairly complicated such as VI:

this gives very complex results when developed, such as:

As for composition itself, I want to broaden the field of polyphony itself as has been done for counterpoint. By that I mean that polyphony will serve as counterpoint – an unequal polyphony, in that answers will be possible between three- and five-part polyphonies or between four, six and seven parts, etc. Moreover the instrumental group will change with each new polyphony.

The first, for instance, is for forty-nine instruments. Seven times seven. The second will be for only twelve, grouped in three times four: four violins, four violas, four cellos. The third will be for brass and percussion divided in four: two pianos, harp, timpani, xylophone, celesta, vibraphone, brass, percussion I, percussion II, etc.

In some polyphonies I should also do as you are doing in the music that you are writing now and make use of sampled [*échantillonné*] sonorities, i.e. aggregates of sounds linked by a constant but movable according to the scale of sonorities. Like you again, I may construct – as I have done in my quartet – with all the possibilities of the material, by which I mean a construction in which the different combinations create the form, and where the form does not therefore arise from an aesthetic choice.

The first polyphony, for instance, opens thus:

Woodwind I: series A^2; rhythm III
Woodwind II: series A^3; reversed rhythm II
Brass: series A^3; rhythm I
Pitched percussion: series A^2; reversed rhythm IV
Non-pitched percussion: rhythm VII

Strings I: series A[1]; rhythm V
Strings II: series A[1]; rhythm VI

As you can see, the complexity of the rhythm is a function of the complexity of the series or the instrumental formation. The architecture of this piece will be based on the exchanges between series and rhythms and the transformations possible on the monoseries and polyrhythms or on the polyseries and monorhythms.

As you see, the work is on a pretty large scale. I want here before all else to get rid of the idea of a musical work meant for the concert hall, with a definite number of movements. My idea is a book of music comparable in dimensions to a book of poems. (Like the totality of your Sonatas or the *Book of Music for two pianos*.)

One foot in front of the other. I hope that I shan't knock myself out by walking on the edge of the pavement!

When I read your letter, you can't imagine how delighted I was to see that we are both on our way to making more discoveries, and in step with each other. Speaking of that, I won't bother you with theories, but Saby and I have been thinking a lot about these questions of organizing sound material. And I think I may well write a little book based on the principle that sound material can be organized only serially, but carrying that principle to its furthest consequences, i.e. that from the whole sound scale (vibration 16 to vibration 10,000) one can take a note series – say A (a b c d e f g . . . n) – that the sound space will be defined by transposing A to all the degrees composing A – i.e. B (b b′ c′ d′ e′ i′ . . . n'), C (c′ b″ c″ e″ . . . n'') and finally N (n b c d e f . . . n) – in the same way as by inverting A, or A (a, b = a + x, c = a + y, d = a + z, etc.) we get V (a, q = a − x, ɔ = a − y, p = a − z, etc.) a being taken as pivot, and all the transpositions based on A. This could result in a schema like this:

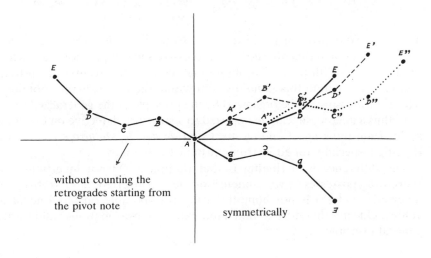

without counting the
retrogrades starting from
the pivot note

symmetrically

Another field of inversion is defined by taking b (or c or d) rather than a as pivot note. (This will not change the transpositions of the original.) This gives us a space defined by a constant and a variable:

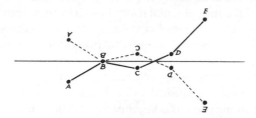

In this way all sound materials can be organized, whatever their nature.

By this means the ideas of modality, tonality and series would be closely combined to form a single whole. The same would be true of the ideas of continuity and discontinuity of the sound material, since this is a choice of discontinuity in continuity. That is what I am working towards with my quarter-tones. In two or three years' time they will be twelfths and twenty-fourths.

Actually I have also found a graphic formula, with quarter- and third-tones, to cover absolutely all the range of sounds [*échelle des sons*] and you will see how: smallest common denominator (simple fractional property between a third and a quarter):

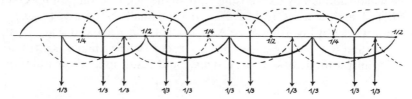

You start your division in third-tones, from the division into semi- and quarter-tones, and each division, by successive superimpositions, gives four intervals of twelfth-tones. To obtain eighteenth- and twenty-fourth-tones you have to operate this same division within the intervals thus obtained. These microcosms can be organized by the principle of the generalized series. And thus a microcosm can be opposed to a structure defective on the grand scale. I am thinking of ending my *Coup de dés de Mallarmé* in this way (having a specially tuned instrument built for the purpose).

The difference with rhythm is that rhythm is (1) not invertible, and therefore possesses two dimensions less (inverted and retrograde inverted), and (2) is not homothetically transposable on any one of its values. One has therefore to find a number of transformations valid for the general principle, i.e.

1 Retrogradation or non-retrogradation
2 Inversion of the rest and the sounded note
3 Augmentation or diminution, regular or irregular
4 Expressed or non-expressed rhythm in units or value or their derivatives
5 Introduction of syncope within the rhythm

So you can see that since we last met theoretical points of view have been confirmed.

POLYPHONIE X AND *STRUCTURES* FOR TWO PIANOS

All my attention this past year has been given to widening the scope of the series and making it homogeneous. With the thought that music has entered into a new form of its activity – serial form – I have tried to generalize the notion of series.

A series is a succession of n sounds, of which no tone as regards frequency is like any other, giving rise to a series of $n-1$ intervals. The serial production from this initial series is made by the transpositions b c . . . n of the entire series, starting from all the pitches of this series. Which gives n series. The inversion also yields n transpositions. The total number of series is equal, therefore, to $2n$.

If one conceives a series between a frequency band F and the double-frequency band 2F, one can speak of serial transposition, multiplying or dividing the frequencies, successively by two, four, etc., up to the limit of audible frequencies.

This is the case (simplified to twelve) with the twelve-note row. In this case, all the transpositions take place between single and double frequency bands: F^1-2F^1, F^2-2F^2, etc. This may be represented graphically by:

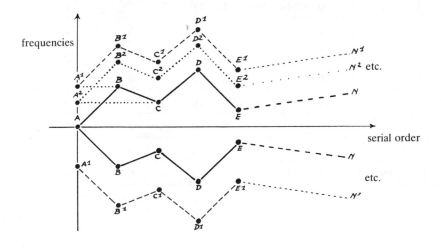

This being assumed, let us look more closely at the twelve-note series. If, as proposed, we make transpositions of it in the order of its components, we have a square, of which the horizontal co-ordinate will be the same as the vertical. We number all the serial notes, following the order of their appearance in the original series. Thus:

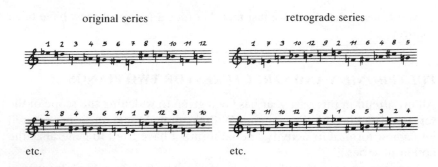

original series · retrograde series

etc. · etc.

Which gives, *in numbers*, the following double serial organization:

A

I	2	3	4	5	6	7	8	9	10	11	12
2	8	4	5	6	11	I	9	12	3	7	10
3	4	I	2	8	9	10	5	6	7	12	11
4	5	2	8	9	12	3	6	11	I	10	7
5	6	8	9	12	10	4	11	7	2	3	I
6	11	9	12	10	3	5	7	I	8	4	2
7	I	10	3	4	5	11	2	8	12	6	9
8	9	5	6	11	7	2	12	10	4	I	3
9	12	6	11	7	I	8	10	3	5	2	4
10	3	7	I	2	8	12	4	5	11	9	6
11	7	12	10	3	4	6	I	2	9	5	8
12	10	11	7	I	2	9	3	4	6	8	5

B

I	7	3	10	12	9	2	11	6	4	8	5
7	11	10	12	9	8	1	6	5	3	2	4
3	10	1	7	11	6	4	12	9	2	5	8
10	12	7	11	6	5	3	9	8	1	4	2
12	9	11	6	5	4	10	8	2	7	3	1
9	8	6	5	4	3	12	2	1	11	10	7
2	1	4	3	10	12	8	7	11	5	9	6
11	6	12	9	8	2	7	5	4	10	1	3
6	5	9	8	2	1	11	4	3	12	7	10
4	3	2	1	7	11	5	10	12	8	6	9
8	2	5	4	3	10	9	1	7	6	12	11
5	4	8	2	1	7	6	3	10	9	11	12

In this table, one may then make use of the numbers, either as notes themselves having this order number, or as belonging to a transposed series having this order number in the transposition. Moreover, having a number as serial origin, one is not forced to start from an initial serial note, but may start from any note you please: provided that a logical process of generation thus defines a structure. Without a structure the process would not be warranted. One may pass, of course, from one table to the other. That is, if in table B, I take the horizontal line beginning with 4, I have 4/3/2/1/7/11/5/ 10/12/8/6/9. I may move over to table A and have the following rows: 4/5/2/8/9/12/3/6/11/1/10/7; 3/4/1/2/8/9/10/5/6/7/12/11, etc.

If in an initial series I define each note by an intensity, an attack, a duration, it is clear that I shall thus obtain other serial definitions. Thus, if I take for the intensities:

1	2	3	4	5	6	7	8	9	10	11	12
pppp	*ppp*	*pp*	*p*	*meno p quasi p*	*mp*	*mf*	*più f quasi f*	*f*	*ff*	*fff*	*ffff*

for the attacks:

1	2	3	4	5	6	7	8	9	10	11	12
>	▾	·	–	⌒	≥	≥·	‑	⋯	^	*sfz* ^	normal

(See Messiaen's *Modes de valeurs et d'intensités*.)

for the durations:

Then I am in a position to refer the three structures to the serial structure proper.

They are not parallel. There can thus be plans of interchangeable structures, counterpoints of structures. Thus the serial structure defines its universe entirely, even that of timbre, if one wishes to extend the procedure.

It is clear that for rhythm one may use rhythmic *possibles*. For instance, if I use the rhythms:

with serial variants of the same number:

(a) simple transformation; capable of reacting upon all the others

etc.

(b) all values expressed

etc.

(c) by omission

etc.

(d) self-generated

etc.

(e) decomposition by its elements

(f) silence of the long

(g) silence of the short

$$| \; \downarrow \quad \gamma \; |$$

(b) to (e) being governed by the others; (a), (f) and (g) capable of reacting on all the others.

Then I can make a serial table with variant (f), which will be different from the serial table of notes. I can consider these cells as *possibles* – in the sense that I can use them in augmentation, diminution, regular or otherwise.

The same for the intensities. One may have variable plans for intensities exclusively designated by a number. Likewise for the attacks.

Tempo itself can adopt a serial structure. If four tempi are being used, for instance, we shall have a serial table with the index four.

It is clear that up to this point we have considered the series only as arbitrarily defined. It is possible to think that a series *in general* can be defined by a frequency function f(F), which may be extended to a duration function f(t), an intensity function f(i), etc., where the function does not change, but only the variable changes.

Finally, a serial structure may be given the global definition:

$$\Phi \; (f(F), \; f(t), \; f(i), \; f(a))$$

Algebraic symbols are employed in order to concretize these various phenomena precisely, and not to suggest any actual algebraic theory of musical relationships.

If the function is applicable to both duration and intensity we may call the serial structure homogeneous. If the functions are not generally applicable (serial structure of the durations being different from the serial structure of the intensities, etc.) then the global serial structure is heterogeneous.

We may therefore conceive of musical structure from a dual viewpoint – on the one hand the activities of serial combination where the structures are generated by *automatism* of the numerical relations. On the other, directed and interchangeable combinations where the arbitrary plays a much larger role. The two ways of viewing musical structure can clearly furnish a dialectical and extremely efficacious means of musical development.

Furthermore, serial structure of notes tends to destroy the horizontal–vertical dualism, for 'composing' amounts to arranging sound phenomena along two co-ordinates: duration and pitch. We are thus freed from all melody, all harmony and all counterpoint, since serial structure has caused all these (essentially modal and tonal) notions to disappear.

I think that with mechanical recording-means (the 'tape-recorder' in particular) we shall be able to realize structures that no longer depend on instrumental difficulties and we shall be able to work with any frequencies, using the serial method of generation. And thus each work will have its own structure and its own mode of generation on all levels.

We shall be able, within a serial space, to multiply the series by itself. That is, if between a and b of an initial series we can express the series in reduction, this would give a great expansion of the sound-material to be used in connection with the other serial functions.

13

'Sonate, que me veux-tu?'[1]

THIRD PIANO SONATA

Why compose works that have to be re-created every time they are performed? Because definitive, once-and-for-all developments seem no longer appropriate to musical thought as it is today, or to the actual state that we have reached in the evolution of musical technique, which is increasingly concerned with the investigation of a relative world, a permanent 'discovering' rather like the state of 'permanent revolution'. My real motive in writing this piece is to go more deeply into this point of view rather than simply to rebaptize the reader's ear into still another state of grace, which might be thought a rather commonplace undertaking.

What impelled me to write this Third Piano Sonata? It may well be that literary affiliations played a more important part than purely musical considerations. In fact my present mode of thought derives from my reflections on literature rather than on music. Not that I had any wish to write music with a literary reference, for in that case the literary influence would have been very superficial. No, the fact is that I believe that some writers at the present time have gone much further than composers in the organization, the actual mental structure, of their works.

I must at once disclaim any idea of embarking on a literary dissertation, something for which I have no qualifications. I simply want to say something about the two writers who have most stimulated my thinking and thus most profoundly influenced me, namely Joyce and Mallarmé.

A close examination of the structure of Joyce's two great novels will reveal the astonishing degree to which the novel has evolved. It is not only that the organization of the narrative has been revolutionized. The novel observes itself *qua* novel, as it were, reflects on itself and is aware that it is a novel –

---

[1] 'Sonata, what do you want of me?', a question attributed to Bernard Le Bovier de Fontenelle (1657–1757). Published in a previous English translation by David Noakes and Paul Jacobs in *Perspectives of New Music*, Spring 1963, pp. 32–44, and in its original French in *Meditations*, No. 7, Spring 1964, pp. 61–75. First published in German in *Darmstädter Beiträge zur neuen Musik*, Vol. III, 1960, pp. 27–40, Mainz, Schott.

hence the logic and coherence of the writer's prodigious technique, perpetually on the alert and generating universes that themselves expand. In the same way music, as I see it, is not exclusively concerned with 'expression', but must also be aware of itself and become the object of its own reflection. For me this is one of the primary essentials of the language of poetry, and has been since Mallarmé, with whom poetry became an object in itself, justified in the first place by poetic research, in the true sense.

In music the difficulty of taking this step is a matter of style. Music has no 'meaning': it does not make use of sounds which hover ambiguously, as words do, between objective sense and reflective significance. In principle both poet and novelist express themselves by means of words taken from the current vocabulary, and can make use of the ambiguity arising from the fact that a word can both denote a utilitarian object and also serve as a cipher of reflective thought. A large part of Joyce's world is constructed from the conscious and rational application of 'stylistic exercises' of this kind. Everyone will remember Stephen's excursus on *Hamlet* in chapter 4 of *Ulysses* and that astonishing chapter 14, where the growth of a foetus in the womb is suggested by a series of pastiches in which the evolution of the English language is traced from Chaucer to the present day.

Words can be used in this way because they possess a power of reference, a 'meaning'. With music the problem is different and, as we shall see, it presents itself in a different guise: here the only 'play' possible is an interplay between styles and forms. I am not setting out to establish a synthesis of general procedures that have received practical confirmation of a tolerably convincing kind. Nevertheless music at the present time unquestionably possesses a large repertory of possibilities and a vocabulary that is once again capable of universal concepts and universal comprehension. No doubt there are many improvements still to be made and it will take time for the language to become flexible and generally acceptable. Even so, all the essential discoveries have been made; there is no longer any questioning of direction and there is even a certain margin of security in the field of terminology, stylistically speaking. There is, however, one major task ahead – the total rethinking of the notion of form. It is quite clear that with a vocabulary in which periodicity and symmetry are of diminishing importance and a morphology that is in constant evolution, formal criteria based on repetition of material are no longer applicable, since they have lost their strength and their cohesive power. This is the task that is plainly becoming increasingly urgent – restoring the parity between the formal powers of music and its morphology and syntax. Fluidity of form must be integrated with fluidity of vocabulary.

It must be our concern in future to follow the examples of Joyce and Mallarmé and to jettison the concept of a work as a simple journey starting with a departure and ending with an arrival. We are assured by Euclidean geometry that a straight line is the shortest way from one point to another, which is roughly the definition for a closed cycle. In this perspective a work is *one*, a single object of contemplation or delectation, which the listener finds in front of him and in relation to which he takes up his position. Such a work follows a single course, which can be reproduced identically and is unavoidably linked to such considerations as the speed at which it unfolds and the immediacy of its effectiveness. Finally, Western classical music is opposed to all active participation, and this sometimes makes it difficult to establish any really significant contact, even if actual boredom does not intervene between the musical object and the listener contemplating it. From beginning to end every marker is carefully emphasized, which virtually eliminates any element of surprise. I will not go so far as to say that this conception by its very nature eliminates masterpieces. That would be untrue, because any work that can in any sense be called a masterpiece is precisely – if such a word is still permitted – one that permits of the element of surprise: and that surprise is nothing else than the evidence, perpetually reiterated in unexpected circumstances, that a straight line is effectively the shortest way from one point to another.

As against this classical procedure the idea of the maze seems to me the most important recent innovation in the creative sphere. I can already hear the malicious retort that I shall inevitably receive – that quite a number of Ariadne's clue-threads may well be needed to make any progress in such a maze possible, and that not everyone feels the call to become a Theseus. Don't let this worry us! The modern conception of the maze in a work of art is certainly one of the most considerable advances in Western thought, and one upon which it is impossible to go back.

(Western thinkers cannot in future forget that their ideas form no more than a part, however undeniably important a part, of universal knowledge, that they possess no unique privilege among the various developments of the human mind, and that the supremacy of Western thought was a ludicrous illusion. I can even speak personally in this matter. When I was a young man I listened to records of the music of other civilizations, especially those of Africa and the Far East. The beauty of this music came as a violent shock to me, because it was so far removed from our own culture and so close to my own temperament; but I was quite as struck by the concepts behind these elaborate works of art. Nothing, I found, was based on the 'masterpiece', on the closed cycle, on passive contemplation or narrowly aesthetic pleasure. In these civilizations music is a way of existence in the world of which it forms an integral part and with which it is indissolubly linked – an ethical rather than simply an aesthetic category.)

As I see it, the idea of the labyrinth, or maze, in a work of art is roughly comparable to Kafka's procedure in his short story 'The Burrow'. The artist creates his own maze; he may even settle in an already existing maze since any construction he inhabits he cannot help but mould to himself. He builds it in exactly the same way as a subterranean animal builds the burrow so well described by Kafka, continually moving his supplies for the sake of secrecy and changing the network of passages to confuse the outsider. Similarly the work must keep a certain number of passageways open by means of precise dispositions in which chance represents the 'points', which can be switched at the last moment. It has already been brought to my notice that this idea of 'points' does not really belong to the category of pure chance but rather to that of indeterminate choice, which is something quite different. In any construction containing as many ramifications as a modern work of art total indeterminacy is not possible, since it contradicts – to the point of absurdity – the very idea of mental organization and of style. Given these facts, the very physical appearance of the work will be changed; and once the musical conception has been revolutionized, the actual physical presentation of the score must inevitably be altered.

Here again I should like to refer to my own personal experience. Reading and rereading Mallarmé's '*Le Coup de dés*', I was greatly struck by its appearance on the page, its actual typographical presentation, and came to realize that this formed an essential part of the new form: the typographical material had to undergo a metamorphosis for Mallarmé. The actual printing of '*Le Coup de dés*' is of fundamental and primary importance, not only as regards pagination – the spatial disposition of the text with its blanks – but also its typographical character. In Mallarmé's own words:

> The intellectual armature of the poem is concealed and resides – takes place – in the space separating the strophes and in the blank spaces in the paper; significant silences as beautiful to compose as the actual lines . . . The poem is being printed, at the present moment, just as I conceived it page by page and this makes the whole effect. A word standing alone in heavy type needs a whole blank page, and I feel sure of the effect . . . Constellation according to exact laws will inevitably produce, as far as this is possible for a printed text, the effect of constellation. The vessel inclines, from the top of one page to the bottom of the next, etc.; because, and herein lies the whole point . . . the rhythm of a phrase concerned with action, or even an object, has no sense unless it imitates that action and, by its appearance on the page and its 'literal' reference to the original image, contrives in spite of everything to communicate something of it.

I could quote the whole of the preface that Mallarmé wrote for the first printing of his work. It is an essential document, and I will mention the points that are of special interest to us as musicians. The poet speaks of a 'spaced reading':

> The paper intervenes whenever an image, of its own accord, ceases or recurs, accepting the succession of other images; and, since it is not a question, as it never is, of regular musical features or lines – but rather of prismatic subdivisions of the Idea, the moment of their appearance and their duration in association in their respective spiritual settings – the text imposes itself at varying points close to, or far from, the latent live wire, according to probability.

Mallarmé considers 'the Page as a unit in itself, like the Verse or the perfect line [of the draughtsman]'. Then he observes that

> The typographical distinctions between a leading motif and what is secondary or subordinate determine the emphasis when the poem is read, and the reader's intonation will rise or fall according to the position of a word or phrase at the top, in the middle or at the foot of the page.

You can understand why I quote so freely. Mallarmé expresses himself so precisely that any paraphrase of these admirable remarks would have been quite useless.

Such formal, visual, physical – and indeed decorative presentation of a poem (though the poet does not include this) – suggested to me the idea of finding equivalents in music. When I started my Third Piano Sonata, I was very suspicious of everything inessential. Altering the physical appearance of a work without any real interior necessity to justify changing the impact of the score on the eye could so easily result in amusing, decorative 'calligrams', fashionable gimmicks in fact. I saw all too clearly the danger of producing musical inanities, such as those we know from various experiments in which the design is pretty and the intention behind it laudable, but there is no feeling that the desire to alter the exterior form corresponds to any interior, structural remodelling.

I therefore tried to avoid fancies of this kind and had in fact completed most of my work when there appeared a book of Mallarmé's posthumous notes relating to his projected *Livre*, accompanied by an excellent essay by Jacques Scherer on Mallarmé's plans. This was, in the strictest sense of the word, a revelation to me, for I found that all my ideas and the objectives I had set myself after *Le Coup de dés* were identical with those that Mallarmé had pursued and formulated but never had time to explore to the full. Jacques Scherer writes:

> Here we find, in opposition to the concept of history as enslaved to succession in irreversible time, an intelligence capable of mastering a subject by reconstructing it in all directions, including the reverse of temporal succession. The same double movement can show, at one end, a book perfectly composed and at the other a collection of sheets that is essentially external, a simple album in fact.

(Mallarmé himself calls the process from book to album an 'unfolding' and the reverse process a 'folding-up'.)

> Before this operation the book may appear to resemble an ordinary book; that is why it is called 'common': but when it has shown, as no ordinary book can show, that it is capable of achieving the clearly sensed diversity of an album and then of recomposing that as a structured whole, it has proved that it is the book. The confrontation is a creative one.

Consider once more Mallarmé's fundamental observation that 'a book neither begins nor ends: at the very most it pretends to do so' and this commentary of Jacques Scherer's:

> The real literary gift is the ability to move with freedom and originality – but without arbitrariness – within the book itself and its elements, which are the page, the poetic line (if it is a poem), the word and even the letter. The book, total expression of the letter, must gather a mobility directly from the letter.

No less astonishing is the idea of holding sessions at which the *Livre* was to be read to audiences of varying sizes directed by an 'operator', in some cases the poet himself. At each of these sessions new possibilities of interpreting the work would be discovered.

This application of combinatory analysis to language must have proved singularly arduous considering the restrictions that it imposes. Grammatical associative logic makes it difficult for words to be interchanged without a phrase losing part or all of its meaning – in fact formal logic is at the present moment concerned with an exact study of this phenomenon. In music, on the other hand, the logic of construction is less rigorously limited in validity: the non-significance and non-direction of the musical object in its primitive state make it usable in structured organisms, in accordance with formal principles much less restricted than those that obtain in the case of words. More than a confirmation, Mallarmé's *Livre* was a perfect proof – of our urgent need for a poetic, aesthetic and formal renewal.

My sonata, with the five *formants* that it comprises, may be called a kind of 'work in progress', to echo Joyce. I find the concept of works as independent fragments increasingly alien, and I have a marked preference for large structural groups centred on a cluster of determinate possibilities (Joyce's influence again). The five *formants* clearly permit the genesis of other distinct entities, complete in themselves but structurally connected with the original *formants*: these entities I call *développants*. Such a 'book' would thus constitute a maze, a spiral in time.

But to return to the five real *formants* – a name that I devised on an analogy with acoustics. Every timbre is, of course, given its individual character by its *formants*, and in the same way the physiognomy of any work is determined by its structural *formants*, i.e. by specific general characteristics capable of generating developments. Each of these characteristics appears exclusively in each of the pieces that comprise the work, so that they may later provide the *développants* mentioned above by means of exchange, interference, interaction and destruction. The titles that I have given to these *formants* underline their individual characteristics:

1 *Antiphonie*
2 *Trope*

3   *Constellation* and its pair *Constellation–Miroir*
4   *Strophe*
5   *Séquence*

Each of these *formants* can be used with a greater or less degree of deter-
minacy according to the degree of liberty taken in relation to the overall
form or local structure. In *Antiphonie* only the general formal scheme is
variable. This is based on two individualized structures, an extended application of the idea of antiphony as found in plainsong and in the music of
certain Central African tribes. These two structures appear on two different
pages and are each performed in a determinate tempo, with its own stylistic
traits: one consists of two fragments, the other of three. These fragments are
copied on to strips of cardboard and disposed thus:

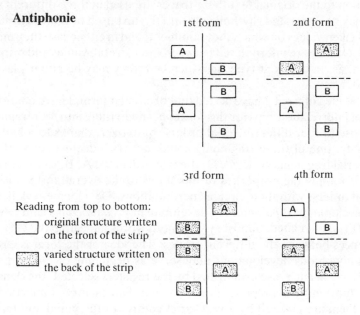

This diagram makes it clear that there are four possible forms of organization. Thus each of the original fragments that appears on one side of the strip
appears in variation on the other side, and in fact *Antiphonie* is divided into
two independent responses. In my physical arrangement of the material any
one of the four forms can be selected by reading one or other side independently, always bearing in mind that within the same response an A structure
must always be answered by a B structure of the same kind. Of course I could
have used the four forms complete and developed them as a function is
developed; but this is made completely unnecessary by the simple operation
of the cardboard strips, an operation itself linked to the structure of the
music.

The title of the second *formant*, *Trope* is a reference to Gregorian chant, an extension of the idea of monody to the formal structure:

Trope

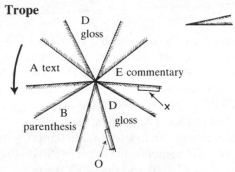

In relation to the original text these tropes are used in three different ways. They may be integrated rhythmically into the text itself or grafted inside the overall given values on which they comment; and in either case they must be played. Or they are interpolated between these overall values and printed in parenthesis, in different type, in which case they may be either played or omitted.

To this idea of trope I have added that of circular form. I have employed a series of interrelationships for this *formant*, subdivisible into four fragments, giving rise to four different serial orders. Moreover, thanks to a harmonic ambiguity, one of these fragments could have two distinct rows. If I call these serial fragments A, B, C, D, the two orders are A, B, C, D and A, B, D, C. If I apply the properties of this series to the overall form, I get two original orders, with their circular permutations. Development A is called *text*, development B *parenthesis*, development C *commentary* and development D *gloss* – related, almost synonymous words indicating the very slight differences between the different tropes. The idea of the form is circular: each autonomous development may serve as beginning or end, a general curve being in each case established by the registers selected, the density of the texture and the preponderant dynamic. Satisfactory connections between them are ensured by a very strict control of the initial and terminal zones. In this way we come back to the idea, which I explained earlier, of a work with neither beginning nor end, able to unfold at any given moment – an idea materialized in this cycle of sheets, which has a direction but no fixed beginning.

The third *formant*, entitled *Constellation*, is reversible. On one side of the sheet is the original form and on the other its retrograde version, entitled *Constellation–Miroir*. It must be performed once, naturally in one of its two transcriptions. Why is this piece a double of itself? Because it occupies an unchanging position at the centre of the *formants* – but I shall be explaining later the relationship between the different *formants*, following a general disposition [*constitution*].

The score is in two colours, red and green: green for the groups marked *points* and red for those marked *blocs*. These two words are exact indications of the morphology of the structures used. *Points* are structures based on pure, isolated frequencies, chords being formed simply by the simultaneous occurrence of two or more points. *Blocs* are structures based on perpetually shifting blocks of sound, and these may be struck vertically or may disintegrate horizontally in very rapid succession, so that the listener's ear retains the identity of the block. In this way groups of points are contrasted with groups of aggregates; or, in other words, an unvarying neutral (pure frequency) is contrasted with a varyingly characterized individuality (sound block). I am only describing the principal criterion by which this piece is organized and there are of course other secondary or subordinate criteria such as timbre (ranging, through an intermediary zone, from a direct to a reverberating sound) and register (restricting the field of frequencies within which any given group is to move) – and so on.

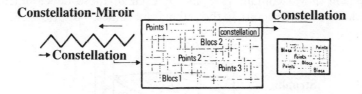

As the diagram shows, there are three *points* and two *blocs*, followed by a final group, which is a microcosm of the large constellation, in which three *blocs* alternate with three *points*, but in inverse order. In this small constellation the *blocs* are in green and the *points* in red, referring to the structural scheme and not to the characteristics of the writing. *Points* and *blocs*, green and red, alternate in the order in which they appear; and within the groups the course taken by the music is extremely diverse, which may or may not modify the tempo. I am absolutely incapable of analysing the mechanism of the piece in detail, nor would this serve any purpose without the text in front of us. I should, however, mention the fact that at the beginning and end of each system there are reference signs to indicate how to proceed from one system to another, and, if necessary, the effect this may have on duration (there may be modifications of tempo *en route* or the tempo may be radically different, but stable) and on dynamics. Some directions are obligatory, others optional, but *all* the music must be played. There is a certain resemblance between this *Constellation* and the plan of an unknown town (such as plays an important part in Michel Butor's *L'Emploi du temps*). The actual route taken is left to the initiative of the performer, who has to pick his way through a close network of paths. This form, which is both fixed and mobile, is thus situated at the centre of the work as pivot, or centre of gravity.

I shall say less about the *formants Strophe* and *Séquence*, since their forms are not yet definitive, having been put on one side and then interrupted by other works.

I adapted the original idea of *Strophe* after reading Mallarmé's reflections on the thickness of the book as a formal 'marker'. Jacques Scherer has given an admirably clear explanation of this:

> Thickness is one of the real qualities of volume and is different from depth. If depth indicates a number of lines, thickness refers to the superimposing of lines or pages, and thus to the possible emergence of a new poetic current, or a new flow of meaning.

This idea helped me to establish a definite relationship between the *formant* itself and its application. In the first place there are four strophes of different length (we will call them A, B, C, D), each capable of being developed independently but on similar lines, and according to the following principle: development 2 will contain development 1; development 3 will contain 1 and 2; development 4 will contain 1, 2 and 3, each of these developments naturally adding a new structure to those that it subsumes. The arrangement is as follows:

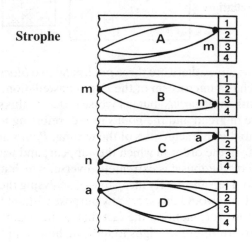

The pagination of each strophe is mobile, independent of all the others. The greater the density of the *formant*, the more complex will it become, since it will subsume all those preceding it. In order to differentiate the four strophes, the work, as it unfolds, will employ only one kind of density at a time, and never the same one twice, so that each strophe illustrates a different stage of development. In this way it will be possible to read A2, B1, C3, D4 and so on. These links affect the register in a direct, obligatory manner: in order to be able to link any 'stage' of any one strophe with any 'stage' of the next there must be a register common to the end of all the stages of this strophe and the beginning of all the stages of the strophe following. These will be register nodes, the antinodal loops of the register being the current of each strophe, where there is no obligation. Only the beginning of A and the end of D can be either a node or an antinodal loop. (I have borrowed these terms from the language of traditional acoustics, since they give an absolutely accurate description of this evolution of registers.)

I shall say least of all about the last of these *formants*, *Séquence*, since it presents the most problems, to which I have still found no practical solutions. Any new elaboration comparable in quality to that in the preceding *formants* demands, in fact, radical innovations in the transcription of variable pitches, this variability being incompatible with our existing system of notation. To give the reader some idea of what I mean I will simply say that the guiding principle is based on reading through a grid – a kind of decoding, in fact – which allows the performer to choose the sequence that he wishes to play. This *formant* will therefore be the furthest removed from predetermined form, while *Antiphonie* will approach it most closely.

As for the general conception governing these five *formants*, it is based on a symmetrical, mobile disposition around the central *formant* of *Constellation* (*Constellation–Miroir*). The diagram below illustrates how this distribution is effected: round a central kernel (which is itself a group of cells) gravitate the four *formants* grouped in twos on concentric orbits, the outer orbit being able to become the inner and vice versa. This provides only eight possible interpretations, given the different symmetries governing the permutations. As Jacques Scherer puts it in his study of Mallarmé's *Livre*, 'The sheets are allowed their freedom, but if this freedom were total, it would take several lifetimes to exhaust the work's content. We can speak only of a "controlled" freedom.'

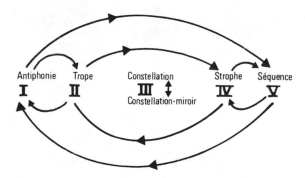

I need hardly say that I did not discover this overall organization at once. My ideas gradually fell into place around the guiding conception of the work as a moving, expanding universe. For this reason the development of one *formant* led me to reconsider another and this in turn reacted on the *formant* following, and even indeed on that preceding! This explains how *Strophe*

and *Séquence* came to be sacrificed almost completely and are being (or will have to be) completely reworked. You will now realize the wealth of possibilities in the interaction of these *formants* – just imagine parenthesis-pages, mobile *cahiers*, constellations of *formants*! The imaginative possibilities are, in fact, endless, provided the craftsmanship is there . . . And, in fact, it is the composer's delight to set out towards a horizon and to find himself in a totally unknown country, of whose very existence he was hardly aware. Composition would be an infinitely tedious occupation if it were no more than a series of trips arranged by tourist agencies, with every stopover prearranged.

One final word. Form is becoming autonomous and tending towards an absolute character hitherto unknown; purely personal accident is now rejected as an intrusion. The great works of which I have been speaking – those of Mallarmé and Joyce – are the data for a new age in which texts are becoming, as it were, 'anonymous', 'speaking for themselves without any author's voice'. If I had to name the motive underlying the work that I have been trying to describe, it would be the search for an 'anonymity' of this kind.

14

Constructing an Improvisation[1]

DEUXIÈME IMPROVISATION SUR MALLARMÉ

I should like to clear up some of the misunderstandings that separate us from
the public, and the best way to do this seems to be to explain how a work is
made, why I have chosen a certain ensemble of instruments and how the
work should be played. I will take as an example the second of my *Improvisations sur Mallarmé*, and will explain it from three different points of
view:

1 what I mean today by 'improvisation'
2 why I have chosen these particular instruments rather than others and
   how these instruments are placed in relation to each other
3 how I have conceived the form of the piece and how I have achieved – as I
   hope – an interaction between the poem and the music

In the first place, then, improvisation. This for me means the forcible
insertion (*Einbruch*) into the music of a free dimension.

In performing a traditional orchestral work the players are dependent not
only on the conductor but also on the laws governing precisely controlled
ensemble playing, which admit of no exceptions. In an improvisation, on the
other hand, two elements become mobile: the actual form and where the
relations between the instruments are to occur. It is only recently that form
has been thought of as anything but precisely defined in every detail. There
was an established musical language based on various agreed hierarchies
with their dependent figures and dispositions. Nowadays the language is
constructed, in essence, of phenomena that are relative, and it is for this
reason that form too must be relative. In other words, elements must be

---

[1] 'Construire une improvisation', lecture at Strasburg (1961) on the second of the
Improvisations sur Mallarmé. The original German text transcribed from tape was published
in *Melos* under the title 'How the avant-garde works today', Vol. xxviii No. 10, October 1961,
pp. 301–8. Revised by Boulez in 1981. Translated here from the French text prepared by J. L.
Leleu for *Points de repère*.

introduced that modify the form from one performance to another and make it impossible for two performances of the work to be exactly identical.

Things were different in the past. According to traditional principles one element, A, was followed immediately by another, B, to which a third, C, was linked directly. The distinguishing feature of the new form consists in the fact that it is in a way created from one moment to the next – in other words it is possible, under certain conditions of course, to move directly from A to C without first passing through B. Imagine a network of railway lines in a station. The disposition of the rails and the points is precisely fixed, but to change the course of any network no more is needed than to press a button or work a lever. In the same way local decisions taken by the players and the conductor enable the form of a work to be modified at any moment in performance.

I will not go beyond these general considerations, because the second of my *Improvisations sur Mallarmé* was my very first attempt to investigate this field of possibilities. Since that time I have examined the problem in greater detail and my improvised forms are now much freer and more relative in character than they were at that time.

My problem in composing this second *Improvisation sur Mallarmé* arose from the dialectic inherent in the juxtaposition of a fixed (verbal) and a mobile (musical) text. To obtain a visual idea of this interplay between freedom and discipline think of two things – the conductor's gestures and the printed score. In conducting a work there are certain traditional gestures that correspond to passages that are notated in an equally traditional manner in the score. But there are also gestures that the conductor makes as it were into the void, signs to an individual player that amount to saying, 'Go ahead – over to you.' The player can then choose his own tempo. The passages concerned are printed in small notes in his part, in the same way as they used to notate ornaments. The maximum time allowed for these mobile structures is marked by arrows.

And now a word on the instrumentation. The work is scored for voice and nine instruments. Five of these – harp, tubular bells, vibraphone, piano and celesta – are fixed-pitch instruments, though this description is not absolutely accurate. A note played by the piano or the harp at a given dynamic is precise, its pitch identifiable among a thousand others. In the case of the celesta there is a confusion between real sounds and harmonics in the lower range, and this is even more noticeable in the vibraphone, on which a *forte* note is a fairly complex sound that sometimes has little to do with the pure note. Finally in the case of the bells the fundamental is notoriously surrounded with a host of partials. The result of this is a complex of frequencies in which the absolute pitch of the fundamental note becomes increasingly difficult to hear. With these five instruments listed above I have also employed others – wooden and metal percussion instruments – whose sonorities are close to the noise category.

On the platform the three different categories of instruments – accurately pitched, partially pitched and unpitched ('noise') – are disposed among each other, and this produces the kind of stereophony that is a function of these instruments' characteristic sonorities. Take the celesta, whose sonority is not very powerful – I therefore place it in front on the right, near the conductor. The sonority of the harp is more powerful but would be covered if it were placed near the piano, and I therefore place it in front on the left. The vibraphone's sonority is of medium power and I place it in the middle of the stage facing the conductor. Since the piano is dynamically powerful, I place it behind on the right. The most powerful are the bells, and these I place at the back on the left. The percussion instruments are disposed among the others.

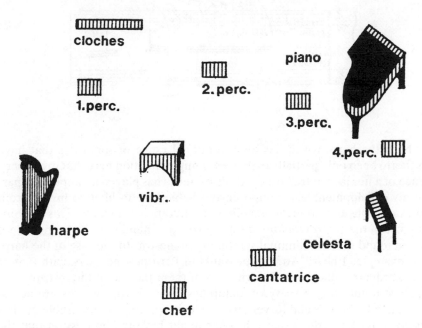

The work is scored for voice and instruments. I place the instruments on the platform in such a way that the three different kinds of sounds – fixed pitch, partially pitched, and unpitched ('noise') – blend with one another.

I should like now to show how I have used these different instruments. First the celesta, which has the shortest-lasting sound – I therefore use it, basically, for rapid figures, passages that 'sound' more or less by themselves. I have also given the celesta rapid successions of short, dry chords, as in bar 66:

The celesta's characteristic virtuosity and brio can be seen in bar 65:

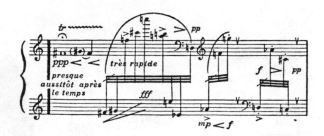

Next the harp, which has an exceptional range of sonorities that have hitherto been only partially exploited. I might mention here that my experience of a number of traditional kinds of music has played an important part in my development as a composer and helped me to liberate myself from Western conventions in the handling of different instruments. This explains my use in the *Improvisations sur Mallarmé* of a number of instruments not often found in the traditional symphony orchestra. In the case of the harp, for example, I heard Andean peasants in Peru playing harps with a most extraordinary sonority and learned from them the use of the instrument's highest notes and a variety of 'dampings'. Our European ears are accustomed to Debussy's and Ravel's use of the harp, which is admirable but has become hackneyed, so that a listener might have the impression that the harp is an instrument conscientiously dusted down at every concert in a series of glissandos.

It is really a pity that such a versatile instrument should be used for such a restricted effect, and for this reason I should like to suggest some possible new methods of playing and new sonorities to be obtained. Harmonics, for instance, have a kind of strangled quality, but they are also quite aggressive in character, as the strings have to be plucked very hard for the harmonic to sound properly. Here, for instance, is bar 66:

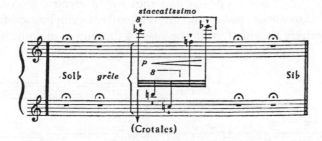

The aggressive quality of which the harp is capable is most noticeable in the highest range (bar 68):

Another method consists of plucking the string close to the soundboard, so that the string cannot vibrate as freely as when it is plucked in the middle. The result is a dry, more piercing sound, rather reminiscent of the guitar. The slight echo following the attack of the note is very characteristic (bar 55):

Finally a possible use of the instrument that I should like to emphasize – short, dry arpeggios instead of chords (bars 48–50):

Many of you are familiar with the vibraphone from jazz. It is not often used in symphony orchestras, where it appeared for the first time in Berg's *Lulu*. Berg, however, made only episodic use of the instrument to obtain certain atmospheric effects or a special symbolical sonority, essentially as a passing colouristic feature. As far as I know, Olivier Messiaen was the first composer to give the vibraphone an independent place in the orchestra; and I shall never forget our amazement as his students when we first heard this instrument taking its place among those of the traditional orchestra. This was in 1945 at the performance of his *Trois petites liturgies*.

The vibraphone consists of a number of sheets of metal backed by resonators, which are alternately opened and shut by an electric motor. This produces a vibrato whose speed – and this is important – can be modified, or the vibrato entirely excluded, as in the case of the simple melodic lines in bars 36–8:

A few words about vibraphone chords. These can be damped by means of a pedal, so that all the metal sheets that have been struck cease simultaneously to vibrate. A much more interesting method, in my opinion, is for the player to damp the vibration with his hands, simply by placing them on one or other of the metal sheets. In this way it is possible to remove notes one by one from a held chord, leaving the rest vibrating, or to remove the chord by degrees (bar 73):

Playing the chord with the pedal produces the kind of 'syrupy' sound that is often held against the instrument. But without the pedal the vibraphone can produce a dry, incisive sound (bar 66):

This matt colour produced by the vibraphone goes very well with staccato passages in the piano or the celesta (bar 66):

Here the dynamics pass by different degrees to and from *forte* and *piano*.

Bars 109–12 show the full sonority obtainable from the vibraphone, whose low trill covers even the *fortissimo* of the piano:

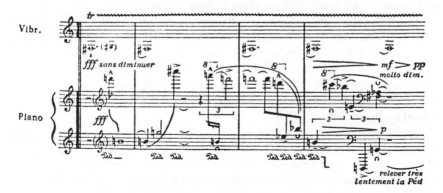

To me the vibraphone is a kind of substitute for the Balinese gamelans, which we cannot procure. I find these a great fascination in Indonesian orchestras, which include forty or fifty 'tuned' gongs; and I like tubular bells for the same reason, because they too recall Far Eastern music. Generally speaking these bells are used only for special effects, as in Mussorgsky's *Boris Godunov* or Debussy's *Ibéria*. There are plenty of other examples of passages in which bells are used in a very significant way, but it is always for dramatic rather than purely musical purposes. Bells are used, one might say, to give musical emphasis to a theatrical situation rather than for their own sake, and they therefore have a certain anecdotal, or even religious, character. My aim has been to free the instrument from these associations, to secularize it and to give it greater importance simply as tone colour.

To return to my composition. Used with the piano and the vibraphone the bells produce a remarkably homogeneous complex of sound. In a passage such as the following (bar 55) it is virtually impossible to determine which instrument is playing which note:

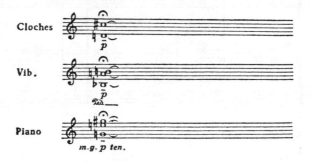

I have already mentioned the fact that in the case of bells the fundamental note is surrounded by a great number of partials. It is this property of the instrument that led me to employ the bells as a link between fixed-pitch instruments and those that produce complex sounds.

And now the piano, which, you may perhaps think, needs no introduction. I think it does, though, because we treat it today quite differently from the way in which it was treated by Debussy and Ravel, by Stravinsky (in *Les Noces*) and Bartók (in *Allegro Barbaro*) who considered it as essentially a percussion instrument. We have not forgotten these lessons, but the piano interests us perhaps even more as an instrument of complex sounds produced by harmonics.

To obtain harmonics on the piano it is only necessary to depress certain notes without sounding them (a simple triad, for instance) and then to play other notes in the normal way – octave, third, fifth, fourth and so on. The strings of the silent notes start vibrating with the others, and the effect can be multiplied by silently depressing clusters of notes with the flat of the hand or the forearm, so that the piano is transformed into a resonator. The case of the instrument then acts as an echo chamber (bars 22–3):

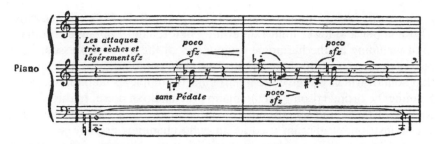

By means of these harmonic effects I can produce sonorities that modify the nature of piano sound (bars 42–3):

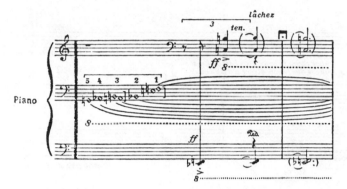

In the same way there are a number of pedal effects that have not been used hitherto. In the second *Improvisation sur Mallarmé* there are only isolated instances of these effects, since the work was not composed specially for the piano. Even so, a short example will serve to demonstrate how the sound spectrum can be modified by means of the pedal. A rapid sequence of chords is played with the pedal, after which the player immediately raises and then immediately depresses the pedal. The strings thus cease to vibrate in some areas but continue to vibrate in others, and there is an audible change of timbre. In this way it is possible to make a chord die away gradually, from the high notes to the low, since the low strings obviously sound longer than the high (bar 20):

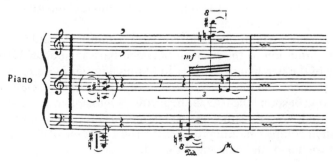

I have already mentioned clusters. If I depress all the keys within a range whose upper and lower limit I determine beforehand I obtain a chromatic total including all the harmonic frequencies of the notes depressed. I can also play clusters of this kind silently and then combine them with clusters that sound, which will give me a particularly complex sound-effect, transforming the ordinary sound of the piano into a halo of noise. In this way the totality of the sound spectrum takes on an *almost tangible* existence. The whole instrument is again used as an echo chamber, and the number of strings vibrating is thus so large that there are interferences and harmonics that never appear absolutely simultaneously (bar 68):

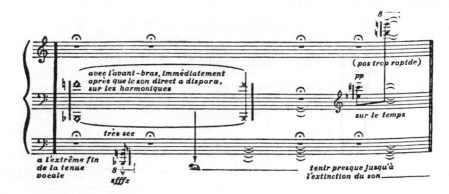

All these possibilities make the piano, as I see it, a particularly valuable instrument, as they make it intermediary between instruments producing notes of fixed pitch and those producing the complex sonorities that verge on noise. This gives the instrument a very wide range of sound qualities.

Now I should like to say a few words about the percussion instruments that I chose for this work. Some of these are of wood and some are of metal. First come the maracas, whose sound is in the nature of coloured noise; and then the claves, whose sound is bright or dull according to the wood of which they are made. My score contains three of these instruments.

Of the metal instruments the crotales are an antique form of cymbals, such as were discovered in the Pompeii ruins. They vary in pitch, and in this work I employ three pairs in order to obtain a sound that, compared with that of the gongs, is rather imprecise.

I need not say anything about the gong or the tam-tam, but I should like to draw your attention to the passage between bars 32 and 44. Here I have made use of the percussion in order to obtain a rather more matt sonority, since the passage contains a large number of highly resonant chords. Above this envelope of sound the listener hears the percussion instruments' 'white' and 'coloured' noises, as they are called technically. These noises are very dry and their complex nature provides the right extreme of contrast with the resonant sounds of the piano and the vibraphone:

*) Assez Vif→Vif (♩=144→♩=231)

Harpe

ne pas étouffer   étouffer ,

Cloches

ne pas étouffer   étouffer ,

Vibr.

ne pas étouffer   étouffer ,

Piano

2/4 ㉜ 3/4   7/8   3/4   2/2

*)
0 ———→ 1   0 ————————→ 3   0 ————————→ 2   0 ————————→ 4
poco accel.   accel.   meno accel.   molto accel.
pp < mp   p ———— f   p ———— mf   mp < ff

1
Mar.
(un seul)

p < f   p < mf   p   < ff

2
2 Mar.

idem.

3 (son
grave)
Mar.
(un seul)

sempre   continuer le trémolo pendant les points d'arrêt
p (sans nuances)   (p sempre)

4
Crotales
graves

f
laissez vibrer

*) *Les accélérandos sont notés ainsi de la vitesse minima à la vitesse maxima une échelle de O (♩=144)
à 4 (♩=231) avec les échelons 1.2.3. intermédiaires — Cette notation ne doit pas être prise au pied de la
lettre, mais la courbe dessinée évoque plus que la notation: accélérando molto ou poco.*

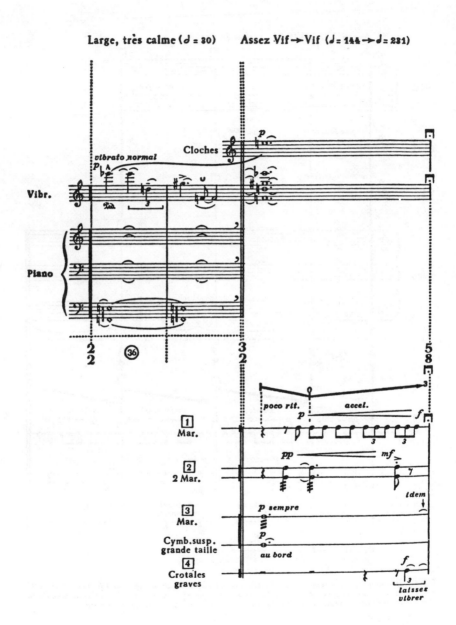

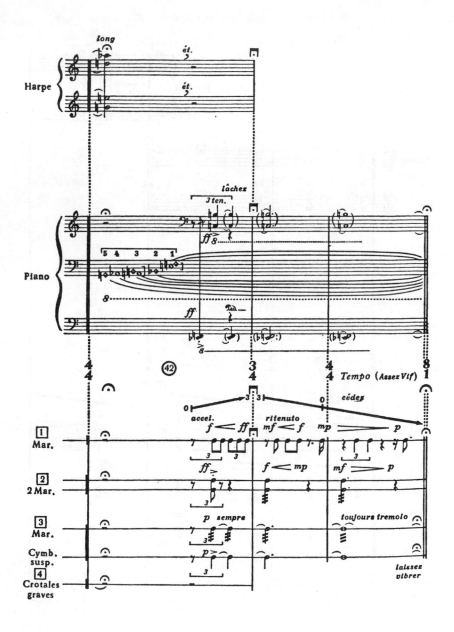

I have already described a number of ways in which the tone of the piano can be transformed. There is a further possibility exemplified in this work, and it consists in the use of the gong and the tam-tam, both of which belong to the same zone of sonority as the lower register of the piano. By making use of this fact it is possible completely to change the way in which we hear the tone of the piano. Exact dynamics are very difficult to determine in this case, since much depends on the acoustics of the individual hall as well as on the particular characteristics of the instruments concerned. The essential thing is to obtain a mixture in which the listener is not aware of the gong and the tam-tam individually, but only of the complete transformation of the character of the piano. There are a great many instances in the second *Improvisation sur Mallarmé* of this mixture principle, too many in fact to list in detail.

After this short lesson in instrumentation we come to the form of the piece, and this corresponds exactly to the structure of the poem on which it is based, the sonnet 'Une dentelle s'abolit':

> Une dentelle s'abolit
> Dans le doute du Jeu suprême
> A n'entr'ouvrir comme un blasphème
> Qu'absence éternelle de lit.
>
> Cet unanime blanc conflit
> D'une guirlande avec la même,
> Enfui contre la vitre blême
> Flotte plus qu'il n'ensevelit.
>
> Mais, chez qui du rêve se dore
> Tristement dort une mandore
> Au creux néant musicien
>
> Telle que vers quelque fenêtre
> Selon nul ventre que le sien,
> Filial on aurait pu naître.

The actual poem is framed, in my *Improvisation*, by an introduction and a coda, both instrumental. The form of the sonnet – two quatrains and two triolets, with the usual pattern of rhymes – provides the exterior skeleton of the middle section, in which the poem is actually 'set to music'. The maximum attention is paid to the form of the sonnet in characterizing it in music.

The whole piece is built on two contrasting structures, which we will call A and B. A is ornamental, and here the melody consists chiefly of melismas and ornaments. In these circumstances syllabic declamation is impossible, and the words are sung with numerous vocalises. This results, of course, in a certain unintelligibility but this is deliberate. The poem is in fact for me an object of musical crystallization.

Let me explain what I mean by this. To my mind Mallarmé's poem has its own beauty, which needs no addition of any kind. In order to enjoy the actual beauty of the text itself, the poem should be recited. At the same time it seems to me a bad plan simply to follow the course of the poem. My idea is to communicate its *internal* structure, and to place this in the closest possible relationship to my music. In order to do this I can – indeed I must – allow myself considerable liberties; I consider that the relationship between poem and music is on a higher plane than that of a mere respect for scansion and rhyme – on the semantic plane, in fact.

So much in parenthesis, and I return to structure A, which is, as I said earlier, ornamental. The vocal accompaniment is collective – that is to say the instruments are not used as solos (bars 12–15):

Structure B begins with the second strophe. Here the declamation is syllabic: a single note corresponds to each syllable of each line and there is no hint of melismatic singing.

The first line of this strophe consists of eight syllables sung, therefore, on eight notes (bar 45):

The second line has 4 + 4 syllables (bars 55–9):

The third line has 2 + 5 + 1 syllables (bars 65–8):

And the fourth line has 2 + 6 syllables. Structures A and B cross here:

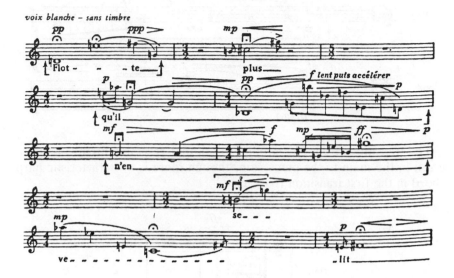

In each line Mallarmé groups his words according to their sense, and I have observed his pattern scrupulously. This has an additional importance because it is here, in the second strophe, that the actual improvisation starts and the conductor signals free, individually chosen tempo.

The two structures are employed in the third and fourth strophes, and the transitions between the four strophes are of course purely instrumental, and nearer to noise than to sound in character.

These, then, are the main features of the work, and I should like to add a few comments on detail, beginning with the introduction and the conclusion, the framework in fact. The mixed sonorities of the first eleven bars give an idea of the ornamental character and the instrumental style of the piece. With regard to the end I should like to point out that there is no 'conclusion' in the strict sense of the word. The last thing that the listener hears is a noise that, musically speaking, has no suggestion of finality. The two maracas close no frontier and the work could perfectly well go on.

In the middle section the two structures, A and B, are frequently superimposed, each penetrating the other. In the sung section, for instance, an increasing number of vocalises may be interposed between the long, held notes of the B structure, as in the last line of the second strophe (bars 71–4):

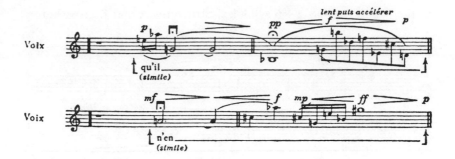

The transitions from one strophe to another resemble breaths and are given in the main to the percussion, though there is a characteristic harp chord in the first transition (bar 41):

A similar harp chord reappears in the passage between the second and third strophes, and the listener is thus made aware of relationships – structural if not thematic – between these sections. In the first transition passage I have inserted a harp chord and a piano chord among the percussion noises; and in the second of these passages the same percussion instruments are interrupted by a similar harp chord and, instead of the piano, the celesta.

Finally I should like to point out once more how, once it has been sung, the text continues to make its effect and leaves the imprint of its structure on the music. In bars 120 and 130, for instance, the five sound structures of the instrumental bar (130) –

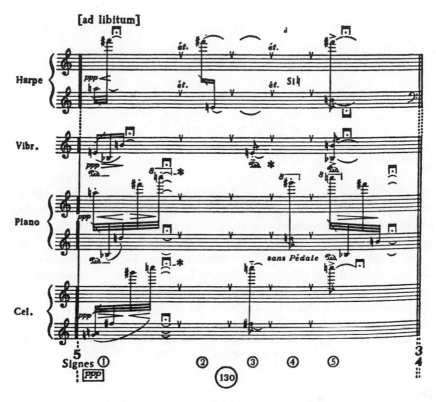

– correspond to the five syllables sung by the voice at bar 120:

In this way the text leaves its mark – its seal in fact – on the instrumental music. The instruments have in fact become song.

15

Pli selon pli[1]

Pli selon pli represents a number of solutions to the problems posed by the alliance of poetry and music, and these solutions range from a simple heading to total amalgamation. They give each piece a meaning and indicate the significance of its position in the complete cycle.

The work consists of five pieces. The first, *Don*, and the last, *Tombeau*, are instrumental and employ the largest forces, the voice appearing only episodically, to present the relevant line of Mallarmé. The three central pieces use smaller instrumental groups and are centred on the voice, which enounces all or part of the poem underlying their musical organization.

The first and last pieces are thus entirely independent of the poem, which appears only in the form of quotation.

DON

The Mallarmé line serves as a heading, and this is the only direct intervention of the voice, since the other occasions on which it appears are quotations from the central cycle, as it were leading up to what the listener will hear later. These musical quotations are suggested by Mallarmé's title 'don du poème', which here becomes 'don de l'oeuvre'. They are not literal quotations, but abstracted from their context, out of place – glimpses of what is to come, as it were. The statement of the opening line, on the other hand, ('Je t'apporte l'enfant d'une nuit d'Idumée') is extremely simple and clear, direct and syllabic.

TOMBEAU

The line 'Un peu profond ruisseau calomnié la mort' appears at the end of the piece. The enunciating of the line conflicts with a very florid vocal style and a demanding tessitura. The only clearly comprehensible words are the last two, which are spoken.

---

[1] Sleeve note for the recording by Boulez, CBS 75.770.

We shall meet this contrast between direct and indirect comprehension again in the three sonnets that form the central cycle: 'Le vierge, le vivace et le bel aujourd'hui', 'Une dentelle s'abolit' and 'A la vue accablante tu'. This contrast is fundamental in any music based on a poetic text; and before saying anything about it I should first make it clear that the form of these pieces is modelled strictly on sonnet form. The relationship between poem and music is not only on the plane of emotional significance: I have tried to push the alliance still further, to the very roots of the musical invention and structure. We should never forget that Mallarmé was obsessed by the idea of formal purity and an unswerving quest for that purity, as both his language and his use of metre show. He entirely rethinks French syntax in order to make it, quite literally, an 'original' instrument. Although the organization of the actual line acknowledges such conventions as the alexandrine and octosyllabic structure, it is dominated by the strict demands of quantity and the rhythm of the sound values implicit in each word, so as to achieve a fusion of sound and meaning in a language of extreme concentration. The esoteric quality almost always associated with Mallarmé's name is simply this perfect adaptation of language to thought without any loss of energy.

Thus, if we take into account the perfect, closed structure of the sonnet as such, we find that the musical form is already determined. In order to make the required transposition it is necessary to invent equivalents applicable either to the exterior form of the musical invention or to the quality of this invention or to its internal structure. The possible forms of transposition cover a wide field, and their diversity is balanced by the rigour with which they are employed.

What point is to be taken as fixed, and what degree to be regarded as a minimum, when considering the listener's actual comprehension of the poem in its musical transposition? The principle I have adopted is not simply that of immediate comprehension, which is only one (and possibly the least rewarding) of the forms of transmuting a poem. It seems to me altogether too restricting, to try to insist on a kind of 'reading in/with music' of the poem. From the point of view of simple comprehension, such a reading will never replace a reading *without* music, which certainly remains the best means of imparting *information* about a poem's content. On the other hand a concert piece based primarily on poetic reflection is quite different from a stage work that demands a minimum of direct comprehension to enable the listener to follow the action, the actual 'events' that, if occasion arise, stimulate poetic reflection.

In my transposition, or transmutation, of Mallarmé I take it for granted that the listener has read the poem, is aware of its direct meaning, and has assimilated the data on which the composer builds. I can therefore work with a shifting degree of immediate comprehension. This will never, on the other hand, be left to chance but will tend to alternate between allowing musical or verbal text to dominate.

Instrumental sonority varies from piece to piece. Percussion is used on a much larger scale than has hitherto been usual, but includes many more fixed-pitch instruments (xylophones, vibraphones, several kinds of bells) than those of indeterminate pitch that come close to 'noise', the former being more easily integrated with 'classical' instrumental groups. The first and last pieces employ a relatively large ensemble, which produces an orchestral sonority, while the style and sonority of the three central pieces are more like chamber music, particularly the second sonnet, 'Une dentelle s'abolit'.

The title of the work – *Pli selon pli* – is taken from a Mallarmé poem not employed in the musical transposition, and indicates the meaning and direction of the work. In the poem in question, the words 'pli selon pli' are used by the poet to describe the way in which the mist, as it disperses, gradually reveals the architecture of the city of Bruges. In a similar manner the development of the five pieces reveals, 'fold upon fold', a portrait of Mallarmé himself.

16

Sound, Word, Synthesis[1]

I

The relationship between the world of our traditional instruments and the universe revealed by electro-acoustic procedures has not yet been established. I have always believed that far from contradicting or cancelling each other these two means of expression must form two sides of one and the same organizing concept, and will thus be able to reinforce each other and form a kind of 'total art', though this expression is a dangerous one. As I have often said, it is my belief that our generation will be concerned quite as much with synthesis as with discovery properly so called – and perhaps even more so. It will be devoted to the expanding of techniques, the generalizing of methods and the rationalizing of the procedures of composing or, in other words, to synthesizing the great creative currents that have made their appearance since the end of the last century. But please do not misunderstand me. I do not imagine such a synthesis as a final consummation, a kind of 'apotheosis' of musical history, or a sort of industrial stage of development succeeding that of the home craftsman. I think of it rather as simply an indispensable starting point from which to embark, with a minimum of intellectual guarantees, on new voyages of discovery, which may very well lead to the reconsidering of all, or part, of our Western musical tradition.

Let me give you some examples. The evolution of Western musical thinking has led composers to normalize all interval relationships in a rigid, definitive hierarchy, having first gradually abolished all exceptions or 'particularisms'. On the other hand these 'particularisms' have eventually reappeared in the form of archaisms, either temporal or geographical; and furthermore the distributive element in this hierarchical scheme has found its way to within the hierarchy itself, which it has first corroded and then rendered powerless. This justifies our saying that, within the serial organization that creates functions only by the fact of its own existence, there is

[1] 'Son, verbe, synthèse', first published in German in *Melos*, Vol. xxv No. 10, October 1958, pp. 310–13. The second part only was included in *Relevés d'apprenti*; the complete text first published in French in *Points de repère*.

absolutely no need for a world of sound in which the scale on which these functions should apply are determined in advance. It would seem rather that serial organization will create, by means of a system of given relationships, a pitch network that varies according to the parameters chosen by the individual composer. An identical organization of *figured* relationships may be applied indifferently – by creating strict differentiations in listening [*écoute*] – to musical worlds tempered according to any given interval or to non-tempered worlds; so that during the course of a work a mobile constitution of the musical material properly so called is obtained. This supposes a similar organization of time, though here we are approaching the question of listening, i.e. problems of form and perception. In the morphological organization of time the relative world of pitch implies consequences not difficult to imagine. There is a curve in the ear's response to the greater or lesser differentiation of intervals, a curve that may be established in relation to listening-time; duration and pitch are linked – 'measurably' – by this phenomenon. In the case of very small intervals time must be considered as stationary, rather as though the ear were listening through a magnifying-glass. Apart from this morphology, we must consider the part played by duration in listening. Western music has ingeniously developed recognized 'markers' within recognized forms, so that it is possible to speak of an 'angle of hearing' as we speak of an angle of vision, thanks to a more or less conscious and immediate 'memorizing' of what has gone before. But with the object of keeping the listener's attention alerted these 'markers' have become increasingly unsymmetrical, and indeed increasingly 'unremarkable', from which we may conclude that the evolution of form characterized by such points of reference will eventually end in irreversible time, where formal criteria are established by networks of differentiated possibilities. Listening is tending to become increasingly instantaneous, so that points of reference are losing their usefulness. A composition is no longer a consciously directed construction moving from a 'beginning' to an 'end' and passing from one to another. Frontiers have been deliberately 'anaesthetized', listening time is no longer directional but time-bubbles, as it were.

This leads us to a conception of artistic creation in which 'completion' is no longer something undertaken by the artist. *Chance* is introduced as a factor in the work, which has no definitive form – this being one of the most important questions and one of the least necessarily understood. Such 'chance' is not a mere gambling with the objects concerned; were it no more than that, it would be pathetic and childish. It is concerned rather with the relationship between time and the individual moment, recognized and utilized as such. A work thought of as a circuit, neither closed nor resolved, needs a corresponding non-homogeneous time that can expand or condense; pitches determined in a mobile manner, and a relative concept of internal structure, including dynamics and timbre. Each performance will thus represent a single, specific option, neither better nor worse than any other.

This intrusion of 'chance' into the form of a work may manifest itself in circuits using multiple nodal points with different probabilities of triggering, or by means of commented structures – 'effervescences' – from which the 'comments' (regarded as being in parentheses) may be removed without altering the general appearance of the structure. (The consequences may be either positive or negative.)

So far we have been speaking of course from the soloist's point of view. As far as ensembles are concerned, we should be thinking rather in terms of sound montages, in which elements may be added optionally and the initiative of one performer triggers off that of another and so on. The days of rigid scaffolding are past, and scores present a number of different possible montages excluding, if necessary, only homogeneity of time.

The word 'montage' immediately suggests electronic or electro-acoustic techniques requiring the support of a tape; and these techniques do, it is true, fit perfectly into the field that is now being explored speculatively. They completely corroborate the idea of relativity in the world of sound, as we have described it above. Even so the precision, the 'definitive' character of actual realizations seems to contradict the most ambitious of the goals we set ourselves, namely the indeterminate nature of the written work (in the case of a text designed for a number of performers). In fact it is precisely this contradiction that we must exploit, conscientiously contrasting the two fields, the electro-acoustic and the natural. In the one we have precision and absolute control of the structures down to the most infinitesimal detail – hence a rigidly determinate realization; and in the other a number of possible structures, a single performance providing no more than a temporary definition.

What, then, is to be the fate of concerts and concert halls? Well, they must be adapted to the new concept of composition. Indeed the question of space is of primary importance, since it can be an essential element in the transmission of the musical 'sign' or 'signal'. The two most important points to be considered in this connection are mobility in the placing of instrumental players and the seating of the audience, which must not be orientated to any particular point. In that case, of course, the listener's perception will orientate itself in a different way from now, and we shall not be far from abandoning the closed space – and its attendant temptation to contemplate beautiful objects in a way that is pointless and no more than half awake – which is the bane of Western music.

II

Does a conception of music such as I have outlined go with the use of words?

If I make the poem of my choice anything more than a starting point for a design of ornamental arabesques, if I establish it as an irrigation source of my music and so create an amalgam in which the poem is 'centre and absence' of the whole body of sound, then I cannot restrict myself to the mere emotional relationship arising between these two entities. In that case a whole web of conjunctions will necessarily arise, which, though including these emotional relationships, will also subsume the whole mechanism of the poem, from its pure sound as music to its intellectual ordering.

'Setting' a poem to music – I am not thinking for the moment of the theatre – involves a whole series of questions relating to prosody and declamation. Is the poem to be sung, 'recited' or spoken? All vocal means are available and it is on their different peculiarities that will depend the communication, the greater or lesser intelligibility of the text. Since *Pierrot lunaire* such questions have been hotly debated among musicians, and I need hardly refer to the controversies about *Sprechgesang*. The typical reflex – a poem set to music should approximate as closely as possible to the same poem when spoken – now seems rather superficial. A good poem has its own sonorities when recited, and there is no point in trying to find an exact equivalent. Singing a poem means entering a world with its own conventions, and it is cleverer to make use of these conventions as such, and to respect their laws, than deliberately to ignore or fake them, or try to distort and divert them from their true purpose. Singing implies transferring the sonorities of a poem to musical intervals in a system of rhythms, and both these intervals and these rhythms are fundamentally different from those of speech; it is not a question of heightening the power of the poem but, frankly, of hacking it to pieces. Very probably the poet at first blush will not even recognize his text when it has been treated in this way, since what he wrote had a quite different purpose. Even his own sonorities will seem strange and alien to him, as they are grafted on to a support that he never foresaw or could have foreseen. At the very best, and bearing in mind the still existing autonomy of his poem, he will recognize that if his poem was to be treated in such a way, this was how it had to be. Between this extreme of pure convention and that of the spoken language lies the whole gamut of intonations the conscious use of which is only beginning to be explored, Schoenberg being the pioneer in the field, as we said above. Since his day we have become acquainted with the theatrical conventions of the Far East, and these have revealed the degree of perfection with which the resources of the human voice may be utilized. In the cases of Schoenberg and Berg there are some questions that have not been fully answered, such as the character of vocal emission according to the different effects required, how long a sound is to be sustained and the tessitura of the different types of vocal emission – all problems that can be solved only empirically. We can be sure that a new vocal technique will be evolved, which will treat each of these problems separately. But what about prosody – that famous prosody about which everyone thinks he is righter than the next man? Are accents and movements of the voice to resemble as closely as possible the inflexions of the speaking voice? This depends entirely on the zone of vocal emission concerned. There are, of course, certain rules that cannot be broken without harm, or on occasion without appearing ridiculous. Punctuation, for instance, in the most general sense, must be observed or the poem will not be raised to a higher power and transmuted so much as destroyed, not only in sonority but in actual substance.

If we accept this, the relationship of a poem to its musical setting may be considered as a kind of function whose variable is the method of vocal emission used.

Once having structured the musical text in relation to the text of the poem, we face the problem of intelligibility. We should ask ourselves without more ado whether the fact that, even in a perfect performance, we 'can't understand a word' is a sure and unconditional proof that the work is not a good one. Against this generally accepted idea it seems possible to act on the intelligibility of a text as 'centre and absence' of music. If you want to 'understand' a text, read it or have it declaimed to you; there is no better method. What you are now undertaking is a more subtle task that implies previous knowledge of the poem. 'Reading to music', or rather reading with music, is unacceptable because it is an only superficially logical solution that shirks the real issue because, again, it ignores the *conventions* of singing and the obligations that these imply. All the arguments in favour of 'naturalness' are foolish, since naturalness is (in all civilizations) quite irrelevant to any amalgamation of text and music.

In that case, you may say, if your first concern is with sonorities, why do you not choose a text in which the meaning is of no importance, or even a meaningless text made up of onomatopoeic syllables and imaginary words invented for the musical context? This would save you from these practically unsurmountable contradictions. It is true that onomatopoeia and words consisting of meaningless syllables can express things outside the range of intellectually constructed language; and there is no lack of examples of this in popular music as well as in art music. The conscientious objectors will not fail to be disarmed by the fact that such a use of words may well be instinctive. In a great number of liturgies, for instance, the ritual chants are in a dead language, which makes it impossible for the majority of the worshippers to understand directly what they are singing. A dead language of this kind, such as Latin in the Catholic rite, may be still known and translated, its meaning perfectly decipherable. In certain African rites, on the other hand, the dialect used for important ceremonies is an obsolete dialect, the meaning of which is totally obscure to those who use it (especially when a whole people has been transplanted, as in the case of Brazilian Negroes). The Greek theatre and the Japanese Noh also provide examples of a 'sacred' language in which archaisms gravely reduce, if they do not entirely abolish intelligibility. At the opposite extreme, in popular songs, successions of onomatopoeias and common words used for their sound rather than their sense are a universal feature. The requirements and delights of rhyme are the essential thing here, coupled with a kind of absurd logic that has a charm of its own, as in counting songs and a number of folk songs, such as those used so effectively by Stravinsky in *Les Noces*, *Renard* and *Pribaoutki*.

According to Friedrich Novalis, 'Speaking for the sake of speaking is the formula for deliverance.' Whether that deliverance is in religion or in play, it is not hard to find examples; and we really should not be astonished to find composers having recourse to this dissociation of words from their meaning. Even so, making this his sole object would mean a composer forfeiting a wealth of other expressive possibilities offered only by texts so organized as to convey a comprehensible message. Comparable to this spectrum ranging from words organized according to their logical meaning to their use simply as sound phenomena is the sound spectrum itself, which offers noises as well as sounds. Although this is no more than a rough comparison, it is still true that the sum total of procedures outlined above will enable music almost completely to satisfy the demands of any text, morphologically speaking. What still remains to be done is to establish an identity between the large structures of organization and composition.

Is this way of fusing music and words – spurting out a phoneme when words literally fail us – no more and no less than an attempt to organize delirium? 'What a nonsensical idea', you may say, 'and what a truly absurd juxtaposition of terms!' Wait one moment. Are the frenzies of the improviser the only ones in which you are prepared to believe, then? Or the powers of some 'primitive' rite? I am increasingly inclined to think that in order to make it really effective we must not only take such 'frenzy' into account but even organize it.

17

Poetry – Centre and Absence – Music[1]

Poetry and music: two sacred monsters often pitted against each other! There was a time (symbolist or mystic?) of transsubstantiation when Mallarmé raised a mortgage in the Wagnerian manner and preached:

> Let us forget the old distinction between Music and Letters, which is no more than a deliberate division of an original unity, with a view to an eventual re-encounter: one of the two evoking the spells belonging to this abstract point of hearing and almost of sight, becoming understanding; which, spreading itself, grants the printed page an equal range.

This mandate was followed by a well-known proposition that has been misunderstood:

> I suggest, at the risk of my aesthetic reputation, the following conclusion – that Music and Letters are alternating faces – one spreading here into the darkness and the other glittering there with certainty – of a single phenomenon. I called it the Idea. One of these modes inclines toward the other and disappears into it, only to reappear with borrowed riches: by this double oscillation a whole genre is achieved.

If I must give this alternating phenomenon a name, I will call it 'centre and absence', though darkness and brightness cannot long remain mere appanages!

What happened to this hypothesis of Mallarmé's, which was put forward, forgotten and then restated? The most flamboyant poetic revolutions have been severe on music as a serious (if not disloyal) rival in the field of dreams. They have regarded music as at best an unusual form of entertainment, a kind of childish finery carelessly dropped in the streets of the commonplace. Listen to René Char's formulation of the poets' complaint:

---

[1] 'Poésie – centre et absence – musique', lecture on *Poésie pour pouvoir* at Donaueschingen in 1962. Published in German in *Melos*, Vol. xxx No. 2, February 1963, pp. 33–40. Translated here from *Points de repère*.

> Until recently music was linked with poetry – or vice versa – only because one of the two admitted defeat in the first bar and adopted a totally subordinate position to the other, to which it served as understudy or frame. And so these two great, inexhaustible and totally different mysteries agreed to appear side by side only to prompt a smile of pity from those who came to enjoy...

And Char goes on to wonder whether their 'tumultuous union' ('interweaving our saps') will create 'a new terrestrial adventure'.

Questioning the foundations of his emotional experience Henri Michaux suggests his own form of exorcism or mediation:

> I surprise it while it is actually happening, this trickle from mood to mood. Suddenly I am aware of joy, unmistakable before I am aware of it. I have only to recognize its presence ... then what? Sadness? About whom? About what? What are these things that suddenly seem numerous enough to cloud the horizon? ... More often than not I feel a sense of uncertainty which it would be wrong to try to overcome too quickly. It knows its own business. That weight of disturbance deep inside me is still too great to find expression, it is for music to determine, the music beneath my fingers. Music will be the first to know the truth ... Tired of images, I play in order to make a smoke screen ... My noise against the other noises ... and I feel alone, deserted by my friends, who now seem to belong so little to me.

Did I say mediation? This active, pragmatic attitude could be described more aptly as 'mediumistic'.

There we have it! The glittering face has found a more or less egoistic expression, and what can we make of it, we, who are the dark face? Are we to give up and lose heart because communication is difficult? Can we really banish this whole concern from our lives?

In everyday language the word 'poetic' is now surrounded by a fog of misunderstanding. Hence, by reaction, the instinctive distrust of all such clichés as 'poet of sounds' and 'poetic music'. We must overcome this handicap, eliminate the element of the picturesque (to which the idea of 'poetry' has quite wrongly been restricted) and set out to discover the Idea.

Music can be linked with poetry at a number of different levels of importance and intensity, from a mere title to intimate fusion and from the anecdotal to the essential. The simple fact that poetry and description have often been assimilated should not necessarily make us suspicious of titles, inscriptions and quotations. The only trouble about 'programmes' is the childish precision of their literal 'correspondences' whose sense is anything but clear. Such 'programmes' divert the listener's attention from much deeper and truer conjunctions by concentrating interest on the success, or evidence, of some 'symbolic' evaluation, some materially tangible system of images. These invite the most primitive and absurd comparisons and have been equally damaging to both poetry and music, which they reduce to so much tinkling and verbiage – a sort of universal code composed of obsolete conventions and employed chiefly in the elaboration of so-called 'functional' tricks.

Does this kind of 'description' imply a plea for pure, abstract music that has its origin and its form exclusively in itself? Is it no more than a quarrel about form? In fact the distinction between 'pure' and 'illustrative' music seems to me to be only a masking and concealing of the essential problem. There is plenty of 'pure' music that may be reduced to illustrative clichés without any necessity for the slightest explicit reference. There are ways of suggesting 'the heroic', 'the tender', 'the whimsical' and 'the pastoral' that need no passport to establish their identity: and there is a whole stylistic arsenal, well supplied and well tested, to assist the conventional poetic imagination both in melodic material and its rhetorical handling. In instances the actual use of a 'pure' form is equivalent to a quotation! (Please do not for the moment take into account the 'dramatic' use of this kind of quotation – in that case it may easily be justified by a kind of *double entendre* in its references . . . But it is without doubt the most complex example of the mechanism of poetry, extremely subtle and delicate and acting directly on 'predetermined' [*précontraint*] semantic elements.) On the other hand there are titles and inscriptions that are sometimes vague in their reference ('Les sons et les parfums tournent dans l'air du soir') or their setting ('La terrasse des audiences du Clair de lune') but stimulate the listener's imagination in a way that the music itself 'realizes'. In the first case we have a fixed code functioning automatically and informing us of the musical 'content', and in the second the real musical substance – with its immediate qualities as sound and its formal elaboration – sends us back to the title or inscription and 'explains' in a totally irrational manner.

Even chorale variations present a problem. Although the original religious text has gone, a direct link with it remains in the syllabic disposition and the periods of the music. As a commentary, it heightens the implicit significance of each verse, thus forming the classical example of the complex esoteric. And what of the *timbres* on which innumerable masses were written? Their original significance has been deliberately falsified; they have been robbed of their origins in order to serve as basic material for a completely different kind of expression in a totally alien structure.

The relationship between poetry and music can take many forms, therefore, and is not simply a matter of employing words. It may range from direct statement to diffuse commentary, but there are a number of constants, and these I should like to try to define.

The first fact to be taken into consideration is that, in its most primitive forms, music is accompanied by words. There are a number of different reasons for this, not the least of which is the primary role played by the human voice. The object of sacred chants is to praise the divinity or divinities concerned, to ensure their favours and to thank them for their past services and protection. Secular singing is either a collective amusement or, in the case of work songs, an accompaniment and alleviation of daily labour. These songs are therefore linked to the different social classes by the direct expression of their existence and the realism of their actual lives, even if they do not go so far as to include onomatopoeic imitation of the sounds associated with different trades such as boatmen. These 'utilitarian' comments make any division between text and song impossible, and instrumental music in such cases is no more than a means of ensuring the continuity of a rite, a way of filling the time until the voices enter.

All poetry was originally designed for singing, and the evolution of poetic forms was inseparable from the corresponding musical process. We should not forget that the Greek playwrights also composed the music for their choruses and melodramas, while nearer to our own time Machaut was an innovator in both fields, so that his name appears in literary as well as in musical history. This unity of conception did not last for long, each 'branch' requiring its own specialized knowledge. We find instrumental virtuosity, in particular, demanding independence and starting to explore its own potentialities. If it is still used as a commentary on settings of poems, it is not long before this bond is broken and our present distinction between vocal and instrumental music established.

There is a vast literature devoted to this antagonism between the two. The quarrel has been particularly violent in the dramatic field, but religious music has not been immune, each party hurling anathemas at the other. From the purely aesthetic or moral point of view music has often been accused of forming a distraction from some essential 'truth', whether it be religious or theatrical. Music has equally been regarded as a necessary evil inseparable from any rite or ceremony but forming an impure element in the action and disturbing contemplation. In the eyes of the orthodox it monopolizes the worshipper's attention and represents an anti-intellectual element, directed to the senses or even actually sensual, and deliberately disturbing by its very nature. The list of hostile philosophers, suspicious writers ('Please do not dump music against my poetry') and uninterested playwrights is interminable. And we still have the nerve to speak of a synthesis of the two? Are musicians so strongly attracted to poetry that they are unable, at some point of their evolution, to do without a text around which to crystallize their music? The very form in which the question is put spells danger, suggesting as it does the profanation of the text (pretext?). What demon incessantly impels composers towards 'literature'? What power obliges them to become writers themselves, if need be? Is it simply the hankering after the lost paradise of this ancient union that they are striving in vain to regain?

On a more prosaic level any use of the voice soon leads to articulation, since vocalization alone soon becomes wearisome and makes the impression, even if it is only an unconscious one, of being a rather restricted use of the vocal mechanism, anything but a full exploitation of its subtler potentialities. This reaction is based on a kind of respect for humanity, the ability to articulate sounds being a distinguishing feature of man as such. Even a consistent use of a variety of phonemes, however, does not necessarily lead to a 'language', for this necessarily implies a system of semantics. Hence we sometimes find composers making use of an imaginary language, invented specially for their own reasons and designed to form part of some instrumental sonority or to create what are properly speaking orchestral effects in vocal ensembles. The method in which this meaningless 'poetry' is employed will depend on its purpose, and this may be either picturesque, esoteric or purely musical. To the picturesque class belong, obviously, all forms of imitative or descriptive onomatopoeia referring either to animals or to the noisier features of human existence – war, for instance, or such daily (and more harmless) phenomena as the old street cries. We are all acquainted with the *Batailles*, *Sièges*, *Chants d'oiseaux*, *Chasses* and *Cris de Paris* of the sixteenth-century *chanson*. At the opposite extreme to this descriptive use of words we find their use for esoteric effect. This may take the form of a sacred language that has become obsolete and lost its direct meaning but preserved a fetishistic character, its verbal formulae reaching immediately the ears of the gods, who understand messages couched only in this archaic form. Alternatively it may be a language whose meaning has been deliberately made obscure in order to ensure that it is comprehensible only to the initiate – either some deformation of everyday language whose normal meaning is distorted or a purely imaginary language, a kind of jealously guarded code. There are cases in which the picturesque and the esoteric are combined for dramatic purposes – in the theatre, for example, a pseudo-secret language is conventionally required for demons or witches, as a hallmark of their essentially mysterious and malignant nature! Finally we have the case of pure inventions, deliberately devoid of any meaning hidden or otherwise, not possessing even a symbolical significance and avoiding imitation of any kind. In this case the composer has precise sonorities in mind and any semantic link would serve as an unnecessary handicap. Every other consideration is subordinate to a strictly auditive logic, and the human voice becomes a species of sonorous material capable of producing phenomena literally unobtainable by any other instruments, though it may also compete with them by imitating or distorting their sounds.

Whatever the object, words used in this way have no direct semantic significance; they either create their own system of references or form part of an organization whose logic is foreign to them. Whether justified ethically or aesthetically, this use of words simply as sounds eliminates one of the regular, outstanding issues in the interminable debate between music and poetry, namely which of the two has prior claim: is the explicit meaning of any text obscured or heightened by the music designed to correspond with it? The theory of poetry underlying the relationship that we have been describing – leaving aside all question of priority – is perfectly adequate for its purpose; and in fact without this theory it is impossible to imagine any exploration of the dark realms of consciousness. Music perfectly fulfils its function either by allying itself to modes of expression that are not directly significant or by appropriating them to itself. It gives an unimaginable power to 'what lies beyond language' and at the same time is enriched by it in that field which concerns it most specifically, namely that of sonority. Music has almost always claimed to possess a 'magic' power, and in the case that we are discussing such power is exercised openly. The power of attraction that it exercises on the unconscious is both acknowledged and employed as such; and that is why musicians will always secretly prefer a 'language' that puts no obstacles in the path of communication by means of sound. The only real danger is that of exoticism, a kind of aural migration that offers too simple a palliative to the longings of minds sick with too much 'understanding', foreign languages taking the place of the unpassable barrier of an unknown dialect. It may be a dream, a kind of economy or sheer exhaustion . . . In any case it is probably a defence mechanism against a society from whose abhorred contact the composer can escape by this magical means. Such an attitude has obvious affinities with the love of folk music simply as a means of escape from the everyday world, an aspect with which our concern can only diminish. The criticism that it implies has been well ventilated by now and that criticism has lost its point. Can it still be called a revolt, or has it not rather become a flight? If non-language and meta-language play an important part in the music–voice amalgam, the written text with its precise significance has always been fundamentally an opposing factor. There is a long 'literary' tradition in music, functioning at different levels, whereas meta-languages have never raised any serious objection – perhaps 'secrecy' exercises a greater fascination than we have been ready to believe? The way in which composers have handled literary texts has aroused controversy in every age.

There are two primary and fundamental questions. Is music capable of communicating the *meaning* of a poem or a dramatic text? And is it possible – and if so, obligatory – by using an appropriate prosody to ensure, at all costs, the intelligibility of that text? And there is a closely connected subsidiary question – whether the language of the original must be preserved in performance or are translations admissible? This age-long dispute about the primacy of text or music has often been conducted with a certain amount of sophistry, and champions of the opposing parties have appeared in the field of the church, the theatre and the concert hall, establishing over the centuries a fairly equal balance between the long succession of 'reforms' and 'counter-reformations'. In fact it is difficult to declare either side to be wholly in the right or wholly in the wrong. It depends on whether the composer's object is to produce a spell-binding effect on the listener, in which case he will give priority to music, or to appeal to the listener's reasoning faculties, in which case he will champion the literary cause. If music is considered simply as an inessential and restricted method of transmitting feelings or doctrines, John XXII and Jean-Jacques Rousseau join hands in their merciless hostility to polyphony. If literary structure is regarded simply as a piece of joinery without which no opera or drama is possible, there will be found to have been quite a number of composers who have happily transferred important sections, and even whole numbers, from one opera to another, or from a cantata to an oratorio, and not been in the slightest ashamed of doing so. The question of translation is of more recent date, but still continues to present problems and to set traps for operatic producers.

But to return to our first question – is music capable of communicating, 'rendering', the *literal* meaning of a poem? We are all familiar with the joke about 'Che farò?' – the total transformation of Orfeo's lament –

> J'ai *trouvé* mon Eurydice,
> Rien n'égale mon *bonheur*!

There is no difficulty with the syllables: 'quantities' are respected; phonetically the second line even ends with a word derived from the same root as the original; the general sonority is preserved. Conclusion – that with a minimum of precautions, in choosing the number and quality of phonemes any text can be sung to any music, music being by its very nature devoid of *direct* meaning itself and therefore unable to communicate any – or, alternatively, to support all – meanings indifferently. There is the even more shocking example of popular – often indeed bawdy – songs being used for liturgical texts, a very common practice until the sixteenth century when, under François I and Henri II the psalms were sung in this way at the French Court...

There is in fact no way in which music can claim the same exact semantic function as the spoken language; it has its own semantics firmly rooted in its own basic structures and obeying specific laws, so that the sense communicated is parallel to, rather than identical with, the sense communicated by words. The explanation of this given by Boris de Schloezer carries conviction. What he says in effect is that, in a mass, 'Non credo' may well be substituted for 'Credo' without making the music absurd; and this is no more a cause for amazement than for scandal. Musical semantics can take no account of affirmation or negation as such, but can transmit only the sense of *conviction* behind either of these professions of faith. It can even distinguish the quality of such conviction, which may be either combative and associated with the will or tranquil and serene; and this is something that cannot be transmitted directly by the written word without specifying the speaker's *tone of voice*, which brings us back to music. The dialectic music–language enables us to understand why there are many different ways of setting 'Credo', which is in itself an abstract, doctrinal notion, whereas such more purely descriptive passages as 'Crucifixus' or 'Et resurrexit' suggest essentially similar musical effects. In these cases the images evoked by the text are images of suffering or joy, and these unequivocally suggest a precise category of musical characterization. It is clear, therefore, that what music loses in immediacy and precision it very largely gains in analytical delicacy. It cannot, on the other hand, be denied that the musical conventions for the unambiguous expression of, say, joy or grief lose their power, and even their significance, with the stylistic changes and transformations that occur from one age to another. The 'symbolism' of music evolves just as the language does, and we shall hardly be aware of this unless we possess the key to the process. ('Realistic' effects, which represent deviations, or often degradations, of this musical symbolism, are so dependent on the style of each age that their representation in music changes quite noticeably over the centuries, although the models – natural sounds, for instance – do not appear to have undergone any comparable transformation.) This evolution in the 'significance' of music shows to what an extent sounds and words are governed by similar linguistic laws.

Let us now go on to the second fundamental question – whether it is possible to ensure the *understanding* of a text by the listener. This question involves both the actual substance of the music and its function. The importance of a direct comprehension of the text will in fact vary according to the part played by music in the overall *form* of the work concerned. In the case of a dramatic work, it is absolutely essential that the listener should understand the literary purport; if he does not, he is not in possession of sufficient information to interest him in the dramatic development, particularly if this is at all complicated. (Programme notes are often useful aids but the need for them should not, on principle, be felt . . .) In actual fact it does not take a very acute intelligence to follow the story of some librettos! Given the conventions of any genre, the listener knows roughly what will happen to the chief characters, and word-by-word understanding of the text no longer serves any real purpose. Once he has grasped the dramatic situation, the part played by words is predictable and their information content unimportant. If, on the other hand, we take the imaginary case of a work that is being seen for the first time and a listener who has no subsidiary 'outside' information about it, a direct relationship between what is taking place on the stage and the listener's intelligence is of primary importance – hence the repeated search for the aptest and most adequate solution. A glance at those attempted, from the *stilo rappresentativo* to *Pelléas* and *Wozzeck* (and including such quasi-theatrical works as *Pierrot lunaire*), will show how various these have been. On the other hand, when there is a pause in the drama and the reactions to the situation of the different characters or groups are given time to develop, we find ourselves faced with the 'parallel semantics' of which we spoke above: once in possession of the necessary dramatic information, music has the right to make its own static commentary, in which words lose their capital importance as the bearers of information.

I have spoken of the theatre and 'dramatic action', and I must make it clear that I am not limiting these terms to actual stage performance, but including oratorios and Passions, where the drama unfolds in the listener's mind rather than on any stage, and a description may be interrupted by individual *reflections* or expressions of corporate *states of mind*. All large-scale musical works with a literary base are built round this alternation of action and reflection (movement and immobility), individual and corporate expression; and this, furthermore, is the most – or in any case one of the most – constant features of all human ceremonies, whatever their nature and to whatever civilization they belong, whether they are popular or the preserve of a cultured minority, secular entertainments or religious rites. ('Music', wrote Mallarmé, 'promises to become the ultimate and plenary form of human worship.')

We have described the process of integrating text and music in order to determine the various ways of using the human voice and the various formal schemes to which these give rise. When it is a question of action or movement, individuals – or individual relationships – will come to the fore and the musical setting will therefore in most cases be syllabic, with a word on each note or several words on the same note. In cases such as these, moreover, the effectiveness of the word–sound relationship will increase the more closely it resembles speech. Attention, however, will be concentrated on the voices and the musical 'scenery' will become correspondingly less important. A perfect example of this is to be found in recitative, or narration, which preserves musical continuity but at a subsidiary level, in order to ensure the intelligibility of the necessary dramatic information. History has witnessed revivals of systems and conventions that have become obsolete and of methods based on rhetorical principles that the evolution of the language has consigned to oblivion; but the fundamental principle remains the same. Different ages and different cultures have devised different conventions, some more realistic in character and others more highly stylized. Thus the problem has been solved in one way by the Noh theatre and in another by Mozart, the recitatives of the Passions offer one solution and Gregorian chant another. The list is endless, but whatever the method of *transcription* employed, we always find the voice being used in a way that is as close as possible to speech, actual speaking. Conventions cloak and unite fundamental dissimilarities, and *Sprechgesang* is only the last metamorphosis in a long series spreading over many different civilizations.

At the opposite extreme we have melismatic song, or polyphony, which either may be purely vocal or may include instruments as well as voices. Here the number of parts, the sheer contrapuntal density, hampers the understanding of the text, though its general meaning is heightened and given a new fascination. Homophonic melismatic chant involves extending words in time, a kind of syllabic dissection that breaks their continuity and destroys their logical sequence. (Tropes, in fact, owe their existence to the difficulty of remembering the words of a text protracted in this way!) If a melisma on a single syllable is long enough, the singer loses the thread and the 'message' of the text escapes him: in most instances vowels are dissociated from consonants and this weakens the ability to discriminate between the multiple possibilities of confusion. The excesses of this flowery style in the Middle Ages were condemned by the Roman authorities, as indeed was the extreme use of polyphony in the widest sense, extended to language itself. In some motets we find three different texts in different languages (Latin and dialects of the vernacular – a sacred and a secular language) superimposed on each other, presenting an insuperable obstacle to any immediate understanding of the text. To make matters worse, the *cantus firmus* was stated in such long note-values that the words were deprived of their natural expression. Even in cases involving a single text the successive 'entries' and independent rhythms of the contrapuntal parts give rise to superimpositions and intersecting verbal rhythms, which present the listener with problems of interpretation. Only a strict observance of syllabic coincidence, as in the homophonic polyphony of the *chanson* and the chorale, can ensure intelligibility.

The various fluctuations of the musical forms in works with a verbal text bear witness to the actual variations in treatment – monody, with or without instrumental accompaniment, and polyphony; syllabic and melismatic writing. The nineteenth-century German *Lied* and French *mélodie*, for instance, present a typical case of a 'musical reading'. The 'significance' of the poem is assured in a number of ways. The tempo at which the poem is sung is roughly the same as that at which it would be spoken, and the modest range of the vocal line excludes all virtuosity. The prosody is as close as possible to the articulation and accentuation of the speaking voice, thus ensuring intelligibility. Accompaniments are for the most part designed to 'set off' the text, although dialogue between voice and instrument is naturally permitted. The form of the song itself, which was at first strophic, became more flexible in order to follow the exact course of the poem and provide, from one moment to the next, an appropriate musical context more or less descriptive in character. The whole attention is concentrated, in fact, on providing the poem with a 'setting', like the setting of a jewel, though this process of identification has proved no insurance against a number of incongruities of quality: excellent music grafted on to mediocre poems and vice versa! I am not for the moment speaking of respective *values* in quality, but simply of the technique of amalgamating words and music.

If we wished to carry our study to its logical conclusion, we might examine exactly how musico-literary forms have reflected social life, for that reflection has been much clearer in these than in any purely musical forms. A ceremony of any kind without singing was unthinkable, and no society has failed to seize the chance of celebrating or describing itself by means of literature (precise in its references) allied to music, representing an escape from everyday existence. Forms may change from court to drawing room, from the concert hall to the radio and the gramophone, but the guiding intention remains the same.

In our own day we are faced with the irksome problem of the original text and translations, something that has only recently become acute, thanks to a wave of 'purism'. This is a stumbling block in every discussion on the comprehensibility of the text, since it involves an argument about ideas. One party claims that the phonetic values of the original language are more important than the literal sense, whose general character is sufficiently indicated by the music. No, says the other party, we want to understand the text immediately, in order better to grasp its relationship to the music. (Problems of synchronization in the cinema have caused the flow of a comparable amount of ink, of the same colour . . .) The exchange of guest artists has led to operatic performances in two, or even three, languages, a bold and risky counterpart of the medieval motet and a sort of Tower of Babel confounding even the strongest adherents of both parties – in fact a demonstration *per absurdum*, if ever there was one. There is no doubt that translations distort the original, as all translations do; but who can manage entirely without translations? In any case the extent of the damage varies. As we have seen, different levels of comprehension are required according to the nature of the scene concerned, which may be active or reflective, commentary or simple statement; and the damage done, or the services rendered, by the translator will vary accordingly. In cases where the music is required to do no more than transmit a verbal message, like a wave bearing a vessel, there seems at first sight no reason why it should suffer from a change of language, given some essential adjustments. Accentuation and grammatical construction (and so, diction) are nevertheless such primary characteristics of the genius of any language that in most cases the 'wave' will no longer correspond to the message that it serves to transmit. This will be delivered in a distorted form, and the words will in fact suffer more than the music. On the other hand translation constitutes an impassable obstacle in cases where music becomes commentary and direct comprehension is therefore less necessary, the vocal line being constructed with reference to verbal sonorities and to the relationship between the emission of syllables and the singing voice exploiting to the full its powers of *cantabile*. Where understanding the text is no longer a primary consideration, the language used is of little importance, provided that the sonorities are chosen with reference to a strictly limited number of equivalents; and in any case the music will suffer more than the words. The arguments on both sides are equally valid and the dialogue between them see-saws backwards and forwards. Without a (necessarily precarious) international agreement there can be no middle course alternating original text and translation according to the character of each passage; and a single language is therefore chosen for each performance, with the necessary explanations provided by the programme. To go to the root of the problem would mean changing the method of composing either text or music. It is quite common today, especially in dramatic works, where 'following' is a necessity, to find two alternative versions, though this reduces the difficulties by only a single unit! It is equally possible to imagine a 'collision' between different languages, and this would be strictly speaking untranslatable, since translation would in that case have no meaning and be entirely pointless. Once again the difficulty would be shifted by only a single unit, the audience's understanding varying with the country in which the performance was taking place.

The problem of translation, which is in fact insoluble, reveals *per absurdum* the force of the meaning–sonority dialectic, and I have raised it less for its own sake than in order to examine this whole dialectic from a new, indirect angle. Listening to a completely unknown work in a completely unknown language comes very close to the phenomenon of an 'esoteric' language, either wholly invented or so obsolete that it has become incomprehensible even to those who use it, simply magic phonetic formulae. This is not a purely hypothetical case, but one experienced in depth by anyone who has ever attended performances in the Chinese or Japanese theatre, in which the European listener has no inkling of the meaning, the style or the conventions of the work and therefore loses his faculties of analysis and judgement and is reduced simply to watching and absorbing without making any use of his reasoning powers.

Thus the same problems reappear wherever these questions arise; and despite the complex relationship between words and sound, between the language of music and the written and spoken language of everyday life, despite the opposed characters of their semantic systems, their differing mechanisms and syntactic logic and their opposed morphological procedures, there is not a moment's hesitation among composers, who busily devote themselves to making a synthesis of the two. They even find collaborators, bold writers or poets, who are happy to work on a common project – not to speak of the dead poets whose reluctance need no longer be feared!

Not that rebuffs and protests are unknown! You may remember the poet who complained of the 'nasty little noise' accompanying his lines. It is worth quoting a letter written by Paul Claudel at the age of 26:

> The company of this mad woman [music] who does not know what she is saying has been so pernicious to so many of today's writers that it is pleasant to find someone [Mallarmé] speaking with authority, in the name of articulate speech, and dictating the limits of her powers. If Music and Poetry are really based in fact on the same principle, the same need to exteriorize an interior noise, and have the same end in view, the representation of an imaginary state

of felicity, the Poet affirms and explains whereas the Other goes about shouting as though in search of something: one enjoys and the other possesses, it being his prerogative to give everything a name.

And Claudel concludes with these words: 'The intelligence has ears quite as exacting as those to be found on either side of our heads.'

Our task is to prove that both pairs of ears can be equally satisfied by this unstable, effervescent association between two savagely authoritarian elements, each defending its independence with jealous and meticulous care.

To begin with, let us distinguish between an already existing text chosen by the composer and a text written specially for the occasion. The difference does not seem to be one of kind. Whether the composer modifies, or selects passages from an existing poem or asks the author of a libretto to introduce changes, his intention is the same; since his procedures and those of the writer do not coincide (even if the composer is also the author of the text) he feels the need to make various modifications as the work proceeds. Although the quality, or intrinsic value, of such corrections is affected by whether the writer plays an active or a passive role, this in no way affects the need for them.

What is it, in fact, that makes a composer choose one text rather than another? What deep-lying needs is he seeking to satisfy, and what are the criteria of his choice? It is extremely hard to give a short answer to such a huge question, and any attempt to generalize is thwarted by endless individual exceptions. The composer may chance on a text or he may equally well have planned it in advance. The impact of a text may be direct and immediate, or it may resemble that of a deep, subterranean explosion, whose effect will take time to reach the composer's consciousness. It may be that the composer wants to write a vocal work and starts looking for a text to set, or it may equally well happen that he comes upon a text that strongly suggests a vocal setting to him. There will be cases in which the free development of a composer's new ideas of form will need the support of a literary theme, so that one form of logical construction can be fertilized by another. There will be others in which the literary theme clashes with the composer's original idea and forcibly modifies it, and in so doing gives it a different direction and a different meaning, both unforeseen. I am personally a great believer in such reciprocal influences between literature and music, not only by means of a direct and effective collaboration but quite as much by the transmutation of modes of thought that had hitherto seemed to be specific to one or other of these two means of expression. All this may be chimerical and simply part of my own personal utopia, but if so it is still a chimera that I value – *ma chimère m'est chère...*

There are several levels of language and meaning at which this transfusion of poetry into music may take place. The first that comes to mind is obviously that of description or expression. This represents the vaguest and most diffuse kind of 'correspondence', the elementary stage of common perception which is still incapable of envisaging the means, properly so called, of achieving any profound contact. It is simply the initial impact, and it may well lead to nothing if at any moment there arise problems of *realization* that cannot be overcome and threaten communication. If we suppose that first phase to have been successfully overcome, the next is to establish the direct grasp of the music on the poem, whether it be in overall form and syntax or in the rhythm and the actual verbal sonority. This 'taking-over' process, from rhetoric to morphology, continues and ensures the faultless transition from one language to another. Communication is in fact established by means of *structure*, whether it be aesthetic or grammatical.

If we start with this idea of structure, we shall be able to extend the existing relations between poetry and music; for, as I see it, it is only structure that can form the foundation of any valuable and lasting *conjunction*. Why do I attach such an absolute importance to anything so abstract? We shall see that it both makes the revelation of the poem possible and at the same time ensures the necessary 'distancing' and the continued autonomy of the original. It does this by making use of criteria common to both, such as time (rhythmic quantity and vocal technique, or prosody in the widest sense) and form (reciprocal structures in determining duration, phonetic regulation and the ordered disposition of the different formal components). If the alliance of music and poetry is free of any suggestion that one is subject to the other in some superficial (and in practice superfluous) manner, and if they can be made to cohere organically deep below the surface, the two can – in René Char's words – 'weave their saps together'.

The time taken to read a poem is a single, exact datum; but musically speaking there are two times, one for the poem as action and one for the poem as reflection. To aim at making the two simply coincide would amount to renouncing a dialectic rich in potentialities on a huge scale. Furthermore the poem as *action* is directly 'taken over' by the music, in which its presence is essential to the resulting form: the concept of time hardly varies in reading music. The poem as *reflection*, on the other hand, may be submitted to a kind of fragmentation or distortion from its original form, may indeed even absent itself from the music, in which it persists in the form of appended commentary. This conception of time affects two main characteristics: the way of treating the voice and the handling of the prosody concerned (which may be either respected or transformed); the overall structure and the essential quality of the writing, more especially the relations between voice and instrument – that is, the real or virtual presence of this mediation between poem and music effected by the use of the vocal mechanism. The variable time of the music derived from the fixed, given time of the poem proves to be a fundamental parameter in the relationship between the two as we see it.

We raised the initial question of how the voice is treated, and in fact the composer will exploit different categories – ranging from speaking to singing, from the unconventional to the completely conventional – according to how far he departs from, or observes, direct transcription. Shall I describe the different stages? Speaking belongs fundamentally to a different order from that of musical structures – and by this I mean all forms of speaking, from the whisper to the shout – different in organization and quality of sound-structure as well as in grammar. The intervals in musical sound belong to a hierarchy arranged according to different degrees of tension, or pregnancy; and this is not true of speech. Rhythmic values are instinctive in spoken declamation, whereas they conform to rule in instrumental music, even in the case of 'free' improvisation. The mere fact of verbal emission makes verbal time different from musical time, two separate phenomena capable at most of imitating each other. They meet as alien bodies; their mixing is only physical; they are perceived on different planes. In rhythmic declamation the fact that both are subject to rule enables them to present a common front; and *Sprechgesang* adds intervals that are, within a narrow range, approximate, though no more than that. Singing, by making use of exact intervals on a much wider scale, leads to voice and instrument coinciding, a coinciding achieved by either suppressing the word or distending its articulation, with the voice extracting from the words their sonorous character – analytically – rather than carrying their meaning. It can thus be seen that meaning, which was of prime importance at the beginning of this scale of values, is progressively replaced by purely phonetic values, since speech is necessarily syllabic with undefined intervals and vocalizing is necessarily non-syllabic with a strict hierarchy of intervals. It follows from this that prosody may range from a servile adherence to the text to complete independence of it, from 'natural' elocution to 'conventional' declamation. How much of the text is understood by the listener will obviously depend on these different uses of the voice. As I explained earlier, 'action' at its most realistic implies a maximum clarity of comprehension, while reflection at its most 'ideal' means sacrificing at least part of the 'message' in favour of non-rational resonances.

There is a similar graduation in the way in which the voice either 'adheres' to the instrumental ensemble or is integrated into it. The vocal line (whether single or multiple) will be *accompanied* by the instruments and will maintain its primacy in the organization of the overall structure, or it will *be (form) part* of that structure, along with other constituent elements. This opens up a whole range of different methods of writing, each with its own properties, functions and laws. We have already described the progression from monody to ,contrapuntal polyphony, this last including all the different combinations from the purely vocal to the purely instrumental. I will not return to this but will add only that the relationship between vocal writing and the use of the different vocal possibilities takes us from the 'presence' of the poem in the most real sense to its latent or virtual presence – when the poem disappears as such but continues to control purely musical features by the continuations of its structure in the music.

Structure and form are the things that I wish finally to emphasize. The structure of the poem and its formal relationships are the basic material of the equivalent musical structure, whether this is simply a support with the minimum of autonomy or a full commentary following the lines (I almost said the 'traces') of the verbal text, like plants that take root on ruined buildings and reduce them to *fragments*.

A poem around which music has crystallized can be, like a fossil, both recognizable and unrecognizable – both a core and yet absent, or, as Mallarmé put it, an alternative facet of the Idea, 'the one reaching into the darkness and the other glittering with certainty'!

18

An Interview with Dominique Jameux[1]

POLYPHONIE X, STRUCTURES FOR TWO PIANOS AND *POÉSIE POUR POUVOIR*

DOMINIQUE JAMEUX: After the first and only performance of *Polyphonie X* at Baden-Baden in, I think, 1951 you declared your dissatisfaction with the work on the grounds that you thought it too exclusively governed by theoretical problems. This was the time when you wrote the article 'Eventuellement', just before the first book of *Structures* for piano. The studio recording of *Polyphonie X* that we are to hear this evening is therefore of exceptional interest. You did not wish to edit this work nor to have it performed again, though there was a question of your returning to it on some future occasion. What are your feelings about it today?

PIERRE BOULEZ: I have in fact had another look at it – more than a look, indeed – and find my opinion stated at the time to be perfectly justified. The statement of the problems involved was correct but their solution far too summary: the principles and ideas of the work were well directed but their exploitation was too schematic to be effective. Let me take an example. The whole rhythmic organization of the work, which is quite complex, is not differentiated by distinct 'motivic' aspects, and this makes it difficult – indeed impossible in practice – for anyone who is not in the picture to differentiate between these rhythmic organizations. This was what I had in mind later – especially in *Structures* and *Marteau* – when I was concerned with giving immediate, exterior consistence to ideas that had remained unrecognized or 'unheard' owing to my insufficient treatment of them.

JAMEUX: Is it possible, away from the score, to state the principle on which the work is organized? As you pointed out in 'Eventuellement', I believe, serialization in this work is total. How does this serialization fit in with the notion of *crossing* [*croisement*] that you have used elsewhere?

---

[1] Interview with Dominique Jameux published as 'Pierre Boulez: sur *Polyphonie X* et *Poésie pour pouvoir*' in *Musique en jeu*, No. 16, November 1974, pp. 33–5.

BOULEZ: I should have to look at the work in greater detail to answer that question. All I can tell you is that what I aimed at here was a complete realization of all the different possible ways in which not only the series but the rhythmic cells could evolve. I have in fact returned to this idea in later works. Here I made use of rhythmic cells rather than durations because it seemed a better idea, more musical, to work with *groups* rather than with *units* of time. The principle is simply that the different organizations change their sense as the work proceeds, i.e. the organizations that have governed, say, one aspect of the sound later in the development of the work govern other aspects and are eventually completely reversed. Hence this kind of x applicable, by the end of the work, not only to the form but to the different functions. It was the first time that this idea occurred to me, although, to be perfectly frank, the very first of the *Structures* was written before *Polyphonie*, in the early spring of 1951, whereas *Polyphonie* itself was written that summer. There is a chronological order, therefore, but it is not exactly the right one: I started *Structures* before I started *Polyphonie* and finished *Structures* after. *Polyphonie* comes exactly in the middle, in fact.

JAMEUX: From the point of view of *timbre* is *Polyphonie* a return to the same principles – total serialization on the one hand and colour crossing on the other?

BOULEZ: Yes, because the groups change. In the score you have a certain number of groups (the instruments are grouped according to affinity, and there must be seven of them), which are determined by analogy. Thus, you have two violas and a double-bass, or a clarinet and a trumpet ... I do not remember the exact combinations. But as the work proceeds and develops, these combinations change – for instance, an instrument from group 7 will be linked to group 6, while an instrument from group 5 will be linked to group 4, and so on. And, at the end, contrary to the picture given by the score, all the groupings are reversed, i.e. they too obey the same general phenomenon. This, too, though, is all rather theoretical; and that in fact is why, after experimenting in this work, I went back to the keyboard, because the keyboard provides much more neutrality. In addition to my lack of experience with some instruments I found it difficult to apply such an abstract conception to instruments whose tessitura and individual characteristics imply, on the contrary, quite specific ideas. It is from this point of view that I should have to reconsider the work, if at any time I feel so inclined. What I mean is, the motivic work of 'justifying' the ideas must be reflected in the instrumental writing, and that would mean a detailed reworking of this idea of 'justification'.

JAMEUX: Might we then say that *Polyphonie X* is a document rather than a work?

BOULEZ: As far as I am concerned it is a document. The work is *Structures* for piano, though that too is a document.

JAMEUX: *Poésie pour pouvoir*, which belongs, I think, to 1958, was your first important essay in the electro-acoustic field. How do you feel about that now, particularly in relation to your most recent essay, *Explosante-Fixe*?

BOULEZ: Well, the first important thing I have to say about this work is that I, personally, have never been much of a believer in taped music played in a concert hall. I have always been painfully embarrassed by the resemblance to a crematorium ceremony, and found the absence of *action* a redhibitory vice. Playing a tape where people are walking about, or for a small group of professionals, is a quite different matter. But for a larger audience – let alone huge crowds – it is a very lame, one-sided affair, with nothing visual to correspond to what is heard. My idea in 1958 was to find a solution that would combine this visual support with an extended hearing space. And the listening conditions for this work were originally quite clearly specified. The orchestra was to be in front of the audience – or to be more precise it was to be a circular arrangement with the orchestra in the middle, on three platforms and in a mounting spiral. The platforms were one above another and there were orchestral groups rising finally to a group of soloists. Hans Rosbaud was the overall conductor and I conducted only at specific points that had their own specific features. I placed the loudspeakers behind the audience, because I wanted to demonstrate that a loudspeaker has no visual significance and can be properly listened to only with one's back to it. The spiral started from the floor, with the orchestra, and at the same level as the upper orchestra there were the first loudspeakers, the remainder continuing up into the roof immediately above the upper orchestra. That is to say, there was also an attempt to make use of 'spatialization' and the relay principle, consisting of a kind of visual refusal / visual acceptance. The performance was, for those days, quite a spectacular one. But here again the electronic material was based not only on a transformation of Michaux's text; there was also purely electronic material (using an oscillator) and material based on chords (or, to be more precise, sound elements) taken from the work and arranged in a different context. I had been trying at about the same time to ensure continuity between orchestra and tape – something that still interests me but that I am now trying to achieve by different means. I do not know how successful I was, but at any rate that was my aim. Right from the start I had been continually struck, in all attempts to combine instruments with taped music, by the heterogeneous character of the two media and the break dividing them. The one consists of a codified harmonic language with a very precisely stratified pitch system, which remained unquestionably powerful, however oppressive it might be felt to be. In electronic, or electro-acoustic, music on the other hand there is no trace of this hierarchical organization; so that the passage from the one to the other suggested that the two had no point of contact. Where the two had most in common was of course in the percussion because there, as in electronic (or more generally electro-acoustic) music, the hierarchical element is comparatively small. It is precisely this fact that explains the wearisome nature of percussion instruments – the fact that you eventually find yourself bombarded on all sides by samplings of sound without any hierarchical pattern. I had tried to avoid this and, after *Poésie pour pouvoir*, I became sceptical about organizing any sound on tape until much better methods had been discovered.

JAMEUX: And do these methods exist at the present time?

BOULEZ: They do. They have been developed by degrees, but developed in practice *apart from* works in which these means have not been used. Although such means have been practically developed by Siemens' engineers in Munich, no really outstanding or interesting work was created at Siemens', though the whole process, (automation in particular) of exchanging sound characteristics – when they are put on perforated tapes to preserve the information, etc. – was progressively discovered at Munich in 1962–3. If there is anything that I regret today, it is that lack of time made it impossible for me at that moment to drop all my commitments, go to Munich and devote prolonged study to the whole question. Whether I really regret it, though, I am not sure, as the Munich studio went through a difficult time after Siemens' withdrew their support, and had to make a lot of film music, etc. It may well be that I should have left very soon after I arrived . . . But what has always seemed to me the most important task of all is to try to discover a means of expansion that is not simply a kind of gimmickry [*bricolage*] – a real expansion of thought, not only logical thinking, in another field – nor merely the astonished discovery of a strange and wonderful toy.

JAMEUX: One last question about *Poésie pour pouvoir*: how does Michaux's poem determine its form?

BOULEZ: I must say that, in Michaux's poem, the form does not determine very much. It was a case of an irrational – or, as the English say, 'emotional' – reaction to the text rather than a desire to incorporate the text in the music formally. This was the exact opposite of my attitude to Char's poem that I used, especially in *Marteau* where the form is closely linked, or the *cummings* that I am working on now, or indeed the Mallarmé,[1] in which the form of the poem is really and essentially linked to that of the music.

---

[1] Boulez had just heard a performance of *Pli selon pli* that had included the three Mallarmé improvisations.

PART TWO
Exemplars

19

Beethoven: Tell Me[1]

Beethoven
a name   – the name
            the least discussed
            most accepted and acknowledged symbol of *our* musical culture
Beethoven – from the philosophic essay to the comic strip
            – from psychoanalytical study to *biographie romancée*
Today   – the cult
              or a parody of the cult
            – between Bach and Wagner
              less austere than the former
              less hysterical than the latter
            – in any case: respected, loved.
            (we must not forget; more serious than Haydn
                               more profound than Mozart
                               less boring than Brahms
                               +, −, +, −, ...)
And yet the story had a strange beginning.
   Delacroix: 'This is the work of a madman or a genius.
              In doubt, I plump for "genius".'
(Not to speak of Goethe and his strong distaste for so uncivilized a hurri-
cane.)
But stupefaction was replaced by delirious enthusiasm:
            plethora of titanism –
            avalanche of catastrophes and blows of Fate –
            bitter tears, and ink of blood –
            lightnings, fires and thunders –
            genius, genius, genius –
Then the too-titanic aspect of genius was left to the common herd.
Refinement befits the ascetic
   as mourning becomes Electra.

---

[1] 'Tell me', written for the bicentenary of Beethoven's birth and published in German in *Die Welt*, 12 December 1970. First published in French in *Points de repère*.

No longer the man of the Crowd,
                but of the future, *the* future, beyond reckoning, eternal;
                the ascetic as terrifying – almost – as the titan.
Beethoven, magic lantern for a host of monkeys.
Can this 'man' have ever been born?
            and two hundred years ago?
                    and in a town – and in a modest house?
Where do we stand, after two hundred years?
                is it really two hundred years?
From one bank to the other – right and left, obviously –
                (as in the birth of Anna Livia Plurabelle)
                the dialogue has produced the river/
                                        /mythical.

Discussion:

Your/my B. is not mine/yours.

My/your B. is – better _____
                – more authentic _____
                – truer _____
                – more profound _____
                – more modern _____
                – more justified _____
                – etc. _____
                – etc. _____
                – more bla-bla-bla _____ than yours/mine

The hero among heroes   – the man amongst men
The classic par excellence – essentially, the innovator
Music made man   – man become music
Turn over and over this many-faceted diamond.
Through it you will see a thousand stars!
    Dialogue – for the deaf; yes. (Kind of dedication.)
Then the tributes – respectful, each in its own way.
    – We go back to the preceding chapter –
I pay tribute to *my* Beethoven, who is not yours.

The   monument   tribute (less respectful than it appears)
       document

The   attack   tribute (more respectable than it appears)
       missile

The dynamic tribute
The state tribute
Frankincense, myrrh ... and gold
Ye Magi bringing your tribute to this newborn child two hundred years old,
to what star do you entrust your expedition?
And in this stable, who will consent to be the ox?
              who can be the donkey? (Thanks for the answers.)
    (The other figures in the picture are recognizable   ⟶

                                  ⟶ excessively.)

    (Joseph [Haydn ??] the carpenter – or the smith's son)
    (Mary Music – and the Holy Spirit, who is not *always* shown in the picture.)
Good. The celebration of the two hundredth nativity is over,
    with all its pomp and ceremony,
            its caricatures,
          and its *tableaux vivants*
(But is it possible to celebratc with such splendour
        THE nativity, ycar O?
Comes to my mind the story – absurd, it seems –:
        Colonel [or General ? / or Captain ?] Hugo arrived in 1802 [month ? / day ? / hour ?]
        at the registry office [in Besançon ? / Dôle ?]
        to register the birth of a son.
          – First name, says the official
          – Victor, answers the happy father
          – All my admiration, exclaims the official
Imaginc the same anecdote in Bonn two hundred years ago.)
So then, we have celebrated and paid our tributes.
We are paying more and more tributes.
There is no anniversary (of death or/and birth)
that is not duly and worthily emphasized.
Provided that it coincides with a round number, symbolic,
a multiple of 5, 10 or 100.
This flux of anniversaries is disturbing.
There comes a moment when, as in Ionesco, death invades
the whole house, contemptuously turns out the living.
Should we be alarmed?
Is it the sign of a civilization in decline,
clinging to its possessions, but in such a way
that the merry-go-round begins to look like a ghost hunt?
Is this a culture so enfeebled that it can no longer
        – tolerate

extensive blood-letting?
– forget
its own wealth?
– go forward without worrying about
its pedigree?
We have paid tribute
an irremediable symbol of our musical culture.
Is that so certain?
Are we quite sure that we are not being deluded by the circumstances?
A little history – very quickly.
First of all, ideas:
It all started with Rousseau (Jean-Jacques).
The utopian revolution – soon followed by revolution in practice.
From idealism to blood – and then back to idealism.
1789 had certainly made an attempt with its revolutionary music and revolutionary hymns – but there was no personality: many whiffs of the old regime and no forerunners to point out the path for us.
In a nutshell, music was not ready to coincide with ideas – we are always being told that musicians lag behind their literary rivals and colleagues.
'Enfin Malherbe vint' – in the shape of Schiller – and Beethoven / still lagging behind. '89 is becoming legendary: all men are brothers. But meanwhile there is no denying Napoleon and the restorations.
The legend lives on and spreads. It will irrigate the whole of the nineteenth century, with its endless proclamations of
faith in hypothetical revolutions
faith in humanity
faith in infinite progress
(ad astra per aspera . . .)
(ad augusta per angusta . . .)
Beethoven still remains the emotional mouthpiece.
Fidelio – the *Ode to Joy*,
those arrows of revolutionary idealism.
Beethoven – the Prometheus punished by the gods
and exalted,
because he gave us the new fire, the divine spark.
As time passed, the ideal was gradually taken over by sections of society that were anything but idealistic.
Generous idealism was used by them as a common screen for much less noble designs.
At the end of the journey it may be doubted whether the original relationship to Rousseau can be said still to exist.
Everything suggests that this revolutionary era, or at least this form of the revolution – this dream? – is now over, finished.
That the future will dream, or 'revolutionize', in quite a different way.

Does this mean that the standard-bearer / Beethoven, here / is doomed to disappear – from lack of relevance?

Do not let us give any answer yet – Listen, and let us go on to
The music, now:
The language is there, more or less collective.

    (This does not mean that there are no structural differences)

    Discoveries are not accepted as quickly as is commonly supposed today – but the increased, later exaggerated search for / expression of the individual? has not yet made its appearance.

Beethoven innovates – increasingly – to a point at which the general public (towards the end of his life) refuses to identify itself with this *individual*.

    Originality entrenches his temperament, unique.

    The language feels the consequences,

        to the point at which what is retained – for convenience? by instinct? – conflicts with discovery.

          The language learns, undergoes, its first distortions.

          Which makes it *interesting*, dramatic,

          The germs of future destruction are to be found here.

          Balance during the years of privilege between

              what is established – what is accepted

              what is destroyed – what is contested

  Difficult equation – a state that might be thought transient

              yet hardens into the definitive form of remolten lava.

Once again: is the volcano extinct?

Apparently not.

And yet once more, the dreams of the future will never again – that is more than predictable – take shape in this landscape.

This era that is coming to an end:

    the individual – imposing his ideas on the collective,

        – revealing independence to it,

        – appearing as a liberator.

Probably, the ideas of the future:

    (guessed at, in the distance)

within the community,

rising from it – but bound to the mechanisms that contain it – the individual (once again, however) acts as function of a collective expression; 'progress' demands a collective effort, a communal participation.

In the past:

    the musical language provided invention with opportunities to make use of its principles and general materials which, if need be, it distorts. (What need have I to consider your violin . . .) . . . a basic *idealism*.

invention finds a place within/against the *rules*.

In the future:
>invention creates both language and material; it can even happen
>that the material distorts the idea by forcing it to be *realistic*.

Even craftsmanship becomes collective.
>invention creates its own *obligations*.

In the past: the individual determines the orientation of the collective
In the future: the collective uses the resources of the individual
>Everything that Beethoven represents,
>this great era in our history,
>is making place for another that is only just beginning,
>in which Europe – and those affiliated with Europe – will no longer
>enjoy exclusive (almost) privileges.
>Is this not the moment to celebrate,
>not an individual birth,
>but a collective death?
>Is it not a way of reassuring ourselves,
>now that we suspect that the supremacy to which we have grown
>accustomed is on the point of collapsing?
>The two emotional states that have annexed Beethoven are in that case
>quite clear.

– A nostalgia for these two odd centuries that have been so decisive,
>a desire to recapture the old splendours.
>Nothing has changed, nothing will change.
>Everything is congealed in a solar radiance that will last for all eternity.

– Let us embark for the unknown, with passion.
>But let us take with us the bust of this ancestor, to reassure us.
>Let us keep him as patron of the expedition.
>He will be our witness with the faint-hearted that our 'barbarism' is
>deliberate.
>What are we to think?
>There comes a moment in history at which every monument, every
>work ceases to teach us anything, directly.
>A Greek temple does not *teach* you how to build a skyscraper of steel
>and glass. But we preserve Greek temples – for our delight, and for the
>apprehension, the mystery of a past existence.

Dead stars that we still see glittering.
So, why insist at all costs on a work being immediately relevant?
It casts its own light, for its own sake.
Its historical supremacy is an illusion.
Its radioactivity has nothing to do with any future status.
Among the voices saying, / tell me, tell me
>>creating it, / elm

the river

      / Beethoven /
                    remains *deaf*
                                to reproaches.
It irrigates.
And there is still no knowing towards what Ocean
                          towards what death it is moving.
Who does not feel relieved to know that
      death – *this death* – is unforeseeable?
      Even if inevitable.

20

Berlioz and the Realm of the Imaginary[1]

What Berlioz brought to music is so singular that it has not yet been truly absorbed, has not become an integral part of tradition. Whereas Wagner, for example, has given rise to fanatical admirers as well as detractors, Berlioz still seems to be isolated. He stands at a point where customary judgements cannot be easily applied. I think we must see the principal reason for this in the fact that a large part of his *oeuvre* has remained in the realm of the imaginary. No one dreams of denying that his works exist or of maintaining that they cannot be incorporated into our musical heritage, for he resembles Wagner in having fully as much practical sense as imagination. One of the permanent aspects of his character is just such a mixture of realism and fantasy – and his realism could be every bit as meticulous as his fantasy could be extravagant.

Berlioz's compositions exist in a sphere that is difficult to define, for they do not respect, and do not claim to respect, the usual conventions in the process of creation and transmission. Depending on circumstances, history required the composer to write works either called for by religious services or intended as entertainment. Such conditions require established forms, which change from one period to another but which respect the social conventions currently in force. Sacred music is one aspect of this ritual, whereas concert and operatic music is the other side of the same ritual. Obviously, there has always been so much stylistic osmosis between the two that it is sometimes difficult to tell which of the two rituals any given piece of music belongs to.

The French Revolution did not change this situation in any significant way, although it did emphasize the lay ritual as being a national duty. Music was to be one of the essential phenomena of the great popular celebrations organized by the French Revolution, under the obvious inspiration of Jean-Jacques Rousseau. The revolutionary ceremonies rejuvenated Christian ritual and imposed different conditions upon it by making it deal once again,

---

[1] 'L'Imaginaire chez Berlioz', from *High Fidelity – Musical America*, 6 March 1969, Vol. xix, pp. 43–6, English translation by David Noakes. First published in French in *Points de repère*.

and urgently, with the needs of society. They used processions and 'abstract' spectacles, which had been the Church's exclusive prerogative for centuries. Replacing God by the goddess Reason was all that was needed; circumstances changed, but the underlying motivation remained the same. Nevertheless, the relationship between music and society was fundamentally different; Berlioz was to remain under the influence of this change throughout his entire life.

It is true that we can see a directly observable revolutionary influence in such works as the Requiem, the Te Deum, or the *Symphonie funèbre et triomphale* (the revolutionary element presents no apparent contradiction with either Roman Catholic observances or governmental devotion), but this influence is not the most mysterious phenomenon found in Berlioz. He has often been criticized for his gigantism and his fondness for ostentatious effects. He frequently did his best to encourage misunderstandings by a certain redundancy in his works as well as in the written commentaries with which he accompanied them throughout his lifetime. Was this not simply to compensate for dreams he had never realized – dreams that, as I see it, were connected with certain aspects of the French revolutionary idea that had been deprived of their meaning by political and social evolution?

To this must be added a devouring need to talk about himself. It shows up not only in the books, which describe his own life as a man and as a musician, but also in numerous works in which, directly or indirectly, he tells about himself. This will be recognized as a need that is inherent in romanticism. What we have here, however, is a very special form of romanticism peculiar to Berlioz, for it is difficult to detect confessions as consistently personal in the other great composers of the period. Even if personal details come constantly to the surface with some of them, these other composers transpose and go beyond the personal in such a way as to create a myth. (I am thinking, obviously, of *Tristan*.)

Under such conditions, everything helped to make Berlioz a predestined victim of the imaginary. His compositions both transcend and fall short of the conventions; it is only with great difficulty that they can finally be inserted into the customary framework of the theatre or the concert. They overrate the latter and underrate the former. The limitations inherent in a social form of transmission have scarcely any *raison d'être* or any logic; we are fully aware of their artificial character, which restricts the imaginary and does not allow it to find expression in an immaterial, fluid dimension. All the circumstances that make the concert and the theatre what they are seem too restricting to this form of the imaginary; they suppress, to a large extent, its reason for existing.

There is an essay by Berlioz that the public knows hardly at all; titled 'The Orchestra', it is the final chapter of his *Traité d'orchestration*, a study read only by professional musicians. It is by far one of his most significant texts because it reflects his attitude towards musical realization. It is typical of Berlioz's character, mixing realism and imagination without opposing one to the other, producing the double aspect of an undeniable inventive 'madness' – a fairly unreal dream minutely accounted for. This chapter begins in a down-to-earth way and simply describes for us what an orchestra is, how it is organized, how it can be installed in a hall. There is nothing out of the ordinary in all that. Soon, however, there are added some revealing observations concerning outdoor orchestras. The open air, which is the typical place for imaginary expansion, is the acoustical enemy of organized sound. Between 'nature' and 'musical *art*' there already exists, therefore, this basic incompatibility. None the less, Berlioz allows them a chance of joining forces in the streets of a city, with the façades of the buildings serving as the approximate equivalent of a closed hall. (His personal reasons for this stand are apparent; perhaps he would not have written so positively after his disappointments in the streets of Paris.) Once past this very symptomatic digression, Berlioz describes the ideal performing conditions for concerts and the theatre. But he cannot stop there, and once again he gives in to the demon of supposition by describing what he calls a 'magnificent Festival orchestra'. He deplores 'the constant uniformity of performing masses' as an insuperable obstacle; in short, he denounces the standardization of symphonic components and considers it in its negative aspects. His reflection, dating from more than a century ago, on the rigidity of the symphonic apparatus shows great insight; this rigidity was indeed going to fix and paralyse the imagination of composers in established, accepted dimensions, allowing them to express themselves only within the same framework and under identical circumstances. It cannot be denied that the standardization of musical conditions brought about, in a certain sense, greater professional competence, built up the repertory, made the concert a social tradition (even a social necessity); Berlioz could not, however, at that time and especially in France, be aware of this phenomenon. On the other hand, he saw very clearly the absolute necessity of a model – musical as well as sociological – to be adhered to by all works intended for symphonic performance.

I pass over certain polemical remarks – unfortunately still pertinent – on the tyranny of economic conditions and come to the heart of the chapter, namely the description of an imaginary orchestra, down to the minutest detail. 'Yet it would be curious', writes Berlioz,

to try once, in a composition written for the occasion, the simultaneous use of all the musical forces that can be gathered together in Paris. Let us suppose that a conductor had them at his command, in a vast hall designed for the purpose by an architect familiar with acoustics and music. He should, before writing, determine with precision the plan and arrangement of the immense orchestra and should keep them constantly in mind while composing.

Berlioz has already called our attention to 'the importance of the *various points the sounds come from*'. Here also he condemns standardization in orchestral disposition since it works against the specific character of each work. His point of view, which surprises us by its acuteness, is essentially modern. Berlioz writes:

> Certain parts of an orchestra are intended by the composer to ask questions, and others to reply; now, this intention becomes evident and beautiful only if the groups between which the dialogue is set up are at a sufficient distance from each other. The composer must therefore indicate in his score the placement he considers appropriate for them.

And certainly we have as a precise example the way orchestras of brasses are placed in the Requiem; this involves not only a spectacular effect but the location of a musical structure in physical space. The position of the brasses in the Requiem was originally descriptive and symbolic, associated with the four points of the compass, but it nevertheless reveals, for the period, a far from customary preoccupation. (I do not believe that Venice, Gabrieli, and Monteverdi contributed anything at all to Berlioz's conception in this respect, for he was unfamiliar with the ceremonies of San Marco.)

Further on, Berlioz foresees and answers the objections that could be raised to the use of great orchestral masses and the way they were going to be abused at the end of the nineteenth century, when musical material not originally designed for such treatment was *fattened up* by doublings. To quote him again:

> Until the present day, in festivals we have heard only the ordinary orchestra and chorus with their parts quadrupled or quintupled according to the number of performers; but here we would be concerned with something quite different, and the composer who wanted to bring out the prodigious, innumerable resources of such an instrument would most undeniably have to perform a new task.

Berlioz then describes in minute detail the entire make-up of this imaginary ensemble, giving us supporting figures; no fewer than 467 instrumentalists and 360 choral singers. The listing of instrumentalists begins with 120 violins and finishes with 4 Turkish crescents (also called Chinese pavilions); in between we find 30 harps and 30 pianos; as for horns, there are all of 16. Including the chorus, we don't quite reach the 'symphony of a thousand' but we are not far from it, since the performers number 827. It is not the entire mass of this enormous ensemble that interests him; what he actually wants is to form a large number of small orchestras within this large orchestra, in order to diversify both style and sonority:

> It would naturally be necessary to adopt an exceptionally broad style whenever the entire mass is called into play, saving delicate effects, light and rapid movements for small orchestras that the composer could easily form and set

to dialoguing within this musical congregation. Besides the iridescent colours that this multitude of different timbres would allow to burst forth at any moment, unheard of *harmonic* effects could be created.

Berlioz then begins to draw up a precise catalogue of the effects that could be created with this orchestra; and I must say that reading this catalogue has always led me to make a most incongruous comparison with the end of *Cent vingt journées de Sodome*, where de Sade, temporarily unable to finish his book, draws up a catalogue of perversions still to be described. There is in de Sade's catalogue as in Berlioz's a sort of obsession with the analysis of different combinations which is ascribable to the same reason: non-satisfaction of desire, compensated for by imagined debauchery. This is, no doubt, the only thing Berlioz and de Sade have in common!

Reading this catalogue imagined by Berlioz when all the instruments would be united in a 'festival orchestra', let us pass in review all of nineteenth- and twentieth-century instrumentation, including not only the instrumental combinations that have already been used but also those that exist in a merely approximate way because of the economic impossibilities about which Berlioz complained (and which have not changed very much up to the present!). I would like to cite a few of those whose chances of being realized remain exclusively within the realm of the imaginary. They are, among others:

> The combination *in a large orchestra* of 30 harps with the entire mass of strings playing *pizzicato*, thus forming, in their ensemble, another gigantic harp with 934 strings, for graceful, brilliant, voluptuous accents throughout the entire range of nuances;
>
> The combination of the 30 pianos with the 6 glockenspiels, the 12 pairs of antique cymbals, the 6 triangles (which, like the cymbals, could be tuned in different keys), and the 4 Turkish crescents, making up a *metallic* percussion *orchestra*, for joyful and brilliant accents in the *mezzo-forte* nuance.

After describing in this way the entity made up by each possible grouping, he wonders 'how to enumerate all the harmonic aspects that each of these different groups would assume when associated with the groups that are sympathetically or antipathetically related to it?' Here again Berlioz's combinative imagination is given free rein. He describes widely used, even conventional, forms, such as 'a song by the sopranos, or the tenors, or the basses, or of all voices in octaves, accompanied by an *instrumental orchestra*'; but he also thinks of less orthodox solutions and reverses the usual situation in order to suggest to us 'a song of violins, violas, and violoncellos *together*, or of woodwinds *together*, or of brasses *together*, accompanied by a *vocal orchestra*'.

Whether because of exhaustion or because of discouragement before such a mountain of future treasures, the description ends with a very prosaic 'etc., etc., etc. . . . .'

De Sade comes to mind again immediately afterwards, for Berlioz is going to give us a minute description of 'the system of rehearsals to be set up for this colossal orchestra'. The conductor and his assistants, sub-assistants, and rehearsal masters are governed by a single set of rules, which cover no fewer than twelve stages. And that is where the *realistic* description ends.

In passing, Berlioz emphasizes the excellent qualities of this orchestra and defends himself against an accusation to which he is particularly sensitive:

> The popular prejudice calls large orchestras *noisy*; if they are well organized, well rehearsed, and well directed, and if they perform true music, they should be called *powerful*; and certainly nothing is more different than the meaning of these two terms . . . What is more: unisons take on real value only when they are multiplied beyond a certain number . . . That is why small orchestras, regardless of the quality of the performers who make them up, have so little effect and consequently so little value.

Discussion on this subject, from Berlioz to Mahler, from Wagner to Schoenberg, has not yet died down. There is not much chance that it ever will. But it is only an episodic aspect over which Berlioz does not linger, and I shall quote his concluding paragraph, which is especially symptomatic:

> But in the thousands of combinations obtainable with the monumental orchestra we have just described would be found a harmonic richness, a truthfulness of timbres, a succession of contrasts that cannot be compared with anything that has been accomplished in art up to the present, and above all an incalculable melodic power, both expressive and rhythmic, a force of penetration unlike any other, a prodigious sensitivity to nuances in the ensemble and in its parts. Its repose would be as majestic as the ocean's sleep; its agitations would be reminiscent of a tropical storm, its explosions would evoke the cries of volcanoes, it would re-create the moaning, the murmuring, the mysterious noises of virgin forests, the clamouring, the prayers, the triumphal and mourning songs of a people with an expansive soul, an ardent heart, impetuous passions; its silence would impose fear by its solemnity; and the most rebellious organizations would shudder upon seeing the roaring growth of its *crescendo*, like an immense and sublime conflagration!

The majestic description winds up with this accumulation of conditionals, and the conditional is indeed the appropriate tense for this project that Berlioz was never to realize but that he carried in his memory. His 'people with an expansive soul' reminds us of Rousseau, Robespierre, the ceremonies in the Champ de Mars. This project, which was to remain in Berlioz's imagination, came to a halt before the contingencies of a closed, withdrawn society. One is tempted to say that Berlioz's written compositions make up only the scattered pieces of a Great Opus that escaped him – an Opus that resembles in this respect that definitive *Livre* towards which Mallarmé was working, the *Coup de dés* being only a stage along the way.

The *Spectacle* that Berlioz constantly dreamed of is a spectacle of himself projected into the realm of the imaginary – an absolute future dimension sustained by an abolished, exceptional past. None of the works in which he consented to respect the limits of theatrical convention – even *Benvenuto Cellini*, the most 'autobiographical' – ever succeeded in taking on a truly scenic appearance. A letter from Wagner to Liszt on this subject is particularly revealing; it already gives an acute definition of the problem:

> If there is a musician who makes use of the *poet*, it is surely Berlioz, and his misfortune is that he always adapts this poet to his musical fantasy and arranges first Shakespeare, then Goethe according to his wishes. He needs the poet because the latter fills him completely, transports him with enthusiasm, forces him, becomes for him just what a man is for a woman. It is with sadness that I see such an extraordinary artist go astray because of this self-centred solitude.

Béatrice et Bénédict and *Les Troyens* contain pages that are among Berlioz's best, but far from bringing about a theatrical rejuvenation, they prove to be incapable of providing the kind of dramaturgy and myth-making quality that would establish them as examples. Very weak scenic conventions often contradict the composer's musical imagination; we do not get beyond 'separate pieces' and 'recitatives'. Although these are admittedly amplified by comparison with the operas of Berlioz's predecessors – Gluck and Weber in particular – they unfortunately do not blend into a new entity that would find its sustenance in a specifically 'Berliozian' conception of theatrical aesthetics. As for such compositions as *La Damnation de Faust*, staging them reduces their imaginary dimension to a painful sham. Berlioz's visual imagination is not essentially of the kind that can be represented *materially*; it is, indeed, a 'vision'. On the other hand, as soon as Berlioz forces himself to write for the theatre, his 'vision' is hindered, clouded over, by the permanent presence of theatrical conventions that he remembers and that he does not create. Instead of making his genius open out, they confine him within limits that cause him to lose his freshness and greatness, sometimes reducing him to picturesque effects. (Could one possibly attribute the same significance to the tempest encountered in the *Ring* and the storm in *Les Troyens*?)

The best of Berlioz's imagination is displayed in an area that, in the final analysis, belongs to no realm determined by precise conventions. In a sense, *Lélio* is the typical example of what the proper field of his poetic invention might have been if the contingencies of musical organization had not quickly led him to give up this kind of project, which, for various reasons, was so difficult to accept, because of aesthetic considerations quite as much as because of economic difficulties. In *Lélio*, there is a unique way of linking theatre and concert by the autobiographical element. It is an intimate journal, sufficiently elaborated upon to be read and played collectively; the author has included himself in the staging, and in his own person. Such a procedure belongs neither to the theatre nor to the concert, but rather to public confession.

This original way of expressing himself anticipates a future time if we look at it from a pragmatic point of view. The conditions imposed upon Berlioz by his period did not make it possible for him to achieve an exact realization of his ideas; that is why he had to put up with substitute solutions that fell far short of satisfying the requirements of his original intuition.

Fragments of a great imaginary project, Berlioz's compositions no doubt require us to find a style of presentation unconnected with any of those that we still accept today, since the latter exist for works conceived in terms of certain predetermined categories. This is an essential condition, I believe, if these works are to find their rightful place, if they are no longer to produce, as they often do now, the impression of an incomplete phenomenon, an erratic creation. After a 100-year delay, the discovery of this point of encounter and fusion between imaginary concert and imaginary theatre remains naturally very problematic, especially since the values represented by Berlioz's works are frozen by history, whether or not one tries to deny this fact.

If posthumous reconstitution remains in all likelihood an illusion, one can with greater profit infer from this suspended dream presentday solutions for contemporary creation. But these solutions could scarcely be *seen*, literally speaking, as having anything to do with the original *vision* of Berlioz.

21

Berlioz: *Symphonie fantastique* and *Lélio*[1]

The *Symphonie fantastique* is familiar to everyone, but *Lélio* is known very little, if at all, although in fact the two works have a single title: 'Épisode de la vie d'un artiste' – *Symphonie fantastique* et *Monodrame lyrique* (*Lélio ou le retour à la vie*)'. Yet Berlioz's preliminary note is quite clear about *Lélio*: 'This work should be heard immediately after the *Symphonie fantastique*, of which it is the end and the complement.' The composer's wish cannot often have been fulfilled, and is not often fulfilled today. Practical reasons? Well, the composer is certainly demanding about conditions of performance:

> The orchestra, chorus and soloists should be on the stage with the curtain lowered, therefore unseen by the public. Only the actor is visible, speaking and acting in front of the curtain. At the end of the first monologue he leaves the stage and the curtain is raised, so that all the performers are visible in the *Finale*. A stand has therefore to be erected above the normal orchestral pit.

But is it only practical difficulties that make *Lélio* a poor relation of the *Symphonie fantastique*? Are there not musical reasons for the work's being banished from the concert hall?

To answer this we must face the problem of Berlioz's genius, which is hard to classify and – probably thanks to the memory of the spectacular musical ceremonies of the Revolution – almost always dominated by the idea of 'singularity', by which I mean *physical* singularity. In almost all Berlioz's works music is linked to some dramatic phenomenon, if not to the actual theatre. It needs gestures emphasized by the *seating* of the orchestra, such as the oboe echoing the cor anglais in the *Fantastique*, the string trio recalling in the distance the Pilgrims' March in *Harold en Italie*, not to speak of the Requiem and other giant works intended to strike the listener's imagination. On this point there is nothing so revealing as the description of an imaginary orchestra that Berlioz gives at the end of his treatise on instrumentation. The list includes, among other things, 120 violins, 30 harps, 30 pianos ... and 4 jingling johnnies! Berlioz describes in detail all that could be achieved with

---

[1] Sleeve note for the recording by Boulez, CBS 32 BI 0010.

these 827 performers (467 orchestral players and 360 voices). How often this has been held against him, this desire to go beyond the purely musical and to strike the listener's imagination by some theatrical gesture! Wagner, and many since Wagner's day, have preferred Mozart's three trombones at the end of *Don Giovanni*.

Of course this need to impress at all costs, this 'lack of moderation' cannot fail to provoke and irritate listeners who are nevertheless prepared to accept in the theatre much showier effects even than those of Berlioz. The piling of one effect on another and unusual seating of the orchestra cannot of course replace real musical substance and interior quality. But surely we are missing the whole point if we do not see in Berlioz's music a persistent amalgamation of theatrical gesture and musical substance.

What I find striking is precisely that – the fact that for Berlioz there was no hard and fast line between the concert hall and the theatre, and that in the last resort – as in the *Fantastique* and *Lélio* – it is the *autobiographical* that by a kind of osmosis links 'music' and 'spectacle'. Even so, autobiography plays a very different role in these two works, which must essentially be heard together if we are to judge them and appreciate their interest. In the *Fantastique* autobiography is superimposed on the movements of a symphony; and although it may give the musical ideas and their developments a precise, individual significance and accentuate their poetic power, it in no way gives a meaning to the specifically musical form of the work. We should still be listening to a symphony, even if the autobiographical framework were non-existent – and a symphony in five consecutive movements: *Allegro*, *Valse* (a kind of scherzo), slow movement, *Interlude* (march) and *Finale*. The necessity of this sequence is essentially a musical necessity and not determined by the autobiographical plan, which is merely superimposed on it. You might say that the plan follows the symphony rather than that the symphony follows the plan.

In *Lélio*, on the other hand, the plan really does determine the sequence. Why? because Berlioz was using a number of 'separate pieces' composed at different times and in very different states of mind. The *idée fixe* appears only twice in this monodrama, as a 'quotation' at the beginning and the end, whereas it appears in each movement of the *Fantastique* – rather artificially, I admit – and also in the form of a 'quotation' in the 'Bal' and the 'Marche au supplice', which were of course composed independently. Since the musical *idée fixe* no longer determined the narrative, autobiography had necessarily to be inserted by some other means – namely the actor. The actor, who now personifies the composer, links the disparate pieces simply by describing his life and his states of mind, and gives them a logical coherence that is not a musical logic, but relates to time and experience. This is a naïve trick, but a trick of genius, by which Berlioz sublimates what is in fact an amalgam consisting of what in the trade are called 'bottom drawer' pieces. (If Bach was doing anything else when he transferred the same piece from one cantata to another, it must be admitted that his motives were not very different . . .)

Thus the shamelessness with which Berlioz makes use of theatrical gestures, so offensive to French 'good taste', often appears to us to be the fundamental motive for his writing.

There are many other aspects of Berlioz's psychology as a composer that should be taken into account. The chief complaints – generally unconscious – of the musicians who find his works hard to accept are rooted in this basic lack of comprehension: they cannot admit autobiographical gestures in a musical work, and they refuse the osmotic identification of theatre and concert hall. From this point of view Berlioz's work is 'a country without frontiers', and it is probably this that gives it its irreducible novelty. In the *Fantastique* the theatre is imaginary and in *Lélio* it is real.

As far as music is concerned, Berlioz was the initiator of this typically romantic vision – which has links with the psychologically unstable element in German romanticism – this deliberate confusion of dream and reality. Once this is granted, there is little point in rehearsing other features of his music that have been, and still are, subjects of discussion, such as his incapacities in matters of harmony and form and his capacities in matters of orchestration and rhythmic invention. But no one can fail to see what an essential link he, and he alone, formed between Beethoven and Wagner – the 'spectacular' link connecting the symphonic composer and the essentially 'theatre' composer. In the *Scène aux champs* the cor anglais looks back to the Pastoral Symphony and on to *Tristan*, while Berlioz's own deepest interests took him along a quite different path from that of either composer.

22

Richard Wagner: The Man and the Works[1]

Hagiographers seize like vultures on the figures of those who have contributed most to forming the character of an age. In their hands mortals become heroes and heroes become saints or gods, gradually disappearing behind the clouds conjured up by the myth-makers. Any rash man who takes it into his head to search for the original facts is rejected as at best indiscreet, if not indecent and immoral. A composer's biography must be made to match his works, and Titans have no weaknesses. The unity of the man and his work is one of the most persistent articles of faith, with very few exceptions.

One of these exceptions, however, is Richard Wagner, who remains the subject of passionate controversy – not his music, but what he represents in the society of his age. His vegetarian proselytism may raise a smile, but it is difficult to disregard his anti-Semitism. On the other hand, although his political ideas are those of an amateur, his views on the reform of education might deserve serious consideration. The most striking thing about Wagner's life has always been the inextricable confusion of ambition, ideology and achievement. The ambition proved illusory in the field in which he believed himself to be a master; the ideology rather confused compared with other philosophical movements of the time, notably Marx; the artistic achievement of such outstanding quality that it called in question and eventually overturned the existing language of music as well as of the opera. Wagner certainly saw himself as a prophet even more than an artist – a prophet who, having received illumination and grace, could claim the right to speak exuberantly and with authority on any matter whatsoever. The artist–redeemer possesses by intuition a universal knowledge, and his task in the world is to present solutions that have been *revealed* to him.

Before Wagner's day, though not very long before, the artist was a servant – religious servant to a community or lay servant to a patron. He then became a witness, jealous guardian of his own independence, even though

[1] 'Divergences: de l'être à l'oeuvre', preface to *Wagner: A Documentary Study*, ed. Herbert Barth, Dietrich Mack, Egon Voss, London, Thames and Hudson, 1975; French version in *Musique en Jeu*, No. 22 January 1976, pp. 5–11.

obliged to make himself a place in a society that only grudgingly accepted him as an exceptional being. Then the artist wished to become a guide, a saviour revealing to humanity its destiny through his genius and intuition. This was a role played in the eighteenth century, on a rational and political plane, by philosophers and more particularly the French philosophers of the Age of the Enlightenment, who considered it their mission to enlighten the world and to lead it towards a better future, a society in love with reason and justice. The catastrophe of the Revolution and its aftermath were followed by a profound and formidable split. Philosophers went on exploring their analysis of society and revolutionary ferment still continued to work spasmodically, as a more or less permanent feature of society. Artists, however, rejected this rational approach and, in their disillusion, cast themselves in the role of redemption symbols. But as this universal ambition proved illusory, the artist turned inward and began to develop his imagination in the direction suggested by his gifts, though infecting with his pessimism the society that had rejected him in his role as prophet. After all, it is painfully disenchanting to be obliged to renounce the idea of reforming the world and to content oneself instead with 'artistic' reforms, or even revolutions. The artist was thus made aware of his limitations, the universality of his ideas was more or less denied, and he was forced to restrict his field of action, to abandon the present for the future. He was left with the privileged role granted him within a society that he could not shape. In our own day this fiction and this inconsistency are still present, except where we have gone back to the idea of the artist as servant, no longer of a patron or a community but of the state. Sacrifice, devotion or necessity have led all over the world to the acceptance of this ideology as a fact of existence; and the artist can do nothing but obey. He must conform to decisions that he has not taken – or often even contributed to – since he has been robbed of this essential responsibility by others considered more efficient and more politic.

Was Wagner himself the servant of the society of which he had aspired to be the prophet? Was he not increasingly obliged to *play* a role that he had once attempted to *live*?

There have been endless accounts of how his existence was transformed – from one of destroying angel to that of court chamberlain, from utopian revolutionary to sour conservative. We have been shown him in his disillusion trying to treat with emperors and kings on an equal footing, keeping up the exterior semblance of the artist's power – a kind of religious, as opposed to temporal, power – and bitterly undeceived when it was made quite clear that he was no more than an actor, a man of the theatre who lived in a world of illusions and myths rather than in the real world, where such dreams were considered of negligible importance, mere games for irresponsible artists. Although Bayreuth had a brilliant start, with all the aristocracy of the day in attendance, it was silenced from 1877 to 1882, and this left Wagner even more perplexed than bitter. Was his dream of German art premature or simply an illusion? How distant and unattainable it seemed, that magic sense of community in Greek tragedy . . . The society on which he wished to confer a unique identity amused itself for a while with this curiosity and then forgot it, until by a series of *misunderstandings* his work was made the narrow, limited symbol of nationalism and racialism. What a sordid irony there is in this posthumous fate! Stripped of this hideous mask, Wagner's work continues to exercise its fascination, for that is what it is: a work – and a theatre. The double nature of this legacy is a fairly faithful reflection of his revolutionary achievement. The work has been, and still is, an essential fermenting element in music even more than in the theatre and, for very good reasons, of universal significance. Its influence has been universal, and the language of music as we know it today is quite simply unthinkable without that work. And what of the theatre and the theatrical practice that that theatre implies by its architecture, its general conception, its location, the changes in its sphere of activity, its functions and its modalities – has there been any evolution in this practice? This is a field in which Wagner has proved to have almost completely failed. His diatribes, written more than a century ago, are still completely relevant, for nothing has changed – the laziness of the repertory theatre, its failings, its precarious functioning, the blind choice of works, the fortuitous casting of singers and players, the lack of rehearsal, the *sauve-qui-peut* routine. Architecturally speaking, the Bayreuth model has remained a dead letter and we still have Italian-style theatres. The proportions of these buildings have become quite absurd, starting with the orchestra pit, which has been disproportionately enlarged in order to accommodate orchestras that continue to grow in size. From the other side of this giant swimming pool – where it is possible during a performance to watch the family life of the orchestra – singers do their best to get through the wall of sound encountered by their voices: and the vanities involved in this contest give rise daily to very questionable, if not disastrous, results. Both visually and acoustically we continue to witness this permanent defeat of what is truly theatrical, Bayreuth having effected not the slightest improvement. The worldwide response that Wagner proposed has remained isolated and individual, lost in the general context in which there has been no fundamental change.

And yet it was the search for a total solution that was the real passion of Wagner's whole existence and provided the justification of even its most ambiguous and unacceptable aspects. We can watch him gradually defining his musical objectives and determining his line of conduct with growing precision, see the progressive inclusion of all his intellectual and artistic interests in a world essentially circumscribed by music whose frontier he came to regard as an absolute and even to accept as a lesser evil. At first there was nothing exceptional in this, far from it: it was the desire to establish his position. Of course the early influences in his music were beyond cavil, but they were equally strong in the best of his contemporaries:

Gluck, Beethoven and Weber, the same trinity that the young Berlioz worshipped. Turning to the theatre we find the models of the day, the normal repertory and a kind of rivalry much less worthy of respect. If we think of Wagner and his historic achievement today, we are inclined to believe that it was inevitable that any genius on such a scale and of such a quality, with such will-power, vitality and ability to survive simply could not fail to produce spectacular results. Yet examining the documents more carefully we realize how precarious and unconfident was his progress from the uncertainties of his early manhood to the absolute assurance of his finished work. The documents confirm the impression, not of mendacity, but of Wagner, once established as a public figure, correspondingly conceiving even his most personal writings with an eye on posterity. In his youth, when he had still to conquer the world and felt no need to be aware of his historical image, his exchanges with his friends were completely spontaneous. When the situation had changed and 'people' had become 'personages', concerned with the impression that they wished history to have of their personalities, their lives and activities, these spontaneous exchanges were replaced by carefully calculated relations, like those between political 'powers'. The old rhetoric of passion often becomes rhetoric for its own sake, and what was once real degenerates into mere appearance. The letters to Ludwig II naturally show this symptom most clearly, although they frustrate their own purpose, revealing the machinations of an intriguer instead of the greatness of a creative artist. Their exaggerated nobility and idealism betray the artificiality of the role assumed and expose – on both sides – the element of parody in this dialogue conceived as an exchange between Pope and Holy Roman Emperor, but becoming a dialogue between two masks, each bent on convincing the other of the genuineness of his disguise. These solemn exchanges were nevertheless carefully observed by a faithful and authoritarian wife, whose respect and admiration obliged her to record every act and gesture of the Master, even his slightest remarks; and it is one of the strangest paradoxes that we are indebted to her total, blind loyalty for the most striking and revealing documents, those that have suffered least from 'editing'. The Master was not on his guard with her, not concerned with sculpting his own statue for eternity; and we can therefore see clearly his real stature, so infinitely greater than what he was anxious to suggest. In fact we become aware of the real stuff of his personality, something far robuster and more durable than the cardboard image that he was anxious to impose on our imagination.

It may be that Wagner himself provides us with the best analysis of his own personality. A number of his writings contain a kind of skeleton in cipher. His genius was both hot-headed – even irrational – and extremely analytical. His correspondence and his writings show a quite exceptional awareness of his own evolution, his importance and his impact on others and also of the workings of his own creative faculty. This self-awareness furnishes us with extraordinarily shrewd insights into the chief characteristics of his artistic invention and the main objectives of his artistic quest. It is true that what he describes in *Tristan* is what we ourselves most commonly perceive, but he also has a very clear picture of what makes *Tristan* historically unique – a music of transition rather than of retrospection and repetition. His ideas about continuity and transition as essential marks of the music of the future reappear many years later in an engaging conversation with Liszt, in which he expresses his wish to renew the symphony along these lines – Beethoven having exhausted the possibilities of thematic struggle and antagonism, it remains for the future to explore thematic fusion and mutation. This ability to analyse, and to make analysis the starting point for invention, is truly fascinating. Particularly in the case of Beethoven, the composer to whom he felt so closely akin, these private conversations reveal his assumption of, as it were, a natural inheritance. Side by side with this Germanic orthodoxy we often find a mixture of fascination and amusement in his attitude to Italian opera, not that of his contemporary Verdi but the opera created by popular actors at the beginning of the nineteenth century. Though quite aware of the flimsiness of the musical content of these works, he still envies their melodic invention and expressive power, and we are aware of his determination to reconcile the two attitudes – the Germanic symphonic tradition and the expressive power of Italian singing.

More generally, he refused to sacrifice expressiveness to polyphony, endowing each part in the polyphonic web with such expressive power that there is almost a conflict of interest: everything sings, and sings 'unendingly'. It was the wealth and density of his music, and its large-scale continuity, that most puzzled his contemporaries, more especially in the world of opera where listeners were not remarkable for their acuteness. Add to this a harmonic inventiveness also springing from his need for continuity, his ideal of endless transition. The further he advanced, the more closely he approached regions in which for long stretches the musical language lost its clear direction; and this uncertainty, the instability of passing resolutions and the discovery of twilight areas in which outlines become blurred, began increasingly to preoccupy his mind at the deepest level. He came to dissolve the immediate absolutes of musical language in order to discover an absolute both larger in scale and more striking in character, and to dissolve finite forms in order to create a fundamental unity in a work, a unity in which successive moments coalesce by means of a memory guided by simple markers – those 'motives' that start as clear identities only to be transformed and metamorphosed to suit each moment of the drama.

Was Wagner's vision of the theatre at the root of this rich proliferation of ideas and concepts? It is difficult to say yes, because the level at which we read Wagner depends on whether it is a matter of musical or literary invention. His music moves confidently and strongly towards the future, while his theatre is obstinately backward-looking. Of course he accomplished an enormous amount in clearing the ground and introducing new ideas in the operatic world of his age simply by opposing to the trumpery so-called 'historical' operas of the day a whole new dimension of myth, with archetypal characters that gave his theatrical works an inexhaustible wealth of meaning. We should realize, though, that the region from which these myths sprang – the idealized Middle Ages to which a large part of his works are related – belonged to the early years of romanticism. Wagner had done practically all his literary work by 1850, by which time his themes were fixed; and although for the remaining thirty years of his life his music continued to evolve in an increasingly singular and striking manner, his theatrical world remained unchanged despite the changes of perspective that he so often emphasized. When, after years of bitter struggle, his work was fully mature, it formed a closed circuit, both literature and music having abandoned the scenes with which he was so deeply concerned. One of the most striking contradictions in his theatrical works is the power of the myths and symbols that he created despite the fact that they were obsolescent by the time that they were given definitive form. In this sense we might speak of Wagner as 'Gothic' in the same way as Bach used to be spoken of as Gothic. It needs, however, an extremely powerful nationalist mentality to accept certain ambiguous aspects of the Wagnerian myths as an alibi, let alone a justification from the cultural point of view.

After alternating between revolutionary activity and conservative repression during the first half of the nineteenth century, Europe inclined towards a patriotic chauvinism heightened by an awareness of national individuality, which was strong in all countries, whether free or oppressed. Wagner did not escape these alternations and, like many other creative artists, claimed to give his work a solid national foundation. That this became something like an obsession with him is shown by his frequent references to German art. Was this perhaps a way of reassuring himself in relation to the cosmopolitan ideals to which he had hitherto subscribed? He himself was certainly a cosmopolitan: but was he ever really a revolutionary? Mikhail Bakunin's dry, laconic remarks hardly confirm the supposition, nor do Wagner's relations with the German exiles in Zurich suggest that he was devoted to the cause of revolution. The impression he gives is primarily theatrical, that of a man who dramatized the conflicts of his day and used them to his own advantage, as a means of nourishing his own work. As a creative artist and therefore egoistic, or at least egocentric, he gave priority to his own creative work; and there is nothing surprising in his overriding desire to establish that work and give it a solid foundation apart from his own individual achievement. The revolution may have provided an initial impulse, but nationalism was to ensure the expansion of his work. This mixture of opportunism and idealism is reflected in even his most trivial preoccupations. German art meant for him performing Wagner's dramas and creating a German school of singing, or in other words teaching young singers how to sing Wagner.

This concern with musical education is not, in fact, difficult to understand. He was convinced of the importance of his work as forming part of Germanic culture, and he found himself faced with the impossibility of finding a place for it in the existing musical world, whose practices and routines he deplored. If there were to be valid interpretations of his works, he must first set about educating the interpreters.

His plans were never to be realized because he died too soon to realize them. German art was never to know its first school, and Bayreuth was soon to become a blindly conservative rather than an exploratory institution. German art was to become the prey of a complacent society with very little interest in new discoveries. Later, when Wagner's works were seized on by political adventurers, his original ideal was as deeply degraded as it is possible to imagine. Perhaps it was only after undergoing this 'purification through infamy' that his myths and symbols could take on their true meaning and escape the chance circumstances of their origins.

There still remains his crude anti-Semitism, shown in its most curious form in the episode that took place between him and Hermann Levi just before the first performance of *Parsifal*. The whole thing would be laughable if it were not so detestable – this conflict between the convenient pose of the pure Christian idealist and the composer determined not to lose a first-class interpreter, this desire to capture a weaker personality and at the same time to humiliate him (was not this in fact the same story as Hans von Bülow's?). To explain Wagner's militant anti-Semitism simply by his personal jealousy of Mendelssohn and Meyerbeer seems rather too easy, though he was clearly irritated by what these two composers stood for, as he saw them, namely the domination of German art by the all-too-clever and the all-too-facile. Nor should we forget that anti-Semitism has been for centuries an endemic disease of European Christianity: nationalism exposed in an acuter form only what was latently present, the national criterion lacking the urgency that it was to acquire at the end of the century. It was not long before the Dreyfus affair would expose these passions and declared anti-Semites would appear among French musicians. Vincent d'Indy, for instance, attempted in his composition classes to explain 'rationally' why a Jew was incapable of writing music of any value. For centuries Jewish culture was totally neglected, just as Jewish religious traditions were ostracized and persecuted. Those traditions were in any case of no wide concern and represented no danger. It was only with the development of a Jewish intelligentsia and the growth of national self-consciousness throughout Europe that Jewish culture demonstrated the incompatibility of cosmopolitan and national ideals and more especially its own long-standing resistance to any real assimilation. The Jewish community has maintained its identity in spite of every kind of pressure; it represents the porous fault in the watertight compartments that exist between states. Wagner, soaked in the romantic idealization of a mythical Middle Ages, superimposed on nineteenth-century politico-cultural reactions the prejudices of a militant Christian church against the people who crucified Jesus. If he is not an exception among intellectual anti-Semites, he represents an amalgamation of ideas on which it was all too easy to draw in order to make him the champion of a particularly virulent crusade. As victim of his own image he was aware of this, because the Nordic myths, which he helped to revive, were forcibly included in an ideological system to which by their nature they were clearly unsuited. The descent from Greek tragedy to racist manifesto constituted a degradation for which he can be held only partly responsible, though responsible even so. This is why it is difficult, even impossible, wholly to disperse the mists, the shadows and the darkness that have gathered round his name.

The hagiographers will therefore never be able to claim him as wholly theirs; he remains vulnerable in some of the opinions that were fundamental to him. But the documents of his life give us a very clear idea of the vague melting-pot of ideas from which this most headstrong of geniuses sprang. It was through his early uncertainties, the exaltations and disappointments of his life that the mystery and supreme accomplishment of his work were brought into existence, until finally his confidence established a code of behaviour, not unlike a Court code. It is not difficult to imagine his impatience to formulate his future plans, the impatience that sent him to pursue his dreams in Italy while he was still in the middle of his battle for German art. As soon as the Bayreuth mould was formed, he seems to have done everything in his power to escape from it, dreading the attendant responsibilities that threatened his work of discovery. The restless king of a domain for which he had fought long and hard, he was doomed – perhaps chose – to be a wanderer. Did death come to him as a surprise? He had finished his work and believed that he had written for the theatre all that he had it in him to write; now his thoughts turned towards the symphony . . . For us he remains a problematical personality and a supreme artistic achievement: the personality has not yet vanished behind the achievement. Can it ever?

23

Cosima Wagner's Diary: 'R. is working'[1]

> This evening the two of us, R. and I, are as usual deep in our memories . . .
> rejoicing at the number of things that we have achieved in these fourteen
> years: *Meistersinger, Ring, Marches, Complete Writings, Parsifal*, the house,
> the theatre, the biography.

That is from Cosima Wagner's entry for Saturday, 1 February 1879 – the
'we' marking her absolute identification with Richard, the identification that
first separated her from the sterile von Bülow and then at last brought her to
create.

Reading that, one might easily imagine a woman calculating with cold
detachment how she can share the life of a genius and bring his gifts to
fruition with a maximum publicity for her own role. Two days later, however, on Monday, 3 February, she wrote:

> As we parted, I said to him, 'Oh! you heavenly creature!' to which he replied,
> 'No, it is you . . .', adding immediately, 'Inexpressible ecstasy!' Oh! how true
> that is for us both . . .

We sometimes find it hard to follow the *grande dame* of Bayreuth from
one extreme to the other, from minute examination of facts to mystical
adoration, and we wonder whether she is not playing some strange, irrita-
tingly exaggerated comedy, with her feet on the ground and her eyes in the
sky.

A number of things about this diary are irritating, and for a number of
reasons; but the most irritating of all is this famous ecstasy, which led her to
accept without distinction everything of her dear Richard's – the last act of
Götterdämmerung and the *Triumphmarsch*, his thoughts on vegetarianism
as well as his reflections on Beethoven, and worse still his anti-Semitism as
well as his utopian socialism.

In this last period, Cosima faithfully noted every detail of their retired life

---

[1] 'Le Journal de Cosima Wagner: "Richard travaille"', review in *Le Monde* 15 December
1977.

and everything that Richard said – from his most trivial puns to his most surprising thoughts – describing all his acts, his manner, his reactions, his enthusiasms, his whims, his rages and his manias. It is probably this faithfulness that makes her diary a unique source of our knowledge of a complex man who was the victim of his own contradictions and the plaything of his own pretentions. I am careful to say 'man', because as far as the *composer* Wagner is concerned, we may just as well go at once to the published sketches of the *Ring* for a definitive picture. These sketches give us incomparably more exact information about the elaboration of a theme, the evolution of a rhythmic figure, about what was essential from the beginning and what was added or transformed in relation to some leading idea, which itself remains unchanged. Here we come in direct contact with the mechanics of musical invention, even though invention itself is beyond our investigations.

To return to *Cosima's Diary* – here we have a uniquely privileged interlocutor whose position and personal stature we can see evolving year by year. True, it was always with the same exalted sense of mission and with a full consciousness of the importance of this mission as something altogether exceptional; but we can see her passing gradually from a state of uncertainty and a profound sense of guilt to the inexpressible joy of redemption. It is also true that the uninterrupted contact with *Parsifal* during the final six years (1877–83) was not without its influence on this attitude of hers – so much so, in fact, that in the extreme state of irritability that marked the last months of his life, Wagner could not refrain from observing bitterly that she took herself for the personification of Virtue ... She herself, in fact, quotes Kundry's famous 'Dienen, dienen ...' ('To serve, to serve ...'). She keeps wondering whether her own personality has not been completely obliterated by this Master whom she only aspires to respect and to serve with total devotion. This personality might cause her to deviate from the Truth, which is her only aspiration. The slightest incidents and the slightest details of Richard Wagner's life were to serve as examples for the chosen son, Siegfried, born six months after the diary starts. It was dedicated to him in the first place and was meant to be primarily an educational document, completed only in a spirit of total self-denial. The moment Richard dies, the diary stops: their son has nothing more to learn from this hagio-biography.

The first thing that she wanted him to understand was her own deliberate flouting of the codes of bourgeois society. She had a mission higher than any convention, however well established: to support genius in its struggle first to create and then to impose itself on the world. In this sense she could justly congratulate herself on 'the many things that we have achieved'. She may not have written the music of the *Ring* and *Parsifal*, but she created the setting that favoured the production of masterpieces. And we can imagine how difficult this must have been with a man so egocentric and so demanding in intellectual matters as well as in the matter of curtains, hangings, stuffs and the like. The nearer we come to the end, the more we share the anxiety of both as to whether he will be able to finish *Parsifal*; and it is touching to see him working desperately for fear of death interrupting him before the work is complete, and to hear him admit his ceaseless anxiety lest death rob him of the works still to be written.

The calendar she kept of *Parsifal* is far more detailed than that of the *Ring*, probably because by that time the children were older and she had correspondingly more freedom. Every detail she mentions can be checked against the final score. Everything is described in the minutest detail – uncertainties in the plan, decisions about its execution, the returning to individual passages and their modification, even the actual circumstances and places in which certain themes were conceived, whether inspired by some garden in Bayreuth or some particular moment of the day. We can follow step by step the gestation, first of the poem, then of the music and finally of the score. However close she is to him, we are physically aware of the mystery of creation in which he encloses himself. The moment he enters his study he is absolutely alone – what he shares with her, and that almost at once, are his inspirations, the product of his thinking, moment by moment. And so we repeatedly read, 'R. is working.' She records the small incidents of the day, 'R. is working'; she busies herself with the children's education, 'R. is working'; she deals with domestic problems, 'R. is working'; she copes with the financial problems of the Festival, 'R. is working.' The sense of this ability to cut himself off is something quite extraordinary in a life so completely shared.

When Richard issues from his own world, Cosima is intensely aware of the aura of creation surrounding him and tries to seize on anything that remains of it or anything that inspired it. In this way we have a better idea of his musical taste and how he spoke about music when unencumbered by rhetoric or the formalities of writing. Not that we learn anything very new: we are almost too familiar with his likes and dislikes, but here we see them in a spontaneous, family setting. There was a great deal of private music-making in the house – that is to say that, among others, Liszt played Bach, Beethoven and fragments of Wagner, either earlier works or something from the work on hand. Cosima immediately enters in her diary the comments of her lord and master on the music itself, but also on interpretation. Wagner having been – with Berlioz, whether he liked it or not – one of the first people to discuss interpretation, consciously distinguishing in orchestral works between what we may call novelty and repertory, it is extremely interesting to learn his ideas not only about his own music but about that of Beethoven in particular, Mozart, Haydn and Weber. Both for his own music and that of others he was extremely demanding in matters of tempo (to which he attached primary importance) of formal continuity and instrumental detail. It seems that his own performances must have been quite exceptional, judging from his conception of the works and his concern with details of interpretation. It is equally clear that what irritated him most was any imprecision in tempo or in the relationship between tempi. It was of this that he openly complained to one of his favourite interpreters, Hans Richter, when the *Ring* was first performed in 1876. The *Diary* reveals how much he in fact invented a style of performance and what importance he attached to it, despite occasional intolerable disappointments. It appears that in Wagner's eyes Hans von Bülow's *Tristan* came nearest to the truth and that, from this point of view at least, he still bitterly deplored the irreparable break between them. He even tried to set up a school of interpretation at Bayreuth, primarily for singers, of course, but also for conductors, in order to create an authentic tradition. The financial disaster of the first Festival, added to the lack of interest among artists, was soon to lead to the abandoning of the project.

Of all the subsidiary activities that should have been centred on Bayreuth none remained in the end except the *Bayreuther Blätter*. These were started with great enthusiasm but soon became an encumbrance, compelling him often against his will to write articles in order to keep the series going. Wagner soon became irritable with the followers whom he attracted and was not often satisfied with the different essays published in the *Bayreuther Blätter*. In the same way stage production of any kind became repellent to him. The experience of 1876 proved a serious warning and he was further disenchanted by the trivial manner in which he saw his dreams realized; so that, having created the invisible orchestra, he came to long for some way of creating an invisible stage ... He could no longer tolerate the material nature of the theatre, and although obliged by financial pressures to hand over *Parsifal*, he did everything in his power to protect it from the vulgarity of actors, the cynicism of theatrical managements and the routine of opera houses. During the composition of *Parsifal* he was always lamenting the necessity of working for the theatre while his head was full of ideas for symphonies. Even after *Parsifal* had been finished and performed, during the last months of his life in Venice, he often returned to the symphony in conversation. This explains why he could find nothing but petty sarcasms to say about Brahms. In his dreams it was he, Wagner, who was really to carry on Beethoven's work and, like a true heir, the first thing he would do would be to abolish the traditional pattern of four movements – something that Brahms certainly never dreamed of doing!

This evolution of his personality in relation to the theatre can also be traced in his earlier enthusiasms during the years between 1869 and 1883, a period of bitter disappointments. We can follow in *Cosima's Diary* the evolution of his political views, largely disillusioned towards the end, partly though not entirely under the influence of his own personal disappointments. Wagner is still regarded in his own country and elsewhere as one of the chief symbols of German nationalism, and this is true if we confine ourselves to the first period covered by this *Diary*. Just after *Meistersinger* he is still talking about German art and the German fatherland. The Franco-

Prussian War, as he saw it from Tribschen, was greeted with hysterical enthusiasm (no need to be shocked – there was plenty of hysteria on both sides of the frontier) Bismarck is the great hero; the Emperor deserves his *Triumphmarsch*. But the vulgar *Wacht am Rhein* was preferred to Wagner's music, and this first artistic heresy caused the first wry face, soon to be followed by many others, so that it was not long before Bismarck was in the pillory, the object of bitter diatribes and violent negative judgements in which the Emperor was also involved.

And where was Ludwig II in all this? Well, there were times when he was no better treated than Bismarck, even worse – ruthlessly condemned as a weak creature, the prisoner of his own foibles, spending on imitations of Louis XIV, XV or XVI money that might usefully have been spent on Bayreuth, on giving his country a genuinely German art. Nevertheless a sort of disillusioned attachment still remained, concealed beneath the pompous rhetoric maintained between the two men, like an artificial code, which preserved the myth by means of falsehood. He did not conceal from Cosima how irksome he found the ceremonious correspondence with Ludwig, and the stylistic exercises involved, which no longer had any meaning – though this may have been to calm her latent jealousy of this powerful protector and greatest of friends to whom the *Ring* was dedicated. Yet when the King failed to keep up even this artificial myth and did not attend the first production of *Parsifal*, Wagner was really wounded, though whether it was his sensibilities or his pride that were wounded would be hard to say. Here too the lights were going out.

All that remained were the twilight terminal anxieties of a life that was deliberately more and more isolated. As the outside world seized on Wagner's work and gradually came to recognize it as that of one of the greatest geniuses of the age, Wagner's own circle shrank, both in numbers and in ideas. Even if his court irritated him, he still had to have a court to tyrannize, while at the same time complaining of its boredom. When members of the family or passing guests stay at Bayreuth, Wagner complains irritably that no one has anything to say to him, that he has to do all the talking and that this tires and exhausts him. This was the time when he embarked on his diatribes on vivisection and vegetarianism and also when his anti-Semitism became most bitter – a narrow, sometimes violent obsession when either his material interests or his intellectual domination seemed to him threatened. He showed his feelings quite clearly to the Jewish members of his circle, such as Hermann Levi and Joseph Rubinstein, and this disconcerting brutality must have been deeply wounding to an intelligent man like Levi. The attraction of genius must have been very strong to overcome such treatment.

But is a genius really a genius if it can sink from Nietzsche to Gobineau? To readers not naturally disposed to be indulgent towards Wagner's personality these conversations in the *Diary* may well seem to be those of a loquacious old man ready to talk about anything and everything and imagining himself to be as well informed on the international situation as on music. Shrewd comments on a Beethoven quartet follow naïve reflections on the future of industry, and an interesting idea about Cervantes or Shakespeare will be followed by a rambling diatribe on vivisection. It is in fact possible that the Wagner a reader may remember from the *Diary* is a Wagner seated in the local Café du Commerce; yet thanks either to Cosima's admiration or Cosima's honesty none of this daily rubbish goes unchronicled.

If we can mentally eliminate this waste matter, we are left with a picture of the intellectual landscape in which Wagner lived. His tastes, both musical and literary, become visibly more stable with the years. First come the peaks, other reading – reflecting a very catholic taste – being reserved for purposes of amusement. Among serious writers the company is very restricted – Homer, Plato, Aeschylus and Sophocles among the Greeks, Calderón and Cervantes among the Spaniards, and finally the great twin figures of German literature, Goethe and Schiller, particularly Goethe. Balzac makes an occasional appearance in this privileged circle. Musically, first and foremost comes Beethoven, the god. Weber often appears, the precursor whom he had seen when a child, and then Mozart, Bach, Haydn. On the theatrical side Auber and Halévy sometimes get a hearing as being the epitome of the French operas that Wagner knew when he first visited Paris and still, despite his persistent francophobia, found seductive with their airy charm and gracefulness . . . but kept in their place of course. The panorama is completed by a number of acid remarks about Liszt, Berlioz and Brahms, not to mention Rossini and Bellini, in whose works he admired a number of things. But with time he became increasingly exclusive and we find Beethoven and more Beethoven, Shakespeare and more Shakespeare.

His lack of interest in contemporary music becomes increasingly marked, and the modern world seems to him sunk in mediocrity. The chief impression is that nobody has really understood his own contribution to the world of music, and that with him a unique secret will be lost. With illness he turns increasingly inward, both his irritability and isolation increase. After *Parsifal* his life closes; he is thinking of symphonies – but is he really, or does he merely talk about it in order to deceive himself?

The last months of his life appear as months of uninterrupted wretchedness. If Wagner shuts himself away, it is only to write letters or a preface, perhaps to start an essay. Was he at last musically exhausted? At the very end we are aware of a great void, the same void that must have been horribly real to Cosima. No, we have not learned anything about the process by which his works came into being, but we have seen its steady reflection. For better and for worse we have made the acquaintance of a really great personality, inextricably tied to a partner indefatigable in her self-sacrifice and her fidelity. The difference between them is still there, and nothing can alter it – 'R. is working.'

24

Parsifal: The First Encounter[1]

Dear Wieland Wagner,

On the eve of the dress rehearsal and with these days of work behind us I should like to sum up for you the results achieved so far.

In the first place I must tell you how effective your letters have been. They aroused some rather bitter reactions at the beginning, but they made everyone ask themselves a number of questions that had not occurred to them before. Thank you for having put all the weight of your authority in the scales and thus contributed so materially to the 'stylistic' renewal of this production.

The principal points on which there were differences of opinion have all been studied and there are no misunderstandings on any important matters.

Gurnemanz's monologue in Act I is now going well, expanding only at important moments and on important words that refer to the immediate dramatic situation. In other words the historical aspect of the monologue is lightened when it is no more than an account of events in the past, which explain the present.

The first chorus is now quite different in character, more mystical. I have insisted on the orchestral *piano*, which is essential at the opening of this chorus and the style is now sustained, suggesting the medieval conception of the monk–soldier.

In the actual rite 'nehmet hin meinen Leib' was too slow, probably on account of the *pianissimo*. I have asked Monsieur Pitz to maintain a tempo at which the melodic phrase remains coherent despite the very low dynamic. But this really presents no problem.

The final male chorus is also now ready and it now has no hint of either the martial or the patriotic song! There again we have a brotherhood of monk–soldiers.

At the first runthrough the scene between Klingsor and Kundry was really not right. All the reworking that we had done in previous rehearsals became

---

[1] 'Parsifal: la première rencontre', letter to Wieland Wagner, 24 July 1966, published in the 1973 Bayreuth Festival programme book for *Parsifal* (which Boulez conducted), pp. 48–51.

very precarious again on account of the depth of the stage. Fortunately all went excellently the second time; it was simply a matter of getting used to the new conditions. I have now achieved greater variety in the tempi and more flexibility in Klingsor's orders and Kundry's faint efforts to resist. Klingsor, especially, is now more *heftig* [violent] throughout.

The Flowermaidens' scene still presents the greatest problems, owing to the depth of the stage, which really necessitates a more flexible tempo. It was only at the third attempt that we got a proper result, but I think that we have really solved the problem now, with all the necessary contrasts and the virtuosity that this scene demands.

The two Parsifals, one echoing the other, are now justified; they keep the action moving and there are no crises!! I was particularly pleased with the change in the scene between Parsifal and Kundry. We worked very hard with K.; and this time I did not let anything pass without saying what I felt. (He was horrified by what you said about the *kitsch* element in his perform-ance and much easier to convince than last time. He was afraid of making the slightest *ritardando* and it was I who had to restore his sense of freedom!!) Kundry's lullaby has now become much more expressive, more 'wheedling'. Among other details I asked for Kundry's 'starb' not to be given the same malicious tone that it has in Act I but to be sung with great tenderness. Without this, the rest of the scene is unintelligible . . . I also got K. to make more distinction between 'Erlösungswonne', 'erlöse' and 'Erlöser', which represent three quite different states of mind.

The whole end of the scene is much less heavy going and went without any hitches in fact.

As you know, Act III presented many fewer problems and it went well with some quite marked improvements. Gurnemanz's 'nobility' is now more natural, less conscious than before, and the whole role has more grandeur, at long last! There is no longer that hint of mawkishness and bad taste about the Good Friday Music. I have insisted on reducing to a minimum the various *rallentandos* and chocolate-box effects.

The first time through the chorus came in much too softly, but we started again and all went well the second time. The end went well too; I should like the orchestra to be even softer so as to obtain a kind of quiet resolution and avoid the 'end of revue' suggestion.

It is a strange thing that the concept of heavenly bliss has never provided either composers or poets with much inspiration – odd that imagining eternal happiness has suggested only bland, vaguely tedious ideas! (Berlioz at the end of the *Damnation*; Schumann in the *Péri*; Debussy in *Saint Sébastien*; not to speak of Claudel, normally so brutal even in his religion, but so conventional when he achieves redemption!)

I should like to avoid that final sea of blandness by giving the orchestral sound an immaterial quality, but I have not yet managed to achieve this. We still have chubby, well-covered angels. I hope that I shall still be able to improve this at the performance. I will certainly pay you a visit after the first night, if you are not too tired, and give you a viva-voce account of my impressions as a 'novice'.

With all very good wishes for your recovery and the assurance of my profound and loyal sympathy.

25

Wieland Wagner: 'Here Space Becomes Time'[1]

It is something of a paradox for me to speak about Wieland Wagner as a producer, having only once worked with him – on the Frankfurt production of *Wozzeck* last spring. I was fated never to meet him actually at Bayreuth, since he was away ill when I went there for the first time. Rather than recounting memories or anecdotes, I should like to pinpoint what attracted me, more or less consciously, about his personality when I actually worked with him. There are some facts and ideas of which I became aware only rather later, particularly when, owing to his absence through illness, I found myself having to give him a fairly detailed account of the work that I had done on the music without him being present.

It is of course a long way from *Parsifal* to *Wozzeck*, or rather, speaking chronologically in our case, from *Wozzeck* to *Parsifal*; and it may be hard to imagine what general conclusions I could draw on the basis of these two works alone. I think, however, that Wieland Wagner was more particularly concerned with seeing music, and even orchestral sound, co-ordinated with the visual aspect of a production in its most 'impermanent' form – I mean, lighting. One of his great obsessions towards the end of his life was the lack of co-ordination common in most opera houses between the stage and the orchestra. There are of course purely personal solutions of the problem, I mean when a work is conducted and produced by the same person; but it must be admitted that the results are not wholly convincing, no single individual being equally gifted in all the departments of such a complex undertaking. In most of such cases the visual aspect of the production is noticeably inferior to the musical, and this tends to destroy the very principle of unity that it tries to establish. In order to realize a fusion between stage and orchestra something more is needed than a mere conjunction of the different aspects or working to a single point of reference; it is

---

[1] *Les Lettres françaises*, 20 October 1966. Wieland Wagner had died on 17 October 1966 and earlier in the year Boulez had conducted his production of *Wozzeck* at Frankfurt. The title of this tribute, originally titled 'Der Raum wird hier zur Zeit', is an inversion of Gurnemanz's observation in the first act of *Parsifal* as the scene begins to change from the forest to the Temple of the Grail, 'zum Raum wird hier die Zeit'. [M.C.]

something that cannot be obtained by simply co-ordinating different personalities or different sides of a single personality. In the majority of cases each partner insists on his own contribution, conductor and singers concentrating particularly on the musical side whatever the stage production may be and the producer generally refusing to be put out by the demands of the musicians. As the saying goes, each man for himself and God for all.

I have often been worried by this separation of powers, or what often amounts to the mutual ignorance of each other's functions. How does it come about? It is perhaps too simple-minded to explain it simply by each individual's self-regard, the egoism of each partner in an operatic production. This raises, in fact, the question of the specific difference between opera and straight theatre. Most operas are based on some anecdote, some story or myth. Librettos are mostly held together by a certain dramatic effectiveness; and even if the literary quality of the text may leave something to be desired, the mere impetus of the action and the disposition of dramatic incident ensure an opera a purely theatrical stage vitality even without the music. Generally speaking, producers stick to the dramatic scheme of an opera, and it would in fact be difficult to disregard it. But the libretto is regarded as the chief armature, which the music, with varying degrees of success, has to fill out. It is a common complaint that operatic productions are static, oratorio-like, and this emphasizes the paradoxical fact that the purely dramatic aspect is determined, basically, by the music. The lesson to be learned from all this is that confining oneself to the anecdotal element in producing an opera constitutes as serious a mutilation as allowing it to clutter up the whole stage.

Opera is in fact the total engulfing of a dramatic anecdote by musical form, and this is achieved by a more or less clearly defined, 'formal' rhetoric. There therefore exists a profound dialectic in opera between action and reflection, between quantity of movement and quality of repose. The reflection may be either individual or collective, but in each case the musical structure at such moments is stronger than the dramatic, since it entirely dominates the situation and carries it to the furthest point of inner awareness. At such moments feeling – the quality of feeling – is the predominant factor, elevating the commentary needed by an audience aware of the dramatic situation at any given point in the evolution of the drama. Contrariwise, when the so-called action is in progress, the musical form is more or less reduced to the state of an agent entrusted with communicating to the audience the maximum of information about the dramatic situation. It is therefore clear that opera is a perpetual transition from strict, formal thinking on the musical plane to strict, formal thinking on the dramatic plane. This dialectic is very often bypassed or else ready-made solutions are accepted which belong to a rather questionable tradition. It can also sometimes happen that even the best composers have hesitated to plump for either of the two solutions, which makes the theatrical problems even more acute.

Take the example of *Wozzeck*. A great deal has been said about its strict construction and Berg's application of symphonic forms to Büchner's play, as though this meant the skilful but artificial imposing of an arbitrary grid on the stage action. We have only to read Berg's own lecture on the subject to be convinced of his profound grasp of the work's dramatic essence and of his success in finding the best possible musical correspondence for this by using a transcendent form of rhetoric. I will not go into details, but merely want to observe that for Berg it was not a question of making symphonic form coincide with the form of the drama, but of creating from the facts of the drama a musical form as strictly coherent as that found in non-dramatic, or so-called 'pure', music. It was thus possible to regard *Wozzeck* as a kind of retreat, or regression from the Wagernian conception, and particularly from the conception of *Parsifal*. The real explanation is both simpler and more complex: the dramatic effectiveness of *Parsifal* resides essentially in the transitions, and does not therefore require the same methods as the dramatic effectiveness of *Wozzeck*, which is achieved by using separate and clearly distinct planes, as in the cinema.

Returning to Wieland Wagner, I think that he had perfectly grasped the fundamental fact that musical and theatrical dialectic are simply two aspects of what is basically a single phenomenon. If I speak further about *Wozzeck*, it is because this was the only opera, as I have said, on which I actually saw him at work. Some faults were found with his handling of precisely such dramatic 'anecdotes', though his critics might well have reminded themselves that he had probably considered such points very carefully before coming to any decision. And in fact it was not simply perverseness that made him neglect these anecdotes, but an original point of view that may well have been different from the author's. I once heard him say, in a television interview, that the dramatic *circumstance* imagined by an operatic composer is possibly the most ephemeral element in his work, linked as it is to the dramatic ideas of his day and not, in most cases, transcending them. There is a typical instance of this in the third scene of Act I. Marie is at her window watching the military band in the distance, led by the Drum-Major. After her quarrel with Margret she slams down her window and Berg matches this dramatic detail with a very realistic effect, a sudden stop in the music. Wieland Wagner transposed this scene from Marie's room to a street bordering the barracks. The barrack gates had a special significance because they reappear at the end of the opera in the shape of the children's playground, where Marie's and Wozzeck's child – now an orphan – is playing alone. In an out-of-door setting the stopping of the military band was not of course in any sense realistic. But Berg's score shows that this break is linked primarily with the violence of the quarrel between Marie and Margret, ending with the word 'Luder' (whore) which constitutes in itself the real break. This term of abuse shuts off the outside world for Marie and makes her turn in on herself and her child – something, as I see it, more important than the slamming of a window. And so Wieland Wagner also felt. I think it seemed more essential to him to underline visually the parallel between the barrack gates and the playground railings than to be guided by a realistic term of abuse that was in itself of less dramatic importance.

He was rather amused by another detail after the first night. Of course there was a complaint that there was no visible moon in the scene where Marie is murdered. There is in fact much talk in the libretto of this red moon, and his refusal to include it in his set struck people as an irritating paradox. In most sets this moon is made very visible and given a rather exaggerated symbolic significance, as in some cheap romantic print. Wieland Wagner rightly thought that premonitions based on strange-seeming natural phenomena really arise from fear and depend on psychological rather than 'real' factors. This was why he refused to use a magic lantern and merely suggested the red moon by the frightened staring of the two characters. Personally I found this infinitely more convincing than any ingenious lighting device, and it provides the main answer to a number of unjust complaints about such details, complaints springing from a rather small-minded pedantry.

I should like to point out something that was, to my mind, a much more important feature of this production of *Wozzeck*, and that is what I should call the displacement of objects. Practically speaking, Wieland Wagner treated objects like musical themes, taking them out of their everyday context and giving them an importance that they do not normally have, in the same way as an absolutely commonplace word may be given an extremely strong significance in the context of a poem, simply by its placing – either by being isolated or displaced or set in an irrational context. Wieland Wagner gave individual stage props an 'exemplary' character by the way he placed them or by their arrangement in relation to each other, this 'placing' giving them structural function and significance. This dramatic conception corresponded closely both to the spirit of Berg's musical forms and to Büchner's text, in which realism is essentially a manifestation of timeless truths. I do not want to speak at any length about my experience of Bayreuth, since I unfortunately never had an opportunity to collaborate personally with Wieland Wagner there; but the letters we exchanged at that time confirm the fact of our complete agreement about the 'desacralization' of *Parsifal*. I want to make it clear that it was not a question of reducing the 'mystery' to a mere Freudian case history, but that both Wieland Wagner and I felt the need to define the precise limits of theatre and religion, the long-standing confusion of the two inevitably causing countless misunderstandings. Owing to his premature death we were never, alas!, able to compare our points of view directly in the theatre, and I bitterly regret that I shall never have the opportunity of working with him on any of the great masterpieces of the operatic repertory. To add a more personal note to these memories, I should like to say that during the short time of our acquaintance I felt no need to exchange many words with Wieland Wagner; we very soon understood one another and words would have seemed to both of us superfluous.

This happens with people whose chief characteristic is a kind of magnetism, and in my own case these are virtually the only people with whom I feel myself to be in instinctive agreement. Short as it was, this collaboration with Wieland Wagner served to draw my attention to a world that I had not been immediately prepared to regard as important or of presentday interest – the world of opera.

26

Approaches to *Parsifal*[1]

For my generation Wagner was a 'forgotten' field of music . . . It had been part of our general education in the same way as the chief works of the musical past, but there was virtually no contact with the world that Wagner represented. The war that had raged round this music and had for years poisoned all judgements of Wagner, was becoming pointless and seemed useless and absurd: partisanship had been replaced by indifference, which was hardly surprising.

Every generation has its own personal quarrels, which have no interest for the next one. Reading the opinions expressed by various composers, we found that both their admiration and their detestation were mixed with purely emotional reactions, and that both their sarcasms and their expressions of respect were not really prompted by Wagner's actual work, by its real interest and importance.

On the one hand Berg had a sentimental attachment to Wagner that could almost be called mystical, however irritated and even outraged he may have been by the narrow conservatism of the Wagnerian cult. On the other hand the scepticism of Debussy and Stravinsky made a negative attitude towards Wagner fashionable. The reason in Debussy's case was clear enough – he had felt the fascination of both the man and his music strongly enough to want to break with both, and forget them. In Stravinsky's case the reasons were equally clear, though they were the opposite of Debussy's – illusion, rhetorical emphasis and any implication of the artist's personality were always anathema to him in a work of art. The generation of 1920–30 merely took over these objections of their elders on a reduced scale.

As a matter of fact *Parsifal* is a work on which Debussy and Stravinsky were in absolute disagreement. Stravinsky regarded it as the apotheosis of the personality cult, attacking its pseudo-religious elements, which he considered particularly detestable, as springing from the most unpardonable of all sins, pride. On the other hand Debussy thought that *Parsifal* was the

---

[1] 'Chemin vers *Parsifal*', from the 1970 Bayreuth Festival programme book for *Parsifal* (which Boulez conducted), pp. 2–14, and 63–8.

exception that justified Wagner, a brilliant contradiction of the *Ring*, free in its invention and unspoiled by the formulae that he found so irritating in the *Ring*. Are we in fact to think of *Parsifal* as a work 'liberated' from the excesses due to an imbalance of theoretical ideas, a building from which the scaffolding has genuinely disappeared, or as the work in which the composer's failings and obsessions are most clearly exemplified? Is *Parsifal* an old man's act of self-glorification or a sublimation made possible by the composer's at last obtaining ideal theatrical conditions?

Without denying that unity of conception which links the musical with the dramatic invention, we may still reconsider *Parsifal* today from two different points of view, either as a theatrical creation or as an elaborate musical construction. The process by which the work came into being is almost an invitation to make this distinction, since Wagner wrote the text first and made no very noticeable alterations to it when he later added the music. It is no new discovery, in any case, that Wagner's two activities were on two very different levels: that the dramatic conception is superior to the purely literary quality of the text, and that the music itself occupies a still higher place.

Wagner's choice of subject in *Parsifal* carries us back to some of the obsessions and the fundamental themes of the early romantics. The legendary Middle Ages, in which the story of *Parsifal* takes place, was a favourite period at the beginning of the nineteenth century, but in the literary world of the 1870s *Parsifal* appears as a belated survivor. Whether in the theatre, in the novel or in poetry (particularly in poetry) there was no longer any novelty in the discovery and resurrecting of the Middle Ages. *Parsifal* is of course more than that, and shows traces of many philosophical or literary influences that were more *modern*. But Wagner's choice of setting is significant and reveals a concern with the past in an intellectual world whose chief concerns were undergoing very considerable change. A single, extreme instance is Rimbaud's work, all of which was written even before *Parsifal* was completed. There are of course other instances of similar divergences when different generations are telescoped together, but the gulf separating two contemporary worlds, as represented by *Parsifal* and *Une Saison en enfer* is quite particularly astonishing . . .

Wagner's drama is built round an idea that all the great romantics after Goethe had made central to their work at one time or another – redemption by divine love. Berlioz came first; Schumann followed and Wagner erected this glittering hyperbola. Without wishing to be sarcastic we may observe that sin suited their purposes better than redemption, which often involved them in an altogether too bland kind of sublimation. The Flower-maidens and their garden temptations seem to us rather simplistic and one-sided as the personifications of Original Sin, the sin against God, chastity alone being hardly able to claim such a unique role in man's breach with the divine.

If there are indeed details that may now irritate us, this should not make us forget the originality of certain characters and certain situations in *Parsifal*. From this point of view the second act may well seem the most relevant to us today, since there we are shown the figure of Kundry in all its complexity and observe the very ambiguous relationship established between the two protagonists of the work, Parsifal and Kundry. Thematically this act glaringly contradicts the sometimes rather stilted 'dignity' of the other acts. Two magic moments stand out – Kundry's calling of Parsifal's name and the kiss, the *revelations* that help Parsifal first to understand and then to cast himself in his true role. These two symbolical gestures are certainly less 'subsidiary' than either the spear or the dove, because they are essential and interior and avoid the conventional symbolism of holiness and purity, which, over the centuries, has lost its telling power.

If *Parsifal* were no more than a theological fable relevant to a definite age and world, its interest today would certainly be limited. The problem is therefore, as it seems to me, not the celebration of some fictional cult reconstituted for purely theatrical purposes, but the presentation of the working of a metaphysical idea that oscillates between being a live and a spent force. In Christian terms this takes the form of man's unhappiness when deprived of Divine Grace and the remorse and pain consequent on this deprivation: for life and strength are communicated to him by that permanent, perpetually renewed contact with his creator. It also appears in the search for Truth, regardless of all obstacles, in order to achieve self-discipline and self-forgetfulness before being reborn in God. The idea of redemption, which is common to many religions, has certainly lost its attraction in any strictly ritual form, but not in the shape of the individual's search for his own self, with all the snares that this implies and the spiritual discipline that it demands. In this sense Wagner has [in *Parsifal*] shed many 'heroic' elements and gone both more directly and more profoundly to the heart of fundamental metaphysical questions than he had done earlier. The *Ring* does not always lend itself easily to transposition, being closely linked to a single mythology. *Parsifal*, on the other hand, like *Tristan*, immediately reveals its essence, recreates a primitive myth and transposes beyond the limits of any clearly defined time or space the doubt and the questioning that are inseparable from being human. Struggle, difficulties and anguish being considered as positive, *productive* factors, any smooth, tranquillizing resolution of these antagonisms leaves us today with a sense of rather diminished ecstasy. The conflict in *Tristan* remains undecided, leaving our imaginations free to roam. Although Wagner stoutly defended himself against this danger, Parsifal seems a little like the *deus ex machina* bringing the happy ending and a feeling of easy satisfaction [*suavité*].

There has been much discussion as to whether the chief characters in *Parsifal* are really Christian (Amfortas presenting the chief difficulty) and whether the work itself is as Christian as Wagner declared it to be. For a believer, 'There is something more beautiful than *Parsifal*, namely any Low Mass in any church.' For an agnostic the whole apparatus of these doctrines and rituals belongs to a sort of prehistory of the human mind. The ability of *Parsifal* to stimulate our interest and our emotions must therefore derive from some source other than its religious character. Inasmuch as the stage presentation remains linked to the conventional gestures of religious devotion – hands joined, eyes gazing upwards, genuflexions – religion in *Parsifal* is hardly more than a caricature, offensive to some and amusing to others. Inasmuch as some of the stage characters are linked to certain episodes in the Gospels, the relationship suggests either sacrilege or, more simply, parody. (The pointless disputes about applause at the end of the acts – pagan actions being approved by applause, other actions not – arise from the spectator's embarrassment in choosing between regarding religion as a dramatic spectacle and making a religion of that spectacle ...) Wagner himself constructed the work on these very ambiguities; and although the dispute is no longer so heated and has become no more than a dispute about a point of etiquette, there is still a feeling of uncertainty about the right attitude to the work. Whatever may be the truth about the religious validity of *Parsifal*, the importance attached to ritual forms and the conception of worship remove the work into a mythical past, a Golden Age that stirs a sentiment of nostalgia, very characteristic of romanticism, and particularly of late romanticism. Here again the date of the work must not be allowed to mislead us about its old-fashioned character. The constant intrusion of the past in *Parsifal* – the past before the 'Fall' – introduces a special sentiment of nostalgia. Claudel spoke of 'this taste for recitatives, in which characters keep on interrupting themselves to discourse about origins and to narrate the past. History as it develops being a continual annexation of the present by the past ...' People have often complained of the long expositions in Wagner, the interminable narrations and innumerable self-justifications. Gurnemanz is high on this list of these complaints by reason of his loquaciousness. But are we really justified in calling him simply loquacious? Can we really say that he is always going back to the Flood and spares us no detail of the catastrophe in his descriptions and his alleging of motives? Is this ruthless tracing of every circumstance of the disaster, and how it arose, no more than a symptom of uncontrollable logorrhoea? What may at first appear prolix and unnecessary – an abuse of the narrative faculty and an over-developed sense of logic – does in fact give us a deep understanding of the leading actors in the drama, grafting on to the actual dramatic situation of the moment a whole number of imaginary situations from the past. A whole network of lines, constantly checked, connects each point in the dramatic action with the various fundamental data that account for it; time is thus always moving on two planes, the present implying the past and the past conditioning the present. In the case of *Parsifal* such retrospection is anything but pointless, since it perpetually quickens the feeling of remorse and

lost powers, and constantly suggests comparisons between present wretchedness and past glories. The future automatically appears in this time-scale
in the frequent references to the promise of redemption and to the hero who
is destined to fulfil that promise.

If time appears in these three aspects – past, present and future, bound
together by remorse and hope – space too takes on a symbolic aspect. The
words of Gurnemanz are of vital significance –

> Du siehst, mein Sohn,
> zum Raum wird hier die Zeit
> [You see, my son,
> how here time becomes space]

– because they bring these two fundamental constituents together to form a
unity. This is an idea adumbrated but never really pursued, though it
reappears incidentally in the magic transformation of Klingsor's domain, in
the evoking of Kundry and in the narrative of Parsifal's wanderings. On each
occasion place and time are linked by a kind of osmosis, explained superficially by clairvoyance and magic but implicit, at a deeper level, in the very
stuff of the dramatic action.

In theatrical terms *Parsifal* is far from being the brilliant exception that
Debussy supposed. On the other hand, Wagner here pushed to its logical
conclusion that unity of conception that lay behind his overall organization of
the *Ring*: incongruities are removed, anecdotes ruthlessly cut and absolute
priority given to the essence of the drama. In this sense *Parsifal* is, indeed,
genuinely *modern*, much more so than either its ideological assumptions or
its theatrical character would lead one to suppose.

And the music? Act II with its glaring contrasts, its extreme tensions, its
showiness, its surprises and sudden ruptures, is plainly *theatrical*; but are Act
I and III really as undramatic as they are generally said to be? The chief
complaint is that Gurnemanz's long narrative paralyses both music and
action and relegates *Parsifal* to some ill-defined category which is neither
opera nor oratorio. This observation is less *critical* than it seems. *Parsifal* is
not in fact an opera; and when Wagner called it 'ein Bühnenweihfestspiel' he
was not, I believe, concerned with inaugurating a ceremony but rather with
explaining – and giving a *name* to – his intentions in the matter of form.
Parsifal is probably the latest work in a tradition that goes back to Schütz and
Monteverdi, and many other less distinguished composers. In fact it is a
synthesis of the Passions and the opera, of Bach and the Mozart of *Die
Zauberflöte*, of abstract, imagined spectacle and the concrete spectacle of
the stage. Wagner's repeated use of the chorus makes it difficult to avoid this
comparison. Although he insisted on the principle of continuity, it is possible to trace in Act I the old forms of recitative, *arioso* and chorale amalgamated into a complex whole. The choruses in this act are not concerned with
action but with reflection – or, to use a more restricted term, prayer. They

refer to the three phases of any ceremonial rite – preparation, accomplishment and thanksgiving – and they frame the action by isolating the three principal characters: Amfortas, Titurel and Parsifal, who is associated in the action by Gurnemanz's violent rebukes. (They are also concrete representatives of the three aspects of time: present, past and future.)

Here as elsewhere the part played by the chorus is extremely important formally. It is entrusted with the contrasts between the areas that precede and follow its appearance, areas in which the forms become simpler, clearer and in fact more *legibile*, and the action scenes in which the music is linked immediately to the text, implying a form that is more complex, more ambiguous and more difficult to grasp. The same is true of the Flowermaidens' chorus, which is not something outside the action but a brilliant virtuoso *intermezzo* between the formally more complex principal scenes of Act II.

The whole work could be analysed in this way as alternating areas of formal clarity and complexity within a single large-scale structure. For this reason *tempo* plays an all-important part, very flexible in what I should call the narrative and the action but firmly stabilized in passages of reflection or comment. Such large-scale alternations carry our minds back still more forcibly to the Passions, *Die Zauberflöte* and the *Missa solemnis*, which were undeniably Wagner's models, the premisses of his own individual syllogism. Once this is admitted all discussion about the spiritual value of a religious ritual transplanted to the stage seems to lose interest and importance. Some people are still shocked, while others snigger at the Communion scene visibly based on the Gospel narrative and its later liturgical adaptation. But we are neither shocked nor amused by Christ singing in the Passions, which is quite as incongruous, unless gesture is reprehensible and singing not. What *Parsifal* amounts to is a staged Passion, which should not be taken for either more, or less, than what it is.

Is Wagner to bear the blame if it is commonly the 'celebratory' aspect of the work that is 'criticized? In part, yes. He was certainly aware that *Parsifal* was not a work of strict Catholic orthodoxy and that it included a number of 'impure' elements about which theologians would no doubt have plenty to say; and he therefore protected himself, tactically, from any untoward comment by insisting on the 'religious festival' aspect of the work, in the literal sense. Hence it happens that productions of *Parsifal* may easily be unbalanced and tend to become slow, solemn ceremonies uninterrupted by any change of tone, since everything must be 'ennobled' in the interests of edification and sanctification. This uniform attitude hardly benefits the work either ideologically or musically, since it abolishes the unevennesses, the ambiguities and the contradictions of the drama and thereby reduces its significance.

Playing down contrasts and forcing every characteristic into a single mould often does no more than emphasize the *length* of the work, which was the chief argument against it and an easy target for Wagner's enemies. Time in the theatre is of course distorted automatically when words are replaced by music. The long sequence of the composer's phrases results in distending the duration of the music, sometimes excessively, time as *speech* being essentially different from time as *song*. As we know, Wagner 'set' his librettos without any great modification of the text that he had already written; and it sometimes seems as though he felt *obliged* to write music to support this already existing text. At such moments skill is needed to bring the duration of the music closer to that of the words, in order to avoid a 'break' between the two. Although the resulting oscillations in the tempo are not marked in the score, they are logically justified by the text and the sense of the declamation, as in the old recitative (from which they certainly derive) in which music serves as a support to the dramatic information provided by the text. At other moments, when the verbal text emphasizes some symbol, some key idea or some turning point in the narrative or the action (the same entities regarded as belonging to the past in the first case and to the present in the second), the text must be given added importance by broadening the musical discourse. In other words, the score must breathe according to the fluctuations of the dramatic text, or there will be a danger of asphyxia . . .

Perhaps the greatest problem about these long scenes is to understand the evidence of their construction. They certainly cannot be explained by any pre-established pattern. I think it was Strauss who observed that Wagner's was the first music in which forms never return literally, are never repeated. As the music progresses, it carries all the thematic elements with it, linking them in new ways, placing them in different relations to each other, showing thcm in unfamiliar lights and giving them unexpected meanings.

This, of course, brings us to the problem of the *Leitmotivs*, which used to be catalogued in the mechanical way that Debussy, in particular, criticized so sarcastically . . . *Leitmotivs* are in fact anything but the traffic signals to which they have been mistakenly compared, for they have a double virtue – both poetic and dramatic, as well as formal. They are essential to the structure of both music and drama as well as to the different characters and situations. Their evolution is a kind of 'time-weave', an integrating of past and present, as I have said before; and they also imply dramatic progression. For their poetic meaning I cannot do better than quote Claudel again:

> Like the *Leitmotiv* that ensures that the actor on the stage is not simply the severed ghost of that blind, distant character, both eternal and ineffable (both existent and non-existent, as in dreams), the wound inflicted on us by a familiar voice. Like those themes which surround us on all sides, repeating and answering each other like confused hunting calls in the woods.

Baudelaire, too, writing in 1861 when he knew only Wagner's early works, was struck and fascinated by the same phenomenon. The structural power of the *Leitmotivs* lies, as I have said, in their linking of present and past. It is absolutely clear how Wagner meant their function to be understood. We first encounter the *Leitmotivs* in their simplest, most elementary and directly recognizable form, either separated from each other by long partition-like silences or quite apart from any other context, so that any fusion between them seems impossible, and the more so because they are presented as absolutely stable musical ideas offering no opportunities for modification or transformation. Melody, harmony and rhythm seem combined to form an entity as striking and as static as possible. This static quality seems to have been deliberately increased by the fact that the motives are repeated sequentially, and are therefore all the more resistant to any kind of change. Their transformability is at first concealed in order to increase our surprise when it is gradually revealed. Particularly in *Parsifal* Wagner in fact makes play with the possibilities of dissociation provided by his material, employing this in many different forms, ranging from allusion to paraphrase. Sometimes it will be an isolated fragment of melody, or even a simple interval, that begins to dominate all the melodic links. Sometimes the allusion will be no more than a harmonic function, or even a characteristic chord. Sometimes a rhythmic cell will suddenly unite thematic materials that had until then been quite unconnected. I have given instances only of transitions from one motive to another; but by a skilful process of first separating and then recomposing basic elements the composer sometimes effects a real change of identity in the motives, so that we find cases of genuine ambiguity in which a motive, at this point in its evolution, can be related to more than one original model. What I said earlier of the *legibility* of some forms and the difficulty of grasping the complex nature of others – a phenomenon that determines the fluctuations in the big overall structure – is equally applicable to Wagner's motive technique. It often happens that the motive is perfectly 'legible', the symbol completely clear; but it happens just as often that the motive is veiled in ambiguity and that the allusion is indirect and to be understood almost unconsciously. These different degrees of reference, ranging from the open to the obscure and from the plain to the esoteric, enrich the musical texture in an organic way. Wagner's technique in this matter is extremely subtle; and as I said earlier, quoting Strauss, no theme preserves its original integrity; Order never triumphs again over the Maze. What we find is a world of cross-references appealing to different degrees of perception and belonging to romantic creation rather than to the theatrical imagination as such. The *Leitmotiv* signifies and implies more than the simple signal to which it has often been reduced in the minds of both admirers and critics. It may of course on occasion serve such a purpose and nothing more, but this still remains one of its most primitive functions.

There is a passage in *La Prisonnière* where Proust expresses how the *Leitmotiv* works on the listener's intelligence and emotions:

I realized to the full the reality of Wagner's work when I considered the insistent yet fugitive themes that appear in an act and vanish only to return. At one moment they may be distant, dormant, almost detached from the whole, but at others they will, despite their vagueness, be so pressing and so close, so intimate, so organic and so visceral that they seem to be the return of a nerve pain rather than a motive.

And he goes on to explain in detail:

In passages where a lesser musician would claim that he was depicting a squire or a knight by giving each character the same distinguishing music, Wagner creates a different kind of 'reality'. Each time his squire appears, he is an individual figure, both complex and simple, making his own contribution to the huge web of sound by a gay, feudal-sounding clash of lines. This gives the music the effect of fullness – the fact that it is indeed filled with so many different musics, each of which has its own personality. A personality, or the momentary impression made by some aspect of nature.

The path traced by the motives as they make their way through the work raises a difficult problem, and one that has not been explored, namely that of *tempo*. I have talked about melodic, harmonic and rhythmic modifications; but in speaking of rhythm I have always confined myself strictly to the sense of the 'rhythmic figure' governing the appearance of motives, the internal metrical relationships implied. But the speed at which they are stated – and at which these metrical relationships are finally regulated, and then perceived by the listener – varies throughout the work. This forms part of the general *ductility*, or lability, of the *Leitmotivs*, which it will be well to discuss initially from this angle of *tempo*, since it probably makes the greatest (and indeed an almost physiological) effect on the listener. I think it was Schoenberg who pointed out that the 'themes' of the classical period were composed with a more or less precise speed in mind, certainly precise enough to need no other indication than their character: any overstepping of the limits determined by the given *tempo* could result only in the various elements of the music becoming meaningless, the harmony becoming confused, the rhythm incoherent and even the intervals of the melody losing their proper relationship. Even in Beethoven, the master analyst of thematic composition, no distending of the tempo is admissible, however simple the form in which figures may appear. It is not until Wagner that we find musical material that is both complete and incomplete, acceptable both as definitive and indeterminate and belonging simultaneously to the categories of past and future, with the present lying between the two, without any distortion of the internal logic of the music. The relationship between the constituent elements is supple enough to permit thematic figures both to preserve their individual character and also to acquire a different *potential*.

Such musical material is, in fact, *neutral* without being in any way devoid of character; and this neutral quality enables the composer to integrate it easily into the different contexts into which it fits and adapts itself. The same is true of melodic intervals and harmonic correspondences. Wagner emphasizes the *interval* and that multiple ambiguity by which it may be adapted to a number of different harmonic contexts. He creates the *event*, which is the conjunction of a melodic interval and a harmonic complex consisting of two hitherto neutral potentialities meeting in a single, unique encounter. This musical material, which is in a perpetual state of 'becoming', is probably Wagner's most exclusively personal invention. Here for the first time we find an emphasis on *uncertainty*, indeterminacy, a definite rejection of *finality* and an unwillingness to stabilize musical events before they have exhausted their potential powers of evolution and renewal.

What about the actual harmonic language within which this 'ductility' manifests itself? The existence of a dualism in Wagner's harmonic language has long been established, the diatonic on the one hand and the chromatic on the other, as in the time of Monteverdi and Gesualdo, whose madrigals provide many examples and employ virtually the same symbolism. The chromatic symbolizing darkness, doubt and grief and the diatonic light, affirmation and joy – this imagery has hardly changed for three centuries, though Wagner may use it more frequently and on a larger scale. I therefore find it difficult to speak of the diatonic as 'archaic' or the chromatic as corresponding to some 'modernizing' tendency. (If we do make use of such terminology, then it must be applied equally to Monteverdi and Gesualdo, which hardly makes sense.) In greatly expanding the tonal vocabulary Wagner makes use of the dialectic movement/rest, stability/imbalance; or, in other words – to employ an expression that I have used in other contexts – the unequivocal *legibility* of the diatonic alternates with the equivocal, ambiguous nature of chromatic structures. This accounts for the varying degrees of difficulty in apprehending the functions of the harmonic language as it evolves from the simple to the complex. It is between these two extremes that Wagner's polyphony moves, as Theodor Adorno has shown in a passage of perceptive analysis:

> We must remember that all the most richly orchestrated works of Wagner's maturity are without exception based on an almost academic four-part harmony. This very often takes the following form – the melody in the top line, a stationary bass interpreted in changing terms – middle parts providing a harmonic paraphrase and moving chromatically.

(He goes on to explain this in a way that I do not find convincing:

> [Wagner's use of] four-part harmony is explained by the respect felt by the dilettante, the 'outsider', for the textbook chorale, and perhaps also by the gesture of the composer beating time. The chorale represents the perfect harmonic scheme in which each beat in the bar coincides with a chord.

If this is true of any composer, it is of Berlioz rather than Wagner.)
Meanwhile Adorno continues:

> The harmonies and their progression, but not the harmonic writing, are full of
> Wagner's liberating spirit, and it often seems as though by his academic use of
> non-academic chords this harmonic revolutionary wished to conciliate the
> masters whom he had deserted.

There is unquestionably an astonishing contradiction between Wagner's
steady four-part writing, this persistent, *residual* use of an academic formula
and the often extreme boldness of his harmonic progressions. Adorno's
analysis ends with these words:

> All these chords refer the listener to the familiar past with its ideas of passing
> notes, alterations and suspensions. But as they eventually become the centre
> of the musical process, they acquire the power of what has never been before –
> of something in fact 'new'.

Described thus, Wagner's language may appear to enjoy a special privilege, an extra dimension. And in fact this complaint has often been made
by those who have pointed to the absence of real polyphony in his music,
despite some spectacular combinations of themes. It has been pointed out
that Bach's combining of *dynamic* themes was a much greater feat than the
manipulating of absolutely static motives that can be attached to an im-
mobile overall scheme. In Wagner's polyphonic harmony the two middle
voices between the top line and the bass are principally used to *give life* to
the overall progressions and this, it is true, has little to do with what is
generally understood by polyphony. But does not the evolution of the
musical language imply an evolution of the very idea of polyphony? Counterpoint and harmony are distinguished academically because at one stage in
the development of the tonal language the two notions did not in fact
coincide except on the hypothesis of a mutual dependence. Harmonic
functions became increasingly differentiated as the language evolved, and
the more they did so, the more necessary it became for counterpoint and
harmony to achieve a kind of symbiosis in order to exist concurrently. (The
fugues in Beethoven's opus 106 and opus 133 are rare examples of counterpoint 'rebelling' against the increasing claims of harmonic functions.)
With Wagner a point was reached at which the two ideas are on the brink
of amalgamating and producing an overall phenomenon in which the vertical and the horizontal are projected on to each other. In this way we find tonal
functions increasingly undermined by the individual power of intervals; and
it was from this point that the style of first Schoenberg, and then Berg and
Webern, developed. Speaking of Wagner's chords, Adorno draws the conclusion that 'they become wholly intelligible only in the light of the most
advanced contemporary musical material in which the link with Wagner's

transitional language has been finally broken'. I believe that this conclusion is even more significant if applied to the fusion, or amalgamation, of counterpoint and harmony, necessitating an entirely new formulation of the idea of polyphony. Of course Wagner's obstinate insistence on uninterrupted polyphonic movement and continuity involves a number of stylistic mannerisms to which others have pointed before me. It is easy, in particular, to recognize in his innumerable broken cadences the seams – one might almost say scars – resulting from amputating the customary clausulae of a 'normal' discourse. It would often be possible to restore if not the first version of a text, at least the traditional idea from which it sprang and which was later *corrected* for reasons of style. There are instances of this 'warping' even in *Parsifal*; but it should doubtless be regarded as an indispensable method of unifying the musical discourse.

The use of the orchestra in *Parsifal* has always been judged by standards different from those used in judging Wagner's other works. Debussy, who was merciless in criticizing the sonorities of the *Ring*, had the greatest admiration for those of *Parsifal*, as can be seen from *Pelléas*. He also expressed his admiration in words when he wrote that, 'In *Parsifal* there are orchestral sonorities that are unique and hitherto unknown, of great nobility and power. It is one of the greatest monuments ever raised to the imperishable glory of music.' Even Stravinsky, who was allergic to the performance that he saw at Bayreuth, nevertheless wrote *Zvezdoliki*, in which the writing for winds is very close to that in *Parsifal* – even leaving on one side the implicit mysticism of Balmont's text. The 'simplicity' of the orchestration in *Parsifal* compared with Wagner's other works is primarily a matter of stylistic evolution, of the quality of the musical material and the general *tempo* of the work. It is more than probable that Wagner reduced the complexity of his sonorities as a result of what he learned from hearing the *Ring* in his own theatre at Bayreuth. It would be natural that he should compose the score of *Parsifal* with Bayreuth in mind and a practical knowledge of its acoustics. He made greater use here than in his other works of the contrast between pure and mixed timbres. There are passages in which the listener *recognizes* an instrument that is clearly emphasized in a solo passage, and the orchestra is *legible*. There are others in which Wagner uses mixtures in order to mask the identity of the different instruments and, by fusing their timbres, achieves an overall sonority within a kind of imaginary *timbre continuum*. Here as elsewhere Wagner boldly pursues his goal – the constant oscillation between knowledge and illusion.

Has my analysis of the constituents of his language been so thorough that I have destroyed its poetry and its mystery? Proust observed wryly that, 'With Wagner, the sadness of the poet, however great, is consoled and surpassed – which unfortunately means partly destroyed – by the sheer delight of the craftsman.' Wagner did in fact lay himself open to many, often malicious attacks by his love of system and his superrational attempts to systematize the irrational. Nevertheless he found a defender in Proust, and for reasons which might seem surprising unless one bears in mind that this was in fact a question of self-defence, Balzac (and by implication Proust himself) having often been accused of working from one day to the next without paying much attention to overall design. I should like to quote the following paragraph of Proust, because it seems to me of capital importance if we are to understand the phenomenon of 'agglomeration' in Wagner:

> The other musician who fascinated me at this time was Wagner, who would select some beautiful thing that he had written and use it as a theme which seemed to him, in retrospect, necessary in a work that had not entered his head when he wrote the original piece: and then after composing first one mythological opera and then another, suddenly realized that he had written a tetralogy, so that he must have felt the same sense of intoxication as Balzac, who considered his works both as an outsider and as their author and, finding in one a Raphaelesque purity and in another an evangelical simplicity, suddenly concluded in retrospect that they would be better as a cycle in which the same characters would recur, and then, to complete this, added a final, finishing touch, which was the sublimest of all.

Examining, rather than simply describing, the aesthetic advantages of this happy chance, Proust continues:

> The unity thus achieved is profound and not factitious, or it would have disintegrated like so many of the systems by which mediocre writers try, by the ingenious use of titles and subtitles, to give the impression of having followed a single transcendent overall pattern. Not factitious, perhaps even more real for being profound and for springing from a moment of enthusiasm when the writer discovers that all that is necessary is to join the different pieces into a unity that has been unconscious and therefore vital rather than logical, and has neither hampered the variety nor damped the ardour of the writing. It resembles (the whole, I mean) a separate, independent work produced on the spur of the moment, not as the artificial development of any plan but taking an organic place among the others.

Although for the argument's sake Proust exaggerates the part played by improvisation and its retrospective justification, the point that he makes so clearly is the organic growth of Wagner's forms. It is true that the potentialities of his thematic material are systematically exhausted – and by thematic material I mean instrumental combinations as well as melodic intervals – but his ideas, in the strict sense of the word, *proliferate*. At the outset Wagner's invention was accused of being nothing more than an exaggeratedly mechanistic idea, and later he was dismissed as a cynical illusionist, overbearing and constricting in effect. Commenting on 'the complexity, the amalgamlike character of not only Wagner's sonorities . . . not only the timbre of his music but his whole work', Claudel continues, in the passage from which I have already quoted:

In the same way as the sound must be such that it leaves none of our auditive fibres untouched but nourishes and paralyses them all, so the music must command and absorb all our powers of attention and imagination and not simply our ears, putting those powers into an enchanted sleep from which there is no escape and in which we simmer as in a magic cauldron.

And in fact it is not possible to listen critically, and to *Parsifal* in particular. This is due not only to its resemblance to a religious rite, but also to the fact that the whole drama takes place in totally unreal surroundings, whether it be Montsalvat or Klingsor's castle, which appear and disappear by magic and belong to what Adorno calls a world of 'fantasmagoria'. And in this Wagner realized the romantics' dream, realized and surpassed it. In Weber and Berlioz the illusion is 'credible', whereas in Wagner it is intended to destroy all illusions, in the same way as Klingsor's domain is transformed into a desert. People have laughed at Wagner's own humour when – probably sick of realistic magic 'effects' and the ludicrous problems they involved ('ladies being hoisted to the roof by strings attached to their bottoms') – he longed for an ideal performance free of such wretched technical considerations. This critical sense of humour showed, at the very least, that he no longer had any illusions about *Illusion*!

As for the interpretation of the work, I can only refer to the various ideas that I have expressed about its individual constituents in the hope that I have been explicit enough on each point not to have to embark on a small manual of practical application . . .

I should, however, like to say something more about the word 'romanticism' and the many misunderstandings to which it has given rise. My attitude may be summed up in a quip I made not long ago – that it was Wagner, not Wilhelm II, who wrote *Parsifal* . . . by which I meant that Wagner's musical gestures do not seem to me either emphatic or grandiloquent; that real greatness can do without the exaggerated demonstrations that amount to parodies; and that since the composer's intentions are as clear as possible in the score, it is pointless to attempt a higher 'yield' with the attendant risk of caricaturing the work. In *Parsifal* particularly, Wagner's romanticism is interior; the impact of the music itself is quite sufficient without any additional 'expressiveness' that contradicts rather than strengthens that impact, by employing a hollow rhetoric that is quite superfluous.

I have no wish to embark on an apologia, but I should also like to say something about speeds, *tempo*. I will not go into boring details, but I have discovered from the Bayreuth archives that the timing of the second act under Levi in 1882 was 62 minutes, against my own 1966 timing of 61 – and this is the fastest-moving of the three acts! The timing for Act III, where tempi are predominantly slow, was 75 minutes in 1882 and 70 in 1966. These variations are, proportionately, not extreme. And they are much the same for Act I (107:100 minutes). I am quite aware that 'absolute' time has nothing to do with the matter and that many other factors – different from, and more important than clock time – enter into the perception of a theatrical whole. Even so, the general balance and distribution of time provide irrefutable evidence; and in a long work this is one of the greatest problems – knowing at each moment, whether consciously or not, where one has got to – what lies behind one and what lies ahead – and thus being able to establish a flexible cruising speed that allows for tension and relaxation. Yes, even in *Parsifal* the 'breathing' of the music must never be inhibited by any vague feeling that the sacred is immovable – or immutable . . .

This incidentally brings me to the question of traditions. Wieland Wagner said all that needed saying about the stage production, in an essay entitled 'Denkmalsschutz für Wagner', and I can only apply his conclusions to the *reading* of the score, i.e. the deciphering of that mass of hieroglyphs and signs. Every performance moves, through this process of deciphering, towards an unknown goal. The work preserves a potential novelty for all those who themselves preserve this desire for novelty, for the unknown. What is the use of an object that is dead and buried beneath the dust of the past? That is, perhaps, the ultimate lesson of the *Gesamtkunstwerk* – that the total work of art exists only as a fictitious absolute that is continually retreating. I would say only this, paraphrasing Claudel: that it is absolutely essential that we should overtake the voice that we hear calling us, without it losing its note of inaccessibility and irreparability, the inexhaustible source of our delight and our despair.

27

The Ring

TIME RE-EXPLORED[1]

Discussions of romanticism, and of Wagner, still proliferate. The taboo word 'romanticism' is understood in very different ways, depending on whether the aim is to rescue its magic or to expose its false claims. There is no doubt that for many people today romanticism represents a lost paradise in a world that has no room for sentiment, dreaming or any kind of poetical vaporizing; the things that arouse nostalgia are shams stylized in accordance with very bourgeois ideas. Romanticism is in that case synonymous with a kind of short-sighted idealism devoid of any social signifiance. 'Artists' enjoy all the rarest privileges, even those of Orpheus, although they themselves drift absently about, any sense of responsibility to themselves or to the rest of the world having vanished. In the eyes of such people genius consists in being beautiful and saying nothing, according to the accepted formula. The longer it persists, the closer this view of romanticism clings to what were the mannerisms of the age, providing a class frightened by thinking and by the pressure of actual events with something to dream about, a refuge from presentday realities, which they find altogether too horrific . . . They discover in romanticism both a pretext and an excuse for rejecting everything in contemporary life that exposes their own appetites and weaknesses.

But what really remains after this obstinate attempt – perseverance being a cardinal virtue in such cases – to analyse romanticism, especially musical romanticism, according to our modern criteria? And what are we to think of this hotch-potch in which sociology finds itself, either by choice or by necessity, confused with aesthetic ideas of which the least that can be said is that they are pretty superficial? Parodying Adorno's followers is an easy game! According to them the chromaticisms that weaken the feeling of tonality in Wagner reflect the doubts and contradictions of a fully developed capitalist society with only one fundamental desire, its own extinction . . . Or

---

[1] 'Le Temps re-cherché', from the 1976 Bayreuth Festival programme book for *Das Rheingold*, pp. 1–17 and 76–80. Boulez conducted the *Ring* at Bayreuth that year in the new production by Patrice Chéreau. [M.C.]

this – the richness of Wagner's instrumentation, the size of his orchestra, his use of unusual instruments in order to extend the range of timbres are simply the hallmarks of a capitalist bourgeoisie hungry for wealth and power and anxious to display its purchasing power by the crudest exhibitionism … Ideas of this kind invite absurd exaggeration, for here deep analysis of stylistic motivation is replaced by examination of the 'physiognomy' of works as in Johann Caspar Lavater's 'phrenology'.

This same approach is naturally most in favour when dealing with something less volatile than music, and the theatre lends itself even more easily, by its very nature, to 'sociological' extrapolations. Wagner's theatre has suffered more than any other from this epidemic, so that with the *Ring* we know everything about mid-nineteenth-century European history from the revolutions of 1848 to the establishment of the German Empire, and may count ourselves fortunate to have so far been spared the colonial age, since Wagner was neither English nor French … His work does, of course, fall within this period of European history and was affected by the repercussions of the chief events of the day. But in the case of the finished work is there any need to have recourse to all these co-ordinates in order to grasp its stature and significance? Do we not run the risk of missing all the essential features that make a 'landscape' if we insist on looking at it through the eyes of geometricians and surveyors? It is really a case of the old commonplace that the beauty of a forest cannot be judged by measuring the height of its trees …

What is more, the insistence on sources that may underlie the creative process but nevertheless remain no more than sources, seems to me clear evidence of a tendency to shirk the real problems, which lie at the heart of the work itself and not in the circumstances that accompanied its birth or even compelled its completion. What a delight it would be for once to discover a work without knowing *anything* about it, like the explorer who discovers a temple in Mexico or in Asia completely overgrown with vegetation, or the archaeologist who embarks on research into a forgotten civilization with nothing to guide him but a fragment of pottery! Such men are really forced to think hard about the work or the fragment, and to discover the really intrinsic nature of the creation of one simple object – it may be no more. Shall we ever make up our minds to disregard context and to forget the time factors so relentlessly insisted upon by the history books? Shall we ever manage to ignore the circumstances, banish them from our memories and bury them in oblivion and take the interior essence of a work as our only guide? Shall we be able *in the first place* to lose 'time' in order to rediscover it later with a new validity?

We are often told that a work is either revolutionary or reactionary, but it is particularly hard in Wagner's case to refrain from facile biographical references and to go beyond mere 'circumstances', which are no more than obstacles to our search. Nothing is easier than to discover a parallel between his dramatic ideology and the evolution of his personal position. Nothing is more misleading and deceptive than such oversimplification and, rather than referring perpetually to Bakunin and Wilhelm, Marx or Krupp, we should ignore them from the outset. Invoking their aid is no subtitute for discovering in the work itself the revolutionary ferment and the reactionary elements as these appear in the actual musical and dramatic structure. After all, Wagner was an exact contemporary of Büchner, but he did not write *Woyzeck* ...

If we look at the vast achievement of the *Ring*, we instinctively use two words not usually found in alliance – romanticism and structure – for the *Ring* represents an attempt to restructure entirely the whole world of myth, drama and music. This restructuring has a natural, logical effect on the actual principles governing performance and on integrating such performance into the life of society. To start with the logic of the situation, we can understand immediately that the *Ring* in particular is quite incompatible with normal performance routines and with the arrangements implicit in the ordinary workings of a theatre. The structure of the work makes it impossible to include it in a day-to-day schedule, in which the product on sale depends on the daily supply. Opera houses are often rather like cafés where, if you sit near enough to the counter, you can hear waiters calling out their orders: 'One *Carmen*! And one *Walküre*! And one *Rigoletto*!' Wagner loathed this system and railed against it, not basically for reasons of personal prestige any more than from purely moral motives. His *amour propre* was no doubt offended, but at a much deeper level he rejected the whole system and the relationship with the public which that system presupposed. The function of a performance, he felt, should be altogether different, since the myths presented had nothing in common with amusement – *divertissement* in Pascal's sense. Performances of Wagner were incompatible with existing theatrical norms and with the conventions in which operatic performance were bogged down. What was needed was an entirely new musical and theatrical structure, and it was this that he gradually created.

Was it in the text that this transformation of the theatre originated? Critics have certainly not spared those texts, rescued though they may be by Wagner's music. Without disputing their dramatic validity, and even recognizing Wagner's attempt to create a language of his own, they have decried their actual literary quality. It must be acknowledged that Wagner's linguistic explorations were very different in quality from those of Joyce; his frequent use of alliteration and his poetic vocabulary in general do not reveal an exceptional literary genius. The sum total is very unequal in quality – a great deal of pedantry, a certain amount of virtuosity, plenty of prosy passages and the occasional magic phrase. And yet these texts were the subterfuge needed in order to introduce into the theatre the world of the epic and the novel, and to present characters whose visual representation is sometimes hard to imagine. There is a perpetual conflict between the world of epic and the world of romance. The stock characters of legend suddenly acquire an extremely pointed and penetrating psychological dimension; and although the dramatic action is motivated primarily by the characters of the protagonists, or the complexity of their reactions, Wagner in case of need – and quite unpredictably – has recourse to the crudest sorts of magic and juggling. The events of the drama and even the physical appearance of the characters – dwarfs and giants, not to mention gods – elude realistic representation. They more or less take for granted an imaginary reader aware of that world of myth which finds more powerful expression in narrative than in dramatic poetry.

It happens thus that any demand for strict homogeneity is damaging to the *Ring* from the outset. Meanwhile, however, it is the music that is actually charged with the structure of these myths and their characters, music that will articulate characters, gestures and actions. The mythical drama will become effective through the musical structure, whether 'thanks to' or 'by means of' it. Conventional elements in the stage action, the dialogue and the subdivision of the acts, will be absorbed by the musical substance, which will transform this primary material, giving it new dimensions and eventually a far more essential significance, an infinitely more striking stature. This is most true of the *Ring*, the perfect instance and all the more interesting because we can observe the evolution of its musical structure as the work progresses. In such works as *Tristan* and *Parsifal*, where the design is clearly circumscribed, the problems are not so great. Moreover those works were written within a single period of time during which the composer's ideas did not change but remained centred on one precise task, swiftly completed.

The *Ring*, on the other hand, provides us with the history of Wagner's evolution as a musical and dramatic thinker. We are often reminded that the creation of this work extended over a quarter of a century, and much has been made of the changes and chances inseparable from so long a period of gestation, and of the difference in musical style between the beginning and the end of this *opus magnum*. It has rightly been emphasized that the text remained mostly unchanged while the music shows profound transformations. This makes the *Ring* an exceptional case in the history of music, whereas equivalents could be found in literature, though probably not in either poetry or the drama. Goethe's *Faust*, for instance, consists of two clearly contrasted panels, and we shall find better examples in Balzac's novels, in Proust and better still in Montaigne's *Essais*, where successive editions contain the same superimpositions, contradictions, additions and cancellations that we find in the *Ring*. The *Essais* constitute a kind of philosophical journal in which the author keeps returning to reflect on the same fundamental concepts, and it is tempting to think of the *Ring* as a kind of journal in which the composer keeps returning to the same thematic material and presenting us with his reflections and variations on these basic ideas.

The case of Wagner is unique in the history of music. It is true that we have Beethoven's sketchbooks, in which we can trace the subterranean work leading from the initial approach to the final form of an idea, and the path is sometimes long and hard to follow – all the transformations of a musical idea being documented in great detail so that we can see, for instance, the theme of the Ninth Symphony's finale developing from the early Bonn sketches to the definitive form that it took in Vienna. But in Beethoven's case these transformations do not occur within the course of a single work; they are employed at most episodically, from one work to the next, in such a way that we can foresee the composer's final decision. The whole process takes place, as it were, below ground and is revealed in sketches that remain strictly preliminary in character. With Wagner, on the other hand, we have musical substance that is determined – and strikingly determined from the outset – being modified under our very eyes during the course of the work, developing, taking on a new coherence and establishing a kind of genealogy, like the characters in a novel.

Wagner's themes seem to my mind to have an existence quite apart from the characters, the actions and the symbols that they represent; and I admit that their intense life and increasing activity often appear to me more extraordinary, more prodigious in their energy and power of radiation than the characters themselves, which are limited in their stage presence and potential existence. It is here that we find the most radical difference between the literary and the musical texts as the work advances: the musical structure proliferates so richly that it annexes, literally absorbs, the characters of the drama, who remain fossilized in a 'previous' existence according to obsolete conventions. Some of the musical themes gradually disappear from the score, as though the composer had lost interest in their musical material, or abandoned them as the victims of whatever detail of the story they represented. Other themes, which may have been comparatively unimportant at their first appearance, develop out of all proportion to our expectations. It seems as though the composer himself only gradually discovered their full significance and all the potentialities of certain figures; looking at passages in the already finished score, he gives them a new perspective, and in so doing confers on them an entirely new significance. Thus it happens that reading the score today we are aware that certain initially important themes are in fact destined to disappear while others, which make only a passing appearance, are destined to acquire increasing importance and even to become essential later in the work. From the outset we see these themes in a light in which the composer himself only later saw them; and this has an intense fascination, infinitely greater than anything in the actual drama, which is, when all is said and done, not very complex!

What, in fact, are the actual stage events, however complicated, compared with the complexity of the musical ideas themselves and their evolution? Watching this vast musical spectacle in which we have become acquainted with each motive, seeing some disappear and others reappear and following their existence and its transformations, we are in the same position as the narrator in Proust returning after years of absence to a party at the Guermantes. The motives that one thought of as still young men are already white-haired . . . It is hard to believe in their transformation; their youthfulness is still deeply impressed on our memories, and here we suddenly meet them on the threshold of old age! Nor is it only this impression of the sudden stopping of time that recalls Proust. Wagner also makes very conscious use of memory, the shock produced by allusions to past situations and events, the famous *madeleine*, so to speak! Debussy's *mot* about *Leitmotivs* being signposts was altogether too facile. Of course *Leitmotivs* used in the simplest way do tell us clearly things that we need to know and the characters of the drama have not yet realized. They warn us of elements in the situation to which they provide a key, furnishing us with additional knowledge that the characters on stage do not possess. But this obvious, placard-like use of the *Leitmotiv* is very far from being the only one: and the further we advance in the work, the more complex and ambiguous the relations become, taking on different meanings to the point at which direct references become the exception. This attitude is reflected in Wagner's technical handling of the motives.

At the beginning of the work he makes considerable use of what may be called a neutral, purely interstitial weave, in which important motives appear from time to time in order to characterize some gesture or emphasize some allusion; or he will employ the same type of motive figuration to organize a scene or give a whole panel its right place in the overall drama. This neutral, interstitial texture preponderates in the recitatives, where it acts as a conventional sign for commonplace, everyday exchanges. But as the work develops, this interstitial texture becomes progressively rarer and is replaced, even in recitative dialogue, by a continuity based on the development and conjunction of motives. There are some scenes composed entirely of motives with no neutral, conventional signs, only a totally significant network completely and exclusively relevant to the work. Instrumental texture in such scenes becomes extremely close – close but not always compact, always in constant evolution and creating a world increasingly independent of the stage. At such moments in the *Ring* there is something like a duality between the worlds of the drama and of the music. The world of the music becomes far richer than that of the drama and tends, by its sheer power of proliferation, to make an exclusive claim on our attention.

The motives show a strong tendency to become autonomous, with the stage action serving perpetually as pretext and providing explanations – in fact the dramatic text becomes, literally, a musical pretext. The worlds of the text and the music, continually corroborating each other, establish an increasingly complex relationship, often to the point of becoming rivals; and in this competition the world of the music often manifests its superiority by the richness of its texture, the multiplicity of its meanings and by its sheer range. Wagner's power of conviction as a composer is greater – spectacularly greater – than his power of conviction as a dramatist, although it remains quite clear that the composer would not have existed without the dramatist and it is incidentally, difficult to imagine the symphonies that he wanted to write at the end of his life, though this is a fascinating subject for speculation. Can we imagine a musical texture so rich in allusions and internal relationships without a dramatic pretext and with no characters or situations as objects of reference? The question can never be answered, and the *Siegfried Idyll* is the only indication we have of Wagner's potential as a symphonic composer . . .

What means did Wagner employ to create the increasingly precise and complex musical network enclosing the drama? If his motives were no more than motives in the classical sense, they would not grip the listener with the same intensity. After all, there are extremely striking and pregnant motives in Beethoven, unforgettable things. But Wagner's motives hold our attention from the outset by something fundamentally different: their malleability in time. Although his motives make their original appearance in some given tempo – at a clearly defined speed, that is – they are never limited exclusively to that tempo on their later appearances, or at least in very rare cases. They are in fact eminently transformable and adaptable in both directions. They may either develop into actual autonomous organisms over a long period, entirely self-enclosed – like the first appearance of the 'Valhalla' theme which is twice repeated in its entirety, first preparing and then supporting the text; or, at the other extreme, they may be reduced to furtive accompaniment figures emphasizing meanings in the text. When Siegfried, for instance, compares the toad to a fish, the 'Nibelungen' and 'Rhine' motives appear for four bars side by side, attached to each other, only to disappear immediately without leaving any apparent trace in the musical web beyond the immediate point of literal illustration.

This oscillation between two extremes is also observable in other areas beside that of structural importance. It is even more noticeable in the actual substance of the motives, which is not definitively stated in terms of musical time, although this seems at first to be the case. For centuries, of course, contrapuntists have made play with such distortion of time, and in fact it was one of the basic principles of *ars nova*. There is no need, however, to go back to medieval texts, probably unknown to Wagner in any case; we have only to turn to Bach in order to realize the importance of temporal transformations of a theme, more particularly in fugues – the *Art of Fugue* itself providing an example of extreme virtuosity. There we see augmentations and diminutions, that halve or double the time, furnishing the fundamental elements of the structure, while the whole polyphonic scaffolding rests on a *cantus firmus* obtained by the expansion of a chorale. But in Bach's case we are dealing with a strict hierarchy in which augmentation and diminution are part of an accepted and recognized formal code and act as an element in unifying the different polyphonic layers. Once established at a certain point in musical history, these strictly academic procedures were always used by composers with unvarying respect for their position in the code. This is certainly true of Mozart; but Beethoven too, although an iconoclast in many other ways, always observed the formal rules of canonic writing even in his freest fugues.

Neither Wagner nor Berlioz saw any need for this codification, which seemed to them absurd, archaic and totally contrary to the fluidity at which they aimed in their own music, which demanded its own musical time. It was precisely this that formed the novelty of Wagner's motifs, which are not only unattached to any definite or definitive tempo but obey no pre-existing formal hierarchy in their transformations. These tempo transformations depend essentially on the expressive needs of the moment at which they are employed. Every reader, listener or interpreter of the score must beware of this. Because we unconsciously associate a theme with the moment at which its appearance seems most significant to us, we easily tend to try to reduce such themes to a single, given speed, the one that seems to us to suit them best. This is to contradict the very essence of most of these themes, which is to remain absolutely untied to any one speed of development. There is no question of any uncertainty in the mind of the composer himself, who was quite capable, when he wished, of firmly etching a complete, finished profile of themes that were to serve a single purpose. The other themes are essentially ambivalent in character, and the fact of that ambivalence obliged Wagner to construct them from elements that were easily transformable and of universal application. This even represents a danger, since any rising chromatic interval, even though divorced from its proper harmonic context, can easily evoke *Tristan*. Reducing the constituent elements of any theme to such simple functions has the disadvantage of making it similar in all circumstances, even those not intended or designed – in other words, all *madeleines* tend to taste alike and thus to release a confused flood of memories . . .

Many of these themes are based on arpeggios, or variations of arpeggios, and on dotted rhythms, which can easily be disassembled. Consequently we can easily see the ductibility of this material and how it lends itself to the composer's wish to adapt it to different contexts. The actual appearances of these motives in time arise from a largely unspecified matrix, in which the accent can easily be shifted from the pitch to the harmony and from the harmony to the rhythm, or vice versa. It was from this technique, so novel in its day, that Schoenberg was much later to draw consequences that tended to reduce the matrix from which themes are drawn to the pure abstraction of simple intervals, rhythmic structure and tempo indications being added only later. Berg started with a single matrix of this kind and, unlike Wagner, constructed the themes and figures needed to characterize the characters in his *Lulu*, giving each a strongly marked profile in order to differentiate them individually from the neutral, abstract matrix.

It is equally easy to see how Wagner's use of arpeggio figures in his motives led to the interpenetration – and in some cases the identification – of harmony and melody. The very beginning of the *Ring* provides a spectacular instance of this fusion, or confusion, of the two. In the famous opening of *Rheingold* the predominating harmony is created by the motionless proliferation of the same melodic material, and it would be hard to say which of these two functions is the more important, the one arising from the other and the latter non-existent without the former until the moment comes at which, by sheer accumulation, the two are indistinguishable. Elsewhere, at the end of *Walküre* for instance, the melody becomes simply the top line of the harmony, each unimaginable without the other and indissolubly linked by the same single function, the articulation of the rhythm. It was clearly a favourite device of Wagner's, and he made powerful use of it more than once during the work, exploring all the possibilities of these ambiguous relationships in order to give them maximum efficacy and to make their fusion, or con-fusion, as spectacular as possible. Wagner naturally exploited the different classical variation procedures, powerfully and often violently expanded – modifying the intervals in a melodic line on its different appearances and altering the harmonies in a succession of chords characterized by the same rhythmic figures and the same pattern of sequences. A good example is the 'Valhalla' motive, in which rhythms, chords and melodic lines preserve the same profile and these elements, however distorted, always remain recognizable. We sometimes find ourselves at the extreme point of recognition, wondering for a moment whether some rhythm or harmony really belongs to this motive or that, questioning our own associations and faced with an ambiguity that has invaded even the identity of the motive.

Wagner, as we can see, pushed the limits of 'variation' far beyond anything done earlier, even by Beethoven. It is true that in order to do so he had to change the concept of musical time and to establish the functions of time by other means, richer and more supple, both more malleable and, once again, more ambiguous in character. This meant a time infinitely capable of expansion and contraction, a perpetually shifting attitude to time-structure, whereby dimensions are fixed the moment they are grasped and then decomposed and reformed in accordance with other criteria, depending on the necessities of the dramatic and musical development. It was *transition* that gradually became Wagner's chief obsession, and this is conceivable only with material virtually divested of stability. Temporal criteria had to be progressively transformed, themes gradually losing that clear definition characteristic of Beethoven, which had exercised such a strong influence on Wagner at first. In this way the themes themselves give rise to new forms of development and radically different methods of organizing their existence and their mutual competition. The hierarchy established by the traditional language gave place to mutual exchanges and to a fluidity in the emergence of musical entities, necessitating formal relationships of a different kind.

How indeed did Wagner effect the transition from a general structure, serving as basis for the themes arising from it – to a structure in which everything is thematic? The *Ring* is the most brilliant demonstration of how this method evolved, because we can observe it actually happening during the course of the work. Such more immediately homogeneous works as *Tristan* or *Meistersinger*, on the other hand, show Wagner's ideas crystallizing at a certain moment during their preparation, while in *Parsifal* Wagner seems to be casting his glance backwards in a striking gesture, deliberately (and now with full knowledge) retracing his original journey from the theme as *statement* to the theme as *Gestalt*. The perspective of his last work, in its abbreviated presentation, seems to be the conscious – and once again retrospective – realization of a procedure gradually revealed in the *Ring* with no initial awareness of its eventual potentiality. The technique, which is unremittingly developed and gradually achieves an extraordinary subtlety, consists in using the different classical methods of thematic aggregation and then deducing from these other more complex and individual methods.

Wagner's virtuosity in the combination of themes has often been admired – in *Meistersinger*, for instance, where it is indeed spectacular. This was, of course, part of the traditional repertory of technical devices always popular with academics and employed by Berlioz himself with a specious *naïveté* – and in *Meistersinger* it was even supposed to be a symbol of academic attitudes. The contrapuntal combination of awkward themes has therefore nothing to do with any new method, even if it may be said to form part of a more general existing repertory of devices. More significant than this is the attaching of one melodic motive to another either by some specific interval or by an articulation common to both, one merging into the other and amalgamating with it to form a unity established by a rhythm, an interval or an articulation. This is the joining of two primary *Gestalts* to form a third, which is secondary and temporary rather than exclusive of either. The respective length of the motives or fragments concerned, and the pregnant nature of their constituent elements, produce an endless variety in the balance of these combinations, and in the shifts of emphasis from one to the other. There are cases in which the melodic substance of one motive is distorted by the harmony of another, obliging it to modify its intervals, harmony being the stronger of the two elements and governing the melodic line, transforming its behaviour without robbing it of its identity. There are also still more novel instances in which Wagner is not content with simply combining two motives, but makes one the *bearer* of the other, one acting as principal figure and the other serving as mere figuration. Here again the importance of the stronger, principal figure may shift at a later point in the music, where it may assume a secondary role when another principal figure makes its appearance. Such motive-work clearly implies a constant mobility and an incessant remodelling of the material, ranging from reduction to the simplest and most neutral element – a kind of lowest common multiple of the motive – to an expansion by which one motive is entrusted with the total control of the polyphonic ensemble and the organization of all the other elements based on its own organization – or to complete the metaphor, a kind of highest common factor . . . This motive-work is sometimes extremely detailed, and Wagner takes a visibly increasing delight in manipulating and arranging his motives according to new rules; yet it gives us very scanty information about the actual form of Wagner's operas, the most disputed and least elucidated of all questions. Is any real elucidation of this point in fact possible?

We might well think that, with such a mass of sound in perpetual motion, it will only very seldom be possible to distinguish anything that, according to clearly defined criteria, may be called form. Everything seems to be in a state of perpetual flux, nothing really fixed: there are times when we find ourselves wanting to grasp the form as something more than the sum total of individual moments. Wagner's time-structures therefore require a different sort of listening, a perception in accordance with the ideas of time underlying his thematic material and his whole system of development and transformation.

Commentators have not failed to emphasize Wagner's contrasting of chromaticism and diatonicism and its symbolical significance as the opposition between light and darkness, certainty and doubt, joy and sorrow. In this sense there is nothing new in such a contrast except the huge scale on which it is employed. Monteverdi and Gesualdo had already contrasted the luminous solidity of diatonic relations and the grief and uncertainty of chromaticism, quite as forcefully and in ways no less striking than Wagner's. In the time category, these two dimensions – the diatonic and the chromatic – take on a quite different significance. In any development in which the drama has a primary function and the old formal hierarchy no longer obtains, the constant transformation of themes, their possible use at any transitional point, the permanent latent presence of a great number of motives – all these contribute to produce a state of instability quite beyond the reach of any listener's attention or memory.

It is for this reason that Wagner inserts at intervals into this perpetually shifting texture certain elements to which the listener can cling as guidelines or markers. This explains his striking use of unvarying themes with immediately comprehensible musical, dramatic and symbolical meanings – Debussy's famous 'signpost' in fact, or what he called, even more maliciously, 'the faces made by the scenery' [*les grimaces du décor*]. Hence, too, the ostinato figures repeated for whole pages of a scene, rightly interpreted by Adorno as a single texture to be taken in at a single glance rather than perceived analytically as simple repetitions of a single idea. Hence the use of diatonic harmony in long stretches where nothing evolves and everything is motionless, anchored in a given tonality with scarcely any exploitation of even the crudest, most primitive possibilities. Hence, finally, those ruthless rhythmic ostinatos that sometimes become almost unendurable, until they are eventually absorbed in the mobility of a texture in which the rhythms are once again fused in ceaseless variation.

There are thus certain points in the musical discourse at which Wagner actually needs stabilizing elements to counteract the almost excessive mobility of other sections of his rhetoric, as this unfolds. He fixes on, and makes use of, at least one main stabilizing element of the musical language, whether it is tonality, figuration, a rhythmic cell or, as sometimes happens, several of these ingredients combined. The diatonic–chromatic contrast is part of a much more general technique making conscious use of the dialectic between fluid and fixed time. In the new time-structure with which Wagner endowed music he first conceived, and then realized, the absolute necessity for fundamental markers based on different, new criteria. Once these markers (which include the motives) are established, the evolution of the work's time-structure will be made clear by their distortion – a brilliant, revolutionary conception if ever there was one! – implying that the work must be thought of as an 'open' structure never 'closed' except provisionally and unwillingly.

This explains why Wagner's conclusions are so difficult and sometimes appear hasty, arbitrary and abrupt – almost brusque gestures of impatience. Yet he may, on the other hand, content himself with the conventional; and if he can find no more convincing final gesture, he will have recourse to some heroic or ingratiating apotheosis, a kind of 'happy ending'. In his strongest works he boldly faces this problem and refuses artificial solutions. Doubt and suspense – the feeling that the whole drama can start all over again – are of the very essence of Wagner's endings: nothing, least of all the musical texture, is finally stopped dead and nothing can ever be absolutely completed. There is no need to go as far as the literal solution adopted by Joyce in *Finnegans Wake* in order to feel that at the end of the *Ring* Wagner has set the scene for a further instalment of the drama. Nor need we necessarily involve Nietzsche if our minds turn instinctively to 'eternal recurrence' . . .

Wagner's conception of musical texture does, of course, entail certain dangers. If there is no other point of reference except a sense of form improvised from one moment to the next to satisfy the demands of expression, and if at the same time the composer refuses to employ already existing schemes on the grounds that their very formalism directly contradicts his dramatic purpose, there is a risk of this mobile form being governed in fact by nothing but instinct. His unwillingness to subject his constantly evolving material to the control of any exterior overriding formal methods clearly involves the possibility of excessive variation, producing an excessive overall homogeneity and resulting in the listener's inability – despite the resources mentioned above – to distinguish the different stages of the musical development. Here again Wagner's starting point was extremely traditional; and what is most striking is the fact that the links are not so much with operatic tradition as with the romantic *Lied*, with which he felt a much closer sympathy. There are scenes in *Rheingold*, and even in *Walküre*, that can be broken down into a series of *Lieder* based on a dominant idea, as in Schubert or Schumann, and articulated into the whole by recitatives, obbligato or otherwise . . .

What he continues to develop during the course of the *Ring*, and particularly towards the end, is the sense of unity in a scene firmly organized in panels, connected with each other by means of extremely elaborate transitions. The principle remains the same from beginning to end, but it is transmitted with increasing complexity and effectiveness. He exploits the contrast between the shorter, more unified and centralized scenes and others that are more deliberately heteroclite in character, where the material is both more varied and more volatile and the impression made is one of marked independence still subordinate, however, to a central control. Furthermore he will on occasion return to elements that have already been used and will either place them in a new context or insert them in the form of long quotations. This integration is most commonly effected by musical elements that are transposed and have changed their original pitch, instrumental presentation and even context. When he employs quotation, on the other hand, the music appears exactly as it did in the first place, at the same pitch and with the same instrumentation and overall context.

It is possible in studying Wagner's technique to trace a whole long German tradition, which he has, consciously or unconsciously, transformed for his own purposes. Whether it be *Lied*, variation or figured chorale, Wagner does not use these forms for what they represented in establishing a formal hierarchy – something that he detested quite as much as did Berlioz . . . They were to him all means that had to be rethought, reinvented in order to fulfil new functions. Berg had a profound understanding of the necessity of a formal scheme, provided that its substance was living matter; and he was to go further along the same road, not being able to share Wagner's aversions, which were provoked by the academic habits of his day. Thus in *Wozzeck* he successfully attempted a synthesis between a formal hierarchy – strict or free – and a musical material that is mobile and not exclusively predetermined; and by making use of this dialectic he solved problems that had hitherto seemed insoluble. He went still further in the same direction in *Lulu*, where he found himself faced with a complete, radical rethinking of the problem of form, making these formal hierarchies and their various transformations depend on the different characters and the multiple phases of the dramatic action. What Wagner conceived at the level of the theme, Berg was to conceive at the level of the formal scheme; and what would have seemed to Wagner an intolerable restriction was transcended by Berg, to become the source of a radical renewal, extending to the whole field of 'form' the same way of thinking that Wagner had applied at the local level of the musical material itself.

It was not only in these 'conceptual' areas that Wagner showed his power of invention and his irrepressible instinct for innovation; his handling of the orchestra shows quite as clearly how deeply he had thought about the subject and what practical conclusions he had drawn. The sheer richness of his orchestration, of course, makes an immediate impression by its profusion of colour and its variety of lighting. Very early in his career Wagner was confronted by orchestral realities and his orchestral practice is for that reason incredibly *realistic*. From the outset the listener is struck by his emphasizing of the different individual structures of the orchestra, by his extending of them and by his wish to separate, quite as much as to unite, their forces. Berlioz had, of course, blazed the trail both in his music and in his writings, for his *Traité* is full of ideas that were never put into practice, magnificent sketches for visionary schemes. But Wagner totally integrated into the web of his music a number of disconnected procedures and sly indications: his use of instrumental resources was logical and closely related to his own musical vocabulary. We have only to follow the evolution of his instrumental style to realize that principles that were in the first place instinctive were increasingly rationalized and gradually established a hitherto unknown relationship between the musical text and its orchestral expression, a relationship in which the functions of the orchestra are of far greater significance than any mere richness of sonority. There is a subtle relationship between the instrumentation and the structure of phrases, emphasizing their articulation and thus giving an immediate, sensory significance to what may be in itself an abstract idea.

As the *Ring* proceeds, Wagner makes increasing use of the contrast between pure and mixed colours, bringing to a fine point the art of transition from one field of sonority to another. Not content with employing real lines in which an instrument is entrusted with the whole or part of a melodic line or a harmonic group, he shows himself a master of ambiguity, creating lines that are not 'real' and do not follow the polyphonic structure closely: these 'virtual' lines intersect the 'real' polyphonic lines and present a kind of mock-analysis of them. Mahler seems to have been the only composer capable of continuing this procedure, which is extremely subtle and demands a greater virtuosity than the more spectacular virtuosity shown simply in his handling of the orchestra. It is in fact a technique of disassociation and recomposition, in which concept and reality may appear to change roles, producing exceptionally rich and far-reaching results. Wagner's use of pure, individual colours is also much more sustained than that of any composer before – or indeed after – him, since he draws the full logical conclusions of this approach, whereas Berlioz had really considered these only in the last chapter of his treatise on orchestration, and there are no more than fugitive examples of them in his music.

This emphasizing of individual groups is probably due to the large time-scale on which Wagner worked. Here again, in order to establish the relationship between static and mobile areas, he makes exclusive use of a single group of instruments, which serves to anchor the music in a clearly defined register, unless he employs the contrary procedure ... Hence we have those long passages entrusted to violins, horns, cellos or deep brass, and hence also the disappearance of some instruments from whole sections of the work. Wagner's awareness of the normal and the exceptional was unusually acute, and he employed both with great care in order to establish the general balance of the work. Every example of his orchestral imagination is perfectly calculated and 'placed' with incredible attention to detail. His sureness of touch and the apparent ease with which he works reveal a natural genius for calculating instrumental effect, something common to composers whose power of purely musical invention is not simply corroborated, but actually amplified and transfigured by instrumental inventiveness.

Does all this mean that there is no dross in Wagner's music and that his legacy consists entirely of marvels and innovations? Would the *Ring* have had such a mixed reception if it contained no contradictions? Of course we can point to clichés, tics, and mannerisms in Wagner's language – his abuse of tremolos, his excessive use of the diminished seventh, the incessant use of sequence, empty cadential formulae and the hollow rhetoric of dotted rhythms. But if it comes to that, we could point to all the other things that have become old-fashioned – heroic compensatory gestures, sentimental commonplaces, primitive martial scenes and the whole formal ritual of processions, funereal and otherwise. Disputes on such subjects were the favourite pastime of the generation that was obliged to be totally intolerant in order to survive, nor is it our intention to make any defence of these features which not only date Wagner's works but actually detract from their value. Just as we have to accept a number of invalid features in Wagner's theatrical practice because they are facts of the situation, so we have to admit that any music as rich, as profuse and as extraordinary as his carries with it a load of dross that in no way either diminishes its greatness or reduces its worth.

Among other composers Mahler presents us with similar problems, if anything more difficult to solve, perhaps because they belong to an age nearer to our own. In the full flowering of any style – not only in the case of Wagner but in every multiple efflorescence, whether it be in literature, music or architecture – contradictions must be accepted and recognized as valid, and even productive. For the last fifty years European art has been polarized in search of a style, and that search has involved a number of perfectly sterile phantoms. Now that we have a clear awareness of the dangers of an enterprise that has proved to be reductive rather than cohesive, we have learned to mistrust all ideas of style that are primarily concerned with 'purity', since they deprive us of that larger vision in which 'impurity' is largely compensated by the extent and the richness of the new territories explored. In saying this, I am thinking not of Nietzsche's classical opposition of 'Apollonian' and 'Dionysian' but rather of the opposition between accepting the fundamental irreducibles of artistic creation and refusing them – or at least reducing them by restrictive disciplines to cohesive norms. It may well be that both attitudes are necessary, according to the point of historical development reached, and that, far from contradicting, they corroborate each other, provided the perspective in which we view them is large enough.

In this way Wagner increasingly appears as a major phenomenon in a century-old synthesis. It is certainly true that his musical message, though grafted on to the dramatic, has gradually outstripped it and become detached and even contradictory. His ideology has been analysed as a passage from revolutionary utopianism to reactionary realism, which implies a betrayal of the self. But is such an analysis not perhaps too superficial? The whole *Ring* reveals a counterpoint that continues to become richer and richer – I mean the counterpoint between ideology in the accepted sense, which does in fact become pessimistic and even reactionary, and the musical ideology, which generates an increasingly subversive fermentation. The language of the musical revolution, affecting time, structures, listening and perception, is confronted by myths reflecting defeat, dissolution and the return to an earlier order. Wagner himself declared that, but for the revolution of 1848, the *Ring* would never have existed. We may accept the fact that in origin the *Ring* is a work of social criticism translated into the language of myth and allegory; but this does not automatically explain the revolutionary aspects of Wagner's drama, still less of Wagner's music.

The different lines followed by Wagner's ideology and Wagner's music make increasingly clear the fundamental contradiction in his grand design despite all his efforts. The *Ring* is in fact a test case, since it states in crude terms the problems of politics and artistic creation, more particularly since National Socialism purged the work of the superficial disruptive elements that it concealed. We are therefore faced with the question of whether revolution and art – to use Wagner's own terms – are in fact compatible; and, if so, in what way? This is a question very familiar today and one to which very different answers have been given, some naïve and others arbitrary and repressive. To put it another way, is revolution an intrinsic or an extrinsic part of a work? It often happens that the artist himself does not have, or at least cannot formulate, an answer to this question, and that the consequences of his work are entirely different from what he had foreseen, as Marx eloquently observed in the case of Balzac. Direct and ineffective propaganda, inadequately formulated, may turn out to be basically reactionary in its effect. On a rather different level from that of Wagner this has been revealingly demonstrated in recent years by American protest songs, in which subversive texts have been set to music employing the current commercial clichés. This ensured them an immediate sale but did a disservice to the cause of subversion, the songs being forgotten as quickly as they were accepted. Wagner's music is the exact antithesis of this, since his music, by its very existence, refuses to bear the ideological message that it is intended to convey.

As a matter of fact, the attempt to employ music to support an ideology, with or without the composer's consent, is centuries old, only what is today a political ideology was formerly religious. The least that can be said is that the result is disappointing. In the case of works with a verbal text, the text expresses the ideology while the music remains obstinately dumb, possessing a huge repertory of resources to express the composer's subjective feelings but none whatever to give a rational explanation of his attitude or his ideological preferences. It can thus happen that a subversive text may be wedded to reactionary music while a reactionary ideology may be belied by subversive music. Wagner does not, despite himself, escape this general rule; and for this reason I have often been puzzled by people's reactions to his attitudes. If the ideology that he claimed to be expressing in his music appears to you grotesque, or even detestable, all you need to do is to listen to the music and you will find that it contradicts what it is supposed to be saying, just as the Woodbird makes Siegfried understand the real meaning of Mime's words . . . The fire of the music purifies the junk of the text and its meaning. In any case, were there not other romantic authors who shared the ideology with which Wagner is reproached? His was by no means the first case of that strange alliance between dream and political action; we need go no further than the Prince of Homburg. As for his anti-French sentiments, they were nothing new and originated, with every justification, under the tyranny of Napoleon. The objection that can reasonably be made against Wagner is that, despite his furtive part in the Dresden revolution of 1849, he was politically behind the times; and that Sachs's famous attack on 'welsche Kunst' is only too applicable – many years later – to the no less famous enemies of Prussia. Nor is this the only area in which, particularly after 1876, we find Wagner behind the times, if we consider what was being thought and achieved elsewhere. Consider only the visual conception of the *Ring* as produced at Bayreuth in 1876, when the Impressionists had already painted some of their finest pictures. In poetry, too, the *frisson nouveau* produced by such things as Rimbaud's *Une Saison en enfer* and Lautréamont's *Les Chants de Maldoror*, which had already appeared in 1876, was something rather different from Nordic mythology, which was closer to the subjects with which writers were concerning themselves at the beginning of the century. It is hardly necessary to quote in this connection the case of Nietzsche and his bitter disillusion with every aspect of Wagner except that of composer. Other names could be added to the list, among them that of Dostoevsky . . .

The Europe in which Wagner claimed to be an ideological force was in fact the Europe of Marx and Engels, and the figure that he cut was far from a brilliant one. Wagner as dramatist and composer was in perpetual contradiction to Wagner as ideologist; on that plane, and that alone, he was and remains absolutely unrivalled and an absolutely subversive force. There is nothing surprising in the fact that two Jews, Mahler and Schoenberg, were the most distinguished heirs of this most blinkered of all anti-Semites, for his musical legacy is the privilege of those who can understand, grasp and make use of it, while his ideological heirs were such nonentities as Ernst von Wolzogen and Joseph Chamberlain – and after them a political power that was far from being a nonentity and made use not only of Wagner's music but of his ambiguous ideology to mask its brutal lust for power. The political power of National Socialism would have existed, of course, with or without music; for like all political powers, its followers were endlessly searching for intellectual justifications and attempting to give themselves a secure historical basis in 'the masterpieces of the national heritage'. Wagner's words certainly lent themselves to that purpose, but his music remains irreducible; and that is why his music is still alive while his ideology has no more than historical interest.

If Wagner's personality has been – still is, indeed – the subject of such passionate controversy, it is because his ambition was great, indeed limitless. So much the better! What we call romanticism was a great adventure, a bold undertaking of the human spirit, and it must be remembered by something more than a few heroic trifles and pathetic nostalgias. People often try to reduce it to nothing more than that – some faintly extravagant mannerisms, some eccentric attitude or cheap and obvious sentimentality. How wrong it is to see romanticism as anything so feeble as a mere consolation – as it were – for living in such hard times as ours. The claims made by Wagner's great undertaking were something very different from that; and if in some ways that undertaking failed – and failed disastrously – there is no denying that in other ways it succeeded beyond all imagination.

Essentially, Wagner stands for myth made effective by musical construction. In order to achieve this he was obliged to change the traditional structures of musical thinking – the most important of which was time; and it is a strange fact that he never refers to this primary component in any of his writings. He does, however, touch on the subject in a veiled way in his letter to Mathilde Wesendonck on the art of transition in *Tristan*. It is in his restructuring, researching of time that I find Wagner's real subversive achievement. It may perhaps seem something trivial compared with the grand revolutionary ambitions with which he set out, but I do not think so. The revolutions that, in the last resort, have the profoundest and most far-reaching results are revolutions in our mental categories, and Wagner initiated, once and for all, the irreversible processes of such a revolution.

A PERFORMER'S NOTEBOOK[1]

I

Purely practically, this Funeral March is to enable Siegfried's body to be removed from the stage. Is this in fact its only function, though sublimated? The commonplace spectacle of a procession actually conceals its real significance, giving it the appearance of a theatrical necessity, part of the musical background. Yet everyone is aware that it actually fulfils much more important functions, not only as music with profound dramatic significance but also as part of the continuous musical *explanation* of the dramatic text. Cosima's diary witnesses to the fact that Wagner himself spoke of the 'Greek chorus', by which he meant a chorus 'sung by the orchestra'. There are not many commentaries of comparable importance, and it is always very difficult to integrate them in the stage action, since they themselves represent a mental 'action' that transcends any stage dimension. The question arises of what is to be done when the composer demands of his audience an imagination that far outstrips material representation? This is the case here. The relating of the music to the stage action is brilliantly conceived and skilfully executed: we hear at the outset the muffled blows of Siegfried's murder and finally his horn, which sounds in Gutrune's imagination. Between these two points the genealogy of Siegfried and his forebears is unfolded in a succession of motives; and this evocation of his birth and his ancestors, this ritual lament for the hero, which will not be silenced through future generations, obliterates all attempts at any visual presentation. Since any literal illustration is impossible, all that we can do is to find the right style for a heroic lament, making the audience play the role of actual spectators at an imagined ceremony, and confronting them with Siegfried's corpse abandoned on the bare ground. This total stripping of the stage can prompt the spectator to reflect, to identify himself with the situation and understand its symbolism, while the absence of all movement adds passion to the collective lament. The orchestral 'words' enable the audience themselves to become the 'Greek chorus' of which Wagner spoke, and there is no trivial play of illusion to stand in the way of Illusion in the absolute. As Claudel puts it, 'the eye listens.'

This uniting in a single performance the theatre of the imagination and visual dramatization is one of the chief problems of opera, and more particularly of Wagnerian music-drama, in which the composer has taken pains to create a powerful continuum whose constituents vary in relative importance and do not observe any fixed order of preponderance. The further the drama

---

[1] 'La Tétralogie: commentaire d'expérience', published as 'Commentary on Mythology and Ideology' in the 1977 Bayreuth Festival programme book for *Siegfried*, pp. 1–16. This was a response to an interview published in the 1976 programme book for *Das Rheingold*, and with which Boulez and Chéreau were not entirely happy.

progresses, the closer and denser the texture of the music, the greater its dependence on the strict organization of musical motives (almost to the exclusion of all that are secondary, anecdotal) and the more difficult – indeed impossible – it becomes to find any stage *equivalent*. All that can be done is to decide what is to remain visible and to separate the spheres of the imaginary and the real. This is no mean task and one that is, by its very nature, unsatisfactory. As is often the case in impossible circumstances, there is no single, ideal solution: all that can be done is to show what seems to serve best to co-ordinate elements that, if not exactly heterogeneous, are at the least centrifugal in tendency. Hence arises the balancing act between happening and symbol, character and ideogram, music of action and music of reflection, fact and commentary.

II

This problem of musical commentary appears again, and perhaps in an even acuter form, at the end of *Götterdämmerung*, where we are faced with stage action that is hard to represent visually (and in fact impossible to present literally), a swift succession of various actions: Hagen's extremely brief exclamation – so brief, in fact, that it seems incongruous in the circumstances – and a torrent of symbols – all assembled and condensed in a few minutes of the most highly 'charged' music of the whole work, though the significance of this musical 'commentary' is anything but clear. There have been endless discussions as to whether this conclusion is pessimistic or optimistic; but is that really the question? Or at any rate can the question be put in such simple terms? Chéreau has called it 'oracular', and it is a good description. In the ancient world oracles were always ambiguously phrased so that their deeper meaning could be understood only after the event, which, as it were, provided a semantic analysis of the oracle's statement. Wagner refuses any conclusion as such, simply leaving us with the premises for a conclusion that remains shifting and indeterminate in meaning. This appears to have been quite deliberate on his part, as we find him saying to Cosima that, 'Music has no end: it is like the genesis of things, always capable of beginning again from the beginning and becoming its opposite, but never actually complete.'[1]

Potential continuity, ambiguity of meaning, transformability into its opposite – these are all characteristics of the provisional truce declared in the final commentary of *Götterdämmerung*. The music employs dramatic elements in order to transcend the drama and give it a versatility and an ambivalence that no words could communicate. The culminating amalgamation of motives is directionless and confronts us with unanswerable ques-

---

[1] '. . . es gibt keinen Schluss für die Musik, sie ist wie die Genesis der Dinge, sie kann immer von vorne wieder anfangen, in das Gegenteil übergehen, aber fertig ist sie eigentlich nie.'

tions, very like an oracle – but what imaginable events could provide the semantic analysis of this particular oracle? This is a conclusion designed to leave us perplexed. And our minds go at once to the 'moral lesson' of *Don Giovanni* (the equivalent, in amplified and more elegant form, of Molière's shocking and trivial 'Mes gages!'), which is equally puzzling. In one case the revelation of the illusion, in the other the illusion of the illusion. But in both cases the public is made to witness the illusion and thus invited to reflect on theatrical illusion in general, the illusion of myth, which is what we are sent back to at the end of the performance, when reality reasserts its rights over the fictitious universe in which we have been plunged for so long.

Are we to listen to the music at the end of *Götterdämmerung*? Most certainly, but the question is, 'How?' As an ambiguous oracle? Music takes on a sibylline character and must be 'heard', and on no account mimed! And so we cordon off this invisible area from which the musical 'word' emanates, a space to include both stage and auditorium, each reflecting the other in the same listening attitude. The drama is resolved in the total identification of these two elements hitherto carefully isolated from each other by the drama-tic and visual illusion, which together form an insurmountable barrier of sound–silence, shadow–light. We must abolish this distance, dissolve this convention of theatrical performance and listen, literally, to the invisible. Let us try, together, to decipher what the author himself is not sure of meaning, or being able to say. It is certainly a more difficult task than abandoning ourselves to some kind of visual charm that saves us the trouble of thinking about what musical language, unaided, communicates. Wag-ner's music itself seems to be telling us that the ultimate form of asceticism is to renounce easy illusion and create in ourselves the void from which a new genesis may spring.

III

It is interesting to compare the three groups of women and their music: the Rhinemaidens, the Valkyries and the Norns. These three groups play lead-ing roles in the general balancing of the *Ring* and are strongly characterized by what may be called very different musical 'styles'. Wagner said amusingly of the Norns, 'A witch's voice cannot be conceived as anything but high and like a child's; the tremulous note of the heart is absent.'[1]

These three 'ensembles' are admirably constructed and composed, but they exercise shifting functions – sometimes engaging in actual dialogue in the action, sometimes influencing other characters, and sometimes estab-lishing a situation statically. Wagner's regroupings and redistribution of voices correspond in detail to these different stages in the evolution of the

---

[1] 'Man kann sich eine Hexenstimme nur hoch und kindlich denken; der bebende Ton des Herzens klingt nicht darin.'

ensemble. Of course it is the Norns' scene, which is not interrupted either by exterior events or by characters outside the group, that is most homogeneous and most properly speaking musical in structure, forming a kind of rondo in which questions about the past, the present and the future provide the refrain.

The Valkyries are in actual fact purveyors of the dead and they laugh like hyenas. All their music is marked by an extreme excitement, a tension that is never relaxed and an unbounded exuberance. Their wild calls and laughter make them terrifying creatures who are reflected in the extreme vocal tension demanded by the music. With the arrival first of Brünnhilde and Siegfried, and then of Wotan, this excitement reaches a hysterical paroxysm. It would be true to say of them what Wagner himself said laughingly about Siegfried: 'The fellow honks like a wild goose.'[1]

The Rhinemaidens are a complete contrast. Their style passes easily and without interruption from the seductive to the mocking, from the plaintive to the reckless. It is the most homogeneous of styles, varying subtly between *Rheingold* and *Götterdämmerung* but keeping the same rhythmic substructure. Their two scenes have a kind of family likeness, and although the musical material is not literally identical its matrix is similar. The air of lassitude and nostalgia that marks their second scene, despite the momentary interest aroused by the appearance of Siegfried, contrasts strongly with the freshness and playfulness of the first.

Wagner does not write 'ensembles' in the old sense, which belonged to 'opera' – though he used these in his early works – but the later scenes represent a revitalizing of group singing, the sharing of a single *character* between different individuals. This dispersing and reassembling of the voices is the clearest indication of an evolution in these stage ensembles, an evolution that literally materializes the different stages in his musical style.

IV

The first occasion on which we are shown Valhalla is in no sense a moment of triumph: Valhalla is not clearly delineated but belongs to a world of dream, phantasmagoria and mirage. The key chosen by the composer, the sonorities, the dynamics and the express marking *sehr weich* all combine to give this dream an extreme mistiness of colour not unlike Turner's painting of Windsor, also seen at sunrise. And when evening comes, after the day's adventures – the bargaining with the giants, the theft of the ring – the 'Valhalla' theme reappears against a floating background of arpeggios, still vague in outline and still soft – *sehr weich* – like a dream that remains hazy and gradually loses its fascination as it becomes reality, soon shrouded in

---

[1] 'Der Kerl schreit wie eine wilde Gans.'

darkness. Two adjacent symbols confirm this impression of vagueness and dream, one by deduction and analogy and the other by contrast, even contradiction. In the first case it is fascinating to see how the theme of the 'ring' – which is harmonically very unstable with its succession of thirds that can form the basis for every kind of tonal ambiguity (properties that Wagner exploits on a large scale later, especially in *Siegfried*, where in the case of Mime the 'Ring' theme is reduced to the first and last of these thirds) – how this theme is designed and intended by Wagner as the initial segment of the 'Valhalla' theme, a very clear symbolic deduction. On the other hand, in the second instance the 'Valhalla' theme takes on its confident, assured character, its rhetorical note of triumph, only when it is supported by the 'sword' theme which, in fact, completes it and puts an end to its existence in *Rheingold*, its peroration actually appearing in the 'Rainbow' theme. There the initial rhythm is also deduced from the 'Valhalla' theme, the opening notes of the 'rainbow' theme constituting a mirror version of the 'Valhalla' theme. There is a still further symbolism in the fact that the only rhetorical certainty is eventual, terminal – the sword being the *fulfilment* of Valhalla, and only the rainbow remaining. A careful study of the music makes it clear that we are a long way from any commonplace rhetoric of amplification and redundance, although we still have the fanfare rhythms with their decorative splendour.

Wagner's working of these themes and their transformation and significance is astonishing enough in *Rheingold*, but it seems simple, indeed minimal, compared with what we find in *Götterdämmerung*. Take the 'Valhalla' theme alone. As the doubts and dangers that threaten its existence accumulate and its decay and disappearance seem increasingly probable, the rhythmic form of the theme changes; it is supported by harmonies that make it almost unrecognizable and it begins to disintegrate, its cohesion undermined by caesuras. When the Ring has been restored to the Rhinemaidens, the theme reappears in its entirety and provides the framework of the final peroration, rising to a climax of power and strength by means of a series of gradations, only to end quietly, dissolving into the dream world in which it first appeared; and the final conclusion of the work is reached only after Valhalla itself is destroyed.

Wagner's motives run through the work like characters in a novel, sometimes vanishing without trace after a single appearance and sometimes taking on a quite unsuspected importance, dominating a whole scene – like the 'Tarnhelm' motive – maintaining their own existence parallel to that of the drama and its characters, like unbelievably active satellites. As the work proceeds, Wagner becomes increasingly familiar with them, 'staging' them with increasing skill, virtuosity and obvious delight. This reminds one of Balzac manipulating, like some primitive creator, the dramatis personae of his *Comédie humaine*. And in fact the complex interior life of these motives links Wagner's dramatic works more closely to the novel than to the theatre of his day, which explains why – quite apart from seeing them performed –

reading these scores is such an absorbing occupation. They represent a confluence of several different currents – the theatre, of course, but quite as importantly the symphony and the novel. It is these 'interferences' that constitute the phenomenal originality of Wagner, who refused to sacrifice any of his gifts, exploiting them all equally in a work whose complexity is primarily a reflection of his versatility. The increasingly subtle transformation of the motives, for instance, is not to be simply explained, either by dramatic necessity or by the pleasure of manipulating them for its own sake, the exercise of an acquired virtuosity. It should rather be related to his need to integrate with his work for the theatre all the most demanding and most essential characteristics of 'pure' music without sacrificing the drama to an alien formal structure.

Towards the end of his life, particularly, he was inspired by the example of Beethoven, which he adapted for his own purposes and in pursuit of his own ideal of theatrical structure. He borrowed from Beethoven's last works the concept of variation, of working on the transformation of motives, of investigating their role and function in establishing a musical discourse, of entrusting them with the continuity and coherence of that discourse. His formal conclusions were different from those of Beethoven; nor did he adopt Beethoven's formal schemes, which would have contradicted his ideas of dramatic structure. One of the extraordinary qualities of Wagner's genius was this ability to draw such totally different conclusions from those of his model, whose extreme individuality was what in fact inspired Wagner. His intellectual kinship with Beethoven is quite clear though his conclusions were quite differently orientated.

Much still remains to be said, in connection with the symphonic current in his music, about Wagner's instrumentation, and more specifically about his instrumentation *of* the motives and his instrumentation *in relation to the motives*. Of course what immediately strikes us is his virtuosity in the use of instrumental colour; but it would be possible to detail the actual function of individual instruments in the orchestration not only of themes but of whole scenes, or parts of scenes. One could almost establish a code of instrumental colour, each colour having its own significance and also its use as a signal [*Signal*]. One remarkable feature is the way in which Wagner uses certain small, strongly characterized groups of instruments in relation to the rest of the orchestra, which is deliberately undifferentiated. Clearly the music owes its character in this sense to the presence of a single instrument or group of instruments; but the *absence* of certain timbres at given points in the action is also a kind of characterization. Long stretches during which a group of instruments either dominates or is absent from the orchestra balance each other in the overall structure, and broadly define the dramatic form in a number of different ways. Although Wagner may have been influenced in such matters by Weber and Berlioz, he was highly original in the way he continued and developed such procedures, which go back to the obbligato groups of the baroque, seen at their most impressive in Bach's Passions and cantatas.

Wagner's development of musical form *by means of* drama was therefore designed to be eventually 'readable' at many different levels, presenting different degrees of significance and different layers of material. In that sense his working of motives and themes is only the most visible, and the most easily demonstrable, aspect of that wider investigation to which he submitted all the constituent elements of the musical drama. Counterpointing all that is visible there is a multiplicity of things that are not visible – the actual material theatre bearing the watermark of the limitless theatre of the imagination.

V

Especially in *Rheingold* and *Walküre* Wagner continues to make considerable use of recitative, and not only in the traditional sense but also in the very explicit way in which the musical texture is reduced to a minimum support of the poetic language, and the supporting intervals draw their principal coherence not from themselves but from their links with the words, their rhythm and the illusion of actual speech. Marked differences of enunciation – which were the very foundation of Mozart's operas, for instance – were absorbed by Wagner in the interests of a continuity in which the relationship between words and musical texture becomes more supple and there is no clear separation between *comprehension* and *expression*. In a way it might almost be said that the dramatic structure of recitative invaded the whole texture of his music, and that pure musical structure was subordinate to the shifting conjunction of the music and the drama. The dividing line between the two became vague, and in *Götterdämmerung* there are virtually no longer any recitatives, properly so called. But, as we have seen, this problem still exists in a very clear form in *Rheingold* and *Walküre*; the verbal information to be communicated is markedly more important than the musical message, which for the most part serves simply as a carrier wave.

I think that the most striking instance of this is Wotan's long self-communing in the presence of Brünnhilde, who is his conscience, if you like, but also in fact the agent of his will. Her role is at first no more than that of interlocutor, necessary in a prosaic sense to his peace of mind and, in a more ideal sense, to the stirring of his memory and to his rehearsing of the past. This is the dramatic artifice of the confidant, something as old as tragedy itself. Wotan's words sometimes have no more musical backing than a single held note, while at others the music emerges in motives that are immediately absorbed into a deliberately neutral background of chords or held notes. As his mind clears and his memories reappear in complete form, the musical texture is developed to a point at which it first becomes one with the words, then becomes thinner again, and eventually, towards the end of the scene, commands all the listener's attention.

As far as the staging of this monologue is concerned, it is essential to co-ordinate the musical and the dramatic intentions, both of which are realized by the *vocal gesture* quite as much as by gesture itself or the disposition of the characters on the stage. Gesture is conditioned by the voice and helps to direct the vocal intention. Even at the outset this monologue implies a reduction of vocal volume, an approximation to speech, followed by a gradual rise to the full expansion of the voice at its most powerful and effective. I take it that Wagner's marking, *mit gänzlich gedämpfter Stimme*, simply means the suppression of all *cantabile*, music properly speaking being here reduced to a thread, or fine mesh, that ensures a continuity – however tenuous – with the general musical texture of the work and its irrigation by the various motives. This momentary reduction of volume while Wotan's memory is at work is reflected on the stage by the motionless attitude of the singer and his concentration on each word. Paradoxically such moments, when everything is reduced to a minimum, demand the maximum collaboration between conductor and producer, since there is no possibility of any counterpointing of music and stage action or any divergence between the two; they must engage together and co-ordinate their respective movements as closely as possible. At other moments this co-ordination can be infinitely more flexible, more specifically moments when the stage action is clearly the primary element, as in the first act of *Siegfried*, where the music provides a continuous rhythmic background and the action is free to assume a certain descriptive, anecdotal autonomy.

It is thus possible and right to explore different aspects of this collaboration between conductor and producer: the work itself invites such exploring, which enables us to trace the convergences and divergences between action and reflection, movement and immobility, the proliferation of ideas and the reduction to bare essentials.

VI

The danger to be avoided in all relations between the stage and the orchestra is, I think, redundance – each repeating at the same moment the same acts only in different domains. This danger is certainly much more present in Wagner than in any other composer, precisely because of his motive technique, which can easily be taken as a system of – as it were – road signs, one theme indicating a turn to the left, another a right turn and keeping one's eye on the road . . . Both musically and dramatically this literal interpretation of the motives can lead to embarrassingly naïve melodrama. But there are other, less extreme forms of redundance, such as underlining musically what is already underlined in the text. This underlining of underlining of underlinings ... is the last thing needed to 'make the listener understand', since it misdirects his intelligence towards elementary objects, when in fact it should be ranging far more widely and subtly.

As I have said before, the actual theatre visible to the audience is counterpointed by a vast, rich theatre of the imagination, which is *by definition* invisible and must remain like a watermark. Such counterpoint seems to me to provide the freest, the most supple and (why not say so?) the most intelligent solution, and also the most effective, since it allows us to absorb rather than eliminate a number of contradictions inherent in the work owing to its great length. This counterpoint also enables us to resolve the questions already raised, of the multiple cross-references between text and music, and of the necessity and quality of these cross-references. There will of course be moments at which the stage action and the musical action will be literally parallel, the two structures coinciding exactly. The relations between the two will sometimes vary and one will achieve a kind of 'concerted' independence – I might almost say a *concertante* independence, in the same way as a soloist may take some liberty, indulge some flight of fancy, in relation to the group with which he is playing, without destroying the organic links between them.

In any case the further we go in the work, the more difficult it becomes to apply any criteria of strict parallelism, taking into account the frequent kaleidoscopic character of the musical texture and its perpetual renewal, matching that of the action. Keeping the two elements in constant proximity can be only forced and artificial, since their two rhythms of action, so to speak, are not the same.

VII

It is often said that the essential element in Wagner is the music and that the stage action distracts the listener's attention from what is of primary importance. Is that why so little attention is paid to the actual level of sound and why an apparently indestructible tradition demands *volume* of sound before all else? Is this impressive noise a major virtue or simply a misappropriation of function?

According to first-hand contemporary accounts, including Cosima's recently published diary, Wagner's own opinions on the subject were much more complex than those of his heroic interpreters. He compared the orchestra to the *cothurnus*, or high boot, worn by the performers in Greek tragedies, giving them greater stature and importance and thus amplifying the drama itself. It is worth bearing this comparison in mind. If the orchestra is a *cothurnus*, it is certainly not a mask, and still less a shirt of Nessus mercilessly burning the voices that it clothes.

There are, of course, paroxysms in Wagner, passages in which he makes extreme use of the forces he employs and their dynamic potentialities, passages such as we should expect from a composer of extreme sensibility and nervous energy. He was preceded of course by the tumultuous din of Berlioz and by Beethoven's hammer blows, and this exaggerated energy was to become not uncommon, especially with the late romantics. But that is no reason to consider such paroxysms as a distinguishing feature of Wagner's music. I should rather say that the most striking feature of his music – and one that leads performers almost to despair – is the constant refining of the instrumental texture during the long course of the work. When I spoke of dramatic characterization by means of instrumentation, I pointed to the profusion of exquisitely sensitive, delicate, subtly calculated textures that mark the irrigation of the orchestra as a whole by currents of chamber music. Wagner's systematic individualizing of these subordinate groupings provides the most striking contrast with his use of large-scale sonorities, and it repeatedly gives the lie to the idea of that monolithic use of the orchestra for which he has received both exaggerated praise and unjust blame. To return to his own metaphor, we may say that Wagner is expert at adapting his *cothurni* to a great diversity of characters and situations, and that he is always subtle in calculating the exact dimensions needed in each instance. He can amplify without overwhelming; and in fact it is just this adaptability that reveals his genius.

VIII

Wagner's use of mythology was very characteristic of the age in which he lived, and the *Ring* was not in fact completed until long after the period when medieval legends and Germanic myths were at the height of their popularity. The birth, or rebirth, of nationalist movements, characteristic of the late eighteenth and early nineteenth centuries, brought an urgent demand for historical confirmation, and the more remote and unreal the history, the better. Some alternative had to be found to the passion for Graeco-Roman antiquity, which had dominated Western Europe for over two centuries but had now lost its original vigour; and this accounts for the popularity of the Middle Ages, preferably the 'high' Middle Ages, which not only provided the new literary movement with fresh sustenance but also proved useful from the political point of view.

On the other hand it was difficult wholly to forget Greek culture, and particularly the dream of a theatre that was truly popular in interest and aspirations. Thus the Greek theatre remained a model until the moment when the theatre of the middle classes came to reflect, more effectively and directly, the problems of the day, and writers felt an obligation to expose these problems in realistic rather than ideal terms – a responsibility completely assumed only by Ibsen.

Despite the use of symbol and myth, therefore, Wagner's theatre represents a halfway house. Wagner concerned himself with the problems of the day while still using the *timeless* convention of gods and heroes, and the inherent ambiguity of this procedure must certainly be respected though not, I believe, simply by respecting the conventions of costume. Now the rub seems still to be felt at one very obvious point – I mean in the fact that the myth extends far beyond the strict framework of its actual origin *in time* – the very time-conditioned setting in which the action takes place.

It is commonly said that this myth can be visualized only in an essentially *timeless* setting. But 'timeless' almost automatically denotes a kind of costume that of its very nature suggests the timeless, i.e. the myth. If we reject vaguely medieval costume as a kind of embarrassed disguise, we find that we have removed the visible mark of the timeless and that the timeless has thus in fact disappeared. It is rather as though Catholics were to refuse to accept as a priest anyone who did not wear a cassock, simply *because* he did not wear a cassock. Can it be that 'timeless' myth is such a fragile concept that it can be obliterated by a costume? Is it not rather an express reflection of the temporal character of these myths, and their comparatively new importance to us, that we still dress them up in the sort of clothes that we consider 'barbaric' because it corresponds to what was then conventionally considered 'barbaric'? In the seventeenth and eighteenth centuries the gods of Greek mythology appeared on the stage in contemporary court dress and lost none of their mythological character by doing so. Is conventional costume to be rejected while conventions of performance are retained?

In this confusion of the temporal and the timeless, the character and the myth, the style and function of the music are, in practice, oddly ignored. What references are there in the music to this mythical past? None whatever, even by allusion. The music is not worried by any of these more or less archaeological considerations, which in fact – as far as costume goes – caused Wagner much bitter disappointment when the works were first performed. If the musico-dramatic reality is to be properly transcribed, a production must not labour under any stylistic prohibitions not strictly imposed by the actual text of the work and only to be found in stage directions intended for specific performance in a specific epoch of time. Should we feel any obligation to play seventeenth-century French tragedy in Louis-XIV costume? Are we forbidden to play Shakespeare except in period dress?

There is a very real difference between the original circumstances in which a work was written and the work itself, which transcends those circumstances even if it bears their mark; and it is this difference that obliges us to free ourselves from this mistaken idea of 'fidelity'. Strictly interpreted, fidelity strangles a work; and what, indeed, does fidelity mean? Does it mean respecting what is ephemeral? Or does it not rather mean considering a work as an inexhaustible source of new truths that will be deciphered differently in different ages, in different places and different circumstances? Literal fidelity seems to me the greatest of untruths and the greatest *in*fidelity towards the actual work, which is obstinately restricted to the circumstances of its original appearance. Everything has changed in the meantime, and we ourselves have greater experience of different stylistic experiments. Are we to reverse our course and forget all this evolution? Every work is a constant shuttle between past and future, and this enriches both it and us. That is why taking refuge in the 'timeless' amounts in fact to no more than switching off this current and interrupting this all-important circuit between past and future. It is a dishonest stratagem designed to arrest the process of history, and to present as timeless a truth that is wholly time-conditioned. Music gains nothing by it and the theatre still less, being far more subject to the contingencies of performance than any other art-form.

The real dimension of myth is not this reassuring 'distancing' by which we remain passive spectators of an unreal 'story' with no dangerous involvements. Myth is something that forces us to think about our present condition, that provokes us to react and forces us to pay attention to the very real problems that it poses. In that sense a performance is satisfactory if it gives myth the impact of presentday reality.

IX

According to Wagner, 'Siegfried is pure Action – though he knows the Destiny that he undertakes to fulfil.'[1] And it is a fact that from his first appearance Siegfried's music is essentially movement and action, forthright, shimmering with colour and light. As a character he is incapable of imagination, never in fact 'imagines' anything. Mime's description of fear, of the terrible Fafner, leaves him completely unmoved because he cannot picture danger to himself, being immunized against it; and when he falls into the trap set by the Gibichungs, Siegfried reminds one of Baudelaire's famous Albatross.

X

It would be interesting to pursue Wagner's musical transcription of the various symbols and observe whether in this transmuting of ideas into sound he follows any consistent plan. There have always been associations of ideas in music, and the traffic between the two has changed with changes in style, while always moving in parallel directions. Pain, darkness and uncertainty are characterized by the use of chromaticism, and their opposites – certainty, light, joy – by the diatonic. But these 'psychological' correspondences are not all; the natural elements have also given rise to a number of imitations. Thus rhythms and rising or falling intervals have been employed in similar ways over the years, falling intervals matching the darker end of the spectrum and rising intervals the brighter. Later, tonalities assumed a sym-

---

[1] 'Siegfried ist nur Aktion – dabei kennt er doch das Schicksal, das er über sich nimmt.'

bolic meaning, though this meaning changed from one period to the next. We have only to compare an eighteenth-century list of key significances with the list given by Berlioz, for example, to see the changes brought about by all the discussion of Beethoven. It is true that such symbolism is a strange mixture of properties that may be called natural (instability of the chromatic compared with diatonic relationships) and characteristics acquired by the impression made on our listening habits by outstanding works in the repertory. In fact our reactions to the whole world of sound are determined by this fusion of innate psychological reactions and the conditioning of our cultural background.

Whether consciously or not, Wagner made use of this phenomenon in creating the musical symbols that we know as *Leitmotivs*. There was a great deal of exaggeration later, when the *Leitmotivs* were given labels that constricted their meaning and reduced them to a kind of coded vocabulary. But there is no doubt that they do in fact refer to a system of natural or cultural perceptions flexible enough to permit considerable breadth of interpretation, yet precise enough to ensure that the listener's perceptions are directed as the composer wishes them to be and coincide with the various elements of the drama. Wagner's vocabulary in this field is extraordinarily rich because it matches the great variety of symbols, perceived as such without the aid of any 'key' to make them intelligible. What gives the motives their striking character is the fact that they are unambiguous, that their form is so precisely calculated that contours, rhythms and general character are almost immediately retained by the listener's memory. Furthermore their instrumental colouring serves as a powerful mnemonic and helps him to keep track of them in their wanderings through the score.

Perhaps the most remarkable feature of these motives is their ductility, or pliability. As the work proceeds and Wagner becomes more experienced, he shows an increasing virtuosity in his treatment of the motives, in disposing them and superimposing one on the other. But if their original material had not naturally invited such treatment, the composer's task would have been much more difficult; and the remarkable feature of both their design – and their designation – lies therefore in the fact that they can be reduced to components that are both neutral and mobile (an arpeggio, for instance), while the combination of these components in the original form of the motive is solid and unmistakable. It is worth observing that this double capacity, of adaptability and persisting identity, is particularly characteristic of the motives that occur most frequently and form, in fact, a kind of Ariadne's thread in the labyrinth of the drama.

XI

As the work progresses, Wagner's expression and style of writing increase in depth and he penetrates still further into a musical universe that is specifically his own and often assumes a twilight colouring. The amazing scene between Alberich and Hagen ('Schläfst du Hagen, mein Sohn?') moves me for reasons that are probably not directly related to the drama. The composer seems here to be conducting a kind of dialogue with his own double and the subject to be something much more general than the Ring: it is a questioning of the future, an uneasiness about generations to come. Will my concerns and my achievement be understood in years to come? Shall I survive in those who follow me? The whole scene reveals a deep uncertainty about communication, and the sense of doubt in the final 'Sei treu!' ['Be faithful!'] is heartrending. Will the future repay my waiting? This may well be a purely private interpretation, altogether remote from the stage reality; yet I cannot help feeling that this anguished questioning, which is ostensibly about the Ring, refers in fact to the whole work and its future validity. Questioning of this kind can be resolved only by that 'Be faithful!' – the call for a faith against all appearances.

28

Gustav Mahler: Why Biography?[1]

Music does not exclude the biographical in Mahler. It may go beyond the anecdotal, which it magnifies in the interests of the imagination, but it remains none the less closely linked to an original experience in real life, so closely indeed that this was for a long time considered an objection. Mahler had no hesitation in allowing his personal experiences, both as man and as musician, to show in his music; and this gave rise to the old and familiar accusation that his was *Kapellmeistermusik*, or in other words music that betrays its origins and is little concerned with being autonomous. It is not very difficult to determine the sources of Mahler's music and this, which might have been a weakness, becomes in his case one of the greatest strengths of the music – that element of narration introduced as such into the hitherto completely autonomous form of the symphony.

Earlier symphonies had, of course, been confidential, descriptive, 'programmatic'; but despite these alien elements composers still respected, in different degrees, the order and the rules established when it was still unthinkable that personal confidences should encroach on the hierarchical framework. The whole romantic movement bears witness to this struggle between pre-established formal constraints and the individual 'feeling' of the moment, an unequal struggle that ended with the defeat of both parties. Mahler's power as confidant and autobiographer lies in his ability to demonstrate that narrative, in order to be valid, must create its own form. For narrative is a constant invitation to enlarge or break the surrounding framework, and thus to eliminate the symmetry that was one of the original elements of the symphony, and to exclude any idea of a literal return to what has gone before – the impression of remembering may be allowed, perhaps, but certainly no actual repetition.

Such essentially personal narrative, linking by an often tenuous thread of descriptions, memories, impressions, avowals, confidences, even atmospheric backgrounds, is always threatened by a number of obvious dangers.

---

[1] 'La Biographie, pourquoi?', preface to *Mahler*, Vol. I, by Henry-Louis de La Grange, Paris, Fayard, 1979, pp. 2–3. (English edition, London, Gollancz, 1974.)

The tension has only to slacken, the internal logic (if indeed any kind of formal logic exists) has only to disappear, and the result will be catastrophic, chaotic. Biography is thus a heavy burden and the very reverse of a support to the listener. A disconnected string of uninvited confidences? A patchwork novel of this kind can hardly be of interest to anyone but the author, who holds the stage and conducts his own defence: it certainly has no interest for us. How faint is the line dividing these admissions, which are uninvited rather than indiscreet, from the confession that compels our interest by its enthralling nature and presentation!

Of course all music is a declaration that betrays the composer in the most indiscreet manner (though there are also composers who have a passionate desire to betray themselves). These self-revelations may often be all too obvious and leave us cold: we do not need them and feel no concern with them. But there are, it is true, a few exceptional cases in which we feel very strongly that this is the only bearable method of musical communication, and that the purer forms of expression lack this potential immediacy, this sheer power of persuasion. The dilemma in which we find ourselves is often whether totally to sink the self in a greater, transcendent whole or to give the self the dimensions of a world. In the former case biography can be forgotten as though it did not exist; in the latter it acquires mythical dimensions and becomes the potential biography of everyman – or, in a sense, an unapproachable model, the ideal geometric *locus*. To achieve this degree of incandescence, this quality of illumination, in revealing our inmost selves, such a confession must be purified and pass through the filter of form – a filter all the more mysterious for having little to do with order and hierarchy, or at least only with an order and a hierarchy contained in the confession itself.

Our first impression of chaos in a confession on this scale, that has been elaborated through the various prisms of form, is accounted for by the fact that we are looking for a manifest order whereas we should be looking for an underlying order, a superficial logic when we should be aware of an organic relationship. We are much happier with a short, well-focused confession in which both outline and sense can be grasped. Thus Mahler's songs are more immediately attractive, since in them we can grasp immediately a human state. Its limits reveal strength and ability, but also weakness or at least some lack, since we miss the superior dimension of what, in academic terms, we can only call development. Confession cannot be simply the lightning projection of a single moment; it must have a continuity in time in order to multiply and proliferate, to become transcended biography. This span of time involves restrictions and surprises, and also an acceptance of the risk – in the long run – of expectation alternating with incident and the danger of the 'trivial' following or contrasting with the 'sublime'. We must accept, also, a lack of homogeneity in both textures and ideas: in fact we must refuse to make a restrictive choice and accept the risks attached to *expansion*, of being *expansive* . . .

What is there to attract us in a factual biography after having once experienced this other biography which, if not totally imaginary, is at least amplified to quite unreal dimensions? It is probably a kind of intoxication, the intoxication caused by witnessing the transcendent nature of all creative activity. Having built up our premisses and piled up our documents, we are sometimes on the point of grasping part of the enigma when we are allowed a clear enough view of the springs of that activity. Yet the moment we carry our investigations any further we invariably meet this break, this gap between life and creation, this shifting and elusive slide that operates between the incidents of an artist's life and their elaboration in his art. In this sense a biography brings no encouragement, only a sense of amazement that so thin and fragile a membrane separating the artist from his work can resist every approach and every enquiry. There are moments when we almost have the illusion that the hermetic seal is breaking, but when we look more closely we see only too clearly our mistake – the gap is still there and still impossible to close, 'the indestructible kernel of darkness' in all artistic invention. The closer we seem to approach it, the further we seem to be from grasping the origin of this invention, which disappears down an endless corridor of magic mirrors. We are both fascinated and depressed by the 'real' biography of the artist, which sends us rebounding with vexation back to the 'imaginary' biography contained in his work.

Are we to abandon hope, then, and to cease wanting to *understand*? We know the circumstances, all the circumstances; step by step we discover the daily routine of work and its setting, mark preferences, whims, amusements, and follow the development of anxieties and the stabilizing of tastes and choices. When we have finished, the enigma still remains. Every reader is at liberty to try to discover a solution, however provisional that solution must inevitably remain.

29

Mahler: Our Contemporary?[1]

What a time it has taken for his name to emerge, not from the shadows, but from purgatory! And a tenacious purgatory unwilling, for any number of reasons, to give him up.

Too much of a conductor and not enough of a composer; at best a composer unable to shake off the conductor in him; too much skill, too little mastery.

And what confusion he brought! There is no direct trace in his work of opera, which he conducted with such passion; on the other hand in the noble field of the symphony he sowed handfuls of theatrical tares, filling what was once a preserve with a noisy and prolix display of sentimentality and vulgarity and an insolent and intolerable disorder. Meanwhile, however, a handful of fervent admirers waited in posthumous exile, admirers easily divided into two camps – progressives and conservatives, the latter priding themselves on being the true defenders of a music which, they believed, the former had betrayed.

On top of that the mistake of being a Jew in an era of intense nationalism – condemned to total silence in his own country, so little remembered that even his (all too revealing) name was almost forgotten.

And that was not all – a mythology arose in which 'Bruckner and Mahler' recur as the Castor and Pollux of the symphony. Impossible to go beyond nine after Beethoven: fate has decreed the doom of any member of the symphonic dynasty who tries to go beyond the magic number. (Since then less gifted composers have achieved the feat . . .)

What was left after this collapse? The memory of a prodigiously gifted, difficult, demanding, eccentric interpreter. A number of scores of which the shorter and easier to grasp were acceptable. For many years this little was enough. The traditional symphonic appetite gorged itself on less complex and demanding prolixities. The few performances given made no conquest and left doubts not only about the worth, but about the quality of the undertaking.

---

[1] 'Mahler actuel?', preface to *Gustav Mahler et Vienne* by Bruno Walter, Paris, Librairie Générale Française, 1979, pp. 11–26.

Meanwhile modern music had continued on its path, leaving Mahler as simply a name on a checklist of out-of-date romantic composers, of no contemporary interest, an object of commiseration. Everything about this *fin de siècle* music went against the grain of the new music: everything about it was abundant to excess while economy was increasingly the order of the day.

A plethora of movements, of instruments, of emotions, of gestures . . . Form crumbled beneath their weight! What worth can there be in music in which the relationship between ideas and form disappears in a bog of *espressivo*?

We are approaching the end of an era surfeited with richness, asphyxiated by plethora: it can end at worst – and at best – only in infatuation, sentimental apoplexy. Goodbye, romanticism with your fatty degeneration of the heart!

Goodbye?

When works insist on surviving, there can be no goodbye . . . You dismiss them? Roughly? They obstinately refuse to go! With pride! And so, after time has done its sifting, there are some real skeletons left. But after this long neglect what is authentic rises again, impels us to reconsider it and questions us insistently on our neglect. Were we guilty or superficial? Had we no excuses? As presented to us, preserved by hands that were certainly pious, but also rapacious – by which I mean lacking in that generosity that opens up the future by means of the past – monopolized by the faithful (at what precise moment do these 'faithful' become traitors?) this music might well inspire a good deal of mistrust. A mistrust that even led us to suspect the composers of the Viennese School of a narrow, local sentimental attachment. Their link with this music was not at first sight obvious, whereas the contrasts between it and theirs were patent.

Meanwhile contemporary music had finished its ascetic period and was turning increasingly towards the luxuriant – so much so that the past began to be explored in the light of new perspectives and with an awareness of modern experiences and the bitter lessons that these had taught us.

Surfeited in all likelihood by the unambiguous and by unilateral meanings, composers began to dream of the ambiguous, of a world in which categories are not so simple that they present no problems of orientation.

Order? A restrictive idea – is it of any importance? Right! Let us turn up our noses at restrictive concepts – order, homogeneity of ideas and style, legibility of structure. Let us lay aside, for a time, these paralysing mental reservations. Is that so easy? By no means, and particularly if one has no desire to submit to the influence of outside circumstances. In this particular case, how hard it is to escape the legend that insists on linking the artist's life and his work, direct experience and that experience transmuted, the melodrama and the anguish. Let us play the double role of interpreter and admirer and examine directly the unequal works that he left us.

We are faced from the start by an awkward ambiguity – the frequent impossibility of drawing the line between sentimentality and irony, nostalgia and criticism. There is no real contradiction involved, but rather a movement like that of a pendulum, a sudden change of lighting by which certain musical ideas that are considered banal and superfluous become, when viewed through this difficult prism, revelatory and essential.

Does that banality – which was initially held against Mahler and even said to show his lack of invention – still strike us as intolerable? Is not this the base of a vast misunderstanding about popularity? 'First degree' listening often rests on comfortable clichés, saccharine commonplaces and fleeting glimpses of a countryside in which the past appears in a series of vignettes. Some listeners find this enchanting; others find it irritating, and both parties fail to go beyond these first appearances, which are no more than preliminary . . .

There is no denying this material. It may often seem to us limited and only too predictable; the sources hardly vary from one work to the next. The march and all its derivatives, military or funereal: dances in triple time (*Ländler*, waltz or minuet); provincial and local folk music – between them these constitute virtually the totality of these 'borrowed' themes and can easily be checked. They represent a glaringly obvious 'fixture' in every work, from the first to the last: clichés inherited from the past, either cultural or social.

In contrast to this stock of 'banalities' there is Mahler's repertory of big theatrical gestures: the heroic and the sublime, the music of the spheres and the infinite; the whole dimension of the grandiose of which the least that can be said is that it has lost its immediate power. But how is it that such gestures, which are powerless when used by other composers, still retain their pathos in Mahler? Is it not because, far from being triumphant, these gestures mask paroxysms of insecurity? What a gulf there lies between them and self-confident romanticism proud of its heroism, between them and the *naïveté* of popular music as apprehended in its original state!

Nostalgia is an undeniable feature of Mahler's musical world, but it somehow coexists with a critical attitude, even with sarcasm. How does this come about, for is sarcasm not the least musical of all attitudes? Music likes frankness and simplicity and does not really lend itself to this double play of irony and sincerity. It is hard to decide between truth and caricature. When there is a verbal text it is not so difficult to get one's bearings, but in 'pure' music . . . ?

Ambiguity and banter can be really understood only with a text based on conventions that are recognized and accepted. Often all that is needed is to distort these conventions by some exaggerated or displaced emphasis, a quickening or dragging of the tempo or some unusual instrumentation that puts a passage in a new light and breaks it up into its constituent elements. Mahler's aggressive humour can even give such passages a character of unreality or fantasy, the smudged outlines of an X-ray photograph that we find puzzling and alarming – a world not of flesh but of rattling bones, realistically described by strange, grotesque instrumental combinations, a nightmare shadow-world, colourless, ashen and insubstantial. And with what savage vigour he presents this universe of spectral memories!

Is this all that attracts us in Mahler's music, the reflections of a world in ruins – some sentimental, others odd or sarcastic – brilliantly etched? Can that be enough to capture and hold our attention? There is no doubt that we today are fascinated by the hypnotic power and passion of this vision of the end of an era – an era that had to perish in order that a new era should be born from its ruins: the myth of the phoenix is here illustrated almost too literally.

Yet beyond this shadow-world there is something even more surprising and that is the revolution that Mahler caused in the world of the symphony – his determined, often savage attack on the hierarchical forms of the symphony as he found them, expanded indeed but frozen into a rigid decorative convention. Was it the theatre that impelled him to create such dramatic havoc among the constrictions of the symphony? Just as Wagner destroyed the artificial order of the opera in order to initiate a far more creative attitude to the drama, so Mahler revolutionized the symphony, ravaging its all too neatly ordered landscape and introducing his hallucinatory visions into the holy place where Logic used to be worshipped. Surely the figure whom he evokes is that of Beethoven, an earlier barbarian who in his day spread similar confusion and disarray and also expanded, beyond the 'reasonable', the forms that he had once taken as models.

Is it possible to speak of an 'extra-musical' dimension? It has certainly been done, and Mahler's own programmes – which he later regretted – began the misunderstanding. Description in music was neither a novelty nor confined to him alone; it was rather a characteristic of an era that, after Berlioz and Liszt, delighted in exciting the musical imagination by means of images – for the most part literary but also including the visual arts and rivalling 'painting' on a more difficult terrain.

In Mahler this extra-musical dimension was no longer a matter of imitation but concerned the very substance of music, its organization, its structure, its power. His vision and his methods have the epic dimension of the story-teller and even more, in both methods and material, the novelist. The name of 'symphony' remains unchanged, as do the principles of the different movements – scherzo, slow movement and finale – though their number and their order constantly change from one work to the next. The frequent inclusion of the vocal element at some point and the use of theatrical effects, such as offstage instruments, weaken the contours of what was once a clearly defined form. Such freedom in the choice and use of material is only possible in the world of romanticism. Once liberated from the visual theatre, which was the obsession of his professional life, Mahler indulged to the full, with a kind of frenzy, in this freedom to mix all the different 'genres', refusing to acknowledge the distinction between what was noble and what was not and using all original material available for constructions which, though carefully planned, were liberated from any irrelevant formal limitations. He brushed aside the ideas of homogeneity and hierarchy as absurd irrelevancies, concerned only to communicate his own individual vision with all its nobility and triviality, its moments of tension and relaxation. He did not select in all this wealth of material: selection would have meant a betrayal, a renunciation of his original plan.

And so in listening to Mahler we encounter a different perception of 'development'. We still, at first sight, have the impression that musical form itself cannot support such an accumulation of facts, and that the musical discourse – and I mean 'musical' – gets lost in pointless digressions; that the composer's intention vanishes beneath the excessive burden that it bears; that the form dissolves in all this complexity; that the direction of the music is lost in this ceaseless succession of incidents, and that these plethoric movements crumble beneath the wealth of their own material and rhetorical excess. These arguments are indeed valid if we listen in a narrowly musical way.

How then are we to listen, to 'perceive' these works? Are we simply to allow ourselves to be carried on the flood of the narrative, to float with the different psychological currents, to refuse to have our attention diverted by the details and keep it fixed on the epic dimension of the work and the stimulus that it gives to our imagination? Yes, that is possible! The music is forceful enough to permit such a purely passive attitude, but is such an attitude really a source of enrichment? Ideally we should be able to trace precisely every strand in the dense musical complex.

A great deal has been said about the *longueurs* of Mahler's music. If we speak of Schubert's 'himmlische Länge' [heavenly lengths], what are we to call the formidable dimensions, the sheer length, of some of Mahler's symphonies? Only those who have not learned to listen properly will find this great length exhausting or boring. (And if this is a problem for the listener, how much more so for the performer, whose perception differs from that of the ordinary listener only in intensity and in the need to look ahead?) There is no sense in looking for the clear markers we find in classical music; what we have to do is to accept the density of the musical events and the musical time, tense or relaxed according to the demands of the dramatic circumstances. All music is of course based on this ductility of musical time, but elsewhere it is not a primary phenomenon of our perception. In Mahler it constantly tends to become a priority and is often more important than any of the other categories, serving as a guide to help the listener to distinguish between what should be listened to in an overall context and what demands an almost analytical attention. The ductility of musical time helps us to distinguish the different planes of Mahler's narrative and immediately to categorize the different elements in the music as it proliferates.

Our way of listening must be adjusted not only within the movements themselves, especially the big epic movements; but in any one symphony each movement requires a different way of listening, since the aesthetic standpoint changes, as does the importance, or rather the density, of each movement within the general design. Mahler's world is not a homogeneous one and always risks incongruities, including quotation and parody as legitimate procedures; and from it we learn how to listen in a richer way, both more varied and more ambiguous.

Mahler's work presents great extremes, so that we pass without a break from the shortest of songs to the longest of symphonies with nothing in between. This may well cause surprise, and it is quite possible to prefer the immediate perfection of the unproblematical snapshots, the fine etching of the short song in which, once the essential idea has been expressed, there is no need for distention, amplification or prolongation. Nevertheless, perfect though the concision of these 'poems' may be, the real Mahler dimension is to be found in the long movements, which are frequently excessive and problematical, Mahler's hard struggle with the epic dimension proving to have a greater fascination than his successful handling of dimensions too obviously restricted by the limitations imposed by a strongly characterized genre. Mahler would probably be less attractive if he were not also on occasion clumsy. The 'hyperdimensional' character of his music has very little of the typical *fin de siècle* turgidity, the gigantism and megalomania, the delight in sheer size for its own sake. More relevant is the anxiety of an artist creating a new world that proliferates beyond his rational control, a dizzy sense of uniting agreement and contradiction in equal parts, a dissatisfaction with the dimensions recognized by musical experience and the search for an order less obviously established and less easily accepted. His ideal work belongs to no accepted category; in fact it refuses to belong to any individual category as such, in order to borrow something from them all. His symphonies are essentially meeting-places of the imaginary theatre, the imaginary novel and the imaginary poem; musical expression asserts its claim to what it has been denied, decides to assume complete responsibility for every possible mode of being, and really becomes philosophy, while escaping the limitations of purely verbal communication.

Can such ambitions be achieved by economical means? Is an ascetic sound-palette suitable to such a conception? It is of course true that prodigious results can be achieved by restriction and discipline, and that the need for external display decreases in proportion to the part played in a composer's invention by the intelligence, which refuses conspicuous wealth for the sake of a profounder communion, in which the actual means of transmission become a matter of supreme indifference. The sound-material, perfectly mastered, not only takes the lowest place but is granted the rarest of all attributes – absence. Such music is addressed to the reflective faculty: it is a book of meditation, a personal hymn of communication beyond the reality of sounds. We are familiar with this from Bach certainly, and in a way from Beethoven, with his intolerance of the 'wretched violin', whereas Wagner even in his most profound reflections still delights in profusion of sound and instrumental richness, which remains – purified, clarified and transparent, subordinate but still powerful – to underpin the very essence of the expression. It is impossible to forget such a model of the fusion, or amalgamation, of idea and means of expression at the very heart of the musical conception.

In Mahler's music do not 'means' occupy an excessive place in relation to the musical idea? Does he not perhaps abuse his power and fall into a virtuosity that, however fascinating, is in fact empty? Immediate reactions to his music virtually all reflect this feeling. It is praised, or blamed, for its virtuosity or its strangeness. No one questions its skill, but Mahler is accused of concealing an absence of content in his music, of diverting listeners' attention and deflecting their musical perceptions to what is superficial and in fact superfluous. Has not Mahler, the conductor, the failing generally considered inseparable from performers as such – concealing the lack of originality (or at best the uncertainty) of his ideas by a process of manipulation with which his profession gives him an almost undue acquaintance? An excessive skill in manoeuvring is held against the whole hybrid race of performers, so easily guilty of cheating, if not of treachery.

Yes, Mahler is a virtuoso of sound, and this virtuosity is constantly visible, though rarely blatant. If it happens to be of a conventional kind, it makes for the most part magnificent use of the composer's repertory. Its place in the perspective of history is quite clear and it explores no, strictly speaking, absolutely new territory. It accepts – if only in order to flout – those romantic instrumental practices which had gradually become the conventions and norms of nineteenth-century music. An obvious instance is Mahler's predilection for the horn, one of many cases that confirm this attitude. The ease with which he handles the orchestra is so great that it might sometimes pass for nonchalance if it were not for the minute detail of his markings, which constantly put us on our guard. Mahler was obsessed, and not without reason, by the effectiveness of his notation. As a conductor he had often seen how 'freely' composers' markings were interpreted by players, how often they were ignored through laziness or mere carelessness. In his notation he does his utmost to counter inertia, just as he mistrusted players' acquired habits, their mechanically 'natural' reactions. As though he knew – as he did – the frequently ambiguous nature of his musical material, lying on the uncertain borderline between irony and sentimentality, he perpetually puts the player on his guard and calls him to order.

There is an inimitably personal note in his numerous markings, positive and negative in equal number – exhorting and warning, encouraging and restraining, urging forward or stimulating the player's critical faculty: What is to be done consists first in knowing what must not be done: the quality needed is first defined by the fault to be avoided. In fact Mahler included a scheme for the performer within the scheme of the composition itself in a way never before attempted. Although he incorporated the players' demands in his actual composing, he never allowed them to dictate anything; his knowledge of them was so great that he was not content with existing practice, but could foresee possible extensions and extrapolations. It was this rather than any empty virtuosity that marked him out as the supremely professional interpreter, the man in daily contact both with the great moments of a fascinating profession and with the detailed tasks and obligations of a demanding technique. The gulf is wide indeed between this attitude and the belief that a minutely careful notation must lead to a rigid interpretation, that a living authority may become a dead hand, that a perpetually shifting musical thought can be captured by mere exactness and correctness, and that any objective observing of the text can take the place of subjective re-creation – and it is one that cannot be bridged by the servile, unimaginative following of Mahler's text.

Mahler may put his performers on their guard, but he does not wish to inhibit them. From all that we know of him he seems to have had no inclination to such inhibition, rather the opposite; but he could not consent to inaccuracy being mistaken for 'interpretation'. It is precisely the most demanding kind of freedom that needs the most severe discipline, without which it becomes mere caricature and is content with approximations – travesties, sometimes blatant travesties, of a truth both more profound and more worthy of respect. All the more so because any rash surrender to the frenzy, or indeed the hysteria, of the moment will destroy the original motivation of the music by destroying its essential ambiguity, thus making it hopelessly trivial and emptying it of its profound content. Furthermore the latent substructure is also destroyed and with it the balance between the different moments of the development – and all in the interests of a chaotic charade by some totally erratic meddler! Mahler's magnetic fields are infinitely more subtle than a mere demonstration with iron filings!

The difficulty of interpreting a score of Mahler's doubtless lies in the divergences between gestures and material, gestures tending to become increasingly 'grandiose' as the material may well become increasingly 'vulgar'. Incoherence may result from this fundamental contradiction, as well as from the impossibility of joining together the many different moments in a work during the course of which musical ideas proliferate around a number of essential polarities. The later the work, the denser the texture becomes, owing to the multiplicity rather than to the thickness of the lines. The polyphony develops in a perpetual crossing of lines or other elements, which are increasingly attached to the principal themes: there is no filling-out or complementing, nothing but cells derived from the main figures. Although it is no easy task to reconcile minute detail with a grand overall design, it is this that restores the unstable balance of forces; and Mahler himself had the same difficulty as his interpreters in grasping these opposing dimensions and forcing them into a single perspective. It is these problems that constitute the deepest and most personal character of his works.

Considering these works in retrospect we can find some justification for the fact that they were not found immediately convincing. Richness and proliferation are more fascinating to us nowadays because they recall that magnificence which was for years forgotten or condemned as superfluous and impure. But this is too simple a reaction and not in itself enough to justify the gradually increasing popularity of music whose ambiguity was originally held against it and is now considered its chief virtue. To attach Mahler to a 'progressive' current leading directly and as a matter of course to the Second Viennese School is to force the facts and to try to give them an interpretation that they will not bear. There is too much nostalgia, too much attachment to the past in Mahler's music for him to be declared, without any qualifications, the revolutionary who initiated an irreversible process of radical renewal in music. His first followers felt this strongly, since it was primarily his nostalgia that attracted them; they were aware of the sentimental aspect of his music and rejected the critical aspect, which must have made them uncomfortable. There is, moreover, a determination to disregard the categories of the past and to force them to express something different from their original purpose, and a persistent extending of limits; and both of these make it impossible to confine Mahler within any 'end of a line' concept. In his own very personal way he had a share in the future, a share that is clearer to us now that a certain purging of our notions of style has done its work (and served its purpose) and we now have to consider a more composite musical language, more complex forms of expression and a more inclusive synthesis. The sources of Mahler's inspiration – even the geography of those sources – may of course seem to us extremely limited and enclosed in a world that far from renewing itself, remained obsessed with certain forms of expression which reflect a form of society doomed to disappear. Now that these sources have virtually ceased to exist, we can regard them with a more indulgent eye, as valuable pieces of evidence that we can no longer directly understand. All this material consequently acquires a documentary value, which, far from rejecting, we may regard as first-degree invention. We are thus in a position to concern ourselves almost exclusively with the process of transformation or transmutation. Throughout Mahler's work we can trace the evolution of his expression based always on the same elements, which provide us with the necessary guidelines. What makes Mahler contemporary is the amplitude and complexity of his gestures, the variety and intensity in the *degree* of his invention – and not only contemporary but indispensable to anyone reflecting today on the future of music.

30

Mahler: *Das klagende Lied*[1]

This is Gustav Mahler's first important work and it is marked by a number of characteristics that appear in everything that he was to write later, becoming increasingly marked and forming our present image of the composer. At a first glance these are of two different kinds: epic dimensions and, technically speaking, instrumental precision. His mastery in these two fields may not yet have reached the perfection of his later works, but it is none the less striking that his personality is here revealed in the fusion of the visionary and the craftsman, a fusion that is not very common.

First, the epic dimension. It is significant that Mahler here employs a poetic text. None of the forms that he inherited from the symphonic past satisfied him. His need for confession and his desire for instantaneous communication made him reject formal ground plans in which 'repetition' was obligatory as part of the architecture. Richard Strauss emphasized the fact that musical form since Wagner has become forward-looking and concerned with 'becoming', and that this has done away with that backward-looking or confrontation with the past which was formerly necessary in order to understand the architecture of a work. If this is so, then Mahler immediately faced the new historical situation and exerted all his energies toward achieving a musical 'continuum'. When themes are recalled they are not actually repeated, but serve as markers, inserted with dramatic effect at important junctures, enabling the listener to follow the work, just as in a novel our interest centres on the characters whose behaviour determines the action and forms, as it were, the thread of the narrative.

There are elements both of the epic and of the novel in Mahler's musical forms, from his earliest works onwards. He 'tells a story in music', quite openly when the music is supported by a literary text but no less when this verbal support is absent. Apart from the epic and the novel, there is often the suggestion of an imaginary theatre in Mahler's works, with real stage effects transferred to the concert hall. An example of this in *Das klagende Lied* is the offstage wind band used with a deliberately *naturalistic* effect, the

---

[1] Sleeve note for the recording by Boulez, CBS 577233.

performers playing *fortissimo* (with the sound quality that this implies) but being heard *piano*. This theatrical gesture goes back beyond Berlioz and Wagner to Beethoven's *Leonora No. 3*.

There is a similar relationship to the past in the text chosen by Mahler. At the end of the nineteenth century he made an ingenious attempt to return to the very origins of German romanticism, using the 'story', or popular legend, which Achim von Arnim and Cleméns Brentano had made the essential element of one type of romantic vision. It was not difficult to foresee his future use of *Des Knaben Wunderhorn*. This return to past origins implies both a nostalgia for a 'paradise lost' and also a calculated ingenuity in searching for a means of retrieving it. Both text and music reveal a deep concern with integrating direct, popular expression with that of the 'learned' professional. This concern shows itself in the literary and the musical vocabulary of the work – hence the contrast between the 'archaism' of some passages and the 'modernism' of others.

Another constant feature of Mahler's sensibility and imagination is the mixture of the marvellous and the macabre, of tragedy and mockery. The poem, which is frequently gloomy and disturbing – and entirely 'interior' – is marked by nervous jolts, shuddering as it evokes scenes of horror, yet enjoying the sensation. Its characteristics are not only marked, but easily recognizable as references to a remarkable period in German literature of the past. The often extreme oscillations of sensibility find feverish expression in the music; and there are moments that come near to theatrical grandiloquence, exaggerated gestures felt to be necessary in order to impress, if not to convince the listener.

From the purely technical point of view the score reveals a mastery in the handling of choral and orchestral masses that is astonishing, particular in so young a composer. This is a natural gift, which some composers possess from the outset, even if they have as yet had no contact with practical music-making. In the present work Mahler shows an acute awareness of timbre and the intuition of a genius in obtaining exactly the effect that he wants. Of course his orchestration shows the influence of earlier models, and it was to be some time before he was capable of some of those audacities that are so surprisingly well calculated. Already, though, we are aware of the perfect aptness with which he chooses the material needed to communicate his musical ideas. The narrative is entrusted primarily to the solo singers, and the chorus are given the verbal commentary that effects the transition from narrative to instrumental comment. Each plane is clearly established and with it the function of each section of the performers.

This is the first of Mahler's epics and it makes us aware of future developments and implications. The great novel has already been roughed out and we shall find a new chapter in each new work. There are in fact artists whose inspiration springs from a single source and develops in accordance with a number of unchanging ideas. Mahler seems to me to be one of these.

31

Reflections on *Pelléas et Mélisande*[1]

Pelléas et Mélisande was an important turning point both in Debussy's career as a composer and in the history of opera. It caused much heated discussion of all kinds without any really important direct consequences. As a masterpiece, its place and its importance were recognized, but apart from that little changed, Debussy's conception occupying a marginal position in the double tradition dating from the middle of the nineteenth century. Within that tradition one party insisted on the immediate impact and the *animal* magnetism of the human voice, while the other attached primary importance to the significance of myth as expressed in music. There was a permanent antagonism between the Italian conception of opera on the one hand and the German idea of 'music-drama' on the other, other 'traditions' constituting no more than episodic and isolated diversions even when they bore the hallmark of genius: Mussorgsky, like Debussy, stands alone. *Pelléas et Mélisande*, therefore, was not an unprecedented incident. While Mussorgsky exercised only a narrowly circumscribed influence, Debussy's influence was manifested on a universal scale, infinitely stronger in the case of his non-theatrical works whose importance was grasped almost immediately, whereas there were reservations about *Pelléas* – or, what comes to the same thing, a preference for *Pelléas* had an obsessive, exclusive character for the 'initiates'.

Did *Pelléas* fail to achieve wide 'popularity' because there is not enough 'singing' in it? Because it contains no great moments of orchestral expansion? Or because the relationship between text and music is too closely dependent on understanding the French language? At a superficial level all these reasons probably played a part, in addition to a heap of misunderstandings, not the least of which was the idea of specifically national qualities. If such qualities really constitute an insurmountable barrier to the propagation of a work, nothing Germanic and nothing Italian would be exportable. Could anything be more deliberately linked to the mentality of a

---

[1] 'Miroirs pour *Pelléas et Mélisande*', on the occasion of the 1969 performance of the opera at Covent Garden conducted by Boulez. Published with subsequent recording of the work on Columbia M3 30119, 1970.

people than the thought that generated works whose universal character is proved daily, whatever may be thought of their actual quality?

No, we must look for deeper reasons.

In the first place, what does *Pelléas* represent in Debussy's life? It was the only work for the theatre that he completed, since he soon dropped a number of other half-formed plans, all of which were centred round some of his basic obsessions. *Le Martyre de Saint Sébastien*, for instance, cannot really be considered as an aesthetic project to which he consciously and totally devoted himself – it was something that was due to circumstance, almost to chance, stage music that became lost in a literary pathos quite alien to its substance. *Pelléas* was therefore a *first* opera with no successor, and it belongs to the composer's youth, the period when he was only gradually becoming aware of his own personality. It is an opera of discovery rather than reflection, and Debussy was not only in search of the dramatic function of music, he was also forging his own musical language, and still subject to influence in both fields. It seems likely that in the first place the dramatic project was the stronger and necessarily took precedence over the musical.

We must remember that Debussy chose a literary text and set to work to 'put it to music' without making any changes. Particularly interesting is the fact that the few cuts that he eventually made were all in the interest of, as it were, *de-familiarizing* the drama, since they involved cutting out domestics and serving women who would no doubt have delighted Mussorgsky by their deformation and distortion of the 'noble' world. These cuts in fact reveal Debussy's deliberate intention of creating a timeless world free of subsidiary contingencies, but they do not imply any modification of the dramatic structure or any reconsideration of the stage language. Thus Debussy grafted his music on to an already existing, self-contained, literary object that did not necessarily imply any other dimension. Given his own aesthetic ideas, the drama was perfectly suited to such grafting, and this is why there was no essential divergence.

Furthermore, Debussy found in Maeterlinck leading poetic themes corresponding very closely to his own sources of inspiration – hair, for example, which provides the title for the second of the *Chansons de Bilitis* ('La Chevelure'), and the sea, which had already formed the background for 'Sirènes' (*Nocturnes*) and was soon to furnish him with the title of one of his chief works. These poetic themes are associated with musical figures that reappear almost literally in compositions of the same date and even in some belonging to a later period. Working on his opera helped Debussy to recognize and explore his own personality and gave him an opportunity to obtain a clear view of the constant elements and characteristics of his own aesthetic. In this way, and thanks to a number of different circumstances, *Pelléas et Mélisande* came to play a leading part in his career as a composer.

The importance of *Pelléas* in the history of opera seems at first less obvious, less decisive. No great changes have occurred, as far as public taste is concerned, in this area, which is before all others one of the most militant conservatism. It has often been said that the failure of *Pelléas* to attract the public is due largely to Maeterlinck's theatrical style, which has been mercilessly described as static and pallid, characteristics that are said to have infected the music. No dramatic excitement and therefore no public. And yet this is in fact a tragedy of middle-class life, with virtually none of the ingredients or the condiments lacking – love, jealousy, violence, a curse and a murder. It all happens for the most part in a kind of padded atmosphere, but from Act II onwards Golaud's behaviour suggests an ill-controlled savagery, which explodes in the hysterical scene in Act IV. Why have Pelléas and Mélisande never become a pair of symbolic lovers despite the exquisite scenes in which they confess their love and affirm it against all odds? It is probably because Maeterlinck's theatrical material belongs to two different worlds: the characters of the story are timeless and possess all the qualities of mythical figures, but at the same time they are involved in a completely everyday drama which seems to lack that very quality of myth.

Think for a moment of all the time and the trouble that Wagner takes to explain, through Isolde, the multiple details of events that occurred before the actual action of the opera begins, describing the antecedents of the situation and informing us about the exact reasons for the attitude of each of the principal characters. Compared with this Maeterlinck's presentation of his characters is not so much elliptical as deliberately vague and allusive, and contains no precise facts, so that whereas we come to believe completely in the dramatic existence of the characters in *Tristan*, the 'spontaneous generation' of *Pelléas* leaves the characters only superficially real to us.

Furthermore the poetic themes in *Pelléas* often remain imaginary in character and their representation on the stage is marked by a heavy realism that contradicts their dream-like quality. Take the first scene of Act III, where Mélisande lets down her long hair. It proves in practice extremely hard to make this symbolism of hair-as-river, hair-as-erotic-symbol visually acceptable, or even plausible. The poetic, *imaginary* vision is difficult to combine with a girl leaning out of a window and hair that is quite obviously a wig . . . On the other hand, in the scene where Golaud, as it were, exorcizes this accursed hair by parodying the sign of the cross – 'à droite, et puis à gauche! . . . en avant! en arrière!' – the ritual must be crudely realistic in order to emphasize its violence and its cruelty. In this case Mélisande's hair is not a poetic transposition at one remove from its origin in reality but is clearly an instrument of torture necessary to the dramatic climax of the scene.

From what I have said it follows, I think, that this ebb and flow of crude realism and fragile dream-life is an important element in Debussy's conception of the theatre, even if it is not *absolutely* original and was borrowed, in fact, from Maeterlinck . . . It is the same overlapping of two apparently contradictory mental approaches that we find in Baudelaire and in one of the authors by whom Baudelaire was most influenced, Edgar Allan Poe. That name recalls Debussy's project of an opera based on *The Fall of the House of Usher*. It is only too clear now why he never completed that project: it could only have been a repetition of *Pelléas*, with the same atmosphere and strikingly similar characters. The literary level was higher, but the imagery had already been exhausted and the idea of reviving it was a pure fantasy.

What constitutes the profound originality of Debussy's aesthetic of the theatre has been for the most part slurred over, so that *Pelléas* has appeared as a kind of disincarnate work verging on what may be described as a 'poetic' tisane in the worst sense, a work in which the conflicts arise for no very apparent reason and can only seem incongruous, since they arise between characters who must never pronounce one word louder than another. A special 'tradition' has given the whole opera an elegant varnish, to which must of course be added the famous French clarity. Well, elegance and clarity in the accepted, conventional sense have nothing to do with *Pelléas*. The atmosphere is sombre, incredibly heavy; there are endless complaints about never seeing the sun, which makes its rare appearance when Golaud and Pelléas ascend from the vaults. As for the 'poetic' character that is wished on to the protagonists, it is enough to discourage – if not to enrage – the boldest dream-fanciers.

Mélisande is made to appear as a kind of dove hovering high above any idea of 'sin', with Pelléas cruising at the same altitude disguised as a noble page; Golaud is a nasty bully without a note of poetry in his character but ludicrously reluctant to hover too; and as for Arkel, he is the incarnation of Poetic Mystery in person, opening his *bouche d'ombre* only to utter oracular statements borrowed from the wisdom of the ages. How can anyone be interested in such silly, bloodless cardboard figures? What has been marketed under the hallmark of mystery is a useless product devoid of that very *mystery* with which Debussy invested his characters, for all ambivalence has been destroyed. It is not only the characters themselves that have been emasculated; the dramatic situations themselves have been defused. The see-sawing between realistic events and their expansion as symbols, the profound significance that links the two together – all that has vanished, leaving something about as solid as a pre-Raphaelite fairy story ... the Golden Damozel on her shaky balcony!

I have already compared Debussy's nature, as a composer, to that of a cat; and the comparison is more than ever true in *Pelléas*, where the swift and deadly sheathing and unsheathing of claws can be seen in at least two of the chief characters, Golaud and Mélisande. Consider the evolution of Golaud and the musical contexts given him by Debussy. At the beginning of Act I he is presented as a robust character, but *lost*; his real weakness can be sensed beneath his masterful appearance. From Act II onwards his anxiety is made clear to us, and also the extreme nervous tension that he can no longer control when he hears of the loss of the ring that he gave to Mélisande. This ill-controlled nervous tension explodes brutally in the tower scene in Act III. In the vaults the oppressive atmosphere strengthens his intention to kill Pelléas and his own anxiety betrays *him* too soon. This anxiety is replaced by the neurotic mentality of an inquisitor when he makes Yniold spy on Pelléas and Mélisande. When he shouts 'Regarde! regarde!' he is almost demented. In Act IV Golaud *must* torture Mélisande, indulging in a sort of ritual exorcism of her hair. As in the scene with Yniold, the music takes on a demented character, suggesting both his frantic willing of the catastrophe and his panic terror as he sees it inevitably approaching: Arkel's cry of 'Golaud!' – his own name cast in his teeth – rouses him, like a spell, from this ritual intoxication. In the last act he is torturing himself quite as much as interrogating Mélisande, and his desperate desire to discover the *truth* ends in a pitiful uncertainty. The diversity of Golaud's music shows the precision with which Debussy followed the evolution of his character, apparently so full of energy but passing in fact from weakness to neurotic obsession and almost to dementia.

The evolution of Mélisande's character could be described in the same way, passing from fear to open hatred of Golaud and finally to a state of obliviousness even harder to bear, just as Pelléas too is transformed, a boy discovering the mystery of erotic love and condemned by his *naïveté* to die an uncomprehending death.

Then there is Arkel, who is generally made up as an old man 'full of wise saws' and gifted with 'clairvoyance', although his predictions fail to hit the mark and are immediately contradicted by events – hence the presentation of him as a solemn, patriarchal figure, as though old age provided an excuse for stupidity . . . Nothing, in my opinion, could be further than this from the Arkel described by Debussy, who is a naïve character given to expressing his ideals rather than to prophesying the future, another frightened person trying to reassure himself by reassuring others. The fact that he has pre- served this *naïveté* despite his age and experience of life links him, by implication, to the youthful, *natural naïveté* of Pelléas – he is in fact a white-haired Pelléas . . . Seen in this light, Arkel's great moments are not his delivering of wise saws, which often prove untrue, but the obstinate *naïveté* that he needs to exorcize and shake off his obsession with physical decay and his fear of death.

The figure of Geneviève shows what, in such a situation as Méli- sande's, resignation can achieve. By her own will rather than by accident Mélisande refuses to accept this fate, and Geneviève disappears from the story.

The constant interaction of realism and symbolism also appears in the music in the form of rapid alternations between action and commentary. These two elements were rigidly separated in the early days of opera, thus assuring the formal framework a maximum effectiveness. The action, which was entrusted to the recitative, was carried on in a vocal style not very different from speech and governed by firmly established conventions, while the instrumental style was limited to the punctuation of the vocal part. There was no possibility of any misunderstanding: the *informative* character of this part of an opera made it very similar to the spoken drama, with its faster speech rhythms, whereas musical continuity was ensured by the harmonic language, which served, like Ariadne's thread, to guide the listener. At due intervals the characters' reflections on the dramatic situation were expressed in *arias* or *ensembles*, at which point the action either came to a halt or else reached a clearly emphasized climax. The form was thus serial rather than continuous until Wagner, who was much more concerned with a continuity designed to give the maximum of illusion. He refused to accept convention as a means of understanding and thus to dissociate action and reflection. This distinction between the two is still occasionally perceptible in his mature works, but then it forms an exception, like the quintet in Act 3 of *Meistersinger*. Even so the alternation between planes of action and planes of contemplation does appear in Wagner in the form of long stretches or 'arches' of time; and we are not often confronted by violent switches except on key words, which suddenly throw a new light on the musical context.

At the other extreme we have Mussorgsky's obsessive concern with transposing into music the inflections of spoken conversation without employing any conventional method such as recitative. His unfinished *Marriage* is significant in this respect, with its careful integrating of the impulses, the lacunae and almost the intervals of spoken dialogue into the musical language. The attempt reveals the composer's ambition, which was nothing less than the unification of two worlds governed by fundamentally different laws and constructive principles. He discovered his own truth in this matter in *Boris* although, more generally speaking, genre (and even bravura) pieces alternate there with musically 'realistic' numbers. There were some absolutely new features in his solution of the problem, but the old dichotomy of the opera still persists.

I would not go so far as to say that Debussy discovered the ideal solution of this basic operatic problem – is there in fact such a solution? – but what he did is well worth studying. Instead of Wagner's long 'planes' he gives us a very closely woven tissue of action and reflection. From the outset a sharp eye and a good ear are needed to perceive these distinctions, or *modulations*, which move rapidly, sometimes with hardly a change in the vocal or instrumental style. In other cases, of course, the contrast is more marked and the differences are more decided. This grafting of the poetic moment on to the dramatic, a sort of instantaneous efflorescence, proves to be the chief characteristic of *Pelléas*: the passage from *information* to *reflection* is often subtle but is none the less clearly expressed. The vocal line detaches itself from the text and assumes an autonomous character; the orchestral texture is no longer supportive but makes a contribution in its own right. These special moments emerge from the general course of the work without disturbing its continuity; there are some cases in which the listener is hardly aware of them before they have vanished. They might be said to be the *revealers* of the dramatic texture.

By seeing in *Pelléas* no more than continuous recitative, the reaction against Wagner's 'unendliche Melodie', the real novelty of the work is slurred over. It is true that the accentuation, the prosody, the speech inflexions, the caesuras and the rhythm of the French language remain a constant concern; but there is no question of attempting a uniquely faithful or exclusively literal transcription. Contrary to the legend according to which every word has its unique place and value in accordance with the laws of French speech, Debussy's transcription of the poetic moments pays absolutely no attention to this aesthetic of imitation; at those points it is the musical inflexion that dominates and the words form a secondary dimension. If this were the only way of detecting Debussy's intention, it would still provide an almost infallible index.

Musical continuity is ensured, if not wholly provided, by the principal themes or motives; but the stylistic characterization of each entire scene is quite as important as far as coherence and unity are concerned. If we are talking of principal themes – musical figures associated with Arkel, Golaud, Pelléas and Mélisande – we immediately think of Wagner and his *Leitmotivs*. In actual fact Debussy's almost cavalier use of this procedure is very unlike Wagner's, both in intention and in execution. We should not forget, as I have said, that *Pelléas* is not only Debussy's first opera, but also his last. His handling of motives, their relation to each other and their transformation has none of the subtlety or the profound logic shown, at its most advanced, in *Parsifal*. What we have in *Pelléas* are more like arabesques associated with individual characters, with no more than decorative variations, easily integrated into the general context and superimposed on each other, but never completely penetrating the whole texture. To find in Debussy any thorough working-out that is entirely individual in character and technique but comparable in quality to that of Wagner's late works we must turn to much later works, such as *Jeux* or the piano *Etudes*. Wagner's only influence of this kind in *Pelléas* consists in the composer's feeling that the chief characters must be musically characterized.

Much more profound, and in fact all-pervading, is the influence of the actual vocabulary, including even the orchestration, of *Parsifal*. It is significant that the passages that reveal this influence most clearly were written quickly: they were in fact some of the interludes added at the last moment to facilitate scene-changes. Even if they date from a later period when Debussy's style was absolutely fixed, haste obliged him to use material that presented itself spontaneously from his memory: the resemblances to *Parsifal* are most striking, almost literal quotations. This literalness is by no means universal, but the close relationship to *Parsifal* is repeatedly marked in some instances. Thus the rhythmic figure associated with Golaud is derived directly from that associated with Parsifal himself; Arkel's harmonic language and the orchestral sonorities that accompany it recall the Gurnemanz of Act III; a certain strident quality in Golaud's anger reminds the listener of Klingsor, whereas the tower scene in which Pelléas envelops himself in Mélisande's hair is a furtive evocation of the love scene in *Tristan*.

I have no wish to undertake a pedantic study of such influences, but I think it necessary to point out that Wagner was in fact one of the chief sources of this opera, which was for many years regarded as an aggressive anti-Wagnerian manifesto. When it first appeared, everyone agreed in discovering a strong Mussorgsky influence, which I find to say the least an exaggeration, since it applies only to very subsidiary points, principally in connection with the character of Yniold. In any case it is much closer to Mussorgsky's *Nursery*, and still more to the nursery scene in *Boris*, than to any other scenes in that opera. As we are speaking of influences, we may close the subject by pointing to the faint echo of *Carmen*, particularly the last act.

In the perspective of today it is easier to identify the sources of the music without denying either the originality or the merits of *Pelléas*; but what of its influence on subsequent operas? This, as far as I can see, is hardly more than superficial or episodic, and relates only to such general features as French *prosody* or lyric *atmosphere*. The next composer who was to achieve an important synthesis between drama and music was Berg, who set out from entirely different ideas about form; at the very most there may be said to be a relationship with the *sonority* of Debussy's music in the scene where Wozzeck drowns himself. Berg defended himself with some heat against the imputation of any other 'impressionist' influence . . . and I am convinced that he was perfectly right.

Since Debussy's ideas about the drama are expressed so pointedly in his music and the means that he employs are defined as precisely as it is possible to define them, why and how did all the misunderstandings arise that have so totally perverted the sense of *Pelléas*? It seems to me the very height of nonsense to associate this opera with a kind of celestial boredom, a pale, remote, 'distinguished' poetry and an imagination that is not so much exquisite as tired, even exhausted. People who use words like 'mystery' or 'dream' when speaking of *Pelléas* are in fact emptying them of all real significance and indulging in an imagery that is insipid, bland, mock-modest, and in fact plain silly. If there is really one fault that one cannot find with Debussy it is wide-eyed silliness, something that he particularly disliked, as can be seen from both his letters and his articles. It is also difficult to see how these cheap mystery-merchants, who are perpetually terrified of seeing their little dream world exploded by the dotting of 'i's and crossing of 't's – a faithful interpretation of the text, in fact – can reconcile this with their other equally obsessive concern with 'French' clarity and light. Unfortunately not only *Pelléas*, but all Debussy's work has suffered from our native thurifers, who have choked their idol with their poor-quality incense. Debussy did not disabuse them, being shrewder and less candid than he was willing to admit; in fact he seems to have composed almost exclusively in the small hours . . .

That is not, of course, to say that he never listened to 'the dialogue of the wind and the sea' and never dreamed of the sirens' song – only that behind those half-closed eyes of his there was a never-winking intelligence busy with works the logic of whose construction was rivalled by very few of the great composers. The apparent nonchalance of their form, the impression they give of being improvisations whose felicitous turns of expression were the result of some miraculous chance – all these were a carefully arranged *trompe-l'oeil*. Any neglect of the exact text, any unguarded surrender to the brilliance of an individual passage, and the famous dream dissolves completely, leaving nothing of the mystery but scented bric-à-brac. In Debussy the ideas of mystery, poetry and dream take on a profound significance only when they are achieved by precision, in full daylight; and in this he resembles Cézanne, who gave his landscapes their secret quality by means of light and plain factuality.

To return to *Pelléas*, the real mystery of the characters is revealed only by a needle-sharp examination of the musical detail. As in every great work, this mystery proves to be more complex and more full of contradictions the more we examine it. Mélisande is a mixture of candour and duplicity; Pelléas shrinks from committing himself to the absolute; Golaud shows a sullen impotence when faced with the ruin of his world; Arkel refuses to abandon his *naïveté* out of fear . . . As André Schaeffner says, this really is a theatre of fear and cruelty. Why will people so often refuse to see the opera in this light? It probably all goes back to Debussy's own day, though this hypothesis is supported only by indirect documentation (as far as the music itself is concerned) – letters, press notices, memoirs.

There is no doubt that Debussy was frankly repelled by the operatic world of his day; Wagner-worship irritated him, he felt no sympathy with the works of the Italian composers and he was impatient with the productions of his French colleagues. He was nothing but sarcastic about the conceited posturing of most singers and took little interest in their vocal capabilities, unless these in some way served musical truth, musical necessity. He was unwilling to admit that their only achievement was a purely physical one and consisted in the successful pitting of their voices against the volume of sound produced by the orchestra. In fact he mistrusted their whole *attitude*. His original idea for *Pelléas* was a short series of performances in an intimate setting, in the fear that a large building would oblige his singers to adopt a grandiloquent style. When this proved impractical, he gave up the idea of a special setting and agreed to a 'normal' theatre and 'regular' performances. But his detestation of any kind of 'theatrical' style, on which he often insisted, led his not very perspicacious followers to sacrifice the drama and its cruelty, and to concentrate on a well-bred 'distinction' and refinement of taste that suggest a smart clothes shop rather than any kind of tragedy.

In order to avoid vulgarity, they plunged – enthusiastically – into a kind of prim affectation. In the same way avoiding the orchestra drowning the voices of these saccharine dolls inevitably involved constant 'discretion' worthy of a footman, with the consequent threat of boring the listener and sending him to sleep. The many contrasts in the work were reduced to a minute scale and this robbed them of their potency and violence. I find it depressing that this so-called tradition of bloodlessness could pass as the very height of 'the French spirit' in music! The real difficulty in interpreting *Pelléas* is to avoid both pointlessly *heroic* gestures and rhetorical attitudes on the one hand and timidity and 'safe' understatement on the other.

Even that, though, is not the chief stumbling-block, as it seems to me. There are other aspects of the score that are infinitely more difficult to realize satisfactorily. Fluid tempo is one of the chief characteristics of Debussy's music. The chief *points of flexibility* are clearly marked in the score and the conductor has nothing to do but follow. Yet if you analyse the score really closely in order to isolate and convey its full significance, there are many fluctuations that are necessary though not in fact noted, since that would destroy their subtlety – fluctuations needed in order to articulate the musical continuity and give the sound/word inflexions the same *variability* as the dramatic action. In order to emphasize these swift changes of mood, these magnetic moments and the transitions from realism to symbolism that I have already mentioned, tempo must be infinitely supple. *Rubato* keeps suggesting itself, a *rubato* controlled by an internal logic and clearly established in its functions yet appearing to be entirely impromptu – in fact a *rubato* that reflects Debussy's own conception of music. This seldom involves actual breaks, so much as a variety of hesitation and holding-back, or else pressing-forward, none of them immediately observable and noticed by the listener only after the actual event. Nothing about this *rubato* must be explicitly deliberate; it must be something more like an irresistible tendency in the music to modulate its gait in accordance with a flexible utterance. Hence the need for a close relationship between singers and orchestra, something at which the general texture, not only the tempo, should aim.

It is a question of *coherence* even more than *cohesion*. It is absolutely vital to establish the interrelationship between the vocal line and the orchestra, both elements achieving real autonomy only when completely united in purpose. There are occasions when their unity of expression is total, others when one element comes to a halt and the other takes the lead. Furthermore each scene can move at its characteristic speed (a major criterion of its intrinsic unity) only if its tempo is precisely defined and moves within the limits that give that scene its individual shape and establish its unique relationship to *every other* scene. Without this firm definition the music will tend to sink into an uncontoured monotony, the elements composing each scene dispersing and becoming isolated moments unless held together by this implicit interdependence and solidarity. The whole score consists of minute gradations in time, which are amplified as the action progresses, and increasingly marked contrasts reveal the deepening of the drama. Debussy's ideas in this field were so completely, so extraordinarily novel that they can be explicated only by a perfect accord between the overall and the immediate, instantaneous conception of the tempo. The orchestra becomes a kind of 'breathing floor' for the singers, as Claudel puts it when describing a ship's movements at sea as experienced by the passengers...

Unlike many operas, *Pelléas* hardly presents any problems of balance between orchestra and voices. The difficulty, if any, lies in avoiding an excessive discretion that makes it impossible for the orchestra to support the voice and ensure essential continuity apart from the vocal dialogue. To reduce the score to a *recitativo accompagnato* is to do the composer a quite singular disservice. There is certainly no need to *exaggerate* the contrasts, but they must in every case be *realized* as imagined and written, and with the emphasis needed to give them significance. Of course the dynamic range of Debussy's music is not the same as Wagner's, but its proper dynamic scale must be respected. It is larger than is generally supposed and variations in dynamics, like changes of tempo and texture, may be very abrupt – another side of that *feline* aspect that I mentioned. As in the case of tempo, I should be tempted to lay down that each scene develops within a certain dynamic scale, which establishes its unity, its individuality and its relation to other scenes. Once again I should like to insist that here too the long-range, overall and the immediate, individual conceptions must be in perfect accord.

I must now, I think, say something about the type of voice demanded by the role of Pelléas. This has so often been given to a high baritone that it may be surprising to find it given here to a tenor. There are, however, two indications – however academic they may seem – that show beyond any possible doubt that Debussy had a tenor in mind, and not a baritone. The first is that he wrote the part in the G clef from the first sketches – which I have examined – to the final version. According to the convention of the day tenor parts (if the C clef is discounted) were always written in the G clef. This convention is still respected today. The second is the tessitura of Pelléas's music, which corresponds exactly to that of the tenor voice as defined in orthodox textbooks of harmony: from low C to high A. I feel certain that Debussy obeyed this law, if only unconsciously following what he had been taught as a student. These arguments may seem 'pedantic', but I still think that everything argues in favour of the tenor voice – from the point of view of colour the tenor is better, whether as a contrast to Golaud or as partner to Mélisande. None of the low-lying passages require great volume of tone, whereas this is needed for high-lying passages where the tenor voice is much more flexible and still has 'reserves' of power, whereas such passages strain the baritone voice to its limits. Both intuitively and logically, therefore, I feel that we should opt for the tenor.

There is no ambiguity about any of the other roles from this point of view.

I think it is clearly better to give the role of Yniold to a child, if possible, both from the vocal point of view – children's voices have a special quality of their own – and for dramatic effectiveness. If there are two or three points at which there is a risk of a child's voice being covered by the orchestra, it is well worth taking for the sake of added dramatic intensity and greater dramatic credibility. With a child in the part of Yniold the last few moments of the final scene of Act III are almost unbearable in their suggestion of terror, whereas they are more likely to be embarrassing if the role is sung by an adult *en travesti*, which makes Yniold's terror quite incongruous.

After living in close contact with an opera for some time, working on it in detail with singers and players and minutely analysing every element before arriving at the synthesis necessary for performance, the work becomes so familiar that there is a danger of its losing its enchantment. It is as though too great an effort to understand is a threat to spontaneity and that you will never in that case recapture an unsophisticated attitude. On the other hand, works that preserve their magic quality seem to become more mysterious the better you get to know them. This is the case with *Pelléas et Mélisande*, which came at an unusual moment in the history of opera and possesses a universal significance. It is a work that has probably suffered from too much 'special treatment', and full justice will be done to it only by restoring its mythical dimension and its dramatic energy. I am quite clear in my own mind that it belongs in the very highest class, the class of works that serve as a kind of mirror in which a whole culture can see itself transfigured.

32

Debussy: Orchestral Works[1]

Except for *Ibéria* Debussy's orchestral *Images* are still underestimated, and neither *Gigues* nor *Rondes de printemps* is often played. These three works are treated as a folklore triptych in which the composer, aware of his failing strength, tried to revitalize his imaginative powers by having recourse to popular themes, in the hope of retrieving the impulse of his earlier works. They are generally blamed for their academic character, resulting from exhaustion, and for lack of invention compared with those earlier works, and particularly *La Mer*.

There is certainly something surprising in Debussy's idea of composing a cycle of pieces based on the 'colours' of three different countries – Scotland (*Gigues*), Spain (*Ibéria*) and France (*Rondes de printemps*) – in view of his often devastating comments on certain uses of folk music. He was very aware of the fact that popular tunes collected at the extreme limit of their vitality do not lend themselves to the kind of symphonic development that was common in France at the time with Vincent d'Indy and the composers of the Schola Cantorum. As he said in so many words, it is no good dressing up helpless peasant women in fine clothes to justify their appearing in the 'symphonic festival': they merely feel ill at ease in such a setting.

The 'Spanish' vein has been constantly exploited in French music since the days of Bizet's *Carmen* and has been an influence comparable to Manet's admiration of Goya. There is no need to give a list of the Spanish-type pieces written by composers from Chabrier to Ravel, and Debussy found a similar inspiration in a number of his piano pieces: 'La soirée dans Grenade' in *Estampes*, 'La puerta del vino' in the *Préludes* and *Lindaraja* for two pianos. The only other reference to Scotland in his music is the rather faceless *Marche écossaise*, while France is represented by 'Jardins sous la pluie', in which he used the same popular song, ('Nous n'irons plus au bois') as in *Rondes de printemps*.

Debussy's use of folksong, then, is not confined to *Images*, but he never

[1] 'Debussy: l'oeuvre pour orchestre', from the booklet accompanying the recording by Boulez, Columbia D 3M–32988.

employed it systematically. Was he not, indeed, more or less aware of how strange any such systematic use would be in his case? The three orchestral *Images* were in fact composed over a long period. *Ibéria* seems to have been composed fairly quickly and 'naturally', but he appears gradually to have lost interest in *Gigues* and *Rondes de printemps*. Léon Vallas, a most scrupulous biographer, tells us that *Gigues* was completed by André Caplet.

Here are some dates. The three *Images* were composed between 1906 and 1912, and the order in which they were published is not the order in which they were composed. The second piece, *Ibéria*, was given its first performance on 20 February 1910; the third, *Rondes de printemps*, a few days later, on 2 March. According to Léon Vallas *Gigues* was begun in 1909, and completed and orchestrated in 1912, and it was played on 26 January 1913. In this connection the question often arises as to the order in which the three pieces should be played in the concert hall when all three are given together. Of course the simplest answer is to follow the order in which they appeared, and this is probably what the composer intended. This is satisfactory in principle, as the short one-movement *Gigues* and *Rondes de printemps* thus frame the longest piece, *Ibéria*, which is in three movements. On the other hand this symmetrical principle seems to clash with the musical quality of the peroration in *Ibéria*, compared with which the peroration in *Rondes de printemps* appears as no more than a pale repetition. The most logical order in performance seems to me to be *Rondes de printemps*, *Gigues*, *Ibéria*. But this, though suitable for the concert hall, has nothing to do with the order adopted for the record, in which the two shorter pieces are used to balance and to provide a contrast with *Ibéria*.

Spanish local colour plays a well-defined role in *Ibéria*. In the first place there is the choice of instruments – the 'characteristic' percussion, such as *tambour de basque* and castanets. Then there are a number of rhythms, or rather rhythmic sequences, that are literally borrowed from Spanish folk music, as indeed are some of the melodic inflexions. What Debussy himself said of Albéniz is relevant here and is rightly quoted by Léon Vallas: 'He does not exactly quote folk tunes, but he is so imbued with them and has heard so many that they have passed into his music and become impossible to distinguish from his own inventions.'

What I find most attractive in this work is in fact not so much the Spanish element (which is not really any more important here than Asia is in *Pagodes*) as the freedom of symphonic invention given to the basic elements selected. I particularly admire 'Les parfums de la nuit', one of Debussy's most inventive pieces, not so much for its thematic content as for the novel way in which he 'creates' the development, and makes the orchestral sound evolve, by the subtlety of the transitional passages. Even when themes reappear, the music never looks back: everything suggests a superior, polished kind of improvisation, so great is Debussy's control of his inventive skill and therefore his ability to do without any immediately recognizable formal framework. This art of transition is particularly noticeable in the passage linking the second and third movements, where 'Les parfums de la nuit' is gradually absorbed as the new elements – particularly the rhythmic elements – of 'Matin d'un jour de fête' become increasingly clearly defined. From Debussy's letters we know that he himself was particularly pleased with this subtle transition from darkness to light.

In the same way I do not find the Scottish element the most significant feature of *Gigues*, but rather the oscillation between a slow melody and a lively rhythm. I use the word 'oscillation', but I might equally say 'coinciding' because, when the two elements are superimposed, they give the impression of a double breathing, and this is most unusual. Timbre plays a primary part in separating the two planes of sound; and by giving the slow opening theme exclusively to the oboe d'amore the composer helps to isolate it in the listener's mind. It is not only that the tone of the oboe d'amore is pretty and unusual, intended to recall that of the bagpipes and excellently suited to the expression in this opening passage. It also makes us aware that the tempo of this tune will not be 'disturbed' by the appearance of other figures in a different tempo.

In *Rondes de printemps* Debussy makes use of a favourite rhythm of five beats in the bar, subdivided into two and three, with repeated notes – the same rhythm that appears episodically in the second of the *Nocturnes*, 'Fêtes'. The Frenchness of this piece is certainly the least noticeable thing about it, at least to foreign ears, and was, I suppose, wholly *absorbed* by the composer's own personality, so that there was no room for the 'exotic'. His different handlings of 'Nous n'irons plus au bois' are not in fact the most remarkable thing about this piece either. It may well be that Debussy felt most free when he was least concerned with the accuracy of his quotations.

Danses for harp and strings may be called an *oeuvre de circonstance* in the sense that it was both commissioned by Pleyel's and also determined by the fact that it was designed to promote their chromatic harp as a rival to the pedal harp, which was then the exclusive property of their Erard rivals. It was believed that the chromatic harp would avoid the frequent pedal changes, which became more and more acrobatic as music became increasingly chromatic; but the difficulties caused by increasing the number of strings prevented the instrument from establishing itself. The first performance of *Danses* was on 6 November 1904. The piece is now played on the pedal harp, and the fact that this is not the instrument for which it was originally conceived presents no major obstacles. The most important reason for this is the nature of Debussy's music, which is quite as much diatonic as chromatic; and the *Danse sacrée* seems deliberately archaic – a tendency to be found in the *Trois Ballades de Villon* and some of the piano *Préludes* ('Danseuses de Delphes'). The harp is treated as a solo instrument, and the orchestral accompaniment is discreet both in musical conception and in actual sonority. In this sense – and this sense only – the work belongs to the baroque tradition of the concerto, in which the 'orchestra' accompanies the soloist and there is no dialogue between the two such as had been the aim of all concerto writers during the romantic period. The piece illustrates the persistence of certain sources of inspiration in Debussy's music and shows them, as it were, in the raw.

After the composer's own words about the *Nocturnes* any further comment seems unnecessary, and in fact futile. He has defined his poetics better than anyone else, and in words unlikely to be forgotten by anyone who has read them. This is not, therefore, the angle from which I shall approach *Nocturnes*, which, with *Prélude à l'après-midi d'un faune*, forms the first panel of an orchestral triptych, the two other panels being formed by *La Mer* and *Jeux*.

A study of this triptych will enable us to trace clearly Debussy's evolution both as a composer and as a writer for the orchestra, and at the same time to note the striking persistence in his music of certain musical and instrumental ideas. The connection between 'Nuages' and *L'Après-midi* is particularly manifest in the middle section of 'Nuages', where the same melodic inflexions appear almost literally and are given to the same instrument (flute) as in the earlier work. In the third of the *Nocturnes*, 'Sirènes', the repeated trumpet call is unmistakably related to the one at the beginning of *La Mer*, where it is also repeated in the course of the work. (In the same way the cor anglais motive in 'Nuages' is very close to the trumpet motive in 'Sirènes').

The second of the *Nocturnes*, 'Fêtes', is more independent, but here too a figure for woodwind and strings, in five time, closely resembles a figure in *Rondes de printemps*. These details are evidence, if evidence is needed, of a constant element in Debussy's imagination, and demonstrate a clear connection between the works.

The handling of the orchestra is brilliant, though the subtleties of *Jeux* are still in the future. In any case forms are very simple and extremely clear. 'Nuages' and 'Fêtes' follow the same pattern, while 'Sirènes' is slightly less symmetrical and more complex.

We should not be misled by the simplicity of the orchestral writing, as the example of 'Sirènes' proves. There are divergences between early scores and the revised version made by Debussy after the first performances. (There are also unfortunately a number of such divergences in the orchestral parts, which does not make it easier for either players or conductor.) When conducting the piece in America, I had an opportunity to compare this first version with the present score containing the composer's amendments. In every case it was a matter of pruning in order to obtain a clearer, more transparent orchestral sound: pointless doublings were removed and various figures either lightened or given a more appropriate form. Another astonishing, and admirable, revelation was the apparent ease with which Debussy composed and arranged his themes. There is sufficient proof of this in 'Fêtes', where a farandole, or jig, theme is followed immediately by a fanfare, and the two seem to have no relationship to each other. In fact the first time that we hear the fanfare beneath the farandole it seems completely alien to the context. But when the fanfare reaches its climax, the tendrils of the farandole surround it so naturally and so expectedly that the listener has to make a conscious effort to realize the fact of this symbiosis.

When in 'Sirènes' Debussy adds wordless women's voices, it is in order to enrich the orchestral colour. Apart from some *bouche fermée* markings there is no indication of the vowel, or vowels, on which the singers are to vocalize. This being the case I have taken no liberties with the text in indicating different vowel colours (oo, o, a) to match the instrumental colours and the nuances of the orchestra. Vocalizing entirely on the vowel 'a' seems in fact to restrict both colour and dynamics and gives the piece a slightly monotonous, even insipid, character compared with the richness of the instrumental texure. As I say, this kind of step does not seem to me in any way to contradict the composer's intentions when these are not expressly indicated in the score.

A composer's total output is commonly divided into three categories – main works, secondary or minor works, and juvenilia. This is certainly a convenient classification, but I must admit that it is also justified by the facts. I may say that the secondary, or minor works – and even the juvenilia – of a great composer often interest me more than the main works of lesser artists! This no doubt betrays an excessive concentration of interest on my part; but I cannot help feeling that a great composer reveals himself – and often most endearingly – in works that resemble family groups or snapshots as opposed to official portraits.

This applies to both *Printemps* and the *Rhapsodie* for clarinet. The *Rhapsodie* was a commissioned work, written for a competition at the Paris Conservatoire. Not many competition pieces are as graceful and poetical as this, half reverie and half scherzo and a good example of Debussy at his least official. There is no dazzling display of virtuosity, but the composer amuses himself by setting the soloist a good number of traps as well as giving him a chance to display his tone and his phrasing in melodies marked *rêveusement lentes*.

Printemps belongs without doubt to the composer's juvenilia, though it contains the first hints of a number of ideas that he was to handle more skilfully later. We are still aware of some 'dated' influences, but Debussy's harmonic genius shows itself in some unmistakably personal characteristics, especially in the first movement. Listening to *Printemps* I can never help thinking of Monet's *Femmes dans le jardin*. Both works have the same freshness, the same lack of sophistication and a sort of delight in embarking on the voyage of self-discovery.

33

Satie: *Chien flasque*[1]

About himself:

'Nothing more to be done in that direction, I must find something else or I am finished.'

'If I fail, so much the worse for me. It means I had nothing to say.'

'How lucky to be old! When I was young, they used to badger me: "You'll see one day! Wait! You'll see!" Well, I have waited and I haven't seen anything. Nothing.'

A case of glandular atrophy – Satie's styles; Satie's discoveries – or inventions; Satie's humour.

Satie's three styles:
   – the harmonic, impressionist style – *Gymnopédies* and so on
   – *style Paulette Darty* – waltzes, sung or otherwise
   – the contrapuntal style – Schola style – 'abstract' clarity, classicism

Some of Satie's inventions:
   – chords of the ninth with unusual resolutions
   – suppression of bar lines
   – 'retour à ...'
   – simplicity
   – his disciples
The only thing lacking to his reputation is to have been the founder of the Lepine Competition (Small Inventors Section.)

He was often up to date, sometimes an anticipator: his music is always dated. The *Sarabandes* date from 1887, in other words fourteen years earlier than Debussy's ...

---

[1] *Revue musicale*, No. 214, 1952, pp. 153–4. The title alludes to three piano pieces published by Satie in 1912 and entitled 'Trois Préludes flasques', one of which is 'pour un petit chien écrasé' ('Three limp preludes', one 'for a small dog that has been run over'.) [M.C.]

The *Valses* date from 1900, just like that...

Socrate dates from 1918, or ten years before *Apollon Musagète*...

Socrate – to be remembered as one of the noble myths of the grand 'abstraction' of old age (along with 'our' Fauré's Thirteenth Nocturne and *Pénélope* and bearing more or less in mind the well-known anecdote about Noah).

Satie's humour, the best of it – 'la maître d'Arcueil'. Wonderful as a title – as long as there is no music attached.

Satie's discoveries and Achras' polyhedra ... Why did no one crop this 'precursor's' ears!

The reader can transcribe according to taste the following passage from Jarry, with reference to the need for a Satie controversy:

MR UBU: Odd's bodikins! Mr Conscience, are you sure that he cannot defend himself?

CONSCIENCE: Absolutely, sir; so it would be very cowardly to assassinate him.

MR UBU: Thank you, Mr Conscience, we have no further need of you. We will kill Mr Achras since there is no further danger and shall consult you more often, as you can give better advice than we should have thought. Into the suitcase! (*He shuts suitcase.*)

CONSCIENCE: In that case, sir, I think that we can, etc., call it a day.

... now and ever shall be, etc.

34

Schoenberg the Unloved?[1]

It must be admitted that Schoenberg inspires more respect than affection . . .
His disciples' admiration was unlimited, uncontrolled in fact. The feelings of
his opponents, the hatred of what he stood for, were no less excessive. Did
he choose this role of the prophet, revered but feared? Was he even
responsible for it? Was he determined on the same 'failure' as Moses?

It looks as though, especially towards the end of his life, he was tired of the
distinguished but thankless role that his century had forced on him. The very
name of Schoenberg calls up ideological quarrels: it was not simply his work
that was disputed, but the very principles of his musical language. Questions
of race and cultural differences also played a part. And to make matters
worse the issues in this already difficult situation were hopelessly confused
by the tensions in his dual personality, half conservative and half adventurous, which alienated a good number of simple souls able to understand and
accept only a clear-cut situation.

My own attitude has remained virtually unchanged. I learned to find my
way about in Berg's labyrinths once I had overcome the lack of natural
sympathy that proved an initial obstacle. I learned to take a detached view of
Webern's all too shining light, despite the fervour that it aroused. In Schoenberg's case I am still fascinated by only one relatively short, but important
period – though I hasten to add that this includes almost all the chief
discoveries of the twentieth century, which have had an influence on music
that cannot be gainsaid.

The chronology of his works suggests that Schoenberg composed rapidly
and by fits and starts, often under the influence of literary texts that stimulated him. The time taken over a work was generally very short – *Erwartung*
is the most striking example of this. Even large-scale works written over long
periods were composed sporadically – abandoned, taken up again, forgotten, restarted . . . The history of Schoenberg's works reveals an impulsive,
discontinuous inspiration – in fact that associated by romantic convention

---

[1] 'Schoenberg, le mal-aimé?', published in German in *Die Welt*, 7 September 1974. First
published in French in *Points de repère*.

with 'genius'. How are we to reconcile this *fact* with the intellectualism of which he is accused? (We should have first to ask ourselves the meaning of what is generally called *intellectualism* . . . but let us for the moment accept its common meaning of arid calculation, the reverse of spontaneity.)

Only one, magic, answer immediately suggests itself, and Schoenberg himself did not fail to provide it when he compared the composer more or less to God . . . The work exists from all eternity, and the primary material has only to be thought with sufficient intensity in order to be created – 'let the work be, and the work was'. There could be no question of 'calculation' for the creator, it was an integral part of the lightning invention. Its organization resembles a thunderbolt, instantaneous and shattering. How easy it is to understand Schoenberg's growing obsession with the figure of Moses! The burning bush and the tables of the Law – there can be no more striking metaphor of human creation as inspired and assisted by God's own creative power.

I am quite ready to admit that I find this messianic attitude irritating – even if it is explained by Schoenberg's lack of 'success'. Finding himself the object of hostility and attack, he took refuge in assuming the attitude of a prophet; and it is hard to find any explanation for that famous assertion, in particular – that he had assured the supremacy of German music for some hundred years – except a mad desire to compensate. Did his work as a teacher simply confirm him in a role for which he had a natural predilection?

He was happy to undertake such work as long as it was at a high level, but found it a heavy burden when it was no more than a demanding and wearisome way of making a livelihood. Even so, few other composers of his stature have spent so much of their time teaching and forming other personalities. But even the best teacher cannot invent personalities: he can only discover them and reveal them to themselves. The two most striking and lasting of those revelations occurred at the very beginning of his career as a teacher – by a small, momentary coincidence that was never to be repeated at the same level. Schoenberg himself, as we know, was virtually self-taught, and the instruction and advice that he received were of only relative importance compared with his own work of assimilating the classical and romantic repertory. It may well be that he wished to spare his juniors this hard experience, in the conviction that a thorough understanding of the musical situation was necessary if he was to find his own place in it as a composer. Innovation is possible only after the completest possible digestion of the past.

Was Schoenberg, then, an explorer in spite of himself? Writings and anecdotes suggest it: 'There had to be a Schoenberg and the lot fell on me . . .' – something like that! What a sense of nostalgia overcame him when he thought of the old order, and how painstakingly he worked in the first place to forge links between his own works and the classical masterpieces that he admired and took for his models! His adaptation and transformation of those models was in fact so intense that his close links with the past were unrecognizable to superficial observers. He himself rather forgot his enslavement to the past during the really explosive period of his career as a composer, a period that lasted a dozen years. The musical culture of the past was always present in his music, but latent, in the background; his inventive powers were so demanding that they hardly left room for historicism. His desire to explore and to renew, and the pleasure this gave him, were stronger than his ambition to win a place for himself in the panorama of history. Once he had taken the first step and freed himself from the constraints of the past, Schoenberg's first concern was to justify himself and then to establish a new order able to bear comparison – victorious comparison – with the old. This explains his sense of triumph when he thought that he had provided music with a new 'eternal' law, and his insistence on presenting his new world parallel to the old. Can such a mirage last?

It is common to consider only two phases in Schoenberg's music – the tonal period and the post-tonal, including the establishment of the twelve-note system – as though his abandoning of tonality were the one fundamental fact of his existence. But is this the only primary question? His earliest works are a kind of introduction that includes prophetic types or patterns in which his ideas and his demands gradually take shape as he creates from the generally accepted language a language that is not only personal but highly individual, flooding his polyphony with an ever increasing number of motives and giving preference to *melodic* rather than the co-ordinating *harmonic* intervals. This had been done before by Beethoven and, more particularly, by Wagner, in whose music the relationship between harmony and counterpoint is so strained that it almost reaches breaking point.

That break occurred in Schoenberg's second period, an explosion as much in form – the method of composition – as in actual language. This period was short and intensely visionary (*voyant* in Rimbaud's sense), and it involved a long, large-scale and rationally planned distortion of all the musical senses. Dimensions are fused and interchanged; the conception flouts order and finds renewal in the extreme tension and effort of instantaneous invention, involving the exploration of both informal continuity and formalized fragmentation. Still, however, as before, the whole process of composition rests on the endless flow of motives and motivic principles and the play of predominant intervals. Invention expands in an anarchical efflorescence troubled by no scruples of economy. It becomes, on the other hand, the central reflecting point in the subsequent transition towards a final codification of the language. The lava cools and we find ourselves facing a crystallization, or geometrization, of forms, a verification of the constituents of the musical organism, a classification of methods and an inventory of the means available.

Some of the works written at this time are almost like demonstrations, confirmations of a link with the past. This codification is more a security measure than a step into the unknown, and the composer's chief concern is with the overall insuring of his place in the context of history from the encyclopaedic point of view. At the same time he continues to pursue his fundamental procedure of flooding his music with motives and basic intervals, only now – in the new context – there can be no more conflict in importance between melodic intervals and their harmonic co-ordination, since both depend from the outset on the same principle of combination. Before we even think of examining the consequences of this, still less criticize them, we must be sure of the unity and the determination of the whole procedure.

We can observe a similar evolution in a number of painters belonging to the same generation as Schoenberg, and two in particular – Kandinsky and Mondrian. There is nothing surprising in the name of Kandinsky, in view of Schoenberg's relations with the Blaue Reiter group, which were more than just an episode in his life, and of the collaboration that was planned with the Bauhaus. As for Mondrian, I do not think that Schoenberg ever showed much interest in him. Even so, if we consider the work of Mondrian and Kandinsky, we can clearly trace the same sequence of prophetic 'type' works, explosion and codification that we find in Schoenberg, the same adventures, the same risks and, I fear, the same relapses and the same disenchantments. In other respects it must be acknowledged that Schoenberg's visual tastes – as shown in his own pictures – were quite different from those of either Kandinsky or Mondrian and (leaving aside all questions of 'professionalism') link him rather with Edvard Munch or Odilon Redon.

Something, however slight, must also be said about Schoenberg's literary affinities. People have inevitably pointed to the rather mediocre quality of the texts he chose to set, or wrote himself, an endless matter of debate not confined to the case of Schoenberg. Cantata and opera texts have seldom figured in anthologies, but what is generally acceptable as dramatic support becomes more of an embarrassment when poor literary quality or dramatic weakness is accentuated by poetic and philosophical pretensions. Schoenberg's choice of 'subjects' nevertheless reveals his profound preoccupations as a creative artist. His exploration of the dream world in *Erwartung* coincides with his plumbing of the deep springs of musical creation in the unconscious. The references to a distant, vanished poetic world in *Pierrot lunaire* correspond to his farewell to a musical language that he considered out of date and inadequate. Later in life he completely identified his own personal crisis with the doubts and anxieties of Moses, his attachment to the new law and his despair of ever seeing it adopted. Although the subjects treated by Schoenberg may not convince us by their literary merits, they remain none the less convincing because they reflect very precisely his general idea of musical invention and describe its evolution – whereas his painting remains, as it were, watertight – static, dated.

Does Schoenberg's power still exist? It has vanished from that part of his work that he considered most worthy to survive, whereas there is still a fascination in what might at first have seemed the most ephemeral of his works. How are we to explain this paradox? I can only repeat what I have already said – that the desire to 'make history' is incompatible with actually being historically important. Wanting to see oneself assuming a historic destiny is – if you will forgive the trivial comparison – wanting to be at the same time both egg and chick. The biological impossibility of such a claim makes nonsense of even the most pious hopes of 'immortality'. The 'desire for immortality' is nothing new, among poets especially – and this appeal to the unknown forces of the future is observable even among the artists who are most bound to their daily tasks. At what precise moment does this precarious balancing act come to grief and prove a failure? At the moment, I think, when a man prides himself on his desire to set a precise limit to evolution and starts to codify it completely in terms of the present, when he confuses prophecy and prevision. It is impossible to codify the awareness of a historic situation and, more specifically, an awareness of the future. It has often been admitted, even proved, that the future never turns out as expected, still less as imagined. This commonsense view is frequently overcome by the hope that the future cannot really escape our grasp and that we can shape it, even if only for a time – an illusion that makes us less impatient with accepting the transitory. But is it not precisely the constant reconsideration of what is transitory that the artist must accept, and with it reconsideration of his own beliefs and attitudes? Surely we must accept this evidence that what is transitory is the very stuff of the historical perspective, of permanence in fact?

If I take Schoenberg as a particular instance of this, it was at the exact moment when he was most acutely aware of the transitory and its impact that he played a unique role as a composer. On the other hand his premature attempt at codification and his convictions about the future represent the most evanescent aspect of his work, the aspect most irretrievably doomed to oblivion. How is it possible to foresee the future, and why should we try? And what is more – is it not essential to live simply in the present moment, even if that is 'the heart of the eternal'? There is no evading the wager – the wager that admits of no deduction, no limitation, no logic and is answered only by the darkest and most obstinately unconscious forces of the self – its 'fiery heart'.

35

Speaking, Playing, Singing[1]

PIERROT LUNAIRE AND LE MARTEAU SANS MAÎTRE

Performing Schoenberg's *Pierrot lunaire* and my own *Marteau sans maître* in the same programme prompts, and will always prompt, certain observations and comparisons. It is in order to avoid all misunderstanding that I have decided to explain as clearly as possible both the resemblances between the two works and the profound differences between them.

I need hardly point out in detail the great stylistic difference, even if only on account of their dates. *Pierrot lunaire* was composed in the spring and summer of 1912, at a time when Schoenberg had already 'suspended' tonality but had not yet embarked on the strict laws of twelve-note composition, which were not to be codified for some ten years. *Le Marteau sans maître* was written between 1953 and 1955, at the time when strict serialism was being abandoned in the hope of discovering more general and more flexible laws governing sound phenomena. This alone constitutes a major difference between the two works – the fact that one was written *before* and the other *after* a period of more radical research in the case of each composer.

Let us examine how much, apart from this personal aspect, the two works may be said to have in common. *Pierrot lunaire* consists of three-times-seven poems, as is stated at the top of the score. Each of these three parts is a whole, clearly distinct and ending with a strongly characterized piece – 'Der kranke Mond' completing the first panel, 'Die Kreuze' the second, and 'O alter Duft', the third. This is an art of contrasts, in which a slightly ironical lyricism is followed by almost hysterical 'possession', followed in its turn by a disillusioned sentimentality. It is not that each part is *characterized* by its concluding piece – far from it; but what all have in common is the passing from one mode of expression to another with great mobility (lability). A good example is the enormous difference of atmosphere between the sombre vision of 'Nacht' and the ingenuous irony of 'Gebet an Pierrot', which follows it immediately, or between the deliberately exaggerated horror of

---

[1] 'Dire, jouer, chanter', *Cahiers Renaud–Barrault*, No. 41, 1963, pp. 300–21. Boulez also writes about *Pierrot lunaire* in his tribute to Roger Désormière, pp. 501–12. [M.C.]

'Rote Messe' and the dry, careless mood of 'Galgenstück'. This extreme diversity of mood is part of the difficulty in performing *Pierrot lunaire*; but the aesthetic problem involved is of such importance that failure to recognize it prejudiced the understanding of the work for many years. I shall return to this later.

Our first observation, then, concerns the division of the work into three parts, a conception of Schoenberg's that may legitimately be compared to that of the romantic song-cycle as realized first by Schubert and then particularly – and more consciously – by Schumann. As a matter of fact only shortly before *Pierrot lunaire* Schoenberg had himself composed such a cycle, based on Stefan George's *Das Buch der hängenden Gärten*. There he had followed earlier examples and used the piano to accompany the singing voice. The really novel feature of *Pierrot lunaire* is the fact that Schoenberg does not use the singing voice in the conventional way, but *Sprechstimme*; and that the piano of the Romantics now forms part of a small heterogeneous chamber group consisting of flute and piccolo, clarinet and bass clarinet, violin, viola and cello. Furthermore a different instrumental combination is used for each piece, and this diversity ranges from a single instrument (the flute in the seventh piece, 'Der kranke Mond') to the complete ensemble (first flute and then piccolo; first clarinet and then bass clarinet; first violin and then viola, cello and piano in the last piece, 'O alter Duft').

This reaction against the inordinately swollen and 'enriched' orchestra of post-Wagnerian composers immediately bore fruit. Schoenberg's immediate pupils developed this idea, Webern in particular, whose opus 14 was strongly and directly influenced by *Pierrot lunaire*. In the case of Berg the influence is actually less apparent, though it is very noticeable in some passages of *Wozzeck*.

Sprechstimme raises quite a number of controversial problems. *Pierrot lunaire* was in fact dedicated to an actress, Albertine Zehme – or more precisely a *diseuse* who used to recite 'melodramas' with a musical background, such as Richard Strauss wrote. As a young man Schoenberg conducted a small orchestra that provided accompaniments at a well-known Berlin cabaret, Ernst von Wolzogen's 'Überbrettl', and he must have written several small works to accompany the *diseuses* of the day. At a concert of his posthumous works given in Hamburg in 1958 I heard two of the cabaret songs that he wrote about 1901 – 'Galathea', to a Wedekind text, for voice and piano, and 'Nachtwandler', to a Falke text, for voice, piccolo, trumpet, snare drum and piano. This, I believe, tells us something about the origins of *Pierrot lunaire* – not that these cabaret commissions are of the smallest interest in themselves, but a musician of genius can make use of anything as a starting point, provided that he then has time to stylize it.

I do not think that there can be any doubt that the 'Überbrettl', which was comparable to the Parisian 'Chat noir' from the 'literary' point of view, gave Schoenberg the idea of a superior, 'intellectualized' cabaret. With this in mind he could not be content with writing vague musical accompaniments for recitations; he had the declared intention of giving instruments an important role and so could not be satisfied with endless vocal 'declamation'. This led him to reflect on the prickly question of how to notate declamation so that it should form an integral part of the music. A very understandable desire for precision led him to notate the speaking voice in exactly the same way as the singing, marking each note with a cross as the conventional indication for the use of *Sprechstimme*. The question then arises whether it is actually possible to *speak* according to a notation devised for *singing*. This was the real problem at the root of all the controversies. Schoenberg's own remarks on the subject (the marginal note in *Die glückliche Hand* and the preface to *Pierrot lunaire*) are not in fact clear, and the interpretation of these rather oracular statements by unscrupulous disciples has thrown no light on the subject but only created a tangled mass of 'traditions', each claiming the authority of the Master. In fact there is nothing to suggest that these disciples, or so-called 'favourite' interpreters, have any better understanding of Schoenberg's intentions than other mortals. If asked to provide a precise and practical solution of the problem, they always refer either to this obscure preface or else to their memories of the 'heroic' past, memories that no one can check. It is therefore better to turn to other Schoenberg texts, particularly his letters (not yet published *in toto*), since his articles have nothing whatever to say on the subject (at least those published under the general title of *Style and Idea*).

A letter to Sándor Jemnitz contains the following passage: 'I must immediately make it quite clear that *Pierrot lunaire* is not to be sung! . . . That would destroy the work completely and there would be every reason to say, "That is not the way to write for the singing voice!"' Schoenberg thus totally rejects anything approaching what is properly meant by singing; and we have further evidence of this in Schoenberg's own recording of the work with the interpreter who seems to have given him the greatest satisfaction, since he chose her for numerous concerts as well as for the recording, Erika Stiedry-Wagner. The recording has now been 'transferred' from 78 to 33 rpm and we might have hoped that this would solve our problems. But, alas!, all that the record gives us is a style of declamation vaguely reminiscent of Sarah Bernhardt and to our ears hopelessly outmoded. Even so – and I think this is particularly important – in the case of the spoken intervals, pitch is more than approximate, while the few notes actually sung are for the most part precise in pitch; on the other hand the perpetual *glissando* from one note to the next soon becomes irritating. I am not forgetting the words of Schoenberg's preface: 'In singing pitch is steadily maintained, whereas in *Sprechgesang* pitch changes by a fall or a rise.' But if he wants *glissandos*, he writes them in the most conventional manner, giving precise instructions. (There are some puzzles here too!) In this recording the nervous expressionism of the voice removes any suggestion of humour from the parody pieces, giving the whole work an unrelieved atmosphere of exaggerated tension quite contradicted by the character of the instrumental parts. Yet parody is quite as important a feature of *Pierrot lunaire* as exaggerated sentiment; so that we must acknowledge the fact that, although we possess authentic documentation on the subject, it is still difficult to form any precise idea of *Sprechgesang.*

We have further evidence that suggests that Schoenberg was not entirely convinced, or very happy, about the legitimacy of his idea or the precision of his notation in relation to actual vocal facts. In later works such as the *Ode to Napoleon* or *Moses und Aron* his notation of the *Sprechstimme* part is basically different: in the *Ode to Napoleon* it has become relative. In *Pierrot lunaire*, as I said earlier, he simply transports singing notation, unmodified and with no precautions of any kind, to speech; adding a cross to each note makes no real difference to the conventional notation. Schoenberg seems to have been aware of this major difficulty, although he never expressed himself openly on the subject. However that may be, the notation in the *Ode to Napoleon* is relative, in the sense that it uses a limited number of signs linked not with precise, clearly marked pitches but with *intervals* – that is to say, relationships – which are themselves relative and need to be 'interpreted' by each individual singer or actor according to the pitch of his or her speaking voice.

It therefore seems as though Schoenberg intended, long after the event, to rectify this original error about the relation between the singing and the speaking voice. There are in fact people the tessitura of whose singing voice is wider and higher than that of their speaking voice, which is more restricted in range and lower. Others – and particularly women – have singing voices of a very similar tessitura and speaking voices with a quite different tessitura. This problem virtually does not arise in *Pierrot lunaire*, and the work is thus both too high and too low. Even so it is worth noting that if the tessitura of the singing voice is almost identical in any one group of singers, this is an artificial, acquired characteristic: indeed establishing the tessitura of a singing voice forms a large part of vocal training. There is therefore always the possibility that we shall one day be able to count on speaking voices whose tessitura has been restricted within a definite range by training, although actors themselves have not hitherto produced an example of this or much hope for the future.

A last point – the speaking voice does not remain on a note, true, but not in the way that Schoenberg imagined when he wrote: 'In *Sprechgesang* pitch changes by a fall or a rise.' In actual fact pitch changes in the speaking owing to the shortness of vocal emission, the speaking voice being a kind of percussion instrument with very short resonance – hence the impossibility of any actually *spoken* sound having any long duration. (Actors who have to sustain a sound use both the natural resonance of the voice and a singing tone in the tessitura which this has in common with their speaking voice.)

There is also whispering, which Schoenberg uses in *Pierrot lunaire* – a sometimes white, or coloured, noise with a very different tessitura, two or three octaves above that of the speaking voice and almost identical in pitch with that of whistling!

I have done no more than outline the many difficulties encountered on the path between *speaking* and *singing*. It was Schoenberg's great merit that he faced this fundamental question, though his analysis of vocal phenomena and the virtually unchanged notation that he employed still leave us with problems that cannot be solved until a number of contradictions have been resolved. Far Eastern theatrical practice (the Japanese Noh theatre, among others) has much to teach us by solutions, both *stylistic* and *technical*, such as have not yet been discovered in Europe.

If I have insisted so much on this vocal aspect of *Pierrot lunaire*, it is because the voice plays an absolutely primary part in the work, in which voice and instruments correspond like actors and stage-set in the theatre. The first performance was really a 'spectacle' with Albertine Zehme, in pierrot costume, 'speaking' the poems alone on the stage and the players hidden from the public by a screen. Any presentation of that kind, especially the pierrot costume, would be found very embarrassing today; so that we are faced with the further problem of how *Pierrot lunaire* should be performed. Should it be given in an ordinary concert setting – the instrumental ensemble in the middle of the stage with the soloist in front of them and on the conductor's right? Or should one attempt a 'historical revival' and reproduce the setting of the first performance? I personally think that a 'concert' setting prejudices the work both aesthetically and acoustically. *Pierrot* is, in its own way, a theatre piece, and the voice is distinguished from the instrumental ensemble by the very fact of being *isolated*. Placing the singer in the middle of the players is an aesthetic contradiction, and as damaging to the visual as to the acoustic effect, quite as strong an objection. The two acoustic planes – speaking voice and instruments – must unquestionably be made absolutely distinct from each other. Otherwise the vocal dynamics will have to be dangerously forced or the players will have to reduce their dynamics to such a degree that the individual 'character' of the pieces will evaporate, dissolving into a kind of monotonous mezzotint. On the other hand the pierrot costume and the screen, though doubtless touching as a kind of souvenir of the past, cannot fail to look rather ridiculous. Stage techniques have evolved sufficiently to make any physical barrier between singer and players unnecessary. This can be achieved by suitable lighting, designed to concentrate 'theatrical' attention on the singer by means of an illusion, or at least the convention of an illusion. The work certainly contains tricky passages in which singer and conductor must not lose sight of each other!

With all these considerations in mind I have decided on the following solution, I place the instrumental ensemble on the left-hand corner of the stage, slightly askew so that instruments like the flute and the cello, who have important parts in some of the pieces, are on the right of the group, thus establishing a 'zone of contact' with that of the singer, who stands slightly to the right of the centre of the stage. From the aesthetic point of view this preserves a sense of theatrical space although the arrangement still suggests a concert; and acoustically voice and instrumental ensemble are clearly distinguished, so that each can evolve on its own proper dynamic plane.

Apart from the lighting by projectors this arrangement is not unlike that commonly used in cabarets or music-halls; and the suggestion is quite deliberate because, as I have already said, I think of *Pierrot lunaire* as primarily a kind of *cabaret noir*. I borrow this excellent phrase of André Schaeffner's with all its implications of cabaret, black humour and even – the 'Chat noir'. Albert Giraud's poems are in fact closely allied to the period of French symbolism, when the Moon and Pierrot were remorselessly exploited by a horde of imitators of Jules Laforgue (giving rise to Mallarmé's irritated 'La lune, ce fromage!')

In his well-documented study of *Pierrot lunaire*[1] André Schaeffner points out that there are 'felicitous liberties' in Otto Erich von Hartleben's adaptation of Albert Giraud's text, which is itself of no great interest.

> A number of coarse images have been pruned away and the medical student's jargon has disappeared. The scene has also been shifted from Flanders, Shakespearean backgrounds and a conventional Italian setting, with its fussy geographical details. Hartleben keeps as cool a head as Schoenberg, both quite consciously flirting with bad taste. The melodrama sometimes verges on a Viennese *commedia dell'arte*, and that is not all. There is a hint of orientalism, in the taste of the day; and in fact Schoenberg's players perform in the shadow of a 'shadow theatre'.

There could be no better definition of the aesthetic embodied in *Pierrot lunaire*, no clearer statement of the feature that offends those who find fault with the work. To say that the text is stupid and that its sentimentality, or 'hysteria', is intolerable – in fact, that Schoenberg would have been a perfect patient of Dr Freud – is to miss the real point of the piece. The flirting with bad taste, the self-ironical sentimentality and the playing with mental anguish and hallucination are all to be taken between inverted commas – 'at the second degree'. The closest literary parallel to the atmosphere of *Pierrot* can be found in the extremes of critical irony with which Robert Musil describes a sentimental, disillusioned world – the world summed up in the 'O alter Duft aus Märchenzeit, berauschest wieder mich!' of the last piece. As for the famous Expressionist *Angst* that people try to discover everywhere in Schoenberg's music – where it does, indeed, play a dominant part but only in comparatively few works – it is virtually absent from *Pierrot lunaire*, really appearing only twice, in 'Nacht' and 'Die Kreuze'. In other pieces such as

---

[1] 'Variations Schoenberg', *Contrepoints*, No. 7, 1951, pp. 110–29.

'Madonna', 'Raub' and even 'Rote Messe' or 'Enthauptung' what we find is something more like *playing* with fear – a process that, once again, André Schaeffner has analysed in detail. He compares it to the Expressionistic features of certain tribal ceremonies that he witnessed in Africa, in which *playing at fear* eventually really produces a feeling of unbearable anxiety and when this climax has been reached, the mood swings from one of surprise to one of irony and then to laughing at the fear that one has acted so well and no longer 'believes in'.

What it amounts to, apparently, is that Schoenberg's aesthetic is much more complex than it at first seemed, and this explains the continuing fascination of *Pierrot lunaire*. If it were merely one of the many *fin de siècle* works, it would no longer attract any attention, any more than Proust or Musil would interest anyone if their works were like those episodic 'psychological' novels describing the emotional lives of members of 'high society' during the *belle époque*! This explains why performing *Pierrot lunaire* turns out to be not so easy, often involving as it does a kind of balancing act on a shaky tightrope.

I must be forgiven for having devoted so much attention to this 'theatrical' aspect of a work long considered either as a model of the purest and driest intellectualism or as the worst example of Expressionist hysteria! It only remains for me to justify *Pierrot lunaire* from the point of view of construction. Technically it is in fact much less 'learned' than people have liked to imagine. Even today people supposed to be 'in the know' will moan about the work's 'learned' nature – with all those passacaglias, double canons, retrogrades and so on. But in fact the *strictly* written pieces are fewer than the *free*. Anyone who studies the score closely cannot fail to be struck by the logical basis of the various musical deductions, and also by the freedom and ease with which Schoenberg manipulates that logic. There are certainly many works of the Renaissance and the Baroque – let alone the Middle Ages – that are much stricter in technique than *Pierrot*. Out of twenty-one pieces one is a passacaglia ('Nacht') and even that is very freely handled; one is a strict canon ('Parodie'); and one a piece with a double canon, retrograde in the middle ('Der Mondfleck'). That makes in all three 'scholastic' pieces, a very small proportion of the whole. How persistent prejudices are can be seen from the writers who even today speak of the 'oppressive learning' of *Pierrot lunaire*. Perhaps it is a matter not so much of prejudice but of simple ignorance!

The shortness of the different pieces is a final complaint. I often wonder what concert performances of the work can have been like in the early days, when one Paris critic compared this series of small pieces to a theatrical reading of La Rochefoucauld's *Maximes*. Schoenberg in fact gives exact instructions as to the relative length of the pauses between the pieces, sometimes indicating precisely that there should be no pause at all. These instructions are either followed or they are not – in which case the composer can obviously not be held responsible. If performed with excessive and ill-chosen pauses even the songs of the *Dichterliebe* might seem comparable to La Rochefoucauld's aphorisms! All this is only to insist that if the forms are small, they are linked in *cycles* and the only real breaks should occur between each of these three cycles – in order to avoid excessive and absurd 'bittiness'.

Finally a word about the instrumentation of *Pierrot* and its significance. Chamber music in which the piano played an important part was an increasingly marked feature of the last decades of the nineteenth century. From Haydn to Brahms piano trios, quartets and quintets figure largely in the catalogues of composers' works. In France Ravel continued the practice whereas Debussy, more musically alert, substituted the marvellous combination of flute, viola and harp. In Schoenberg's case the use of a chamber ensemble with piano was closely linked with this tradition, though he employed it in a completely different spirit, if only in the relationships of the instruments to each other and what might be called the style of those relationships. The instrumental formation of *Pierrot* is not *monovalent*, in the sense that the whole ensemble is not used continuously. In old piano quartets and quintets (whether the other instruments concerned were strings, winds or a combination of both) the instrumental writing remained clearly defined from beginning to end, emphasis being laid on the cohesion of the ensemble as a whole. In *Pierrot* on the other hand – and this may have something to do with the theatrical aspect of the work – each piece draws attention to an individual colour, a special instrumental combination; and in some cases the instrumentation emphasizes the form or highlights some structural detail. There is no need to insist on the virtuosity of Schoenberg's instrumentation, some features of which (the *Klangfarbenmelodie* in 'Eine blasse Wäscherin', for instance) are linked directly to others of his works, such as the orchestral Five Pieces op. 16.

This brief account of *Pierrot lunaire* has involved us in a 'circular tour' that has included the aesthetic views implicit in the work and the technical aspects of a musical mind in full evolutionary spate. The work has, of course, a number of very clear links with the past and I have tried to point these out. But it is not derived simply from 'expressionism'. The ambiguities that it contains and Schoenberg's bold ideas about the relation between words and music represent an inexhaustible wellspring for the future.

I am not going to attempt such a 'distanced' analysis of *Le Marteau sans maître*, but I believe that I can give a sufficiently objective description of the work – at any rate as far as its aims are concerned – to point out the similarities and dissimilarities to *Pierrot lunaire*.

Let us go through it point by point, as we did with *Pierrot*.

In the first place the work consists of nine pieces attached to three poems by René Char, three cycles in fact. The poems are entitled:

1 'L'Artisanat furieux'
2 'Bourreaux de solitude'
3 'Bel édifice et les pressentiments'

The voice is not necessarily employed in each piece; in fact I make a distinction between the pieces in which the poem is directly included and rendered by the voice and the development pieces in which it has, on principle, no role to play. Thus the cycle built on 'L'Artisanat furieux' comprises: BEFORE 'L'Artisanat furieux' (instrumental); L'Artisanat furieux' proper (vocal), and AFTER 'L'Artisanat furieux' (instrumental). The cycle built on 'Bourreaux de solitude' comprises 'Bourreaux de solitude' (vocal) and Commentaries I, II and III on 'Bourreaux de solitude' (instrumental). The cycle based on 'Bel édifice et les pressentiments' is composed of the first version and its double.

But the cycles are not heard in succession; they interpenetrate each other in such a way that the general form is itself a combination of three simpler structures. If I give the order in which the pieces succeed each other, their relative importance will be clear without further comment:

1   BEFORE 'L'Artisanat furieux'
    2   Commentary I on 'Bourreaux de solitude'
3   'L'Artisanat furieux'
    4   Commentary II on 'Bourreaux de solitude'
        5   'Bel édifice et les pressentiments' – first version
    6   'Bourreaux de solitude'
7   AFTER 'L'Artisanat furieux'
    8   Commentary III on 'Bourreaux de solitude'
        9   'Bel édifice et les pressentiments' – double

The first thing that is clear is that a single poem is enough for the organization of a cycle; and then that the cycles interrupt each other, in a regular way, whereas the number of pieces varies with each cycle. 'L'Artisanat furieux' is a purely *linear* piece in the sense that the text is here treated, 'set to music', in the most direct way. The poem is sung straight through in an ornate style, with a single flute counterpointing the vocal line – a direct and deliberate reference to No. 7 ('Der kranke Mond') of *Pierrot lunaire*. The poem here unmistakably occupies the foreground and, as I say, is literally 'set to music'.

'Bel édifice et les pressentiments', first version, inaugurates another kind of relationship: the poem serves to articulate the big subdivisions of the general form. The vocal element remains important, though it is not primary as before, since that primacy is disputed by the instrumental element. This antinomy will be resolved in 'Bourreaux de solitude' into a total unity of voice and instruments, linked by the same musical structure, the voice emerging at intervals from the ensemble in order to enunciate the text. Finally the role of the voice undergoes a further metamorphosis in the double of 'Bel édifice et les pressentiments' – once the last words of the poem have been pronounced the voice (*bouche fermée*) melts into the instrumental ensemble and ceases to exercise its specific function of verbal articulation. As the voice assumes an anonymous role, the flute (which had accompanied the voice in 'L'Artisanat furieux') takes its place in the fore-front of the scene and, as it were, takes over the part of the voice. Thus the roles of voice and instrument are gradually reversed by the disappearance of the verbal text. This is an idea that I find valuable, and I should describe it as the poem being the *centre* of the music though it is in fact *absent* from the music – just as the shape of an object is preserved by lava even when the object itself has vanished – or like the petrification of an object which is both RE-cognizable and UN-recognizable.

Different methods of vocal emission are used in *Le Marteau sans maître*, from singing to speaking. Singing is given its decorative function and words their dramatic efficacy according to the demands of the context. To quote extreme instances – 'L'Artisanat furieux' is virtually one long vocalise and the opening of 'Bel édifice et les pressentiments', double, is a kind of recitative in which speaking and singing closely overlap each other. The role of the voice is in fact extremely variable and ranges from primacy to absence, in accordance with a kind of 'stage setting' in which emphasis alternates between direct expression of the text and expression of the poetic world that the text evokes. This might be described as intellectual drama prompted by reading the poem and the echoes that it creates in a world that is, properly speaking, interior.

Such being the case, it is pointless to plan any external, explanatory arrangement, which is quite unnecessary. This brings me to the instrumenta-tion of the work, which requires six players: flute in G, viola, guitar, vibraphone, xylophone and a variety of percussion instruments. Although, of course, a chamber ensemble, this has very little to do with any classical or romantic grouping, being distinguished by the use of instruments designed, for the most part, to give a special, even exotic colouring to a given ensem-ble. If you ask me why I chose this particular instrumentation, I might simply say, 'Because I liked it!' But this immediately prompts the question: 'Why did I like it?' I will try to explain my reasons, which are partly a matter of natural affinities and partly logical.

As a start I would point out that all these instruments have a medium pitch register, an important consideration since they are to accompany a contralto voice. If I chose a flute, it was an alto flute, a fourth lower than the ordinary flute and with a more veiled tone; and in the same way I chose the viola for my stringed instrument, halfway between its more brilliant neighbours. Both guitar and vibraphone have a very 'central' pitch range, and the only exception is the higher-pitched xylophone. The percussion instruments that

I selected are also medium-pitched except for the gong and the tam-tams, which are used only right at the end in a low, sometimes a very low, register. In this way the nature of the instrumentation supports the nature of the voice in both tessitura and colour. But what link is there between these different instruments, which differ so greatly in appearance? Is there any continuous thread of resemblance between them? I think it will be enough if I explain a number of features shared by these instruments and thus forming a continuous passage from voice to vibraphone, however absurd this may sound at first.

The link between the flute and the voice is simple: the performer's breath, and the fact that both are monodic 'instruments'. The flute and the viola – when it is played with the bow – also have this monodic character in common. On the other hand if the viola is plucked it has a link with the guitar, whose plucked strings have a longer response than those of the viola. This resonance forms a link between the guitar and the vibraphone, an instrument based on the protracted vibration of metal bars when struck. When the bars of the vibraphone are damped, i.e. not allowed to resonate, they are directly related to the wooden bars, or strips, of the xylophone, which have no resonance when struck. We have thus established a chain linking each instrument to the next by a feature common to both. Let us look at it again: voice–flute, breath; flute–viola, monody; viola–guitar, plucked strings; guitar–vibraphone, long resonance; vibraphone–xylophone, struck bars of metal or wood.

I have deliberately said nothing about the percussion, properly so called, because its role is marginal compared with that of the other instruments. In the first part it appears in only one of the cycles, 'Bourreaux de solitude', in which it marks the time. It would involve too many technical details to explain exactly my use of the percussion, and I will give only a general account of the way in which it is inserted into the polyphony. When the other instruments are playing, the percussion is silent; but as soon as there is a pause, the percussion fills it with one or several strokes, according to the length of the pause. The percussion thus plays a complementary part, filling with indeterminate pitches the void left by the determinate pitches – a kind of architectural time game.

The instruments used vary from one piece to another, and this is another deliberate, direct reference to *Pierrot lunaire*. The whole ensemble is never used continuously except in 'Bourreaux de solitude'. I have already explained the shifting preponderance of voice and flute and need to give, as it were, only an anecdotal account of my reasons for using some instruments. Many listeners' first impression is primarily exotic; and in fact my use of xylophone, vibraphone, guitar and percussion is very different from the practice of Western chamber music, closer in fact to the sound pictures of Far Eastern music, though the actual vocabulary used is entirely different. Without being entirely mistaken this first impression is superficial: instruments that still seem 'exotic' because unfamiliar to our Western tradition will lose their 'special' effect as soon as they have been incorporated into our music. I must however acknowledge that I was influenced by non-European models in choosing this particular combination of instruments, the xylophone representing the African balafron, the vibraphone the Balinese gender and the guitar recalling the Japanese koto. In actual fact, however, neither the style nor the actual use of these instruments has any connection with these different musical civilizations. My aim was rather to enrich the European sound vocabulary by means of non-European listening habits, some of our traditional classical sound combinations having become so charged with 'history' that we must open our windows wide in order to avoid being asphyxiated. This reaction of mine has nothing whatever to do with the clumsy appropriation of a 'colonial' musical vocabulary as seen in the innumerable short-lived *rhapsodies malgaches* and *rhapsodies cambodgiennes* that appeared during the early years of the present century.

The seating of the performers on the stage helps to highlight the acoustic relationships between the different instruments. In front, sitting in a semi-circle from left to right, are the viola, the guitar, the singer and the flute, and behind them the xylophone, the percussion (slightly further back) and the vibraphone. This seating gives physical expression to the dynamic distinctions and makes it easier to obtain the correct balances. The voice is *included* in the ensemble and able either to stand out as soloist or to retire into anonymity when replaced by the flute.

Then a few words about the form of the work. The pieces vary considerably in length, and the cycles in both length and importance, each having its own individual constitution. To give a full account of their development would mean a detailed technical analysis, which would be out of place here. But I should like to point out that the three Commentaries on 'Bourreaux de solitude' form a single large piece directly linked, from the formal point of view, to 'Bourreaux de solitude'. BEFORE and AFTER 'L'Artisanat furieux', two short developments, frame the central piece. In 'Bel édifice et les pressentiments', the first version forms a completely isolated unit; the double mingles elements taken from all three cycles, either textually (in the form of quotations) or *virtually*, as it were, by exploiting their potential developments. This last piece, therefore, represents an overlapping – both actual and potential – of the work's three cycles, thus forming the conjunction that concludes the whole work.

The handling of the relationship between poem and music is novel, the verbal text serving as a *kernel*, the centre around which the music crystallizes – as I explained above. There are two distinct stages, first presentation and then indirect reflection. The temporal dimension of the poem bears no comparison with the chronometric time of the music; and I think it is significant that none of the three poems consists of more than a few lines – René Char being, before all else, a master of concentrated expression. It is in fact this density of the poetic material that makes it possible to graft on to it musical structures that are to burgeon and proliferate, so that there is no place for the descriptive element as such. For the same reason no play is made with the ambiguities of an aesthetic situation, and any quotations refer to the work itself, of which they are reflections. There are only two 'abstract' quotations and both – the pairing of voice and flute and the changing of the instrumentation from one piece to the next – refer to *Pierrot lunaire*.

Now that I have thrown some light on the various aspects of *Pierrot lunaire* and *Le Marteau sans maître*, you may still want to know why I wanted to perform the two works in the same programme. That I did particularly want to do so is, of course, an unanswerable reason; but the fact that they have a number of points in common, at least exteriorly, justifies the confrontation. The two works are of roughly equal length and demand a similar number of players, including a soloist. There is also a lot to be said, I believe, for a programme that *demonstrates* something – in this case the fact that, in spite of some striking similarities and the deliberate references that I have mentioned, the two works are based on different points of view and thus on opposite aesthetic principles.

Whereas *Pierrot lunaire* is a theatre piece with instrumental accompaniment and the voice always preponderating, *Le Marteau sans maître* develops from the cell of a poem which is eventually absorbed *in toto*. This seems to me a fundamental difference even in the conception of the relationship of text and music – the text being always directly present in the one case and alternating, in the other, between presence and latency. Hence the contradiction between the part played by the voice in the two pieces. In *Pierrot lunaire* the singer *narrates*, and her role is to *speak* and to *act* a text. In *Le Marteau sans maître* she *sings* a poetic proposition, which sometimes occupies the forefront of the picture and is sometimes absorbed into the musical context.

Then there is a fundamental difference in the conception of the cycles. Schoenberg's three cycles succeed each other as in the romantic cycles, their structure remaining essentially unchanged; one piece follows another without any change of direction. (The only thematic reminiscence, recalling Schumann's *Dichterliebe*, occurs at the end of No. 13, 'Enthauptung', in a commentary containing a textual repetition of elements taken from No. 7, 'Der kranke Mond'). In *Le Marteau sans maître*, on the other hand, I tried to make the cycles overlap in such a way that the course of the work becomes increasingly complicated, using both actual reminiscence and 'virtual' relationships: the last piece alone provides a sort of *solution* or 'key' to the maze. I was in fact carried much further afield by this conception and totally abolished any predetermined form, after taking the first step by rejecting 'one-way' form.

The choice of instruments in the two works is in itself a revelation of two quite different sets of aesthetic principles. Schoenberg picked a chamber ensemble typical of the post-romantic era, with the piano as centre of gravity. (As I have pointed out, Debussy proved much more acute in this matter of instrumental inventiveness when he wrote his Sonata for flute, viola and harp; and we know that just before his death he was planning a sonata for oboe, horn and harpsichord . . .) On the other hand I selected a group quite unfamiliar to European ears in an attempt to extend our sound conceptions and to 'normalize' instruments that had hitherto been regarded exclusively as 'picturesque'. There were examples of similar instrumental combinations in European music, among others Stravinsky's *Three Japanese Lyrics* (especially the second piece); a number of songs and orchestral pieces by Webern; Schoenberg's *Serenade*; Bartók's *Music for strings, percussion and celesta*; and Messiaen's instrumentation after his *Trois petites liturgies*. This list makes it clear that there was no lack of models for the new instrumental evolution of our own time.

Finally, speaking of taste (if we must) we have to admit that *Pierrot*, following Hartleben's text, is full of stylistic and aesthetic ambiguities – 'coquetry flirting with bad taste', as Schaeffner calls it – whereas the purity of René Char's language forbade anything of that sort (which, in fact, did not attract me then any more than it attracts me now) – and obliged me, on the other hand, to discover a style 'as such' free of any oblique references.

36

Kandinsky and Schoenberg[1]

The position of Kandinsky is comparable in more than one way to that of Schoenberg, and this is of interest, I think, to others beside musicians. Each represents an important and decisive liberating force which, in both cases, was only belatedly recognized in France, where attention was at that time distracted by more immediately striking or more superficial phenomena.

Emancipation from tonality might well be considered as parallel to emancipation from the object – or the 'subject' – each favouring an important progress in the theory and practice of their respective arts. I am quite aware that the two artists were deeply aware of this similarity of appearance and procedure, and the Blaue Reiter published things by Schoenberg as well as by Berg and Webern.

During the first years of the century Kandinsky represented a great spiritual force that furnished painting with new premisses more fundamental than any based on sense data, and this key fact applies to Schoenberg also. He emphasized the contrast between deep reflection on the need for means of expression and direct artistic gifts, which soon lose their significance. The artist does not only derive a superficial pleasure from his pictures: they impel him to contemplate and adopt an attitude to existence.

Too many painters are content with being just painters . . . Yes, you will say, but what an eye he has – an eye, indeed, but nothing more! We are charmed but soon become indifferent, the fascination is quickly exhausted and such painting may easily be classed as what Pascal calls 'divertissement'. It is an unsatisfactory situation if one thinks of the outstanding gifts that, if pruned, might have been put to a better use, and it seems a waste of life itself. You saw the picture? Yes. And have you forgotten it? I have – it is a permanent disappointment, like watching fresh water seeping into the desert sand.

With Kandinsky it is different: his pictures are not so easy to take in. However long you look at them, they yield their secrets only if you really

---

[1] 'Le parallèle Schoenberg–Kandinsky', published as 'Parallèles' in a special number ('Hommage à Wassily Kandinsky') of *XXe Siècle*, No. 27, December 1966, p. 98.

soak yourself in them. They present an imaginary landscape in which the spectator comes and goes along paths determined either by a definite choice of his own or by some latent influence. He will certainly cease to be the prisoner of any kind of reality, however transposed; his ideas will be inflected by those of Kandinsky, who will lead him into his labyrinth. I enjoy this timeless wandering when I look at pictures, and always hope that the pure 'painterly' gift will not spoil 'the rest' for me and return me to the outer darkness of a loud and empty virtuosity. Yes, what I really like best is spirit speaking to spirit; I cannot be content with the gestures of a conscious rhetorician. And this is the basic experience I have whenever I look at a picture by Kandinsky.

I remember particularly the Munich collection of his works in which this liberating force explodes with a youthfulness and an audacity that penetrate the depths of my being, like the brutal, sumptuous, dazzling blossoming of some sudden, wild spring. It is impossible not to think immediately of the sumptuous, dazzling quality of Schoenberg's *Erwartung* and *Die glückliche Hand.*

Like Schoenberg, and for the same reasons, Kandinsky later went through a difficult time, and the awareness of this only emphasizes my considered admiration for him. Faced with the undeniable fact that no artist can go far simply by means of brilliant improvisations, Kandinsky divested his art of most of its exterior fascination and embarked in sober earnest on a quest for THE RULE. Firework displays are short-lived, it is true, and nothing could be more risky than to devote one's entire existence to them. A stricter spiritual obligation is inevitably forced on one – the acceptance of an iron rule, the search for an order that has been proved, a new formulation of balance and weight. All research must be founded on the essential antinomy between doubt and law: challenge and caution. There is no denying the existence of hard stretches of desert along this demanding route! But let us recognize that at the end of this high adventure we shall have an altogether larger conception of painting, a new point of view and a fresh way of looking at pictures.

Of the three painters who determined the character of their age – Kandinsky, Klee and Mondrian – Kandinsky seems to me the one who represents the ingenious alliance between delicacy and geometry. It is a far cry indeed from any kind of *divertissement* and that charge has been silenced for good!

37

Bartók: *Music for strings, percussion and celesta*[1]

Between 1934 and 1937 Bartók produced three wonderfully mature works, which achieve an extraordinary degree of balance. They are the Fifth String Quartet (1935), *Music for strings, percussion and celesta* (1936) and *Sonata for two pianos and percussion* (1937).

Of the three, *Music for strings, percussion and celesta* is probably the most impressive, although this rating cannot be too dogmatic. Bartók's early works represent a kind of synthesis between late Beethoven and mature Debussy – a very curious and very endearing synthesis – and he then went through a phase in which his researches led him towards an organic chromaticism not far removed from that of Berg and Schoenberg. This in turn led him to a wholly personal style that represents a balance between folk and art music and between diatonicism and chromaticism.

It is hardly necessary to say that Bartók's compositions were deeply indebted to his researches in folk music. He started as a fairly conventional nationalist composer and was led by his desire for authenticity to look for new materials and unfamiliar techniques. These were profoundly to revolutionize his whole aesthetic outlook and obliged him to find a solution of the problem of 'Hungarian' music very different from that of any merely provincial exoticism.

Music for strings, percussion and celesta was commissioned for the Basle Chamber Orchestra by Paul Sacher, who conducted the first performance of the work at Basle, on 21 January 1937.

Quite apart from the musical success of the work, of which we shall speak later, it represents a great instrumental achievement – two string orchestras used antiphonally and contrasting with a third group consisting of piano, celesta, harp, xylophone, timpani and percussion. The opening fugue is certainly the finest and most characteristic example of Bartók's subtle style, in which a great number of small intervals overlap and intersect each other within a persistently chromatic framework. The writing is predominantly contrapuntal, strict or free, and this continues in the canonic imitations of

[1] Sleeve note for the recording by Boulez, Columbia 7206.

the various developments. Rhythms constantly fluctuate, with odd and even metres alternating, and have an individual character which is also properly speaking contrapuntal.

Bartók always wrote admirably for the piano, which was his favourite instrument, and also for strings. His use of the celesta and the xylophone is always effective, the celesta's arpeggios lending colour to the strings' tremolos and trills, and the xylophone accentuating and giving a dry quality to the percussive tone of the piano. In writing for the strings Bartók makes use of all the usual effects, even those that were rare before his day (such as the *pizzicato*, now known by his name, in which the string is touching the fret) and he varies these different sonorities with great skill. The bow here regains that fresh, even aggressive quality of attack which it had lost in romantic music. The piano is used chiefly for its percussive, *martellato* quality, more rarely for trill effects, like a Hungarian cimbalom, and only on much rarer occasions for its resonant quality or for *cantabile* purposes. Bartók's piano-writing, like Stravinsky's, is one of the chief hallmarks of their generation.

The four movements of *Music for strings, percussion and celesta* are clearly differentiated, although there is a parallel between Nos. 1 and 3 (*Andante* and *Adagio*) and between Nos. 2 and 4 (*Allegro* and *Allegro molto*). The two odd movements (1 and 3) might be quoted as evidence of Bartók's 'interiority' and the even numbers (2 and 4) of the vigorous, even violent character of his music. There is no trace of any 'national' character in the first movement, which is probably the most *timeless* in all Bartók's works – a fugue that unfolds like a fan to a point of maximum intensity and then closes, returning to the mysterious atmosphere of the opening. The third movement is one of the nocturnal pieces to be found elsewhere, though not very frequently, in Bartók's work. It opens with a xylophone solo – something quite novel at that time – and the string phrases show a direct folk-music influence, assimilated and transcended no doubt and chiefly noticeable in the *rhythmic gait* of the music. Another characteristic, and equally novel, feature is the use of timpani glissandos, a poetic effect that Bartók was the first to discover. The two fast movements (2 and 4) are more popular in character, although they show a concern with form that is not typical of so-called 'national' music. The thematic material may be directly folk-inspired, but the way in which the composer uses and transforms it serves to 'distance' it from its origins and to integrate it into a universe genuinely *invented*, as opposed to merely *observed*.

One of Bartók's constant concerns was the conscious opposing of chromaticism and diatonicism in the structure of a work. A good example of this is the subject of the first movement fugue, which returns in the coda of the fourth, with the intervals literally doubled. In the same way the four phrases of the fugal subject are used to articulate the five sections of the third movement, almost like quotations designed to ensure continuity.

Bartók occupies a very special place in contemporary music as the chief modern composer, after Stravinsky, to be completely accepted. Immediately after his death his music in fact achieved great popularity, and after a long period of neglect his name became one of the symbols of the contact between the modern composer and the public. There is a certain amount of misunderstanding in this unusual case of a composer who died in straitened circumstances, even poverty, and was then, immediately after his death, promoted to the first rank of 'comprehensible' composers. In fact the triumph of his music is due to the ambiguity attaching to the use of folk music and national symbol. Bartók unquestionably belongs with Stravinsky, Webern, Schoenberg and Berg to the 'great five' of contemporary music; but his exceptional position in the twentieth century is not due to those aspects of his music that have been most assimilated by presentday audiences. It is much more probable that his success lay in the fact that his poetic genius enabled him to realize his ideas effectively. Whether it is in a brutal violence animating a 'sound material in fusion' or in a tranquil gentleness glowing in a 'halo of grating sounds and rainbow colours' Bartók is incomparable and remains unique.

38

Stravinsky: Style or Idea?[1]

In Praise of Amnesia

I have been familiar with Stravinsky's works for more than a quarter of a century, and despite – or perhaps because of – this my point of view has remained virtually unchanged. If the polemical element in my attitude has vanished, it is probably because time has confirmed the affinities and erased the discrepancies between this music and my own feelings. It may well be also that in perspective, it is a generation that I see rather than an individual.

If I say that my point of view has not changed, I should add that the intensity of my feelings has changed a great deal. The works of Stravinsky's that have always struck me as essential are now so much part of me that my identification with them has become second nature. The works that at one time irritated me I can now approach in a detached way as fragments of history, which are linked to other very similar fragments and constitute a historical document, which as such can hardly inspire feelings of irritation.

Twenty-five years ago we were in the thick of the fight and a clear dividing line separated the musical world into two camps. It was an inherent feature of the situation that sharpshooters attached to neither camp were few and far between. The very survival of the language demanded choosing between what Adorno called 'progress' and 'restoration', and nothing seemed more urgent than to make this choice since *in principle* the situation appeared frighteningly clear.

Even so I had my doubts about this simplistic, Manichaean attitude that laid undue stress on categorical classification; and I thought that the 'Cathars' – the 'pure ones', the élite of the revolution – were not wholly free of that very sin of 'historicism' of which they considered the pariahs of the 'restoration' to be exclusively guilty. I gradually came to the conclusion that a whole generation, Stravinsky's generation in fact, took the same path, which was not, as used to be said, 'regression' but something altogether more complex. This is worth considering since it involves the whole notion of *style*.

---

[1] 'Style ou idée? – éloge de l'amnésie', *Musique en jeu*, No. 4, 1971, pp. 4–14.

Were Stravinsky and his generation victims of 'codifying' *style*, or was it rather that they gave the whole concept of style a new, hitherto unknown, importance, raising it to the rank of an absolute symbol?

If my memory does not deceive me, I think it was Baudelaire who said enigmatically to Manet, 'You are the first representative of the decadence of your art.' This has been called unjust, over severe and lacking in perspective, since decadences start a long way back. Do they in fact come from the function allotted to style – or, in other words, is it for style to generate ideas, or vice versa? We must consider the words, which so often appear with capital letters, in the context of their absolute supremacy . . . Decadence, for example.

During the *fin de siècle* period a number of spent forces enjoyed the spectacle of their own wilting away, and the revolutions of the first quarter of the present century seem to have been the result of a spontaneous impulse, both savage and furious in character. Anything was preferable to the total desiccation that seemed to be quickly approaching – and there began a feverish exploring of the limits of areas that, despite their luxuriant glitter, seemed intolerably restricted. There were two alternatives – either to carry that luxuriance still further, to exaggerate it and let it strangle itself, or else to take up the barbarian's axe and proceed to sack Rome, to burn Alexandria. These two reactions were visible in every field – literature, music and the visual arts – and there are striking parallels between the personalities engaged in both 'exaggeration' and 'simplification'. The former may have shown themselves the cleverer and the latter the more naïve, but the reactions of both were dictated by the irrepressible instinct to survive. Decisions were imposed by circumstances rather than calculated. There was no question of consciously analysing the value, let alone the spell of 'style'. The ideas of destruction and sublimation demanded their right to exist and little attention was paid to appearances. The whole mass of creative artists seemed for some years bent on exhausting every possible kind of invention. Style was the last thing that entered their heads – the opposite extreme to the immediately preceding years, which took a morbid delight in precisely that field.

Stravinsky was heart and soul engaged in this hectic activity, as *The Rite of Spring* proved in the most explosive way. To simplify the picture, I should count him as one of the great *simplifiers* and Schoenberg as one of the great *exaggerators*, with *Erwartung* as typical of the 'exaggerating' tendency. In actual fact there are traces of this same 'exaggeration' in Stravinsky too, though they belong to a quite different tradition from that of German chromaticism and are linked with Debussy and Skryabin – strange as it may seem to associate those two names. Works like *Three Japanese Lyrics* and *Zvezdoliki*, and some episodes in *The Nightingale* and *Firebird*, contain tentative suggestions of a path of development that Stravinsky did not follow, either deliberately or otherwise. Basically however his work oscillates between violence and irony, which are the two faces of *simplification*, both of which reduce the musical object in the same categorical way. *Les Noces*, which came at the end of a crucial period in Stravinsky's development, presents an unusual synthesis of violence and irony, the only earlier instance of which seems to be Mussorgsky.

Irony was to account for Stravinsky's overt use of parody and – like Picasso at roughly the same time – of *objets trouvés*, which act as distorting elements in a complex style. The very oddness of his quotations, their *naïveté*, the different level of the languages employed and their absolute disparity have an integrating function. Stravinsky does not try to reduce these divergences and unify these incongruities by grammatical synthesis as Berg – who belonged to the 'exaggerating' school – was to do in *Wozzeck*. He made the incongruities still more pointed, on the other hand, and exploited linguistic absurdities, writing as it were in inverted commas in a way that foretold his almost hostile attitude toward stylistic integration. This hinted at what was in fact to come – Stravinsky's appropriation of elements already existing not simply in popular music, as hitherto, but in so-called 'art music', the finished products of musical culture and thus the supreme repositories of Style with a capital letter.

However profound the differences between the 'simplifiers' and the 'exaggerators' who between them discovered a whole new potential field of invention between 1910 and 1920, both displayed a remarkable lack of interest in any general discipline, any overall attitude. This was by no means due to any lack of reflection. All the convulsions of these years were very precisely motivated, and among the 'exaggerators' Berg and Schoenberg particularly – Kandinsky, Klee and Joyce, too, in their different fields – were quite unusually explicit about what they were trying to do. Stravinsky and Picasso may have been more impulsive temperaments, less aware of the need to know and analyse their resources in order to make the best use of them, but they were quite as acute in their actions and their works. Their decisions were so careful simply because their aims were conceived with such radical lucidity.

After the first 'savage' explosion, in which their initial objectives were achieved – sometimes surprisingly quickly – there was a clearly observable pause, a kind of breathing space for introspection, self-examination, and naturally also for an examination of their work and its validity. Their actual creation had a markedly individual character, and they now seem to have wanted to view it in a wider, more universal context and to extend the field of inventions linked, in the first instance, to various individual features. Each of them seemed to feel a real nostalgia for some conception that would enable them to extend their imaginative efforts beyond the limited aims of an individual work. They longed to discover general components that would allow them to invent within a firmer, more 'comfortable' framework. It was not that they were no longer prepared to take risks, but it was felt that there would be greater validity in discovering collective solutions rather than in treating each work in isolation. In fact they were aware of the danger of chaos and the sterility in which chaos might result, and felt a growing desire to discover some *rule*. The need for this was particularly clear in the case of two of the most enterprising, Schoenberg and Kandinsky, but it is also clear in the case of Stravinsky. The *rule* was not to be a safeguard against the spirit of adventure but a reinforcement of the spirit of invention, facilitating its task and assisting the examination of future possibilities. Obedience to some law would help to forge a style – even a collective style – typical dreams of order and regulation after a swift and sometimes chaotic revolution!

This search for a rule or law, however, was gradually to lead to a number of misunderstandings, and especially in the matter of *style*. Is there not something presumptuous in thinking that style defines idea? Something dangerous in choosing deliberately to see oneself in a historical context, which means adopting a teleological view of evolution? This danger has arisen on more than one occasion; and it is clear to us today that the composers and painters of that generation did indeed achieve a style that belongs to the history of their art while they were not consciously trying to be 'historical', and that they were misguided when they claimed to be creating stylistic models. Did not their longing for a future closely modelled on an idealized vision of the past distort their search, however honest, and direct it towards a conception of style that was totally defective because erroneous? And finally to what extent are style and invention compatible with the experience of history that we all slowly gain during our lives?

The increasingly persistent intrusion of the past, which is a relatively new phenomenon, tends to become a serious handicap for the creator, the *inventor*, who allows himself to live exclusively in a universe of *references* and feels himself safe and comfortable among the products – or more grandiloquently, the monuments – of a past culture. The problem is not a wholly new one, particularly in the case of literature, since literary documents are preserved without too much being lost, and the same applies to architecture and sculpture. Painting and music, on the other hand, have generally been able to refer only to such second-degree documents, in the case of music, as theoretical treatises and obsolete instruments whose use is not precisely known. In this way music was a long time preserved, by its very nature, from any but aesthetic references. This is no longer the case, since musical memory is today free to range over several centuries of references and first-hand documents.

The time when Mozart could pay conscious homage to Handel by making restricted use of a number of stylistic procedures is long past, and it was an isolated episode. But it was different when Mozart assimilated Bach's contrapuntal technique and so gave his music a texture that it had not hitherto had, or had only *in potentia*. Mozart's fugal writing, to say nothing of any actual fugue, makes implicit reference to a pre-existing style, and this may really be regarded as an *archaism* despite the fact that it was absorbed and that the grammar of Bach and Mozart is governed in principle by the same fundamental rules.

At a further remove in time synthesis and absorption of this kind became more problematical, both grammatically and aesthetically, as we can see from two very different instances – Berlioz's *L'Enfance du Christ* and Wagner's *Die Meistersinger*. In both cases historical quotation – the appeal to the witness of the past – is literary in origin and proves, if proof be necessary, the absence of any real conception of 'history', and hence the absolute predominance of the 'contemporary' language. It would not occur to anyone with even a relatively good knowledge of eighteenth-century music to compare it stylistically with that of Berlioz. His deliberate archaizing reflects the nostalgia for an idealized past – the past of 'the old illuminated missal' and the 'mystery play', which never in fact existed. Berlioz's own admission of the hoax ('Pierre Ducré') merely emphasized his contempt for the 'authenticity' of any orthodox reconstruction. He took refuge from the anguish, the doubt and problems of his own day in creating the artificial paradise of this 'old style', which had no precise connection with any definite period.

In Wagner's case it was the 'querelle des anciens et des modernes' all over again, only in medieval Nuremberg – and the Middle Ages are oddly absent from this battle of styles! (And this, incidentally, is why it seems to me absurd to insist on reproducing the Gothic 'reality' of Nuremberg on the stage . . .) What we are in fact witnessing behind this conventional façade is the confrontation of two languages – Wagner's own and his conception of an academic language, which in fact goes back no further than the eighteenth century. This play of stylistic mirrors both serves a dramatic purpose and emphasizes the composer's polemical intentions: the question of authenticity is never overtly raised, and indeed the references to the past in the drama differ from those in the music.

How do matters stand in the twentieth century, or at least in those years of which we are now speaking? Before saying anything about Stravinsky's attitudes, I should like to touch on the case of Schoenberg, which may perhaps help us to a deeper understanding of the whole matter of stylistic idealization, which has been so important in the evolution of music during the recent past. It will probably also help us to clear our minds about 'classicism' and tradition, and to see how Stravinsky approached these same facts, if not these same concepts.

Paradoxical as it may seem, Schoenberg was a traditionalist: his writings prove this, and his music makes it even clearer that, though adventurous, he was never a declared rebel. His wish was to create a music that extended, rather than contradicted, existing musical experience, even if he drew more radical conclusions from his analysis of any given situation. Until his 'exaggerating' period there was nothing in his music that could not be traced to the recent past. Everything was new, and everything was recognizable. There could be no problem of historical relationship, since his adherence to the past was absolute and complete. It was only that within this process a number of the fundamental hierarchies existing in the traditional language of music were dissolved and replaced by a provisional function and order. This involved the risk, clearly envisaged by Schoenberg himself after a certain period of exploration, of a chaotic situation arising from so unconditional a submission to the present, and indeed to the future, of musical evolution. He refused to see the *immanent order* of music escaping his control and was soon to modify his attitude profoundly. In order to avoid the task of discovering an individual, provisional, temporary solution of each linguistic problem as it arose, he set out to establish a basic rule that would impose a firm discipline on the anarchy of chromaticism, and establish an order and a function.

Not content with seeking a *new* rule in the elaboration of words, he was inclined to confirm this by an *old* rule that he imagined to be valid and so proceeded not to *adopt* the old forms, but rather to transplant or graft them. Within a framework that seemed to him firm he pursued a traditional utopia, forgetting the fundamental contradiction between a form picked up like an empty seashell and the living organisms of the language, which proved incompatible with such an arbitrary proceeding. The result was that, in order to adhere to these forms that he had borrowed from the past, Schoenberg's musical ideas were gradually adapted. His relationship to his models was no longer direct, as it had been before, but came to reflect an image of the past as a golden age of invention whose legacy was a code, a system of conventions that was good in an *absolute* sense. His adopting such an attitude is a clear sign of respect, but still more of a lack of confidence in his own age, in the value of its discoveries and its still undreamed-of potentialities. From now on Schoenberg's invention was to operate as a function of this world of 'references': and there was to be an intolerable discrepancy between conventional phrases and original words, between historical modes of thought and contemporary expressions. We become aware of the awkwardness, even falsity, of a situation within which there is a conflict between pedantry and *naïvité*; but the most fascinating thing of all is the almost complete transformation of the musical conception itself, involving a reversal of the idea of style. The presence of the past, the continual awareness of re-exploiting a revered tradition, the intrusion of old forms – all these lead us to conclude that Schoenberg was searching for an ideal 'classicism' deduced from some perfect *model*.

Ideas no longer generate style – style imposes the idea.

I should like to say something more about this last point. Style does not seem to me to be a quality (an essence?) that can – or more importantly, should – be sought for its own sake. I see it as the inevitable consequence of language, when that language has managed to unify its different composing elements, both at the most elementary level and also on the most elaborate formal plane. The composer's task impels him to establish a homogeneity and to forge a unity between the different elements with which he is dealing; and these elements have a strong centrifugal tendency, which increases by reason of the disparity and dispersion of the materials with which he is working. Style is what will eventually appear as the *operative* element *par excellence*, even if achieved with recalcitrant materials. On the other hand any dependence on an *adopted* idea of style – something extracted artificially from its historical context and applied like a pre-existing pattern to the process of invention – will produce a superficial homogeneity perpetually exposed by the deep distortion between a gratuitous stylistic intention and elements that reject, and may even nullify, that intention. When the composer thinks that he has achieved a 'classical' ideal of beauty and necessity, he has in fact been playing with a mask.

This analysis of Schoenberg's position has not taken us so far as it might seem from Stravinsky. Despite the labels attached to his work during one period of his career, Stravinsky's music reflects much less clearly than Schoenberg's the neo-classical ideal that I have just described. Stravinsky's aims in attaching himself to history were not the aims of a traditionalist like Schoenberg. From the outset his whole situation was entirely different from Schoenberg's. Stravinsky was a rebel who, far from ratifying the legacy of romanticism and absorbing it to the last drop, rejected it out of hand. This was not simply a matter of personality, but probably also one of nationality. In rejecting the aesthetics of romanticism, however, Stravinsky also largely deprived himself of the resources provided by the evolution of the musical language, and he therefore found himself on a more primitive plane of invention with virtually no access, most importantly, to the formal complexities characteristic of the late-romantic period. Far from taking up his inheritance, he simply destroyed it; and hence there arose that series of works that still fill us with astonishment, works in which he gave a new meaning to the language of the tribe. I would even say that he gave a new meaning to the most trivial words and that elementary phenomena suddenly acquired a note of necessity, an urgency that had been either forgotten or lost. At the opening of his career as a composer he carried out a masterly *reduction* of the musical vocabulary by temporarily abolishing all cultural references – or at least all elaborate cultural reference, since ethnic references persist in an absolutely natural symbiosis. The only explicit reference is reduced to caricature and the *objet trouvé* whose poetic appeal he magnified by means of mockery.

The question now arises, however absurd it may seem, how long it is possible to avoid a confrontation with the past, particularly in an era in which we are perpetually obliged to use our memories? Stravinsky's way of 'discovering' history or tradition was initially by means of anecdote. His handling of Pergolesi[1] suggests a chance visit to a museum by a wandering visitor, quite unprepared for what he finds. The museum is for the moment empty, although it will soon be crowded with people. This chance visit whetted his appetite and he soon began to vary his itineraries, exploring other museums that aroused his curiosity but without any serious purpose. (It was not a matter of respect, but of love.) He was in fact no ordinary visitor. Between him and the pictures at which he looked there existed the immeasurable gulf that separates commitment from simple investigation. If we try to explain this attitude – the attitude of a rebel amusing himself and allowing himself to fall under a spell – it came, I suspect, from the French (or rather Parisian) intellectual world of the day, with Cocteau certainly playing a part and perhaps, at a deeper level, Valéry. They shared a considerable number of paradoxes and actual attitudes – a tight discipline in the handling of material (the virtue of the imitator), the necessity for painstaking workmanship, a desacralized view of poetry and a cultural aestheticism. There was, however, one essential difference between Stravinsky and them: intellectualism. Although the opposite has often been maintained, Stravinsky was not an *intellectual*, by which I mean that he did not enjoy speculating about the phenomenon of culture as such. Nothing could be more alien to him than the obsession so common in France from the end of the nineteenth to the middle of the twentieth centuries, that sense of delight and torment caused by the sense of being enclosed in a cultural space that was becoming increasingly 'precious' and increasingly uninhabitable. No! Stravinsky was essentially a realist, and from this point of view his contacts with the French intellectual world had not the slightest effect on him. He always liked manipulating any musical objects upon which he came even if they were in future to be museum objects. He had an almost childlike curiosity in taking any toy to pieces – and that toy might be a musical masterpiece – and then showed an almost unsophisticated delight in putting it together again 'differently', giving it an individual significance. In this way he 'collected' a number of historical objects, choosing elements from them that he needed for his own purposes, and in any order he pleased.

To return to the ideas of style and idea, it seems that in Stravinsky's case style was not so much a preoccupation as a *game*, if we understand game in the widest sense of 'play' – an activity of the speculative intelligence based on the inherent human need for diversion. Play is sometimes amusing, but it can also be deadly serious, since it questions the necessity of creation. Play may help us to shirk fundamental issues; it may also go to the very heart of the truth, and of our own uneasiness, by revealing the huge accumulation of culture with which we are more or less bound to live, and indeed to 'compose': playing with this culture means trying to abolish its influence by

[1] The attribution to Pergolesi of the eighteenth-century music on which Stravinsky based *Pulcinella* has subsequently been shown to be, in part if not in whole, doubtful. [M.C.]

making it quite clear that one has mastered all its mechanisms – from outside – even the most perverse.

What is not so certain is whether anyone who adopts such an attitude can find it satisfying in the long run; before he can hope to attain any truth it is necessary to have passed through the final stage of asceticism. Ideas cannot ultimately be reduced to a game: the interchange between style and idea lies beyond this transitional antimony, this visitor's attitude.

Should we perhaps be right in finding the explanation of Stravinsky's final metamorphosis – the change in his musical personality that was at the time found the most astonishing of all and to most people the least convincing – in his transcending of the play principle? That change was greeted with incredulity, and even with sarcasm. Stravinsky was often accused of wanting to remain young at all costs, of clinging desperately to remaining 'contemporary', and he certainly found himself surrounded by a new generation whose ideas made a deep impression on him. I can see nothing reprehensible in this, let alone indecent, but I think that it reveals something more than a passing influence, something much more fundamental: abandoning the 'play' principle meant, in fact, the rejection of illusion. It has often been suggested that this final appropriation of a new style was a mere going into reverse, and that the principle remained the same. I do not think that this is true, any more than I think the different proportions of diatonicism and chromaticism of fundamental importance. These are all external features and not difficult to decipher. What is much harder to understand is the profound necessity for this apparent volte-face.

In the last resort 'play', 'the game', simply amounts to one huge quotation: we are back in Alexandria, and even in that library that somehow still survives the flames. Moreover, if this contact with the literature of the past is designed simply as a series of shock effects, it loses its interest. As soon as one period has been appropriated another must be selected, and then another, mechanically, until the supply is exhausted. This inexorable repetition brings us to the moment when history has been finally 'resumed' – or rather turned into a 'synopsis' – and the need to bring it up to date is no longer felt. At that point there is nothing for it but to forget the historical heritage that has been so inquisitorially inspected and rifled, more from *ennui* than in any spirit of irony. You are forced to remove the mask and show your own face, even if the process prove uncomfortable, painful perhaps, and the transition ambiguous, almost amounting to another 'borrowing'. The necessary return to facing the problems of the musical language, which are the only source of any real vital power, means rejecting all aestheticizing motivation, abandoning all superficially literary pretexts and drawing the drastic conclusions of this surgical operation with the sole object of mastering the bitter problem of how to compose.

That is the fundamental truth, whatever the circumstances may have been – abandoning the 'game' in order to rediscover the idea, or in other words rejecting the preoccupation with style as something a priori and once again regarding style as the consequence of idea. In spite of a number of finger-prints and certain dominant traits of character, Stravinsky's profound self-confrontation during the last years of his life, his reconsideration of all his basic concepts, clearly shook him profoundly. They made him appear in the role of penitent, asceticism and austerity being an absolutely essential condition of his change of position. Every means had to be readjusted, every structure reconsidered. The 'game' was over, and it was the turn of the 'idea'! The dilemma in which he found himself was so serious that Stravinsky had the courage to face it probably because, with the help of his vitality, he saw no other valid solution.

Why was it that the world of quotation and reference (a shrunken and accepted form of death) exercised such a fascination on the most brilliant spirits of the day, and why does that same fascination persist today though the borrowed clothes are new and the masking ideology has lowered its claims? Can it be explained solely by the character of *inventors* at the present time or does this obsession cling, like the shirt of Nessus, to our whole era, our whole civilization in fact, the better to burn and destroy it? Klee, I think, was already murmuring 'too much culture!' or something like it. How good it would be to wake up and find that one had forgotten everything, absolutely everything! As it is, we all have an encyclopaedia of culture at our fingers' ends – all the memory of the world at every moment of the day . . . It has become practically impossible to ignore the history not only of one's own culture but of that of any other civilization however distant or however, close, in time or in space. This plethora is not without its effect – unless the material itself makes new forms necessary, stultifying any form of imitation or appropriation. We have seen this happen in architecture, but what of music? And especially for a generation working exclusively with traditional instruments – with means, that is, invented for different musical needs from our own?

Doubtless Stravinsky, like Schoenberg and all the innovators of the early twentieth century, began by making history without being aware of it. The need to create was too strong for them to be hypnotized by the idea of finding their own niche in some future gallery. They were intent on finishing with certain ways of thinking and certain modes of existence. The process of transformation was all the swifter for being prompted by impulse; each of these men who did, in effect, discover a huge area of potential novelty, was seized by a kind of frenzy. After the brilliant firework display given during those few years by both Stravinsky and Schoenberg, they were haunted by History (with a capital h) and by an obsessive desire for order and classification based on absolute models. The conviction in each case may have been of a different order and their attitudes antithetical, but the concept of a *model* comes from a profound motive that is exactly similar: the tendency to shrink history by making a transfer of it, to claim a premature place in it by enclosing it. It was forbidden to consider a composition purely in the category of 'becoming': memory and invention were both given a place in the hope of achieving absolute continuity. In this way it was possible to belong to the present – the actual moment and its various episodes – rather than to the past, and certainly more than to the future.

If there is in fact a (?moral) lesson to be drawn from this state of affairs, it is the primary importance of what may be called 'wild' discovery. Just as Klee feared, there is no escape from the knowledge of our own culture, nor nowadays from meeting the cultures of other civilizations – but how imperious a duty we have to volatilize them! Praise be to *amnesia*!

39

Stravinsky: *The Firebird*[1]

The Firebird today seems to us inseparable from the first great days of the Ballets Russes and Stravinsky. The ballet had its first performance on 25 June 1910 and the musical world was to pay particular attention to the work, although its successors, *Petrushka* and *The Rite of Spring* both outstripped (as they say) all the expectations of even the most attentive observers! These three works might be compared to three leaps of a dancer, and they established 'historically' both Stravinsky's reputation and his importance in twentieth-century music. *The Rite of Spring* is certainly the most prodigious leap of the three, but as a first attempt *Firebird* was a real masterstroke. It has often been said that it reveals the influence of Rimsky-Korsakov, and especially of his *Golden Cockerel*, but this does not prevent us from being struck by its originality, and all the more so in perspective. It is impossible not to recognize in this music the *youth* of a genius, and I believe that, however much may have been said to the contrary, this youthfulness is the most fascinating aspect of the score.

Stravinsky's mastery of the orchestra asserts itself with a vigour and a tartness comparable only to those of Berlioz's *Symphonie fantastique* (though I know that Stravinsky was not particularly fond of Berlioz . . .). I would say that the modernity of nineteenth-century orchestration was revealed in the *Symphonie fantastique* in the same way as it was revealed in *Firebird*. The two composers both reveal an innate virtuosity that also displays their poetic genius.

This, in fact, is why I have chosen the original version – because it seems indissolubly linked to the musical thought behind it. (Stravinsky himself may well have been better satisfied with the more rigorous control of the later versions, but I hope that he would have allowed me my own point of view, even though it was not absolutely identical with his own. I am still persuaded, even as regards my own works, that the composer composes and his listeners dispose . . .)

In the present version there are five movements:

---

[1] Sleeve note for the recording by Boulez, Columbia 7206.

1. Introduction, Kashchei's enchanted garden; appearance and dance of the Firebird
2. The Firebird's entreaties
3. The Princesses' game with the golden apples
4. The Princesses' round-dance
5. Infernal Dance of Kashchei's subjects

This suite does not include either the *Berceuse* or the *Finale*, which will probably surprise those used to the other version. It may well be that, at that particular time, Stravinsky preferred the more brutal ending with the Infernal Dance to the apotheosis that concludes the ballet.

Stravinsky's harmonic style is inimitably personal from the very outset, intervals fluttering with perfect balance and settling on one dominant after another – to borrow a metaphor from the bird world. There are of course more traditional moments, but even in them the more or less 'exotic-sounding' model passages give the music a colour that is not only Russian but specifically Stravinsky's own. His rhythmic energy and the very individual cut of his phrases already appear as earnests of future developments, which were completely to renovate twentieth-century music. I would take as an instance Kashchei's Infernal Dance, in which we can immediately recognize the same energy, or rather the same principle of energy, of certain passages in the *Rite*. The markings of some of the movements, such as *Allegro feroce* and *Allegro rapace*, are characteristic of this rhythmic aggressiveness.

In fact I see in *Firebird* a kind of greed to take possession of already existing music and transmute it into an aggressively personal object. This virulent determination to take possession of music and transform its whole aspect and appearance, and the youthful zest of the whole conception, are very remarkable; and all the more so because the historic antecedents of the musical material are so plainly visible. This places us in a perfect position to appreciate the passion with which the ferment of a creative idea impels a composer to embark on his first work.

40

Stravinsky: *The Rite of Spring*[1]

The Rite of Spring serves as a point of reference to all who seek to establish the birth certificate of what is still called 'contemporary' music. A kind of manifesto work, somewhat in the same way and probably for the same reasons as Picasso's *Demoiselles d'Avignon*, it has not ceased to engender, first, polemics, then, praise, and, finally, the necessary clarifications. In seventy years, its presence has been felt continuously. Paradoxically, until recent years, the *Rite* has made its career much more as a concert piece than as a ballet; even today, despite a few resoundingly successful stagings, symphonic performances far outnumber ballet productions.

In the same way that the name of Schoenberg remains identified primarily with *Pierrot lunaire*, the name of Stravinsky remains attached to *The Rite of Spring*, or, I should say, to the phenomenon of the *Rite* in which both the work and the context are united. This 'piece' has become (of itself and by the legend quickly spread around its creation) the cornerstone of modern music.

Even if today the historical landscape seems more varied and the personality of Stravinsky more complex, nothing can dilute the physical excitement provoked by the tension and the rhythmic life of certain sections: it is not difficult to imagine what amazement these sections caused in a world in which a 'civilized' aesthetic often exhausted itself in dying affabilities. It was the new blood of the 'barbarians,' a kind of electric shock applied without tact to chlorotic organisms. In algebra, the term 'simplification' is applied when the terms of an equation are reduced to a more direct expression. In this sense, the *Rite* may be spoken of as a *basic*: it reduces the terms of a complex language and allows a new start.

This simplified language permits the decisive recapture of a long-neglected element; from the very start, and throughout the most important episodes of the *Rite*, this right is aggressively claimed. Harmonic relations or melodic figures are reduced to striking formulae, extremely easy to remember; they serve to support a *rhythmic invention* the like of which Western tradition had never known before. Unquestionably, the music of Western Europe already contained the seeds of rhythmic preoccupation, especially at

---

[1] Sleeve note for the recording of Boulez, CBS, MS 7293, HM 47293. Translated by Felix Aprahamian.

the outset; but in the quest for solutions in the areas of polyphony, melody and form, the role of rhythm had gradually been reduced to that of a necessary substratum, sometimes refined, based on a certain number of archetypes, or 'models'. Nevertheless, rhythm followed the general evolution of musical writing in the direction of subtlety, flexibility and complexity.

But with Stravinsky, the pre-eminence of rhythm is shown by the reduction of polyphony and harmony to subordinate functions. The extreme and most characteristic example of this new state of affairs is furnished by the 'Dances of the Young Girls', where *one* chord contains, literally, the entire invention. Reduced to its simplest and most summary expression (because a single chord cannot imply any functional relationship), the harmony serves as material for rhythmical elaboration which is perceived by means of accents. The orchestration helps us to hear these accents more clearly, by the 'barking' of the horns above the continuity of the strings. This is how we perceive music so conceived: before worrying about what chord we are hearing, we are sensitive to the *pulse* emitted by this chord. 'Glorification of the Chosen Victim', or 'Sacrificial Dance', though they are less simplified moments, impress us initially in the same manner; for, beyond melodic fragments (which repetition allows us to grasp so quickly as to neutralize them), what we hear is the rhythmic impulse almost in its pure state.

Stravinsky changed the direction of rhythmic impulse. Musical writing until his time relied essentially on a basic metre, within which were produced 'conflicts,' due to overlappings, superimpositions and displacements of rhythmic formulae attached mainly to melodic invention and to harmonic functions. There was thus a kind of order and regularity momentarily disturbed by foreign elements. With Stravinsky, and more particularly in the *Rite*, there exists primarily a basic pulse, felt almost physically. (Not without reason, his music is always conceived exactly in relation to a given metronome marking a phenomenon much rarer among composers than one would think.) This basic pulse, according to a given unit, is multiplied, regularly or irregularly. Naturally, the most 'exciting' effects are provoked by the *irregular* multiplication, for this gives a certain proportion of the 'unforeseeable' within a 'foreseeable' context.

As to the composition itself, it does not *depend* on the argument of a ballet; and that is why it has no need of any modification in passing from the theatre to the concert hall. One can state that the plot of the ballet blends with the musical form into a single entity: the form of the ballet *is* its argument. This quest for coincidence between form and expression was often pursued by Stravinsky in the ensuing years; here, in *The Rite of Spring*, he stumbled upon the solution almost unaware, and rendered null and void the distinctions (however sterile they may be) between pure and 'programme' music, between music that is formal and that which is expressive.

This ritual of 'Pagan Russia' attains a dimension quite beyond its point of departure; it has become the ritual – and the myth – of modern music.

41

The Stravinsky–Webern Conjunction[1]

There is, of course, such a thing as 'contemporary interest'. But of what use is such feather-pated curiosity? The very flexibility of the word 'conjunction' will allow me to gather either a bouquet of rhetorical flowers or a nice little bunch of thorns. No need, therefore, to put oneself out much in order to pick a quarrel with those whose business is supposed to be to think.

The watertight compartments into which they divide all activities (like retired soldiers) form a rigid hierarchy. Anything resembling a cataclysm knocks them silly, and they resent this as a personal insult, as an attack on their idea of the ant-heap. Any excuse is good enough to attack the victim! He is either too young or too old, too ready to adapt himself or too out of touch, his friends are evil or destructive influences. In short, they are hot on cold scents, for frantic witch-hunting of this kind gives the witch-hunters a mad desire to cook themselves in the cauldron of their own inhibitions.

Then there is the fossil brigade, whose ferociously superior smiles brand any outsider caught interfering with their marbles and their ivories. If their nostrils twitch, it is not from pain or virtuous wrath but from a sort of uncontrollable nausea provoked by alien sweat. You must forgive their squeamishness: they suffer from a perpetual hysterical pregnancy but never give birth.

We may set one conjunction against the other, the mediocrity of the one balancing the level of the other. Contemporary interest is something that has to be experienced.

STRAVINSKY–BACH: Variations on the Chorale 'Von Himmel hoch'

These are the famous canonic organ variations that Bach wrote in 1747 in order to become a member of the Sozietät der musikalischen Wissenschaften, founded by Mizler and including Telemann and Handel among its members. In them he displays all his knowledge of counterpoint, because

[1] 'La conjunction Stravinsky/Webern', sleeve note for the recording by Boulez, Véga C30 A 120.

counterpoint is the very foundation and method of controlling the music. In the original text the variations – without the actual chorale – succeed each other in the same key of C major, and each presents a different problem or complexity of canonic writing, in ascending order of difficulty. This virtuosity takes on a high significance, which gives these variations a place beside *The Goldberg Variations*, *The Musical Offering* and *The Art of Fugue* in what may be called Bach's contrapuntal *summa*. They are much less known than the three other works and Stravinsky's orchestration is a welcome contribution to the task of making them more frequently heard.

According to the information supplied by Robert Craft (to whom the work is dedicated) Stravinsky completed the work quickly, between the end of December 1955 and the beginning of February 1956. There are five variations in Bach's work:

Variation 1   In canone all'Octava
Variation 2   Alio modo in canone alla Quinta
Variation 3   In canone alla Septima
Variation 4   In canone all'Octava per augmentationem
Variation 5   L'altra sorte del canone al rovescio: alla Sesta, alla Terza, alla
              Seconda, alla Nona

Stravinsky orchestrated the variations for woodwind (no clarinets), brass, violas, double-basses and chorus, and the chorale itself, with which he opens the work, for brass. Finally he gave the work a tonal plan – C–G–D flat–G–C – according to the five variations; the instrumental and vocal design is one of the chief reasons for this plan, which was not in Bach's mind.

It would take too long to list the various additions that Stravinsky made to the original text. Some have an instrumental or acoustic purpose connected with the problems of orchestrating music originally conceived for the organ; others are designed to emphasize the already existing canonic structure by reinforcing it with other counterpoints of the same kind.

The significance and import of this act of homage are best understood if we compare it to the 'copies' that painters used to make of masterpieces. That is to say, we should not regard it as a simple instrumentation, such as Bach himself might have made, but rather as the grafting of one personality on to another. Did not Stravinsky add at the end of the manuscript, after his signature, 'Mit der Genehmigung des Meisters' ('With the Master's consent')?

STRAVINSKY: *Canticum sacrum ad honorem sancti marci nominis*

This work was written for performance in the Basilica di San Marco in Venice and employs solo tenor and baritone, chorus and orchestra. The orchestra consists of woodwinds (no clarinets), brass (including a bass trumpet and a double-bass trombone), organ, harp, violas and double-basses. The absence of violins and cellos gives the strings a markedly matt sonority, without any brilliance.

The work opens with a dedication to the city of Venice, and the five movements then follow an architectural plan that is worthy of note. Movements I and V, which resemble each other, are in a vigorous harmonic style recalling that of the *Symphony of Psalms* and are intended to provide a massive framework for the three more finely worked inner movements – a tenor solo, a triptych celebrating the Three Theological Virtues (the centre-piece of the work) and a baritone solo with choral responses. This architectural structure is plainly symbolic and in fact recalls the five domes of the Basilica. There is also a close connection between the musical form and the subject matter.

The first movement describes the will of God and the last the carrying-out of that will: one is therefore musically the retrograde of the other, suggesting according to Robert Craft the idea of the future-in-the-past and the past-in-the-future. The style of the second movement matches the stylized lyricism of the text and is ornamented with long melismas, almost Byzantine in character. In contrast to this the third movement, setting out the Three Theological Virtues, is in a severe contrapuntal style and the writing is strict, note-for-note. Finally, in the fourth movement, the Christian apostolate is symbolized by an antiphonal construction in which the congregation responds to the priest's declaration of belief. Only his words 'adjuva, adjuva' emphasize the isolation of this prayer for faith, the chorus remaining totally silent.

Although the outer movements (I and V) are in the composer's normal harmonic style, the other three are serial. It is impossible to give a complete analysis of the music from this point of view, and it can only be said that Stravinsky has here fully faced the problem of dodecaphony in its most rigorous aspects, and that the present coupling with the canonic variations is therefore not a matter of chance.

In the *Canticum sacrum* some commentators have discovered the influence of Webern's *Cantatas*, and this is plain in the canonic structures and the superimposition of the series. On the other hand Stravinsky's horizontal interval structure, and the vertical sonority resulting, are entirely different; and his use of melismas and ornaments reveals a desire to stylize that was never a concern of Webern's.

A word in conclusion, simply to say that where a host of others have continued to stammer and to pontificate, to chatter and to prejudge, to simper and to haggle, to rage, to threaten, to mock and to torpedo, Stravinsky has simply *acted*.

WEBERN: *First Cantata*, **Op. 29**

The text of this work is by the Viennese poetess Hildegard Jone, and there are three movements. The first is choral, the second a soprano solo and the third choral, with a soprano solo at the end. The music shows all the suppleness of thought and writing characteristic of Webern's late works but is neither as large-scale in conception and forces employed nor as imaginative in construction as the second *Cantata*, Op. 31, though it marks an advance on Webern's first essay of the kind, *Das Augenlicht*.

The chamber orchestra consists of woodwind and brass employed as soloists (no bassoon or tuba); harp, celesta and glockenspiel, all favourites with Webern; and there is also a timpani part and an unusually important percussion section consisting of triangle, cymbals, tam-tam and bass drum. The small string section does not include double-basses. The second movement includes a mandolin, rarely used by Webern; and the choral writing is in four parts.

The first movement is based on a constant alternation of a slow tempo and a fast which is exactly double the first; and this alternation is often marked dynamically, the fast tempo being generally *forte* and the slow *piano*. This infrastructure serves as the basis for a larger plan in which a purely orchestral introduction and conclusion entirely enclose the choral section. This is the movement in which the percussion is the most important, underlining the text with violent jolts designed as almost 'realistic' illustration – as when the words 'Lichtblitz' [lightning] and 'Donner' [thunder] are immediately preceded by the timpani, the bass drum and clashed cymbals.

In contrast to this the second movement is marked by an almost unbroken continuity. The strophic structure is easily recognizable thanks to the vertical or horizontal character of the accompaniment, and the instrumentation is light and airy, even at strong points. Mandolin and glockenspiel give it the bright, sharply defined colour that is its hallmark and only metal percussion instruments (triangle and tam-tam) are used.

Finally the third movement contains three developments, which gradually combine elements from the two preceding movements. This ends with soprano and chorus singing antiphonally, either in counterpoint or in harmony. In the last bars there is a rhythmic *rallentando*, a fall in the pitch of the music and a *pianissimo* that gradually fades to nothing.

WEBERN: *Second Cantata*, **Op. 31**

The *Second Cantata* opens up infinite perspectives and must without doubt be considered one of the key works of the contemporary movement by reason of its potentialities for the future. A whole generation will acknowledge this work as one of its essential starting points: both poetically and technically it stands at the origin of a new conception of music itself. It may also be considered as the involuntary testament of the composer, since it is the last work that he completed. He was to be killed a year later in brutally stupid circumstances.

The movements are as follows: two bass arias (movements I and II) corresponding with a soprano aria (movement IV) and a purely choral piece (movement VI), with two movements (III and V) for soprano solo and chorus, women's voices only in III and mixed voices in V. All these movements are based on a single pulse, i.e. whatever the rhythmic unit, it always has the same metronomic value (168 and its ternary or binary subdivisions).

The orchestration is denser than in the *First Cantata*. The woodwind consists of piccolo, flute, oboe, cor anglais, bass clarinet, alto saxophone and bassoon (an instrument rarely used by Webern). A tuba is added to the three normal brass instruments and Webern also uses his favourite celesta, harp and glockenspiel. Of the strings, the violin is used as solo instrument in movements I and V, and the double-basses appear only in the first bass air. The use of the bell is almost Berliozian, sounding the twelve strokes of 'stiller Mitternacht' [calm midnight] in movement II.

In movement III the three-part writing for women's voices is deliberately and strictly contrapuntal, whereas in movement V the chordal writing for mixed chorus recalls the organist's *plein jeu*. Movement VI is again contrapuntal. In order to safeguard intonation the chorus is always doubled by the instruments in contrapuntal movements (III and VI) but never where the writing is purely harmonic (V).

Without going into great detail, I will indicate the chief characteristics of each movement.

I   Bass aria in three symmetrical verses. Here the chords of the orchestral accompaniment are all composed of the same notes and only the disposition of those notes changes. In this way Webern achieves a strange effect of simultaneous movement and immobility.

II   Bass aria, in perpetual canon. As in the famous canon in *The Musical Offering* the text returns – very varied – each time one tone higher, right through the chromatic scale. The last notes are directly related to the first, so that the piece eventually represents a cycle that can run straight on. (On the other hand the cycle in movement VI has two new beginnings.)

III   This movement is in four successive parts – for chorus; for soprano solo; for chorus and soprano; and for chorus with a single word sung by the soprano soloist. When the choral writing is in three parts, the orchestra has the fourth, in canon; in the soprano solos the orchestra has the three other parts – hence there is a reversible relationship between the density of the orchestra and that of the chorus. On the other hand the contrapuntal answers in the orchestra may be concentrated in chords, thus providing a contrast that is more thoroughly explored in the last movement.

IV   Soprano aria in two symmetrical verses. This is based on approximately the same principles as the first bass aria, but employing a greater variety of chords.

V   This movement is in three parts. In the first the chorus (chordal) alternates with the soprano solo, who has the second part to herself, while the third returns to the alternating pattern of the first. We have here an example of one of Webern's most important innovations. The chorus being written in four-part chords can generate four-part counterpoint, so that the chord is considered as the 'degree zero' of the counterpoint, when time has ceased to be successive and become simultaneous. On the other hand Webern either conducts this counterpoint strictly, i.e. with exact answers, or distorts it by shuttling one answer into another – in other words he achieves an ingenious 'fading' of both intervals and time.

VI   This is a more traditional four-part canon recalling the choral writing of the Renaissance. The metre of each part is noted separately. In other words the four parts have no common bar line, a clear reference to the old masters of vocal polyphony. The three verses of the poem involve a triple repetition of the musical text.

42

Varèse: *Hyperprisme, Octandre, Intégrales*[1]

Edgard Varèse was born in Paris in 1883 and studied at the Conservatoire and at the Schola Cantorum with Widor, d'Indy and Roussel. In 1915 he emigrated to New York, which he then made his home. The works recorded here were written after working for several years in the United States as a conductor, and *Intégrales*, *Octandre* and *Hyperprisme* were performed, in that order, in New York during 1923–4.

These works form the 'terms' of Varèse's whole career as a composer, which was radical and many-sided, concerned with melody, harmony, rhythm and acoustics. From the outset all three can be seen to spring from a single source and to be articulations, as it were, of different facets of a single intuition – its 'crystallization', as Varèse himself liked to call it. These were the years immediately after the First World War, when Debussy was dead and both Schoenberg and Stravinsky seemed to have already made their essential contributions to music. A large section of the Western musical world was taken up with the futile disputes between 'fauvism' and neo-classicism, while Varèse himself was unaware of Webern's serialism; and he made his totally unexpected appearance as a composer capable of making an irresistible affirmation of contemporary reality in sound.

There is a certain dialectic in the material that is of primary importance in this case. Varèse felt under absolutely no obligation to refer his music to any 'tradition' (and this was true in an almost physical sense!) and he finally rejected the classical (academic) conception of the orchestra and of tonality, even indeed of equal temperament, re-forming in its stead an ensemble that would answer the 'spatial' and 'rhythmic' demands of his music. This meant completely forgetting the archetypal 'romantic' orchestra, virtually doing away with the strings and reinforcing the dynamic element with an enormous percussion section. Massed brass and woodwind form the main body of sound, with piccolos, piccolo clarinet, trombone and double-basses completing the pitch range at each end of the spectrum.

This represents the acoustic plan of *Hyperprismes* and *Intégrales*, which are very similar in formation. As regards percussion, Varèse went far

---

[1] Sleeve note for the recording by Boulez, Véga C30 A 271. For Boulez's tribute to Varèse at the time of his death, see p. 497.

beyond the merely picturesque usage found in the post-romantic orchestra. He structured and ordered his material, thereby achieving a huge 'work force', both aggressive and static in character – stretched skins (drums), deep-toned metals (cymbals, tam-tam), high-toned metals (anvil, triangle, bells), dry-toned wood (whip, Chinese block), scraped wood (rasp, rattle) and even breath (siren).

He made the same complete break with tradition in the matter of rhythm and, conjointly, form. We find on the one hand what might be called melodic rhythm – very minute articulation of an almost essentially chromatic melodic process; a new plasticity of line around certain poles that serve as accents (the oboe solo at the opening of *Octandre* or in the last part of *Intégrales*); a rhythmic chromaticism moving parallel to pitch chromaticism.

On the other hand Varèse grafted on to these features their logical opposite, a contrapuntal rhythm based on pitch ostinatos, repeated notes and constantly varied forms of attack. The whole orchestral ensemble is, as it were, watermarked by the 'characteristics' of the percussion.

The powerful sense of enchantment that strikes the audience at a performance of *Intégrales*, for instance, comes from the uninterrupted combination of these two rhythmic worlds. There is certainly no other work in which the melodic (and even the 'formal') thematicism, which is still latent, is no longer dissolved or drowned in the raw projection of the compact blocks of timbre and register complexes.

One last observation on the harmonic use of these blocks. Following his own musical logic Varèse echoes harmonically all 'conflicts' of register and timbre, and this meant using the tensest relationships within the chromatic scale, in the shape of aggregates consisting of two or at most four sounds. Hence the listener is immediately aware (in addition to the aggressive havoc of these frictions) of the differentiation and order of importance in these relationships: acoustic *evidence*, in fact.

In listening to these three essential works of Varèse's, we should bear in mind his constant concern with form. This was no doubt a legacy from Busoni with whom he was at one time in contact – a very fruitful contact – and it is a determining factor in his music. Varèse and Webern were the first to learn the lesson of Debussy's last works and to 'think forms', not – in Debussy's words – as 'sonata boxes' but as arising from a process that is primarily spatial and rhythmic, linking 'a succession of alternative, contrasting or correlated states' – that is to say, intrinsic to its object but at the same time in complete control of it.

Hyperprisme is the most masterful projection of this state of mind, in its refusal of all thematicism and in the fluctuating plasticity of the tempi.

It is good (or is it?) to recall finally that all the works recorded here had their first performances at New York in 1924 and 1925 conducted either by the composer (*Hyperprisme*), by R. Schmitz (*Octandre*) or by Leopold Stokowski (*Intégrales*).

43

Berg: *The Chamber Concerto*[1]

Berg's personality is fascinating in more ways than one, but what I find most striking is the combination of immediate expressiveness with outstanding structural powers. He was certainly a romantic, even to excess: what he communicates are feelings of fascination, nostalgia, often paroxysm. His music expresses his whole personality and reflects the epoch in which he lived. Yet this orgy of sensations is organized in such detail that it needs the work of a detective to trace the endless ramifications of his ideas. These are scattered in abundance throughout all his scores and even include certain esoteric features such as numerical relationships and cryptograms, difficult to decipher unless one has the key. This formal, even formalistic, symbolism, which might seem to contradict the expression of the feelings that inspired the composer to write, in fact confirms Berg's expressive power, giving it an unusual dimension and an incredible strength and durability.

The *Chamber Concerto* is one of the most typical examples of the fundamental 'contradiction' in Berg's music between the elaboration of the formal scheme and the expressive character of the musical material. At the very outset we find an idea that seems ludicrously constricting – the whole work is based on the number 3, a symbol of his friendship with Schoenberg and Webern. Furthermore part of the thematic material consists of the musical transcription of the letters of their three names; and finally one rhythmic ostinato figure is based on the initials of their first names. All these extra-musical conditions must surely form a kind of straitjacket, one would think; but Berg seems to have delighted in such symbolic *correspondences*, the constraint that they impose exciting his imagination and stimulating his brilliant powers of invention to create the music and the forms of the overall symbolic structure.

The *Chamber Concerto* also clearly marks a transitional stage in the evolution of the composer's language towards the twelve-note technique. It is typical that this evolution appears initially not in the linguistic sphere – the actual vocabulary of the music – but in the relationship between each musical phrase and its placing in the overall form of the work. A good

---

[1] Sleeve note for the recording by Boulez, DGG 2531007, 1977.

example is the first movement – variations for piano and winds, in which Berg employs the four classical contrapuntal forms in which a melodic line can be presented.

The work also contains an example of one of Berg's favourite obsessions, the palindrome. Thus the second movement (violin and winds) is divided into two halves of which the second is a 'mirror' of the first. In the third movement the forms of the first two are combined, either in succession or simultaneously, a symmetrical form thus combining with a non-symmetrical.

Finally there is an echo of *Pierrot lunaire* – each movement, or part of a movement, having its own individual instrumental character and a tutti occurring on only one occasion. This large outer casing is naturally both the simplest, and the most striking feature of the work for those who are not familiar with it – piano and winds; violin and winds; piano and violin; piano, violin and winds – the cadenza being given to piano and violin.

The content of the *Chamber Concerto* includes evocations of all Berg's private fantasies – the Viennese waltz; nostalgia for a lost paradise; the symbol of midnight marking the central point of the symmetry; the taste for dramatic gestures as in the fading of the final bars into silence. Here, no doubt, lies the secret of Berg's 'contradictions' and of his success is resolving them; he felt these gestures – formal, structural and esoteric even in their number symbolism – as dramatic features demanding expression in musical texture.

There are quite a number of these dramatic gestures in the *Pieces* for clarinet and piano, but they do not require such a highly organized framework. Compared with Schoenberg's relatively short pieces of a similar kind, and even more with Webern's extremely short pieces, Berg's gestures are of quite a different kind. Where Schoenberg condenses and Webern creates a perfect microcosm, Berg's gestures are *sketches*, and the listener feels that they might be continued, diffused or multiplied. In this they resemble the sketches for *Novellen* in Kafka's *Journal*, which suggest continuations that are not expressed, beyond the actual, 'closed' text – forms that, though complete, yet remain in a sense open.

The Piano Sonata differs from the *Chamber Concerto* and the *Pieces* for clarinet and piano in that it shows Berg adapting himself to the world of composition and does not raise the question of his originality. He is absolutely himself in some features, which are already very characteristic, but not yet quite wholly himself. He is adapting himself, making preparations for his voyage, still on the shore and scanning the distant countries that he is going to explore. He feels the attraction of the distant future but is still tied to the recent past. He is collecting his arms and making his preparations. The nostalgia of this opus 1 is the nostalgia of a boy. What labyrinths lay before him, between the Sonata and the *Chamber Concerto*, before he was to become wholly, completely and irredeemably himself!

44

Wozzeck and its Interpretation[1]

Wozzeck marks an important date both in Berg's evolution as a composer and in the history of music, constituting a major contribution in the field to which it belongs. It shows the same preoccupation with form that marks Berg's principal masterpieces, and indeed almost the same obsessions.

Schematically the opera may be said to consist of (a) *Exposition*, which, with the five first scenes, forms the first act; (b) *Peripeteia*, which includes the next five scenes, forming the second act, and (c) *Catastrophe*, with the five last scenes, which together form the third act.

The solid formal armature with which Berg had provided Büchner's text was to be a great help in establishing the architecture of the music. There is a certain parallelism between Acts I and III enclosing the longer and more important Act II, which also uses stricter forms than those used in Acts I and III. Finally, each act ends with a cadence on the same chord, though with certain modifications in its layout.

A brief analysis reveals that the five scenes of Act I are character pieces (*Suite, Rhapsody, Military March* and *Lullaby, Passacaglia, Quasi Rondo*); the five scenes of Act II constitute the five movements of a symphony (*Sonata, Fantasia* and *Fugue, Largo, Scherzo, Rondo con Introduzione*); and the five scenes of Act III may be considered as *Inventions* (on a theme, on a note, on a rhythm, on a chord, then on a tonality, on a moto perpetuo).

It might seem from this that Berg was returning to the old pre-Wagnerian opera of separate 'numbers', but in fact his genius lay in resolving the antinomy existing between the idea of closed forms and Wagner's continuous music-drama. In this sense *Wozzeck* presents a résumé of the opera as such and may indeed have finally closed the history of this particular form; it certainly seems that after such a work music theatre will have to find different means of expression.

From the thematic point of view the *Leitmotiv* (*Erinnerungsmotiv*, to be more precise) plays a much more distinct role than in Wagner, really serving

---

[1] 'Situation et interprétation de *Wozzeck*', on the occasion of the first performance of *Wozzeck* in France at the Paris Opéra in 1963. Published with the complete recording of the work by Boulez, CBS 3003.

to elaborate forms and thus integrating the dramatic and the musical thought in the most satisfactory possible way. It is impossible in a short essay to give examples of Berg's many different uses of this procedure – the multiple variation of a motive serving as a major link throughout all fifteen scenes of *Wozzeck* – but Berg himself regarded it as so important that I have felt obliged to emphasize this use of musical forms throughout the work. He even wrote an article on the subject, defending the idea with great warmth:

> You can believe me when I tell you that all the musical forms used in the work are used successfully. I can demonstrate their justification and their aptness in great detail and in a way that allows no denying.

He also wrote elsewhere, still on the subject of *Wozzeck*, that

> Each scene and each entr'acte must therefore be considered as possessing its own, clearly identifiable musical physiognomy, a coherent and clearly defined autonomy. It was this overriding consideration that determined the much discussed use of old or new musical forms normally employed only in abstract music. Only they could guarantee the wealth of meaning and the clear outlines of the different pieces.

Not the least important of Berg's declarations on the subject is the following:

> However aware the listener may be of the multiplicity of musical forms employed in this opera, of the rigorousness and logic of their elaboration and the skill in combination revealed in even the most minute details from the rise of the curtain until it falls for the last time, there can be nobody in the audience who can distinguish anything of these various *fugues* and *inventions*, *suites* and *sonatas*, *variations* and *passacaglias* and who is not still wholly absorbed by one thing, and one thing only – the fundamental idea of the work, that transcends the individual fate of Wozzeck.

We thus see Berg pursuing the most direct dramatic effectiveness by means of the most recondite formal elaboration. How is an interpreter of the work to resolve an apparent contradiction of such magnitude? Is he to give all his attention to making clear to the listener Berg's symphonic forms, or should he concentrate his whole attention simply on the dramatic power, the expressiveness of the music? Should he abandon all idea of making the listener aware of what Berg calls his 'skill in combination'? How can he keep his eyes fixed always on the fundamental 'idea' of the opera when he is beset by so many formal problems? And finally should he too follow the advice that Berg gives his potential audience and put out of his mind all theoretical explanations, all questions of aesthetics? Berg was particularly proud of having reconciled musical rigour and dramatic potency; but he was anxious not to be considered either a pedant or an academic . . . hence the excessively precautionary nature of his observations! Personally I believe that what he really meant is this: if you are perspicacious, you will know the subtle character of my opera and the secrets of its construction; if you are even more perspicacious, you will know them so well and will have assimilated them so thoroughly that you will realize that they are one and the same thing as the dramatic expression. In any case this was the line I decided on for my own elucidating of the 'secret' of *Wozzeck*.

I will take a few simple but unusually striking examples. In the *Invention on a Note* (Act III scene 2) the note itself (B) is always present underlying all thematic developments, varying in importance and in 'audibility' up to the moment after Wozzeck murders Marie, when the monstrous expansion of this B fills the whole orchestra while at the same time the obsession of the following scene – a rhythmic obsession – makes its appearance. I think that the conductor must concentrate on emphasizing the fluctuations of this central note, which correspond to the presence in Wozzeck's mind – sometimes vague (the growling of the double-basses at the opening) and sometimes terrifyingly clear (the steady, ruthless hammering of the timpani towards the end) – of the idea of murder, right up to the moment of astonishment and horror, at the resolution on C, when he realizes what he has done: 'Tot!' ['Dead!'] If the fluctuations and the different forms taken by this central note are given exactly the right value, there can be no doubt that even the least aware of listeners will grasp, if only unconsciously, Wozzeck's doubts and hesitations and his final decision that nothing can now thwart. This purely musical precision is a perfect decription of the dramatic situation and of each minute step in its development.

If we now turn our attention to the next scene, we find both instruments and voices subordinated to a single, obsessive rhythmic figure. We have entered a nightmare world in which nothing can ever be natural again and everything combines, as in some automatic mechanism or 'truth machine', to crush the wretched Wozzeck. For this reason it is important to lay particular stress on the verbal contortions imposed by the all-powerful rhythm and to make glaringly obvious the absurdity of the resulting prosody:

> Ich glaub' / ich hab' / mich / geschnitten . . .
> Wie kommt's / denn zum / El . . . / . . . len bogen?

> [I think I've cut myself . . .
> But how is it right up to my elbow?]

The more clearly the rhythmic structure stands out, the more immediate the audience's awareness of the automatic nightmare of the accusation that leads Wozzeck to the fact of the murder, and to its expiation.

In the same way the even quavers in the final scene – the *Invention on a moto perpetuo* – must give the end of the work a kind of indifference, only slightly disturbed by the news of Marie's murder, an indifference felt in the movement of the music (well named 'perpetual'), which perfectly reflects the children's indifference to the grown-ups' deaths and also suggests the everyday fact that 'life goes on' unchanged, untouched by any sense of outrage and marked by a sense of pity that is only momentary and evanescent. The audience must realize clearly that the opera has, properly speaking, no real conclusion but ends precariously balanced, as it were, in the air . . . and that another drama of the same kind may begin, is *ready* to begin again at any moment and in any place . . .

I have deliberately chosen the most immediately striking examples from Act III, but I might just as well have delved into the less obvious treasures of Act II – scene 4, for instance, in the beer garden, which is formally a scherzo interrupted by three trios. The scherzo itself is related to the waltz by which the crowd is gradually carried away in a kind of frenzy that finally reaches a hallucinatory climax. The trios that interrupt it, on the other hand, are linked to the 'happenings' that suddenly create small islands of interest round precise, individual points – the two apprentices, the chorus of apprentices and soldiers and the stranger, more irrational intervention of the Madman. These 'happenings' distract Wozzeck's attention and crystallize his obsession, so that each time the waltz returns the dramatic tension increases, right up to the final paroxysm. The dramatic sense of these interruptions and returns will be clear to the audience only if the conductor pays particular attention to the 'structuring' of the musical form.

I could easily take other scenes of the work and show how, in every case, doing justice to the construction and organization of the music means doing justice to the organization of the drama and the analysis of the different characters. More especially, whenever a situation or even a word – even if used in a different context – suggests by association a parallel with an earlier occasion, Berg makes use of 'quotation'; and it is most important to underline this in order to stress the links, however tenuous, between the two moments in the drama. In fact Berg makes very conscious use of a kind of overall *symbolism* in matters of form, in motives and even in intervals (the fifth A–E, for instance, symbolizing death), and the emotional power of this symbolism must be made as clear as possible. *Wozzeck* is in any case an extremely complex work, and these are the lines of force that immediately impress themselves on the memory, strengthening the drama and giving it a directly perceptible additional aural sense [*une épiphonie auditive*] since they knit the tissue of acoustic phenomena to that of the dramatic states, forming in the listener a single durable amalgam that whets his sensibilities and keeps him perpetually on the alert. I believe that this *symbolism* should be one of the principal concerns of all the performers in *Wozzeck*, but particularly of the conductor.

This brings with it, of course, a number of obligations, chief among which is orchestral clarity. In order to grasp these numerous allusions of Berg's an 'overall' rightness is not enough; Berg himself expressly asked for a chamber-orchestra clarity. This will, apart from anything else, ensure that the singers' voices are not drowned and that the maximum of expression is held in reserve for the orchestral commentaries that provide a kind of reflection on the foregoing scene and at the same time foreshadow what is to come. They are not simple 'interludes' but integral parts of the overall musical form, only without stage action or anything corresponding visually to the music. The sequence of certain scenes often recalls the *fondu-enchainé* of the cinema, and Berg's overall technique often suggests to me Proust's handling of the novel.

Speaking of technique, I should like to say a few words on the controversial subject of *Sprechgesang*, a problem that will perhaps never be solved really satisfactorily. In his preface Berg refers expressly to the examples of Schoenberg's *Die glückliche Hand* and *Pierrot lunaire*, virtually repeating the explanations given by Schoenberg in these two scores. The problem is therefore the same in each case – in *Sprechgesang* the performer has to avoid both any suggestion of 'singing' and also natural, realistic speech.

It may be that the heart of the difficulty in exactly following the composer's wishes lies in a mistaken analysis of the relation between the speaking and the singing voice. In some performers the tessitura of the singing voice is more extensive and higher in pitch than that of the speaking voice, in which the range is smaller and the pitch lower. On the other hand many singers have a very similar tessitura (after all, voices are trained in order to achieve certain 'norms') but the tessitura of their speaking voices is quite different – and this is particularly true of women, so that passages of *Sprechgesang* can be both too high and too low for them. Finally, the speaking voice ceases to sound because its actual emission is short. You might say that the pure speaking voice is a kind of percussion instrument with a very short resonance – hence the impossibility of pure speaking tone of long duration.

To give some idea of the innumerable difficulties in this ill-defined area I should like to quote the opening scene of Act III. Berg uses *Sprechgesang* when Marie either reads the Bible or tells a fairy story; she sings when she thinks about herself and her situation. The difference between the two symbolizes very precisely the difference between Marie's attitude to the written word or a remembered narrative – to a world of 'quotation', that is – and her attitude to her own personality and the events that directly concern her. To renounce this vocal contrast would mean forfeiting the translation of this antinomy into sound and would make nonsense of the dramatic situation and of Marie's psychological reaction to that situation. In *theory* there is no problem: *Sprechgesang* and *Gesang* must be differentiated. But the tessitura used by Berg makes one wonder whether there is any convincing way of performing the written intervals of his *Sprechgesang* ... In the fairy tale, particularly, the high Gs and A flats can easily produce terrible results! Shirking them will lead to the suggestion of a child-wife's harmless simpering, while emphasizing them will suggest the hysteria of a badly placed voice that is being forced. Both are out of character and can easily become ridiculous, and thus totally 'anti-dramatic'! The high notes, which are relatively easy when sung, suddenly become a major problem, since it is impossible to abandon *Sprechgesang* simply in order to perform the notes as written. We are faced with a delicate situation, a dilemma in which the choice seems to be between singing the notes as written or using *Sprechgesang* and altering the musical text.

Personally I am strongly in favour of the 'dramatic' solution, while at the same time deploring the necessity of departing from the strict letter of Berg's score. I point this out only in order to avoid any suspicion of negligence on my part and to make clear my own feeling of uncertainty in finding a practical solution for a problem that I believe to be in fact literally insoluble.

The profound organic complexity of Berg's works and their intense dramatic potency enable him to invest his forms with the highest degree of significance. In the case of *Wozzeck* the means he employs to describe the most tense situations involve extremely rigorous techniques. The need he feels to quote – whether it be a musical passage, an instrumental combination or a popular song – emphasizes the discrepancy in his mind between music that is genuinely 'composed' and what may be described as 'idealized' musical clichés. This discrepancy argues a double standard of intrinsic musical value applied, in each case, according to the aesthetic quality, or 'reference', demanded by the context and the emotive, anecdotal power intended by the composer. This amounts in fact to an *ars poetica* designed to establish a system of composite styles; and it is essential to bear all this in mind in conducting a work with so many ambiguous and complex echoes. The ramifications of the drama and the stylistic divergences of the music will achieve real unity only in an aesthetic vision synthesizing all the heterogeneous elements. On the other hand it is the formal strictness of the music that constitutes the centre controlling the various centrifugal forces, which, if unchecked, would disperse in mere anecdote. And finally the dramatic potency of the work is amplified by the symbolism of the musical language, an element that is always present at every level.

It would be a mistake in any case to see Berg as no more than a hero torn by contradictions or as the logical conclusion of the romantic movement. If we transpose the contradictions that are the key to his work and discount the actual circumstances from which those contradictions arose, we can learn a very valuable aesthetic lesson from Berg. Conducting his music implies essentially assimilating this point of view and demands a transposition into practical terms of the complexity that is the hallmark of his theatrical ideas, a complexity that is both widely dispersed and strictly unified.

45
Lulu

THE SECOND OPERA[1]

Let us first settle the quite unnecessary dispute about the third act of *Lulu*, which is a question of doing justice to a hitherto mutilated work. Coming chronologically between two known works, this act does not cause any upheaval in the landscape of Berg's music, but merely completes an opera that has suffered for forty years from being performed incomplete. In the light of Berg's obsessive attention to the formal aspect of his music there is every reason to think that *Lulu* is much more distorted by being performed incomplete than by the instrumentation of the already existing music.

From posthumous documents we can be sure that Berg completed the work, that a number of subordinate details could be restored without any fear of error, and that the numerous thematic relationships and correspondences linking this act to the other two give us an exact idea of the instrumentation intended by the composer. Friedrich Cerha has done the necessary work with great care, competence and mastery, finally carrying out what Adorno had urged so warmly and clear-sightedly – and he was unquestionably the best placed and the best equipped judge of the matter. This third act is no longer a myth but a reality, and in future it is in this completed form that *Lulu* must be given.

It is interesting to see Berg's determination in the choice of his two opera texts and his friends' amazement as he picked first *Wozzeck* and then *Lulu*. Schoenberg's astonishment with the choice of *Wozzeck* can be seen from the following passage, which dates from 1949:

> I cannot tell you how surprised I was when this soft-hearted, timid young man had the courage to engage in a venture that seemed to invite misfortune: to compose *Wozzeck*, a drama of such extraordinary tragedy that it seemed forbidding to music. And even more: it contained scenes of everyday life that were contrary to the concept of opera, which still lives on stylized costumes and conventionalized characters. (*Style and Idea*, p. 474.)

---

[1] 'Lulu: le second opéra', from the complete text published in *Alban Berg: Lulu*, Vol. 2 (no ed. given), Paris, Lattès, 1979, pp. 13–37. Extracts from it were published in the booklet accompanying Boulez's recording of *Lulu*, DGG 2740 213.

What Schoenberg says about *Wozzeck* is equally applicable to *Lulu*, and there were members of Berg's circle who were very nervous when he embarked on what appeared to them such a doubtful enterprise.

We must remember the circumstances in which Berg selected *Lulu*. He had given much thought to the subject of a new opera. He was tempted by a sort of fairy-story divertimento of Gerhart Hauptmann's, *Und Pippa tanzt* [*And Pippa Dances*]; but he also remembered a play by Frank Wedekind, *Die Büchse der Pandora* [*Pandora's Box*], which Karl Kraus had shown him when he was 20. Hauptmann was at that time one of the chief figures of the German theatrical establishment, while Wedekind was the exact opposite, a writer associated with scandals. Berg wrote to Adorno, 'I shall do one of the operas, if not both, but they will belong to two absolutely different worlds.' He settled on the one that flouted the conventions of the day and constructed the libretto of *Lulu* from Wedekind's two plays, *Die Büchse der Pandora* and *Erdgeist* [*Earth Spirit*].

He was certainly influenced in his choice by what was then the fashion in Berlin. Brecht and Weill had set the tone with *Die Dreigroschenoper* and *Mahagonny* and Hindemith's little operas *Cardillac*, *Neues vom Tage* and *Hin und Zurück* were having a *succès de scandale* – musically uneven works but representative of the deliberately provocative mood of the day. Like others of his contemporaries, Berg was disturbed by the mood of violence and provocation in Berlin. But what was common currency in Berlin did not yet pass muster in Vienna, and Schoenberg's circle – in spite of Karl Kraus – could see no direct relation between the 'nobility' of opera and a description of the *demi-monde* and the dregs of society, with all that this implied in the way of situations and dialogue.

Webern's mystic pantheism was at the opposite extreme to the spirit of perversity that was to attract Berg. Schoenberg's own use of the theatre in *Erwartung* and *Die glückliche Hand* was eminently 'noble', and he was soon to start work on *Moses und Aron*, showing how remote his interests were from Wedekind's plays, which might well shock his profoundest convictions, as Beethoven was shocked by *Don Giovanni*. Yet in spite of those feelings Schoenberg's links with Berlin were the cause of one of the few mistakes in his career as a composer when he wrote *Von Heute auf Morgen*. This was a comedy written in the hope of achieving success with a light, easily approachable piece, though it was in fact closer to the old *buffo* tradition than to Brecht's sarcastic social criticism. What Schoenberg conceived as a satirical operetta like *Neues vom Tage* proved to be old-fashioned, both musically and dramatically, and so pedantic that it effectively damped all high spirits.

The original manuscript of his *Suite*, Op. 20, in the Los Angeles Library confirms the Berlin influence already shown in *Von Heute auf Morgen*. Schoenberg's choice of sources and models reveals that, like all composers of the time, he had been attracted by jazz and the dance music that in different degrees derived from jazz. It is strange to see the transformation that occurred in Schoenberg during his last period in Berlin, in the twenties. This leader of the Vienna avant-garde, who saw himself as the classical example of a *poète maudit* – seems to have lost his head when transplanted to Berlin, and to have been suddenly put 'out of phase' with contemporary trends. Yet, although he may then have appeared in the role of impenitent romantic, the mastery of his writing and the complexity of his invention still assured him unquestionably a place high above his rivals. The 'Dance round the Golden Calf' and the final chorus of Act I in *Moses und Aron* are superb examples of a neo-classicism that a Hindemith never managed to rival.

Realism was far from being a novelty when Berg wrote his two operas. Alfred Bruneau had already set Zola, and a clear line ran from Leoncavallo's *verismo* to Charpentier's *Louise*. No doubt the practitioners of this realism were small fry musically, although the balance may be redressed if we count Mussorgsky among them; the first scene of *The Marriage* consists of no more than trivial, everyday conversation, and the same is true of some scenes in *Boris Godunov*. Our judgement of this whole period is too often clouded by the overshadowing figure of Wagner, whose genius wrought havoc in operatic history, not least because by his choice of subjects he prolonged artificially the romanticism of the early nineteenth century at a time when a number of lesser composers were laying the foundations of twentieth-century theatre, if not of twentieth-century music.

Berg seems not to have felt the general pull of operatic history except in the matter of forms and titles, which he used when they suited his purpose. He took his place, musically speaking, in the line of Mozart, Beethoven and Wagner, that is to say in the same line as Richard Strauss . . . and yet neither mythology nor a nostalgia for the past attracted him.

It was 'disturbing' subjects that fascinated him, but this fascination shows only in his two operas. His chamber music and the texts that he chose for his songs rather suggest a 'sublimating' artist, particularly the *Lyric Suite* – written immediately after he immersed himself in the brutally realistic world of *Wozzeck* that seemed so 'out of character' – and the Violin Concerto, a virginal requiem written immediately after *Lulu*. Are we to explain this by the attraction that he felt towards the morbid, or should we regard these rather as works of social criticism? Berg represents Wozzeck and Lulu as victims and lays the greatest emphasis on the wretchedness of their lives, their progressive social degradation and their increasing enslavement by forces that they have not the strength to combat.

The Passion for Symmetry

Lulu is without doubt a 'morality play', a kind of *Rake's Progress*, showing Lulu's rise in the social scale up to the death of her rich protector Schoen, followed by her gradual fall, which ends as a London prostitute. Berg accentuated the symmetrical character of the story by doubling the parts of Lulu's three London clients in the third act with those of the characters who owe their deaths to her in the first two acts – the Doctor, the Painter and Schoen reappearing as the Professor, the Negro and Jack the Ripper – while Lulu is actually killed by the same character (Jack) as she had herself killed (Schoen). This is not simply a matter of economizing in a work which needs a large cast! The parallelism does not exist in Wedekind and was Berg's own invention, and the musical reminiscences by which he establishes it are so clear that their meaning is unmistakable. Furthermore, he remodelled and adapted Wedekind's text in order to accentuate the dramatic 'arch' formed by Lulu's rise and fall.

The general structure of *Lulu* is quite clear, with the three acts divided into two parts – one rising, the other falling – grouped round a central interlude. Berg explained his idea in a letter to Schoenberg:

> Since I have been obliged to cut four-fifths of Wedekind's original text, the difficulty lies in knowing what to retain in the remaining fifth. And it is only increased if I try to subordinate everything to the musical forms (large and small) and still preserve Wedekind's individual language ... Anyway, although these problems of detail have been troublesome, I have long ago decided on a general plan for transforming the play into an opera. This involves musical as well as dramatic proportions, and most of all the scenario, which looks like this:

The Two Plays		The Opera
	Act I – Painter's studio, in which Dr Goll, Lulu's husband, dies of a stroke	
Erdgeist	Act II – The apartment of Lulu and her second husband, the painter, who commits suicide	Act I (three scenes)
	Act III – The dressing room of Lulu, now a dancer, whom Schoen promises to marry	
	Act IV – Schoen's apartment, where he is killed by Lulu. She is arrested	Act II (two scenes divided by a long interval)
	After one year in prison, Lulu is released by the Countess Geschwitz and returns to	(In Berg, one year in prison)
	Act I – Schoen's apartment (same set as before). She becomes Alwa's mistress	
Die Büchse der Pandora	Act II – Gambling club in Paris. Lulu has to escape	Act III (two scenes)
	Act III – A London attic	

By means of paying my respect to both parties you see how (in my Act II) I have brought together the parts that are separate in Wedekind; there are two plays there. The interlude by which I have joined the last act of *Erdgeist* and the first of *Die Büchse der Pandora* is actually the pivotal point of the tragedy, as it is there that the rise of the first part is replaced by the fall of the second.

This pivotal scene, Lulu in prison, is not shown on the stage (Berg conceived a film sequence instead) but is the formal axis of the whole opera. Wedekind balances the two plays by a different division, and it is interesting to observe how the symmetrical disposition of Berg's three acts shifts the dramatic emphasis from Schoen's death to Lulu's temporary absence in prison, the point of non-return in the opera.

Berg's taste for formal symmetry showed itself very early, but the more his work progressed, the more this mere interest took on the character of a fundamental obsession. All his last compositions are based on more or less strictly symmetrical patterns. It is true of the *Lyric Suite*, in which three increasingly slow movements alternate with three increasingly fast and the second of the fast movements is itself symmetrical. It is true of the *Chamber Concerto*, in which the symmetry of the two first movements is implicit in the third, which combines the first two. It is true of *Der Wein*, where the middle movement acts as pivot to the two outer movements, which mirror each other. It is true of the Violin Concerto.

It would nevertheless be a mistake to exaggerate the importance of this principle, which Berg employs very loosely. In *Lulu* he often uses it to establish moments of balance, and there are mini-forms, which are a model of this restricted use of symmetry, such as the sextet in Act I scene 3. This opens with a stroke on the bass drum (bar 1, 177), crescendoes to the pause (bar 1, 190) and subsides in a symmetrical diminuendo to the end, which is marked by another stroke on the bass drum (bar 1, 203) – thirteen bars on each side of a central bar, which is marked by a pause. This forms a small parenthesis in the general movement of the scene, a kind of bubble suspended in time, and Berg marks it *quasi a tempo, ma più tranquillo*. When I conduct the work, I adopt a noticeably slower tempo here, in order to emphasize the momentary suspension of the action during which each character is, as it were, frozen.

There are many other passages constructed on this same principle of formal balance, only applied less rigorously. To use symmetry systematically would be terribly uninteresting and Berg repeatedly avoids any regularity of this sort.

The Invention of Forms

It is not so much the use of symmetry as the exploiting of multiple musical forms that is one of the most complex and attractive features of Berg's music in *Lulu*. Büchner's *Woyzeck* was a posthumously published fragment, and although its language is powerful, it lacked a final form. Berg could therefore feel free to arrange the scenes in an overall scheme in which the structure of the drama would be created by that of the music.

The problem with Wedekind was quite different. Here Berg was faced with two complete plays in a discursive style quite unlike that of Büchner, who concentrates a situation in a single lapidary exchange. He was therefore compelled quite literally to reduce and at the same time to avoid any kind of anecdotal dispersion of interest.

The first time I read the text my reaction was negative – what, from a stylistic point of view, could music do with such a work? When I spoke to Adorno, he said, 'Wait until you get to know it better.' And I must admit that the text does go much deeper than would seem at first sight to be the case; and, most importantly, Berg's condensation gives it a pointedness that I should never have supposed possible.

The reduction had to be made on two planes, in the actual dimensions of the work, of course, but also within the whole dramatic 'phenomenon', which Berg pares down to its essential features. In doing this he always allowed himself to be guided in the direction of clear formal correspondence. What he felt important was to preserve the narrative impulse and the dramatic flow and at the same time to place them in a formal 'safety network'. He was very well aware of the constant danger of falling into mere anecdote and said so quite openly from the outset – yes, there is indeed anecdote, but it will be contained in such a tight network that it will never be felt simply as anecdote, but raised to a higher power by the formal aspect of the music. This determination can be seen even in the generalized names by which he calls the secondary characters – not Rodrigo but 'an Athlete', not Puntschu but 'a Banker', not Hugenberg but 'a Schoolboy'. The action is focused on the chief characters: Lulu, Schoen, Schigolch and Geschwitz, while the others become anonymous.

In this way Berg seems consciously and deliberately to have combined two parallel traditions in German opera – one represented by Mozart (and of course Beethoven) that may be called 'number opera' and the other represented by Wagner, continuous opera. *Wozzeck* itself was an essay in formalizing the relations between music and text, but much less complex than *Lulu*. Throughout *Wozzeck* each scene was given a corresponding musical idea, whether this was strictly formal – sonata, preclassical forms – or purely tactical – invention on a note or a chord.

The great advance from *Wozzeck* to *Lulu* lies in the fact that, although the scenes are still separated by interludes, there is now no 'passage' between them: there is a kind of complete fusion between continuity and formal separateness. Berg achieves this most notably by what might well be called 'collage'; and this is not a fortuitous encounter but a structural fretwork that employs as formal elements the dramatic relationships between the different characters in various given situations considered as prototypes of the action.

A dramatic structure that is not divided up into short scenes as in *Wozzeck*, but develops over long periods involving intersections and repeats, demands more suppleness and greater resources. In *Lulu* the forms are more versatile, telescoping even in the same scene and sometimes replacing each other, particularly in the first scene of Act III. Some of Berg's forms are so flexible that they are almost non-forms (melodrama or recitative) always involving direct conformity with the text. Others are strict, and these compel the text – with varying degrees of violence – to take its place in a musical dialectic based on different types of criteria, linked to the rhythm or to traditional patterns.

It is thus possible to distinguish 'accepted', historical forms such as sonata and canon, and 'invented' forms in which a specific hierarchy, such as that of rhythm, dominates the other dimensions of the musical language.

The characters of the drama are not identified with individual forms. Schoen is not sonata or Lulu arioso . . . The relationships are not as rigid as that, although there are correspondences, which are clearly emphasized. For instance, all the passages relating to marriage or engagement, to flirtation and all the other superficialities of social life in this particular milieu are marked by features from the past, such as gavotte or musette. This neo-classicism disappears when it is not required either by characterization or situation. And the use of these obsolete forms can be misleading. Thirty years ago I used to think, 'Why on earth does Berg find it necessary to write a gavotte? He can express himself perfectly well in *Wozzeck* without making use of this old rubbish!' Later I realized that it was impossible and a mistake to accept such forms as these at their face value, and that Berg used them for the critical analysis of a dramatic situation. The gavotte, as I have said, is linked to the idea of an eventual marriage between Schoen and his fiancée and to the flirtations of Lulu, with her dream of being married. There is a clearly sarcastic reference in its obvious 'prettiness'.

Berg never allows us to forget his skill in handling irony. Even when he is characterizing someone like Alwa, for whom he feels a real sympathy, he often manages to give his sentimentality an ironical note, and this was very characteristic of his whole personality (particularly in the *Altenberg Lieder*). With other characters, including Lulu, he is more acid and mocking, adapting his manner to the nature of the character concerned. In the case of the Athlete the mockery is brutal and direct, and blatantly boorish in expression – attacking the piano with his fists and forearms in a welter of black notes, white notes and *glissandos* – all typical of a character who is before all else a blackguard.

But there are also more subtle kinds of mockery – particularly the use of the forms of the past, old-fashioned rhythms and turns of phrase that are too insipidly sweet to be acceptable today. In this way the whole 'neo-classical' aspect of this opera, Berg's use of canzonetta, duettino, gavotte and arietta and the express references to things borrowed from early nineteenth-century Italian opera, his stylistic parodies and his flirtation with obsolete devices – all this is to be understood as a kind of mocking description of the characters on the stage rather than as 'back to' Bach, or whoever it may be.

Berg was no exception in being caught up in the neo-classical wave of the 1930s. But just as Stravinsky after 1918 began to use a number of contemporary dance types, Berg too used a whole repertory of *objets trouvés* taken not from the distant past but from everyday life. He certainly knew Stravinsky's works, which were often performed in Germany at the time, and the ragtime from Act I of *Lulu* is more or less directly derived from Stravinsky's. On the other hand the influence of Berlin was infinitely greater throughout the German-speaking world – and Berg's world particularly – during the years when he was working on *Lulu* than when he was writing *Wozzeck*. The whole perspective of the theatre had changed, especially in the use of vulgarity both as a way of destroying vulgarity and as an instrument of critical analysis. In fact Brecht, Weill and Hindemith had given the coconut tree of respectability a good shaking.

This can be seen in Act III of *Lulu*, where the 'circus' theme (which appears in the prologue and is quite deliberately 'plebeian') is used as the foundation of the three ensembles that form the skeleton of the opening scene in the Paris casino. Another instance is the marquis–procurer's *chanson*, which is taken from a collection of Wedekind's and is used with the same purpose, something clearly suggested by Kurt Weill and Bertolt Brecht. This third act contains more criticism of a decadent society than the other two.

Oddly enough Berg's sarcasm is closely related to his sentimentality and, as with Mahler, it is hard to tell when the one changes into the other. Even in his early works this anomaly is present both in his choice of song texts (*Altenberg Lieder*) and in the music, where there is always a suspicion of sentimentality. Both characteristics appear still more strongly in *Wozzeck*. Berg was in fact a sentimental man, a soft temperament, which he sublimated in his music; and his choice of brutal texts revealed a certain brutality and vulgarity in his own personality. In the same way the 'crudeness' in *Lulu* is one of its most unusual aspects, coming from such a composer.

The Manipulation of Time

Side by side with an aesthetic of parody, justifying references to obsolete or popular forms, we find in *Lulu* other formal structures that exercise varying degrees of constraint on the music. The exceptional complexity of some scenes brings a risk of destroying continuity by dispersion, and in these it seems as though Berg carefully made the setting of the action sufficiently rigid to be effective and sufficiently supple to allow dramatic incident. The scene in Act I where Schoen reduces the Painter to a suicidal state is a good example of this. Their conversation is carried on against a rhythmic ostinato (*La Monoritmica*, always associated in the opera with the idea of death), which constantly accelerates. This reaches its maximum speed and intensity at the actual moment when the Painter's body is found, and then gradually decreases up to the supposed arrival of the police. This scene is very complex formally and contains elements that have already been heard in the preceding scene; they return now in apparent disorder and will reappear later, but they are all harnessed to this rigorous rhythmic scheme. Rhythm in fact dominates the whole scene, forming, as it were, the envelope of the form though not creating it.

Similarly the second scene of Act III, which takes place in London, begins at a hectic pace with the visit of Lulu's first client, the Professor, and gets slower and slower until the death of Lulu, where the tempo suggests the frozen horror of a nightmare. One might have supposed that as Lulu's death drew nearer the tempo would become faster, but Berg shows his extraordinary perspicacity and acuteness in exposing Wedekind's dramatic intentions in this way. Lulu's death is inevitable; she herself begs to be killed and her longing for annihilation is communicated by being thus extended in time.

Here as elsewhere Berg's manipulation of time is one of the most significant ways in which he reacts to anecdote: he uses slackening or speeding up of the tempo to 'formalize' the realistic discourse and so gives it a resonance far beyond that of its literal sense. In Act II the first scene (Schigolch, the Athlete and the Schoolboy, bar 94) and the second (Geschwitz, Schigolch and the Athlete, bar 788) have the same musical text, and Berg expressly says that the second should be a kind of 'slow motion' [*quasi Zeitlupe*] of the first, an extending of the time in order to formalize this repetition and give it an entirely new expressive power.

Generally speaking Berg is extremely meticulous about changes of tempo: his markings are very precise and detailed. There is a good example of this in Act I scene 3, where the continuity between two moments of the drama is insured by a very characteristic gradual shift of tempo. After the sextet (crotchet = 120; bar 1, 204) triple becomes duple time and the tempo of the sonata returns (crotchet = 80; bar 1, 209) when the very lively dialogue between Lulu and Schoen begins. There is another slowing down (crotchet = 52; bar 1, 237) – i.e. the previous dotted crotchet becomes a crotchet – to mark Schoen's reaction to the news of Lulu's eventual departure for Africa. Then the tempo of the sonata returns by means of a linking bar in which the quaver moves from 104 to 80, i.e. the previous crotchet (bar 1, 248):

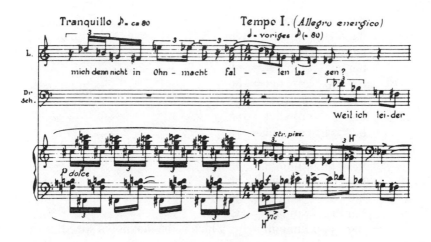

Berg manages in this way to control the tempo changes, all of which correspond to some dramatic point. He will often superimpose movements that fit together – for example, the 2/4 stage-music ragtime corresponds to the preceding movement by taking three quavers for two:

Here Berg doubtless had in mind a model with which any Viennese would be familiar – the stage music in *Don Giovanni*, where the three different tempi of three different orchestras are combined. In *Lulu* some tempo transformations spread in regular progressions over long stretches. Thus *La Monoritmica* in Act I, to take an obvious example, is constructed over a stretch of almost 300 bars. Once again Berg is remarkably precise in his calculations:

bar 669   quaver =   84
bar 675   quaver =   92
bar 675   quaver = 100

bar 679	quaver = 108
bar 687	quaver = 120
bar 694	quaver = 132
bar 702	crotchet = 76
bar 710	crotchet = 86
bar 717	crotchet = 96
bar 724	crotchet = 106
bar 732	crotchet = 118
bar 739	crotchet = 132
bar 748	minim = 76
bar 766	minim = 86
bar 788	minim = 96
bar 812	minim = 112
bar 833	minim = 132 which is the maximum speed.

In the other direction *ritardandos* are scaled in the same way. To perform a movement of this kind absolutely accurately proves in practice extremely difficult, especially for singers, who have a tendency to accelerate more quickly in the theatre.

Examples of this kind reveal Berg's clear wish to control the progress of the dramatic discourse by the text of the score so closely that it becomes impossible to separate the two. It is also worth observing how Berg sometimes employs various forms as signals of certain conflicts or situations. If *La Monoritmica* is the signal of death, the sonata is the signal of conflict and canon of agreement between two characters, while variations denote an ambiguous relationship between them. Stated in this way, such a repertory of signals may seem somewhat naïve but it proves most effective in practice.

The Liberated Style

Berg's musical language is based of course on the technique of the twelve-note series. How important is this? From the disciplinary point of view, very important. As a faithful disciple of Schoenberg Berg accepted the dogma of unity as preached by his master and in principle, therefore, a single series governs the themes and their elaboration. In actual fact Berg pays no more than respectful lip-service to this principle, and the original series soon becomes a mythical reference point to which he has only precautionary recourse. There is in fact something ironical about the moment when it makes its appearance, which is when the Animal-tamer observes to the audience 'Es ist nichts besondres dran zu sehn' ['There is nothing special about it']! These words are set to the notes of the series in its original form:

There is also something ironical in Berg's breaking-up of the complete chromatic scale into three diminished sevenths in the fifth bar, and he makes systematic use of this in Act III! This is the only sly reference to an obsolete operatic convention by which a diminished seventh automatically suggested dramatic tension.

From the very beginning of *Lulu* Berg made it quite clear that he meant to use the twelve notes of the chromatic scale with more respect for his own needs than for the rules. What does he in fact do with the series? Unless one is acquainted with the mechanisms of serial writing it is difficult, if not impossible, to follow in detail the ingenious – often impossible-seeming – devices by which he creates the thematic figures belonging to the different characters – Lulu, Schoen, Alwa or Schigolch – and the complex situations and feelings that criss-cross the action. In this sense the single series generates real *Leitmotivs* in the Wagnerian sense, strongly characterized and even emphasized by being confined to a single instrumental timbre, which helps the listener to recognize them as signals – such as the piano for the Athlete, the violin for the Marquis and the saxophone for Alwa. Simplicity is a remarkable feature of most of these elements, which lend themselves to the most complicated combinations and yet remain always recognizable. They are in fact *Erinnerungsmotive*, as Berg called them, reminiscence motives.

Berg's attitude to the dogma promulgated by Schoenberg was both to respect and at the same time to ignore it; his handling of the series is so free that he takes from it simply what he wants. Some of his musical figures could exist quite as well without it – the chromaticism of Schigolch's music, the pentatonic character of the Athlete's and Geschwitz's fifths are all extracted from the series with no other justification than Berg's wish to enclose his chosen dramatic symbols within Schoenberg's magisterial framework – the ultimate stratagem of an obedient disciple turning the law to his own ends.

Then there are the questions raised by the vocal writing. Berg followed operatic convention in his choice of voices – Alwa, the lover, is a tenor and his father, Schoen, a baritone – it could hardly be the other way round – Geschwitz, with her rather masculine personality, is a mezzo and the Schoolboy, a *travesti* part, a contralto ... Berg was quite content to follow the traditional operatic rules, if only to make his characters credible and to have the complete range of the human voice at his disposal.

On the other hand there was a quite definite reason for his making Lulu a coloratura part. In the operatic repertory that he knew and loved there was only one coloratura role, the Queen of the Night, who is a symbol of seduction, danger and darkness and thus has points in common with the figure of Lulu. But the two are not really linked by anything more than a vague evocation or simple allusion, such as Berg himself liked to make in his smallest gestures.

The vocal writing in *Lulu* is very complex, and it is often difficult to satisfy Berg's demands. He distinguishes six different forms:

1 unaccompanied dialogue
2 free prose (accompanied)
3 prose in which the rhythm is indicated by the tails of the notes and their ligatures, but the pitch is not exact
4 *Sprechstimme*, in which both pitch and rhythm are precise (Berg refers to Schoenberg's explanations in *Pierrot lunaire* and *Die glückliche Hand*)
5 half sung
6 wholly sung

The most problematic of these is *Sprechstimme* – whether the pitch is to be exact or not. *Sprechgesang* is comparatively simple when the pitch of the speaking and the singing voice are similar, as in the case of a baritone for instance. On the other hand if, as in the case of Teresa Stratas, the speaking voice is very low, the problem is insoluble since dramatic truth is attainable only at the sacrifice of musical truth, I prefer, if necessary, to ignore the notes in the interest of expression, as in the Act I dialogue at Lulu's 'Meines Mannes' ['My husband'] to Schoen (bar 615):

Berg dreamed of using the voice like a violin, with its repertory of *arco*, *col legno*, *sul ponticello*, *sul tasto*, etc. His difficulty – which was also in fact Schoenberg's – lay in the fact that he found himself excluded from everyday musical practice, condemned to isolation by the musical establishment of the day. Wagner had had his own theatre and knew by direct experience what was possible and what was not, the virtues and the faults of those who sang the existing repertory. In the same way, any score of Berlioz's will always be playable – though the *Queen Mab* scherzo is terribly difficult – because he wrote from personal orchestral experience, whereas there are some things in Berg and Schoenberg that remain unclear. These are things prompted by speculation rather than practical experience, and it may seem an illusion to hope to solve them satisfactorily. Although Berg was fiendishly precise, it is sometimes necessary to adopt compromise solutions for the problems that he poses. However that may be, simply from the point of view of difficulty *Lulu* is a more accessible work than *Wozzeck*, and this cannot be explained by Berg's greater experience. The complexity lies deeper than that and must be sought in the formal ordering of the music and the multiple relationships established during the work between the different themes, patterns and rhythms; for the deceptive simplicity of the writing conceals a wealth and a profusion that are virtually inexhaustible.

The references to jazz and ragtime may remove *Lulu* from the 1900 era of Wedekind's original, but they show how open Berg was to his own contemporary world and its cultural trends and the by no means negligible examples of Stravinsky, Hindemith and Weill.

It would be pointless now to try to return to Berg's sources and to concentrate our attention on the years around 1900. Berg has, as it were, destroyed those sources by his own progress as a composer and they remain his own secret, which cannot ever be discovered, though we may clear the surrounding landscape. We should be on our guard against nostalgia for the past: the work grown richer with time, as a river is enriched by alluvial tributaries. The interesting thing is to regard the composer's labour as the point of departure for another adventure, the adventure undertaken by those who make the work their own. What is valuable is not discovering the composer, but discovering ourselves through him. The difference hardly matters as long as it is fruitful.

If we are to insist on the historical aspect of *Lulu*, we can quote it as the first instance of the modern world intruding into opera – the last occasion on which modern opera could be considered as a valid search in a form inherited directly from the past. And if we insist on the difference, we are entitled to ask the question, absurd in itself, 'What would a third opera of Berg's have been like?'

A catalogue of the themes in *Lulu* could be compiled in the same way as has been done in the case of Wagner. H. F. Redlich has analysed them and revealed their mechanism in his *Alban Berg* (London, 1957). Here are some of these themes based on the original series:

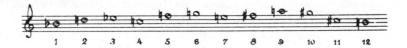

In its basic form this series appears only at the opening of Act II, in Lulu's *Lied*. In the form of four chords it becomes the motive of Lulu's portrait:

The dance theme of *Lulu* is obtained by reading the three parts of these chords in the following order – top line, middle line, bass line:

Berg also works several permutations based on a repetition of the series. Alwa's theme is obtained by taking every seventh note in such a repetition:

By taking every fifth note Berg obtains Geschwitz's series, while another principle of permutation gives him Schoen's theme and that of the sonata:

It will be observed that most of the themes are announced in the Prologue, in particular:

– the *Erdgeist* motive played by the trombones in the first bar, a kind of fanfare that reappears with the same intervals reversed at the end of Act II (bar 1,149) and condensed into chords at the moment of Lulu's death cry

– the Athlete's clusters (bar 16)

– Schigolch's chromatic intervals (bars 34–5)

– the theme of Lulu's power of attraction, a long phrase in several sections (bar 44 *et seq.*) in which the twelve-note series appears for the first time (bar 63)

– Alwa's theme (bars 73–5), heard at the words 'und nun bleibt noch das Beste zu erwähnen . . .' in the vocal line –

– and in bars 74–5 in the orchestra (cor anglais and saxophone):

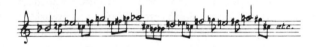

QUESTIONS OF INTERPRETATION[1]

With an opera like *Lulu*, the first problem is one of form, which was a major preoccupation of Berg's whole life. *Lulu* contains a number of closed forms borrowed from 'absolute' music, among others the sonata associated with the meeting of Schoen and Lulu in Act I, the choral variations that articulate the dialogue between the Marquis and Lulu in Act III and Schoen's five-verse aria in Act II before Lulu kills him. There are also more indeterminate

---

[1] 'Lulu: questions d'interprétation', from the booklet accompanying Boulez's recording DGG 2740 213. See also p. 380.

forms – such as *La Monoritmica* (based on a single rhythm) that constitutes the scene between the Painter and Schoen in Act I. There are also a number of more discursive passages in which the form depends directly on the text, the music playing no more than a supporting part, as in the old recitative.

Our first essential task, therefore, is to find a meeting point between these different types of expression, which at first seem to be mutually exclusive, whereas dramatic continuity was in fact Berg's chief concern. We shall find anecdote enclosed in a formal framework, sometimes strict and sometimes flexible, and no transition from one to the other must be allowed to prejudice the fundamental unity of the work. Berg's thinking was always extremely complex, and he grew increasingly attached to cross-references or what might even be called formal arabesques. Whether it is his taste for symmetry, his passion for allusions and secret references or his wish to combine apparently disparate forms, his musical universe seems unquestionably to depend on direct expression despite the presence of multiple underground streams, the tracing of whose unexpected courses never ceases to astonish the student.

The orchestral writing in *Lulu* is admittedly simple compared with that of Berg's earlier works, particularly the *Pieces for Orchestra*, Op. 6, and *Wozzeck*. Even so, the texture is often fairly dense, and it is important to bring out as clearly as possible the various thematic references, which serve as markers and are indispensable to our following the work as a whole. But we must be on our guard against an excessive 'demonstration' of the interaction of motives, the return of themes and the various formal articulations, and thereby neglect the overall power of expression – what these themes and motives actually convey and represent, the very reason for their existence in fact. It would in any case be useless to try to reveal these numerous allusions, to cast too bright a light on the innumerable recesses of the labyrinth and to give away all the secrets of the work. This could only be a monstrously artificial undertaking, and one that would simply emphasize the problems of Berg's music instead of his solutions of those problems. The very act of demonstrating would, I think, contradict the intention of the composer, who said in so many words, about *Wozzeck*, that he wanted the work's construction to be forgotten, its ground plan taken so completely for granted that it did not interfere with the drama and its naturalness.

This direct ability to express himself is Berg's exceptional gift as a composer, coupled with his determination to sustain this expressive power by a radical investigation of the formal means by which it can be achieved. What is necessary [for the conductor], therefore, is an ability to achieve spontaneous expression without neglecting his intellectual resources.

As I have said, the instrumental writing itself does not present any insurmountable difficulties. Of course any score composed with such attention to detail needs careful study, but *Lulu* contains nothing for the players that lies outside what is normal and traditional. Much more demanding is the relationship between the characters and the colours of the orchestra; there are moments in fact when either a single instrument, or a group of instruments, is linked to one particular character, which it must literally 'characterize'.

Throughout the work the piano is clearly associated with the character of the Athlete, just as the violin is associated in Act III with the Marquis. Alwa is characterized chiefly by the saxophone and the asthmatic Schigolch – very properly – by a group of wind instruments. When the instrumental colours are not mixed, there is of course no difficulty in highlighting them; but when the motives cross each other – i.e. in a dramatic dialogue between two or more characters – different instrumental timbres are superimposed, combine and either reinforce or threaten each other. The conductor must at every moment be aware of the dramatic structure of the music, which depends on both thematic development and instrumental invention. In order to achieve correct characterization he must bear in mind the coinciding of character and situation, voice and instrument, motive and form, texture and density. Berg's dramatic structure makes constant use of such references, whether conscious or no, according to how precisely they are expressed; and to ignore this would be to ignore the energy of his ideas and the strength of his expression.

Then there is the vocal writing. Berg gives a precise description in the score of the six different uses of the voice, from unaccompanied dialogue to singing proper, passing though the intermediary stages of rhythmic recitation and the famous *Sprechstimme*. These different vocal 'degrees' are notated differently and should remain distinct. But such distinctions are not easy to realize in practice, given the fact that not all vocal registers are equally apt, the spoken register being obviously unable to compete with the singing register. And halfway solutions are difficult to find . . . In any case I do not think that these vocal 'degrees' are to be taken too literally; they relate essentially to the enunciation of the text, with the dividing lines *deliberately* left vague. An exaggeratedly literal following of Berg's indications is quite unreal and would probably result in something that he had not meant and did not want.

And so there are really no insoluble problems! Like every work too rich to yield all its secrets at a first reading – or indeed a second – *Lulu* demands a detailed grasp of the composer's complex intentions, a watchful eye on the details to which he himself devoted such intense thought – and, finally, a conductor who has become so at home in this musical world that he is justified in forgetting all the work of preparation in order to recapture the spirit of freshness and even *naïveté*.

A SHORT POSTSCRIPT ON FIDELITY[1]

Every work is a proposition, and no more than a proposition; and this is particularly true of any work conceived for the theatre, and therefore linked to the ephemeral at its most elusive.

The visual side of a work for the theatre is the quickest to perish.

The author proposes – the reader, the performer, the producer disposes.

Is there such a thing as fidelity? And, if so, fidelity to what? To a historical truth? Or an absolute truth?

In Berg's case fidelity may be thought to be possible, even indispensable in view of his obsession with detail, which determines the structure.

Should not the anecdotal structure of the stage action correspond to the patent structure of the music? If so, it is always redundant.

What is my position? As a musician I am better able than anyone to sympathize with Berg's obsession with detail, really to understand the intention behind his musical and stage directions and to grasp their rational relationship to each other, to judge the need for them to coincide. How, then, can I possibly accept a solution that so obviously belies the famous 'author's intentions'?

And in the first place, before accepting these famous 'composer's intentions', do we never think of questioning their validity, the ephemeral nature of everything appertaining to that most fragile of all the aspects of a work – its stage representation?

Why try at all costs to reproduce textually the anecdotal structure of the work by means of a blind fidelity? Why not accept the fact that this ephemeral aspect of the work belongs to the past, Berg's past and that of the theatre? Why not question the validity of Berg's own conception – his stage conception, I mean – which always consists essentially in maintaining an exact parallel between stage and orchestral pit?

According to Chéreau, Berg's choice of Wedekind's text and his setting of it already make him a 'producer'. Are we to regret the fact that he radically 'reduced' the original plays, changing their drift and actually adding something wholly alien to Wedekind's intention? Was Berg 'faithful' to Wedekind? Did not his 'reduction' – his literal infidelity – give the text a latent dimension obtainable only by his reconstruction of the work?

We must face the fact that literalness kills invention and anaesthetizes intelligence.

The important – no, the essential thing in the theatre, as in every other art form, is the actual grafting, the new creation sparked off by the proposition

[1] 'Lulu: court post-scriptum sur la fidelité', a riposte to remarks sharply critical of Patrice Chéreau's production made, at a public discussion at IRCAM, by Dominique Jameux at the time of the first performance of the complete version conducted by Boulez at the Paris Opéra in 1979. Published in *Alban Berg; 'Lulu'*, Vol. 2, Paris, Lattès, 1979, pp. 13–37.

inherent in the origin. This grafting of one man's idea, one man's attitude on to another's produces amazingly rich results.

We should remember, too, that a composer is not necessarily a 'professional' in every field. He may of course give a lot of thought to the theatrical problems that his work presents; and the solution that he puts forward will depend on the theatrical circumstances of the day. In the event that he has professional knowledge of the theatre, his solution may well be cleverer and more acceptable – acceptable for longer, and even now, at least partially – but it will still inevitably remain linked to the theatrical circumstances of a past age. In fact, however, composers are dilettantes in theatrical matters and the solutions of visual problems that occur to them cannot fail to reveal this.

The fashion of Berg's day – as clearly seen in the works most likely to have influenced him, such as Schoenberg's *Erwartung* and *Die glückliche Hand* – was a precise correspondence between stage detail and its musical description, an identification of the musical and the stage gestures, a sort of amalgamation of symbols effected by the two texts, literary and musical. This was probably suggested, or revived, by the cinema and by film music. Before that production had not been of such importance, and it was only in the 1920s that the producer began to play a leading role and production was deliberately given an autonomous character. Today, producers' names are sometimes remembered while the works and the authors with whom they were specially associated are forgotten. Reinhardt, Piscator and Meyerhold represent a whole period in the history of the theatre; these were the first producers to be remembered for themselves and what they represented quite apart from the actual works they produced, works that had often been inspired by their theatrical ideals.

It is not surprising that a composer aware of the contemporary theatre should give his mind to these problems and visualize if not the actual production, at least the close, clearly defined relations between his music and its stage realization. Another factor to be taken into account is the spoken cinema, which introduced a new mode of 'seeing' during exactly those years when Berg was composing *Lulu*. What a temptation it must have been to form an unbreakable link between the listener's eyes and ears by establishing a network of correspondence that both must obey in order to obtain an overall perception of the theatrical whole. Is this no more than the *Gesamtkunstwerk* in a new form, and thus a restriction? Of course it is; but was there not something dilettantish and utopian even about the *Gesamtkunstwerk*, as Adorno has pointed out?

In Berg's case the misunderstanding was even more fundamental. It is not only a question of gestures coinciding, but of the general formalization of the work. In both of his two operas it is the formal structure that, either flexibly or rigidly, dominates our understanding of the work, indeed our whole approach. The problem, then, was apparently – or rather naïvely – to reproduce on the stage the structure of the music, to 'stage' the sonata, the rondo and the variations. What a paradox, and what delight to see the stage equivalent of those strict forms! What a superb discipline, what a lesson for all those theatrical people who could never get beyond the anecdotal!

And yet . . . is it quite as simple as that? Exactly why should we consider as the most spectacular of achievements what can in fact be nothing more than an embarrassing redundance, a kind of caricature? Structure shows itself by means of music as in, let us say, the sonata. Does repetition of that structure strengthen its significance? No, it weakens that significance because it attempts to explain, to explicate it. Suppose that I hear Schoen's theme as the first theme of the sonata – whether it be in its simplest form, as in the exposition and the re-exposition, or in its more diffuse form, as in the development – and suppose that I identify it with the character of Schoen, will not my theatrical experience be on two planes, and will not their counterpointing of each other tell me much more about Schoen's character than making the two exactly parallel and thus oversimplifying the issue? My theatrical and my musical experience are both important to me, and I need the divergencies between their two specific messages in order to obtain a conception of each character in the round, with all its ambiguity, its deviousness, its passionate outbursts and its weakness. Counterpointing the two messages will give me a multidimensional view of a character, whereas making them coincide will literally 'flatten out' that view. Any transcription of the sonata, or of any other movement, must be something more subtle than mere repetition or parallelism, which spell impoverishment.

In any case there are no real arguments in favour of a literal visual transcription of the musical structure, which is based on nothing more than a piece of elementary knowledge and the snobbish supposition that if I possess that knowledge – the existence of a sonata, a rondo and variations – I know all there is to know about the work's musical substance. That would argue a fairly primitive idea of both music and the theatre, one quite inadequate because it equates knowledge with what is no more than an elementary piece of information. The mystery of Berg and the depth of his obsessions lie far beyond this trivial knowledge and this 'wretched miracle'.

What a load of codswallop it all is, in fact – this obsession with the time and place of the action, and this minute following of stage directions! What contempt it shows for the real meaning of the work! What a demonstration of Pharisaical literal-mindedness! What a failure to understand the autonomous existence of the work itself in relation to its creators!

Only the letter of the original must be adhered to, it would seem, and it is not admitted that no work is eternally bound by its initial co-ordinates! Such a restrictive attitude suggests nothing less than necromania, for it must surely be obvious that it is just the ability to escape from its own contingent character that constitutes the greatness of a work! Imagination can destroy and rebuild on what the work proposes, while the work itself is a heap of iron filings to be ceaselessly rearranged and reorientated by the magnet.

Was not this the kind of fidelity that Berg himself exhibited [in constructing his libretto from Wedekind], a fidelity that refused to be weighed down by mere literalness? Did he not give us the example of a cannibalism that he felt quite easy about practising?

What exactly are the complaints against Chéreau? That he used a larger space than is suggested by Wedekind's stage directions? That he replaced Wedekind's attic by a basement public lavatory? That he changed the date from 1900 to 1930? That he made the Medizinalrat and the Professor two different characters? Leaving out the circus? The business with the portrait? The uncomfortable position in which the letter was dictated? The 'marriage'? Leaving out the film? Bringing in the crowd unnecessarily? Anything more? It sounds like a chemist's list, or a list of chemist's complaints; and I cannot help feeling that if 'fidelity to the text' means righting such 'wrongs' as these, said to have been done to Wedekind and Berg, then fidelity is nothing but a nauseating kind of servility. As if the real structure and significance of the work were not more clearly revealed by a single one of Chéreau's modifications than by any slavish following of Berg's stage directions! I can only repeat that the specific nature of all stagecraft is its provisional character, and that in both Wedckind and Berg everything directly related to actual stage presentation can be considered as temporary and open to change, the same of course being true of Chéreau's own production.

That is why the production that I find satisfying is one that makes no claim to any lasting, absolute value and does not worry about being ephemeral – or at least only enough to ensure that the ephemeral is up to date. Surely the very essence of theatrical experience is 'bringing things up to date' – making them relevant today?

If we need an unusually large, unusually bare space to represent the way people are crushed by their surroundings, then it must be deliberately made unusually large and bare, as in Richard Peduzzi's sets. This basic decision once taken, who is going to worry their heads about the details of a 1900 artist's studio or a 1900 middle-class drawing room? Why dwarf the image and tie it inextricably to its original form? The stage is the scene in which the drama occurs, and it cannot simply reproduce a distant, faded version of reality. If the misery of prostitution shows up more glaringly and more embarrassingly in a basement public lavatory than in an attic, forget the attic and leave Sherlock Holmes in the cupboard. If the crowd in Schoen's flat accentuates the emptiness of the flat after Schoen has gone, bring in the crowd, and life with it. Set all these puppets working, and you will suddenly find yourself face to face with Geschwitz, Schigolch, the Athlete and the Student, all playing hide-and-seek at this party at which Schoen is trying to 'catch' them. But, for heaven's sake!, no more blind-man's-buff in an empty flat! 'Culture' has vanished and all that remains is a number of isolated individuals desperately cruising about in the dark.

Berg may have been concerned with establishing parallels by making characters who were formerly husbands return as clients, the parallel between the situations is more important than the literal observance that it demands. In actual fact Berg's transformation of the painter into a Negro prince is neither more nor less plausible than Chéreau's idea of transforming the normal-sized Medizinalrat into a dwarf professor. In fact the only convincing transfer of identities is from Schoen to Jack. I should not at all object to dropping the two other transformations and concentrating exclusively on the identity of the two situations, which has deep roots in the score.

And what about the film? Oh! I had forgotten that – the wonderful film that was to reveal the structure of the opera on which Berg was so keen and that was suggested by music in which the second half mirrored the first. Was not the film to have been the visible pivot of the whole work, the keystone of this model arch?

'But there is only three minutes' music!'

'Make a short film then.'

'There's a lot of incident to get into three minutes. Aren't you afraid that a film showing a series of events in quick succession will be more like Charlie Chaplin than Wedekind or Berg?'

'Berg wrote film music and so we must have a film.'

'Yes, but what if Berg were equally mistaken about the timing and the impact on the audience of these three minutes, which occur with no sort of preparation and are really nothing more than a kind of visual entr'acte, more like an advertisement than a contribution to the development of the drama?'

'We must make a film, Berg said so!'

Those who know least know most, and vice versa, as Jarry might have said!

While we are on the subject of fidelity to the score, I must say something about the five revolver shots that kill Schoen. No, they have nothing to do with the knocking on the door in *Macbeth*! But they do prompt some reflections on literalness. As a musician, I can see that they involve a distortion of the regular rhythm at a tempo fast enough to make the passage precarious even if the revolver were entrusted to a member of the orchestra. Lulu must kill Schoen 'in time', since the revolver shots punctuate the articulation of the musical phrase. But this precision is an illusion, bearing in mind the stage situation, which is at fever pitch and totally absorbs the listener's attention. What does 'fidelity' in fact mean – attempting to follow Berg's perilous notation of the passage to the best of one's ability, or firing five absolutely regular revolver shots and adjusting them approximately to the orchestral phrase? I suggest this as a subject – an inexhaustible subject – for a discussion on synchronism or regularity by the champions of fidelity ... and others.

Joking apart, though, and trying to come to a serious conclusion, I can only say that I personally have no nostalgia about the historical sources of the work, by which I mean the composer and the author. I believe, in fact, that it is essential for any creative artist whose invention is directed towards producing a finished work to burn the original. This hides his first attempts and destroys his traces. Is it even right to ask what the composer had in mind? That is a secret that nothing will reveal, though of course it is quite possible to obtain a clear view of the circumstances and, as it were, the countryside surrounding a work. If there were no secrets, there would be no work. The essential thing is to re-create another secret based on the existence of the work – not to rediscover the author, but to discover oneself. *Possessing* a work and making a provisional transcription of it in our own language is something that makes one both perfectly humble and perfectly proud, free in relation to the author and the past and responsible only to one's own deeply considered options. There is no such thing as *truth* – that is something that 'masterpieces' call upon us to discover and to accept: they command our disrespect, our vandalizing even. 'If the seed perish not...

Why are we still so intent on sterilizing seeds? Oh!, those closely guarded silos and their grim guards!

46

Olivier Messiaen

A CLASS AND ITS FANTASIES[1]

In the wastes – and wastings – of the Conservatoire a single personality stood out as a clear beacon, teaching only harmony but having a reputation to which more than a hint of sulphur attached. Choosing such a man as master meant, as you can imagine, already isolating oneself from the majority and making oneself out as a rebel, because in those days people were very ready to speak of 'the Messiaen class', in inverted commas. Both name and inverted commas were quite justified in fact, because Messiaen's class (harmony was later dropped from its schedule) was the only one that gave its members that conspiratorial feeling beneath all the excitement of technical discovery for young people devoted to 'l'artisanat furieux'.

It is hard to date exactly this unique experience and harder still to place it in a precise context ... Dates seem irrelevant to what was rather an atmosphere – an epic birth, heroic days, an intellectual idyll! It was a time of exploration and liberation, an oasis of simplicity in the surrounding desert of contrivance and fabrication. Names that were all but forbidden, and works of which we knew nothing, were held up for our admiration and were to arouse our intellectual curiosity – names that have since made quite a stir in the world. It was not only Europe that was honoured in our spirit of enquiry: Africa and Asia showed us that the prerogatives of 'tradition' were not confined to any one part of the world, and in our enthusiasm we came to regard music as a way of life rather than an art: we were marked for life.

Such, briefly, was the Messiaen experience, which also meant the friendship and solidarity of a small group gathered round a master whom public opinion either rejected or accepted with hesitation and reluctance. There were of course scenes at a number of concerts! Such were 'our' young days, stormy and impassioned but with a single focus.

---

[1] 'Une classe et ses chimères', tribute to Messiaen on his fiftieth birthday from the programme for the Domaine musical concert of 15 April 1959 (sixth concert in the 1958–9 season).

IN RETROSPECT[1]

It is interesting to observe the fidelity of Messiaen's pupils to their master, something unusual enough to be emphasized. I have not personally any great faith in the virtues of teaching above a certain level, and yet I cannot fail to recognize that Messiaen was the determining influence of my student days.

What did we expect of a teacher in those days?

It is a rather awful habit to tell stories about one's time at the Conservatoire and to draw unconvincing conclusions from them. But if I think back, I can very well remember my first composition classes with Messiaen. At that time he had a harmony class, outside strict teaching hours. He used to take a number of pupils and analyse for their benefit important contemporary works, thus revealing to them the world of composition. I have a very clear memory of these 'organized meetings' and of the generosity shown by Messiaen in these voluntary sessions whose timetable obeyed no fixed rules. We started early in the afternoon and finished ... whenever the analysis finished.

Messiaen's influence on his pupils is also explained by the fact that even in his harmony classes he never confined himself simply to setting work to be done – something demanded by the examination system and by the need to learn the actual craft of music. He devoted the necessary time to this, but ensured against the danger of sterility by strictly limiting the period of pure instruction and then going on to a live analysis of the works on which that instruction was based.

After all, what is the use of doing laboured exercises divorced from their real purpose? What Messiaen had grasped and made very clear to us was the necessity of referring to actual works rather than to theoretical treatises.

Thinking of musical life as it was twenty years ago (1943–4) we can see how intent he was on revealing to us the modern world of music. The models he gave us were Bartók's violin sonatas, quartets and *Music for strings, percussion and celesta*; Berg's *Lyric Suite*, and Schoenberg's *Pierrot lunaire*, none of which were at that time in the concert repertory. They became known to us purely through his agency.

Furthermore, he was not content with putting us in contact with other men's music and making us realize its importance for contemporary developments; he also allowed us to share in the evolution of his own musical thinking, his discoveries and his day-to-day progress. In this way it came about that conversations at the end of a class, after a rehearsal, in the street or wherever it might be influenced me perhaps more profoundly than the actual teaching.

There was something else about Messiaen, too, something much more

[1] 'Rétrospective', *L'artiste musicien de Paris*, No. 14, first and second series, 1966, pp. 8–10.

unusual – and that is that he understood the necessary break between master and pupil once the pupil has served his apprenticeship. In order to establish his own personality he has to face the image of himself that he has seen being formed by his relationship with his teacher. Standing back in this way generally involves clashes and a certain amount of violence. Looking back after all these years to my own birth as a composer, I can see the healthiness of such a reaction and of the outbursts that it involved. Once free of an influence that threatened to become overwhelming and to dull my critical sense, I found it necessary to cut to the quick, as it were, in order to re-establish myself on a footing of equality.

The anecdotes and all the ins and outs of the story have become vague in my mind, but what remains is the personality of a teacher who revealed modern music to us and made us understand the absolute necessity of research and discipline. But what stands out most vividly in my memory today is Messiaen's generosity as a teacher. I am not thinking only of the generous way in which he devoted his time to us – that is something superficial, the vocation of a teacher being among other things a kind of apostolate, as often becomes clear. No, the generosity I mean is something more profound – his generosity in comprehending a young, malleable human being, and in refusing to regard him simply as an object to be moulded, though impressing on him the necessity of both determination and curiosity.

Personally I rejoice at having had the benefit of Messiaen as a teacher at a time when his novelty was fresh, and I can say without fear of seeming banal that this experience at the outset of my career as a composer was not only something that left its mark, but something irreplaceable.

VISION AND REVOLUTION[1]

Messiaen occupies a strange position. It seems in some ways limited by his use of traditional instruments but in other ways the exact opposite. For thirty years he has exercised a strong influence on a large number of composers by his works and probably even more by his teaching. He has remained active as a teacher as well as a composer, and this proves how important he himself regards teaching, feeling that his inventiveness lies partly in that field.

Yet compared with those of another teacher of the first rank, Schoenberg, Messiaen's attitudes are clearly anything but consistent or homogeneous, however much he may insist on certain aspects of musical thinking. His theoretical position, if he can be said to have one, is not based on any decisive ideas about the evolution of the musical language and its logical consequences, but on a strict eclecticism. By eclecticism we generally mean a series of superficial options dictated more or less by circumstances, oppor-

---

[1] 'Messiaen: vision et révolution', text of a BBC Television programme directed by Barry Gavin, 13 May 1973.

tunism or necessity; but there is nothing superficial about Messiaen's eclecticism, which raises questions about the validity of certain survivals and the relevance of historical contexts.

Looking at his work as a whole, we can see that it has its roots in the music performed in Paris during the twenties and early thirties. In addition to the classical and romantic composers an important role is played by Debussy, a rather less important one by Ravel, while Stravinsky occupies a leading place – other influences may for the moment be considered as merely episodic. He was only much later to be seriously interested in Schoenberg or Berg, and even then only to borrow certain expressive mannerisms rather than to adopt their progressive ideas. The whole German–Austrian musical tradition is fundamentally alien to him in its need to express *evolution* and *continuity* in the handling of musical ideas – what the Germans themselves call *durchkomponieren*. (Just as we can speak of eclecticism in his choice of composers, so his actual style of writing – juxtaposing and superimposing rather than developing and transforming – may be called eclectic.)

What was novel and important was the way in which he was to amalgamate with this limited Western tradition heterogeneous, if not heteroclite, elements that were profoundly to transform his musical point of view. In the first place he looked back to Gregorian chant, very understandably in view of his attachment to Roman Catholicism and the active part that he played, as organist, in Catholic ceremonies. A considerable number of other, much less important French composers interested themselves in rediscovering Gregorian chant, but without Messiaen's imagination and without learning from it what he learned. He was influenced by the melismas, the phrase structure and the monodic character of the chant, and these account for the long, flexible vocalises that are a regular feature of his music, for his unfailing instinct in ornamentation and melodic order for its own sake. Also Gregorian in origin are the many quotations and montages composed of slightly modified elements of the chant.

Messiaen was to discover what was – at least up to a certain date – the basis of his general vocabulary by allying pre-polyphonic Western musical tradition to those of India – namely the use of the modes. Like the Greek modes transposed in Gregorian chant and like the Indian ragas, Messiaen's language is founded on different modes, which he has described at length, with an explanation of how he employed them. If his language is sometimes not properly speaking tonal, it always refers to a polarization of the different modes that he uses and transposes. His contact with Indian musical theory and his deep study of some of Stravinsky's works formed him rhythmically as a composer, and his attitude towards questions of rhythm has always been the most consistent of all his attitudes. He has provided a sufficiently solid theoretical foundation for options that he himself considered arbitrary and in so doing has largely revolutionized modern ideas about rhythm.

Perhaps the most remarkable sign of Messiaen's eclecticism is to be found in his contact with the natural world and his notation of it in his music. Of course there are descriptions of landscapes that remain on the purely symbolical plane, but there are also actual sounds – such as those made by a stream – and most important of all innumerable examples of birdsong. These made episodic appearances quite early in his work, becoming increasingly important and eventually forming the centre of a series of works based entirely on the transcription of birdsong.

It will be clear from this list that the sources of Messiaen's music are very various, and anyone who listens to his music will realize that he has never attempted to reduce them to any basic unity, preferring to leave the different elements in open conflict or, as he calls it, to pass from one style to another. Meanwhile he moulds all the elements in his music to suit his own convenience, and this often involves considerable distortion and placing them in quite different perspectives. It is quite clear that when he uses the rhythms of Greek poetry, it is purely for their *metric quantities* and not in order to obtain a codified language parallel to that of the Greek poets. The same is true of his use of birdsong, which he transcribes for our existing instruments, which means using the tempered semitone – an interval quite unknown in birdsong but a safeguard against its ambiguous character, half sound and half noise. In this case we might perhaps speak of Messiaen as an *eclectic reformer*.

An eclecticism of this sort, like his lack of 'taste' in the conventional French sense, is not unique in the history of French art. Although the common hallmark of French art remains 'good taste' – moderation and clarity – this general rule is confirmed by a series of important exceptions. In the case of music we think at once of Berlioz, but there are also famous instances among writers and painters – Claudel and Léger among many others. Messiaen in fact belongs to the line of French artists whose very last concern was with *restriction*.

To move from the general to the particular, let us first examine the material of Messiaen's original language. As I say, he developed a modal system based on intervals whose immediate impression on the listener is vaguely exotic or fantastic. These modes, which are in some ways related to those of Indian music, have certain well-defined characteristics that are reflected not only in the melodic lines to which they give rise, but also in the harmony and more generally speaking in the whole harmonic language. In this sense Messiaen is visibly concerned with coherence and unity of expression. The modes give rise to sequences of what may be called chord clusters, and Messiaen's use of these is almost more characteristic than his melodic writing. Is this explained by his training as an organist and the use of mutation stops? However that may be, the function of these chords is not to *accompany* a melodic line but to become *identified* with it and to give it substance and colour. This feature appears very early in Messiaen's music and the use of harmonic 'mutations' of this kind was to increase and to become in his latest works such a favourite procedure that it absorbed all others in this particular field. Linked with it was his very strong sense of the colours corresponding to these families of chords. He writes *in colours*, not in Skryabin's sense – attempting to achieve a correspondence between light and sound – but *kinaesthetically*, sound evoking a colour response in the individual. Certain chords in his scores are accompanied by a description of the combination of colours that he attaches to them, thus providing the listener with a 'key' to these correspondences. (I must admit that I have never personally felt any need for this literal transposition.)

As in the Indian tradition, the modes form part of the organization of a piece, governing the actual sounds that we hear. Another feature of these sounds – their duration or rhythmic relations – is governed by laws that Messiaen was gradually to formulate with increasing precision and eventually to build into a logically coherent system. There are a number of general characteristics worth observing. In the first place Messiaen's rhythm becomes increasingly freer of traditional metrical conventions, in that he no longer employs a modula, or basic formula, for governing the rhythmic life of a movement. Not only does he frequently use rhythms that may be considered irregular, but if he uses more-or-less regular bar lines it is often only to make things easier for the performer. In works for solo piano or organ he dispenses entirely with numerical indications and often uses bar lines simply to mark rhythmic phrasing when possible. The idea of regular metre gradually disappears from his music and is replaced by two fundamental principles. The first of these is the inequality of basic note values starting from the smallest pulse (a point on which he was greatly influenced by Stravinsky); and the second is the rhythmic sequence based on a type series in which the initial cell determines the rhythmic construction and is no longer obliged either to take its place in, or to counter, a regular rhythm. Detached from any obligatory and limited periodicity, the idea of duration becomes increasingly supple and subtle. Periodicity becomes variable and can be long term as well as short term. (Here Indian rhythmic pattern played an important part.)

It should be observed that this overall conception of duration becomes pre-existent to the writing of the actual *notes*. Of course the regular metres used by classical composers also 'pre-existed' as patterns, and even in some cases as genres (as in various dances, such as the 3/4 minuet). In this case the rhythmic sequence is a primary datum ready to receive its embodiment in sound, whereas in the past invention, within the limits of a strict framework and a number of laws accepted as *natural*, was *spontaneous*. To find a parallel instance in the musical tradition of Western Europe we should have to go back to the ambitions of *ars nova*, the most recent innovation having been the intellectual use of Greek metres by some of the French polyphonic composers of the Renaissance.

Other obsessions of Messiaen's in the matter of duration include his use of very long note values contrasted with very short; the importance he attaches to the symmetrical or asymmetrical character of rhythmic figures, and a number of others arising not so much from the system as from personal taste.

In a work rightly considered to be a document of primary importance Messiaen was the first to attempt a synthesis between his modal and his rhythmic ideas, extending these in a manner that was entirely novel in the field of rhythm and performance. Instead of defining a mode solely by its pitch – as is the case with all scales, whether traditional or otherwise, which exist as it were *in abstracto*, 'outside time' and with no temporal function – he defines each component equally by a duration, a dynamic, and a characteristic manner of performance. Each note in its context is thus an unchanged entity; and it is the confrontation of these multiple entities that creates both the sound world *and* the composition. The stability of the actual element is now to be integrated in the multiplicity of its encounters. This stroke of genius was quite noticeably to change the course of his music, directing it towards a greater integration of all the sound elements in a work, at least for a time. But after a number of works more specifically centred round this main idea Messiaen's fundamental eclecticism was to lead him to think that this technique was no more than a means – and sometimes a very secondary means – of composing. In his latest works (1973) he seems to be looking for a close correspondence between linguistic and musical laws, a further amplification of the means at his disposal.

The organ occupies a primary position in his music, and in this he is unique, the organ having been (with very few exceptions) relegated to the church and, as it were, to history. Messiaen's organ works make him a church composer, but he is not interested in giving them a liturgical character. There are virtually no liturgical works of his but many inspired by a religion that has no need of rites and ceremonies. He makes a virtuoso use of all the instrument's resources and every kind of registration, based on his practical experience. The character of his music is generally speaking not polyphonic, and his harmonic tastes therefore make him favour a powerful, opulent instrument capable of providing a large number of combinations, from the most refined to the most massive. Thanks to him the organ now has a repertory that professional organists have for many decades failed to provide despite the many 'renaissances' of organ music.

The piano is equally important in the list of his solo works; and here too he writes as an expert, using a style in which we can trace important influences, such as that of Debussy, and marginal influences like that of Albeniz, not to mention Liszt, whose mark appears on many works.

His only chamber work, properly speaking, is the *Quatuor pour la fin du temps*, which he composed in a prisoner-of-war camp where he was inevitably obliged to write for whatever instruments were at his disposal.

It is therefore not surprising that, apart from the piano and the organ, his important works are all orchestral. I emphasize this because even his works for smaller forces are orchestrally conceived. His conception of the orchestra is often grandiose, different groups of instruments being entrusted blockwise with the different motives or the various components of a work. As against this *stratified* style, he also made use of an extremely individual style of which *Chronochromie* is the most interesting example – an 'Épode' for nineteen solo strings. By accumulating these multiple individualities and superimposing their different lines he achieves an overall impression in which all individuality is neutralized. Another characteristic feature of Messiaen's orchestral writing is his stubborn ignoring of certain instruments, such as the harp, which he rejects for its lack of volume. What attracts him to the organ, the piano and the orchestra is their potential massiveness, their rich, full texture.

Examples of his vocal writing are to be found in the cycles for voice and piano (only one of these, *Poèmes pour Mi*, has been orchestrated) and his works for chorus and orchestra, the most recent of which is his monumental *Transfiguration*.

Messiaen's position, as we can see, is not easy to grasp, still less to sum up. Though very attached to a number of traditional attitudes, he is very adventurous in fields hitherto virtually unexplored; and it seems that he has been influenced by the contradiction not only of his own personality but of a whole generation of French composers who, at a crucial point in their careers, were simply starved of information about the revolutionary events that were taking place elsewhere ... Does this mean that his music would have been different if he had come in contact with the Second Viennese School? Probably not. On the other hand if our attention had been entirely directed elsewhere, we might well have failed to benefit from those discoveries that we owe without the shadow of a doubt to the personality of Messiaen, and to Messiaen only.

THE UTOPIAN YEARS[1]

Messiaen's evolution has a quite special interest for me, far exceeding that of an old pupil. It was thanks to him – sometimes even more than to his music – that I obtained an idea of contemporary music and its evolution, the personalities who played a part in that evolution and in the elaboration of a new language in which certain factors – rhythmical factors, for instance – had assumed a far greater importance than they had previously had. Although

---

[1] 'Messiaen: le temps de l'utopie', text of a broadcast by the Südwestfunk (Baden-Baden), October 1978. French text first published in *Points de repère*.

Messiaen's personal interests had given rise to some interests of my own – particularly in matters of time and rhythm in general – they still left unresolved a number of linguistic problems for which I thought the music of the Viennese School provided more satisfactory solutions.

Messiaen's music sprang from a systematic viewpoint determined by a number of personal choices in which certain ideas played a dominant role. As far as pitch was concerned, he attached great importance to modal organization and harmonic relationships, sometimes employing the most traditional tonal relationships in order to polarize one particular aspect of the music. A number of his important innovations in the matter of time and duration appeared to me, in this single instance, to complete and to provide a counterweight to the discoveries of the Viennese School. Few earlier composers had attached so much importance to time, and the wholly original means that he employed to organize time liberated rhythm from traditional metre. Rhythm was so important to him that he sometimes organized this before any other aspects of a work, regarding this as permissible on the grounds that these other aspects were in a way no more than a revelation of the rhythmic datum.

Messiaen furthermore enriched the rhythmic repertory by adapting to his own musical language elements gathered from exotic sources, Indian features or forms of Greek prosody. He was always remarkable for his systematic concern with his actual tools and for his wish to co-ordinate the elements of his language, to map out a clearly defined universe from which he could draw the actual material of his works as he needed it. In fact he very soon felt a need to summarize his choices and put them in clear theoretical terms, which he did in his *Technique de mon langage musical.* In this book he describes his own method of composing and quotes the sources of his language, explains and gives reasons for his working methods, providing an overall account of the different aspects of his work and attempting to relate them to each other. This he does so thoroughly that at the time when he wrote the book it seemed that his work had thoroughly crystallized and was not likely to produce any real surprises in the immediate future. We had the impression that he would continue still further his investigation of certain features and factors of works that he had already written, simply following the methods outlined in *Technique de mon langage musical.*

Then in 1949–50 Messiaen went through a period of intense self-questioning, possibly as a result of the explorations carried out by some of his pupils (of whom I was one) who had made a more-or-less radical break with his personal predilections. I should call this his 'experimental' period, in the best sense of the term; and it is significant that the two works dating from 1949, *Mode de valeurs et d'intensités* and *Neumes rythmiques*, were written at Darmstadt and Tanglewood – symbolical names associated with the teaching of composition – at the very time when his work as a teacher was becoming known to the larger public outside its normal setting, the Paris

Conservatoire. The works that reveal his new interests were composed between 1949 and 1951 and written exclusively for Messiaen's favourite instruments, piano and organ, which were his own instrument and therefore the best available for his researches. The piano works soon became known as *Quatre Etudes de Rythme* because they were published at the same time, though they in fact consist of two quite distinct groups – *Mode de valeurs et d'intensités* and *Neumes rythmiques* dating from 1949, and *Iles de feu 1 and 2*, dating from 1950. The organ pieces are *Messe de la Pentecôte* (1950) and *Livre d'orgue* (1951). This series of works, written fairly close together, is unified by an identity of interest and represents a number of radical transformations in Messiaen's language. It would be safe to say that he had never made such an attempt to 'radicalize' his language – to go as far as possible, that is to say, in discovering and exploiting new resources. This spectacular effort was followed by a synthesis of the new elements with more traditional methods, which he did not wish to abandon, in order to achieve greater fullness of expression.

What is the chief characteristic of these works of Messiaen's adventurous years? Their total freshness and their radical, exploratory appearance? One takes for granted, of course, the broadening of his views on the technique of his musical language, but is that all? Does not this broadening mark a serious breach with some of his previous procedures? And what is more, would not the most hasty and superficial glance give us some indication of the way his musical thinking was evolving? If we compare these with Messiaen's previous works, the most striking point is his use of disjunct intervals and his relinquishing of his highly melodic, highly conjunct form of modal writing. We are aware of the influence of the Viennese School and of the consequences that a younger generation had already drawn from that music. So far as Messiaen is concerned, the consequences vary in nature. He had always attached great importance to harmony – and was to do so again in the future – and to a vertical conception of music, yet here we see him virtually abandoning chordal writing. Some of these pieces are exclusively, even aggressively, 'non-harmonic', with a preponderance of horizontal lines, which – as in serial works – are not controlled by any harmonic considerations and do not obey harmonic laws. In this matter at least Messiaen seems to be questioning everything that had been most personal, and probably most dear to him, in his previous music. If this is the most obvious and tangible feature of this 'experimental' phase, there are quite a number of others. Even so, before listing and examining these, there is a more general fact that will explain these transformations, which are so surprising in view of Messiaen's earlier musical thinking. Through his disciples, and through a return to sources that had hitherto played only a secondary part in his musical formation, he had been brought face to face with a formal systematization of the language, and he was therefore confronted by the problem of *spontaneous* and *calculated music* and the problem of what sort of relationship was possible – even desirable – between the two. This I believe to be the dilemma that lay at the root of his activity and his thinking during this crucial phase.

As I have said, Messiaen had always felt the need for a certain systematization of the different aspects of his musical language – the codification of his use of the modes and of his ideas about rhythm – but this had been essentially concerned with certain fundamental notions, invention retaining its free and spontaneous character in relation to the whole arsenal of means at the composer's disposal. At this point in his development he seemed to be confronting the problem of these means much more explicitly. He did not dissociate the exploration of new means from their use. The idea of the series was engaging his maximum attention during these years, and it was probably the influence of this fact that caused him to reflect on the possible strict, and strictly calculated, relationships on which his music might depend; there are many instances in these works of a clear conflict between spontaneity and organization, the one unwilling to abdicate and the other determined to become all-powerful. This conflict, or antinomy, is reflected even in the titles of the different pieces written between 1949 and 1951. In some cases these are poetic, biblical or otherwise – *Les Yeux dans les roues*, *Les Mains de l'abîme*, *Iles de feu*. In other cases they are almost aggressively technical, denoting an exclusive concern with grammatical aspects of the language, as in the case of *Reprises par interversion*, *Soixante-quatre Durées*, *Neumes rythmiques*. I do not think that this question of titles is a frivolous one, since each seems like an open declaration of the dilemma in which the composer found himself – whether he was to preserve his poetic vision or to surrender to the intoxication of linguistic problems. In other words, would his poetic instinct prove able to make free use of the new technical means that thorough (and in some cases one-sided) research had put at his disposal? Or would these technical means, sought in many instances for their own sake, generate a new musical poetics by the very fact of their existence and importance?

In some of these pieces it looks as though his use of a circumscribed form, having both a beginning and an end, had been a secondary consideration with the composer, as though the essential reason for writing the piece were the actual manipulation of the material. No more than an 'arithmetical' diagram is needed to describe the piece and to justify it in the typographical sense. Messiaen takes, for instance, an initial idea with a certain number of interversions and chosen permutational principles, and once these interversions have run their course the piece can be considered as finished. Almost all the pieces in the *Livre d'orgue* 'run out' in this way, and it is precisely for this reason that they end with such surprising abruptness. In some cases the composer emphasizes this. The end of *Les Yeux dans les roues*, for instance is marked *couper brusquement*, and that of the second trio *sans ralentir*. But whether he uses these markings or not, it is clear that these 'pieces' do not have an end, in the rhetorical sense; they simply *stop*. Their strict organization means that they are like fragments of some larger whole that is tacitly understood. The actual beginning and end of a piece do not constitute its real limits, with a 'before' and an 'after'. Forming parts of a larger whole that we do not hear but which has an absolute existence, they are no more than symbolic moments or favoured episodes in the existence of a great whole more securely defined by numbers than by the composer's wishes. What we hear are fragments of an overall movement of which the composer gives us a glimpse virtually prolonging the mechanisms that he has momentarily set in motion for our benefit. The question for Messiaen was to be whether to surrender entirely to this cosmogony of numbers and structures, or to make it *one* element of his language, an important element no doubt but one whose claims must be combined with those of other sources of invention. There were two possible solutions. He could adorn these numerical structures with ornamental figures that were essentially alien to their nature and reveal the structures only to make the listener forget them (in fact what the composer himself calls 'colouring time', *chronochromie*). Or he could alternate calculated numerical structures with spontaneous elements, emphasizing still further their purely musical nature by the fact that they had no relation except that of alternating with what might be called the 'non-musical' or 'not exclusively musical' elements.

There are beyond any doubt two different desires in Messiaen himself. He wants discipline, a discipline that transcends his own personality and refers only to itself, implying its own justification by means of a numerical order that has to be obeyed. He wants as it were to decipher in his own way the secrets of the universe, just as a scientist can transcribe natural laws in numerical terms. In this way a composition strictly observing numerical laws would reflect a transcendent order in which personal desires have no place and are annulled by explicit laws that override any individual purpose. But at the same time he wishes to express himself with greater immediacy, feeling vaguely that these laws may well be a means of deciphering certain secrets but are not, in any case, *the* absolute way, and foreseeing that beyond the formal law there is a more important order both more difficult to discover and also less reassuring, because it cannot be codified numerically. In this Messiaen shares both the joy of discovery and that fear of formal chaos especially characteristic of the composers of the Viennese School and the origin of those radical questions that Messiaen began to ask himself at the beginning of the fifties. His case is by no means unique, but it is interesting because nothing in his earlier work led one to foresee his being 'engaged' in this way or asking these fundamental questions. A close inspection of the musical or para-musical means by which this dilemma is communicated enables us to reconstitute the struggle between the two systems which they so clearly exemplify.

It is also a curious fact that, especially in the works that we have been discussing, Messiaen's invention takes two different directions: his formalism is more evident in all matters concerning the organization of time and duration, while his pitch vocabulary shows a much more explicit freedom. The ground plan of the 'structural' pieces depends primarily on a diagram of permutations and interversions more closely linked to duration than to pitch, these being governed by a fairly free serialism rather loosely formalized. Pitches, on the other hand, follow a strict hierarchical selection and their development is organized according to restrictive laws; they predominate over the other constituents of the work and also determine the formal architecture to which the other elements are subject. In fact we can see Messiaen embarking on a new voyage of linguistic discovery, but not totally committed to it. He is not looking for a unification of all the elements of a composition in the way that some of his disciples had already done, by modelling themselves on Webern's last works, and particularly the *Variations*, Op. 30.

In his choice of the series and its different transpositions, his treatment of the basic rhythmic cells, his thematic work and formal positioning, Webern had set out with determination to deduce all the possible consequences of a certain number of elements rigorously selected and generated by a mind obsessed with the idea of uniqueness and the organic development of these elements. To speak of going one better than Webern is almost a euphemism for what resulted; all that Webern had inherited from the classical tradition, his use of thematic work and his formal schemes, were rejected in the interests of a construction springing entirely from the extension of recent techniques to all the sonorous elements of the work. In this way, it seemed, maximum unification would be achieved and there would no longer be any divergence between micro- and macrostructure, between the final form and its initial elements. It became clear that a synthesis of this kind was not so simple to achieve; but nevertheless, beyond this 'zero point' of composition, there remained a desire to give the language of music a new coherence.

These were not Messiaen's intentions, as his later development has clearly shown. Not only had he no interest in unification – the total reduction of the multiple elements of the language to certain common denominators – but he was clearly attached to a diversity of means, to their heterogeneous character and even (if the word had no pejorative flavour) their heteroclite accumulation. I have already referred to the obvious conflict between spontaneity and calculation in these works. Perhaps, indeed, I should not speak of 'conflict' so much as alternation, cohabitation! In this sense no music could be less 'purist' than Messiaen's, which absorbs and makes use of everything. Its materials are drawn from every azimuth and their very diversity, their contrasts, their contradictions and even their irreducibility justify their use in a single complex. The composer does not claim to reduce their disparate nature or to conceal it: he exploits and thereby produces the tensions that serve his purpose, always avoiding the technique of collage, the mere assembling of unorganized material.

His musical language exercises a sufficiently unifying influence to hold together constituents that would naturally fall apart, as in the case where he subjects 'Hindu' rhythmic cells to a system of permutations or augmentations and diminutions that is in origin totally alien to their nature. The same is true when he starts with the melodic definition of neumes and adapts their characteristics to suit his rhythmic vocabulary, thus giving them an entirely different dimension and even significance. Or take his transcriptions of birdsong, which may preserve a certain realistic character but are none the less governed by a hierarchy of intervals much more closely related to his own harmonic language than to any literal reproduction of the intervals actually heard by any birdwatcher. I could give many other instances of this double tendency – accepting materials or techniques from every quarter and then subjecting them to a radical stylistic treatment that enables them without too much difficulty to be integrated in a total overall conception.

Despite appearances these few years in Messiaen's development therefore show not so much any radical change as a further exploration of certain techniques, a concern with examining more thoroughly a number of clearly limited dimensions of the musical language. The other elements of his own personal language were, as it were, laid on one side: if they appear less frequently, more sporadically and in less essential form, they are none the less present. Although the composer concentrates his attention for the moment on a number of clearly defined fundamental problems and relegates other elements to the background, he is far from forgetting these and soon gives them pride of place in many works. The more 'calculated' elements in his musical thinking increased the repertory of means at his disposal and he was unwilling to forgo any of them, although he felt little or no inclination to make any formal synthesis, remaining content to secure the unity of a piece by means of a convergence of different styles. It is this feature of Messiaen's musical thinking – or rather the sum-total of his personal predilections – that reveals the unchanging nature of his attitude – the consistent search for an amalgam of styles and the choice of conditions best calculated to achieve this.

Is this period of his development, then, marked on the whole by more interesting characteristics than any other, and why have I chosen to consider it in isolation? Is it a matter of personal preference? Yes, because Messiaen's chief interests during this period are closest to my own, in spite of obvious differences that still exist. Yet quite as important as this personal preference, if not more so, is the fact that what we have observed as symptomatic in Messiaen's case was typical of a general evolution involving at that time a new awareness of the radical transformation of the musical language, its structures and meanings. It was a time of utopian exploration of which the technical aspects were no more than symptoms and need not be considered too literally or too exclusively – a time when composers were concerned with discovering the secrets of number, with a rigorous expression of the universe and, transcending that rigour, with achieving an essential freedom of self-expression. Surely no one will deny that the most extreme and agonized moments of that utopian quest produced a number of esoteric works that may be ungrateful or difficult to perform but possess a unique fascination and, at their best, give a momentary illusion of being able to go beyond *les barricades mystérieuses* of knowledge.

THE POWER OF EXAMPLE[1]

Olivier Messiaen was to have been with us for his seventieth birthday today. He is still in hospital after an operation, but I know that he is listening to the broadcast of this concert, and so I want in these few words to convey to him our thoughts and affections, all the warmer for his absence.

Of course the most obvious way of paying homage to a composer is to perform his music, to bring his music to life among us, with us, in us. Even so it is permissible on an exceptional occasion like today's to want to add something more definite, a more personal note.

My own link with Messiaen, with all its memories, goes back to that spring of 1944 when I presented myself at his house to become his pupil. At the Conservatoire he was just another member of the staff – the most recent member in fact – a professor of harmony with the reputation of being something of a revolutionary and of standing apart from the reigning orthodoxy of the day. That reputation was based on his works, which were not often performed though an almost chance hearing of one of his earliest – *Thème et variations* for violin and piano – was enough to inspire me with an immediate wish to study with him. I felt the force of his attraction immediately, as I say, at a single hearing.

I do not much care for veterans' reminiscences, but I should like to recall an experience that must have been shared by many others, both before and after me – that sudden feeling of attraction to a master of whom one knows, with an inexplicable sense of certainty, that it is he, and only he, that is going to reveal you to yourself. This is a kind of magic exercised partly by his music, but also by the power of his personality, by his immediate appeal and by the overwhelming force of his example. This chosen master acts as a stimulus by his very presence, his behaviour, his very existence and the glimpses that he gives of what he demands of himself. He sees and listens, understands the clashes in the pupil's personality as he tries to discover himself in a fog of contradictions and resentments. The master is prepared to accept ingratitude and injustice, rebuffs and rebelliousness, if these reactions mean the momentary loss of the pupil in order to establish him firmly as

---

[1] 'La toute-puissance de l'exemple', speech given at the Paris Opéra on 10 December 1978 on the occasion of Messiaen's seventieth birthday. First published in *Points de repère*.

an original, independent personality. Attention and detachment are needed for this, and a sense of the adventure of preparing all the details of a long voyage without knowing its destination, a desire to set out for goals that are never clearly defined. Giving an example is as necessary as learning to forget it: 'Throw away the book I have taught you to read and add a new, wholly unexpected page!'

The miracle lies in the teacher combining this generous giving with the ability to preserve intact his fundamental egoism as a creative artist, which is the sole guarantee of his generosity. For how can one be generous without having anything to give? This is a problem that Messiaen has shown an enviable determination in solving: he has enriched himself by enriching us. The evidence for this is to be found in the present series of retrospective concerts, which enables us to sum up his work in all its profusion and variety, covering a very wide range that includes not only the composer's own instruments, piano and organ, but the most varied groupings, with a marked preference for the unfamiliar.

Today is not the occasion for drawing up a detailed balance sheet, but we can still pick out a number of the more specific characteristics that have made Messiaen the outstanding figure that he is at the present time. In the first place I should like to say that he has the great merit of having freed French music from that narrow and nervous 'good taste' inherited from illustrious forebears whose greatness has been reduced to the dimensions of their panting followers. Then I should like to point to his boldness and calm courage in treating music as a worldwide, universal phenomenon and his refusal of any obligation to retain any characteristics simply because they were considered the property of some national group. He has opened windows not only on Europe, but on the whole world, on civilizations as remote in space as in time. He has thought of the distinguishing marks of any civilization not as barriers but as possible links. Living in a world so much inclined to exclusive nationalism that neighbours, by their very existence, were thought of primarily as enemies and aggressors, Messiaen has been willing to accept freely everything that could enrich him, broaden his vision or increase his potential strength. Instead of harping on the genealogy of French music he pointed out that a 'tradition' is nothing if it does no more than preserve its own prerogatives – in fact he was 'ecumenical' before that word became popular in other contexts . . .

In fact there must be a predator in every creative artist; he gives, no doubt, but he also takes. Before he can give *his* vision of the world he must grasp that world in its entirety; if his adventure is at first an interior one, there is still no reason why it should not come from without. Messiaen's openness to all the musics of the world has greatly enriched his own powers of expression, both in the matter of sonorities and actual instruments and in the theoretical field of rhythmic concepts and musical time. In this field specifically his originality and his contribution have been enormous and his influence unparalleled, the more so for his being the first to venture into these hitherto unexplored regions.

Finally, we should not forget the characteristic that makes him absolutely unique – his deep love of nature expressed in forms virtually unknown to the more artificial world of music. That love is so demanding that it can transpose in detail not so much what birds, rocks, colours, landscapes and mountains inspire in him, but what they actually dictate to him.

Were it not for the fear of being taken for a bad punster I would add that 'composer' is exactly the right word for Messiaen, in that it suggests the word 'composite'. His personality resembles some great baroque building: he fascinates us by the diversity of his options and the elaborate simplicity of his choices. Beneath the very real complexities of his intellectual world he has remained simple and capable of wonder – and that alone is enough to win our hearts.

Olivier Messiaen, I know that you are listening to me and I want to repeat to you the gratitude and the affection that we all feel for the example you have never failed to set both as a composer and as a teacher. We thank you for *your* adventure, which has also become ours, and we wish you a speedy recovery so that you may continue to share that adventure for many years to come. Happy birthday!

47

Oriental Music: A Lost Paradise?[1]

I am against this talk of parallels, this system of comparison. I find that people form a too sentimental and emotional idea of Oriental music. They now dive into it like tourists setting off to visit a landscape that is about to vanish. For they know very well that these musical civilizations are on the verge of extinction and so set out to sight-see while they still can. Such people imagine that they are deriving from these forms of music a measure of wisdom and contemplation, supposedly in relation to our Western world of movement. But movement is life. There is a great foolishness in the Westerner who goes to India, and I detest this idea of a 'lost paradise'. It is one of the most odious forms of affectation.

The music of Asia and India is to be admired because it has reached a stage of perfection, and it is this perfection that interests me. But otherwise the music is dead. In the course of time other languages arrive at the same maturity, but what is important is that which endures.

The musical art of the Orient that has attained perfection is now frozen, and if there is no modern Oriental music it is because those peoples have lost their vigour. I know the Andean regions and the Indians of Peru, and there the same problem exists: a physical inertia, a loss of energy closely related to political, economic and social conditions that have brought to a standstill the artistic development of civilizations such as those of India and the Andes.

I came to know Peruvian music during the course of a long journey with Jean-Louis Barrault, and also the music of Black Africa. I have carefully studied and also transcribed Indian music, but if knowledge and study of these civilizations have influenced me they have done so only on the spiritual level. I have found an ethics of existence rather than an aesthetics of enjoyment. The influence is on my spirit and not on my work. The main points are as follows: the time structure, the conception of time being different; the idea of anonymity; the idea of a work of art not being admired as a masterpiece but as an element of spiritual life.

---

[1] 'Musique traditionelle – un paradis perdu?', from an interview with Martine Cadieu, trilingual French/English/German text in *The World of Music*, Vol. IX, 1967.

The technical aspects, which are always analysed and regarded as being of primary importance when a contemporary European score is studied, are here a completely secondary matter. We are well aware that Asia has attributed the utmost significance to the organization of intervals, and with a unique sensitivity. I would be happy to acquire this acuteness of listening, this fineness of the horizontal interval disengaged from the thickness of polyphony, but this would involve working out a different kind of polyphony.

The precision in the organization of rhythmic structures also interests me. It is very great in the music of India and Bali. Certain intermediary dimensions in improvisation, especially in the wonderful Gagaku, I also find of great interest. I like this not wholly defined dimension, which gradually becomes defined. There is here no masterpiece achieved for all time; one learns to live within the music and to make one's choice there. The influence of India and Japan is thus an influence of thought.

But there is no sense in trying to build specimens of Oriental music into contemporary music; no influence is good except when it is transcended. There are no exact illustrations in contemporary music of which one can say that they are derived from this or that raga. This would be folklore. To transfer such elements – as is done by some – is completely mistaken; it is the quest for the lost paradise of which I have already spoken. There is something of 'Paul et Virginie' in people who ransack contemporary music for such illustrations and make of it a journey to the East. This is in fact nothing new. A diffuse influence has made itself felt since the eighteenth century, the era of chinoiserie.

The composer who received this influence at the deepest level and transcended it in the most marvellous way was Debussy.

I am thinking not of *Pagodes* but of 'La lune descend sur le temple qui fut'. Here the concepts of time and sonority are clearly determined. But Schaeffner has said everything on this subject, and how Debussy was impressed by the Annamese theatre.

The most profound contact between Orient and Occident is seen in the work of Claudel. He has understood the Asian world better than anyone else. It is not a matter of a purely musical influence but rather an influence in the realm of thought. Consider Van Gogh, and also Debussy enthusing about Hokusai. There have always been deep relations between civilizations. What is important is universality. A Japanese discovering the perfection of Gregorian chant undergoes a similar experience.

Take John Cage, who is a particularly interesting case. Before he became infatuated with Zen and employed a technique of rhythmic sequences borrowed from the raga, he wrote interesting works.

But when I say that one cannot transfer the perfection of a dead civilization to our own civilization, I mean that one cannot preserve and exhibit at the same time. The sense of the music is falsified before it is exhibited in strange surroundings. This is why, when outside their own country, so many Indian musicians and dancers lose themselves and their art becomes distorted.

A further important point: just beating gongs and using a gamelan orchestra signifies nothing. This is a superficial procedure. But there is a lesson to be learnt from Oriental tradition. Our Western instruments have tended to become standardized and to have specialized uses. They all produce a pure sound and give the same C in all registers. There is no individualization of sound. In the Orient, however, an instrument has no absolute tuning. A relativity exists between the instruments, a relativity not only of timbre but also of tuning, dependent on the creation of the moment. To me it seems important to use instruments not as a master key to open all locks but in relation to their individual qualities.

I feel that an interesting contribution could be made here through a study of Oriental music. For me, however, the Noh remains the peak of Oriental art. I would like to study it more closely, also the relations between Noh and *Sprechgesang*, and hope one day to be able to spend a long period in Japan in order to do this.

A new vocal technique should now be created based on the Noh style. There are serious problems here, since no real starting point for a new vocal technique, or for a new method of vocal training has been found. Schoenberg wanted to combine speech and singing (a combination of which has always existed in musical theatre), but did not realize that the tessituras of the two mediums were different. The tessitura of speech has become, so to speak, anarchical, while the tessitura of singing is now more or less rigidly determined. The only system I know that has solved this problem is the Noh. If I have the time – and that is always the difficulty – I would like to investigate all the Noh schools, to make a thorough study in Japan of the techniques, and to take lessons long enough to discover the secret of the Japanese, the ease with which they pass from speech to singing.

Regarding the different time conception and the cyclic works that apparently have neither beginning nor end – in India and Japan a performance lasts a very long time, people come and go, listen or not as they please – I would say that on a creative level I live in a kind of plasma that enables me to change my location by moving from front to rear. I remain in the same material and project my thoughts in several directions at once. I now have a flexible material that permits these shifts in time and these diversions. Because of this I have made several versions of *Pli selon pli* and am thinking of extending *Eclat.*

If we enthuse over Indian music we must beware of an ethics that leads us to attribute a magic power to this universe of sounds. I would regard it a pity if the Oriental influence became a refuge for young musicians in a world allegedly threatened but which is our living and real world. The devil take all religious taboos!

You say that the ragas appear to you to present an excess of formalism on account of their correspondences with certain times of day (dawn, evening, etc.) and with classified spiritual states. Do not forget that this formalism also exists in our own music. We do not play a cha-cha-cha in a church. Also, the music of the Middle Ages had its equivalents to the ragas. But time effaces and obliterates. In the Middle Ages polyphony was banned from the church as a vehicle of unspeakable and indecent sentiments. We no longer have moral categories, but instead aesthetic categories. Even our assessment of Bach's cantatas is distorted. It is really difficult to distinguish a secular cantata from a church cantata; only the fundamental language remains. A language very quickly closes in on itself, and this phenomenon will become universal.

All distant civilizations exhibit one feature in common: a historical dimension to which we no longer have the key. In the same way that a Japanese could well confuse Meyerbeer with Berlioz, so can we confuse, and very easily, two different Oriental creations. We should look with mistrust on all approximations, superficial acquaintance and infatuation.

Apart from a few specialists who know more, there is a danger that others who are less well informed will spread mistaken ideas, for culture is viewed through a microscope: each person looks only at that which interests him, and therefore there is so little co-ordination of the results.

The musical systems of East and West cannot have any bearing on one another, and this will be quickly realized by experienced composers of character.

The myths and legends whose origins are lost in the mists of time are doomed to extinction. This is but the course of history, and we see it more clearly every day. What is of lasting value is that the enrichment yielded by any study of the various musical languages is positive in so far as it has the power to exert a fructifying influence and is transcended.

PART THREE
Looking Back

48

First and Second Hearings[1]

It used to seem that contemporary music was before all else esoteric – at least that was the chief complaint about some contemporary music, which would apparently never be able to stir great enthusiasm in any audience owing to its extreme intellectualism. Excessively complex and overambitious, these works were condemned to be admired by snobs or to pander to the vicious tastes of unrepentant abstractionists: they would never delight the heart of any decent citizen with a taste for clarity and feeling.

Well, during the last two years we have had the experience of audiences making the enthusiastic discovery of these monstrosities which they had heard described in such unflattering terms; we have watched them reacting with deep feeling to works considered hitherto totally frigid. The years of isolation are over. The public has had enough of sham masterpieces and muddled thinking, enough so-called 'clarity' (there was certainly no mystery about it), enough of perpetually throbbing hearts, and is charmed to make the discovery of a new kind of poetry, unfamiliar sonorities and – in a word – composers who have been honest in their search for truth.

It is reassuring that this new understanding – which showed itself first in the case of the Second Viennese School – is not an isolated phenomenon due to any individual effort. All over the world there have sprung up similar organizations, which have initiated currents of sympathy – Heinrich Strobel's programmes at Baden-Baden, Herbert Hübner's 'Das Neue Werk' at Hamburg, Wolfgang Steinecke's International Courses at Darmstadt, 'Musica Viva' founded by Karl Amadeus Hartmann at Munich, the concerts sponsored by M. Bartomeu in Barcelona, the 'Monday Evening Concerts' in Los Angeles, the 'Agrupación Nueva Musica' founded by J.-C. Paz in Buenos Aires; the 'Fylkingen' association in Stockholm; the concerts sponsored by Serge Garant in Montreal; and finally our own 'Domaine musical' concerts in Paris.

It is not by chance that all these organizations reveal an international tendency, since they all arose in answer to a single need – the need to make

---

[1] 'Première et seconde audition', *Cahiers Renaud–Barrault*, No. 13, October 1955, pp. 122–4.

known and loved works that were starting points for the generation that attained its 'majority' ten years ago, at the end of the war.

That should be the aim of contemporary music concerts – to get this music known and loved. First, though, to get rid of the artificiality and the amateurishness that had gradually grafted themselves on to an idea that was, originally, vital and vigorous; and silence a damaging form of propaganda undertaken by 'disciples' more notable for good will than for talent. That, you may retort, is purely negative. On the positive side there are two objectives that must be achieved immediately. First, to show that contemporary music does not represent a historical 'break', as has been too easily admitted, but that there is quite clear evidence of historical continuity. Second, to make up the balance sheet of the artistic generation immediately preceding our own. Once this ground has been cleared, the listener will find his bearings much more easily when faced by the boldest of today's experiments.

Then a word about interpretation. If contemporary music has been generally cold-shouldered, the fact is that the difficulties presented by these scores have not been properly met – not merely the mechanical difficulties, but those concerning comprehension, the true penetration of the composer's intention. It is only when a performer is completely familiar with a work that audiences can really grasp its musical veracity.

We must also take into account the shock of actual novelty, a shock that paralyses memory and immediate appreciation. It is impossible for the listener to get his bearings and to latch his attention on to something that has already appeared, music having finally escaped from all those more-or-less literal repetitions that once formed so familiar a feature. If in addition to this the listener is put out by a vocabulary with which he is ill acquainted, it is easy to see how little of the pleasure of appreciation he can hope for from a first hearing.

It is for this reason that 'second performances' seem so important to us, making it possible for audiences to reacquaint themselves every season with great figures like Webern and Schoenberg, each encounter becoming richer with increasing familiarity. Repeat performances also make it possible for listeners to become accustomed to the sound world of the younger generation of composers and to realize, behind the superficial aggressiveness, the real qualities of imagination, even when the craftsmanship shows a certain hesitancy.

The 'Domaine musical' will remain faithful to this programme since its plans include:

a Schoenberg Festival: *Ode to Napoleon*, *Serenade*, *Pierrot lunaire*
important works such as Berg's *Lyric Suite* and the *Piano Studies* of Debussy and Bartók
an important selection of Webern's works

a complete performance of J. S. Bach's *The Art of Fugue*
first and repeat performances of new works by Maderna and Nono (Italy),
Stockhausen and Henze (Germany), Pousseur (Belgium), Messiaen, Le
Roux and Barraqué (France)

The 'Domaine musical' has invited Herman Scherchen, Hans Rosbaud
and Rudolf Albert to conduct a number of concerts, and the Parrenin
Quartet and the pianist Paul Jacobs to contribute to the chamber music
series.

Let us hope that this season's five concerts will attract as immediate an
interest as last year's, which amazed even the most sceptical. In this way we
shall gradually hear the last of the bad old legend of the unintelligibility of
contemporary music.

49

Experiment, Ostriches and Music[1]

What is experimental music? There is a wonderful new definition that makes it possible to restrict to a laboratory, which is tolerated but subject to inspection, all attempts to corrupt musical morals. Once they have set limits to the danger, the good ostriches go to sleep again and wake only to stamp their feet with rage when they are obliged to accept the bitter fact of the periodical ravages caused by experiment.

'Messieurs nos Consciences, et ainsi de suite, dans vos valises!' Your disapproving, masochistic yelps might well discredit you. 'What!' they will say to us, 'We have just *seen* a great moment come to life, *undergone* a shattering experience. Like true catechumens, we have organized *congresses* to promote the true faith; for years we have eaten locusts and preached to our own reflections in the desert. And now that our breath has at last created a slight mist and doubt has shrunk, you want to rob us of the reward of our penitential exercises?'

Seraphic souls! Be so good as to hook your phantoms on to any portemanteau you like. The time has come for you to do away with the austere ghosts and to exorcize your little devils. We had known for days that you were obsessed by high-water marks and safety railings; there is nothing surprising to us in the fact that you are now raising your voices to assert your possession of these precious attributes. All that irritates us is the shamelessness of your protestations, and above all the cause for which you are fighting.

You pride yourselves on belonging to the race of *Homo discipulus*; you boast of having been pupils of some great master or other, of having enjoyed his unique advice and known his first (or his last) wishes. You feed your collection of polyhedra on vague memories and imagine that you exist in a tradition by your funeral wakes and odours of decay. Is there any tradition but that of the funeral parlour in which you would not choke, you dear transparent people!

By way of conciliating us you will be said to have been useful. Yes, indeed, you have despite yourselves served as necessary stepping stones. But is there

---

[1] 'Expérience, autruches et musique', *Nouvelle Revue Française* (*NRF*), No. 36, December 1955, pp. 1,174–6.

anything more ludicrous than an empty staircase, the only evidence of the fact that the plane has taken off?

Why should I not develop further this notorious personification! What a dialogue we could dream up between these staircases against an empty sky! Or even something like snatches of conversation between these two empty (and stinking) shoes the sight of which opens the second act of *Waiting for Godot*. From one personfication to another we should probably soon tire of this larval existence that calmly bases its self-assurance on tumuli.

Having played the roles of John Baptists, our admirable empty-shirts now wish to enjoy the prerogatives of Pius, excommunicating as 'experimental' all the new music that they no longer pant to decipher. They note as on the right path the class of 'journalists' who play the part of the dead dogs of music, going from one concert hall to another – as others go from one commissariat to another – for the daily harvest.

And they decide that the Grand Master of the Order is AS–74, not AW–83; they proclaim that AW–83 himself considered himself inferior to AS–74 and that this humbler path is therefore the right one to take; they declare that AS–74 and his satellite AW–83 have discovered (finally and overwhelmingly) so many possibilities that it is useless, 'experimental' to quarter them; and finally they set out on the rocky search for Offenbach and Verdi, if it is not divinely to establish the green lucidity of IS–82.[1]

The most harmless of these common marionettes generally have at least a 'presence'; but these transparent barkers are totally without anything of the kind. As long as these shabby-wretched clowns do not make of contemporary music a kind of Versailles with a code of behaviour drawn up by a mad Saint-Simon. As long as they do not forget that they are nothing – 'and nothing, as you know, means nothing or very little' – which they have not learned in twenty or thirty years, which means no longer being disciples or epigones – as long as they do not start blaming a new generation for having realized it. Seniority has never been an enviable privilege: all that count are the evidences of activity, actual works. So let these poor shrimps who have achieved nothing but pale plagiarisms (anything, indeed, but 'experimental') shut up. For the future, silence is their only salvation – allowing themselves to be forgotten.

There is no such thing as experimental music, which is a fond utopia; but there is a very real distinction between sterility and invention. The ostriches demonstrate to us the existence of *danger* – with their heads tucked under their folded wings.

---

[1] Boulez is of course referring to Arnold Schoenberg, b. 1874, Anton Webern, b. 1883, and Igor Stravinsky, b. 1882. [M.C.]

50
Mini-Editorial[1]

The fame of the 'Domaine musical' concerts has been provoking certain scratchy pens to search for explanations – more emotional than logical – that fall into four chief categories: snobs, socialites, members of a clique, and even the politically interested.

We began at the Petit-Marigny: small clique. We went on to the Salle Gaveau: still a clique. We have just started our season with a packed Salle Pleyel: still a clique. If we filled the Vélodrome d'hiver, we should doubtless still encounter the same accusation, *clique* and *politique* providing an easy rhyme.

And who form these small, medium-sized and large cliques? Two categories of people. First the socialites of whom it is well known that they (particularly the *dames du monde*) have no intelligence but plenty of money. Then the bearded brigade, who are generally dirty, wear picturesque things like roll-neck sweaters and are well known to attach their enthusiasm, like a kettle, to the tail of any dog as long as he barks. It should be added that according to our critics the success of the 'Domaine musical' concerts is due to the fact that they are meant for the deaf.

And so, socialites and beardies, it is up to me to undertake your defence and to emphasize in the first place the regularity with which you practise your frivolous and irritating deafness. That is indeed your chief fault – that you insist on finding Webern a more important composer than the estimable X, on taking more interest in Stockhausen's works than in those of the incomparable Y. You refuse to give up your deplorable tastes, and that is why . . . your daughter is deaf! Do you grasp the full point of that reasoning? And its probability?

But cheer up! Your numbers, my dear snobs, increase from year to year, while your pathetic critics are themselves moving into a category that threatens to go on shrinking. What a see-saw – they will soon be the snobs, the 'unhappy few' . . . Until then, justify the prerogatives that the world allows you, and continue your snobbery!

---

[1] 'Petit éditorial', programme of the Domaine musical concert of 14 December 1957 (fifth concert of the 1957–8 season).

As a matter of fact your ludicrous critics have for the last five years been scratching together the most monumental nonsense book – there are a number of real gems on the subject of Webern alone! This nonsense book would be quite enough to justify your snobbery, and a good deal more beside. One day we will publish an anthology from it and will dedicate it to you.

Go on being snobbish, then, about the so-called *juste milieu*, which is in fact both mediocre and insincere!

Be snobbish about the virtues that are sold to you as outstandingly national, though they are in fact simply the signs of a mean and narrow-minded provincialism! Be snobbish about everything supposed to be 'human', which is in fact no more than going into sham ecstasies over the smell of an old slipper! Beardies and society ladies – and all the *rest* of you who attend our concerts, be snobbish as we are about stupidity – you can never be snobbish enough about that!

51

Ten Years On[1]

What is a concert? How should a series of musical events be conceived?

The first thing is to have a guiding idea communicated by performers to a definite public.

The lack of a clear idea of this means of communication condemns the majority of concerts, whether 'classical' or 'contemporary', to zigzagging about in what may literally be called a 'no man's land'. If you make a musical gathering a sick museum or an unreadable panorama, you can be quite sure of not attracting or interesting anyone except statisticians, and even then . . .

In principle concerts should be regarded as means of communication, a live contact between active people, whether they are listeners or creative artists. But can this be said of most of the musical events that we are offered? Leaving on one side purely athletic displays (which are less interesting than the circus or the sports ground) the endless rediscoveries of the past, and friendly 'celebrations', Paris concerts are not exactly calculated to excite the appetite of the amateur. This is due to a multiplicity of causes any deep analysis of which would quickly lead to bitter differences of opinion. Personal influence, chronic lethargy and official lack of interest would each provide the title of a chapter and represent so many Scyllas and Charybdises.

It would take more than a journalistic battle to conquer this inertia. Jellyfish remain quite undaunted. They may occasionally be washed up on the shore and become dangerously dehydrated, but as soon as the tide comes in again, they float off gorged with salt and self-complacency!

The aim is to prove that we are moving by actually walking. But any toddler will tell you that walking is not as easy as it seems to adults! Of course one can learn to move, once one has got one's balance. As for tumbles, we know that the 'Fall' is something common to us all.

After giving my great mind to these matters I decided ten years ago to give concerts aimed at re-establishing communications between the composers of *our own* time and a public interested in promoting *its own* age. This

---

[1] 'Dix ans après, *Cahiers Renaud–Barrault*, No. 41, December 1963, pp. 360–9.

explains the lack of eclecticism for which the 'Domaine musical' is often blamed, but which is in fact its virtue and its strength. What made me shoulder this responsibility? I am quite ready to admit that circumstances forced me to do so; for even without any exact idea of the forced labour inseparable from the organization of concerts, it is clear that one's personal repose will seriously suffer. I confess that I have always felt – and still feel – a strong repugnance to the idea of a composer embarking on such an activity as the organizing of a series of concerts.

Composers belonging to the Establishment, considering themselves well protected in their well-fortified positions, refused to have anything to do with what they considered ludicrous, pathetic, despicable, uninteresting, anti-French, abortive, insignificant, low, pointless, harmful, dangerous, cosmopolitan, Middle European, ectoplasmic, inorganic, inconsistent, invertebrate, Freudian, inopportune, gloomy, sad, morbid, degenerate, spectral, unhealthy, etc. (All these adjectives have in fact been applied to us at one time or another!) Arguments of this kind have often been repeated by writers who, having played the trumpet too much, have taken to gobbling like turkeys. Composers and writers of this description have hardly even noticed that the fortified positions in which they supposed themselves to be so well protected from the sight and the attacks of young undesirables are in fact no more than wretched aquariums: it was not very difficult to follow the clumsy manoeuvrings of these squids (who even lacked ink!) and to gauge the deficiencies of their organic radar systems.

Facing them there were the failed explorers whose highest qualification was that they were somebody's 'disciples' (though anything but 'beloved' ones) and proud of it. They were patently amateurs, though passing for 'wise men' thanks to their strangeness and rarity; they have since been revealed as simple charlatans.

As a result of this state of 'things' concerts of 'contemporary' music were either the concern of petty princelings prepared to defend their false currency to the last or the apanage of feeble heirs who wasted and devalued the true currency. Could we be happy with such a charade as this? I can remember feeling really ashamed at some concerts of contemporary music in which the masterpieces of today were grossly caricatured by the hands and shoulders of conductors as grotesque as they were incompetent. And I can also remember the feeling of uncontrollable hostility aroused in me by the activities of the forgers who were determined to confuse the issues. No shred of intellectual honesty or of manual dexterity – that was the fine dilemma into which they were determined to force us!

Were we going to surrender to an opposition apparently so powerful but in fact so weak? Could we be happy to be regarded as suspect theorists? Our music was discussed but dismissed as nothing more than a matter for discussion: it was apparently unplayable and completely non-viable because there was no public for it. And with that 'the subject was closed'. It remained for our generation to show that it could get its music played and find a public, *the* public; it had to prove that all discussions of the matter were artificially conducted by 'seigneurs' anything but sure of their 'droits'! More simply, could we do without the elementary means of communication, concerts? How much longer were we to tolerate being forbidden contact with the outside world? Confident in the justice of our case and in our youth, we wanted to cut short these absurd theoretical discussions and to achieve two things – to propagate at long last a knowledge of the contemporary classics by means of performances that no one could accuse of incompetence or amateurishness, and to perform the works of genuinely contemporary composers with proper care and preparation. At least one point would then be gained: the discussions would no longer be about press articles but about the works themselves. We even felt justified in hoping that, once this negative side had been dealt with, the music itself would seem different to the public. People were afraid of 'modernism' yet hankered after it; for by its very nature modernism possesses an astonishing propulsive force. Once given an opening, it will burst into a fossilized world, corroding everything (though of course once the initial erosion is complete, the resulting void must be filled in . . .) Oh!, yes, everything would be simple if we could find an answer to the billion-dollar question – *who* is going to perform these works and demonstrate their recent, all-too-vulnerable immortality?

This was the urgent problem, then: to find performers with the necessary technical qualifications and the ability to adapt themselves to new styles. At first, I think, there seemed to be no answer except in the alliance of a group of musicians who all knew each other well, having first proved themselves professionally at the Théâtre Marigny as performers in the various pieces of stage music that Jean-Louis Barrault never failed to include in his productions. This group of friends immediately solved many of the difficulties – no discussions about likes and dislikes but perfect agreement on quality of performance. The list of players who took part in the first ten years of our concert giving must be seen as, before all else, a list of our supporters, a register of solidarity! But it is more than that. These performers were the principal auxiliaries in our whole work of prospecting and have helped us to discover the instrumental style of our age. It is certainly true that the virtuosity of some of these players inspired composers to write for some instruments more than others, and vice versa – modern composers have given some instruments a quite unexpected repertory of their own . . . In this way modifications have arisen that have changed this whole aspect of musical practice and built up a style of performance that faithfully reflects contemporary musical thinking. Furthermore the performances of contemporary classics, especially the works of the Second Viennese School, were scrupulously prepared with all the necessary rehearsal; so that the purely technical problems posed by these works were fully assimilated and there was still time to devote to the actual interpretation of the music. In this sense we tried as far as possible to put on model performances that gave each work its maximum value. Before discussing the aesthetic principles involved or the value of certain historical positions, we had to have irreproachable examples. In the past it has often needed nothing less than a blind faith to believe in the worth of some masterpieces when performed without any respect for tempi, dynamic nuances and other absolutely essential markings. Performances of that kind were no real introduction to a work, but positively misleading – hence our primary concern with quality of performance. If 'accidents' occurred occasionally, they were all the more noticeable for their rarity and for being out of our 'general line'.

A list of the twentieth-century classics given their first Paris performance by us reveals a time lag that is not very creditable to an international capital; and it furnishes an unanswerable proof that even after the Second World War our musical 'pastors and masters' did not even bother to acknowledge the good faith of the only real contemporary values.

If we take the example of Webern, twenty of the thirty-one opus numbers in his output owe their first Paris performance to the 'Domaine musical'. The *Passacaglia*, Op. 1, composed in 1908, had its first Paris performance in 1958 – a time lag of half a century! The *Second Cantata*, Op. 31, composed between 1941 and 1943, reached Paris in 1956, only thirteen years later! The case of Berg is not much better: his Quartet, Op. 3 had to wait forty-five years, and his *Three Pieces for Orchestra* forty-three, before being honoured with a Paris performance.

These figures are appalling and prove better than anything else the indifference of the musical 'ruling class' in France. Are they not an ample justification of our revolt against such a state of things and of our revolutionary ardour in the face of this organized lethargy? In other words, we felt it our duty to 'inform' the public about contemporary music by performances that were not disgracefully garbled. This simple information alone would prick the bubble of certain over-inflated values and remove many of the prejudices fostered by pointless discussion.

We have pursued that course without flagging and it has proved rewarding and effective.

Once we had re-established a more accurate picture of the historic period immediately preceding our own, we could perform the works of our own generation in a climate purged of ignorance. Putting the historical record straight was by no means enough: what we wanted to do was to promote a 'new' music, so that composers would no longer have to wait forty years to hear their works performed. This should not be taken as a kind of publicity hunger; having his works performed is quite essential to a composer, who gets his experience from direct contact with problems of performance . . . or performers! Checking technical points – whether certain instrumental combinations sound as he meant them to; whether certain difficulties are worth the risks involved – verifying not only details in the score but the actual sense of the piece as a whole, finding by practical experience forms of communication that he had not suspected – these are the immense advantages that the performance of a new work gives a composer. What is more, this direct contact automatically dissolves the insidious, unreal question of the relationship between music and the public. As an experience shared by the composer and the public, the new work takes its place in a network of relationships, more or less harmonious, more or less tense but unique in the give-and-take that they initiate. We shall not be so bold as to maintain that we have presented a series of masterpieces, should not indeed dream of making such a claim for the very good reason that we consider it quite unnecessary. In choosing works to perform we are naturally guided by criteria of quality, but not by these alone. We are not a museum for future generations; we perform what seems most likely to arouse interest. Our realizations often fall short of our intentions, as we know, but we still present certain works because they indicate a direction. Other performances, more convincing ones, may well follow and justify by their perfection certain attitudes towards which we groped our way among all the uncertainties inseparable from all pioneer work.

The list of composers whom we have introduced to Paris audiences shows that from the start our choice has not been bad. Some names in particular have become universally established, personalities without whom it is hard to imagine the evolution of contemporary music, though ten years ago they were hardly even names . . . I could give a detailed list of the most important works that we were the first to perform, but no attentive and intelligent reader of that list will need any commentary.

Hitherto we have been speaking of the 'intellectual' heights, but concerts are also economic problems. Even if composers 'charge' nothing (and they really are the least demanding of people . . .) the actual material organization, rehearsals, instruments, etc., involve a considerable budget. Particularly in our case, because we were anxious to give polished performances and these presuppose a considerable capital. No begging, no charity! There was absolutely no question of relying on the support of the musical Establishment, whose attitude was either uninterested or hostile; nor did we want to ask musicians to keep *giving* their time for rehearsals that meant a lot of hard work. On the other hand we were anxious to have a completely free hand in the matter of programmes, experience having shown how fatal *committees* can be, quickly degenerating into 'spheres of influence' in which anonymity favours every kind of 'under-the-counter' activity. Personal responsibility, undertaken in the full light of day, was essential.

These different claims were not easy to reconcile, since they involved the problem of patronage and, still more, of patrons! I have been fortunate in encountering friends and patrons willing and able to deal with every situation. That the 'Domaine musical' owes its existence to two well-known actors is, perhaps, one of its least paradoxical features.

The original plan for the Théâtre Marigny included music, and there was no question of returning to the old routine of a moderate eclecticism: it was to be a fight for the recognition of a really modern attitude. The only really responsible enthusiasm that I found was that of Madeleine Renaud and Jean-Louis Barrault, and I am not likely to forget it. I use the word 'responsible' because they never for a moment blinked at my lack of experience as an organizer or the vagueness of my budgeting. They had promised their support and they gave it whole-heartedly. All my warmest gratitude to them today for 'launching' us by their powerful and flexible support...

Mme Suzanne Tézenas has bravely consented to carry on their work and has been good enough to undertake the presidency of the 'Domaine musical', which is much more of a responsibility than an honour ... For patronage has to be *organized*, and this needs a great deal of patience, perseverance and tact. But for this organized patronage our concerts could not have gone on for more than two years: I feel a great sense of gratitude to all our 'benefactors' and should like to express my thanks to all of them in the person of Suzanne Tézenas, to whom the 'Domaine musical' owes an enormous debt.

Since I am on the subject of thanks, I must express my gratitude to the general public, and particularly to the regular subscribers, whose names have always been a comfort in all our worries and vicissitudes ... I really must say something about this public of ours, which has literally *made* these concerts. We began with a hall that held at the most about 200 people, a modest beginning for a town of the size of Paris. Now, at the Odéon, we have concerts that are sold out. Since it is no longer possible to dismiss such concerts as 'private and confidential', people sometimes still try to insist on their cliquishness ... Must we resign ourselves to the persistent dishonesty, echoes of which appear in the press? Certainly not! The past ten years have seen an evolution in our musical life and finally proved that these pygmy obstacles are powerless against the vitality of a movement. We should have preferred enemies who were intelligent enough to provide at least a stimulus, but no – our opponents are uniformly commonplace and conventional. A word should be said about outside observers who have followed our developments with a scrupulous and sympathetic eye, because no reservations they may have had – and some of these have been considerable – have ever stopped them admitting the positive side of the new ideas and the new works.

All this definitely adds up to a 'movement'. Unlike most movements, ours was not preceded by a manifesto. Of course there were fighting articles, theoretical essays, deliberate attitudes adopted, but we never thought of signing a common declaration of the usual flamboyant kind. More effectively, I think, we have made musical history from one day to the next. We thought (and when I say 'we', I mean the generation of composers who *recognized* each other, in the years immediately after the war, by certain attitudes) that the days of manifestos were long past, and we therefore set ourselves – sensibly, you must admit – to demonstrate the 'movement' by going straight ahead.

52

Why I Say 'No' to Malraux[1]

André Malraux has just made a cavalier decision about music in France, one that I believe to be ill considered, irresponsible and illogical. In doing so he has deferred to the wishes of the 'Comité national de la musique', which claims to be fully representative of all branches of our corporation. In fact this committee, as I see it, represents only its own members, who have time for forming committees ... The personality of their president, Jacques Chailley, only increases my suspicion of this committee; and this suspicion is only further increased by the last-minute juggling of Nestor ('Old Man') Milhaud. It needed a cleverer conjuring trick to make the illusion convincing, and the present masquerade emphasizes only the main outlines.

Malraux's was a compromise decision, which is always the worst of all: unwilling to disown Biasini,[2] but anxious to appease the 'official' representatives of music, he cut the pear in two – one half, the theatres, remaining in Biasini's hands and the other going to Landowski's claws. And the third half, by which I mean radio and television music, is still entrusted to the white fingers of the Ministry of Information.

A real reform, in fact, both positive and productive! It is not a matter of 'dividing and conquering', but dividing in order to have a quiet life.

Two fundamental questions are involved: (1) Is it good to separate music from general cultural affairs? and (2) Is it good to entrust the administration of music to a composer?

I answer both questions with a categorical 'No!'

The organization of music cannot now depend on ossified, out-of-date methods. Use must be made of more general organisms, which also deal with dramatic performances and exhibitions of paintings as well as concerts – and indeed 'magazines' – as organized by the Théâtre de l'Est Parisien. This is the price that must be paid if we are to contact the young, a public that is new both in social formation and aesthetic aspiration. It is sheer idiocy to try

---

[1] 'Pourquoi je dis non à Malraux', *Le Nouvel Observateur*, No. 80, 25 May 1966.
[2] Emile Biasini, entrusted with responsibility for theatres and music (until music was given to Landowski) at the Ministry of Cultural Affairs. [Editor's note in the *Nouvel Observateur*]

to ignore a collective phenomenon of this size and to continue the present partitioning-off of music, which is injurious to the actual development of the art and also risks creating a caste system in which each caste is totally ignorant of the other.

On the other hand the basic work of reorganizing the structures of our musical life needs a specialist, and therefore an administrator. Nobody could be less suited to the work of general administration than a composer; he will always remain an amateur working half-time, unless he gives up composing and learns this specialized job from A to Z.

In the present case separating the theatres from the concert-giving organizations is tantamount to giving up, without more ado, any attempt to solve the musicians' employment problem – the only possible solution lying in avoiding the perpetual coxing-and-boxing between theatres and concert-giving organizations. If these two services continue to be independent of each other, it is quite clear that we shall simply perpetuate the present basically sterile anomaly, which is at the root of all the absurdities and endless illogicalities that determine musical life in Paris. Finally, Malraux's choice has fallen on a dim, inconsistent individual, who shows very little imagination in his music and is hardly likely to show any more as an administrator.

Furthermore I simply cannot divide a personality into separate slices like Bernardin's melon.[1] Musicians like Chailley and Marcel Landowski have always been extremely reactionary, and I cannot for the life of me see what sudden inspiration from above will make them change their deep-seated conservatism the moment they attack the problem of organizing French music. We can rest assured of the scruples with which they will preserve academicism and its dusty traditions.

These are my reasons for saying a firm 'no' to Malraux's plan; and I draw my own conclusions. It is not my role to reverse the common saying and justify these new directives: 'What you see in the shop window you will not find in the shop!' *And so until decisions are taken that are not simply jokes, I shall refuse to collaborate with anything that, remotely or otherwise, in France or abroad, depends on the official organization of music.*

If Malraux chooses to ask Robert Bordaz[2] to send Landowsky to the Montreal Exhibition with the Orchestre National to play the complete works of Chailley, they will laugh in his face. If he asks these same individuals to take the same orchestra on tours of the USA and Germany or to Lucerne, they will laugh in his face again. And if he asks the public to form

---

[1] Bernardin de Saint Pierre (1737–1814) maintained that the melon was designed by providence as a family food, being divided into ready-made slices. [M.C.]

[2] In charge of organizing the French contribution to the forthcoming World Exhibition. [Editor's note in the *Nouvel Observateur*]

popular associations in support of these eminent musicians, they will laugh in his face a third time (one of the possible forms of Saint Andrew's denial...)

He will then realize that music is something too important to be entrusted to the hands of the feeble and incompetent or abandoned to 'showcase' musicians...

I take it that the coming season will be hastily given some liberal financial injections, but these doses of morphine will do nothing to cure the malady from which music is suffering, which will very probably have become more serious in the meanwhile.

All that concerns me is that it should be known that I am not playing any more, and that I consider the present solution the worst, the laziest and stupidest possible.

I am therefore on strike against the whole of French musical officialdom. There is nothing heroic, in fact, about such a strike, since it by no means threatens my livelihood. It is no secret that I have gone to Germany, having been unable to achieve anything on any decent scale in France. My only difficulty has been to choose which of the many invitations that I have received I should accept. I am well able to do without official French invitations with so many foreign ones to chose from.

I do not want to play the demagogue, but there is one regret that I must express – that for a time at least I shall not be working with French players. They and I have had opportunities to appreciate each other and some evidences of this, at least, will remain. Neither the cavalier behaviour of a minister nor the intrigues of the 'showcase' musicians will make me forget the quality of these players. I protest – by default – in the name of this French potential that every step is being taken to annihilate. Since I am not dependent on my livelihood for any official employment, I can afford it, and I insist on declaring publicly that I disclaim all association with the minister's weary cavalier gesturing and the jiggery-pokery of the old men's committees.

I have already been accused of using Führer-like methods. The official grapevine, aiming below the belt and using soft words, has already caused a few ripples and other sticky bubbles. Coriolanus' name may be invoked... good, I'll settle for Coriolanus.

I am still quite convinced that there will be no improvement in the situation of music in France as long as it is controlled by failed composers. The control of music is neither an honour, nor a trust, neither a *voie de garage* nor a privilege; it is a function... and a function that needs specialists. Until this is understood, France will remain a country where everything is improvised – more often than not, badly – and Paris a capital in which music has become a ludicrous appendage. I refuse to associate myself with this situation, knowing as I do the untapped resources that exist both in Paris and in the provinces, and very aware that disinterestedness is not exactly the cardinal virtue of the doctors provisionally summoned by Malraux to attend the sickbed of music.

The position that I have adopted involves nobody but myself personally, certainly not the 'président d'honneur du syndicat des artistes musiciens de Paris'. I am not anxious for the general secretary of this union to become once again the object of telephone pressurizing on the part of Landowski or any other member of Malraux's cabinet. In this way he will not therefore be forced by these gentry to make a public disavowal of his president. (Such unsavoury blackmailing methods really have to be shown for what they are . . .)

On the other hand, if the union is to discuss purely material questions with the new directors of music, it must not feel handicapped by my fundamentally hostile attitude. Free of all collective responsibility and speaking for myself alone, I feel all the more independent and at liberty to express my own opinions on certain aspects of a situation that I find both sordid and contemptible.

Is this the only future to which we can look forward – one of regrets, bitterness and desertion?

53

Where Are We Now?[1]

I belong to a generation that is no longer young and has probably played its part in changing the face of contemporary music. I am both a composer and a performer, which means that I have had occasion to concern myself a great deal with practical questions, particularly with the way in which contemporary music is developing and with establishing contact between new music and the public. This means that I am in an intermediary position, both as regards age and function, and therefore find it necessary to ask myself where music is going today. I am not trying to determine the future, because the future can never be determined and would-be prophets are bores, because they deprive themselves of the privilege of innovation and adventure. Even so, we have passed the stage at which we were still clearing the ground and making belated discoveries. Things have settled down to a certain extent and we have reached a point at which we need to reflect a little – composers, that is, as well as listeners – in order to go forward.

Immediately after the war there were great hopes for a generation (and especially for the generation that had realized the failings and weaknesses of its predecessors and immediately marched ahead, full of enthusiasm), to make its own discoveries on what amounted to a *tabula rasa*. I must first remind you that in 1945–6 nothing was ready and everything remained to be done: it was our privilege to make the discoveries and also to find ourselves faced with nothing – which may have its difficulties but also has many advantages. As a teacher (I am not a very good one, but I have had two or three years' experience), I have seen the great difference between the problems facing the next generation and those that we had to face. Our first thought was unity of action.

The discoveries we made between 1945 and 1950 were comparatively easy: it was simply the primary effort needed to lay the foundations of the new language, starting from the existing sources, which we had chosen afresh for ourselves. This language developed in a way that might have

---

[1] 'Où en est-on?', transcript of a lecture given at Saint-Etienne on 13 May 1968. Published in part in *Le Monde de la musique*, No. 2, July–August 1978, pp. 20–2, but not complete until in *Points de repère*.

resulted in a new academicism. It was to avoid this that every composer began to explore his own world, which is the normal and desirable way for things to happen, the most serious fault that could be found with composers of the same generation in different countries being too great a mutual resemblance, a following too closely of the same path. There were cases in which this accusation was justified, though not for long, individual person-alities developing and becoming more marked with age, and divergencies with them. There finally appeared temperaments able to express themselves with the freedom that all of us had striven so hard to achieve.

I do not want now to start justifying (primarily because it is too late and nothing remains to justify) the steps that brought us to the position in which we now find ourselves; but I should like to point out that, in relation to the older generation, our chief concern was the discovery of the grammar and the form necessary for the establishment of a solid and reliable language, one not merely linked to more-or-less vague speculations. What seemed to us characteristic of our immediate predecessors was the multitude of aesthe-tic speculation, slogans and passwords, none of which had any precise bearing on the musical language or any long-term stabilizing effect on it. What we were looking for was not simply a fashion to be worn for a single season – such as the big fashion houses produce every year – but a real language and long-term solutions of formal and linguistic problems. Some of our solutions were no doubt exaggeratedly strict in character, a discipline that irked but represented a necessary stage. Why necessary? Because in order to forge a language strict disciplines are necessary and so is a know-ledge of the *via negativa*, the phenomenon of negation. If you do not negate, if you do not make a clean sweep of all that you have inherited from the past, if you do not question that heritage and adopt an attitude of fundamental doubt towards all accepted values, well!, you will never get any further.

I once wrote a piece to which I gave a title (later withdrawn) that I had borrowed from Klee – 'à la limite du pays fertile', on the border between ploughland and desert. If you know this picture of Klee's, you will realize that he too went through periods when geometry was almost more important to him than invention, because at that time invention had to be codified in a certain particular way in order to recapture a new simplicity and a new codification of the language. That is what happened to our generation. After a certain time it became clear that this was not enough and that the search must continue, that after the precise codification of the language we must once again concern ourselves with questions of aesthetics. At first we had neglected these, laid them on one side, at least for a time, finding them less important and full of awkward problems. Moreover we wanted to be quite frank about the solutions that we were seeking, and not to embarrass ourselves with pseudo-problems of aesthetics, which would have been at that time premature. In spite of this, once the language – or at least the constitution of the language – was established, each of us returned to his own personal problems and the different directions in which these led us. Now we need to get a kind of second wind, and it is quite clear that a new generation is turning in a number of different directions, the youngest of them particularly. The great unity that seemed a possibility twenty years ago has proved a myth, a snare and a delusion; what we have instead is different personalities each taking their own courses, sometimes in violent opposition to each other.

A certain amount has been said about different sectors of the contemporary scene being unable to understand each other, of contradictory procedures having destroyed the primary unity that had been our original aim. Might there not in fact be new ways of finding and defining a new unity, which had no reference to the old order of things, but could co-ordinate activities in very different fields? These ways, it seems to me, still have to be discovered and certainly do not at present exist; but individuality plays a part in a much more general procedure, a synthesis of which we can catch a glimpse even if it is not yet realizable. What am I in fact trying to say about contemporary music? That there are a lot of different tendencies – but I must eliminate from the start all that are backward-looking, all 'restorations', which are not so much tendencies in fact as nostalgias. When one has had one's fill of experimenting, there comes a nostalgia for the past, a nostalgia for childhood, and attempts are made to camouflage this nostalgia by returning to certain things and integrating them as best one can in the world of today by means of a clumsy dialectic. Well!, I can only say that such nostalgias have no interest for me; they are purely individual phenomena, of purely individual interest and quite unable to contribute to a future in the framework of history. I think that, quite the opposite, what we must face at the present time is a return to the future, seeking a way out of our strict disciplines and imagining the future with a certain freedom, which, combined with voluntary discipline, will give our contemporary language a chance of becoming more truly universal. The major problem at present lies in the fact that each composer is busy in his own corner of the field, hoping in some way to achieve a universal expression: that is why contemporary idioms are less divergent than they seem at first sight. You probably hear a lot about the contrasts between electronic, electro-acoustic and instrumental music in particular. This contrast is to be found in the theatre and in the organization of concert life, and it is in fact a phenomenon of growth in one individual area. What point have we reached, then, in the general organization of music and its relationship to the public?

I will not say that contact with the public is the primary problem, but it is one that concerns you directly. Before saying anything about the individual problem of each composer, I should like to say something about this contact which he refuses in one sense but could accept in another, and also to insist that creation in general has become much more a collective than an individual phenomenon. The creative artist and the public still communicate by means of what we call 'concerts' and there is of course a great gap between the creative artist and the mass of the concert-going public that interests itself in orchestral music and great artists. There is a deep discrepancy here, and I believe that music is perhaps the most conservative of all worlds, certainly much more conservative than that of the theatre and more so than the museum world. A glance at the individual efforts made by museums (even in Europe and certainly in America) and by theatres, will reveal just how desperately music lags behind. This is because its organization is based on routines and on contacts that are completely irrelevant to life as it is today. Knowing my own situation, you may very well ask me, 'Why do you go on directing concerts if this means still working within a conventional framework where the only change that you can make is by introducing slightly bolder programmes and where you can never radically alter the framework itself or the sense of communication?'

It is obviously difficult to find a solution to this problem, or at any rate it is easier to solve verbally than factually. It is simple to say that new concert halls should be built, that orchestras should be reorganized or that the orchestra should be replaced by a kind of consortium of performers that could be drawn on for *ad hoc* purposes. All that is very easy to say; and it is true that solutions of this kind can well be imagined, such as have been discovered in the theatre, although there the problem is either different or non-existent. As I have said, there is an economic factor in music, and this factor always tells in favour of conservatism. By this I mean that in any organization qualified for an activity of this kind it is very difficult to persuade people – simply from the point of view of intrinsic organization – that things can be organized differently without creating major problems in any well-regulated economy. Meanwhile an orchestra consists of so many violins, so many flutes, so many horns, etc., according to generally accepted norms, which I can only call expanded nineteenth-century norms that we have inherited. These norms were accepted a hundred years ago, with a certain vocabulary and a certain style of expression in mind, and have since then been gradually enlarged to meet new demands. This has landed us in the completely absurd situation of being unable to perform anything but a repertory extending over the last century and a half, and being obliged to embark on quite unrealistic extra expenditure in order to play contemporary works, which are not economically rewarding. Performing early music involves similar additional expenditure, which proves similarly uneconomic.

This proves the absurdity of the situation: we have progressed further and further towards an encyclopaedic knowledge (though encyclopaedic is a big word) of music history and now, having a kind of imaginary museum of music, certainly want to hear more than what has been composed during the last century and a half. The reference points in music history that we need are not in any sense limited by space or time. For many composers beside myself European music, though naturally a primary experience because we were born in Europe and belong to the European tradition, is not enough: we are anxious to hear other forms of music. Listening to Japanese Gagaku or Noh, Indian, Balinese or Aztec music, is to me as satisfying an experience as listening to European music. That is to say, the present tendency (very belated in music compared with the plastic arts) is to regard European musical culture as only one of the developments capable of interesting and enriching us. From this point of view the communication between the public and musical origins is very incomplete and impossible to justify except from the point of view of a historical museum and museums, though certainly of interest, are not of prime importance! I still admire Descartes – or whoever it was – who installed an ox in his library instead of books. It is always interesting for a creative artist to burn his library and forget absolutely everything that he has read or been taught. We should, in fact, regard this culture of ours as one among many, and musical life today makes this quite impossible: not only have we no opportunity to encounter other cultures but we are not allowed to form an opinion of examples of our own contemporary evolution. Believe me, I am speaking with fifteen years' experience of concert giving. It is really impossible to put today's audiences in contact with the creative forces at work at the present time without totally altering our present conception of musical life. This is an absurd paradox.

I cannot see why each public should exist in a kind of ghetto – the opera public, the classical symphony orchestra public, the public interested in baroque music, the public interested in choral music, the public interested in contemporary music. For the most part – and I feel very strongly about this – these specialized publics, whether it be for contemporary or baroque music, specialist conductors or specialist performers, are all specialists in nothing, because they are incapable of seeing what may be happening in other cultures, incapable of corroborating their own special interest with present-day activities. And until we have the means for this practical synthesis, our musical life will continue to lack any real sense. It is not possible to judge simply as a specialist, as one might judge Chinese prints. Musicians, for instance, who are interested only in the interpretation of some single work, a single period or a single composer, are, as far as I am concerned, a race of aesthetes not destined to survive for long. That is why our musical life, in so far as it is an affair of famous performers and works that belong in museums, is a rapidly dying culture and one that will die even more rapidly if it receives a blow or two. And we must hasten its death because culture has nothing to do with these sham phenomena of knowledge. The worst people of all are the semi-cultivated, who think they are connoisseurs but really know absolutely nothing. Yes, the musical world is indeed one of the most conservative of all and almost the most enclosed. You cannot expect such a world to be quickly transformed, because it is governed by economic imperatives extremely difficult to control.

Try, for instance, simply as a matter of organization, to modify the constitution of an orchestra. You will see that you will almost certainly encounter deep hostility, from both public and players, who will tell you that it has worked very well as it is: why should it not continue to do so, with a few adjustments? The fact that must now be faced is that it will not continue unless a profound remedy is discovered – and how is that to be done? By organizing either concert halls or actual concerts in a much more flexible way. There is a great deal of talk about free music, music in a state of 'becoming', from the point of view of composition, but as soon as this music 'in the state of becoming' reaches the stage of practical performance, we all come up against the fatal rigidity of structures. From a simple, practical point of view anyone who has ever attended a concert of contemporary music must have been horrified by the amount of time spent moving chairs and players' desks compared with that spent actually on the music. This means that our concert halls are a completely aberrant phenomenon. They were built of course for nineteenth-century performances in which the music was presented as an object of contemplation. You watch someone playing, you watch without taking any part; of course, you are contemplating the masterpiece. This conception is quite inapplicable to contemporary music. In the first place the 'masterpiece' no longer exists as a norm; there are no obligatory formal norms, no obligatory norms deciding the number of performers and how they are grouped. So that one ensemble and one grouping will demand one arrangement of the stage and twenty or twenty-five minutes later this will be followed by another ensemble, another grouping and another arrangement of the stage. In so rigid a framework as this the concert form is no longer really necessary, as performance is perpetually interrupted and any desire for communication will simply be frustrated.

The same is true in the case of electro-acoustic or pure electronic music (and this is quite recent) – you sit facing a number of loudspeakers, which are in fact devoid of all interest, and after a few seconds you really do get to know what they look like. Such so-called concerts are really more like cremations: the tape takes about twenty minutes to be, as it were, cremated but no one even considers what possible visual interest there can be for anyone attending the ceremony. There is no need of a visual interest if two or three people simply listen to the recording in a room. But as soon as this listening takes on a group character, a point of focus is absolutely essential and without it everyone will simply shut their eyes and do as Mme Verdurin did – pretend to listen but in fact sleep. Everyone is more or less asleep interiorly unless there is really something to see or some deduction to be drawn.

This has given rise to a misunderstanding about contemporary music because in the last resort, unless you are a real fanatic on the subject or in any case know what the problems are and can surmount the absence of communication, the first things that strike us about this music are its faults. These are so manifest that anyone without a profound attachment to music as such – and after all it is quite possible to be more attached to painting or to literature than to music, I admit that – anyone who takes only an occasional interest in music and is interested in other things, sees only the ridiculous side. People going to the Opéra for the first time are primarily aware of the singers' mouths rather than the sense of the music. Without seeing or knowing the conventions of an art (and I must say, in parenthesis, that all expression depends on a certain number of conventions) – if these conventions are evident to the eye and produce good results, we admit them and accept this means of expression: this is universally true of all means of expression. If on the other hand the means of communication is not 'in phase' with the matter to be communicated, all that appears to the outsider is this failure to communicate, this kind of embarrassment caused by an attempt to communicate that proves ineffective.

There are different ways of dealing with this, different palliatives (and I have used them myself, I admit) – particularly synchronizing the performers with the loudspeakers. The musicians play and what you hear are the loudspeakers. You look at the performers but the sound comes from elsewhere, producing a kind of false perspective rather like that of the eighteenth-century Italian mannerists. You feel pleased because you have seen one thing and heard another. You are self-satisfied and feel more intelligent than you in fact are; it is a *trompe-l'oeil* (or *trompe-l'oreille*) solution of the problem.

Attempts have also been made to relate the concert formula to a kind of gesticulation (rather than gesture), to get music accepted for secondary reasons that really have nothing to do with music, making musicians 'play' like actors, something that they are unfortunately quite unqualified to do. Some theatre music has been like the caricature of a concert. It was not justified for its own sake, as we were shown the gesture separate from the action, an arrangement that simply does not work. It was all very well meant and very nice, but it gave no idea of the right reaction or of how properly to reconstitute a gesture that has some meaning in the context of today.

This is of course the business of architecture, not architects but architecture. Architects should interest themselves in this problem but have not been given many opportunities. The only example of a modern concert hall is that of the Berlin Philharmonic which, as an adventure, is on the quiet side. Concerts are conceived visually in a rather more modern way there than elsewhere but, that apart, the whole central conception remains unaltered – the conception of music as an object of 'worship' and so presented. Each individual worships in his corner and the architecture of the hall makes any participation impossible.

I do not want to claim to solve the problems of either architecture or the social functioning of music, but I do claim that it is time that we faced these problems really seriously. It is time, for instance, that we refused to build new halls copying or simply updating the old models, with facings of concrete instead of wood and moquette instead of plush but no structural modification whatever. Putting a large piece of modern sculpture in the main foyer or having a flying-saucer ceiling will not alter the 'sense' of a hall. The reforms that have been attempted hitherto are inadequate and have not been planned in relation to the music of today. It is almost tragic to see everyone working away in their own corner and no one trying to strengthen their vision of the world today. On the one hand we have concert halls with completely conservative specifications, belonging to the last fifty years, and on the other musicians complaining that they have no adequate place for their experiments or their performances (because I hate the word 'experiment' – everything is an experiment) – with the result that there is a general feeling of dissatisfaction, whether it is in the organization of music, of concerts or of musical life in general.

So what is the result? Inevitably, a number of small ghettos. (Not that I am against 'action cells', which are essential – new movements always start with a central, directing group.) No one undertakes the direction of the new movement. There are simply scattered, isolated searchers, whose searchings ultimately give an age its character, form its profile; but it remains difficult to escape the problem of how to make an overall contact with the public. I think that it is always much better to set out in search of a public (understood in the most demagogic sense), in search of communication and contact, than simply to satisfy a small group, which is always possible. I have often been accused of cliquishness, and indeed do not resent the accusation, which is only one of many. But real cliquishness, for me, consists in being content with the approval of a small group; and from this point of view I must admit that my analysis is not so much bitter as fulminating.

Any public always includes a number of people who long to be creative and are not. As soon as these people find a way of latching themselves on to any creative personality, they always form a group round him to make up for their own lack of activity. We must face the fact that any activity will always find its public and everyone is anxious to prove that they are right; and it is in this way that misunderstandings arise. As soon as a public falls out with the individual who is set up as an idol, there are inevitably hisses and rebellions. As things are at present, people attend concerts to see how clever and gifted they are themselves. They go to hear a great virtuoso play some work that they have heard times without number and will, of course, not be hearing any more as soon as they are in their baths. (Of course I am generalizing and oversimplifying, because to discover the truth one has to simplify and caricature.) They pride themselves on attending the concert and, with a few exceptions of course, their applause is the expression of self-approbation. You pride yourself on what you take to be your culture: it is a personal reflex. (You have only to observe the way people judge each other. Without exception everyone says, 'Yes, he is really clever; he agrees with me.') You yourselves are satisfied with this reflex, which you have most of the time.

If you go and see something (and I am speaking about music as I would about the theatre or a museum or a book) what you are after is self-approbation. It needs a great deal of goodwill and a kind of permanent self-criticism to be able to say, 'No, I am not satisfied with that; it is not good enough and I want to go further than I have got so far.' This kind of sense of dissatisfaction is common throughout music generally, not only in France but all over the world, as far as I can see; and with it there spring up small personal groups whose chief delight is experiment, hostile to the rest of the world, and who go to one place because they find satisfaction there and not to another, where they find none. These small groups spring up round some individual personality or group; everyone defends his own small piece of territory and regards himself, in the fashionable jargon, as a *groupuscule*. This really is the death of music in the wider sense and of expression as such. As I say, it is always possible to satisfy a small group, or even a large group, according to how much you are prepared to abdicate; but the interesting thing is to promote musical expression to a point at which it becomes a means of *general* communication, and is not simply confined to a number of individuals.

Of course I am not such a demagogue as to maintain that anyone who achieves communication with the real public has found a real solution. There are plenty of false solutions here as elsewhere. Apparently obvious solutions are sometimes accepted because they have been easy, but there again one must use one's critical faculty both on oneself and on others. Organizing even a series of avant-garde concerts (and I have fifteen years' experience) can sometimes be amusing, if only to see the final upshot. My idea has been to let the public itself judge certain things, and this was my chief principle during the final period of my activity as concert director. It seemed to me altogether too simple to aim at producing a disciplined, well-educated public – which really means a public that is bored but dares not say so. There were a number of experiments of which I did not personally much approve (that is the wrong word – 'approve' does not mean anything; but I did not quite agree about the meaning and value of these experiments) but in the last resort I thought it better to present something to be judged, rather than to make my own judgement and present it as a kind of orthodoxy. This has for years been the failing of all avant-garde manifestations – that in the end they become rearguard and always remain 'guard' actions. This is really no good!

Generally speaking, I believe that the organization of any expression must have two senses. Some periods – even recent ones – are fixed, and some works – even recent ones – absolutely beyond discussion. These form the 'museum' part of the repertory, consisting of models to be imitated, definitive models of which there is nothing further to be said. A tree is a tree, and if you look at it, you are not going to call it a weathercock! That is therefore one part of our necessary activity; but on the other hand we must not lose the sense of experiment and of communication between these models, which are there and can always be viewed in different lights according to how they are interpreted and to the sense in which they are models of experimentation.

This brings me back to the phenomenon of the composer. The composer is simply each person's image. In every listener there is a creator, who asks to express himself by means of another personality only because he himself lacks the creative gift. The composer is exactly like you, constantly on the horns of the same dilemma, caught in the same dialectic – the great models and an unknown future. He cannot take off into the unknown. When people tell me, 'I am taking off into the unknown and ignoring the past' it is complete nonsense. Only if one were an Eskimo and found oneself in the middle of civilization, would it be possible to ignore the past. A certain modicum of civilization is needed, of course, in order to be able to share in our means of expression. Anyone born here, anyone whose first experiences of expression and of culture have been in Western Europe, is completely conditioned and cannot help himself. It will be possible for him to escape and to discover ways of eluding his formation, but he will never be able to escape his basic conditioning.

When he shuts his eyes in order to escape, he is simply behaving like the ostrich – knocking in open doors with his head in the sand. It seems to me very difficult but it can be successful all the same. The composer finds himself in exactly the same dilemma, a prisoner of this same sense of dissatisfaction, and in the most immediate sense. If he is commissioned to write a new work, he asks himself, 'Am I to remain within the existing framework? I shall have so many players, so many rehearsals, the use of this or that concert hall, the work will either be played at once or, if it is difficult, I shall get a German radio station to play it, because they have plenty of rehearsals.' Up to this point it is always possible to imagine the new work in terms of the data with which you are presented. There have been works written for unusually difficult media, for rare combinations and halls other than conventional concert halls – and they have been played once, perhaps twice. But it soon becomes clear when budgeting for such a concert that the carpenter and the scene-shifters will get much more money from it than the musicians – in fact two-thirds of the sum budgeted will go to the former and only a third to the latter, which is pretty silly in the case of a musical work!

The composer therefore finds himself from the practical point of view – and right up to the actual conception of the work – in this kind of dilemma: 'Am I to accept a compromise solution, or shall I refuse to compromise and run the risk of being played and heard only by a small group?' Of course it is quite easy to set up a few loudspeakers and have a group of between five and ten players; but it is quite clear that we are not going to return to baroque formations nowadays. In the first place, our concert halls are too big, and in the second, taste has evolved in a quite different way. It is a strange thing, but after a period of restriction we are now returning to big forces. It is noticeable among composers, and I am not speaking of myself but of the

20–25-year-olds, who have a new taste for size as such, for noise and volume. This is presenting them with problems that they have never faced before. How are they going to resolve the difference between contrary dialectics, between the forces of the past and this force that propels them towards new discoveries, towards a future that they cannot wholly foresee, though they feel its pull?

What we need today is to rediscover aesthetic and technical problems in relation to each other, which has hitherto been extremely difficult in practice. Is this possible for a single individual? I do not think that it is. I think that musical vocabulary tends to appropriate new territories but can do this only by means of a common effort, by working together. Invention, of course, will always remain purely individual rather than communal, but work conditions can be shared. Why have almost all electronic music studios failed hitherto? Simply because there has been no co-ordination between the experts, the inventors and the musicians. If music is to discover a new vocabulary, it is essential that it must be the concern of others beside musicians, whose musical culture makes it impossible for them to work practically and naturally with certain new concepts that are none the less extremely useful. When musicians use these new concepts, they do so very naïvely, establishing relationships between science and music that are, to say the very least, unconvincing. Actually no serious work has yet been done on the relationship between music as a science and music as a means of expression. In logical sequence the most recent studies in this field go back to the eighteenth century, since when there have been nothing more than studies in acoustics, nothing really new, no basic investigation of the structural relations possible between the language of music and the language of science, though the one is founded on the other. I think that all today's discoveries, whether in the instrumental or the electro-acoustic field, demand a much wider basis, and to achieve this we need a kind of general school, or laboratory, where researchers in different disciplines can study these problems with a view to finding solutions applicable to music. This would at least avoid a great many misunderstandings.

You may well object – as many others have done – that music is not a science. It is indeed a purely individual means of expression reflecting an interior expression, not just a putting-together of mathematical structures. But, as I say, the language has not really been investigated for almost two centuries, and it is high time that this should be done. And what will the musician stand to gain from all this? At the present time he is faced, I believe, with a numer of problems relating both to language and to expression. Let me say a few words, not too technical, on the linguistic problem, under three headings:

i   instruments and the instrumental world, in which real possibilities have become very restricted

2 the world of intervals, which of course depends on instruments and has also become very limited, no longer corresponding in any way to musicians' desires

3 the electro-acoustic world, which is of course entirely new and has been taken over, in a way, by a kind of curiosity-shop aesthetics, this bastard descendant of a dead Surrealism – everything happening fifty years later in music than in the other arts, as usual

It is my belief that these problems can be solved only by being co-ordinated. Take for example the first two of those listed above – instruments and intervals. Instrumental music, as is well known, has always been linked with intervals that are now obsolete – I mean tempered semitones. People have given their minds to the subject but have still not succeeded in finding any solution but these semitones. Everyone is, I am sure, aware that there are musical cultures, such as that of India, that use different intervals from the semitone and have their own instrumental culture, their own conception of instruments. In Africa there are pure and impure sounds, whereas everything in our Western culture tends to the standardization of intervals and of sounds in general. We have *deliberately* sought the pure sound, in other words the sound that can be mistaken for another. If, for instance, I use a D or an E, it will be a D or an E that is absolute, not relative, and will have no individual characteristics.

Thus the whole Western musical vocabulary has tended towards an abstract conception of intervals and of pitch independent of the instrument concerned. Thus sound has become a material independent of its own existence and has an existence that is quite independent of its essence. All our instrument building has of course been guided by this concept and with this aim. Wind and stringed instruments, instruments like the piano, all tend to produce a determinate, *abstract* sound destined to be used as an abstraction, in fact as an abstract concept. Other civilizations, on the other hand, are founded on individual scales – by which I mean that an instrument, at one pitch, will have one colour and at another pitch another colour. Everything is individualized. Of course I am quite aware of the objection that the whole direction and progress – the evolution, in any case – of Western music has been towards an *abstract* convention, a dimension capable of projecting music in the absolute. Indeed all individualism represents a link with some given phenomenon and hinders its evolution or at least hinders the establishment of a certain distance or dimension in relation to its origin. It is an observable fact that this abstract dimension in musical evolution has given rise in Europe to the following phenomenon: instruments have ceased to develop and have become entities considered as ultimate models of our civilization, unalterable because 'perfect'. Added to this is the fact that pupils at the Conservatoire learn to play their instruments in a certain way that never changes for the rest of their lives – which amounts to saying that an education of this kind, given at a certain moment in musical history, prejudices musical life and musical education for the next forty years. This is a serious consideration involving, as it does, long-term results.

Look, on the other hand, at the world of show-business, which is revealing on a minor scale; where there is no dearth of experiment, since there are no traditions or repertoires and no one cares a fig for instrumental propriety. In that world instruments do evolve: ten years ago, for instance, the electric guitar did not exist, and now it is manufactured in hundreds and is evolving in the process; and in the same way the vibraphone appeared and has also evolved. All the instruments in the variety orchestra have evolved because they are not, as it were, handicapped by a repertory that condemns instruments to remain fixed in form, because in relation to one tradition they are 'perfect'. In variety orchestras nobody worries about the exact number and specification of players; they make do with what they have, or what they need for any individual occasion. There are no set rules, no abstract ideals of perfection.

Classical music today is still governed by abstract ideas of the setting and resources needed for concert giving, and it is time to reconsider our whole system of musical education and the actual *invention* of instruments. Obviously the violin, which is tuned in fifths, is quite unsuited to music that is totally uninterested in fifths or semitones. It is quite clear that instruments must be adjusted and invented to produce the scales that a composer needs for any given work. It is the composer's object, in fact, to invent a universe of its own for each new work, a universe that is in complete contradiction to that which he encounters when he turns to the instruments at his disposal.

The present development of percussion instruments presents an unreal problem – a kind of flight into the future, because we have not really grasped the problem involved and we are dealing with instruments that have no history themselves and no place in History with a capital H. These instruments have no tradition and virtually no repertory; they are not associated with any definite aesthetic system and their charm is basically exotic, belonging to Asia or to Africa rather than to our own European culture. This, I think, is a characteristic 'false' problem, a typical instance of a problem that has been shirked. What in fact do we find in the case of these percussion works, which have been grossly abused? Very summary descriptions of scales that are not accepted. If, for instance, you play five tom-toms, you cannot go back to five fingers on the piano, and if you had a five-note piano, you would be considered a pretty elementary pianist. The problem is shirked rather than solved because we are using instruments in the wrong way. It is quite right that they should be used, but not in silly, elementary ways. Composers need to take a longer view and only a technician can help them to do that.

Turning to another problem, not concerned with percussion instruments, let us consider the harp – a seven-stringed instrument that is really made for diatonic music and is, in a way, an expression of that music. It is an instrument with many possibilities, and can be tuned as one likes, thus escaping from its diatonic character, though not from the number seven – there will still be seven strings, which will be doubled or, if tuned without in a way considering octaves, will produce an extremely irrational instrument. Thus we find ourselves back with the problem of the individual character of instruments, which cannot be expanded into an abstract phenomenon. It is no use simply returning to the instrument's individuality as we and other cultures have known it hitherto, because it also fails to promote the culture to that level.

General solutions must be found with the help of technicians who have studied these complex questions under the direction of composers. I take the example of the harp – as you probably know, it has been said that harpists spend half their time tuning and the other half playing an instrument that is out of tune – but much the same is true of all other instruments. If you want them to play strict intervals, you must find a new way of tuning them depending not on hydrometry but, for instance, on electronic control, in order to cease being dependent on a tuner who spends three hours on the job and produces disastrous results. Instruments must be conceived and tuned in new ways and only then will they take their place in today's conception of music.

So far I have spoken about instruments, but I might just as well speak about the way in which instrumental ensembles are conceived. Why, for instance, should an orchestra have eighteen violinists and one timpanist? Suppose a work needs three violins and six clarinets and you pay four extra clarinettists and give seven violinists the day off because they have nothing to do – does not this mean that such an organization is completely absurd and out of date, given the work that is being done at present with different groupings? Yet that work is absolutely fundamental to any reorganization of our conception of music and of the education of violinists. A solo player, for instance, can be made to play quarter-tones or tune his instrument in different ways, but this will involve a great effort of control and a manual and mental re-education that cannot be undertaken from one day to the next: education of this kind is a long process. Musicians are, in practice, highly specialized workmen, and it will need much time and thought to train them in some other kind of specialization.

The search for new means of expression, even if it is only in the purely practical field, is a collective, not an individual undertaking. For, as you know, written music exists as a model, but not as a fact. I personally believe that in addition to the effort of the composer, who writes what he must and, with luck, hears what he hopes to hear, there is a mirror effect between what he composes and what he hears. What he hears can suggest to him what he has to create, and in the same way what he creates may suggest to him, in other words, something quite new. There is a perpetual contact, a perpetual exchange between him and his interpreters, and he should not be thought of as the maestro who invents everything.

I have spoken about instrumental problems because they are probably the most accessible, and many of you will certainly have studied an instrument and will have an idea of instrumental music, so that you will be immediately aware of the urgency of these problems. The existing means are years behind the times and at the present moment we can find no way of remedying this because we have never really faced the problem in its general aspect, though we are obliged daily to face its purely practical aspects. We must really give our minds to it if we are to change our point of view.

A lot has been talked about electro-acoustic and electronic music, an extremely important phenomenon of the present time, although it is treated automatically as a phenomenon of civilization: 'We have astronauts, we have rockets, we have motorways (yes, it boils down to that in the end) so we have to have electronic music.' In fact this is a much more important problem, because if it were simply a matter of linking astronauts or rockets to the problems of electronic music, it would be a fairly simple matter. There are always a few electronic *glissandos* in science-fiction films, enough to suggest the 'leap into the future'. They play, in fact, a pretty stupid role and one that is much too facile to be accepted as a role at all. The point of electronic and electro-acoustic devices is that they will expand our instrumental means.

At the present time there is no opposition between future and past, the natural and the artificial because – as I think I said earlier – language, whether musical or any other, is for me a convention – and any convention implies artificial means. If there in fact existed a naturally given truth, it would have been discovered for music and would be the same in all cultures, with the same intervals and the same methods of investigation. In actual fact, however, each culture has used the natural means that it found to hand and created a certain number of artificial means so disposed as to satisfy the aesthetic aims of that particular culture. That is why it is not possible to speak simply of the evolution of a technique hitherto used to obtain the sonorities obtainable from a vibrating object now that it is being transferred to obtaining from an electric vibrating phenomenon other sonorities, other sources of communication and other sound sources. For me, then, this is not a problem for the future, and I am anxious to make this clear because people generally envisage a kind of gap between the past and the future when an electro-acoustic instrument or electro-acoustic means are used. In fact it is only the expansion, possible at the present time, of a convention that may be called either artistic or artificial (the two are in fact identical) aimed at expanding the field of enquiry and the field of expression of the individual who creates musical objects.

That, I believe, is where all the misunderstandings start. Machines are very fascinating objects to those who work them – which is sometimes easier and sometimes more difficult than working with an instrument or so-called 'natural'-sounding object. One tends to be less demanding with machines, because the solutions they offer smack a little of science and definitive orthodoxy, and this seems at first sight satisfactory. If we look more closely, however, it soon becomes clear that electronic or electro-acoustic material involves exactly the same basic problem as we meet elsewhere – that of the *means* – 'Is this sound, or this sounding object [we speak of a sounding "body" in the same way as we speak of celestial "bodies"] adaptable to a musical idea?' That is the real heart of the problem. A really fundamental consideration of the matter will reveal that not only is there no difference in the size of the means of investigation, but there is also no basic difference in our approach to the musical object and its use. What electronic and electro-acoustic studies have always – and sometimes disastrously – lacked is an aesthetic standpoint, not from the angle of the composer (which is a later stage) but simply from the angle of the actual material itself. As I was saying just now, the abuse of percussion instruments is an error of aesthetic judgement, in judging the actual material; and in the same way it is an error of aesthetic judgement to make irrational use of electro-acoustic or electronic means.

It is a satisfying experience to discover sounds and sonorities and to transform them into something that has (quite literally) never been heard before, in a way that no instrument or combination of instruments can do and is possible only by electro-acoustic transformation of the sound source itself. Everyone is agreed on that point – that this method really does give us new sonorities, and that they must be capable of a dialectic of construction and musical composition.

In instrumental music we are also faced by the opposition between the individuality of the sounding body and the possibility of employing it in a composition. Though this may sound paradoxical, I will give you concrete examples. Composers are constantly faced with this problem – are we to aim at a maximum individualization of our sound sources, making a kind of sample book of sound objects carefully individualized, but in the last resort always recognizable? Or are we to adopt the opposite line and look for sound objects that can easily melt into each other and thus take their place in the composition? The same problem arises in painting and in audio-visual matters. In the case of mobile sculptures we are told that it will be 130 days, or even a year, before the same combination occurs again. You are obviously not going to spend a year watching the millions of combinations that occur before your original combination is repeated, because your imagination intuitively reconstitutes and analyses the whole process and reconstructs the whole family of objects that will present themselves to your vision. Exactly the same is true of music where, if you are presented with samples of objects, you have no need to hear all their possible combinations, because you can imagine them for yourself without too much trouble. It is very easy to suppose that recognition plays an extremely important role at that moment; if these objects are highly individualized, you recognize them, you are 'sensibilized' as you are for drawings of faces. If you see thirty people in five minutes, you will recognize their faces: and in the same way you will recognize these musical objects because they are extremely individualized and cannot be cast in different roles, as it were.

This brings me to another important problem that has been much discussed – I mean aleatory music. 'Aleatory' is a word that is frequently used, rightly or (more often) wrongly, when speaking of 'chance'. It means a directed, or controlled, chance, one that you have yourself chosen. For example, instead of a form that goes from A to B, you have one that goes from A to Z passing through a whole number of points that can be changed and structurally modified by you; so that whereas if you go from one point to another, there is only one path on the plan that is given you, you can now choose your own itinerary and make your own form. But to call this 'chance' is quite absurd, because chance – whether it is in the material used or the form that it is given – can give you only one satisfactory solution out of the 10 million that are possible; and this after all is not the object of composition.

What actually happens, for instance, when players are given vague diagrams? I have a lot of experience here, and I know that if you give them schemes or diagrams, or even a number of notes to arrange themselves, you can be quite sure that they will always produce clichés, contemporary clichés but clichés none the less. If the player were an inventor of forms or of primary musical material, he would be a composer. If he is not a composer, it is because he is by choice and capacity a performer; so that if you do not provide him with sufficient information to perform a work, what can he do? He can only turn to information that he has been given on some earlier occasion, in fact to what he has already played. Since he cannot play C, D, E, F, G, A, B, C, he plays something 'modern' that he has played before and attaches precise schemas to the vaguer ones he has been given. It is the same phenomenon of 'flight forwards', and an unreal problem.

In stating the problem of so-called 'chance' music, the material cannot be dictated by chance, because it is impossible to take the 10 million to one chance of success, of happening on some interesting combination. Everyone has been in a railway station or a law-courts waiting room. For the first ten minutes the noise of talking seems interesting, even exciting; but after that you would like the volume to change or people to talk more loudly in one corner. If you shut your eyes at a bullfight, all you hear is the noise of the crowd, and you can follow the fight simply by the noise people make. This gives you the dimension needed to see the work and the play of pure chance. You may find yourself in a corner and hear a simple conversation that may well be interesting, a phenomenon entirely due to artistic sense, but an organized phenomenon.

That is what is interesting about today's music – its lack of determinate form, the fact that it does not oblige you to select it but does oblige you to make your own selection of the form that you wish to give it. This is all within certain limits; when we say that a work is structured in such and such a way and can be played a hundred times, the same is true as what we said earlier about mechanical objects. No two solutions will ever actually be the same; it is a plural solution; a multiple phenomenon in which a path has always to be discovered. In fact no structure is sufficiently modifiable as to become unrecognizable; hence the many misunderstandings about aleatory music like the misunderstandings about electronic and instrumental music.

The trouble is that these problems are stated in far too simple terms and the different categories are far too naïve. For my own part I always consider a work as something essentially ambiguous – that may be a question of temperament or character, but I know that any picture that I have exhausted after three minutes' inspection I find unsatisfying. Similarly if the first hearing of a work gives me a shock, and that shock is repeated at a second hearing but is replaced by comprehension at a third hearing, that work does not interest me. It interests me *qua* shock and for the effect that it may have on me for a certain definite length of time. What really interests me (and it is there that actual form may give a work its maximum effectiveness) is a work that contains a strong element of ambiguity and therefore permits a number of different meanings and solutions. This profound ambiguity may be found in a great classical work, though there it is limited by precise length and basic structural data. Even so such a work does contain ambiguities in its deeper meaning and has many more meanings than the one revealed at a first hearing or a first performing.

On the other hand in today's music and today's means of expression it is possible to investigate this ambiguity, giving the work multiple meanings that the listener can discover for himself. In this way the listener – the person who reacts to the work – will assume an active role, selecting from it what suits him. Now you can understand why concerts in their present form absolutely contradict music as it is today. Contemporary music in fact demands the intelligent participation of the audience, which is 'making' the work at the same time as the author. You can understand a work only by passing through it and following its course with total, active, constructive attention; but our concert-hall arrangement, and indeed the whole character of our musical life, implies, as I have said, an attitude of worship, the proposing of an object to be adored or, if the worst comes to the worst, chewed over. Everyone is now, I think, aware of this, certainly all composers who take any part in musical life.

I believe that solutions to this problem can be found only in a common undertaking in which each individual will have his own part to play. I am quite clear in my mind that musicians by themselves cannot solve these problems, which are scientific, economic and sociological as well as musical; but they alone will be capable of determining the direction of any new discovery. It is essential that musicians should be at the centre of all these researches, but in fact the problems of past/future, instrumental means/electronic means, theatre/non-theatre, concert/non-concert are all typically unreal problems. They are flights, failures to synthesize, and nobody is to blame; it is simply that we have not yet learned how to make the necessary synthesis. Some twenty years ago we passed through a kind of narrows and it was fairly easy to grasp all the problems, but now that everyone is aware of these ideas, it is very hard to unite them all in a single person. For this reason I consider it quite indispensable that our approach should be highly disciplined and quite ruthless about the possibilities of music, rejecting absolutely all the easy options represented by ready-made or purely superficial solutions. This is why I believe that the time has now come to prepare this synthesis and to look to other methods, other means of investigation and other means of communication. Only in this way will music be able to progress.

54

The Bauhaus Model[1]

We can see for ourselves the enormous difference between musical life conceived as 'the retailing of masterpieces' and musical life linked to the lives of contemporary composers. The divergence between these two conceptions is such that the real concern of composers today is the problem of transmission; and this is so not only because of the failings of concerts as institutions but because we have no research organizations to explore the transformation of instruments, the nature of composition, the development of electronic techniques or the sociological implications of concert giving. We seem condemned to continue in the same old treadmill as long as we possess no specialized institution to study a number of fundamental problems.

I imagine that you are all familiar with the story of the Bauhaus, a quite exceptional institution whose existence was cut short by the advent of National Socialism. The Bauhaus exercised an enormous power of renewal in all the visual arts, starting of course with painting, since two outstanding painters – Klee and Kandinsky – attached themselves for a time to the institution and were joined by others of quite unusual gifts. But it was not only painting: the Bauhaus influenced architecture, the graphic arts, glass and furniture as well. We are still living today – and particularly in the graphic arts – on ideas systematically explored by a small group working in an institute in which research was carried on for its own sake.

At the present time performers and composers are educated separately, and whether they get their final diplomas or not neither emerge properly prepared for music in its present state. They find themselves obliged to make their way as best they can and under their own steam, both performer and composer having to find their feet in a world that is incapable of evolving because their education is supposed to have provided them with an equipment that will last them for life. This is totally mistaken, especially nowadays when we all have to be perpetually questioning our own skills and presup-

[1] 'Le modèle du Bauhaus' based on an interview with Maryvonne Kendergi (19 March 1970) published under the titles 'Pierre Boulez interrogé' in *Cahiers Canadiens de Musique*, Spring–Summer 1971, pp. 31–48. Rewritten by Boulez in 1980. See also p. 467.

positions and aware that the gap – or at least the lack of identity – between the demands of the present situation and our own contribution can grow only larger. This is in fact the explanation of the misunderstandings, the delays, the inertia and the impression of paralysis that we all perpetually experience in the functioning of our musical life. I therefore believe it essential to found an institute in which all these problems can be studied and analysed, one where there would be time for the unprejudiced consideration of even the most radical solutions.

Let me give you some examples. The great majority of the instruments in presentday use were conceived and constructed for the music of the eighteenth and nineteenth centuries. It is primarily economic considerations that make the whole world of instruments a stationary one: the market is very restricted and therefore conservative, linked almost exclusively to that of Louis-XV furniture! We should obviously interest makers of stringed and other instruments in the present situation and make them consider a number of modifications and even invent new solutions suited to contemporary techniques in the matter of scales and sonority. We are so tied to the semitone that we have nothing but meagre, makeshift resources when dealing with more delicate and variable scales. It would be the business of an institute such as I have in mind to consider this problem from an entirely unprejudiced point of view and one at which intellectual necessity takes priority over economic considerations.

Or take another example – the sociological aspect of concert giving. In the institute that I have in mind it would be possible to do research studies on the different kinds of audiences, on how to organize the actual space of concert halls in accordance with new demands, i.e. the relationship between the actual work, the performers and the public – on the place of concerts in the cultural life of today and hence on the methods of arousing the interest of different kinds of audience. These purely material problems of actually transmitting music would demand plenty of imagination and, subsequently, even more action. The need for such an institute would soon become apparent, because it would represent a common meeting place for the closed structures of musical education and the open world of musical life, a continuation from the point where a musician has completed his studies and is faced by the mobility and variety of actual musical experience. That is why I believe that any solution of today's problems must involve not only the reforming of our orchestras, the statutes governing our broadcasting services and the question of whether or not to accept the present system of state subventions. It must also involve the creation and promotion of research institutes quite independent of the official powers that hold music anchored, as it were, to routine.

I am also convinced that composition today presents problems that can really be solved only by teamwork. In the electronic field no one composer in isolation, working without any help from experts and associates, can decide satisfactorily such questions as the aesthetic suitability of different sound objects, the relation of technique to invention, the mutual dependence of structure and automation and the problems of transmission. Some individuals will always be more gifted than others, of course, but even they will be obliged to accept the discipline of a certain amount of teamwork. I believe that this is a fundamental change that we must learn to accept in future.

In these circumstances we shall have to consider the possibility of working with the firms that actually produce electronic equipment, without whose co-operation no research institute will be able to carry on specialist work for lack of the necessary materials. Finally, an institute of this kind should enjoy a total autonomy and a very flexible internal structure despite its many external links and ramifications. With no immediate obligations it should be able to manifest a true *disinterestedness* and pursue objectives unattainable by any organization too deeply engaged in 'mundane' matters.

55

Orchestras, Concert Halls, Repertory, Audiences[1]

In the transitional period in which we are living the traditional function of the orchestra is largely a thing of the past. The orchestra as we know it today still carries the imprint of the nineteenth century, which was itself a legacy from Court tradition.

What we have to face now are problems of multivalency. I believe that our aim should be polymorphous groupings; within the larger group formed by the orchestra we should make it possible to tackle all the different repertories – solo, chamber music, normal orchestra, very large formations and vocal ensembles of all dimensions. This would restore to the orchestra – which would in fact be a co-operative of performers – its sociological function, because it would include all the different sectors and in addition provide a certain mobility, an ability to move about. As things are at present, orchestras resemble spiders sitting at the centre of their webs, waiting for clients and pouncing on any that allow themselves to be caught. It is a case of 'if Mahomet will not go to the mountain, the mountain must come to Mahomet' and I am convinced that nowadays the mountain must indeed become mobile. I am only too aware that for this to happen faith is essential ... Even so we are approaching a point at which everything will have to be reconsidered in terms of mobile structures.

The conservative structure of our concert halls makes matters worse. The first thing that people did after the wholesale destructions of the war was to rebuild concert halls on the old plan. There may have been less plush and gold, but plywood, cement and nylon hardly made any change in the setting of concert halls, opera houses and theatres. If some exceptional 'object' was in fact built, it was little used or not used at all, as in the notorious case of the Mannheim theatre, built in the middle fifties according to Piscator's theories. This had a movable stage, which could be adapted to the Italian or Elizabethan model and also be transformed into a central arena. For a very short time after the theatre was first built these potentialities were

---

[1] 'Orchestre, salle, répertoire, public', another piece rewritten by Boulez from the interview (19 March 1970) with Maryvonne Kendergi. See note on p. 464.

exploited, but since then the old routine has prevailed because rapid changes of scene proved too difficult, too much effort to carry out.

There was another instance at Grenoble, where they built a superb arena in which concentric rings could move simultaneously in different directions and at different speeds. The comment of a member of one of the first audiences accurately summed up the result. After a series of these revolutions there was a moment's silence and a student, mimicking a child, called out, 'Just one more turn, Mummy!' He was absolutely right: the hall was just a toy and the spectator the captive of an object that functioned for its own astonishment; the performance became secondary and all the audience's attention was concentrated on the smooth functioning of the mechanism. It is no use building a hall as an eccentric object that obliges those who make use of it to accept ludicrously restrictive forms. The problem for the future is how to build adaptable halls in which that very adaptability does not impose restrictions.

Organizing the repertory? In the first place I do not use the word 'repertory' in the narrow sense of the conventional, existing repertory but in the widest possible acceptation of the word. The first essential is a maximum diversification of the fields of activity. As things are at present we suffer from a far too rigid framework and our idea of concerts resembles a plastic lunch – a roll, a slice of ham and an ice in a sterilized packing – your portion of dream, ready to take away. I am sure that this can be improved, if it is only by following the example of the visual arts. Some museums are devoted to preserving 'historic' works, others specialize in the twentieth century, while art galleries concern themselves with contemporary works and organize exhibitions of groups, individuals or 'retrospectives'.

Organizations of this kind prove that concerts too could be retrospective, perspective and prospective. Everyone should be given freedom of choice. As things stand, we are blocked by the way rehearsal times are arranged. These are insufficient because they lack flexibility and are not adapted to individual needs, with the result that any difficult, complex piece that needs maximum rehearsal has to be sandwiched between the most familiar repertory works. These will be read through at top speed, chiefly at the dress rehearsal, to ensure that everyone agrees on the conventional interpretation. People whose main interest is in the new piece have to listen once again to repertory works with which they are only too familiar, and the others, those who come to spend an hour of pleasant digestion, will be roughly disturbed from their nice little dreams by the sudden eruption of this horror that they are obliged to swallow. You think that you have struck a blow for contemporary music only to find that in the last resort you have done it the greatest disservice.

Is it possible that there is an element of snobbery in those who show an interest in new works? In any large town there will always be 200 genuine 'believers' who are relatively easy to discover, in fact only too easy in the case of events carrying a whiff of scandal. Starting with this nucleus, we have to create a wider public and continue to build up interest. It is not enough simply to arouse curiosity, we must know how to sustain it. This means perpetually sowing new seeds, of which fifteen will rot and one will bear fruit. Sow the fifteen: that is what you are there for.

What sometimes enrages me about those who cling obstinately and exclusively to the traditional repertory is their attitude to the masterpieces they are supposed to be so passionate about. Of course everyone is at liberty to listen to these as he likes, in the way that suits him. But I am quite certain that a little serious enquiry would reveal that the pleasure that many people get from listening to music is linked to a sterile nostalgia for the past, for a youth that is remote and irretrievably lost. At the root of this deliberate stagnation is a kind of physical process not difficult to analyse. Generally speaking, it is between the ages of 16 and 18 that people open their eyes to the world and, if they belong to a certain class, discover the arts – theatres, concerts, operas, exhibitions – and become aware of what is wrongly and possessively called their 'heritage'. At the same time their hormones are working with results that are familiar to every adolescent. It is a time of life that seems, in retrospect, happy. By association – almost by a Pavlovian reflex – when they listen to the music that they discovered and loved at the age of about 20, such listeners recall their youth when their hormones were more active. A plague on this sleepy audience that goes to concerts simply in order to relive a time when they were less sleepy!

That is very different from the way that I regard our musical 'heritage'. In the case of the most familiar works we have to bypass our memories and use our imaginations to discover new potentialities. Nothing is so frigid, so dull and so repugnant as to regard the masterpieces of the past as so many inert blocks congealed in the historical process. What interests and attracts – even fascinates me – as a performer is the incandescent glow of these masterpieces, a glow that can always be made to burst into flame again. There are some scores that awaken no response in me, and these I never conduct. If on the other hand a score arouses an echo in me and chimes in some way with my own musical interests, I unhesitatingly undertake to conduct it, in the belief that I shall be able to communicate what I have found in it. When I accepted an invitation to conduct *Parsifal* at Bayreuth, even the least prejudiced expressed surprise at my risking my neck in such a stronghold of German music. Meeting Wieland Wagner halfway, I thought that the most useful thing I could do was to achieve for the music of *Parsifal* what he had achieved for the production – namely, free it from the pompous and funereal ritual with which it had been weighed down. It used to be the correct thing to go into raptures about the 'wonderful chiaroscuro' of pictures that were in fact covered with a layer of bituminous dirt. When these pictures were cleaned and restored to their pristine condition, the astonishing brightness, even violence of the colours forced people entirely to revise their original ideas of the picture.

The same is true of music, where the first thing to be done with a masterpiece of the past is to clean away the accumulated dirt, which has been all too readily accepted.

56

Arousing Interest in New Music

It is difficult for an outsider to have any clear picture of exactly what is demanded of a musical director and of the qualities that he needs. His functions seem enigmatic, a mixture of dictatorial omnipotence and 'artistic' volatility, not to say inconsistency. He is a performer, but obliged to make choices involving more than those of a performer. He is not an administrator, but his projects implicitly require a good grasp of administration. When these projects are successful, they are taken more or less for granted as the results of a good general management. When they fail to achieve their expected results, this is explained directly by the personality of the director who initiated them. So true is this that it might be said of the musical director as used to be said about film music – good if unnoticeable. Should his object in fact be to remain anonymous?

Even after a first season with the New York Philharmonic – and particularly after that season – I do not think that is the answer. Nor am I revealing any major secret when I say that, even if he cannot hide behind anonymity, a musical director is not personally responsible for all the decisions taken in the course of a season, and there are quite a number of these – from altering the order of works in a programme to choosing an important new orchestral player. In the first case, of course, all that is needed is a simple exchange of views with the president and the performers concerned. But in recruiting a new member of the orchestra there is no doubt, as one of the players pointed out to me, that the director's choice implies a long-term view affecting more than his own term of office and also involving extremely important human factors. The same is true when it comes to deciding on programmes, when he must bear three different things in mind:

1 the subscription system, which must ensure a balance in the choice of different works and players
2 the organization of concerts and rehearsals according to a system laid

---

[1] 'Pour éveiller la curiosité de la nouvelle musique', *New York Times*, 6 August 1972, but here translated from the French text in *Points de repère*.

down by contract and necessarily implying clearly defined working methods

3 the relation of guest artists to the works in which they are invited to perform and the ensuring that their wishes and preferences can be observed throughout the whole season

Bearing this in mind we can hardly imagine the musical director making his decisions in a spirit of cynicism, aggressiveness or intolerance. Even if he wished to do so, it would be impossible. And in any case why should he wish to? Rather than being a manifestation of a desire for personal aggrandizement, his directives must show one overriding concern – ensuring vitality and movement in spite of being bound by restrictions that, although necessary, make for excessive stability and can lead to asphyxia.

It is quite clear that the times in which we live oblige us to reconsider all our means of expression, whether in music or any other field. Our philosophical concepts are changing, and so is our perception of the universe. Can there be any preserve in which all these enormous changes can be simply ignored? It sometimes looks as though we thought so. Probably from nostalgia, fear or sheer despair people often like to cherish the illusion that ART will be preserved from PROGRESS, hoping to preserve one inviolate, unassailable corner of paradise in an otherwise apocalyptic world. This is quite a normal reaction when faced with the unknown – even the hardiest explorers have had their moments of panic and second thoughts, and yet they have gone on under the stimulus of a force even stronger than fear – curiosity.

Why should we not arouse this curiosity in music too? And how is it to be done? Is there no hope of intolerance vanishing and being replaced by a common will to discover some new form of musical life and to share in it even more passionately than before? Before such an ideal can be realized there are many dilemmas to be resolved and many difficulties to be overcome. Why not face them and see what we can do here and now?

Let us start with the reactions of the ordinary listener, which vary between two extremes when faced with any difficulty – immediate rejection and what may be called 'positive doubt'. Everyone will remember the remark of the elderly Parisian figure at the first performance of *The Rite of Spring*: 'This is the first time in sixty years that anyone has dared to make fun of me.' Less familiar perhaps is a note in Delacroix's *Journal* after hearing a performance of one of Beethoven's last quartets in the 1860s, which ran roughly thus, 'It is the work of either a madman or a genius; in doubt my bet is genius.' Of course a chance to bet for genius or to feel floored by a new masterpiece does not occur every week, and we must feel able to count on doubt rather than intolerance in the case of works in which the fruits are no more than the promise of flowers, leaving aside any question of genius . . . Many suggestions have been put forward of how to break down the resistance of the public to twentieth-century composers, and the simplest of these can in fact be stated very simply: 'Perform good contemporary music and the public will follow.' This idyllic vision is not very well founded in historical fact, examples in its favour being outweighed by those that tell against it. And in any case, is the attitude of the public to contemporary works to be considered in isolation, or is it not simply part of a general attitude to music? I am not disputing the love of music, the preference for certain works or the pleasure obtained from them, nor do I think that masochism is ever demanded as a discipline essential for the appreciation of masterpieces – whether future, past or present. I even believe, despite what I am often supposed to believe, that musical satisfaction begins and ends with a satisfaction with the sheer richness and quality of the actual sound itself.

Between this beginning and this end there are a great many other sensations that make the end of a musical experience more interesting, more complete, more perfect than the beginning. What is important therefore is this persevering in musical expansion that enables us to appreciate works in all their fullness. For the same reason, too, it seems to me important to remove the ambiguity surrounding 'the public', which may suggest either a stable but conservative public or one that is adventurous but flighty. There are good reasons for establishing categories of this kind. There does in fact exist, quite apart from those who enjoy being lulled by the same memories, a sector of the public that has gradually acquired a deep musical culture and a knowledge that provides, as it were, an anchorage to which they have a good right. As against these, there are more adventurous spirits for whom music as such is less important, but who are quick to grasp correspondences between composition and painting or literature; such people are more immediately open to what is new, but less exclusive in their interests and quickly attracted to other fields. A synthesis of these two kinds of 'public' is surely exactly what we want to achieve, but the problem is how? The solution probably entails a great variety of musical activities. It could mean enormously enlarging the panorama presented during a concert season and making each individual *absolutely* conscious of the fact that music is not summed up in a number of masterpieces that become increasingly fossilized by interpretations immutably based on a single set of references.

Alban Berg gave a rather humorous answer to one enquiry: new music, he said, should be played as though it were classical, and classical music should be played as though it were new. This expresses the profound necessity of not seeing music as finally and absolutely stabilized in a series of *tableaux vivants*. (Why are they called 'vivants' in any case?) It also implies a reconsideration of what we generally mean by 'tradition'. The better one comes to know the problems of interpretation, the more aware one becomes of the ephemeral character of the models that have been established, which were essentially determined by their epoch. This is clear in the theatre, where the visual aspect of a play is so closely linked to the present day that it hardly survives more than a very few years. A cursory glance at any theatre or ballet album will reveal how much is ephemeral in the visual imagination of any age and the visual interpretation of any work. In the same way we can now compare recordings made over a period of some fifty years, which show very pointedly how interpretations vary not only according to the temperaments of performers but according to their date. I am not speaking simply of cases in which the progress of musicology has made it possible to achieve a greater authenticity. What I mean is the change in the general attitude to a composer according to which aspect of his music appeals most to the taste of the period. In this way we have heard Bach's music highly 'dramatized' and then reduced to the dry and rather trivial, while Mozart's, once presented as charming, is now tragic. There are innumerable instances of this, and all give the lie to the idea that there is any one, exclusive *tradition* that represents the single, eternal aspect of any masterpiece.

Would these same masterpieces indeed continue to arouse our interest unless they continued to express our subjective feelings? It is their adaptability that has kept them alive: they are like Hamlet's cloud, large enough to furnish our imaginations with innumerable starting points. As far as interpretation is concerned, we must of course maintain a high technical standard but should not be afraid of new ideas and attitudes even if we find their novelty disconcerting. This is probably what Alban Berg really meant. There is no doubt that listening at the same time to so-called classics and to contemporary works prevents *specialist* reactions, both in performers and listeners. It establishes fruitful exchanges between the two, and if this could become a permanent feature of our musical life – a steady alternation between discovering the new and renewing acquaintance with the old – there would be many fewer reservations.

As it is, performers have quite as many reservations as members of the public, not only about new works but about any interpretations that are not 'traditional'. Perhaps the reservations of the public are dictated by those of performers. Their origin is in any case the same – a fear of the unknown, a fear of losing something that has been acquired over the years. There are many instrumental players, and even more singers, who complain that contemporary music ruins their sound quality or their voices. New works certainly make great demands on those who perform them, but do they – in the best cases – demand much more than established works? As far as virtuosity goes, the difficulties can hardly be said to be greater since the physiological capabilities that composers have to bear in mind are limited, even if there is no limit to their own inventiveness. It is therefore a question of using different resources of the performer rather than actually stretching them beyond certain norms. It is a question of a different approach rather than of 'inhuman' difficulties. History is wholly reassuring on this point. Works that once seemed impossible to perform have only needed a period of adaptation and then come to seem natural until new works have appeared, which, in their turn, question the accepted traditions. Neither singers nor instrumental players have anything to lose by this constant exploration of their potential powers; they stand rather to gain by the enrichment of their repertory, whereas repeating the same repertory – even if they perfect their approach to it – restricts their potentialities, some of their powers simply atrophying like muscles that are not exercised.

And what is the place of composers in all this? We have said a great deal about audiences and performers, but seem to have forgotten them. They certainly present a problem for everyone, including themselves; they are neglected, but those who neglect them often have bad consciences, which are betrayed in aggressive form by blunt refusals or more timidly by weak excuses. Composers certainly do not have the best of it in their lifetimes, and even when they are dead they are often made use of for personal advantage. Is it composers who need rehabilitating, or perhaps composition itself? In fact neither is given much chance by our rigid organizations. A pre-established format, an inflexible rehearsal system and hurried working conditions do not exactly promote easy and agreeable relations between the composer and his eventual performers. Added to this is the indifference or hostility that he will encounter if he offends against the prevailing habits of thinking, performing or listening – in fact any of the norms governing his professional activity. Composers feel rejected, not only as people, but in their very function, which is so manifestly 'useless'. And so they tend to reject this whole world, to live within a closed circuit and to put all their confidence in organizations that show a more immediate understanding of their work, thus increasing the gulf between themselves and the public. This state of affairs has now been accepted – with resignation or fury – for a considerable time; but are we really to give up all hope and allow different bodies to continue specializing? To rely simply on goodwill will provide no solution of the problem, any more than the hard-and-fast separation of musical genres.

On the other hand we might be on the right road towards solving this problem if the relations between composer, performer and public were considered within a freer and more flexible organization, one less bound by formal constraints. As so often, the principle may be simple, but putting it into practice is quite another matter. Changing our attitudes is of course the most difficult part; a new frame of mind would automatically mean revising the way in which we organize our musical life. Any transition from one stage to another always needs a period of adaptation and that period might seem lengthy, but there would be no turning back once embarked on the new course. To put it in a nutshell, the ideal that we are pursuing is a greater variety in our approach to different audiences in a number of different contexts. What we are trying to escape from is the sterile standardization that imposes on the present – and indeed the future – norms suited to the past. We want the creative spirit to be re-established at every level of musical life.

History shows that evolution, however slow, is inevitable; but rather than allow it to take its course as passive spectators, oblivious or unobservant, we should play a conscious role. Our first task is to widen our horizon in the field that is already familiar to us – seeing works, even masterpieces, as mobile objects. We should be more concerned with what they suggest than with what they sum up and should look, even in the most universally accepted composers, for some feature particularly relevant to our own times. There is certainly more life, more joy and more excitement to be had from active listening of this kind than from passive, automatic absorption in a work. Furthermore, active listening and real participation of this kind in the case of a performer, will make us more curious about the future. Seeing the works of the past as monuments of man's restless desire to progress, to go beyond what has already been achieved and to discover new worlds, will make us less intolerant towards modern works and towards everything that makes our own epoch, like those of the past, an important moment in the history of music.

57

What's New?[1]

Does our musical life today pay enough attention to living composers, I mean anything comparable to that paid to new works in the theatre or to the many exhibitions of contemporary art in the picture galleries? The theatre, of course, is not bound by any cumbrous and expensive machinery subject to numerous restrictive regulations; and at that level experiment can be spontaneous, with no need to go through any organization. Painting, sculpture and the plastic arts in general are created by individuals and appreciated by individuals and therefore entail no major problems of presentation; and in addition to that, the financial speculation aroused by new works facilitates, if it does not actually cause their entering circulation. The same cannot be said of music, which cannot be presented so freely or independently, except in the case of electronic works. Far from being the object of commercial speculation, music has for many years involved formidable financial problems. It may be possible within a small group to count on goodwill and thus obtain the same atmosphere and the same liberty that is found in theatrical groups, but when it comes to large formations the case is different, since these inevitably involve quite complex organization; and in the case of opera the size and difficulty of these problems are considerably increased.

The situation with which we are faced is certainly a difficult one, but the difficulties are not insurmountable. The musical world in general, whether performers or members of the public, is more apt than any other group to rely on the visible advantages of convention. Music appears to be, and in fact is, a largely irrational phenomenon: musical communication has no verbal logic, scores are composed of cryptic signs that mean nothing to the vast majority of people, and the actual performance of music is becoming increasingly a specialized field. This being the case, it is easy to understand why most people surrender to the pleasures of a convention that they have gradually mastered and never think of broadening or superseding. It seems as though once having reached a certain stage of musical understanding

[1] 'Quoi de nouveau?', published in English in *Celebration of Contemporary Music*, programme of a week of contemporary music at the Juillard School of Music in New York (5–13 March 1976), but translated here from the French text in *Points de repère*.

determined by their education, people find that progressing beyond this stage requires an effort that is disproportionately great in relation both to what they have already achieved and to the rewards that they can expect from new discoveries. They therefore prefer to remain ignorant of contemporary music – and even less recent works – and obstinately take refuge in the illusion of a vanished Golden Age whose comfort and fascination they bitterly regret, though of course both are in fact illusory.

Whatever we may think of this very common attitude, the worst response to it on the part of the composer is to accept the role of *artiste maudit* and to form a kind of experimental ghetto, parodying the normal processes of publicizing music and addressing himself exclusively to a safe audience of already converted listeners. A small, deliberately closed world of this kind is of no real interest because it shirks the essential element of confrontation. For confrontation willed, provoked and accepted by the composer is the indispensable element that gives composition its fundamental *raison d'être*. We must never give in and simply follow the existing rules, which are not difficult to observe – each man for himself and God (in other words music) for all – but take action as direct as possible to transform those rules, which have often become nothing more nor less than the conventions of an established swindle. This means the composer losing in security what he gains in adventure. The liberalism of the society in which we live is a matter of common knowledge and generally regarded as a matter of congratulation . . . though there are a number of exceptions to this, since people's conceptions of what is meant by liberal are not necessarily the same. Our society therefore tolerates the most adventurous activities, at least in the field of the arts, because there subversion can easily be kept within bounds . . .

For this reason our musical society, properly so called, is quite prepared to have its jesters, as kings used to have, though they may arouse surprise rather than admiration: their role is an exceptional one and they are allowed freedom of speech as long as their relations with the rest of the world are governed by a strict unspoken code. After all, jesters cannot expect to enjoy royal powers. And so each of us has his place and there is no threat to the government – you have your audacious follies and I have the real artistic power. Considered in such terms as these musical life, and composition itself, would be a humiliating failure because all new experience would automatically be regarded as invalid. This is a state of mind that must be avoided at all costs, and we should guard against it by making the most established institutions equally responsible for the music of today as they are for the cultural heritage that is clearly entrusted to them.

That, you may say, amounts to the same thing as attempting to make circles concentric that can never be so, circles of interest that are by their very nature eccentric. This tendency to see the musical universe as one of concentric circles must be countered by an attitude that is sufficiently flexible and fluid to take divergencies into account and to organize that diversity. It is certainly possible to integrate contemporary music in any musical life that is not excessively partitioned; but to do this effectively all our musical institutions must be reconsidered, not only in their functioning (which would be comparatively easy) but in their very essence, something much more difficult to achieve. Until comparatively recently to organize concerts with programmes of contemporary works was enough to give an air of modernity to musical life; the idea and function of concerts were no more questioned than was hanging pictures in a gallery, as the only means of exhibiting them. Recent developments have made it impossible to go on accepting these convenient notions; many things hitherto accepted as natural now seem dated and everything is called in question – the actual nature of a work, its presentation, the method of communicating with the public and the approach of performers. This universal questioning is sometimes chaotic and its object may seem vague, but never mind. We shall find ourselves increasingly discontented with concerts, as a well-meaning form of communication that we have in fact inherited from the late nineteenth century. Why should we not try to foresee the situation in the future and forestall the growing divergences between the disruptive forces and the comfortable, lazy routine that exists at present?

There is no doubt that our musical enterprises lack flexibility, and their rigid organization prevents any free expanding of the musical field, which ought to combine unity with diversity. How then should we ideally organize that field, so as to take into account musical life as it actually is today, and do it justice? First, I think, we should realize that all musical functions are inseparable and interchangeable, execution being only one part, however important, of a field in which other tasks are also capital. Execution, research, experiment, propaganda and teaching should all radiate from a single central point. Every musician should be able to pass from one of these activities to another in accordance with his own personal engagements and thus lead a varied and free-ranging life. I personally think of all these different branches of musical activity as essential to any musician anxious to get away from the routine of the past and to avoid specialization, which represents a threat to the individual by its limited character – any musician, in fact, anxious to take part in a real musical culture rather than to be simply a cog in a machine that is cultural only in name.

Isolated individuals do of course pass from one field of activity to another – from research to performance, for instance, and from teaching to propaganda – and much of their energy is expended on moving from one institution to another and trying to avoid wasting their time in occupations that are bound to overlap each other. Such people appear as eccentric idealists in institutions whose aims and methods are too narrowly defined. Education, for instance, is for the most part obstinately separated from research and experiment and concentrated on handing down a clearly defined heritage, on 'forming' a student for life, rather than instilling in him a sense of the transitory and ephemeral and of the irresistible pressure of evolution. Such an education seems to me to be a deflection from what should be its fundamental purpose and may even become a counter-education, producing specialists of limited powers, manifestly warped in their reactions and likely to become essentially sterile. On the other hand, if research and experiment are carried out as it were behind locked doors, and without the communication that only teaching and propaganda can give, research and experiment themselves become, if not sterile, at least overprotected, pleading their absolute necessity in a spirit of false martyrdom, whereas organized confrontation is beyond any doubt the only form that benefits from live and genuinely productive exchanges.

I obviously have not space to describe in detail the steps necessary to release or to precipitate this essential evolution. I will say only that all the necessary conditions exist, chief among them being the state of uncertainty that is to be found at the heart of most of our present societies. Uncertainty of this kind is by no means always negative, since it forces us, both individually and collectively, to ask ourselves a number of fundamental questions about our cultural heritage and our cultural ideology. We should not complain too much about our problems: how dull life would be without them! The word 'crisis' is too often used for situations that are no more than necessary and inevitable transitional stages. Taking the long view simply means regarding our present situation as a link in the process of evolution; and if we identify past attitudes and their results, we must also clearly analyse what is obsolete and transitory about them. Only thus shall we be able to see the gradual emergence of those new lines of conduct and new lines of force that some of us welcome so gladly and others reject so timorously. The history of music, as of anything else, is made *of* individuals *for* individuals: it exalts them as much as it crushes them beneath its weight as it progresses towards an absolute future, even though it means passing through our present state of uncertainty. We can at least make up our minds not to be crushed *for nothing*!

Postscript

I realize that I have not mentioned Europe or America, and the fact is that geography, so to speak, seems to me of little importance. I would no more think of denying the occasional need for solidarity within an ethnic group than I would of concealing the fact that I regard this as something narrowly confined to local and temporary conditions. In our day, and in the field of music proper, this does not seem to me an urgent matter. I believe that the characteristics of individuals, regardless of their geographical situation, are far more important: and perhaps I should add that cosmopolitanism has never seemed to me a sin.

58

Freeing Music[1]

Every truly creative artist is always consciously or instinctively guided by one overriding idea that directs his work. During the course of his life he may give the impression of changing direction, of hesitating and even of going back on that idea. But behind those appearances we shall always find the same motive and the same theme, which is identical with the man himself.

In my own case that idea has been breaking down the wall – or rather the series of walls – that separate the artist from the public; this has been true ever since I became aware of the existence of the wall. Dividing life into watertight compartments means certain death, as I see it: interpenetration is essential to effectiveness of any kind. We need today to achieve more fluid relations between our various activities, and this means that the watertight compartments in which we have kept chamber music, symphonic music, opera house and concert hall – each with its own equally watertight public – must be broken down if music is to be made free and available to the majority.

What I want to do is to change people's attitude. They have inherited their tastes from the past and look only to the past – to museums, as it were – for their music, while all the time there is live, living music in the world around them. My aim is to promote in every field the ideas of today. We cannot spend our whole lives in the shadow of the huge tree of the past. People nowadays have developed a kind of defence mechanism and are more interested in preserving than creating, like the Romans in the third and fourth centuries. No generation that fails to question the achievements of the past has a hope of achieving its own potential or exploiting its vital energies to the full.

In the past some of my quips have caused surprise – when, for instance, I suggested that it was not enough to add a moustache to the *Mona Lisa*: it should simply be destroyed. All I meant was just to urge the public to grow up and once for all to cut the umbilical cord attaching it to the past. The artists I admire – Beethoven, Wagner, Debussy, Berlioz – have not followed

---

[1] 'Libérer la musique', *Preuves*, second series 1972, pp. 133–8.

tradition but have been able to force tradition to follow them. We need to restore the spirit of irreverence in music.

I am looking for new ways of promoting new music, and this explains what I have been doing for the last few years. When I accepted the musical direction of two orchestras simultaneously, the New York Philharmonic and the BBC Symphony, I was bombarded by a host of malicious questions and insinuations: 'So, you've stopped composing and come down to conducting – back with the Establishment in fact? Is that where a quarter of a century of fire-eating has brought you? What's happened to Boulez the Robespierre of the 1960s?' And so on.

I like being attacked: it is invigorating and forces one to be absolutely honest both with oneself and with other people. I think of myself as a gardener rather than as a woodsman: if I sometimes use an axe, it is only to cut out dead wood and give a tree a better chance of surviving. Christ said, 'I came not to send peace, but a sword' but since I am not Christ I prefer Brecht, who laughed at people who ensured theatre audiences their daily bread.

Only a quarter of a century's fighting will make it clear to a man that to have achieved something as a start, however modest, is better than a whole lifetime of rejection. I am 46 and the time has come when I ask myself, 'What offers me most chance of achieving my aims? I need to communicate and to act: who will give me the opportunity to do both?' Must I go on barking at the moon, or is it more sense to put my trust in the musical world and establish my professional reputation in such a way that I shall be given an opportunity to take real action? Faced with the famous choice between changing things by a hypothetical revolution in some vague future and trying to modify them here and now from inside, by influencing existing organizations, I chose the second.

I had been hoping for years for the post of musical director, something more far-reaching than that of conductor and this has now been offered me. I am now in a position to attack the rigidity of musical life, and I am busy developing an audience for contemporary composers. This cannot be done overnight in the 'protectionist' climate of our musical life, which has hitherto been restricted to specialists.

People have turned to me in the hope that I would develop a new general line. As far as programmes go, I have introduced two important innovations. In the first place I am trying to encourage listeners to have their own, personal point of view about works by taking, for example, Stravinsky's evolution over a period of ten years and constructing programmes of the most representative works within that period. The listener is puzzled and wonders why two particular works have been placed next each other. In this way he can begin to grasp how the composer evolved instead of listening passively to a succession of apparently unrelated works.

Every year I arrange two complete 'retrospectives', as is done for painters

– one a twentieth-century classic, such as Berg, and the other a composer of the past either forgotten or little played, such as Haydn, a number of whose neglected works – such as the Masses and operas – I gave in London. I am trying at the same time to promote chamber music (bearing in mind no less the diversifying of the orchestra's activities and attracting different sections of the musical public, which have hitherto been 'compartmentalized'). In London and New York, for instance, some of the big orchestral concerts have been preceded by half an hour of chamber music related to the main programme of the evening.

Another thing that I have tried is going out to meet the public, not confining music to the conventional concert halls. In London I have had regular audiences of a thousand at the Round House, which normally attracts members of the theatrical avant-garde and the National Film Society, a younger audience than is to be found at concerts. There is of course a marked division between the Establishment and the inverted snobbery of 'unattached' intellectuals, who refuse to go to 'official' places where they find the atmosphere too thick for them. These people are much more interested in the theatre and the cinema than in music, and it is quite a challenge to undertake their conversion.

I have tried the same thing on several occasions in New York and taken my players dressed in mufti, with conductors like Bruno Maderna and Michael Gielen, to play and explain new music to young audiences in Greenwich Village. On these occasions the audience falls into groups round the players and performances are preceded by talks, often given by the composers themselves. Works are generally played twice and then there is a quite lively discussion. George Crumb, Charles Wuorinen, Eric Salzman and Earle Brown have all appeared on such occasions, when the audience consists of artists, students and people who are simply curious. In this way we hope to revitalize one public by another and to re-establish the circulation between the two. Thus BBC2 is broadcasting at 8.30 on Sunday evenings talks on Varèse, Bartók, Berg and myself with graphic as well as musical examples. By 1974, when my present contracts come to an end, I hope that contacts of this kind will have become permanent, that the orchestral players will have become used to a much wider repertory, that contemporary music will have gained a much more broadly based public and that the distrust between professional players and the avant-garde will have disappeared. This is vital if music is to survive.

I sometimes hear savage attacks on contemporary music, as though it had come to a halt in a kind of cul-de-sac. 'You yourself have stopped composing,' people say. In my own case my work during the last ten years in Germany, at Cleveland and elsewhere has certainly not favoured composing because I have been perpetually on the move; but I have after all written works like *Eclat* (1965) and *Domaines*, both played in London and Paris; and at present I am working on a piece for chorus and orchestra. No, music is not in a state of collapse. It is our vision of music that has changed with the appearance of new means of expression, electronic and others. Technical developments and freedom from tradition have between them brought an almost embarrassing abundance of new possibilities and an explosion of the language that obliges the composer to rethink all his categories, including the whole conception of 'concerts'. The divisions that once existed between the different genres have disappeared, leaving the composer with a virtually unlimited freedom, which he finds confusing.

In music, as in architecture, new materials necessitate new structures. At first cement was used to imitate stone, but the new material proved too strong to be treated traditionally. In music, too, we shall have to discover a system of expression suited to the new material. Since concert halls alone can provide listeners with the excitement of coming into direct contact with music, their design will have to be altered, including the seating of orchestra and audience. Hitherto music has been 'contemplated', like a picture. Now we must adopt flexible methods of presentation, as museums do, in order to ensure that each work has the benefit of an individual presentation. Concert halls will of course have to be based on acoustic considerations, but they must include adaptable features.

I have accepted in principle the directorship of the centre for acoustic research planned at Beaubourg, in Paris, purely in order to attempt a radical reconsideration of the world of music as it now stands. Those who believe that I am prejudiced against Paris and against working in France are mistaken. What I cannot tolerate is the mediocrity of narrow-minded and incompetent officialdom wasting money and blandly proclaiming that everything in the garden is lovely. In three years' time the Beaubourg experimental centre will be examining all the possibilities in the instrumental and electronic fields. We shall aim at a permanent alliance of musicians and scientists such as exists in a number of American universities. My object is to create an organization modelled on the Max Planck scientific institutes in Germany, based entirely on the principle of research.

The present musical crisis is due to the fact that our ideas are more advanced than the sound material required to realize them. We need on the one hand to explore the vast number of new technical resources and on the other – taking into account the greater contact between the composer and the public – to sharpen the listener's critical faculties and stimulate his interest by allowing complete freedom of reaction. Musical education is unsatisfactory in every country in the world, containing no live element and no permanent link between theory and practice, whether contemporary or not. Composition will be promoted by establishing a lasting exchange between composers and the public, the lack of this exchange being one of my chief complaints. Composers must be made aware of the extent of the new sound resources and the public must be given a sense of responsibility and a taste for exercising it.

I have great hopes for the future of some kind of alliance between music and the theatre. I once said that the most elegant solution of the problem of opera was to blow up the opera houses, and I still think this true. Opera is the area before all others in which things have stood still. Yet I have been willing to conduct certain operas under certain conditions – *Parsifal* at Bayreuth, *Pelléas* in London, and *Wozzeck* in Paris and Frankfurt. As I see it, *Wozzeck* is the last 'opera', extending and completing the traditional form. With *Parsifal* I had the delight of working in the only opera house in the world where the actual building has been intelligently taken into account, and in collaboration with Wieland Wagner, a figure of outstanding importance responsible for the destruction of an obsolete mythology. (I never declared, by the way, that I would never conduct Wagner, as I am supposed to have done.)

Conducting *Pelléas* gave me a chance to get away from the so-called 'traditional' interpretation, which I found impossibly sentimental. I was able to choose my singers and to discuss the whole stage presentation of the work. A musical director's responsibilities are not confined to the orchestral pit. Moreover I have quite unorthodox ideas about the relationship between a work and those who perform it. Reconstituting the past is a snare and delusion. What matters to me is what a work means today, its validity for the present; and I go back to the text in the light of the present day without worrying myself about the accretion of mannerisms from the past.

I think that certain dance companies are now more advanced than the opera, because they are less stifled by rigid protocol. They are certainly pointing the way towards the theatre of the future. A collaboration with a Maurice Béjart or a Peter Brook might enable us together to cut a path leading to new theatrical forms. But we must begin at the beginning, which means taking two singers and ten players into a barn and working out a new style for a new musical form. The studio idea, as used by Peter Brook with actors, is important because it is a way of getting to know the tools with which one has to work and how to use them, before embarking on large-scale undertakings. As things are, one is paralysed by the scale on which opera houses are built, the conditions they impose and their lack of flexibility.

What chiefly interests me is communication; and we need first to experiment on a small scale with different means, since music is unquestionably becoming multifunctional, with performers always able to diversify their work. Thus an orchestral musician may spend one month with a big orchestra, the next on a research experiment, then return for some weeks to his original job and so on. It is only by this continuous search for flexibility that we shall achieve that interpenetration essential to any real effectiveness.

59

Technology and the Composer[1]

Invention in music is often subject to prohibitions and taboos which it would be dangerous to transgress. Invention must remain the private, exclusive property of genius, or at least of talent. Indeed it is hard to find any purely rational explanation for it; by summoning up unpredictable results out of nothing it escapes analysis. But is this nothing really the total void appropriate to miracle-workers? And does the unpredictable come to exist in a totally unpredicted context? Invention cannot exist in the abstract, it originates in contact with music of the past, be it only the recent past; it exists through reflection on its direct or indirect antecedents. Such reflection concentrates naturally on the spiritual approach, the mental mechanisms and the intellectual development displayed by the work it takes as models, but it concentrates also on the sound material itself, without whose support music cannot exist; musical material has evolved over the centuries, providing for each age a typical sound profile that is continually renewed – slowly perhaps, but inevitably.

Yet invention is today faced with a number of problems particularly concerned with the relation between the conception, we might even say the vision, of the composer and the realization in sound of his ideas. For some time now, the composer's mental approach, his 'wild' invention, has been free to follow very different paths from those that the medium, the sound material, can offer him. This divergence has caused blockages dangerous enough for invention to lose all its spontaneity; when either the material or the idea develops independently, unconcerned whether or not they coincide, a serious imbalance develops, to the detriment of the work, which is tugged this way and that between false priorities. Underlying these blockages there are undoubtedly causes that are beyond the composer's power and over which he has little control, but of which he is – or should be – aware if he is to try to overcome them.

We think at once of blockages of a social kind. Since at least the beginning

[1] *The Times Literary Supplement*, 6 May 1977. Original French text in *Passage du XXᵉ siècle*, *Iᵉ partie*, January/July 1977 (Paris, IRCAM) under the title 'Invention/Recherche'.

of this century, our culture has been orientated towards historicism and conservation. As though by a defensive reflex, the greater and more powerful our technological progress, the more timidly has our culture retracted to what it sees as the immutable and imperishable values of the past. And since a larger – though still limited – section of society has easier access to musical culture, having more leisure and spending power, and since modes of transmission have increased enormously and at the same time are cheaper, the consumption of music has considerably increased. This leads to a growing boredom with pieces that are frequently heard and repeated, and to search for an alternative repertory – one within the same radius of action as the well-known works and providing a series of substitutes for them. Only too rarely does it lead to a genuine broadening of the repertory by giving fresh life to works that have become the exclusive property of libraries. The search for historical peculiarities of interpretation also serves to divert energies that are all too likely to be swallowed up by it. Thus the 'museum' has become the centre of musical life, together with the almost obsessive preoccupation with reproducing as faithfully as possible all the conditions of the past. This exclusive historicism is a revealing symptom of the dangers a culture runs when it confesses its own poverty so openly: it is engaged not in making models, nor in destroying them in order to create fresh ones, but in reconstructing them and venerating them like totems, as symbols of a golden age that has been totally abolished.

Among other consequences, a historicizing culture has almost completely blocked the evolution of musical instruments, which have come to a disastrous halt for both social and economic reasons. The great channels of musical consumption which exploit, almost exclusively, the works of the past consequently use the means of transmission appropriate to the past, when they were at their most effective. It is hardly necessary to add that this state of affairs is faithfully reflected in education, where the models selected for teaching are drawn from an extremely circumscribed period in the history of music, and consequently limit – from the outset – the techniques and sound material at the musician's disposal; even more disastrously, they give him a restricted outlook whereby his education becomes a definitive, absolute possession. The makers of musical instruments, having no vocation for economic suicide, meet the narrow demands made on them; they are interested only in fiddling about with established models and so lose all chance of inventing or transforming. Wherever there is an active market, in which economic demand has free play – in a field like pop music where there are no historical constraints – they become interested, like their colleagues who design cars or household appliances, in developing prototypes, which they then transform, often in quite minimal ways, in order to find new markets or unexploited outlets. Compared with these highly prosperous economic circuits, those of so-called serious music are obviously impoverished, their hopes of profit are decidedly slender and any interest in improving them is very limited. Thus two factors combine to paralyse the material evolution of the contemporary musical world, causing it to stagnate within territory conquered and explored by other musical periods for their own and not necessarily our needs – the minimal extension of contemporary resources is thus restricted to details. Our civilization sees itself too smugly in the mirror of history; it is no longer creating the needs that would make renewal an economic necessity.

In another sector of musical life that has little or no communication with the 'historical' sect, the musical material itself has led a life of its own for the past thirty years or so, more or less independent from invention: out of revenge for its neglect and stagnation, it has formed itself into a surplus, and one wonders at times how it can be utilized. Its urgency expresses itself even before it is integrated into a theme, or into a true musical invention. The fact is that these technological researches have often been carried out by the scientifically minded, who are admittedly interested in music but who stand outside the conventional circuit of musical education and culture. There is a very obvious conjunction here between the economic processes of a society that perpetually demands that the technology depending on it should evolve, and that devotes itself notoriously to the aims of storage and conservation, and the fall-out from technology, which is capable of being used for sometimes surprising ends, very different and remote from the original research. The economic processes have been set to produce their maximum yield where the reproduction of existing music, accepted as part of our famous cultural heritage, is concerned; they have reduced the tendency to monopoly and the rigid supremacy of this heritage by a more and more refined and accessible technology.

Techniques of recording, backing, transmission, reproduction – microphones, loudspeakers, amplifying equipment, magnetic tape – have been developed to the point where they have betrayed their primary objective, which was faithful reproduction. More and more the so-called techniques of reproduction are acquiring an irrepressible tendency to become autonomous and to impress their own image of existing music, and less and less concerned to reproduce as faithfully as possible the conditions of direct audition; it is easy to justify the refusal to be faithful to an unrecorded reality by arguing that *trompe-l'oeil* reproduction, as it were, has little meaning given that the conditions of listening and its objectives are of a different order, that consequently they demand different criteria of perception. This, transposed into musical terms, is the familiar controversy about books and films on art: why give a false notion of a painting in relation to the original by paying exaggerated attention to detail, by controlling the lighting in an unusual way, or by introducing movement into a static world? Whatever we make of this powerful tendency towards technological autonomy in the world of sound reproduction, and whatever its motives or its justifications, one sees how rapidly the resources involved are changing, subject as they are to an inexorable law of movement and evolution under the ceaseless pressure of the market.

Aware of these forms of progress and investigation, and faced at the same time by stagnation in the world of musical instruments, the adventurous musical spirits have thought of turning the situation to their own advantage. Through an intuition that is both sure and unsure – sure of its direction, but unsure of its outcome – they have assumed that modern technology might be used in the search for a new instrumentation. The direction and significance of this exploration did not emerge until long after the need for it arose: irrational necessity preceded aesthetic reflection, the latter even being thought superfluous and likely to hamper any free development. The methods adopted were the outcome either of a genuine change of function, or of an adaptation, or of a distortion of function. Oscillators, amplifiers, and computers were not invented in order to create music; however, and particularly in the case of the computer, their functions are so easily generalized, so eminently transformable, that there has been a wish to devise different objectives from the direct one: accidental conjunction will create a mutation. The new sound material has come upon unsuspected possibilities, by no means purely by chance but at least by guided extrapolation, and has tended to proliferate on its own; so rich in possibilities is it that sometimes mental categories have yet to be created in order to use them. To musicians accustomed to a precise demarcation, to a controlled hierarchy and to the codes of a convention consolidated over the centuries, the new material has proposed a mass of unclassified solutions, and offered us every kind of structure without any perspective, so affording us a glimpse of its immense potential without guidance as to which methods we should follow.

So we stand at the crossroads of two somewhat divergent paths: on the one hand, a conservative historicism, which, if it does not altogether block invention, clearly diminishes it by providing none of the new material it needs for expression, or indeed for regeneration. Instead, it creates bottlenecks, and impedes the circuit running from composer to interpreter, or, more generally, that from idea to material, from functioning productively; for all practical purposes, it divides the reciprocal action of these two poles of creation. On the other hand, we have a progressive technology whose force of expression and development are sidetracked into a proliferation of material means which may or may not be in accord with genuine musical thought – for this tends by nature to be independent, to the detriment of the overall cohesion of the sound world. (Having said which, one should note that long before contemporary technology, the history of musical instruments was littered with corpses: superfluous or over-complicated inventions, incapable of being integrated into the context demanded by the musical ideas of the age that produced them; because there was no balance between originality and necessity they fell into disuse.)

Thus inventors, engineers and technicians have gone in search of new processes according to their personal preferences, choosing this one or that purely by whim, and for fortuitous rather than for musically determined reasons – unless their reasons stemmed from their more exclusively scientific preoccupations. But musicians, on the whole, have felt repelled by the technical and the scientific, their education and culture having in no way given them the agility or even the readiness to tackle problems of this kind. Their most immediate and summary reaction, therefore, is to choose from the samples available, or to make do at a level easily accessible to manipulation. Few have the courage or the means directly to confront the arid, arduous problems, often lacking any easy solution, posed by contemporary technology and its rapid development. Rather than ask themselves the double question, both functional and fundamental, whether the material is adequate to the idea and the idea compatible with the material, they give way to the dangerous temptation of a superficial, simple question: does the material satisfy my immediate needs? Such a hasty choice, detached from all but the most servile functions, certainly cannot lead far, for it excludes all genuine dialectic and assumes that invention can divorce itself from the material, that intellectual schemas can exist without the support of sound. This does not even apply to the music of the past, which was not, properly speaking, written for specified instruments, for its writing assumes absolutely the notion of the instrument, even of the monodic instrument within a fixed and limited register. If invention is uninterested in the essential function of the musical material, if it restricts itself to criteria of temporary interest, of fortuitous and fleeting coincidences, it cannot exist or progress organically; it utilizes immediate discoveries, uses them up, in the literal sense of the term, exhausting them without really having explored or exploited them. Invention thereby condemns itself to die like the seasons.

Collaboration between scientists and musicians – to stick to those two generic terms which naturally include a large number of more specialized categories – is therefore a necessity that, seen from outside, does not appear to be inevitable. An immediate reaction might be that musical invention can have no need of a corresponding technology; many representatives of the scientific world see nothing wrong with this and justify their apprehensions by the fact that artist creation is specifically the domain of intuition, of the irrational. They doubt whether this utopian marriage of fire and water would be likely to produce anything valid. If mystery is involved, it should remain a mystery: any investigation, any search for a meeting point is easily taken to be sacrilege. Uncertain just what it is that musicians are demanding from them, and what possible terrain there might be for joint efforts, many scientists opt out in advance, seeing only the absurdity of the situation: that is, a mage reduced to begging for help from a plumber! If, in addition, the mage imagines that the plumber's services are all that he needs, then confusion is total. It is easy to see how hard it will be ever to establish a common language for both technological and musical invention.

In the end, musical invention will have somehow to learn the language of technology, and even to appropriate it. The full arsenal of technology will elude the musician, admittedly; it exceeds, often by a big margin, his ability to specialize; yet he is in a position to assimilate its fundamental procedures, to see how it functions and according to which conceptual schemes – how far, in fact, it might or might not coincide with the workings of musical creation and how it could reinforce them. Invention should not be satisfied with a raw material come upon by chance, even it can profit from such accidents and, in exceptional circumstances, enlarge on them. To return to the famous comparison, the umbrella and the sewing machine cannot create the event by themselves – it needs the dissecting table too. In other words, musical invention must bring about the creation of the musical material it needs; by its efforts, it will provide the necessary impulse for technology to respond functionally to its desires and imagination. This process will need to be flexible enough to avoid the extreme rigidity and impoverishment of an excessive determinism and to encompass the accidental or unforeseen, which it must be ready later to integrate into a larger and richer conception. The long-term preparation of research and the instantaneous discovery must not be mutually exclusive, they must affirm the reciprocity of their respective spheres of action.

One can draw a parallel with the familiar world of musical instruments. When a composer learns orchestration, he is not asked to have either a practical, a technical or a scientific knowledge of all the instruments currently at our disposal. In other words, he is not expected to learn to play every one of these instruments, even if out of personal curiosity he may familiarize himself with one or other of them and even become a virtuoso. Furthermore, he is not expected to learn how the instruments were made, how they reached their present stage of development, by what means and along which path their history has evolved so that certain of their specific possibilities were stressed to the neglect of others; here too the composer can study and reflect on whichever aspect is particularly important to him – it remains his personal choice. Still less is the composer expected to learn the acoustic structure of the sounds produced by a particular family of instruments; his curiosity or his general, extra-musical education may lead him to concern himself with these problems in so far as scientific analysis can confirm his impressions as a musician. He may have none of this literal knowledge, yet nothing in the functioning of an instrument, either practical, technical or scientific, should be beyond his understanding. His apprenticeship is in a sense not a real but a virtual one. He will know what is possible with an instrument, what it would be absurd to demand of it, what is simple and what is out of the question, its lightness or its heaviness, its ease of articulation or difficulty in sound production in various registers, the quality of the timbre, all the modifications that can be made either through technique itself or with the aid of such devices as the mute, the weight of each instrument, its relationship with the others; all these are things that he will verify in practice, his imagination abandoning itself to the delights of extrapolation. The gift lies in the grafting of intuition on to the data he has acquired. A virtual knowledge of the entire instrumental field will enable him to integrate into his musical invention, even before he actually composes, its vast hidden resources; that knowledge forms a part of his invention.

Thus a virtual understanding of contemporary technology ought to form part of the musician's invention; otherwise, scientists, technicians and musicians will rub shoulders and even help one another, but their activities will be only marginal one to the other. Our grand design today, therefore, is to prepare the way for their integration and, through an increasingly pertinent dialogue, to reach a common language that would take account of the imperatives of musical invention and the priorities of technology. This dialogue will be based as much on the sound material as on concepts.

Where the material is concerned, such a dialogue seems possible here and now: it offers an immediate interest and is far from presenting any insurmountable difficulties. From our education within a traditional culture we have learned and experienced how instrumental models function and what they are capable of. But in the field of electronics and computers – the instrument that would be directly involved – models do not exist, or only sporadically, and largely thanks to our imagination. Lacking sound schemes to follow, the new field seems exaggeratedly vast, chaotic, and if not inorganic at least unorganized. The quite natural temptation is to approach this new field with our tried and tested methods and to apply the grid of familiar categories to an unexplored domain – categories that would seem to make the task easier and to which, for that reason, we would like to resort unthinkingly. The existing categories could, it is true, be helpful at first in mapping out virgin territory and enabling us, by reconstitution and synthesis, better to know the natural world, which we think we know so well and which, the nearer we get to it, seems to elude the precision of our investigation. It is not only the question 'what is a sound made of?' that we have to answer, but the much harder one of 'how do we perceive this sound in relation to its constituent elements?' So by juxtaposing what is known with what is not known, and what is possible with what will be possible, we shall establish a geography of the sound universe, so establishing the continuity of continents where up until now many unknown territories have been discerned.

It goes without saying that the reasoned extension of the material will inspire new modes of thought; between thought and material a very complex game of mirrors is set up, by which images are relayed continuously from one to the other. A forceful, demanding idea tends to create its own material, and in the same way new material inevitably involves a recasting of the idea. We might compare this with architecture, where structural limitations have been radically changed by the use of new materials such as concrete, glass, and steel. Stylistic change did not happen overnight; there were frequent hesitations and references back to the past – to ennoble, as it were, these architectural upstarts. New possibilities triumphed over imitation and transformed architectural invention and concepts from top to bottom. These concepts had to rely much more than before on technology, with technical calculations intervening even in aesthetic choices, and engineers and architects were obliged to find a common language – which we are now about to set off to look for in the world of music.

If the choice of material proves to be the chief determinant in the development of creative ideas, this is not to say that ideas should be left to proceed on their own, nor that a change of material will automatically entail a revision of concepts relating to musical invention. Undoubtedly, as in the case of architecture, there will be caprices and hesitations, and an irrepressible desire to apply old concepts to the new material, in order to achieve – perhaps *ad absurdo?* – a kind of verification. But if we wish to pass beyond these immediate temptations, we shall have to strive to think in new categories, to change not only the methods but the very aim of creation. It is surprising that in the musical developments of the past sixty years many stylistic attitudes have been negative, their chief aim, need or necessity being to avoid referring back – if there has been such reference it has been produced in a raw unassimilated state, like a collage or parody, or even a mockery. In trying to destroy or amalgamate, reference in fact betrays the inability to absorb, it betrays the weakness of a stylistic conception unable to 'phagocytose' what it takes hold of. But if one insists on stylistic integrity as a prime criterion, and if the material, through previous use, is rich in connotations, if it stimulates involuntary associations and risks diverting expression into unwanted directions, one is led in practice into playing, if not absolutely against the material, then at least to the limit of its possibilities. Coincidence no longer exists, or can exist only in the choice of a specialized area – in the rejection, that is, of many other areas that would impose references that were eccentric and too powerful. It would seem that this excessively cautious attitude could not persist in the face of new material from which connotations have been excluded: the relationship between idea and material becomes eminently positive and stylistic integrity is no longer at risk.

Creative thought, consequently, is in a position to examine its own way of working, its own mechanisms. Whether in the evolution of formal structures, in the utilization of determinism, or in the manipulation of chance, and whether the plan of assembly be based on cohesion or fragmentariness, the field is vast and open to invention. At its limits, one can imagine possible works where material and idea are brought to coincide by the final, instantaneous operation that gives them a true, provisional existence – that operation being the activity of the composer, of an interpreter, or of the audience itself. Certainly, the finite categories within which we are still accustomed to evolve will offer less interest when this dizzying prospect opens up: of a stored-up potential creating instant originality.

Before we reach that point, the effort will either be collective or it will not be at all. No individual, however gifted, could produce a solution to all the problems posed by the present evolution of musical expression.

Research/invention, individual/collective, the multiple resources of this double dialectic are capable of engendering infinite possibilities. That invention is marked more particularly by the imprint of an individual goes without saying; we must still prevent this involving us in humdrum, particular solutions that somehow remain the composer's personal property. What is absolutely necessary is that we should move towards global, generalizable solutions. In material as in method, a constant flow must be established between modes of thought and types of action, a continual exchange between giving and receiving. Future experiments, in all probability, will be set up in accordance with this permanent dialogue. Will there be many of us to undertake it?

TRIBUTES

60

Wolfgang Steinecke

ACCIDENTAL[1]

from behind a white paper screen there rises, uncertainly, the outline of a figure who finally breaks through the screen, appearing with a quiet laugh, which is followed by this dialogue between shadows, both shaking with the same quiet laughter:

'so!'

'quite!'

'good lord!'

'I know!'

'so much talk!'

well, one must do something.'

'true enough ... but even so – who'd have thought it?'

wolfgang steinecke's death somehow stirred a memory of the 'screens' that jean genet used to 'express' accidental death.

the ludicrousness of it, the odd moment of surprise – it is all familiar. the sense of being stunned grows gradually less: the irretrievable has, by pure chance, happened.

our sympathetic forces gather in an attempt to exorcize the whole event, to return to zero point after the rocking of the machine!

'who would have thought it? have I been a long time, then?'

there is a flood of anxious questions; and suddenly the awareness of an indelible burn. the whole thing has scraped us clean, split us in half: our friable experience of the past, the cladding we are tempted to take for granted in a false sense of security, has been brutally stripped away.

all we can do is to dispute the absence that has made such a cavalier appearance in our lives, halt this whole mechanism of 'so – quite – good lord!', the whole spiral of pointless astonishment.

let us save from mere accident the presence in us of the friend dismissed by

---

[1] 'L'accident.' Wolfgang Steinecke (1910–1961) was the founder of the Darmstadt courses. This text was spoken at his funeral and later appeared in *Darmstädter Beiträge zur neuen Musik*, No. 5, 1962, p. 6. First published in French in *Points de repère*.

life with such aggressive insolence: we owe him this revenge on the blindness of a 'fate' that abuses its power to interrupt and to intrude.

FROM THE DISTANCE[1]

wolfgang steinecke

we are here this morning to recall you. not to go over the past, so prematurely and finally truncated; not to recall your work, or to talk of what, since your death, has become a historical epoch. no. to recall you, directly, to call up your presence here, today, among us.

you have crossed that 'much abused, the shallow stream'. respond to our urgent thoughts and cross that ford again: return and look. the part of you that you left to us is still intensely alive – just that part of you so generously expended on others' behalf, the part of you sacrificed to yourself. look: we are here today to prove it.

the lectures and the rehearsals still go on; the discussions are as lively as ever, everyone contributes something, some new interest, some new passion. new arrivals cannot wait to make their first contacts; old hands go straight on to talk shop. groups form and scatter. will it be a good year? memories are exchanged, there is a heap of new plans. next year, we will do this . . . no, perhaps in two years' time.

well, wolfgang steinecke, don't you feel at home in this maze? what's that? i'm not with you? i can't hear you now . . .

what poor creatures we are, unable to do without a physical presence.

no need for the cock to crow to dissolve this conversation. i see you in the distance, moving further and further away, irretrievably. and yet it is certainly your voice that I hear pursuing us, like the ghost in *Hamlet* with its – 'swear! swear! swear!' and we too will answer 'rest, rest, perturbed spirit!' but what are we to swear? it is as simple as impossibility itself: to go forward, and together.

---

[1] 'Dans la distance', tribute published in French in *Melos*, Vol. xxix No. 2, February 1962, pp. 55–6.

61

Edgard Varèse[1]

Varèse,

In the heady days when we were musical apprentices we thought of you as something strange, erratic, distant, mythical and apart, removed from us by vast dimensions of time and space.

A legendary hurricane still remembered for its wild destructiveness. You were summed up in a few oracular words, highly prized by us, on the transmutation of the material of music; in a faded record of *Ionisation*.

Seen in retrospect: a skeleton from a junk shop!

In the meantime we hope that we have filled the gaps in our knowledge by continuous study, exploring the full extent of your work in so far as we have been able to lay our hands on it.

Let me spell out the progress of our acquaintance:

Hyperprisme 1960
Octandre 1954/1958/1962
Intégrales 1958
Ionisation 1954/1960
Ecuatorial 1963
Densité 21.5 1954/1964

and this evening, designed as an anniversary celebration:

Offrandes
Déserts

We have deciphered your works one by one – not large in number, energetic, thickset, close-textured – and enjoyed, by default, the privilege of exclusivity.

'For Edgard Varèse on the occasion of his eightieth birthday, loner and outsider, unique erratic.'

This was how we planned to present our homage in a programme agreed with you at a recent meeting – our last meeting.

Because our gesture of friendship encountered a commonplace obstacle.

---

[1] 'Arcanes Varèse' [Varèse Mysteries], published on the occasion of Edgard Varèse's death in the programme of the Domaine musical concert of 24 November 1965 (opening concert of the 1965–6 season).

Death. On 6 November 1965 there disappeared a human being much given to grumbling and banter, surly and abrupt, that is to say obstinate in friendship and rich in sympathy, a sympathy so deep that it discarded words and gestures as superfluous.

You remain very close to my heart, Varèse, because you are an *outsider* – forming the 'margin' that justifies the lines on the page,

and because you are a *loner*:

you have the deliberate wildness of the animal that does not go with the herd,

the rarity of a diamond in a unique mount,

an untiring patience in the elaboration of your sound combinations.

'Varèse mysteries'?

No, you show no trace of any tendency to the esoteric as something artificial and obligatory. Your power of conviction is manifest, you force the listener to share the secret of your vitality and of that profound committedness that springs from the depths of your being, overcoming the mirages of the surrounding desert.

I find a tonic in the ozone of your scores, and in your example.

Your legend is deeply rooted in our era; we can now scrub the chalk (and water) circle of those magic or ambiguous words 'experimental', 'precursor', 'pioneer' . . .

Have you not had enough of the 'promised land', which always remains a promise? And that qualified honour that is often as much an embarrassment to you as it is to the honourer?

You have s' own yourself to be one of the few cursors of your generation; only our acknowledgement of the fact is post-dated.

Farewell, Varèse, your day is over, and is just beginning.

62

Hermann Scherchen: the Adventurous Patriarch[1]

when i started organizing concerts devoted to the discovery of contemporary music at the Theâtre Marigny – the concerts that later became the 'domaine musical' – i was inexperienced and had neither the right nor the authority to conduct works that demand a solid craftsmanship in order to achieve an impeccable standard of performance.

my dear friend désormière being laid low by illness, the name of scherchen occurred to me. armed with the initial advantage of a close relationship with the three viennese and of having given the first performances of some of their works, scherchen showed himself to be one of those rare personalities naturally at home with novelty, something he needed for the full expansion of his vital powers and for the expenditure of his superfluous energy. he lived up to his reputation; i might describe him as a slow proselyte, a solemn promoter: both adventurous and patriarchal in character; persuasion and conviction were deeply rooted in those recesses of the soul where agitation is clearly ridiculous and superfluous; a groundswell unconcerned with surface eddies. he was certainly not what is called an easy person: the tenacity of his opinions either carried you with him or left you stranded. with him even the unforeseen took on the colour of eternity.

'calm block', or frontal moraine – only a geological metaphor will serve to express the natural, elemental impression that scherchen gave me; a phenomenon whose intuition had no need of subtlety, whose effectiveness had nothing to do with perspicacity: a self-taught phenomenon. might we use of him the same image as gide used of claudel, a powerful image with no hint of cruelty in it – a 'frozen cyclone'?

---

[1] 'Un patriarche aventureux', *Nouvel Observateur*, 22 June 1966.

63

Roger Désormière: 'I Hate Remembering!'[1]

'Don't be sceptical. Have faith, fight against indifference' – those words perfectly sum up Roger Désormière's attitudes and if they were unusual – as indeed they were – it is probably because he had given up composing for some time in order to devote himself entirely to conducting.

I found those words after his death among a lot of miscellaneous lecture notes for the orchestral class at the Conservatoire, which he took over for a time after Charles Munch, and they were certainly not meant for publication. Not that they provide us with the only evidence of Désormière's real personality. He did not confide in many people; even those who brought their problems to him sometimes had the impression of a man who, whether deliberately or not, kept a certain distance between himself and the rest of the world and seemed to be on his guard, reserved, as though defending his own secrets. In this and many other ways he was like Hans Rosbaud, although there were many points of difference between them, owing to their different origins and backgrounds. As with Rosbaud, there was something fascinating and 'mysterious' in the way Désormière combined open friendship with a kind of 'absent' quality on which it was hard to put one's finger. This almost certainly came from both men's profound dissatisfaction with their profession, whose exterior resources they had exhausted, and from their search for music beyond 'conducting' – hence that hunger for what was new and that need for different forms of expression which gave them a youthfulness not common among composers of their generation.

Also among the notes left by Roger Désormière I found this: 'The goal to aim at is extreme sobriety, the gradual shedding of everything superfluous. Sobriety of gesture does not mean a failure to carry expressiveness to its highest pitch, nor a lack of strength or dash.' And this: 'Don't think of the effect on the public, but achieve a moral authority that gives you an ascendancy over the members of the orchestra.'

There is of course nothing new in that. We are well aware that the best conductors are not necessarily those who make the wildest gesticulations.

[1] 'J'ai horreur du souvenir', in *Roger Désormière et son temps* (ed. D. Mayer and P. Souvtchinsky), Monaco, Editions du Rocher, 1966, pp. 134–58.

The idea of conducting as a kind of physical demonstration belongs to the past, and a man like Pierre Monteux was a lifelong demonstration of the fact that sobriety pays, and often achieves a greater moral authority over orchestras than that obtained by those 'good dancers' – as Désormière calls them – 'who put on a dance routine'! This is proved not only by the conductors who worked with the Ballets Russes, like Monteux, Ansermet or Désormière himself. Richard Strauss is still remembered in Germany for his ability to conduct Mozart or Wagner without the slightest parade of gesture, unlike those mad semaphors who have specialized in Wagnerian 'expressiveness'; and in our own times Knappertsbusch became legendary for conducting without any external dramatization by gesture.

These few names prove that sobriety is not an isolated phenomenon but a characteristic of personalities coming from widely different backgrounds, their platform gestures developed in some cases in conducting Debussy and Stravinsky and in others Wagner, Strauss and Mahler.

But I should like to return to Désormière's 'The goal to aim at is extreme sobriety, the gradual shedding of everything superfluous.' This seems to me something more than a useful, but not very unusual piece of professional advice. It is more like a general rule of life that sums up a whole attitude to music, Désormière's own attitude, so far as I could make out from observing him, the goal that he had set himself but was prevented from reaching by the premature paralysis of his faculties. Of course he was 'conditioned' by his early experiences of musical life in Paris, and we often discussed the necessity, the opportuneness and the value of some music to which he felt himself drawn by his memories quite as much as his taste. (Is not taste itself often a function of memories – the choices one makes during one's formative years, in fact? A publisher friend of mine once told me that after the age of 40 a conductor can be written off as far as contemporary music is concerned: he goes on living on what was contemporary when he was young! If he has not passed 40, he is 'recoverable' to the end of his days, or his powers! That joke probably contains the truth about a 'conductor's' attitude to the music written during his life . . . Verify, and check!) Désormière, like the rest of us, was dependent on the choices he had made first as composer and then as interpreter. If pressed hard, he would take refuge behind an amused smile and preserve his ironical secret, no doubt making a mental note of the eternal generation gap and perhaps thinking that this involved misunderstandings that were inevitable.

Other papers discovered after his death include an interesting piece written for the *Courrier musical* in 1922 – when he was 24 – after the first Paris performance of *Pierrot lunaire* in a concert organized by Jean Wiener, conducted by Darius Milhaud and with Marya Freund as the soloist. The article expresses great admiration for Milhaud and describes the work, listing the instruments concerned and paying special attention to certain contrapuntal features that seem to have been found particularly striking by all those who wrote criticisms of the work or otherwise discussed it, although we should remember that this 'learned' style does not play a particularly large part in *Pierrot lunaire*. But in general it is interesting to observe how much more strongly all the commentators reacted to some of the secondary features of the work than to its fundamental assumptions! Surprise played an important part in distorting the perspective of these first audiences, and it would be wrong to forget this factor in our judgement of them. Even so what is striking about Désormière's notice is not so much his mistaken judgement of various aspects of Schoenberg's music as the embarrassment caused by the poetic aspects of *Pierrot lunaire*, an embarrassment that was to poison the relations between French (and not only French!) music and the whole evolutionary process represented by the Second Viennese School.

Désormière speaks first about atonality, which he calls 'one of the greatest revolutions in the history of music', and then goes on with disarming *naïveté* to say that, 'This constitutes the boldest affirmation and the most dazzling proof ... that in music everything is possible' as long as it is musical and sensitive. (The fatal consequences of the general mentality of certain people were realized only later in the endless sophistries that swarmed in the treacherous area of 'freedom of expression', a favourite quagmire never-ceasingly defended, protected and maintained...) Désormière goes on to observe that,

> After much previous study, during which Schoenberg has shaped this new language, giving it suppleness and refinement, it has become so natural to him that he uses it without affectation, effort or embarrassment, subordinating and adapting it in the most extraordinary way to the depth and delicacy of the feeling that it is to express.

These lines prove that Schoenberg's work was genuinely appreciated for its purely musical qualities, and it is strange that within a short time – and under the influence of a number of different events – it was forgotten, apparently for good. If we read Désormière's article to the end, we shall see how divergences originated, explaining what appeared to be the final disappearance, indeed the end, of *Pierrot*.

There is one particular passage that reveals more precisely the background against which Désormière was writing and gives us a glimpse of the general lack of any detailed information about Schoenberg's other works – the prejudices based on second-hand information or national feeling (a stumbling-block for even the best intentioned) and the various adverse currents of feeling that were actually reasons for establishing a new perspective, in fact for seizing the opportunity to praise *Pierrot* more enthusiastically and to emphasize the injustice done to Schoenberg's music hitherto.

> His Opus 10 (Second String Quartet, 1908) marks the beginning of Schoenberg's second manner; and since then he has seemed uniquely concerned with

forging his new language in works that reveal simply that determination. These works often resemble laboratory experiments in which the exclusive concentration on ingenious and laborious research seems to shrink and freeze the composer's sensibility.

If we consider that these 'laboratory experiments' include *Das Buch der hängenden Gärten* songs, the Five Orchestral Pieces, *Erwartung* and *Herzgewächse* – Schoenberg's best works, in fact – we have every right to express surprise, and to consider the gap that existed between Schoenberg's works and even the most professional musicians. By this I mean the information gap, since none of these works had been performed in Paris, I believe, except the Five Orchestral Pieces given by André Caplet – and these were to suffer a particularly prolonged oblivion before their next performance in Paris, which was in 1957. This gap, prolonged by political events, was to be one of the chief features of the period between the two wars: 'But don't let us anticipate,' as Lucky would say . . .

After these complaints we come to the laurel wreath – what Claudel calls 'cette branche militaire' whose leaves confer honour 'amère, le triomphe, et verte, le mystère'.

And in fact there is a good deal of mystery in the sort of honour paid by Désormière to Schoenberg and his *Pierrot*!:

> With *Pierrot lunaire* everything changes. Schoenberg is now master of his new language, which is no longer a kind of end in itself but a flexible means of expressing a rich sensibility which has for too long been repressed. *Pierrot lunaire* is full of that romanticism that Schoenberg inherited from the great German composers of the nineteenth century, and with which his early works were overflowing.

How was it possible to appreciate this German 'romanticism' in the Paris of 1922? All heads had then been turned by contemporary events of a very different nature. The Ballets Russes had taken on a new lease of life, dada was gesticulating wildly and the cubists were occupying the daily scene. What Paris was producing threw into the shade everything else, at least in the eyes of the hypnotized visitor. In the hubbub of 'modernist' activities what chance was there for the aesthetic ideas of such a work as *Pierrot lunaire*, when *L'Histoire du soldat* had meanwhile operated its stylistic marvels? A very slender chance, one must admit ('mince comme un cheveu, ample comme l'aurore', to draw on the stock of unexplained metaphors) so slender that there is nothing to astonish us when Désormière continues:

> For this work is purely German and, it must also be admitted, its sentiments are often nothing but those of the old romanticism with its misty moonlight, *Brocken* spectres and *Walpurgis* nights. Thanks no doubt to the shortness of the pieces this sentimentality is almost always expressed with a sobriety, a

purity and an absence of everything declamatory and unnecessary, which are wholly delightful and mask the rather impoverished soil chosen by the composer. But in the end the enchantment fades and it is impossible not to be struck by the contrast between Schoenberg's musical language – which is the most novel and original of the day – and the polytonality of M. Milhaud; and by the fact that Schoenberg represents a stage of human sensibility that belongs to the past.

This had been the opinion of Stravinsky, the 'big brother', when he heard *Pierrot lunaire* some ten years before; and it was owing to the works that he had written in Paris during these years that his opinion had so deeply influenced his French contemporaries. It was inevitable, since there had not yet been time for a new generation to make its appearance. Désormière's article ends unexpectedly with an expression of 'no surprise', which we today should reverse, since our own surprise is still lively! Writing of the first performance of *Pierrot* in Berlin, Désormière says: 'We have been told that at the first performances in Berlin and Vienna the orchestra played behind a screen and that the singer, Madame Zehme, wore a Pierrot costume. We are not at all surprised to hear it.'

This laconic conclusion reveals more than it appears to and more than Désormière meant – both screen and Pierrot costume were in fact 'alerting' . . . and on this occasion Paris was not alerted: 'We are not surprised.'

Full stop, a final judgement, and its implications were to follow: certain ways of understanding music were curtly dismissed. Roger Désormière had to travel a long way before he found himself again confronting historical 'traces' emerging from oblivion. Time certainly played a part, for time is a 'reviser' with a rather bitter sense of humour. Political isolation and cultural constriction also contributed, let alone the appearance of a younger generation that had no interest in the judgements of their elders and no involvement in their collective decision, only a keen curiosity about this inexplicable (inexpiable?) rejection, to which their attitude was far from friendly.

You may well wonder why I have devoted so much time to Désormière's notice of *Pierrot lunaire*. After all, it does not occupy a very large place in his activities, and the fact that it was among his papers does not necessarily prove that he attached any particular importance to it. To try to 're-create' the course of a life from an ephemeral article written under a first impression would be to make unjustifiable use of hindsight. I have no desire to do that; but I did say before how much Désormière seemed 'conditioned' by his early experiences of musical life in Paris; and this document reveals an individual instance of what we knew to be true of an epoch in general. Désormière's article is simply a document that helps us to understand what happened later. For me, and for those of my generation who shared my ideas – or more precisely the members of Messiaen's class in 1944–5 – Désormière was the personality we most admired among the conductors of the day. I suspect that in the first place it was Messiaen himself who was more or less responsible for this noble sentiment! Désormière's performance of *Pelléas* at the Opéra Comique gave the final edge to our enthusiasm, which was total, prejudiced and unqualified! What is more, we knew that he was very interested in new scores – such things are quickly known and the news spreads even more quickly. Désormière was in a way 'our' conductor.

Looking back over my many memories of him, I would pick out two occasions on which I had an opportunity to make my first contacts with this man whom hitherto I had seen only 'from afar'. The first time that I attended a rehearsal of his was on the occasion of the first performance of *Trois petites liturgies*, when I was still a member of Messiaen's harmony class. He had given us leave to attend all rehearsals, and it was an opportunity that I certainly did not miss. One thing struck me most forcibly and dominates my memories of the occasion, and that was Désormière's rhythmic exactness, the vital precision of his metrical impulse (a magnificent feature of his Stravinsky performances). I was equally impressed by the kindness with which he answered my questions about the technique of conducting, his willingness to enter into the problems of the youngest of us, and the charm with which he shared his knowledge. I was struck, too, by the moral rectitude of his attitude towards both works and composers. At a time when disputes about Messiaen's music were at their height and no criticism was too low, too facile or too insultingly expressed, he was the only person beside the composer to know what was really at stake; and he had taken on his responsibilities in that knowledge. His own personal taste might well have made him hostile to Messiaen's musical opinions, but he devoted himself completely to performing the *Liturgies* with the greatest possible brilliance and sonorous power. He gave a wonderful example and gave it with a total lack of pretentiousness.

The second occasion was a concert conducted by him and containing the first performance of a work by Stravinsky, at which we had banded together to hiss loudly, at the same time receiving a work of Dallapiccola's with the greatest enthusiasm, in order to show – one way and the other – which we preferred. Since we admired and loved Désormière, as I have said, and did not want him to be offended by our prejudices, we all went round after the concert to explain our attitude and to make it absolutely clear to him that our violent, if not untimely, demonstration was not in any way directed against him. We were not quite sure how to make our case plausible . . . But I can still remember the amused look on his face – 'Things are moving,' he said – and I believe that he felt sympathetic towards our rowdy behaviour rather than hostile. He scented in it a new spirit and was himself perfectly aware that musical life was not going to go on just as it had before, that 'post-war' was not going to be just a return to 'pre-war' in music any more than it was in cooking, clothes or drinks . . . There was to be no return to the fusty habits of the past – and whether he was relieved or excited by the new prospects, he was certainly pleased. His reaction showed interest, quite unlike the hostility of most of the Paris musical establishment. (I wonder whether we should still appreciate today the comicality of some of the vindictive articles written at that time? Our rebellion was noted with amazement and severely condemned in the terms of a schoolmaster reprimanding insolent schoolboys...) Désormière, on the other hand, wanted to know why it had all happened and what had made us feel so strongly? It could not have been mere irritability, as he realized – and from this he was led to re-examine his own position and to decide whether he himself was so sure of that position that he was justified in anathematizing the troublemakers.

There is one passage in these posthumous notes that actually refers to interpretation, but tells us much about the 'magnetic pole' of his whole personality, which was keyed to open-mindedness, independent reactions and uninhibited reflexes: 'Have the courage of your opinions. Acknowledge your mistakes rather than persist in error. Do not be afraid of changing your ideas. Self-criticism ... preserving one's enthusiasm...'

I have deliberately abbreviated this quotation in order to remove it from its context, which was the conducting class that he had temporarily taken over. What he has to say about an interpretation class is perfectly applicable as a description of the writer by himself. These jottings do in fact provide a self-portrait, and they are valuable as clearly revealing the characteristics of a personality that we can conjecture behind the veil of discretion and cordiality, the friendliness and the polite reserve. Writing, in fact, about working with an orchestra and speaking of chording, he says, 'Precision, a mark of aristocracy.' Like many of us, he aimed at this difficult kind of aristocracy: personal precision – and he realized that it could be achieved only by sacrificing one's accumulated prejudices and passing one's intellectual faculties, phoenix-like, through the fire, if they were to be revivified in the powers of a youth renewed...

And so Désormière recanted, burying the feelings of his generation, which he had partly shared, and set out in search of the values that had been too lightly dismissed, devoting himself to the study of a mode of feeling that was naturally alien to him; and he was thus in a position to give performances of the works that we had been so anxious to hear him conduct – truly *professional* performances of works by the Viennese School which, by force of circumstance, had hitherto been massacred by 'ghastly bunglers'. These included the concert extracts from Berg's *Wozzeck* and the *Chamber Concerto* and Webern's *First Cantata* and *Concerto for Nine Instruments*. How grateful we were to him for sharing our new discoveries and actually performing music that we knew, in some cases, only by reading! I take it, of course, that this entailed obtaining more exact information in order to convince himself that our enthusiasm for this music was well founded and not exaggerated. I can well imagine that there was quite an element of scepticism in his approach ... But honesty cannot be deceived indefinitely and music fairly examined is in the end fairly accepted.

I can hear a hum of objections – that I make Désormière's life and his interests revolve round a very strange centrepoint and that my view of them is a grossly personal one. You may well say that his life was not built around the thesis that I have put forward; you may well raise a number of definite obstacles in the path that leads from him to me and contrast the eclecticism that he showed in practice with the single-mindedness with which I am in vain trying to credit him. You may, in fact, accuse my portrait of showing partiality and tell me that I am an author in search of a character . . . And my reply is this – do we never want to remodel the faces of those to whom we feel in some way drawn to suit ourselves? If we are ever tempted to do this, may it not be for very good reasons? Perhaps because the person concerned invites the attempt?

It is easy to say that no particular conclusions can be drawn from an article on *Pierrot lunaire* forgotten among a heap of papers from the past – or from notes made hastily in the first place and unlikely to contain any unique revelations . . . but I can nevertheless sense the presence of certain stable factors in these occasional writings, if not in the field of ideas or tastes, at least in the personality of the writer, his actions and reactions. And so I am quite deliberately interpreting these documents as far as I can – as far as they permit, that is – in my own sense. I shall be careful not to forget that Désormière was far from being wholly devoted to the cause of 'modernity' and that, like all of us, he had his special favourites among the composers of the past, just as in the contemporary field we are conditioned in our preferences. We remember his frequent forays into French music of the seventeenth and eighteenth centuries. As a matter of curiosity and without narrowing our interpretation of his character, we cannot forbear to mention a similar trait, which showed itself in a less immediately relevant field – I mean his wish to find national equivalents for names that belong to the universal human heritage, a sort of childish satisfaction that Mont Blanc was French, just as Everest, Aconcagua or Kilimanjaro 'belonged' to other countries! What a naïve delight he took in such things, a legacy from dear old Plutarch . . . The idea of certain peaks as 'captured' and frozen into a historical heritage now arouses an affectionate smile. There is a touching 'family' feeling, in fact, about the procession of his chosen ancestors, though when it comes to territorial claims this feeling is not quite so innocent: for although it reveals the same deep-lying emotional candour, there is always the danger that, given the right circumstances, this may take a more aggressive form . . .

Whatever the motives behind these 'elective affinities' of Désormière's, they were fruitful in practice, since they acquainted us with a number of little-known composers and with works that were virtually unknown. Such works provide admirable historical documentation and enlarge the national repertory: and if they were later given an exaggerated importance, this was the inevitable result of a precarious alliance made in the unreal atmosphere caused by a passion for contradiction. If Désormière's instinctive taste led him to specialize in works from the French past (he was to be followed by others whose claims on behalf of minor Italian and German composers became little short of a menace) he was also deeply concerned to revive any works that had been unjustly neglected. Monteverdi's *Vespers* are a good example. These were first performed piecemeal in a succession of concerts (like some superb serial) and then given complete in an unforgettable programme. It was not by chance that in Désormière's posthumous notes we find the name of Monteverdi under the heading of craftsmanship – namely instrumentation. 'Study the history of instrumentation. Families of instruments. The wealth of Monteverdi' and then, 'Take an interest in historical documentation', 'Study sources of inspiration ... the age in which a composer lived, his life, his psychological make-up.'

I had the good fortune to follow very closely Désormière's rehearsals of Monteverdi's *Vespers*; and I saw how carefully he collated the two editions then in use, correcting falsifications of the text, restoring the order in which pieces were performed and collating with the original when in doubt – work that musicologists rather than conductors are trained to do. It was simply a matter of respecting the music, something elementary no doubt but by no means common practice and always slightly astonishing when one comes upon it.

I appreciated his 'taste for hard work' – which he recommended in those words – when I followed every stage in his rehearsing of Stravinsky's *Les Noces*, from his work with pianists, soloists and choruses separately right up to the superb performance, above all the amazing peroration! It was on this occasion that Désormière told me about the exercises that he had devised for himself and recommended, in order to be able without any difficulty to beat the 'bar changes' rightly feared by conductors. His method was to start from a metre expressed in equal values and then gradually to do away with the regular subdivisions of the bar until he reached a point where he could do entirely without them, except at occasional control points. He thought that the first problem was to learn to feel the double pulse *naturally*, the rhythmic feeling for the two basic units combining to give all the figures arising from the multiplication of the smallest unit. (Constantin Brăiloiu, who approached the matter from quite a different angle – that of folk music – was at this time calling this the 'giusto syllabique bichrone'.) When the basic tempo is relatively slow, it is easy to master and the inequality between binary and ternary impulses is quite clear, but above a certain tempo the difficulty increases at a staggering rate. Only solid training will enable the conductor to maintain, in the first place, his own mental control of the rhythm and then to ensure that his arm and his wrist are in complete control of the act of *communicating* that rhythm, and that this action is always absolutely, visibly clear to the players.

(This suddenly reminds me of the amazing virtuosity, of a similar kind, with which the conductor–percussion-player in a Balinese ensemble communicates to his players an enormously prolonged *accelerando*. Our European achievements in this field are very modest compared with the swiftness and precision of the reflexes of traditional musicians in Bali or Japan. I can imagine the sort of conversations that Désormière and I would have now about exploring new ways of conducting, of co-ordinating musical performance – rather like those I used to have with Rosbaud about the need for certain gestures, how to make them unambiguous and effective, and the way they serve the musical text. Hitherto not much virtuosity – in the sense in which we use the word of an instrumentalist – has been demanded of the conductor in ensemble works. He is the centre of the action, the man who combines some hundred different energies into a single unit: in fact, he 'directs'. But it seems likely that in the future co-ordinating a performance is not going to be quite so simple an affair, and that conductors will not simply combine, but also disperse the energies of the music in different directions – and not only in a spatial sense but in ways of giving the music different effects. It is possible to imagine a kind of 'score' of gestures co-ordinated with the musical score and loosely linked to it – action on an already existing object that needs the conductor only incidentally, to determine its place within the framework of the whole, and that depends on him for such accidental things as the timing of its appearance and its relationship to other musical entities. In fact the whole science and technique of conducting needs to be rediscovered . . . It must actively corroborate the mastering of a new musical universe, which it will help to explore, something urgently needed, as can be seen from the present state of musical poetics. Real problems, imaginary conversations . . .)

Yes, imaginary, alas!, and (as with Pascal and Cleopatra) we may well wonder sometimes what Désormière would have achieved if his activities had not been brutally, and finally, truncated. The question is pointless, because his life did 'continue', and insidious, because he would have had to make even more painful choices. It is also bitter since his life did in fact continue in a descending scale of 'choices'. Questions . . .

Shortly before he was struck down, he and I planned with Pierre Souvtchinsky to give some programmes that – to say the least of it – would be new to Paris. We had passionate, though always friendly, discussions about works, programmes, and concert halls, and Désormière, accepting our suggestions, began to consider the practical side of the plan. Then came his illness; and after that – and without him, alas! – the 'Domaine musical'.

When, after many remissions, he died in November last, I heard the news while I was actually correcting the proofs of the first programme of the season. I at once wrote this short piece, thinking of all that might have been and of French musical life robbed of his rich personality:

For the last eleven years he was immured in a silent nightmare world from which there was no waking, and he had become a lucid and impotent spectator of his own life, which had exploded beneath him, leaving his activities in fragments. And so, many young composers and new concert-goers who have come to contemporary music after 1952 know him only by his reputation, that enduring reputation that began to be something of a legend . . . For the rest of us his performances have remained more than precious memories, something better than unforgettable models.

His death rekindles the bitter regrets aroused by the illness that condemned him to the absurd role of a gagged witness and a disabled fighter. Contemporary music lost a unique source of inspiration and his empty place was a perpetual rebuke to frivolity, indifference, prudence, small-mindedness. Roger Désormière was never afraid of making a choice, of showing his independence and his courage, whether it was in his public or his private life.

Death has now destroyed this absent figure, already cruelly excluded from life. We of the 'Domaine' salute his shade, paralysed for ever but 'standing in the distance'.

There is much that I could say about Désormière's personal courage and his political views, of the bold choice he made when he joined the Communist Party, though not sharing its blunders or being unaware of the insoluble problems that bedevilled the years between 1947 and 1952. His reaction to inconsistent squabbling and dictated attitudes was simply that of an honest man determined to resist the imposition of any narrow, anti-historical conception of musical evolution: and he never had any truck with those reactionary 'ideologies' justified by the dictator miracle – later known as 'the cult of personality' – which accused the most important among today's composers of cosmopolitanism or the vices coming under the general heading of 'cultural decadence'. He was fond of commenting ironically – when he was not enraged by the odious police methods involved – on the idiotic propaganda for 'progressive' music dictated by Zhdanov; for Désormière was not one of those who allow themselves to be duped and try to conceal the necessities of the artist beneath the so-called claims of society – the shameless degradation of a real and fundamental problem. Even when Stalinism was at its height, he went on conducting any music that he thought worth performing, though he risked being treated as suspect by 'comrades' who were more servile, less honest and, in fact – as later events were to show – less perspicacious than himself.

He was guided in his political views by those ideas of 'hard work', 'spirituality' and 'humanism' to which his notes on conducting refer. But his was not a conventional humanism with its squally conventional aesthetic imperatives, the 'ready-made' spirituality of commandments and prohibitions or the hard work of a narrow-minded and unthinking labourer doing his job to order and in fear of the withering reproof that any chance deviation would incur. This was still, for Désormière's generation, the generous ideal – the utopia – of 1936 strengthened by the fight against ideological and nationalistic oppression. Freedom of choice, open discussion and critical analysis – those were the ideals that he meant to make the 'foundation and summit' of his life, both professional and private. They can be summed up in the word 'integrity', which also appears in his notes . . . It was not an easy path to tread, the path between the precipices of servility on the one hand and 'treachery' on the other, with smart customers watching his every step until their smartness proved vain and their wretched activities brought them public disgrace. And when the reaction came how perfect his moral attitude was. How we love him for being generous-hearted yet refusing to be dictated to, and for grasping the necessity – and acknowledging the duty – of cultural exchange and mass communication yet rejecting the easy hypocritical solutions tainted with nationalism and the worst kind of conservatism! We can understand how he detested the stale smell of the *petit-bourgeois* stables! If he had adopted that hideous disguise, he would not have been Désormière but one of the countless parasites who like to parade their high-mindedness while all the time devoting themselves in fact to the most utter mediocrity. His empty place was indeed, as I have said, a rebuke!

What can I say of his last years, of his friends' despairing efforts to re-educate his nerve centres, already partially destroyed, and of those moments when there seemed to be some hope of his being able to work again professionally? When he was first ill, he made every possible effort to recover the movements that he had lost, and it was heartbreaking to see him endlessly confronted by the difficulties that arose every time he tried to make use of physical mechanisms that had lost their use and had to be restored one after another.

Talking to him, you would be surprised by his lucidity and his memory, his enjoyment of old anecdotes and the old jokes, but this only made it harder to accept his total inability to communicate directly. One often had the agonizing feeling that one was talking to a perfectly lucid person enclosed in a glass cage. It was like being in a recording studio when one has forgotten to switch on the connecting microphone and the person in the actual studio can hear and understand you perfectly though you can only gather what he is saying from his gestures and his facial expression. This was Désormière's plight – still passionately interested in the outside world with which he could only with the greatest difficulty maintain active communication.

The quiet dignity with which he faced this terrible predicament imposed a similar discretion on all those who saw him, and this was perfectly in accord with the Désormière we had known in his active days. His personality in this ghastly existence remained absolutely true to the principles established in the first instance by his sense of rightness. In the terminal prison to which he was condemned he still retained a distinction and an elegance that refused to surrender to illness: he would not accept the easy solution of admitting to being 'a sick man', with all the pity and commiseration that this entails. And so he made a firm decision – simply to disappear from the professional musical world that had so often surrendered to his charm, admired his gifts and his performances and benefited so enormously from his spell – the world to which he was attached both emotionally and professionally. It was the highest form of respect that he could show that world, physically to conceal his disfigurement and thus to leave intact in everyone's memory the figure of the Désormière they admired and loved. It was a deliberate act of self-effacement and one that, while he was still living, his legend was to transcend, obliterating all trace of his illness.

It was cold and foggy that November morning when we finally took leave of him and its very commonplaceness made it unbearably sad. The 'dead season' of absence! Forgotten ... I can see it again in my mind, and my answer to it lies in the words that I have already quoted: 'The goal to aim at is extreme sobriety, the gradual shedding of everything superfluous.' Fate prescribed that he should verify literally this purely professional observation about his work: his life had been in effect stripped – and cruelly slowly – of everything superfluous, and the hearse provided the last bitter touch of that sobriety ... No passing-bell could have been more apt than the last page of *Les Noces* as he had once conducted it, giving an extraordinary reality to the 'paralysis' of the final chord, where sound melts into silence. Dissolution and farewell – I can find no better words to express the meaning of the rite than those which I have borrowed from Claudel's *Soulier de satin*:

> J'ai l'horreur du passé! j'ai l'horreur du souvenir! Cette voix que je croyais entendre tout à l'heure au fond de moi, derrière moi,
> Elle n'est pas en arrière, c'est en avant qu'elle m'appelle; si elle était en arrière elle n'aurait pas une telle amertume et une telle douceur!

> [I have a horror of the past, a horror of remembering! That voice which I thought I heard just now inside me, behind me,
> It is not back that it calls me, but forward; if it were back it would not have such bitterness and such sweetness]

Now, dear friend Désormière, you are no longer with us, for ever!

64

Hans Rosbaud

THE CONDUCTOR AND HIS MODEL[1]

There has been much talk of the gap between composers and performers, and particularly between composers and conductors, unwilling to devote their time to the study of new scores likely not only to present difficulties of purely musical comprehension but also to set technical problems, and for that very reason to rouse more or less open hostility among players. Overcoming this handicap needs great perseverance and patience, a great deal of self-abnegation, psychological skill and also a large dash of humour, the sort of humour that relaxes the latent tensions that arise when long work sessions make everyone irritable . . . not to mention a subtle mixture of authority in handling players and deference towards composers. It is often a case not only of avoiding clashes or 'getting round awkward corners', but of getting a body of individuals to share in understanding a work and therefore appealing to its origin – the author.

I have drawn a kind of ideal portrait of the conductor; and do we not sometimes find a model of this ideal interpreter in real life? In actual fact my description of this dream figure was based on Hans Rosbaud.

Since his death I have had time to think about his gifts and his stature as an artist, which absence and time have only confirmed. Everyday life sometimes interferes with perspectives obtainable only at a certain remove in time. Some figures then become dim; others appear in their true dimensions.

To find a place for Rosbaud in the everyday world is not easy: it is in fact a paradox, since he was the very opposite of an everyday personality. He has been compared to a figure from Hoffmann, and this is an image of him that certainly appeals to me. His habitual affability did not preclude a kind of distance from the rest of the world, a permanent self-absorption: it was

---

[1] 'Le chef d'orchestre et son modèle', broadcast given on the Südwestfunk (Baden-Baden) on the seventieth anniversary (1965) of Hans Rosbaud's birth. Published in German in *Anhaltspunkte* by Pierre Boulez, ed. and trans. Josef Häusler, Stuttgart/Zurich, Belser Verlag, 1975. First published in French in *Points de repère*.

impossible to be sure of really understanding him, so surprising were the unexpected recesses and the elliptical attitudes of his personality. There was a part of him that he shared with no one: an enclosure carefully protected from all intruders. The clearest proof of this lay in his incredible reserves of energy, which, right up to the end, made him refuse to admit the existence of the obvious malady that was sapping his strength. He would have felt it indecent to mention this as anything more than a commonplace indisposition. A sort of fanaticism of the spirit compelled him to ignore 'Brother Ass' and his shameful demands.

Very occasionally – and then, as it were, in a moment of elegant obliviousness – a hint of the intensity of his inner life would appear in his relations with the outside world – a reference to something he had read, a chance reflection astonishing in its cool passion and its very brevity. He would immediately regain his self-control and all that remained was a short silence, quotation marks finally closing this reference to his interior life.

I have chosen to speak about Rosbaud's personality before discussing him as a musician, because I believe that the musician was only one facet – the most obvious one – of his personality. His 'cultural' interests were by no means confined to music, as could be seen from his taste for languages and his curiosity about new scientific discoveries. Minds such as his are not attracted by the routine of musical life, because they are fond of exploring other fields of human knowledge, which make them permanently aware of the limitations of their own profession and anxious to launch out into the unknown.

Rosbaud's personality was thus divided between the habits of a professional and the aspirations of a man outside his profession. Those who saw a lot of him found in this shifting balance between a sedentary and an adventurous life, between the established and the improbable, the real key to his character, the motive behind his actions and the explanation of the attitudes he adopted. This might well surprise anyone who had only a superficial acquaintance with him, but to those who knew him better it seemed a biological synthesis essential to his intellectual health.

I will not say much about his gifts as a conductor, because our memories of his prodigious powers are still fresh – he was a marvellous score-reader, an indefatigable worker and devoted interpreter. I am too aware of what as a composer I owe to him not to acknowledge that without him my music would never have been performed as it was. I have a very clear memory of his rehearsals because I learned so much from his extraordinarily 'professional' attitude to whatever he was working on. I learned the practical side of conducting from watching him, from talks with him and I came to understand the essential relationship between the score as written and the score as performed.

This is the final point that I should like to make – the possibility of professional discussion with Rosbaud. Nothing suited him less than easily pleased composers, of whom he was immediately suspicious. He wanted composers to have their say – thus showing clearly that professional experience alone, whatever its quality, is not enough. Performers have a right to demand of the composer the same initiative in invention as that which will determine their own shaping of the music.

The very existence of music at the present time depends on this dialogue between composer and performer. There are many other things that we can learn from Hans Rosbaud's example, but none more important than this fundamental collaboration.

'... TO CUT ME OFF BEFORE NIGHT'[1]

hans rosbaud's death will be a major loss to contemporary music, with which his name is closely associated.

writing immediately after receiving the cruel news i do not intend in these few lines to rehearse the career of this indefatigable worker or to list his achievements. hans rosbaud had an impressive number of first performances to his credit, more in fact than i could hope to enumerate.

i am more concerned to speak about him personally, because i was fortunate enough to know him well and because several of my works were given their first performance by him, at the südwestfunk, after preparation such as would nowhere else be possible.

when a composer speaks of rosbaud the conductor, he is speaking in the first place of a friend who would put you at your ease immediately by his own way of talking and his kindly humour. still more important he put you at your ease when working with him, generously putting at your disposal his immense experience and his incredible craftsmanship. i was always amazed by his supreme mastery of his craft – the ease with which he read difficult scores at sight, the elegance of his beat in the most unusual music, the agility with which he adapted himself to the new conducting techniques demanded by the different grouping of performers in contemporary works.

two things in particular delighted me about him.

first: he was never happy rehearsing unless the composer was present at the birth of his own work. very few conductors can have with better reason questioned the composer to discover the overall conception of a work, its precise intention, or have been more concerned about the relationship between performance and original conception. he liked to have precise information about any problems of interpretation in order to solve them as exactly as possible. in fact he asked to be convinced so that he, in his turn, could communicate that conviction.

second: he was a man of exceptional energy, who manifested inexhaust-

---

[1] Written on the occasion of Rosbaud's death (1962). First published in French in *Points de repère*.

ible resources both in music and in life. he liked action; even when unconvinced, he would always give the future the benefit of the doubt.

and so his name will live, engraved on the title page of countless scores, a witness to the high esteem in which he was held by so many composers – and a witness, in my own case, to that friendly gratitude which links me for ever to his memory.

65

T. W. Adorno[1]

what is true of a man's personality is true of his work
what exercises a fascination is simply what is still, and will always remain,
           unexplained
           what resists all attempts at investiga-
           tion,
           what, clearly, provides the evidence.
in an attempt to pin it down, we generally make use of neutralizing words:
                    ambiguit/y(-ies)
                    contradiction(s);
        we try different keys – they fail to fit the lock
        of the enquiry.
it only remains to imagine the discrepancies within an individuality:
    : he who observes a divergence in his gifts and does not
       refuse the divergence –
       – not only, but –
       tries, despite flagrant incompatibilities, to use it as a
       lever;
    : he who, indivisible, preserves and provokes – does not
       give up the soil, though aware of the phenomenon of
       rotting destined to sustain it,
       he who aspires to shelter and stability, though this means
       fire and burning;
    : he who amasses knowledge, and endeavours not to envy
       innocence.
specifically due to circumstance, (though have pogroms no precedent?)
           the wandering life,
           median section of this existence,
           definitive break,
                confirming
                confirming

---

[1] Published in French in *Melos*, September 1969, pp. 85–6, with the subtitle 'en marge de la, d'une, disparition' (with reference to a, or the, disappearance).

ties and homesickness, exalting the wrench and the determination.
the hosts of contradictions – unresolved,
      ambiguities – unexplained,
      which the subtlest, the craftiest dialectics will not pierce;
      which the craftiest, the subtlest of dialecticians
      will make his hoard!
            (the hoard that fieldmice and other vermin will not
            fail to visit, and to pillage . . .)
the intelligence, the perspicacity, will now be transmitted *viva
voce* (*acuta*):

      he who establishes the privilege and the advantage of com-
      munication with a basic marker;   a point not fixed, *moving*
                                     – leading out beyond the
                                     enclosure, the handrail,
                                     to a country of multiple
                                     dimensions: where peak
                                     and abyss may be *one and
                                     the same*.

66

Heinrich Strobel

THE FRIEND[1]

The sudden death of Heinrich Strobel leaves me at a loss, and I find it hard to sum up exactly what he meant to musicians of my generation. During almost twenty years of friendship I got to know him not only in his professional capacity – in which he won a worldwide reputation – but also as a man, with whom I had many unusually close links.

Some men try to express themselves by writing or composing, or some other direct means. Others – who are a rarer breed – express themselves through other personalities, whom they shape, helping them to overcome their problems by their own understanding and perspicacity. This involves great self-abnegation, an observation always on the alert and a natural gift for shaping personality. Heinrich Strobel belonged unquestionably to this category of what may be called 'clairvoyants', whose friendship – if one is lucky enough to win it – is enormously valuable and profound, but masked by irony in order to make any question of gratitude superfluous. Thanks to him I have had experience of a mutual exchange, I might even say sharing, of ideas that would be an enrichment of any life.

I had almost daily experience of his extreme and never-failing sensitiveness, his desire never to repeat himself and his vocation as a discoverer; and these were always an example and an inspiration to me. His scepticism simply served as stimulus to a fundamental optimism and a profound faith in the future. Trust was one of the chief features of his friendship, and I myself have had so many proofs of it that without this quite unusually generous man my life would have been both poorer in experience and less stable.

With the friends he trusted he was extremely spontaneous and very frank; and I particularly appreciated this double gift of being intensely *there* yet never imposing himself. This was so true that after a time it became hard to distinguish his personality from your own in those fundamental things that you shared in common. It was one of Heinrich Strobel's secrets that any

---

[1] 'Visage de l'amitié.' Heinrich Strobel (1898–1970) was head of music at the Südwestfunk in Baden-Baden, to which he invited Boulez in 1959. This text was spoken at his funeral on 20 August 1970 and appeared in French in *Melos*, October 1970, pp. 368 and 388.

friendship as alert as his becomes so completely identified with your own being that when it is suddenly removed by death, the blow is all the greater, because you cannot make out what has suddenly disappeared from your life after having been so completely identified with your everyday thoughts. After that, what are 'presence' and 'absence'? Nothing can destroy his genius or the mirror that he will always be for anyone who had the privilege – through identification and demand – of his friendship.

THE INTERMEDIARY[1]

Music is composed: but musical performance has to be organized, even provoked, and that is why side by side with composers one always find these 'second personalities' whom we call 'artistic directors' . . .

The personality of an individual artistic director may well determine the character of an epoch, for there is every chance of such personalities being *real* people – people, that is, who are not simply concerned with organizing other people's works but who, at a deeper level, are genuinely concerned for the various personalities whom they encounter and may almost be said to create, moulding them to events.

Such people adopt a cause which is both *theirs* and that of the talents that they serve. We find this in every field. The lives and works of some painters have been inextricably linked to friends who, for their sakes, have become 'dealers' and thus spared them some of the burden of material cares, at the same time directing their activities to fields that might never have occurred to the painters themselves or which they might only have discovered later, perhaps too late . . . Theatrical and literary history is full of instances of the same kind.

Music clearly offers many opportunities to unusual people of this kind, who combine a natural flair with great determination and a gift for organization.

It is the composer, of course, who makes the 'proposition' in the first place; but, as with the playwright, it is not enough to have realized his 'propositions' on paper. If these are to be given total reality in time and space, they need the further 'realizing' of performance. At that stage there may be considerable problems that thwart the artist who (quite rightly) has not considered ways and means. His vision of his work needs a corresponding realization, and this can be achieved only within a certain framework, at a certain time and in certain circumstances.

Even when these have been arranged there will still be plenty of obstacles to overcome, of an everyday kind; but these present no real problem.

---

[1] 'L'intermédiaire', a broadcast early in 1971 on the Südwestfunk (Baden-Baden) in memory of Strobel. Published in German in *Anhaltspunkte* ed. and trans. Josef Häusler, Stuttgart/ Zurich, Belser Verlag, 1975, pp. 395–8. First published in French in *Points de repère*.

Practical difficulties, personal differences and clashes of temperament occur in all professions and have to be dealt with by everyone who leads an active life of any kind.

In this particular matter of artistic selection and artistic option the hard thing is *to keep going*. By this I do not mean simply surviving, but possessing the necessary reserves of vitality and keeping one's eyes open to every opportunity without losing the ability to analyse, preserving one's critical faculty without losing a certain capacity for 'wonder'. And this, after long years of activity, is not as easy as it might seem.

This youthfulness of judgement (even more than of character) contains a strong element of the irrational, what Baudelaire calls 'the right to contradict oneself' . . .

Though he may not admit it openly and may even find brilliant disguises for it, everyone is to some extent tempted to remain wedded to a number of early experiences dating from some decisive period of his life (generally the years immediately after adolescence). It makes little difference whether one's subsequent attitude to these experiences is negative, an attitude of defiance, or one of sentimental attachment, even enthusiasm: the fact remains that this period occupies a definitely privileged position. One needs great energy, and what is more a very unusual power of self-detachment, to achieve an habitual self-forgetfulness without self-betrayal.

A constant self-forgetfulness is in itself a fundamental problem for any creative artist. It might be supposed that this is relatively easier for an intermediary, and that for him it is in no way a matter of life or death. But remember that the intermediary lives in complete symbiosis with the composer, or rather with the composer's work – whoever the individuals may be with whom he is concerned at the moment. If he drops the work, or the work loses sight of him, his choices very soon deteriorate, and the famous flair (so much talked about and so hard to define, so easy to recognize and so hard to explain) wanders off on fresh, imaginary scents . . .

The symbiosis of intermediary and creative artist may go so far that there are times when the intermediary – a very modest word for so essential a function – appears indirectly, as the creator. It may even be such that with the disappearance of the intermediary there disappears a certain form of activity that it would be useless to try to continue in his image. Without him it could be no more than a kind of shadow play; and at every individual disappearance the whole question of the function of an intermediary has to be reconsidered. With him a period of history comes to an end, and with it the form of creation that was directly linked to him.

We may welcome or lament this transitoriness, but it is an unavoidable fact, which we must learn to take into account.

Everyone's ambition is, roughly speaking, to *remain a presence* in the affairs of his day and in future utopias. Has the *individual* intermediary any future role, or will his personality perhaps be replaced by a kind of collective consciousness? Will not the needs of the situation tend increasingly to crush any individual rebellion, or, without completely annihilating it, at any rate integrate it in very reduced form into this collective consciousness? We still have to find definitions for all these new relationships between inventors (even inventors of inventors) and society, for whose good (if not profit) they *function*. Will the idea of personal responsibility be replaced by group decision?

Hitherto the 'artist' has gained access to the 'world' by means of intermediaries who were the first to recognize his specific, or exceptional, gifts. But the whole conception of '*the* single artist', and therefore of his intermediary, or spokesman, is now being more and more radically questioned. It is not a matter of suppressing individual qualities, but of providing them with a new field of action and an essentially different manner of acting.

A solution will be found, beyond any doubt. Every age finds its own solution, because it must; and because, models being never repeated, a solution is implicit in the very existence of the age.

Seen in this light, the great individual intermediaries will certainly have been of the greatest importance as precursors. Sometimes without being fully conscious of it, sometimes against their wills but often with an instinctive sense of the future, they will have shown that artistic creation is a collective phenomenon – not in the naïve, narrow sense but within the framework of a complex social organization.

67

Bruno Maderna: A Portrait Sketch[1]

Our careers ran parallel. Starting in Germany, we succeeded each other in Great Britain and finally met again in the United States. In 1958 we both took part as conductors in the première of Stockhausen's *Gruppen*. Later on we alternated with each other as conductors of the Residenzorchester at The Hague . . .

In the heroic days after Walter Steinecke founded the Darmstadt Ensemble we shared the innumerable first performances that had to be kept up all through the summer. Planning rehearsals was a nightmare. It did not worry Bruno too much, and there were times when he did not hesitate to turn up late. He enjoyed life and always got away with it.

In fact to get any real idea of what he was like as a person, the conductor and the composer must be taken together; for Maderna was a practical person, equally close to music whether he was performing or composing. The first time I saw him, at Darmstadt, he was rehearsing a work with one percussion-player short, so he sat by the tam-tams and bongos playing and conducting at the same time, and with equal facility. It was rather like a monkey agile enough to jump from one musical tree to another with incredible ease.

This direct, instantaneous and profound contact with the stuff of music gave all his performances a special flavour of their own. Physically Bruno looked like a small pachyderm, but his good-tempered bulk seemed paradoxically light. He was compact of intelligence, finesse, humour and imagination. The pachyderm was an elf.

His meeting with Scherchen was certainly a turning point in his life. He had always had an unbounded admiration for his old master. But that did not prevent him from spending long evenings telling us every kind of anecdote about him, all marked by an affectionate disrespect. There was one, I remember, about bathing with Scherchen on the Lido – both of them puffing like grampuses and discussing, as they swam, the right way to conduct the

---

[1] 'Esquisse d'un portrait', published as 'Salut à Bruno Maderna' in the *Nouvel Observateur*, 26 September 1973, on the occasion of Maderna's death.

Eroica, Scherchen producing mnemonic devices as surprising as they were infallible – such as putting the words 'Das ist Napoleon' to the theme in the finale!

Bruno Maderna was someone who knew what it meant to be rigorous but had never decided to apply it to himself, simply because it did not appeal to him. One day when he was conducting a new work which had very precise metronome markings and changes of tempo, such as 'from crotchet = 118 to crotchet = 80·5', he turned to the composer and me who were sitting in the hall, and shouted '"crotchet = 80·5!" Right?'

His kind of rigorousness had nothing to do with numbers, it was simply the knowledge that he could express his personality only by disregarding punctilio of any kind.

The best things in his own music, the prize moments, sprang from this immediate, irrational musical sense, and for this reason his most successful works are those that leave the most initiative to the players. At the end of his last work, an oboe concerto, he wrote: 'I hope that I have provided enough material for soloist, conductor and orchestra to come to terms and enjoy playing what I have written.' In a way he gave birth to a music that he carried, like a mother, and then absolutely trusted.

His *Satiricon* was commissioned by the Holland Opera and forms a kind of link between the new music and the tradition of bawdy; and it was while he was engaged on this that he discovered how ill he was and how short a time he had to live. Coming at that particular moment, this blow was characteristic of the contrasts of which his life was full. I am glad that he died quickly: nothing is more painful than the slow decline of someone bursting with life.

BY WAY OF CONCLUSION

68

The Elliptical Geometry of Utopia[1]

Without going as far as Sartre, with his 'l'enfer, c'est les autres' I would still say that there is no escaping other people's attention, the scrutinizing glances that analyse you and sum you up. Sometimes there is no avoiding their ill will; but there are other times – such as today – when there is no escaping their good will.

I am reminded of Charlie Chaplin's gesture when faced with a judge accusing him of some terrible misdeed – how he turned round to see the monster whom the judge was describing as being him, and saw nothing but the wall of the courtroom. Listening to the kind exaggerations in your words about me, I felt the same inclination to turn round in order to catch a glimpse of this more than life-size paragon, and should no doubt, like Chaplin, have seen nothing but the wall of this hall.

Outside ourselves, therefore, there is the image that other people form of us; and this makes us realize, now and then, that outside the daily routine of our work – though closely linked to it – a profound change is taking place in our personalities. In the words of my friend Clytus Gottwald, every hour of every day of every year we are transforming our routine subjective experience into an objective reality that rises above its origins which thus become if not unrecognizable, at least 'forgettable'.

And so the great pleasure that I have in accepting the honour that you are doing me today is less for what I am than for what I have been trying all these years to represent. I do not represent – in the purely external sense – the forces that pass in and through me. I manifest them rather, try to make my action ensure that they are successfully realized in one way or another. And I know only too well, from experience, the charge that can be made against me – the charge of dispersing my activities in different fields and thus running the risk of being deflected from the one important object, creation. There is a Portuguese proverb that Claudel uses as the motto of *Le Soulier de satin*: 'God writes straight with crooked lines.' In no sense do I take myself for God, still less for Jesus Christ – Nietzsche preserve me! But this is still a

[1] 'Géométrie courbe de l'utopie', speech made on receiving the Siemens Prize on 20 April 1979. First published in *Points de repère*.

proverb that I would happily apply to myself. I have been perhaps only too
fascinated by this strange geometry in which straight lines are achieved by
means of curves; but I simply cannot imagine a life without the exaggerations and the risks inherent in dispersion, provided that at the centre of
a multiplicity of activities there is always a firm guiding idea and a clear
vision.

And so it can happen that what may well have seemed a pointless sidetrack and a dangerous dispersion of energy has been simply the multiple
manifestation of a single central obsession – the need to communicate this
mystery, or at least fragments of the mystery, that one thinks one has
discovered oneself. Even now, in fact, in this newly founded Institute
[Institut de recherche et coordination acoustique/musique, Centre Georges
Pompidou, Paris], I may be giving the impression of being ready to sacrifice
everything to rational research – an ugly word in anything to do with
inspiration and creation. People often quote a remark that Picasso is supposed to have made as being a definition of the free artist, a Prometheus in
his claim for total liberty: 'I do not search, I find.' Without going so far as to
invert this aphorism and proudly proclaim: 'I do not find, I search' I still
think that claiming to find without searching is simply an illusion that may
flatter the artist's self-esteem but has the effect of a drug. There is no more
dangerous illusion for a man than to think that he has 'found' when he is not
questioning himself at every moment of his existence.

The illusion of 'finding' is perhaps the most pleasant kind of vertigo and
one to which one would like to surrender if one did not know that, like the
euphoria produced by cold or depth, it can be fatal. Even if research involves
manoeuvring a number of awkward corners in our rational processes, it is
not simply the destroying of illusions or the sacrificing of untamed faculties;
it is certainly not the sterility of the well-tarred road. Far from it: for me
research is the toughest, and sometimes the maddest, kind of utopia or – to
quote a remark of mine that Clytus Gottwald took as a motto – research
enables me, urges me irresistibly in fact, to dream my revolution quite as
much as to plan it. Any man who simply trusts his own powers can abandon
himself, in the midst of plenty, to his own mental habits, take pleasure in the
quirks of his own personality, accept not being scarified by his own sensibilities as by a new shoe, accept the comforts and conveniences of a personal
universe that he has finally arranged to suit him, only adding a pretty
ornament or a house plant here and there.

But no – research is not the dry desert of logic, not the cramping and
imprisoning of live forces, not the squared-out plan of a town that no one
could be interested in building, not the security of a universe hedged in by
definitions. Research is like hunger: it grips you until you satisfy it; and then
returns. This hunger cannot be satisfied once and for all and then be got rid
of and forgotten.

And at this point it is my turn to become Promethean . . . as I believe that the mission entrusted by the gods to the vulture that gnawed the hero's liver was quite simply to be hungry . . . just hungry.

I am not for a moment supposing that the fate from which you wish to preserve me by awarding me this prize was that of either Prometheus or the poor vulture . . . But I should like to believe that in choosing me it was not simply myself but also a certain form of the utopia that I represent, or should in any case like to represent. I feel sure that you have discerned, apart from the conscious tasks that I may have fulfilled, the large element of unconsciousness needed to persevere along the path dictated by circumstances (with a little help from me) during all these years. And so I am grateful to you for what I consider to be your great – and flattering – perspicacity: for having discovered, marked out and even rewarded my gifts as a sleepwalker.

Index